THE BOOK OF SECRETS

Editor
Marion Buhagiar

BOARDROOM® CLASSICS

Illustrations: Daniel Pelavin and others.

Completely Revised Edition
10 9 8 7 6 5 4 3 2 1

Boardroom Books publishes the advice of expert authorities in many fields. But the use of this material is not a substitute for legal, accounting, or other professional services. Consult a competent professional for answers to your specific questions.

Library of Congress Cataloging in Publication Data Main entry under title:

The Book of Secrets

1. Handbooks, vade-mecums, etc.
2. Life skills—Handbooks, manuals, etc.
I. Buhagiar, Marion.
AG105.G666   1986b   031'.02   86-31050
ISBN 0-88723-150-0

Boardroom® Classics, a division of Boardroom®, Inc.
55 Railroad Ave., Greenwich, CT 06830

Printed in the United States of America

TABLE OF CONTENTS

1. The Smart Consumer

2. In and Around the Home

3. You and Your Car

4. Enjoying Your Leisure

5. The Skilled Traveler

6. Your Personal Best

7. Family Life

TABLE OF CONTENTS

8. Relationships

9. Sports and Fitness

TABLE OF CONTENTS

10. Eating and Dieting

11. Staying Healthy

12. Solving Health Problems

13. Brain Power

TABLE OF CONTENTS

14. Self-Improvement

15. Communicating Clearly

16. Kids and College

17. Career Strategies

18. Management Skills

TABLE OF CONTENTS

19. Successful Collecting

20. Smart Investing

21. Real-Estate Money Makers

22. Smart Money Management

23. Financing Retirement

24. More Insurance for Less

25. Tax Strategies

TABLE OF CONTENTS

26. Handling the IRS

27. Personal Legal Tactics

How to be a bargain shopper

The biggest problem most shoppers have with bargaining is a feeling that nice people don't do it. Before you can negotiate, you have to get over this attitude. Some ammunition:

☐ Bargaining will not turn you into a social outcast. All a shopkeeper sees when you walk in is dollar signs. If you are willing to spend, he will probably be willing to make a deal.

☐ Bargaining is a business transaction. You are not trying to cheat the merchant or get something for nothing. You are trying to agree on a fair price. You expect to negotiate for a house or a car—why not for a refrigerator or a winter coat?

☐ You have a right to bargain, particularly in small stores that don't discount. Department stores, which won't bargain as a rule, mark up prices 100%–150% to cover high overhead costs. Small stores should charge lower prices because their costs are less.

The savvy approach:

☐ Set yourself a price limit for a particular item before you approach the storekeeper.

☐ Be prepared to walk out if he doesn't meet your limit. (You can always change your mind later.)

☐ Make him believe you really won't buy unless he comes down.

☐ Be discreet in your negotiations. If other customers can overhear your dickering, the shop owner must stay firm.

☐ Be respectful of the merchandise. Don't manhandle the goods that you inspect.

☐ Address the salesperson in a polite, friendly manner. Assume that he will want to do his best for you because he is such a nice, helpful person.

☐ Shop at off hours. You will have more luck if business is slow.

☐ Look for unmarked merchandise. If there is no price tag, you are invited to bargain.

Tactics that work:

☐ Negotiate with cash. In a store that takes credit cards, request a discount for paying in cash. (Charging entails overhead costs that the store must absorb.)

☐ Buy in quantity. A customer who is committed to a number of purchases has more bargaining power. When everything is picked out, approach the owner and suggest a total price about 20% less than the actual total.

☐ If you are buying more than one of an item, offer to pay full price on the first one if the owner will give you a break on the other. Or, ask to have an extra, probably small-ticket, item thrown in.

☐ Look for flawed merchandise. This is the only acceptable bargaining point in department stores, but it also can save you money in small shops. If there's a spot, a split seam or a missing button, estimate what it would cost to have the garment fixed commercially, and ask for a discount based on that figure.

☐ Adapt your haggling to the realities of the situation. A true discount house has a low profit margin and depends on volume to make its money. Don't ask for more than 5% off in such a store. A boutique that charges what the traffic will bear has more leeway. Start by asking for 25% off, and dicker from there.

☐ Buy at the end of the season, when new stock is being put out. Offer to buy older goods—at a discount.

☐ Neighborhood stores: Push the local television or appliance dealer to give you a break so you can keep your service business in the community.

Source: Sharon Dunn Greene, co-author of *The Lower East Side Shopping Guide*, Brooklyn, NY.

What goes on sale when

A month-by-month schedule for dedicated bargain hunters:

January

☐ After-Christmas sales.
☐ Appliances.
☐ Baby carriages.
☐ Books.
☐ Carpets and rugs.
☐ China and glassware.
☐ Christmas cards.
☐ Costume jewelry.
☐ Furniture.
☐ Furs.
☐ Lingerie.
☐ Men's overcoats.

- ☐ Pocketbooks.
- ☐ Preinventory sales.
- ☐ Shoes.
- ☐ Toys.
- ☐ White goods (sheets, towels, etc.).

February
- ☐ Air conditioners.
- ☐ Art supplies.
- ☐ Bedding.
- ☐ Cars (used).
- ☐ Curtains.
- ☐ Furniture.
- ☐ Glassware and china.
- ☐ Housewares.
- ☐ Lamps.
- ☐ Men's apparel.
- ☐ Radios, TV sets and phonographs.
- ☐ Silverware.
- ☐ Sportswear and equipment.
- ☐ Storm windows.
- ☐ Toys.

March
- ☐ Boys' and girls' shoes.
- ☐ Garden supplies.
- ☐ Housewares.
- ☐ Ice skates.
- ☐ Infants' clothing.
- ☐ Laundry equipment.
- ☐ Luggage.
- ☐ Ski equipment.

April
- ☐ Fabrics.
- ☐ Hosiery.
- ☐ Lingerie.
- ☐ Painting supplies.
- ☐ Women's shoes.

May
- ☐ Handbags.
- ☐ Housecoats.
- ☐ Household linens.
- ☐ Jewelry.
- ☐ Luggage.
- ☐ Mothers' Day specials.
- ☐ Outdoor furniture.
- ☐ Rugs.
- ☐ Shoes.
- ☐ Sportswear.
- ☐ Tires and auto accessories.
- ☐ TV sets.

June
- ☐ Bedding.
- ☐ Boys' clothing.

- ☐ Fabrics.
- ☐ Fathers' Day specials.
- ☐ Floor coverings.
- ☐ Lingerie, sleepwear and hosiery.
- ☐ Men's clothing.
- ☐ Women's shoes.

July
- ☐ Air conditioners and other appliances.
- ☐ Bathing suits.
- ☐ Children's clothes.
- ☐ Electronic equipment.
- ☐ Fuel.
- ☐ Furniture.
- ☐ Handbags.
- ☐ Lingerie and sleepwear.
- ☐ Luggage.
- ☐ Men's shirts.
- ☐ Men's shoes.
- ☐ Rugs.
- ☐ Sportswear.
- ☐ Summer clothes.
- ☐ Summer sports equipment.

August
- ☐ Back-to-school specials.
- ☐ Bathing suits.
- ☐ Carpeting.
- ☐ Cosmetics.
- ☐ Curtains and drapes.
- ☐ Electric fans and air conditioners.
- ☐ Furniture.
- ☐ Furs.
- ☐ Men's coats.
- ☐ Silver.
- ☐ Tires.
- ☐ White goods.
- ☐ Women's coats.

September
- ☐ Bicycles.
- ☐ Cars (outgoing models).
- ☐ China and glassware.
- ☐ Fabrics.
- ☐ Fall fashions.
- ☐ Garden equipment.
- ☐ Hardware.
- ☐ Lamps.
- ☐ Paints.

October
- ☐ Cars (outgoing models).
- ☐ China and glassware.
- ☐ Fall/winter clothing.
- ☐ Fishing equipment.

- [ ] Furniture.
- [ ] Lingerie and hosiery.
- [ ] Major appliances.
- [ ] School supplies.
- [ ] Silver.
- [ ] Storewide clearances.
- [ ] Women's coats.

November

- [ ] Blankets and quilts.
- [ ] Boys' suits and coats.
- [ ] Cars (used).
- [ ] Lingerie.
- [ ] Major appliances.
- [ ] Men's suits and coats.
- [ ] Shoes.
- [ ] White goods.
- [ ] Winter clothing.

December

- [ ] After-Christmas cards, gifts, toys.
- [ ] Blankets and quilts.
- [ ] Cars (used).
- [ ] Children's clothes.
- [ ] Christmas promotions.
- [ ] Coats and hats.
- [ ] Men's furnishings.
- [ ] Resort and cruise wear.
- [ ] Shoes.

The best factory outlets ✓

Factory outlets are often part of the manufacturer's old warehouse or factory, and furnishings are sparse. Credit and return policies are stricter than in retail stores, and fitting rooms are makeshift at best. However, the money you can save should make up for the lack of customer services.

Guidelines for factory outlets:

- [ ] Go regularly to the outlet store of a manufacturer whose goods you particularly like. If you frequent an outlet, you'll learn the types of goods available and how often they come in.

- [ ] The best buys at a manufacturer's outlet will be its own goods. At a Palm Beach outlet, for example, the resort

clothing may be a real bargain—but other manufacturers' goods on sale there may not be as sharply discounted.

- [ ] Irregulars can be a great buy if the flaw is fixable or unnoticeable. But beware of prepackaged items if you can't open them to check. One pajama leg could be six inches shorter than the other!

- [ ] Always check merchandise for quality. For example, make sure plaids match at seams in skirts and shirts, seam allowances are generous and the material used in clothing and linens is not flawed.

Top factory outlets:

Clothing

- [ ] *Barbizon Lingerie Factory Outlet,* 20 Enterprise Ave., Secaucus, NJ, 201-867-1714.
- [ ] *The Company Store,* Factory Outlet Bldg., Rowan St., E. Norwalk, CT, 203-838-9921.
- [ ] *Factory Stores of America at Nut Tree,* I-80, from east Monte Vista exit, from west I-505 Orange Drive exit, Vacaville, CA, 707-447-5755.
- [ ] *Pacific West Outlet Center,* Highway 101, Leavesley exit, Gilroy, CA, 408-847-4155.
- [ ] *Polly Flinders Factory Outlet,* 2700 State Rd. 16, Suite 104, St. Augustine, FL, 904-824-5057.
- [ ] *Vanity Fair Outlet Store,* 801 Hill Ave., Wyomissing, PA, 610-378-0408.
- [ ] *Warnaco Outlet Store,* 130 Gregory St., Bridgeport, CT, 203-579-8164.

Home furnishings & housewares

- [ ] *Anchor Hocking,* 621 N. Memorial Dr., Lancaster, OH, 614-687-2500.
- [ ] *Dansk Factory Outlets,* 7024 International Dr., Orlando, FL; Route 1, Kittery, ME; junction of routes 202 and 31, Flemington, NJ, 207-439-0484. There are also other locations. Look in your local telephone book.
- [ ] *Corning Revere Factory Store,* 638 Queshend St., Fall River, MA, 508-676-0066.
- [ ] *Stonehenge Mill Shop,* 30 Canfield Rd., Cedar Grove, NJ, 201-239-9710.

Candy

- [ ] *Russell Stover Candy,* Highway 722, Clarksville, VA, 804-374-2172.
- [ ] *Wilbur Chocolates' Factory Outlet,* 48 N. Broad St., Lititz, PA, 717-626-3249.

Shoes

☐ *Bally,* 20 Enterprise Ave., Secaucus, NJ, 201-864-3422.

☐ *Bass,* 531 Amherst St., Nashua, NH, 603-889-6000.

Source: Jean and Jan Bird, authors of *Birds' Guide to Bargain Shopping,* Andrews, McMeel and Parker, Fairway, KS.

Saving at supermarkets ✓

☐ Complete your shopping within half an hour. *Why:* Customers spend 50 cents a minute after they have been in a supermarket longer than 30 minutes. The almost-empty shopping cart invites impulse buying.

Look for:

☐ Generic products. *Most popular:* Paper goods, canned fruits and vegetables, laundry products and soap, soft drinks, canned soups and canned tuna.

☐ Don't be taken in by advertisements pushing premium paper towels (those that are extra-strong or super-absorbent). For most uses (wiping up small spills or drying your hands), the typical supermarket economy brand probably does the job equally well.

☐ Domestic seltzers. Have no added sodium, and they are less expensive than most imported mineral waters. *Insight:* Price seldom parallels the taste and quality of various brands of bottled waters. Often the least expensive have the cleanest taste. *Basic types:* (1) Sparkling mineral water is carbonated water from an underground spring. (2) Seltzer is carbonated tap water. (3) Club soda is also carbonated tap water, usually with mineral salts added.

☐ Buy milk in cardboard containers, not translucent plastic jugs. *Reason:* When exposed to fluorescent lighting in the supermarket, milk in jugs oxidizes. It develops a flat taste and loses vitamin C.

Source: *Family Practice News;* Tom Grady and Amy Rood, co-authors, *The Household Handbook,* Meadowbrook Press, Deephaven, MN.

How to choose the right checkout line

Successful people play to win. They know the rules, devise plans of attack and follow their plans with discipline, whether it's on the job, in the stock market—or just doing the grocery shopping. To spend less time in the supermarket…

☐ Look for the fastest cashier. Individual speeds can vary by hundreds of rings per hour.

☐ Look for a line with bagger. A checker/bagger team will move a line up to 100% faster than a checker working alone. When the supermarket uses optical scanning equipment, the bagger increases line speed by more than 100%. *Note:* Two baggers in the same line are barely more helpful than one.

☐ Count the shopping carts in each line. If all else were equal, the line with the fewest carts would be the quickest. But…there are other factors to consider. Look for…

A) Carts that contain many identical items. Two dozen cans of dog food can be checked out faster than a dozen different items. They don't have to be individually scanned or rung into the register.

B) Carts that contain a lot of items. Because each new customer requires a basic amount of set-up time, it's better to stand behind one customer who has 50 items than behind two customers who have ten items each.

C) Carts that contain a lot of produce. Each item has to be weighed.

D) People with bottles to return. This can take a lot of time.

E) People who look like they're going to cash a check. This too can take a lot of time. *Most likely check-cashers:* Women who clutch a purse.

Source: David Feldman, author of *How to Win at Just About Everything,* Morrow Quill, William Morrow & Co., 105 Madison Ave., New York 10016.

Shopping for bargains in luxuries

☐ Get to know your neighborhood stores and be known in them. In foodstuffs, ask for what is in season—even for items such as imported cheese.

☐ Visit a new store in the neighborhood promptly. Early customers will be remembered. And new stores generally have the most competitive prices.

☐ Shop at smaller clothing stores where the owner selects merchandise, generally providing better quality fashion at lower prices than department stores.

☐ Select clothing essentials when stock is fresh—even though prices are highest at the start of a season. Fill in with bargains later in the season.

☐ Look into resale shops (better than thrift shops) as a good source for items such as evening gowns, furs, etc.

☐ Look at the fabric, workmanship and country of origin on clothes before trying them on. (*Good ones:* Italy, France, Germany, Ireland, Scandinavian countries.)

☐ When buying appliances, electronic goods or big-ticket items, know exactly what you want when you walk into a store—make, model, options, colors, etc.

☐ Ask the salesperson the price on unmarked goods and then ask for a discount for cash, for travelers checks, for taking the floor model, for carting away the goods right then and there, etc.
Source: *Money,* New York.

If you're thinking of mink

If you are thinking of purchasing any fur, consider buying in Canada first. Buying even the best furs in Montreal costs only a fraction of the US price. Typical savings range from $5,000 to $15,000 plus. As a rule, Canadian furs are of a higher quality than their US counterparts. The pelts are denser because the animals grow thicker fur as insulation from the colder climate.

You are better off buying your fur from a furrier—especially from a member of the select professional Fur Council of Canada—than from a department store. Furriers are more knowledgeable and better trained than department store personnel. And they are more flexible on prices. Since furs are a major investment, they should look magnificent and fit perfectly. There is no reason purchasers should decide to settle for less.

In order to choose the best fur, think of its function. Some furs are more fragile, others more durable—a characteristic of the fur itself that is independent of its price. *Most durable:* Mink, beaver, raccoon and fisher. *More fragile (not for everyday wear):* Sable, lynx, fox, chinchilla, broadtail and squirrel. Except for the more expensive kind (over $5,000), avoid dyed furs. Sooner or later, dyed furs oxidize, turning an unforeseeable color.

Furriers process the necessary paperwork and provide free shipping to your home so that you can avoid the national and Quebec sales taxes, which presently total 14%. (There is no longer any US customs tax on goods brought in from Canada.)

Source: Judith H. McQuown, author of four investment books, writes about fashion, travel, shopping and antiques for many national magazines.

How to buy caviar

Tips for getting the best for your money when you buy caviar:

☐ If you want top-of-the-line caviar, buy one of the three grades that come from sturgeon.

☐☐ Beluga: Biggest grained; black or gray in color; most expensive.

☐☐ Osetra: Grains almost as big; brown to golden color; somewhat less costly.

☐☐ Sevruga: Much smaller grains; least expensive of the sturgeon caviars.

☐ The freshest, best caviar is packed with mild salt, labeled Malossol. Also excellent is pressed caviar, which is top-grade but too "ripe" to be packed in whole grains. This kind can be frozen.

☐ Avoid bottom-of-the-line caviar that comes in jars; among other negatives, it is strongly salted.

☐ For good value and flavor, don't overlook red-colored caviar from salmon. Best choice is the smaller-size grains from silver salmon rather than the more common Ketovya or chum salmon caviar, which is often artificially colored.

Buy & enjoy the best cognac

Cognac is a complex liquor from the Cognac region of France. It is made by twice distilling a white-wine base and then placing it in oak casks to age. Different batches are blended to make cognac.

Classification of a cognac is determined by the youngest batch in the blend. (Other parts can be up to 20 years older.) The older the rating, the smoother and better tasting the cognac.

☐ Three Star: Aged 2½ years.

☐ VO (Very Old): Aged 4½ years.

☐ VSOP (Very Superior Old Pale): This is also aged 4½ years, but the blends are superior to those used in the VO.

☐ XO (Extra Old): Aged 6½ years.

☐ Buy cognac from a reliable producer. This insures quality, since most good producers age their cognacs far beyond what the law requires.

☐ Favorites: Delamain, Hennessy, Remy Martin and Martell.

☐ Drink cognac slowly to appreciate the flavor. Use a medium-sized brandy snifter, and warm the glass in your hand while you sip. Don't warm the glass over a flame, since too much heat will damage the liquor and hide the nuances of its flavor.

Source: Mary Ewing Mulligan, International Wine Center, New York.

Gearing up for auctions

Depending on the kind of auction (country, indoor) and the type of merchandise sought (bric-a-brac, tools, furniture), assemble the appropriate gear. Suggestions:

☐ Cash, travelers checks, credit cards or checkbook. (Be aware that many auctions accept only cash.)

☐ Pens, pencils and notebook.

☐ Pocket calculator.

☐ Rope for tying items to car roof.

☐ Old blankets for cushioning.

☐ Tape measure.

☐ Magnet (for detecting iron and steel under paint or plating).

☐ Folding chair and umbrella (if auction is outdoors).

☐ Picnic lunch (auction food is unpredictable).

How a Postal Service auction works

A US Postal Service auction is an exciting combination of Las Vegas and a flea market. Anything that can be sent through the mail might turn up at a post office auction. *Items typically available:* Stereo equipment, TVs, radios, dishes, pots and pans, tools, typewriters, clothing, books, coins.

The Postal Service holds regular auctions of lost, damaged or undeliverable merchandise every two or four months in all major US cities. (The New York City Postal Service has an auction once a month.) Call the main post office in your city for time and date.

Basic ground rules:

☐ Items are sold by "lot." Similar articles are often grouped together, such as a dozen jeans, or four typewriters, or three radios. The items must be purchased together, so bring friends who might want to share a lot with you.

☐ Lots are displayed the day before the auction for viewing. Lots are in compartments or bins that are covered with netting. Nothing (except clothing on hangers) can be handled or tested. Many compartments are badly lighted, so bring a flashlight to get a good look.

☐ All lots are listed by number on a mimeographed sheet given out on the inspection day. They are auctioned off by number, and each has a minimum acceptable bid listed next to it (never less than $10). But the minimum bid is no indication of how much the lot will sell for. Some go for ten or more times the minimum bid listed.

☐ All lots are sold "as is." There is no guarantee as to quality or quantity. The Postal Service tries to mark items it recognizes as damaged. *Remember:* All sales are final.

☐ You must pay a nominal fee the day before the auction to obtain a paddle for bidding. Each paddle has a number on it, which the auctioneer recognizes as your bidding number. To bid, hold up your paddle. The cost of the paddle will be refunded if you don't buy anything. Otherwise, it is applied to the purchase price.

☐ You must deposit 50% of the purchase price in cash or certified check 30 minutes after buying a lot. Bring several certified checks in different amounts so you won't have to come up with large sums of cash.

☐ Merchandise must be picked up a day or two after the auction. Bring your own container.

The bidding at Postal Service auctions is extremely unpredictable and quirky. Some lots are overbid, while others go for the minimum bid, often with no obvious relations to actual value. A set of inexpensive plastic dishes may fetch more than the retail price, while a much more valuable and lovely set of china dishes goes for less than the plastic ones.

Sample prices at recent auctions:

☐ Sanyo cassette deck: $100.

☐ Sansui amplifier: $100.

☐ Brother electronic typewriter: $120.

☐ Oriental jewelry chest (very large and ornate): $85.

☐ Hamilton beach blender and hand mixer: $28.

☐ Persian lamb jacket with mink-trimmed sleeves (brand new): $40.

How to bid:

☐ Go through the list of lots carefully while looking at the merchandise, and write down your maximum bids. During the actual auction, bidding is confusingly fast, with prices rapidly increasing by $2 at a time as bidders drop out. Listen carefully to the bidding, and don't exceed your maximum.

☐ Sit in the back of the room so you can see who is bidding against you.

☐ Take someone knowledgeable to the visual inspection, especially if you're planning to bid on something like electronic equipment. Find out how much that particular piece is worth, and calculate your top bid by including the cost of repair.

☐ If you can't find someone who is knowledgeable, stick to bidding on lots that you can see are in good shape. *Best bets:* Dishes, cutlery, pots and pans, hand tools, furniture, clothing sold by the garment. (Much of the clothing is sold in huge bins and can't be inspected.)

How to save money on almost everything

It's easy to cut costs by taking advantage of discounts and freebies. One woman we know saved enough in a few years to buy a new car!

Worthwhile: Keep track of your savings —and enjoy watching them grow.

Utilities/energy

☐ For free evaluation of your energy usage, call your local utilities company. In addition, many utilities companies give away free energy-saving devices, such as low-flow shower heads, water-heater blankets and fluorescent bulbs.

☐ Repair major appliances yourself instead of paying for a costly service call. *How:* Call manufacturers' customer-service repair hotlines for instructions.

☐ General Electric, 800-626-2000.

☐ Whirlpool, 800-253-1301.

☐ White-Westinghouse, 800-245-0600.

☐ Gather free firewood from any of our 155 national forests. Contact your regional office of the US Forest Service for a permit, which allows you up to six cords of downed or dead wood. At the going rate of about $150 a cord, this will save almost $1,000.

☐ Install a water restrictor for your shower head. That saves an average family thousands of gallons of water a year. Check with your local utility for a free water-restrictor head.

Home- and health-care products

☐ Coupons are not just for food. Some of the very best coupon savings are for cleaning supplies, tissues, toothpaste, shampoo, batteries and other home-care and health-care products. Keep an eye out for "Free with Purchase" offers…stores that pay double coupon values…coupons printed on product packaging.

☐ Take advantage of refund/rebate offers. You must take the time to save UPC symbols, labels and receipts, but the savings can easily reach hundreds of dollars a year. *Good source of offers:* Supermarket and drugstore bulletin boards.

Refund request forms are often mounted as tear-off pads where products are shelved. Don't overlook offers in hardware and home-building stores, pet stores and appliance stores.

☐ Ask for free samples at department store cosmetics counters. Just say you need to try products before you buy, and you'll walk away with handfuls of high-priced makeup, skin-care products and fragrances.

Watch for: Fine print in magazine ads offering free samples of perfume or moisturizer simply by writing or calling an 800 number.

☐ Have your hair cut, colored, permed or styled at a cosmetology school. Students have spent hundreds of hours working on mannequins and each other, and are closely supervised by expert instructors. Customers are usually pampered.

Savings: About 60% less than a salon. The average American woman spends $238 a year at hair salons, so expect to save $143.

☐ Get routine dental care at a dental school. Services at the country's 57 dental-school training clinics, including orthodontics, are high-quality and 60% less expensive than normal dentists' fees. To find one, check the phone book for your local dental society.

☐ Ask your doctors for free samples of medications whenever you are given a prescription. Most doctors have plenty to give away.

Home entertainment

☐ Take advantage of free magazine offers. Don't throw away subscription invitations from periodicals. Most publications will send you a free issue, then begin your subscription unless you cancel.

Key: Remember to write "cancel" on the invoice they send, and mail it back to them. The postage is almost always paid, and you owe nothing.

☐ Use your public library to borrow books, records, audiotapes, videotapes, even posters and artwork.

☐ Order free publications from your favorite manufacturers. Almost every food product company offers a free cookbook, including Quaker Oats, Dannon, Kikkoman, Goya's Seasonings and Nestlé…as does almost every trade organization, including the American Mushroom Institute in Kennett Square, Pennsylvania, the California Raisin Advisory Board in Fresno and the Idaho Potato Commission in Boise.

Examples: Eastman Kodak of Rochester, New York, offers three free booklets on photography…the Chicago Roller Skate Co. has two free booklets on roller skating how-to's…United Van Lines of Fenton, Missouri, offers a free booklet called *How to Hold a Garage Sale.*

To find offers…check package labels for the location of company headquarters, or call 800-555-1212. Then contact the company's customer-service department.

Source: Linda Bowman, author of *The More for Your Money* series of guides, including *Free Food & More* and *Freebies (and More) for Folks Over 50*, COM-OP Publishing, Malibu, CA.

How to buy at flea markets

Flea markets can be a bargain-hunter's dream—but let the buyer beware. Here are the best ways to make great deals at flea markets—and have fun while you're hunting.

How to find the best deals

☐ Evaluate a variety of flea markets to find your favorites. Flea markets are unpredictable—anyone can rent a table and sell whatever was in the attic, closet or basement. But no matter where they are located, the best flea markets offer a wide range of used and new merchandise, antiques, collectibles and good, old-fashioned "junque." Many include a farmer's market as well.

To evaluate a flea market: Look for diversity. Cruise the market quickly before deciding to stay. Do you see merchandise that interests you? Or is it just a show of cheap socks and knock-off designer watches?

Example: I visited a flea market in North Carolina that was stocked almost entirely with used computer equipment, office supplies and stationery overruns —good deals, but not what I was interested in at the time.

☐ Familiarize yourself with market values of collectibles and antiques. Flea markets are not geared for people who know exactly what they are looking for —they're for fun and surprises. But the more you know about the values of many types of items, the better you will be able to identify and bargain for a treasure when you see it. If you are serious about antiques and collectibles, check price guides and retail dealers regularly to develop an eye for authenticity, condition and prices.

☐ Be prepared to bargain for the merchandise—but don't feel obligated to bargain. Most vendors will bargain, some won't. Usually, if a flea-market vendor senses you know what you are talking about, he/she will move on the price. Many dealers "build in" a cushion so they can come down in price, so that you feel as though you are getting a deal and both you and the vendor get what you want.

☐ Talk to the vendors—especially if you have an item to trade or are looking for something special. It is boring to sit at a table all day, and flea-market vendors generally love to gab. Most vendors network among themselves and exchange merchandise and business cards. Many are knowledgeable antique professionals or collectors themselves. Most of them buy as well as sell and know what everyone else has to offer. Many vendors have a shop or store items at home that they would be happy to bring to the market the next week.

☐ Come early and stay—or return late. As a general rule, you can find the best buys very, very early in the day. But if an item is unsold at the end of the day, you may be able to negotiate a better price. *Best strategy:* Visit your favorite markets regularly. Go early in the morning and pass through quickly, to scout out anything new and interesting. Swoop down on the treasures you must have immediately or that you believe will sell by the end of the day. Then return for the last-minute bargains near closing time. The strongest buyers arrive when the booths are being set up—and bring flashlights with them.

What to avoid when shopping at flea markets

Mistake: Thinking you are getting a steal. Most flea-market vendors are reputable, well-informed on the value of their merchandise and want happy, repeat customers. But there are always a few who intend to thrive on credulous tourists.

Mistake: Buying the first thing you see. This may sound as if it contradicts the "come early" rule—but flea-market vendors often have overlapping wares. That is, you may buy a "unique" Maltese falcon statue, only to find a whole tableful further on.

Buyers can often find real steals at small, out-of-the-way markets that are not hit regularly by bargain-hunters. But there are also excellent deals to be found at the large, well-publicized markets.

Source: Albert LaFarge, author of *The Confident Collector: US Flea-Market Directory,* Avon Books, New York.

Secrets of big-time food-bill savings

Most of us have had the thought, "I can't believe I'm paying this much for one bag of stuff," as the supermarket cashier finishes ringing up the "few things" we ran to the store for.

"Did I really buy that much?" we wonder. Usually, we haven't bought that much—just paid too much. Here are some ways to save big on the family food bill.

Supermarket savings

☐ Shop with a list…or you'll spend more than you save.

☐ Clip coupons—and keep them organized. Don't throw money away with the garbage. Coupons can easily save you $1,000 a year.

Be willing to give up brand loyalty in favor of a meaningful discount. One brand of tomato paste or dish detergent is much like another.

File coupons in envelopes by category —canned goods, cereals, pet foods, paper products, etc. Put coupons you plan to use right away and those with short expiration dates in the front. Take them with you to the store, along with an empty envelope to put coupons in for the items you select, so you don't have to sort them at the check-out counter.

Shop at a supermarket that honors double the value on the face of coupons. You can also increase your savings by combining in-store sales with coupons. Be sure to calculate the per-unit price of products when using coupons.

Example: A 6-ounce jar of instant coffee may cost $3.29, or 55¢ an ounce, and a 10-ounce jar $4.99, or 50¢ an ounce. Normally, the larger size is the better buy. But with a 75¢ coupon, at a double-coupon store, the 6-ounce jar costs $1.79, or 30¢ an ounce, while the 10-ounce jar is $3.49, or 35¢ an ounce.

☐ Companion product offers. Companies and supermarkets often issue coupons for a free item, with the purchase of a companion item.

Examples: A free gallon of milk with the purchase of a breakfast cereal…a free box of pasta with the purchase of spaghetti sauce.

☐ Refund and rebate offers. You may need to clip UPC symbols or save register receipts as "proof of purchase" to send for these offers. They are worth the trouble—and can be very lucrative, whether you get a cash rebate, additional coupons or free products.

☐ Senior discounts. Many large chain stores and some independent markets issue senior discount cards that allow cashiers to subtract as much as 5% to 10% off the final bill.

☐ Generic brands. Not only are they here to stay, they are growing and growing. Generics can provide substantial savings, especially on grooming products, cereals and canned goods.

☐ Track savings. Most supermarkets total the amount saved with coupons at the bottom of the register receipt. You can deposit monthly savings from coupons, refunds, etc., in an account earmarked toward a goal.

Supermarket alternatives

☐ Join a wholesale or warehouse shopping club. These huge operations are springing up in metropolitan areas nationwide. Shopping is a no-frills enterprise, and products must often be purchased in bulk or large sizes. Brand selection may be limited and may change at any given time. But savings can be excellent. *Key:* Know your prices. Some warehouse-club prices are not significantly better than prices at the discounters.

☐ Shop at farmers' markets, where vegetables and fruits are fresher, tastier and cheaper. Buy in bulk in-season, then can or preserve.

☐ Shop at bakery outlets and "thrift stores." Thrift stores are one-brand outlets for companies such as Entenmann's, Pepperidge Farm, Arnold's Bakery, Sunbeam Bread and Wonder-Bread/Hostess. Prices run 30% to 50% off retail for day-old goods.

☐ Food co-ops and buying clubs. Consumer cooperatives are run by members and usually buy food in bulk and then repackage it for buyers. Members can save 15% to 50% on most items, because brokers, middlemen and costly packaging are eliminated from the exchange.

☐ Do it yourself. Grow a vegetable garden, make your own frozen dinners from leftovers.

Source: Linda Bowman, professional bargain hunter and author of the *More for Your Money* series of guides, including *Free Food & More and Freebies (and More) for Folks Over 50,* Probus Publishing Co., Chicago.

Wintertime money savers

Winter is the season of higher electricity and gas bills, car maintenance and repair bills, bills for cold and flu medications and so on. But there are several ways that you can cut down on expenses without sacrificing great comfort.

Avoid costly car repairs

☐ Keep your gas free of water. The most frequent problems mechanics see in winter are caused by water in the gas. To prevent problems, add a drier (such as Prestone Gas-Drier or Heet) to your gas every few fill-ups.

☐ Check your radiator fluid and the condition of the radiator hoses. If the fluid is low, add a 50/50 mixture of antifreeze and water. In the coldest parts of the country or when an extreme cold snap strikes, you may want to alter this by using more antifreeze. *Best:* Use a mixture of 70% antifreeze and 30% water. Muddy-looking fluid should be changed. Make sure that the rubber hoses leading from the radiator to the engine are not cracked, brittle, bulging or mushy when they are squeezed.

☐ Keep your battery terminals clean to avoid starting problems (and costly towing bills). Clean the battery terminals occasionally with baking soda and then reduce the corrosion problem by smearing them with a thin coating of petroleum jelly.

☐ Promptly repair any nicks in your windshield. Stop those smaller than a quarter from spawning spider legs and ruining the windshield by covering them on both sides with transparent tape (duct tape works, too). Then get the car to a windshield-repair specialist. Cost for a nick ranges from $30 to $50, compared to the $300 to over $600 it can cost to replace the whole windshield.

☐ Check tire inflation every few weeks with an accurate gauge. Changes in temperature alter tire pressure, and underinflation increases tire wear and gas consumption by as much as 5%.

Important: Check the pressure while tires are cold. Know how many pounds of pressure they require. Then check them again at the gas station (after they've warmed from being driven on) and add the pounds of pressure that were needed when they were cold.

Save on heating

☐ Put on an extra sweater and modify your heating habits. Keep the daytime thermostat at 65 degrees Fahrenheit and the nighttime temperature at 55 degrees Fahrenheit. This can reduce your heating bill 15% or more. And turn down the heat when you leave to run errands.

☐ Keep fireplace dampers closed when not in use. Install glass fireplace doors. Then heat won't escape through the chimney.

☐ Have your home's insulation checked by your utility company. Many utilities perform this inspection service free or for a nominal fee. Make sure your home's insulation meets the US Department of Energy's recommendations.

☐ Wrap fiberglass insulation around heating ducts and hot water pipes in basement, attic and crawl space. Putting 2½ inches of insulation around these ducts and pipes will pay for itself in one season.

Save on lighting

☐ Replace incandescent lights with fluorescent lights in areas that need light for hours each day. Today's fluorescent tubes produce warmer hues that won't make your home feel like a factory, and they're three to four times more efficient. If you don't want to install the tubes, use compact fluorescent bulbs. They screw into standard sockets.

☐ Use outdoor light fixtures that turn on and off by means of built-in heat/motion detectors and timers. They're far more economical than those that burn nonstop.

☐ Don't turn lights on and off frequently. Turning the lights out every time you leave the room for a few minutes may seem like it's doing good, but it shortens the life of the bulbs. So don't turn out the light unless leaving for more than a few minutes.

Grandma's remedies

☐ Get an annual flu shot if you're 65 or older or suffer from cardiac or respiratory problems. It's cheap insurance against the major problems a flu can precipitate.

☐ Have prescriptions filled at a discount drugstore. It is much cheaper than using your hospital's pharmacy.

Miscellaneous money savers

☐ Freeze your credit. This is a good idea any time of year, but works especially well around the holiday season. Put your credit cards in a bowl of water and place them in the freezer. It sounds crazy, but by the time the ice melts enough to retrieve the cards, the urge to buy may have passed. And writing checks or paying cash for items forces you to do a "reality check" on how much you really have to spend.

☐ Put rubber half-soles on the bottom of your shoes. In damp or wet weather, the leather soles of your shoes are constantly absorbing water, which slowly damages the leather and reshapes the shoe. Half-soles cost $12 to $15 and add years of life to your shoes. *Also:* Alternate the shoes you wear each day. Having a day to dry and air between uses greatly extends shoe life.

Source: Andy Dappen, author of *Cheap Tricks: 100s of Ways You Can Save 1000s of Dollars,* Brier Books, Mountlake Terrace, WA.

Determining if wooden furniture is well made

Before buying a piece of wooden furniture, answer these questions:

☐ Is the piece stable when you gently push down on a top corner or press against the side?

☐ Is the back panel inset and attached with screws (not nails)?

☐ Do drawers and doors fit well and move smoothly?

☐ Are corners of drawers joined with dovetail joints?

☐ Do long shelves have center braces?

☐ Are table leaves well supported?

☐ Are hinges strong and well secured?

Source: *Better Homes and Gardens,* Des Moines, IA.

Great buys by mail and phone

Why settle for the best deal in town when you can get the best deal in the United States? You can save big, big bucks off the price of major appliances, top-of-the-line furniture and large equipment by telephoning a price-quote company.

For a broad spectrum of items—lingerie, high-quality art supplies and name-brand sporting goods, you can thumb through a wide variety of very attractive, specialized direct-mail catalogs, mail or phone in your order and save.

Big-ticket items

The average consumer doesn't know much about price-quote companies because they don't spend a great deal of money advertising—but their sales-people are eager to receive your call. They require that you know what you want, the name of the manufacturer, model number and other descriptive details of the item you intend to buy.

Here's a sampling of the kind of merchandise offered by price-quote companies handling calls from around the country:

☐ Furniture. Cedar Rock Furniture carries all major brands of furniture at up to 50% below retail.

Cedar Rock Furniture, Box 515, Hudson, North Carolina 28638.

☐ Appliances. EBA Wholesale offers dozens of products from more than 50 top-name manufacturers, including Admiral, Panasonic, Litton, KitchenAid, Westinghouse and General Electric at up to 60% less than list price.

EBA Wholesale, 2361 Nostrand Ave., Brooklyn 11210.

☐ Automobiles. Nationwide Auto Brokers will send you a form ($9.95) showing all the operational equipment available for the car you want and then arrange delivery with a local dealer. You save from $150 to $4,000 by allowing the broker to negotiate a dealer-to-dealer price break that eliminates the salesperson's commission.

Nationwide Auto Brokers, 17517 W. 10 Mile Rd., Southfield, Michigan 48075.

☐ Computers. CMO offers name-brand computers like IBM, Epson and Hewlett-Packard as well as systems and software at savings as great as 40% off retail.

CMO, 2400 Reach Rd., Williamsport, Pennsylvania 11701.

☐ Fitness equipment. Better Health and Fitness will help you complete your fitness center with name-brand equipment at savings of up to 25%.

Better Health and Fitness, 5302 New Utrecht Ave., Brooklyn 11219.

To locate a price-quote firm in your area, turn to the Yellow Pages for the type of item you're looking for, but understand that there are tiers of discounters, with those who do the highest volume buying getting the best prices. Your best bet by phone will be a company with nationwide delivery. But shop discounters, too.

Example: If you want a new stove, look in the *Yellow Pages* under a major heading such as Appliances:

☐ Household.

☐ Major dealers.

You often will find promotions for "top brand names" at "wholesale prices to the consumer."

Smaller items

There are hundreds and hundreds of fabulous catalogs you'll never know about unless you watch for their rare ads in the back of newspapers or magazines or you learn about them through word of mouth.

Yet, these catalogs offer you the opportunity to buy your favorite brand of merchandise at a great price without spending money on gasoline and sacrificing hours out of your day to trek to the mall.

There are catalogs for just about anything you might want—from the mundane to the exotic. Here's a sampling of nontraditional catalog types:

☐ Art supplies. Cheap Joe's Art Stuff. Save 30% on paint, canvas, brushes, mat cutters, books on art. Free catalog.

Cheap Joe's Art Stuff, 300A Industrial Park Rd., Boone, North Carolina 28607.

☐ Fragrances. Essential Products Company lets you save up to 90% on perfumes. Essential Products buys them from a company that copies designer scents. Free brochure.

Essential Products Company, 90 Water St., New York 10005.

☐ Bed and bath. Harris Levy, Inc. Save up to 50% on Wamsutta, J.P. Stevens, Springmaid and Fieldcrest, etc. Free catalog.

Harris Levy, Inc., 278 Grand St., New York 10002.

☐ Collectibles. Quilts Unlimited. Save 20% to 30% by buying from "America's largest antique quilt shop." *Catalog:* $5.

Quilts Unlimited, 440-A Duke of Gloucester St., Williamsburg, Virginia 23185.

☐ Boating supplies. Goldberg's Marine Distributors. Save up to 60% on boating equipment and nautical clothing, and receive your shipment in three to seven days. Free seasonal catalog.

Goldberg's Marine Distributors, 201 Meadow Rd., Edison, New Jersey 08818.

☐ Camera equipment. Porter's Camera Stores. Save up to 35% on equipment, cameras. Free catalog.

Porter's Camera Stores, Box 628, Cedar Falls, Iowa 50613. 800-553-2001.

☐ China. Greater New York Trading Co. Save up to 60% on Lenox, Waterford, Wedgwood and just about every other major manufacturer of fine china. Free brochure.

Greater New York Trading Co., 81 Canal St., New York 10002.

Basics:

☐ Whether you are calling a price-quote company or a direct-mail marketer, always know the return policy before you make a commitment—sometimes there is a charge for returned items.

☐ Use a credit card so you have recourse if you need to return an item.

☐ Keep records of your transaction by noting the date the order was placed and the name of the order-taker.

☐ Save your receipts.

☐ If you ask for a price quote through the mail, it will help to send a business-sized, self-addressed, stamped envelope to speed the response.

Armchair shopping pays off

Not only do you get great convenience by checking with price-quote firms and ordering through direct-mail catalogs, but you get big savings. Sometimes those calls are free with the 800 number, and with high-ticket items or quantity purchases, shipping charges may be waived.

Source: Sue Goldstein, author of *Great Buys by Mail (And Phone!)*, Penguin Books, New York.

How to care for leather clothes

Leather and suede garments need the same careful treatment as furs. Otherwise, you may lose them.

☐ Buy leather garments a little bigger than you need, because they can never be enlarged. This is particularly important in women's trousers.

☐ Be aware that leather and suede may shrink in cleaning.

☐ Avoid wearing your leather garment in the rain. If the garment does become wet, dry it away from heat.

☐ Use a dry sponge on leather occasionally to remove the surface dust.

☐ Wear a scarf inside your neck to prevent oil stains from your skin.

☐ Don't store the garment in a plastic bag. Put dust covers over the shoulders.

☐ Never put perfume on a suede or leather garment. Even putting it on the lining is risky.

☐ Don't pin jewelry or flowers on leather garments. Pinholes do not come out.

☐ Store leathers in a cool spot.

Source: Ralph Sherman, president of Leathercraft Process, New York.

What dry cleaners don't tell you

The dry-cleaning process is not mysterious but it is highly technical. After marking and sorting your clothes on the basis of color and material type, the cleaner puts them into a dry-cleaning machine. This operates like a washing machine except that it uses special solvents instead of water. After the clothes have gone through the dryer, the operator removes stains from them.

A good dry cleaner will use just the right chemical to remove a stain without damaging the fabric. Pressing correctly is next—also a matter of skill. With some fabrics, the garment is put on a form and steamed from the inside to preserve the finish. After pressing, the clothing is bagged.

What to look for:

☐ Suits should be put on shoulder shapers.

☐ Fancy dresses and gowns should be on torso dummies.

☐ Blouses and shirts should be stuffed with tissue paper at the shoulders.

☐ Except for pants and plain skirts, each piece should be bagged separately.

Taking precautions:

☐ Examine your clothes before leaving them with the cleaner. Point out stains and ask whether or not you can expect their removal. For best results, tell the cleaner what caused the stain.

☐ Don't try to remove stains yourself. You may only make them worse. Bring stained clothing to the cleaner as soon as possible. Old stains are harder to remove.

☐ Bring in together all parts of a suit to be cleaned. Colors may undergo subtle change in the dry-cleaning process.

☐ Check all pockets and remove everything. A pen left in a pocket can ruin the garment.

☐ Read care labels carefully. Many clothes cannot be dry-cleaned at all. Do not dry-clean clothing with printed lettering or with rubber, nylon or plastic parts. If in doubt, ask your dry cleaner.

☐ Make sure your dry cleaner is insured if you intend to store a large amount of clothing during the winter or summer months.

☐ Don't wash clothes and then bring them to the cleaner's for pressing. The saving is minimal.

☐ Ask if the dry cleaner will make minor repairs as part of the cleaning cost. Many cleaners offer such service free.

☐ Don't request same-day service unless absolutely necessary. Rushed cleaners do a sloppy job.

☐ French cleaning means special handling for a fragile garment. The term used to be applied to all dry cleaning, since the process originated in France. Now it indicates shorter dry-cleaning cycles or even hand cleaning. *Best:* Alert your dry cleaner to the term "French cleaning" on the label.

35 mm SLR camera basics

The 35 mm single-lens reflex (SLR) camera is the most versatile, all-around-useful photo tool ever invented. You can fit virtually any lens to the camera body and through its unique viewing/focusing system, see the exact picture that's going to appear on the film.

Keep in mind that although you may be buying a camera at the moment, you are investing in a system down the line. Try to anticipate your photographic growth, and consider the overall system in making your choice.

☐ Standard features: Self-timers, exposure information in the viewfinder, exposure compensation ("backlight") switches, "dedicated" autoflash, optional autowinders, autofocus (AF), zoom lens.

☐ More exotic features: Switchable spot or averaging metering systems, super-high shutter speeds and multiple exposure capability.

☐ Shutter speeds in excess of $1/1000$ second are of dubious value at best... virtually unnecessary and notoriously inaccurate.

☐ A built-in autowinder saves bulk and weight—if you really want that feature.

☐ Multiple exposure is a function that will go unused by most photographers.

Available auto exposure (AE) systems include:

☐ Aperture-priority auto exposure (a-p): You set the aperture (f-stop) and the camera sets the shutter speed. (This is the easiest to manufacture.)

☐ Shutter-priority (s-p) auto exposure: You set the shutter speed and the camera sets the f-stop. (Most photographers feel this is the better system.)

☐ Programmed (prog.) auto exposure. The camera sets an "optimum" combination of speed and f-stop.

☐ Multi-programmed auto exposure. It's designed to circumvent the problems of a general-purpose program. Consists of two programs...one favoring fast shutter speeds for stopping motion, the other favoring small f-stops for increased depth of field—with or without a "normal" program. (Multi-programming begins to defeat the goal of simplicity, but can certainly be of use.)

☐ Through-the-lens autoflash (TTL flash): Reads light off the film plane and shuts off the flash at just the right instant. This excellent feature greatly simplifies all flash photography.

Hot weather hazards to camera gear

Humidity is the summer photographer's nemesis. Here are some defensive maneuvers:

☐ Don't open new film until you are ready to load and shoot. (It is packed in low-humidity conditions in sealed packets.)

☐ Have exposed film processed as soon as possible. Don't leave it in the camera for long periods—it may stick.

☐ Use slow advance and rewind to avoid moisture static.

☐ Keep equipment dry with towels or warm (not hot) air from a hair dryer.

☐ Store film and gear with silica gel to absorb excess moisture. (Cans of silica gel have an indicator that turns pink when the gel is damp. They can be reused after drying in the oven until the indicator is blue.)

Source: *Modern Photography*, New York.

Protecting your eyes from the sun

No matter how much you pay for your nonprescription sunglasses, there is no guarantee that the lenses will adequately protect your eyes.

Biggest traps: Lenses that do not filter out 100% of all ultraviolet radiation (UV-A and UV-B), which can damage retinas permanently…lenses that are not optically correct—this can blur vision or cause headaches…buying lenses with tints other than gray, green or brown (other colors can distort visual images)…wearing nonprescription sunglasses if you regularly wear prescription glasses.

Your optician, optometrist or ophthalmologist can easily confirm the optical quality of your sunglass lenses. If there is a problem but you prefer the frames for fashion reasons, have the optician replace the lenses.

Many people only buy "cheap" sunglasses because they keep losing them. If you buy good sunglasses, you will be more responsible with them.

Source: Melvin Schrier, OD, 539 Park Ave., New York 10021.

Picking the right running shoes

Running shoes do not need to be broken in. They should feel good the moment you try them on. Look for:

☐ A heel counter that holds your heel in place and keeps it from rolling in and out.

☐ Flexibility in the forefoot area so the shoe bends easily with your foot. (If the shoe is stiff, your leg and foot muscles will have to work too hard.)

☐ An arch support to keep the foot stable and minimize rolling inside.

☐ A fairly wide base for stability and balance. The bottom of the heel, for example, should be as wide as the top of the shoe.

☐ Cushioning that compresses easily. (Several different materials are used now.) The midsole area absorbs the most shock and should have the greatest amount of padding. However, the heel (which, particularly for women, should be three-quarters of an inch higher than the sole) needs padding, too. Too much causes fatigue, and too little causes bruising.

☐ Start with the manufacturers' least costly shoes first. Try them on. Then keep trying up the price range until you find the one that feels best. Try on running shoes with the same kind of thick socks you will be wearing with them.

☐ Adequate toe room (at least one-half inch of clearance). Running shoes, particularly in women's sizes, run small, and women often need a half-size or whole-size larger running shoe than street shoe.

Source: Gary Muhrcke, proprietor of the Super Runner's Shop, New York.

How to buy ski boots

First rule: If a boot is not comfortable in the store, it will be worse on the slopes.

☐ Toes should be able to wiggle while the heel, instep and ball of the foot are effectively, but not painfully, immobilized.

☐ Buy in a shop with an experienced shop technician who can expand the shell and modify the footbed and heel wedge.

☐ Check forward flex. When you bend your foot, you should feel no pressure points on your shin or upper ankle.

☐ Look for a high boot with a soft forward flex. Low, stiff boots concentrate loads just above the ankle, which can be painful for the occasional skier.

How to buy the right bike

For city use, make sure the bike has:

☐ Fenders to keep yourself clean. A rack on the back for a newspaper or side racks for your briefcase.

☐ Rubber pedals. (They are less durable than steel, but preserve your leather soles.)

☐ A topnotch lock. (The U-bolt models by Kryptonite and Citadel are among the best ones.)

☐ Touring bikes are right for most people. They have a longer wheel base for a "Cadillac" ride.

☐ With racing bikes, you feel the road more, but you get better handling and efficiency.

☐ Consider a Japanese brand. A European bike of equivalent quality will cost at least 20% more. (Although there are 30 different Japanese makes, they're all produced by one of two corporate families, so they're about the same.)

☐ For more comfort, look for new anatomically designed saddles. These seats, made of leather with foam padding, feature two ridges to support the pelvic bones, with a valley in between to avoid pinching.

☐ Buy a low-impact, plastic shell helmet. In a typical biking accident, this will protect the head better than a high-impact motorcycle helmet.

☐ Padded bike gloves make good shock absorbers. Sheepskin bike shorts provide added comfort. Bike jerseys with rear pockets will keep your keys from digging into your leg with each push of the pedal.

☐ Female bike riders should point the seat slightly downwards to avoid irritating the genital area. Men should point the seat upward, to avoid problems such as irritation of the urinary tract and injury to the testes.

☐ Sizing up a new bike. Straddle the frame with your feet flat on the floor. There should be an inch of clearance between your crotch and the top tube. *If you can't find an exact fit:* Buy the next smaller size, then adjust seat and handlebar height. A frame that's too big can't be adjusted.

Sources: Charles McCorkell, owner, Bicycle Habitat, New York; *Physicians and Sports Medicine* and *How to Select and Use Outdoor Equipment,* HP Books, Tucson, AZ.

Best family camping tents

☐ Allow about 25 square feet of floor space for each adult and half that for each child. *For a family of four:* At least 80 square feet.

☐ *Best:* An umbrella tent. It folds up neatly to fit into a car trunk. And it weighs only 24–40 pounds. *Best material:* Nylon.

☐ Make sure tent provides good cross-ventilation. Look for openings with sturdy mesh to keep out insects, windows that close during a storm.

☐ Seams should be double-stitched with 8–10 stitches per inch. Look for lap-felled construction (the material folded back on itself for extra strength and waterproofing). Good tents have extra stitching at points of stress.

☐ Before taking the tent on a trip, set it up in the yard and douse it with a hose. Check for leaks (particularly at the seams).

Choosing a sleeping bag: Down vs. polyester

Although waterfowl down still offers the best warmth-to-weight performance as padding, the newer, lightweight, polyester-filled bags are preferred by many campers.

Take into consideration that:

☐ Down is worthless when wet. It takes hours to dry and must be refluffed before reuse.

☐ Polyester keeps two thirds of its insulating capacity when wet. It absorbs very little moisture, and dries much faster.

☐ Down bags must be dry-cleaned.

☐ Polyester bags are machine-washable.

☐ Down is a magnet for dust, the real culprit for those who think they are allergic to down.

☐ Polyester is nonallergenic and doesn't collect dust.

☐ Down is much more expensive. Most polyester-filled bags cost about half as much.

The best board games

☐ *Trivial Pursuit.* Still "the" game for trivia buffs, despite the 100-plus copycat games now on the market. It's easy to learn and can be played by almost any number of people. Supplements to the original 6,000 questions are introduced periodically, to keep the game lively and fresh.

☐ *Scrabble.* The ultimate word game. Scrabble (or "Scrabble Brand Cross-word Puzzles," as it is officially known) is a subtly complex game that rewards both knowledge of words and strategic thought. Like many other board-game classics, it has engendered clubs and tournaments and even a newsletter. Computer and video games are also available for kids. It's also available in a more congenial *Duplicate Scrabble* version.

☐ *Diplomacy.* Players make and break treaties in an attempt to conquer Europe on the eve of World War I.

☐ *Clue.* The well-known murder-mystery game.

☐ *Boggle Master.* A more challenging version of the original *Boggle.* This is the best word game for large groups. Whoever comes up with the greatest number of words wins.

☐ *Civilization.* Each player tries to forge a primitive nomadic tribe into the most advanced civilization on earth. Along the way, decisions concerning philosophy, science and other hallmarks of civilization make the difference between success and failure. Requires six or seven players—and up to ten hours. *Best idea:* Start at noontime on a rainy Saturday and play all day.

☐ *Yahtzee.* A classic game of knowing when to stop trying to improve your score.

☐ *Cosmic Encounter.* Fast-paced, funny game suitable for family play. Games seldom last more than 90 minutes.

☐ *Blockhead.* One of the few games that can be played almost equally well by adults and children. Tests dexterity, coordination and judgment.

☐ *Shogi.* Unlike chess, draws are virtually impossible. There is also a handicap system that allows experienced players and novices to play exciting games with one another.

☐ *Sherlock Holmes, Consulting Detective.* Really a board game without a board—there's no dice-rolling and no tokens to move about.

☐ *Risk.* A somewhat long but very engrossing game of world conquest, one country at a time.

Source: Burt Hochberg, senior editor, *Games,* New York.

Choosing a long-distance telephone service

Guidelines to help make the decision easier:

☐ Choose a service that offers the cheapest rates for your calling pattern. (Analyze your last year's telephone bills to see where you called, when you called and how long you talked to each location.) If you are a heavy long-distance phoner, a company's minimum monthly charge won't hurt you. If you make few long-distance calls, however, the minimum charge might be more than your average telephone bill.

☐ Some companies also have minimum monthly usage requirements and/or volume discounts. Again, choose according to your needs. If you make only a few short calls a month you'll be hard pressed to justify the minimum. If you have high long-distance bills, a volume discount may offer big savings.

☐ Consider whether a company charges by distance or according to its service abilities in the areas you call most frequently. If you tend to call distant or hard-to-reach places, a "cheap" service with fewer connections may end up costing you more.

☐ Rounding off the number of minutes per call can add as much as 10% to your phone bill, especially if you make a lot of shorter calls. Check to see if the company you are considering rounds to the minute or to the tenth of a minute.

☐ Test each long-distance carrier that you consider for line clarity and ease of connection. There is still a big difference among services.

Source: Robert Krughoff, author of *The Complete Guide to Lower Phone Costs*, Consumers' Checkbook, Washington, DC.

Testing your water

If you have your own water from a well or other source, you should check its purity. The old-fashioned tests for biological impurities are not enough.

☐ The basic tests for natural contaminants and for trihalomethanes are a first priority.

☐ The test for trihalomethanes will also pick up common industrial pollutants such as benzine.

☐ If you have a shallow well in a heavily agricultural area, consider tests for pesticides.

☐ If you buy a new house that was recently treated for termites and it has a well, you should test the water for traces of chlordane.

☐ If untreated sewage is a problem in your area, order tests for biological pollutants.

☐ If you are near an industrial complex, you might want to check out chemical waste products in your water.

☐ If the first analysis shows nothing to be alarmed about, wait a year and test again. If the results are the same, you can rest easy for another ten years unless, of course, the environment of the house changes radically.

Taking delivery

☐ Before accepting your car from the dealer, allow him enough time to "prepare" the car. Before you buy, find out what the dealer's preparation includes. Engine tune-up? Emission checks? Installation of optional equipment and a test drive? Some automobile dealers charge extra for every step of the preparation.

☐ Inspect the car yourself. Check paint and body moldings. Examine the car in daylight. Look for imperfections and mismatched colors. The car may have been damaged in transit and repainted.

☐ Compare the list of options on your bill of sale with those actually on the car. Be sure they are the options you ordered and not inferior substitutes.

☐ Examine doors, latches and windows to see that they are operating properly. Inspect tires for cuts and bulges. Look at the interior finish. Test the heater, the radio and the air conditioner.

☐ During the first week of ownership, test drive the car under as many conditions as possible. If the car does not perform satisfactorily, then you will have a better chance of getting the car dealer to make adjustments than if you wait a month or two before complaining.

Ways to cut the cost of moving

☐ Schedule the move between October and May, or around the middle of the month, the moving companies' slack periods. Better and faster service can save as much as 10%–15% of cost.

☐ Reduce poundage involved in the move by selling or giving away unneeded items. (Give to charity and keep receipts for later tax deductions).

☐ Collect refunds due from local utilities before leaving.

☐ Arrive at the new location before the van does to avoid charge for waiting time.

☐ Have enough money to pay the exact amount of the estimate plus 10%. That's the maximum customers can be required to pay before goods will be released. Payment must be made in cash, or in a certified or traveler's check. A personal check may not be accepted. Get a receipt.

☐ Useful Interstate Commerce Commission publications include: *Household Guides to Accurate Weights; Arranging for Transportation of Small Shipments; People on the Move;* and *Lost or Damaged Household Goods.*

Source: *How to Move Your Family Successfully,* HP Books, Tucson.

How to complain effectively

Basic rule when dealing with defective merchandise:

Save receipts, warranties and all other papers. Then:

☐ Have your facts straight before you act. Be clear about dates, prices, payments and the exact nature of the problem.

☐ Meet with the salesperson or store manager. Describe the problem. Give him copies of the relevant documents. Then ask for a replacement or other compensation. Be polite but firm.

☐ Be specific about what you want done—repair, replacement or refund.

☐ In response to whatever excuse the merchant uses, repeat your demand like a broken record.

☐ Give reasonable deadlines for action you expect to be taken. (A week for store personnel to look into a problem, for example.) Deadlines move the action along.

☐ Write to the manager, going over the points made in the conversation. Include in the letter copies of the sales slips as well as a statement of intention to refer the matter to the Better Business Bureau, a consumer agency or the manager's superior.

☐ Send copies of receipts. Keep the originals for your records. File copies of all correspondence and notes (with dates) on any telephone dealings. Those records may be the pivotal factor if negotiations are prolonged or you must take your complaint elsewhere.

☐ Be businesslike in your attitude and make it clear you expect a businesslike response.

☐ Find out where you can go if the seller fails to make good, and indicate your intention to follow through. Government agencies, such as a state attorney general's office, may need the very kind of evidence that your case provides to move against chronic offenders. Licensing boards or regulatory bodies are good bets for complaints against banks, insurance companies or professionals.

☐ If that fails, write directly to the president of the company, *not* the customer-relations department. Manufacturers of products are listed in the *Thomas Registry.* Names of executives and addresses of companies are in *Standard & Poor's Register of Corporations.* You can find both these books at the public library.

☐ Recount the facts and the demand for compensation. Include copies of paperwork. Make sure to send a carbon to the store's local manager.

☐ As a last resort, call a consumer agency. State consumer offices are generally in the attorney general's office. There are 140 Better Business Bureaus in the country and more than 100 consumer hotlines.

Additional recourse:

☐ Consumer action centers sponsored by local newspapers and radio and television stations often get swift results.

☐ Small claims court. If you can put a monetary value on your loss, you may get a judgment by suing in small claims court. Collecting can be a problem (you must take the initiative yourself), but the law is on your side and the psychological benefits are enormous.

☐ Trade associations can be effective with their member organizations but not with outside companies.

Source: Nancy Kramer, co-author with Stephen A. Newman of *Getting What You Deserve: A Handbook for the Assertive Consumer,* Doubleday, New York.

How to change your mind after buying from door-to-door salespeople

Impulse buys made from door-to-door salespeople or at houseware parties need not be binding. Under Federal

Trade Commission rules, you have three business days to reconsider at-home purchases of $25 or more.

What to do:

☐ When you buy something from a door-to-door salesperson, always ask for two copies of a dated cancellation form that shows the date of sale and a dated contract with the seller's name and address. The contract should specify your right to cancel.

☐ If you wish to cancel, sign and date one copy of the cancellation form and keep the second copy. Send the cancellation to the company by registered mail (return receipt requested).

☐ You can expect the seller to act within ten days. *Their obligations:* To return any signed papers, down payment and trade-in. To arrange for pickup or shipping of any goods. (Sellers pay shipping.)

☐ You must make the merchandise available for pickup. If no pickup is made within 20 days of your dated cancellation notice, the goods are yours.

☐ If you agree to ship the goods back and then fail to do so, or if you fail to make the goods available for pickup, you may be held to the original contract.

☐ Be aware that the same rules apply at a hotel, restaurant or any other location off the seller's normal business premises. They do not apply to sales by mail or phone, or sales of real estate, insurance, securities or emergency home repairs.

Protect yourself against hospital billing errors

According to the New York Life Insurance Company, which has been auditing hospital bills for the past three years, the average hospital bill contains $600 worth of erroneous charges.

Typical mistake: Because of a clerical error, a $100 electrocardiogram is entered onto your bill as a $1,000 charge. Since you may not know the typical cost of an EKG, the error goes undetected.

Major mistakes:

☐ Respiratory therapy. Equipment, such as oxygen tanks and breathing masks, isn't credited when it's discontinued.

Sometimes it's not even removed promptly from the room.

☐ Pharmacy charges. Credit isn't given for drugs that were returned, or unused drugs are not returned.

☐ Lab tests. Cancellations of tests aren't noted.

☐ Central supply items. Hospital staff or nurses may run out of something and borrow it from another patient. They intend to give credit or return the item, but often they don't get around to it.

What to do:

☐ Keep track of the most basic things, such as how many times your blood was drawn. *Suggestion:* If you're able, jot down what happens daily. *Note:* If the patient is too sick to keep track of services rendered, a family member should try to keep track of the charges.

☐ Ask questions. Ask the doctor to be specific about tests. If he orders X rays, ask him what type of X rays. If he doesn't answer the question to your satisfaction, ask the nurse. The newer generation of doctors is more willing to involve the patient in his own care.

☐ Insist on an itemized bill, not just a summary of charges.

☐ Check room and board charges. Count the days you were in the hospital and in what kind of room. Are you being charged for a private room, even though you were in a semiprivate? Some hospitals have different semiprivate rates for two-bed and four-bed rooms. Check your rate.

☐ Review the charges for TV rental and phone.

☐ Be equally careful with doctor bills. Often these bills are made out by the doctor's assistant, who may not be sure of what was done. *Most common errors:* Charges for services in the doctor's office, such as a chest X ray or an injection, that weren't actually performed. Charges for routine hospital physician visits on days that the doctor was not in attendance.

Source: Janice Spillane, manager of cost containment in the group insurance department of New York Life Insurance Co., New York.

How to get the most for your medical dollar

While it's no surprise that Americans spend too much on medical care, few consumers are aware of just how much money they're wasting on diagnostic tests, drugs, doctor's visits, etc. Biggest areas of overspending:

Doctors' fees

Patients often forget that doctors are businesspeople. While the services they offer are different from those offered by car dealers and real-estate brokers, your goal should be to get the best service for the lowest price.

Every day we negotiate prices with suppliers. The same should be true with those who supply our medical care. Ask questions and negotiate with your physician. The more you ask, the more information you'll receive—and the better decisions you'll make.

If you think you're being overcharged by your doctor for office visits or medical procedures, discuss your concerns with the doctor. Try to get a better price. Don't allow yourself to be steered to an assistant or bookkeeper. The physician is supplying the services, and he/she is responsible for what they cost.

Diagnostic tests

Even the most routine examination often results in the physician suggesting one or more diagnostic tests.

Some tests are useful and necessary—for example, an X ray or MRI scan to check for a broken bone. But 40% are unnecessary. Close to half of the $20 billion a year Americans spend on diagnostic tests is wasted.

Scandal: Many doctors have a financial stake in diagnostic labs, either through direct ownership of the lab or because they may receive a payment for each referral patient.

To protect yourself: Never leave the doctor's office without asking the rationale for the recommended diagnostic test. Find out what the test is intended to find—or to rule out. If you're told that one test might prove inconclusive and that a second test might need to be done, ask your doctor to consider skipping straight to the second test.

Also, make sure you receive a copy of test results directly. Don't let your doctor call you "only if there's trouble." Reviewing test results with your doctor will help ensure that no problems have been overlooked.

Be especially careful if you are hospitalized. When patients check into their rooms, staff doctors often order a new round of diagnostic tests—without first checking to see if these patients have already undergone these tests.

Trap: Hospital patients wind up having to pay for duplicate tests—which can easily cost thousands of dollars.

To avoid duplicate tests, ask your physician to share with the hospital staff the results of all medical tests he/she ordered. And double-check with the hospital physician about what any newly ordered test is supposed to do.

Follow-up office visits

Doctors often suggest a follow-up visit just to check up on a patient's progress —and they often charge the standard fee even if no additional treatment is necessary.

Example: A pediatrician prescribes a drug to treat your child's ear infection, then tells you to bring the child back for an office visit in 10 days. You pay $40 for the first visit and $20 to $30 for the follow-up—even though it consists of nothing more than a 10-second peek in your child's ear. If that's all there is to the follow-up visit, ask your doctor if he/she would be willing to accept a reduced fee. Rather than haggling, many doctors will agree to look in an ear or listen to a set of lungs for $10 or less—perhaps even for free.

Prescription drugs

There are several ways to save money here…

☐ Buy generic drugs. They cost as much as 80% less than brand-name drugs.

Caution: A generic drug may be slightly more or less potent than its brand-name counterpart. If you have a chronic heart condition or another ailment that requires a very precise level of medication in the bloodstream, be sure to ask your doctor if switching medications is safe.

Bottom line: If your doctor insists on a brand name, ask why. If you're not convinced, go generic.

☐ Buy only a two- to three-day supply of drugs. Doctors often prescribe 10 days or more of a particular drug— even though you might have an adverse reaction to the drug after only a day or two. *Result:* You wind up being stuck with a week's worth of a drug you cannot take. Lesson: Don't overbuy.

☐ Inform your doctor of any medical condition that might affect your tolerance to a particular drug—or if you're taking another drug that might interact with the newly prescribed drug. About $2 billion a year is spent on drugs that treat the adverse effects of other drugs.

☐ Comparison-shop. Call several pharmacies, especially those in discount stores. Some offer prescriptions below cost to entice customers into the store. Your doctor might have some ideas on finding the best deals.

Medical specialists

Just because you've used a high-cost specialist in the past doesn't mean you must return in the future.

Examples: If you consult an ear, nose and throat specialist for a difficult sinus problem, there's no need to go back to that specialist for a simple cold or allergy. A general practitioner (GP) can take care of those problems for far less. Women often go to gynecologists for complaints that a GP could easily handle—doubling or even tripling the cost of the office visit.

Bottom line: Pick your doctor on the basis of your problem—see a general practitioner whenever possible. If the GP recommends a specialist, ask why. Doctors occasionally "hand off" patients to specialist colleagues—just to give their friends a little business.

Billing errors

Common mistakes: Being billed for a private room when you actually had roommates…being billed for a circumcision—when you gave birth to a girl. And hospitals routinely charge thousands of dollars under the category of "pharmacy" with no itemization of the drugs for which they're billing you.

Many patients are so intimidated that they blindly pay bills—squandering hundreds or thousands of dollars.

Better: Delay paying the hospital bill until several days after the day you are discharged. When you check out, tell the billing office you'll pay it after you've had a chance to scrutinize the bill. For any charge you don't understand, call the billing department and request an explanation. Be sure to get an itemized list of all charges—and don't pay up until you're satisfied that all charges are accurate.

Source: Charles B. Inlander, president of the People's Medical Society, a consumer advocacy group based in Allentown, Pennsylvania. His most recent book is *Good Operations, Bad Operations,* Viking Books, New York.

Is your home environmentally safe?

☐ Does the neighborhood appear on any government hazards lists? This is not something that the owner of the property is likely to know. The information is available by calling your regional Environmental Protection Agency (EPA) Superfund office. It will tell you whether the EPA has targeted the area for cleanup. In some cases, you must rely on the Freedom of Information Act, which can take six weeks or more. If the EPA is unable to help you, there are several fee-based information groups. They include:

☐☐ Environmental Risk Information and Imaging Service (ERIIS). *Information:* 800-989-0403.

☐☐ Vista Environmental Information Inc. *Information:* 619-450-6100.

☐ How has the property been used during the past 40 or 50 years? Not all hazardous sites are listed in state or federal records. Check with the city's or town's zoning records. Speak with people who have lived there for a long time.

Harmful: Was the property ever used as an auto-repair facility…a pottery, art or photo studio…a dry cleaner…a printer…a farm…or a junkyard? The chemicals used by these businesses may have leached into the ground, raising the chances of health hazards from contaminated soil.

☐ Is the property—or adjoining properties—built on a former landfill? Landfill dirt can contain asbestos and other outlawed substances. Over time, these substances can create harmful gases or contaminate the surrounding land. Check with your state's Solid Waste Management Office or Landfill Office.

☐ Is there, or was there ever, a gas station, chemical plant or factory within one-quarter mile of the property? The underground storage tanks for facilities built in the 1950s and 1960s are prone to leakage. There have been cases in which leaks went undetected for years and gasoline or chemicals permeated the soil of entire neighborhoods. The locations of such facilities will appear on a Fire Insurance Map—available at most public and university libraries, at your fire department, in the databases of ERIIS and Vista, in city or county site records or on the federal government's Leaking Underground Storage Tanks list.

☐ Has a radon screen been performed on the property? Many states require the seller to do a radon test on behalf of the buyer. Your state or regional radon office will tell you if radon is a problem in your area. Home test kits, available in hardware stores, are adequate. Or hire an EPA-certified radon inspector. The EPA will send you a free list of all certified radon inspectors in your state.

Source: Gary T. Deane, EdD, executive director, National Society of Environmental Consultants, 303 W. Cypress St., San Antonio, TX 78212. 800-486-3676.

Instant revenge against obscene phone caller

Forget blowing a whistle into the receiver or slamming down the phone—this only serves to antagonize the pest.

Better: Electronic voice boxes, available with a preprogrammed joke script by comics such as Henny Youngman and Jackie Mason. Hold it up to the phone, press a button and have the last laugh. Available through many novelty mail-order houses.

Home appraisal basics

Retain only an appraiser with formal appraisal education and references… pay an appraiser an hourly rate or a contract price—fees based on a percentage of value, or a contingency fee, are unethical…make sure the appraiser will be willing to defend his/her work in court, if necessary…ask for a formal, written report.

Source: Velma J. Miller, Certified Appraiser of Personal Property in Beaverton, Michigan, writing in *AARP Bulletin*, 3200 E. Carson, Lakewood, California 90712.

Better housecleaning

Establish a halfway house for those items (clothing, books, papers, etc.) that you haven't used in years but can't bear to part with. *How it works:* Pack everything into cartons, marking the boxes with a date two years from now, and store it all away. After two years, review contents.

Source: *365 Ways to Save Time* by time-management consultant Lucy H. Hedrick, Hearst Books, 1350 Avenue of the Americas, New York 10019.

Burglary prevention

Do:

☐ Secure all windows and doors.

☐ Leave drapes open to a normal position.

☐ Engrave your Social Security number on all valuables that can be removed from the house.

☐ Arrange to have the lawn mowed and the newspapers and mail rerouted or stopped when you go on vacation.

☐ Trim shrubbery to eliminate hiding spots for prowlers.

☐ Leave your car lights on until you have opened the garage door.

☐ Have a house key ready when you arrive home.

☐ Instruct family members about these security precautions and procedures.

Don't:

☐ Let the telephone go unanswered or give any inviting information over the phone, such as the fact that you are not at home during the day.

☐ Advertise valuables by making them easily visible through your windows.

☐ Leave a key outside the house.

☐ Leave notes on doors.

☐ Leave a porch or front foyer light on. It advertises that you are probably not home.

☐ Leave a ladder outside.

☐ Enter your home if anything appears suspicious. Call the police from a neighbor's telephone. Don't lose your life trying to save items that can be replaced.

Source: Vertronix, manufacturer of electric burglar-detection systems, Larchmont, NY.

Warning signs burglars fear

If a burglar sees warning signs, no matter how outlandish, on your house, he will think twice before breaking in. These signs should be handwritten, in large, clear print, on six-inch by eight-inch cards posted above each door-knob. Don't put them on the street or in your yard where passersby can see them. You don't want to give a burglar a reason to case your place and find out they are not true. Make up your own wording. Just be sure the signs look fresh and new. Some suggestions:

☐ *Danger: Extremely vicious, barkless German Dobermans.* In his nervous frame of mind, a burglar probably isn't going to wonder if there is such a thing. He won't want to take the chance.

☐ *Knock all you want. We don't answer the door.* Most burglars check to see if anyone's home before breaking in. About 95% of those questioned said they'd pass up a house with that sign.

☐ *Carpenter: Please do not enter through this door. My son's three rattle-snakes have gotten out of the cage, and we've closed them off in this room until he returns. Sorry for this inconvenience.*

☐ *Attack dogs trained and sold here.* Again, 95% of those questioned said they'd pass up a house with that sign. Have one engraved, and post it on your front door (so it can't be seen from the street).

☐ Leave extremely large bones and two-foot-wide dog dishes near all entrances. A person up to no good will think a very large dog lives there.

How burglars say they break in

Some burglar-survey results:

☐ 75% were more likely to go through windows than doors. (Sliding glass doors are easier to open than wooden ones.) *Remedy:* Storm windows. No one surveyed would bother with them at all.

☐ 85% cased out a house before hitting it. *Recommended:* If you see a stranger hanging around, call the police.

☐ Only 20% picked locks or tried to pick them. It takes too much skill. There are so many faster ways into a house.

☐ 63% cut the phone lines before entering. *Remedy:* A sign saying that the police will be notified automatically if the phone lines are cut.

☐ 65% said that a large, unfriendly dog would scare them away. *Most frightening:* Dobermans.

☐ 80% looked in garage windows to see if a homeowner's car was there. *Remedy:* Cover your garage windows.

☐ 50% said that neighborhood security guards didn't deter them.

☐ 72% made their entrance from the back.

☐ 56% continued to burglarize if they were already inside when they realized people were home sleeping.

Choosing the right lock

There are two major components to a truly thief-resistant lock system: Strong, tamperproof basic hardware and a key that is impossible to duplicate without your knowledge and permission.

Assuming that the main access door to your house or apartment is structurally sound and hinged on the outside, the standard mechanism for keeping it securely closed is an interlocking deadbolt latch. What makes the latch burglarproof is the outside lock that controls it and the plate that protects the lock.

Best: The 3Ms of locksmithing— Medeco, Miwa and Multilock. All use high-security, state-of-the-art cylinders, and require signature cards and presentation of a registration card before key duplication. All three brands have selected dealers in most areas.

Add-on security devices:

Steel gates for windows near fire escapes or at ground level (gates must be approved by the fire department).

Source: Neal Geffner, vice president, Abbey Locksmiths, New York.

Choosing a locksmith

☐ Go to the locksmiths' shops to size them up.

☐ Make sure the store is devoted exclusively to the locksmith business and isn't just doing locksmithing on the side.

☐ Ask to see the locksmith's license if it's not displayed. There are a lot of unlicensed people doing business illegally.

☐ *Best:* Locksmiths who belong to an association. They are keeping up with the latest developments. Look for a sticker in the window indicating membership in a local or national locksmiths' association.

A secure door

☐ If you're buying a door, buy a metal flush door without panels and get an equally strong frame to match it. *Cost:* About $500. *What makes a good frame:* A hollow metal construction, same as the door.

☐ On a metal door, use a Segal lock on the inside and a Medeco on the outside with a Medeco Bodyguard cylinder guard plate. If it's a tubular lock, get Medeco's D-11. It gives you the option of a key on the inside, and you don't need a guard plate.

☐ If your door has panels on it, put a piece of sheet steel on it. If the panels are glass, replace them with Lexon, an unbreakable plastic.

☐ If you have a wooden door, get what the industry calls a police lock. This is a brace lock with a bar that goes from the lock into the floor about 30 inches away from the base of the door. Also, get a police lock if your door frame is weak. It keeps the door from giving because of the brace in the floor. Even the best regular locks won't protect you if the whole frame gives.

☐ Jimmy bars: Don't bother with them. They're psychological protection only. If you have a metal door, a good lock is sufficient protection. Use a jimmy bar on a metal door only if the door has been damaged through a forcible break-in and is separated from the frame. The bar will straighten out the door and hide some of the light shining through. On a wooden door, a jimmy bar can actually help a burglar by giving him leverage. He can put a crowbar up against it, dig into the wood and break through the door.

☐ If your door opens out instead of in, get a double bar lock—one that extends horizontally on each side. With a door that opens out, the hinges are often exposed on the outside, allowing a burglar to remove the door from its hinges. With a double bar lock, he can't pull the door out.

Source: Sal Schillizzi of All-Over Locksmiths, Inc., New York, is a national safecracking champion.

How to protect yourself against your drinking water

Americans are concerned about their drinking water—and rightly so. Roughly 20% of households have dangerous levels of lead in their tap water…and the once sporadic cases of bacterial and industrial-chemical contamination seem to be occurring with increasing frequency.

Yet despite the real and ever-growing threat, there are effective ways to protect yourself and your family.

What's the biggest threat? By far the biggest threat is lead. Ingestion of lead causes a wide variety of serious health problems. Children who drink lead-tainted water often sustain irreversible brain damage—resulting in reduced IQ scores, short attention spans and other mental problems. (These problems are also common among infants born to mothers who drink lead-tainted water while pregnant.)

In adults, lead poisoning can cause kidney damage, high blood pressure and brittle bones. It can also cause brain damage, although adult neuro-logical tissue is less sensitive to lead than children's neurological tissue.

Exposure of skin to lead-containing water—during a bath or shower, for example—is not considered dangerous.

How does lead get into tap water? It leaches into tap water as the water passes through lead-containing pipes or plumbing fixtures. Homes of all ages can show lead contamination from leaded solder joints or lead-alloy pipes.

Even if your water pipes are made of plastic, however, faucets may still be leaching lead into your drinking water. Reason: Even faucets touted as "lead-free" are allowed by federal law to contain up to 8% lead.

The lead can also come from outside your home. In some parts of the country—including parts of New York City, Boston, Chicago and the Pacific Northwest—the municipal water systems are built with lead-jointed pipes. Even water from private wells can be contaminated with lead.

Bottom line: Any home can have lead in its water.

What can I do to protect myself? Have your tap water tested. Your local water utility may provide you with a free test kit—or may be able to recommend a water-testing agency in your area.

Test kits are also available from…

☐ Suburban Water Testing Labs, 4600 Kutztown Rd., Temple, Pennsylvania 19560. 800-433-6595.

☐ National Testing Laboratories, 6555 Wilson Mills Rd., Cleveland 44143. 800-458-3330.

☐ Clean Water Lead Testing, 291/2 Page Ave., Asheville, North Carolina 28801. 704-251-0518.

A typical test requires two water samples. The first sample is taken early in the morning, when the water has been sitting overnight in your home's pipes. The second is taken after the water has been running for one minute.

Even if the first sample contains dangerous concentrations of lead, the second sample will not in nine out of ten cases.

So I can eliminate the threat of lead simply by purging my water for one minute? Yes, in most cases. But purging your faucet once in the morning—the old advice—is not really valid. Reason: Lead leaches into water much more rapidly than previously thought. If it's been more than a few minutes since the last time you drew water, purge the tap again. To save time and water, keep a gallon pitcher of water from a purged tap in your refrigerator.

Can't I just boil my water? No. Although boiling water generally gets rid of bacteria, it does not eliminate lead or other heavy metals.

What if purging my tap water doesn't get rid of lead? Get a water-purification system…

☐ Cation-exchange filters remove 80% to 90% of lead. Cost: Less than $200.

☐ Reverse-osmosis filters remove 90% to 95% of lead. Cost: $300 to $400.

☐ Distillation units remove nearly 100% of lead. Unlike cation-exchange or reverse-osmosis systems, they do not need periodic filter-element changes. But unlike these other systems, distillation units do require electricity. *Cost:* $200 to $300—plus about $100 a year for electricity.

Caution: Filter makers generally specify a schedule for changing the filter elements on cation-exchange and reverse-osmosis units. But an element that lasts six months in one home might last half as long in a home with higher concentrations of lead.

Self-defense: Until you get a sense of how long the filter element lasts in your home, have your filtered water tested for lead every four months or so. Periodic testing is no longer necessary once you know how long the filter continues to work.

What about bottled water? Bottled water is another safe—and generally less costly—option. We've tested a variety of brands. All have proven safe with respect to lead. Just to be sure you're getting pure water, however, choose bottled spring water over bottled water from a municipal water supply. *Even better:* Distilled water. It's cheaper than spring water and should be absolutely free of lead or any other impurities.

What about germs? Very rarely do water supplies become contaminated with E. coli or other potentially harmful bacteria or parasites. When this happens, local water authorities are generally quick to alert people to the problem—which is easily solved by boiling your tap water or switching to bottled water until the microbes are eliminated.

Bacterial contamination is uncommon in the US because almost all municipal water is now chlorinated. Unfortunately, when chlorinated water comes into contact with dissolved organic matter commonly found in municipal water systems, trihalomethanes (THMs) and related compounds are created.

THMs are suspected of causing cancer of the colon, rectum and bladder. Federal regulations now set the maximum allowable THMs at 100 parts per billion (ppb), and this will likely be reduced to 50 ppb within the next couple of years.

How can I tell if my water contains dangerous levels of THMs? Contact your local water authority. If levels of THMs have approached or exceeded the 50 or 100 ppb level in recent months (or if you're simply worried about the accuracy of the water authority's records), just let water stand in an open container for at least six hours before using. Most of the THMs will dissipate if the water is exposed to air in this fashion.

Another way to get rid of THMs is via a granulated activated carbon (GAC) filter. *Cost:* $80 to $200. GAC filters remove more than 80% to 90% of THMs…and they are equally effective at filtering out most organic industrial pollutants that may have found their way into your tap water.

Caution: GAC filters do not remove lead.

Source: Richard P. Maas, PhD, associate professor of environmental studies, University of North Carolina, Asheville, and director of the university's Environmental Quality Institute, the nation's largest research center on tap water purity.

Best places in your house to hide valuables

Even if you have a safe, you still need a good hiding place for the safe key or combination. It should not be hidden anywhere near the safe. And, if you don't have a safe, you should hide your jewelry and other valuables where they won't be found.

☐ Don't hide things in any piece of furniture with drawers. Drawers are the first place burglars ransack.

☐ Don't hide anything in the bedroom. Thieves tend to be most thorough in checking out bedrooms. Find hiding places in the attic, basement or kitchen. In 90% of burglaries, the kitchen is untouched.

☐ Don't be paranoid. If you have thought up a good location, relax. A burglar can't read your mind.

Try hiding things in the following spots:

☐ Inside the phony wall switches and generic label cans sold by mail-order houses.

☐ In a book, if you have a large book collection. So you don't forget which book you chose, use the title to remind you (for example, *The Golden Treasury of Science Fiction*). Or, buy a hollowed-out book for this purpose.

☐ Inside zippered couch cushions.

☐ In the back of a console TV or stereo speakers (thieves usually steal only receivers, not speakers) or in the type of speakers that look like books.

☐ Under the dirt in a plant. Put non-paper valuables in a plastic bag and bury them.

☐ Under the carpet (for small, flat things).

- ☐ In between stacks of pots in the kitchen, or wrapped up and labeled as food in the refrigerator or freezer.
- ☐ Inside an old, out-of-order appliance in the basement.
- ☐ In a pile of scrap wood beneath the workbench.
- ☐ In the middle of a sack of grass seed.

Source: Linda Cain, author of *How to Hide Your Valuables*, Beehive Communications, Medfield, MA.

What to do if you come home during a burglary

- ☐ If you walk in on a burglar by accident, ask an innocent question. *Example:* "Oh, you're the guy who's supposed to pick up the package, aren't you?" If, at this point, the burglar tries to run away, it's smart to step aside.
- ☐ Resist the temptation to yell or otherwise bring on a confrontation. Go as quickly and quietly as possible to a neighbor's and call the police from there.
- ☐ Avoid walking into your home while a thief is there by leaving a $20 bill conspicuously placed, near the door. If the bill is gone when you return home, someone else may be there. Leave at once and call the police.

Sources: Margaret Kenda, *Crime Prevention for Business Owners*, AMACOM, NY, and *How to Protect Yourself from Crime*, Avon Books, NY.

Home emergencies

Vital information about the house should be known by everyone in the family in case of emergency. *Key items:*
- ☐ The location of the fuse box or circuit-breaker panel.
- ☐ Placement of the main shutoff valves for the water and gas lines.
- ☐ The location of the septic tank or the line to the main sewer.
- ☐ Records of the brands, ages and model numbers of the stove, refrigerator, freezer, dishwasher, furnace, washer and dryer.

Source: *Woman's Day,* New York.

House-sitting checklist

To decide what kind of sitter you need (to live in or to visit regularly, long-term or short-term), determine your requirements. Typically, sitters should:

- ☐ Make the house look lived in, so it won't be burglarized.
- ☐ Care for plants, pets and grounds.
- ☐ Make sure the pipes won't freeze.
- ☐ Guard the house and its possessions against natural disasters.

Where to find help:
- ☐ Some communities have sitting services or employment agencies that can fill the job.
- ☐ *Better:* Someone you know—the teenage child of a friend, a cleaning woman, a retired neighbor.
- ☐ Placement services at colleges.
- ☐ When interviewing, test the resourcefulness and intelligence of the candidate.
- ☐ Check references.
- ☐ If you find a writer looking for a place to stay or a person from the place you are heading to who would like to exchange houses, you might make a deal without any money changing hands.

Before you leave:
- ☐ Walk through every sequence of duties with the sitter.
- ☐ Put all duties in writing.
- ☐ List repair, supply and emergency telephone numbers and your own telephone number or instructions on how to reach you.
- ☐ Make clear that no one is to be admitted to the house or given a key without your prior consent.

What to put in a home improvement contract

Plunging ahead with major improvements or additions to your home without a carefully thought-out contract is asking for trouble.

Here's what to get in writing:
- ☐ Material specifications, including brand names, and a work completion schedule.

☐ All details of the contractor's guarantees, including the expiration dates. Procedures to be followed if materials or workmanship should prove defective. *Trap:* Do not confuse manufacturers' guarantees with the contractor's guarantees of proper installation.

☐ An automatic arbitration clause. This provides that an impartial board will mediate if problems of excessive cost overruns arise.

☐ A clause holding the contractor responsible for negligence on the part of subcontractors. Check with your lawyer for specifics.

☐ A clean-up provision, specifying that all debris be removed.

Getting your money's worth from a home improvement contractor

☐ Consult a lawyer before signing a complex contract.

☐ Don't sign a contract with any blank spaces. Write *void* across them.

☐ Don't sign a work completion certificate without proof that the contractor has paid all subcontractors and suppliers of materials.

☐ Don't pay in full until you are completely satisfied.

☐ Don't pay cash.

When serious problems arise with a home improvement contract

☐ Contrary to popular myth, an attorney is not necessary to modify a contract with a home improvement contractor. Just write on a separate sheet, "Notwithstanding anything else in the contract to the contrary, we agree as follows… (specify the contract modification)." Then, both parties sign the modification.

☐ The contract should have a clause that describes how changes will be made. Typically, all changes above $100 must be agreed to in writing by both parties to the contract.

☐ If an unforeseen problem crops up (for example, subsurface boulders obstruct the laying of a new foundation), or if the contractor honestly underestimates his costs, renegotiate terms. If

you try to hold a contractor to unreasonable terms, he will cut corners, stall or walk off the job.

☐ It's possible to insert a clause saying what damages you will pay if you cancel a project before work begins. But once work does begin, you should see it through to completion. Courts favor contractors in cases where homeowners want to break off a project halfway through.

Protecting yourself in home improvement contracts

Improving a home has become more attractive than buying a new one for many people.

The key to protecting yourself when hiring a contractor for a major alteration is thoughtful contract negotiation. Even contractors with good reputations sometimes get in over their heads.

☐ Always do your own financing. Terms of lenders working with contractors are usually stiff. Often they give the lender a second mortgage on your house—sometimes without your realizing it. That can leave you without leverage to force correction of bad workmanship.

☐ The contractor should show you the document from his insurance company covering workers' compensation. Standard homeowners' policies do not cover workers (except, in some states, an occasional baby sitter).

☐ Fix responsibility for repairing wind, rain or fire damage, as well as possible vandalism at worksite.

☐ Include a payment schedule in the contract. Typically, a contractor gets 10% of the negotiated fee upon signing a contract, then partial payments at completion of each stage of succeeding work. You should withhold any payment until contractor actually begins work. Then hold down succeeding payments as much as possible, so that contractor does not earn his profit until his work is completed.

☐ Make sure the final payment is contingent upon approval of the work by municipal inspectors.

☐ Make the contractor responsible for abiding by local building codes. If you assume this responsibility, make the contract contingent on your ability to get all necessary building permits.

Be specific about what work you want done, how and with what materials:

☐ Don't settle for normal contract language about the project's being done in "a workmanlike manner," because homeowners' standards for work they want done is often higher than common trade practice.

☐ To avoid misunderstandings, refer in the contract to architect's drawings, where possible, and actual specifications.

☐ Include a schedule against which to measure work's progress. *Use calendar dates:* For example, foundation and framing to be completed by March 1; roughing-in by April 1; sheetrock by May 1; woodwork and finish work by June 1.

☐ Push for a penalty clause if the work is completed unreasonably late. For example, all work to be completed by June 1. If, however, work is not completed by June 1, the contractor will pay the homeowner $100 a day thereafter.

When you need an attorney for a home improvement contract

Consider an attorney when:

☐ The job is very complicated or expensive.

☐ Modifications to an existing house will require a structure to be open to the weather for an extended period.

☐ The nature of the property (swampy, rocky) makes unforeseen difficulties likely.

☐ A thorough check on the contractor's references is impossible.

Source: Birger M. Sween, attorney, Hackensack, NJ.

Cost-cutting steps for construction work

☐ Set up a separate bank account for control of expenditures. This also provides a record of expenses to offset future capital gains.

☐ Check preliminary drawings against all deed requirements. Also check with government authorities that must issue any permits.

☐ Be sure that utilities are available at the site and are adequate for your needs.

☐ Budget for surveys, professional fees, permits, financing costs, bonds and insurance. When possible, include these costs in your long-term loan.

☐ Obtain at least three bids for every area of the job—carpentry, plumbing, etc. *Best:* Bid and build when others aren't doing so.

☐ Once bids are accepted, never pay in advance.

☐ Be sure no outdated drawings or specifications are left on the job site.

☐ Have the work checked regularly by a knowledgeable person other than the contractor.

☐ Before making final payment to a contractor, be certain all corrections of completed work are made. Set a date for a one-year-after guaranteed inspection.

Source: Werner R. Hashagen, author of *How to Get It Built Better—Faster—For Less*, La Jolla, CA.

The best way to schedule a home remodeling

☐ Complete as much work as possible in summer. At that time, you can send children to camp or to visit relatives. Workers can leave bulky supplies and equipment outside. Don't hold off until winter in the expectation that it will cost less because it's off-season. Interior renovation goes on all year long. And prices seem to go only up.

☐ Get a couple of rooms finished, clean and livable quickly. The best first choice are children's rooms. Children are very adaptable, but they do best when they know where their clothes and toys are.

☐ Keep a spot clear for the children to play in and get out from underfoot while the rest of the work goes on. If the renovation is easy on the children, the parents will have it easier, too.

☐ Make sure supplies and workers are ready at the same time. This is especially important when doing the kitchen. If the job is well coordinated, you will be without a functioning kitchen for only two weeks.

☐ Order kitchen cabinets well ahead. If they are custom-built, plan a six-to-eight-week leadtime.

☐ Don't tear out wiring and plumbing until you know the cabinets are on the way.

☐ Keep the place relatively clean. Sweep up every evening, even if the workers are coming back the next day to make a new mess. You will feel better.

☐ When bedrooms are being redone, move all your clothes and belongings out. Even if you put your things in drawers, the plaster dust will infiltrate.

☐ Every week or so, invite friends over. If there is no place to sit, spread a table-cloth on the floor and have a picnic. If there is no kitchen, serve take-out food.

Living through a home renovation

Remodeling has become even more important recently because of high purchase prices and mortgage interest rates and the growing trend toward restoring old homes nearer to city centers.

Too many people have an idealized notion of what a renovation entails. To minimize frustration and disappointment:

☐ Budget realistically. Renovations tend to cost more than you expect. You may find that you are paying much more than your neighbor paid to remodel just two years ago. Add 20% to the most conservative estimate.

☐ Assume that everything that can go wrong will.

☐ Be ready to deal with more disruption to family members' lives than you can possibly imagine. Renovating, especially if several rooms are involved, is very messy. And there is no way to make it neat.

☐ Use a professional you can communicate with and trust to get the job done in a reasonable period. This could be an architect, architect-builder, builder-designer or designer-contractor. The most important qualification is rapport with you. The problem with some architects is overoptimism, which can take the form of not leveling with clients about how time-consuming, costly and messy the project will be.

☐ If you have a competent supervisor, stay away from the house as much as possible.

☐ Be realistic in deciding what to have professionals do and what to do yourself. Almost all the jobs required in a remodeling can be done by an intelligent, reasonably handy amateur. Few are exceptionally difficult. But each task can take an enormous amount of time, in some cases months, especially if you hold down a full-time job.

☐ Use experienced workers for heavy work such as demolition, basic carpentry, wiring, plumbing and masonry, floor scraping and refinishing.

☐ If you want to cut costs by doing some things yourself, stick to wallpapering, painting, wood-stripping, sanding, tiling (vinyl, asbestos, ceramic) and laying parquet-wood floor squares (messy, but not hard).

☐ Find the best skilled workers by asking for names from the previous owner of the house or apartment, neighbors, realtor, bank.

Source: Richard Rosan, president, Real-Estate Board of New York, who has lived through several restorations.

When renovation pays off

Rehabilitating and then renting older buildings in areas undergoing a renaissance can lead to quick profits.

☐ Buy on a block where a third or more of the buildings show some signs of recent renovation or improvement. Don't make the mistake of assuming that one or two efforts, even major ones, indicate a trend.

Signs that an old neighborhood has comeback potential are:

☐ A low crime rate and a declining ratio of low-income families.

☐ Below-market rents because of poor property maintenance. If you improve conditions, you can raise rents.

☐ Avoid areas where rents are cheap because tenants don't want to live there.

☐ Parks, lakes, rivers, colleges, shopping areas.

☐ More owner-occupants than absentee landlords.

☐ Neighborhood organizations that actively promote community interests and activities.

☐ *Also:* Government concern for clean streets, regular trash collection and visible police protection.

☐ Be sure that banks are willing to lend money for purchase and rehabilitation of buildings.

Source: Jerry Davis, author of *Rehabbing for Profit*, McGraw-Hill, New York.

Building a tennis court

There are four types of tennis courts: Clay, Har-Tru (pulverized clay with a gypsum binder), asphalt and cement. Clay and Har-Tru are soft and need daily maintenance. Asphalt and cement are hard courts that require little upkeep.

Here are the major considerations:

☐ Choosing the right court. Soil and rock conditions can dictate the best type for your yard as much as your playing preference. Sandy soil with good drainage makes an ideal base for any kind of court. Heavy clay soil holds an all-weather court easily but requires additional excavation and filling for a soft court. Rocky areas may need blasting to create a proper base for any kind of court.

☐ Construction time. A tennis court needs time to settle, particularly the hard surfaces (asphalt and cement) that might crack if the base were to heave. In the northern part of the country, where winters are severe, the ideal building schedule for hard courts is to excavate in the fall, let the base settle over the winter and finish the surfacing in the late spring or early summer. With soft courts, settling is less of a problem because cracks can be filled in with more clay or Har-Tru. A soft court can be built in six to eight weeks, with three weeks for settling.

☐ Space requirements. Home tennis courts require much more space than commonly believed. While the actual playing area of a court is relatively small (36 by 78 feet), adding the out-of-bounds areas pushes the total required to 60 by 120 feet, about one-sixth of an acre.

☐ Zoning and permits. Property owners must provide an up-to-date survey of their property and be sure that the proposed court fits within the set-back requirements—or get zoning variances if necessary. Contractors obtain the building permits. Many communities require fencing.

☐ Costs. Prices vary considerably from one part of the country to another. Special excavating problems create only one of the price variables. In general, however, a clay court with sprinkler system and fencing is less expensive than a similar Har-Tru court. All-weather courts (asphalt in the East, cement in the West) are the least expensive of all.

☐ Maintenance. Soft courts must be swept and relined daily, sprinkled and rolled periodically and refurbished annually (or more often in climates where they get year-round use). Hard courts must be resurfaced every five to seven years. Many builders offer maintenance-service contracts.

Source: Ray Babij, tennis-court builder, Remsenberg, NY.

Supersavers

☐ Rubber gloves will last longer if you buy them one size larger than you need. Place a cotton ball in each fingertip to protect the gloves from your fingernails.

☐ Cut down on drying time. If you only have a small load of clothes to dry, toss in a dry bath towel to absorb moisture and speed drying.

☐ Your local printer is a great source for scrap paper. Ask if you can have some of the excess paper that is usually thrown out. You'll get paper that has been trimmed to shopping list size, full sheets with printing on one side, etc.

☐ If your cedar chest has lost its cedar smell, rub the inside with very fine sandpaper. Then vacuum to remove the dust. If that's not enough, wipe only the inside lid of the chest with oil of cedar. Lay a protective covering over clothes to protect them from the oil.

☐ Don't waste the last half-inch of bottled salad dressing. Add two teaspoons of lemon juice and shake vigorously. Add a half-cup of fat-free mayonnaise, putting in a little at a time and shaking.

☐ Save money and frustration by keeping track of things that you have lent to friends. In a small notebook, record the item, date borrowed and name of the borrower. Check the notebook every month or two, and give gentle reminders when appropriate.

☐ Save on directory-assistance charges. When you move to a new town, take your old telephone book with you in case you need to call former associates or businesses.

☐ Use area rugs instead of wall-to-wall carpeting. Save on the cost of carpet and installation. And if you move to a new house, you can take the area rug.

Source: Jackie Iglehart, editor, *The Penny Pincher*, Box 809, Kings Park, New York 11754.

How to keep cool without busting your budget

Utility costs continue to rise—so it's more important than ever to keep your air conditioning energy-efficient this summer.

Keys to a cool house and a low electric bill:

☐ Look for an air conditioner with an EER (Energy Efficiency Rating) of at least nine of a possible twelve. Although an efficient unit may cost more, it will save you 3¢–10¢ an hour. Even if you pay an extra $100, you'll get the difference back in as little as two years.

☐ Get the right size. Too small a unit won't cool the room. Too large a unit will cool the room quickly, then go off before removing the humidity, leaving cold clammy air and damp rugs.

☐ Buy an air-conditioner timer. If you will be out all day, set it to switch on an hour before your return.

☐ Keep your air conditioner's temperature control at the lowest comfortable setting. A unit set at 10 won't remove humidity any faster than one set at five.

☐ See if you can remain comfortable at a higher temperature. It costs 25% more to keep a room at 74°F than at 78°F… 39% more to keep it at 72°F. People can generally live with higher temperatures when they are sleeping, since their bodies are throwing off less heat.

☐ Be conscientious about maintenance. Keep the filters and outside fins clean (check them every two weeks). Keep outside vents closed when trying to cool a room (but open when it's cooler outside than inside). Direct the cooled air toward the ceiling (it will naturally sink and circulate). Fill the space between top and bottom window sashes with insulation or foam. Seal doorways with weatherstripping. Close fireplace dampers.

☐ Close blinds and drapes in any room facing south or west, to keep the sun's heat out. Direct sun pours up to 4,350 Btu through a single three-foot by five-foot window every hour—enough to overmatch a room air conditioner. Or, install awnings above windows and doors to reflect the sun.

☐ Install ventilating fans to substitute for air conditioning on all but the most humid days. A fan consumes only 1¢–3¢ worth of energy per hour. An air conditioner swallows 8¢ an hour—and up. The most effective fans have retractable panels that seal the window. They work best when they exhaust hot air through west-facing windows while drawing in cooler air from an open window on the east side of the house.

☐ Make sure you have adequate attic insulation. It keeps summer heat out as well as keeping winter heat in.

Source: Robert Peterson, Con Ed Hotline representative, Conservation Center, New York.

Increasing natural ventilation

Before air conditioning, home builders provided architectural features that promoted natural cooling. *Examples:* High ceilings (heat rises), indoor and outdoor shutters, floor-to-ceiling double-hung windows. For natural ventilation:

☐ Open windows at night to let in cool air.

☐ Close shutters and draw curtains where sun hits the house during the day.

☐ Use the stack effect: Open a window low on the cool side of the house and another high on the hot side. Cool air will flow in on the low side, and hot air will exit on the high side. If possible, open that window from the top. Transoms between rooms serve the same ventilating function.

☐ Install shutters, and curtain liners tightly sealed to window frames. The liner creates a dead-air space, reducing heat entry.

☐ Old-time canvas awnings, let down during the heat of the day, are very efficient. *Bonus:* Shading a room from direct sun prevents fading of furniture and fabrics.

☐ *Key to super-efficient cooling:* A whole-house fan. *Needed:* An electrical source and a large roof ventilation area.

Air-conditioning secrets

Room air conditioners mounted in a window or through the wall are ideal for keeping small, comfortable havens against the worst of summer's hot spells. They can be more economical than central air conditioning because they are flexible—you cool only the rooms you are using. But even a single unit can be expensive.

To keep a room cool with minimum use of the air conditioner:

☐ Limit the use of the air conditioner in the "open vent" setting—it brings in hot outside air that the machine must work hard to keep cooling.

☐ Protect the room from the direct heat of the sun with awnings, drapes or blinds.

☐ Close off rooms that you are air-conditioning.

☐ Turn off unnecessary lights. They add extra heat (fluorescent lights are coolest).

☐ Turn off the unit if you will be out of the room more than 30 minutes.

☐ Service room air conditioners annually to keep them efficient. Replace filters, keep condensers clean and lubricate the moving parts.

☐ Supplement central air conditioning with a room air conditioner in the most-used room.

Source: John D. Constance, licensed engineer specializing in home maintenance, Cliffside Park, NJ.

Using fans to save on air conditioning

Ventilating fans can cool a whole house—or a single room—at a fraction (about 10%) of the cost of air conditioning. The trick is knowing how to use them to move in cooler air and to move hotter air out.

☐ Control the source of the cooler air by manipulating windows. During the day, for example, downstairs windows on the shady northern or eastern side of the house are most likely to provide cool air. All other windows should be closed and shaded from direct sun with blinds and drapes.

☐ At night, shut lower-floor windows for security while upstairs windows provide cool air.

☐ Attic fans are permanent installations above the upper floor. They are powerful enough to cool a whole house. The opening to the outside must be as large as the fan-blade frame in order to handle the air flow properly.

☐ Louvers, bird screening and (particularly) insect screening all reduce the exhaust capacity of a fan.

☐ A doorway or other opening must allow the fan to pull cool air directly up from the rest of the house.

☐ Direct-connected fans are quieter than belt-driven fans.

☐ Some attic fans have thermometers that automatically turn them off and on when the attic temperature reaches a certain degree of heat.

☐ Window fans have adjustable screw-on panels to fit different window sizes. Less powerful than attic fans, they serve more limited spaces.

☐ Box fans are portable and can be moved from room to room to cool smaller areas.

☐ Ventilating fans are rated by the cubic feet per minute (CFM) of air that they can exhaust. For effective cooling, engineers recommend an air-change rate of 20 per hour (the entire volume of air in the area to be cooled is changed 20 times every 60 minutes).

☐ To calculate the required CFM rating for a particular room, calculate its volume in cubic feet. Then multiply this figure by 20/60 ($\frac{1}{3}$). *Example:* A room 20 feet by 15 feet with an eight-foot ceiling contains 2,400 cubic feet of air. This, multiplied by $\frac{1}{3}$, gives a CFM rating of 800 for a proper-size fan.

☐ The CFM rating of an attic fan is done the same way. Total the cubic feet of the rooms and hallways you want cooled before multiplying by $\frac{1}{3}$.

Source: John Constance, licensed engineer specializing in home maintenance, Cliffside Park, NJ.

How to save water

Whether you live in an area plagued by periodic droughts or simply want to save money on rising water bills:

☐ Install flow restricters in your showers and take shorter showers. (A normal showerhead sprays up to eight gallons per minute, so even a short, five-minute shower uses up to 40 gallons.)

☐ Get in the habit of turning off the water while shaving, brushing teeth and washing hands, except when you need to rinse.

☐ Put a weighted plastic container into the toilet tank to cut the normal amount of water used in flushing (approximately six gallons per flush) by as much as half. Some people use bricks to displace water in the tank, but this may damage the tank.

☐ Wash only full loads in your dishwasher and clothes washer. Running these machines half empty is a big water waster.

☐ Fix all leaks. Dripping water, even if slow, can cost you a lot of money over the course of several months.

☐ Use buckets of water to do outside chores like washing the car and cleaning the driveway. If you must use a hose, turn it off between rinsings; don't just let it run.

Home energy savers

After you've insulated your home, here are some smaller steps that can trim added amounts from your heating and electricity bills:

☐ Air-conditioner covers. Outdoor covers not only block drafts, they also protect the machine from weather damage during the winter. Check the caulking around the outside of the machine, too. Indoor covers can be even more effective draft stoppers than outdoor ones. You can make your own from heavy plastic or buy Styrofoam-insulated ones.

☐ Door and window draft guards. Sand-filled fabric tubes effectively prevent uncomfortable drafts from entering around doors and windows. Easy to install and to remove.

☐ Light dimmers. The newest solid-state dimmers consume little energy themselves but allow reduced lighting levels and lower energy consumption. Some dimmers are installed in the wall in place of conventional switches. Others simply plug into existing sockets or are inserted into lamp cords. A dimmer can save you approximately 50% a year on a single light fixture if you dim it halfway.

☐ Air deflectors. Used in homes heated by forced air, these direct air from the vents away from walls and into the room. Depending on the location of your registers, significant savings can result.

☐ Heat reflectors. Reflectors direct radiator heat into the rooms to save energy. Very inexpensive ones can be made by covering a sheet of plywood or foam board with aluminum foil and placing it between the radiator and the wall.

☐ Storm-window kits. You can make your own storm windows with sheets of plastic and tape. Kits are available to install them either inside or outside your existing windows. The cost ranges from as low as 85¢ to $35 per window. Removable rigid plastic storm windows in permanently installed frames are also big energy savers. Some companies will cut them to fit any window at a cost of $4–$5 per square foot. For city dwellers, they also reduce noise levels significantly. Storm windows reduce heat loss by as much as 30%, so an investment in permanent storm windows may pay off in the long run.

☐ Energy audits. Your local utility may offer free home energy audits. For absolutely no cost or obligation, it will inspect your home and suggest ways you can reduce your energy costs. Also, more and more utilities are acting as general contractors in making energy-efficiency changes on houses, ensuring that the work is done properly and on time.

Accurate radon testing

Radon testing isn't conclusive the first time unless the reading is very low—below four picocuries per liter. But if you get a reading higher than that, don't panic. It may be a temporary wave of radon, not a permanent condition. You need at least a year of follow-up testing to get a conclusive picture of high radon content. *Recommended:* If your area is reported to have a high incidence of radon, contact your state environmental protection agency's listing of companies that provide reliable long-term radon testing kits.

Home insulation contract

The best time to negotiate a contract to insulate your home is spring, when contractors are not as busy as in the fall. Your first saving can come on air-conditioning bills. *Biggest saving:* Heat bills next winter.

The contract and estimate should:

☐ Specify exact areas to be insulated.

☐ Specify type and brand of product to be installed in each area (including the number of packages or bags that will be needed).

☐ Give the R-value (resistance to heat loss) of the products, which is the most important measurement.

☐ Break down the total cost into materials, labor, cleanup, service charges and taxes.

☐ Provide written guarantees of product claims, including inflammability, moisture absorption, shrinkage, settling, odor and soundproofing.

☐ Provide an adjusted-cost clause that gives you the savings if less than the estimated amount of materials is needed.

☐ Provide a written guarantee of workmanship, including the contractor's responsibility for any future damage caused by the insulation.

Source: John D. Constance, licensed engineer specializing in home maintenance, Cliffside Park, NJ.

New rules on home insulating

You may be surprised to learn that adequate insulation is still the most effective way to save money on your winter heating bill.

A six- to eight-inch layer of insulation in the attic floor (the easiest place to install insulation) can slash 30%–50% off your fuel bill. Similar savings result from insulation on the attic ceiling. Adding insulation to outside walls, pipes and hot-air ducts will add substantially to your savings, too.

☐ Those inclined to stay with the tried and true can choose among several insulating materials. Cellulose, rock wool, glass fiber, perlite and vermiculite all have withstood the test of time. Their R values (the measure of insulating effectiveness) run 3.8 to 4.2 per inch. (The higher the number, the better the insulating properties. In contrast, urea-formaldehyde foams had a slightly higher R value—about 5.)

☐ Regardless of your choice of materials, your now cheaper-to-heat home will nonetheless suffer from indoor pollution. Energy experts say that the properly insulated house no longer "breathes." *Solution:* An air-to-air heat exchanger, a new appliance that looks like an air conditioner. It's installed in a window or wall. Essentially, before the hot air leaves the house, it's used to heat the cooler, fresher air coming in.

Making certain insulation is well installed

For attics:

☐ A good contractor will provide proper ventilation above the attic insulation to prevent water condensation and moisture damage.

☐ Never apply attic insulation directly to the underside of the roof.

☐ Apply a vapor barrier on the warm side of the insulation.

For side walls:

☐ Holes for blowing in the insulation should be drilled between all studs and above and below every window.

☐ The contractor should drop a weighted string through each hole to check for obstacles in the wall. (Holes should be drilled below an obstacle as well.)

☐ Require a thermograph (heat picture) to check the finished sidewall insulation. X rays do not give an accurate picture of total insulation.

Cleaning your chimney without messing up the house

☐ Clean the chimney at least once a year, and more often if the fireplace or airtight stove is used continuously. If your flue contains a buildup of creosote, a tarlike substance created by fire, more than one quarter of an inch thick, you run the risk of a chimney fire.

☐ Get the right equipment for the job—a special brush the right diameter for your flue and a set of flexible rods to push the brush up and down the chimney.

☐ Contain the falling soot by sealing off the fireplace with sheets of plastic held by duct tape.

☐ Spread plenty of newspaper around to protect rugs and furniture.

☐ Slit the plastic covering to allow the brush access to the chimney. Run the brush up and down the length of the chimney about six times.

☐ If you really want to avoid a mess, hire a professional chimney sweep.

Woodstove safety

Fire, injuries and deaths are rising rapidly with the increased use of woodburning stoves. Faulty installation, poor maintenance and careless use are to blame.

Installation musts:

☐ Have a professional mason check and repair the chimney before you put in a stove.

☐ Place the stove on a fireproof base that extends 18 inches on all sides. There should be 36 inches of clearance space between the stove and combustible walls and ceilings. *Alternative:* Sheet-metal protection for those areas.

☐ Seal off the fireplace where the stove connects to the chimney. Don't use the chimney for other fireplaces.

Maintenance guides:

☐ Check the stove and stovepipe annually for cracks and defects.

☐ Have the chimney professionally cleaned once a year.

☐ Burn only dry, well-seasoned wood. Apple, red oak, sugar maple, beech and ironwood are the most efficient. (Green wood, aged less than six months, causes creosote buildup in the chimney and stove.)

☐ Never throw trash in the stove.

☐ Never use a starter fluid.

☐ Put ashes in a metal container outdoors.

Burning wood more productively

Heating a home safely and efficiently with wood requires more than a stack of logs and a fireplace. The ground rules:

☐ To be cost-effective, one cord (128 cu ft) of wood should cost no more than 150 gallons of fuel oil.

☐ Prices vary widely. Four-foot-long green logs are much cheaper than shorter dry ones. But the latter come ready for the fireplace. (The other must be dried and cut.)

☐ *Best bet:* Buy green wood in late spring or summer. It will dry in six months, in time for winter use.

☐ Harder woods, such as oak, ash and beech, yield more heat. Less efficient are magnolia, cherry, Douglas fir. The least efficient are poplar, spruce, willow.

☐ The most efficient stoves use baffles, long smoke paths and heat exchangers to extract as much heat as possible. They are more expensive than simpler types. But, in the long run, they save money.

☐ Make sure to check local restrictions on furnace types. A wide variety of wood-burning (and multifuel) furnaces are available for central heating systems, but not all are permitted everywhere.

☐ Except for emergency use, fireplaces are mainly for aesthetic value, since they are essentially poor heaters. Homeowners who want the best of both worlds should consider efficiency-improving modifications or combination fireplace-stove units.

Source: *Heating with Wood*, US Department of Energy, Washington, DC.

Keeping street noise out of your home

Noise intrusion is a constant and nagging problem in many buildings because of thin walls and badly insulated floors and ceilings.

How to noise-proof walls:

☐ Hang sound-absorbing materials, such as quilts, decorative rugs, carpets or blankets. *Note:* Cork board and heavy window draperies absorb sound within a room but do not help much with noise from outside.

☐ If you don't want to hang heavy materials directly on your walls, consider a frame that attaches to the wall. Insulation goes on the wall within the frame, and then a fabric is affixed to the frame.

How to noise-proof ceilings:

☐ Apply acoustical tile directly to the ceiling with adhesive for a quick and inexpensive fix.

☐ If you can undertake more extensive work, put in a dropped ceiling of acoustical tile with about six inches of insulation between the new and existing ceiling.

How to noise-proof floors:

☐ Install a thick plush carpet over a dense sponge-rubber padding.

☐ *Key:* The padding must be dense, at least three eighths of an inch thick. Your foot should not press down to the floor when you step on the padding.

Appliances and your electric bill

Do you know how much your appliances cost to run, and which ones cost the most? Heating is the biggest energy expense; other big energy users are the refrigerator, dryer and lights. The figures here are estimates—so use them only as a general guide. Your actual costs will vary based on factors such as:

☐ Your appliance models.

☐ Your appliance usage patterns.

☐ Your home's size and insulation.

☐ The weather.

The figures here are based on 1994 average residential rates (which will vary depending on where you live).

Appliance	Cost
Hair dryer	$.01/5 minutes
Incandescent bulb (100 w)	$.01/hour
Compact fluorescent bulb (27 w)	$.01/4 hours
Portable heater	$.09–.20/hour
Digital clock	$.10–.50/month
Vacuum cleaner	$.09/hour
Cooling	
Window system	$.18–.33/hour
Central AC (3 ton)	$.55/hour
Fan	$.01–.07/hour
Entertainment/Education	
Color TV	$.02–.06/hour
VCR	less than $.01/hour
Radio	less than $.01/hour
Stereo system	$.02/hour
Personal computer	$.01–.02/hour
Kitchen	
Microwave oven	$.15/hour
Range-top burner:	
A. Electric	$.15/hour
B. Gas	$.04/hour

Oven:	
A. Electric	$.16/hour
B. Gas	$.06/hour
Dishwasher:	
A. Hot water/electric	$.37/load
B. Hot water/gas	$.10/load
Refrigerator/Freezer:	
A. Frost-free 16 cu ft	$12–18/month
20 cu ft	$13–22/month
B. Manual defrost	
10 cu ft	$4–8/month
Toaster	$.01/per use
Toaster oven	$.06/hour
Utility Room	
Clothes washer	$.03–.07/load
Clothes dryer:	
A. Electric	$.67/load
B. Gas	$.16/load
Freezer	$16–20/month
Water heater:	
A. Electric	$20–70/month
B. Gas	$7–19/month
Heating	
Furnace:	
A. Smaller home	$16–40/month
B. Larger home	$41–200/month
Electric central heater:	
A. Smaller home	$56–110/month
B. Larger home	$114–400/month

When you need an exterminator and when you don't

Bug problems can usually be solved without an exterminator. *Keys:* Careful prevention techniques, basic supermarket products and apartment-building cooperation.

Insects

Roaches are persistent pests that are the bane of apartment dwellers. The problem is not that roaches are so difficult to kill but that the effort has to be made collectively, by every tenant in a particular building. Roaches cannot be exterminated effectively from an individual apartment. If one apartment has them, they'll quickly spread throughout the building.

Most landlords hire exterminating services that visit during daytime hours when most tenants are at work. They wind up spraying just a few apartments, which is totally ineffective.

Recommended:

☐ Apartment dwellers have to get together, contact their landlord and arrange for all apartments to be exterminated at the same time. If the landlord is uncooperative, the Board of Health should be notified. If you live in a co-op, the co-op board should make arrangements for building extermination. *Best:* A superintendent or member of the building staff should perform regular exterminations, since he can get into apartments at odd hours when the tenants are not home. A professional exterminator should be called only as a back-up, in case of a severe problem in a particular apartment.

☐ Incinerators that no longer burn garbage are a major infestation source in large buildings. Many cities, to cut down on air pollution, have ordered the compacting rather than the burning of garbage. Garbage is still thrown down the old brick chutes, which have been cracked from heat, to be compacted in the basement. Roaches breed in these cracks, fed by the wet garbage that comes down the chute, and travel to tenants' apartments. *Remedy:* Replacement of the brick chutes with smooth metal chutes which don't provide breeding places. *Also:* Compactors must be cleaned at least once a week.

☐ Rout roaches without poisoning your kitchen. Boric acid or crumbled bay leaves will keep your cupboards pest-free. *Another benign repellent:* Chopped cucumbers.

☐ Homeowners do not need regular extermination for roaches. Since a house is a separate unit, a one-time extermination should do the job. Food stores are the major source of roach infestation in private homes. People bring roaches home with the groceries. Check your paper grocery bags for roaches before you store them.

☐ Ants and silverfish can be controlled by the homeowner himself, unless there is a major infestation. Don't call the exterminator for a half-dozen ants or silverfish. Try a store-bought spray first. *Exception:* Carpenter ants and grease-eating ants must be exterminated professionally.

☐ Clover mites come from cutting the grass. They look like little red dots. The mites land on windowsills after the lawn is mowed and then travel into the house. *Remedy:* Spray your grass with miticide before cutting.

☐ Spiders don't require an exterminator. Any aerosol will get rid of them.

☐ Termite control is a major job that needs specialized chemicals and equipment. Call an exterminator.

☐ Bees, wasps and hornets should be dealt with professionally. Their nests must be located and attacked after dusk, when the insects have returned to them. If the nest is not destroyed properly, damage to your home could result. *Also:* Many people are allergic to stings and don't know it until they are stung.

☐ Clothes moths can be eliminated by hanging a no-pest strip in your closet and keeping the door tightly closed.

☐ Flies can be minimized with an aerosol or sticky strip. An exterminator is of no help getting rid of flies. *Best:* Screens on all the windows and doors.

☐ Weevils and meal moths can be prevented by storing cereals, rice and grains in sealed containers. *Also:* Cereals are treated with bromides to repel infestation. The bromides eventually break down. Throw out old cereals.

☐ Wood storage and insects. Firewood kept in the house becomes a refuge and breeding ground for insects. *Risky solution:* Spraying the logs with insecticides. (When the sprayed wood burns, dangerous fumes could be emitted.) *Better:* Stack the wood (under plastic) outside and carry in only the amount needed.

Mice

There is no 100% effective solution for exterminating mice. Try these alternatives:

☐ Trapping is effective unless you have small children or pets.

☐ Poison should be placed behind the stove or refrigerator where children and pets can't get at it.

☐ Glue boards (available in supermarkets) placed along the walls can be very effective. Mice tend to run along the walls due to poor eyesight.

Pesticides and prevention

Many of the residual (long-lasting) sprays have been outlawed because they don't break down and disappear in the environment. The old favorites, DDT and chlordane, are generally no longer permitted. *What to use:*

☐ Baygon, Diazanon and Dursban are general-purpose, toxic organo-phosphates meant for residual use in wet areas. They're recommended for all indoor insects, including roaches.

☐ Drione is a nontoxic silica gel, which dries up the membranes in insects. Recommended for indoor use in dry areas only, it is especially effective on roaches.

☐ Malathion is helpful in gardens, but it should not be used indoors.

☐ Pyrethrin is highly recommended, since it is made from flowers and is nontoxic. It has no residual effect, but is good for on-contact spraying of roaches and other insects. If there is a baby in the house, Pyrethrin is especially useful, since children under three months should never be exposed to toxic chemicals. Don't use it around hay-fever or asthma sufferers.

☐ When buying products in the store, look at the label to determine the percentage of active ingredients. Solutions vary from 5% to 15%. The stronger the solution, the better the results.

☐ Prevention is synonymous with sanitation. If you are not scrupulous about cleanliness, you will be wasting your money on sprays or exterminators.

☐ Moisture is the main attractor of insects. If you live in a moist climate, you must be especially vigilant. Coffee spills, plumbing leaks, fish tanks, pet litter and pet food all attract bugs. Clean up after your pets, and take care of leaks and spills immediately. If puddles tend to collect around your house after it rains, improve the drainage.

☐ Word of mouth is the best way to choose a good exterminator. Don't rely on the *Yellow Pages.*

☐ Contracts for regular service, which many exterminators try to promote, are not recommended for private homes. A one-time extermination should do the trick, but apartment dwellers must exterminate buildingwide on a regular basis.

☐ To remove a bat from your house at night, confine it to a single room, open the window and leave the bat alone. Chances are it will fly right out. Otherwise, during the day when the bat is torpid, flick it into a coffee can or other container. (Use gloves if you are squeamish.) Release it outdoors. Bats are really very valuable. A single brown bat can eat 3,000 mosquitos a night. *Note:* Bats, like other mammals, can carry rabies. If you find a downed bat or you are scratched or bitten by one, call your local animal control agency and keep the animal for testing. However, very few people have contracted rabies directly from bats. *More likely source:* Skunks.

Source: Tom Heffernan, president of the Ozane Exterminating Co., Bayside, NY, and Clifton Meloan, chemist, Kansas State University, writing in *Science.*

Oil vs. water-based paint

☐ Water-based paint (also known as latex or acrylic) has many distinct advantages over oil-based. It dries in less than an hour, has no paintlike smell, doesn't show brush or roller lap marks as openly and makes for an easy soap-and-water cleanup. It also wears longer, is washable and holds color best.

☐ Latex can be used on all interior surfaces including those with existing oil-based layers. *Exception:* When there is a water-soluble substance underneath the oil, such as calamines or sizers. The water in latex softens these substances, which leads to peeling. Enough coats of oil-based paint usually shield underlying water-soluble surfaces from the water in the latex. *Test:* Paint a small area with latex. If there is no peeling within a couple of hours, continue with latex.

☐ Latex exterior paints are ideal for surfaces that have never been painted. *Why:* They allow the surface to breathe. And their flexibility during the freeze-thaw cycle enables them to adhere better to the surface. (If you have latex over an oil-based layer that is holding, continue with water-based.)

☐ Stick with oil-based paint if the exterior surface is already painted with an oil-based paint (alkyd resin). *Reason:* Latex expands and contracts more easily than oil during the freeze-thaw weather cycle. This action may pull off any underlayers of oil-based paint that aren't locked onto the surface.

Source: Neil Janovic, Janovic Plaza, a paint and paper concern founded by his grandfather in 1888, New York.

Painting trouble areas

Often, paint peels in one section of a wall or ceiling. Causes:

☐ A leak making its way through the walls from a plumbing break or an opening to the outside.

☐ The plaster is giving out in that area due to age or wear and tear.

☐ The layers of paint may be so thick that the force of gravity, plus vibrations from outside, make the paint pop and peel in the weakest spots.

How to fix the problem:

☐ If it's a leak, find and correct it first.

☐ Otherwise, remove as much of the existing paint as you can.

☐ Scrape away any loose, damp or crumbling plaster.

☐ Spackle and smooth the area.

☐ Prime and paint it.

For real problem areas:

☐ Spackle, then paste on a thin layer of canvas. Apply it as though it were wallpaper.

☐ Smooth it out so it becomes part of the surface.

☐ Then prime and paint it.

Safe food storage

☐ Yellow bananas can be held at the just-ripe stage in the refrigerator for up to six days. Although the peel might discolor slightly, the fruit retains both its flavor and nutrition. Ripen green bananas at room temperature first. Mashed banana pulp can be frozen.

☐ Nuts in the shell keep at room temperature for only a short time. Put them in a cool, dry place for prolonged storage. Shelled nuts remain fresh for several months when sealed in containers and refrigerated. For storage of up to a year, place either shelled or unshelled nuts in a tightly closed container in the freezer.

Storage times for frozen meats vary significantly. Recommended holding time in months:

☐ Beef roast or steak, 12.

☐ Ground beef, 6.

☐ Lamb, 12.

☐ Pork roasts and chops, 8–12.

☐ Bacon and ham, 1–2.

☐ Veal cutlets and chops, 6.

☐ Veal roasts, 8–10.

☐ Chicken and turkey, 12.

☐ Duck and goose, 6.

☐ Shellfish, not over 6.

☐ Cooked meat and poultry, 1.

Keep an accurate thermometer in your refrigerator or freezer. *Optimal refrigerator temperature:* 40°F for food to be kept more than three or four days. *For the freezer:* 0°F is necessary for long-term storage. *Note:* Some parts of the freezer may be colder than other parts. Use the thermometer to determine which areas are safe for keeping foods long-term.

Freezing leftovers:

☐ Raw egg whites. Freeze them in ice-cube trays.

☐ Hard cheeses. Grate them first.

☐ Soup stock. Divide it into portions.

☐ Stale bread. Turn it into crumbs in the blender.

☐ Pancakes, french toast and waffles. Freeze and reheat in the toaster oven at 375°F.

☐ Whipped cream. Drop into small mounds on a cookie sheet to freeze and then store the mounds in a plastic bag.

☐ Citrus juices. Freeze in an ice-cube tray.

☐ Freezing fish. Make a protective dip by stirring one tablespoonful of unflavored gelatin into ¼ cup lemon juice and 1¾ cups cold water. Heat over a low flame, stirring constantly, until gelatin dissolves and mixture is clear. Cool to room temperature. Dip the fish into this solution and drain. Wrap individual fish pieces in heavy-duty freezer wrap. Then place them in heavy-duty freezer bags. Use within two months.

☐ If you do your own food canning, preserve only enough food to eat within one year. After that time, quality deteriorates.

Sources: Tom Grady and Amy Rood, co-authors, *The Household Handbook*, Meadowbrook Press, Deephaven, MN, and Joan Cone, author of *Fish and Game Cooking*, EPM Publications, McLean, VA.

Secrets of quick cooking

Knowing your way around the kitchen will help you get your meals on the table in minutes. Here are some hints to help you along the way:

☐ To use your food processor more efficiently, first chop all dry ingredients, such as bread crumbs, in the processor, then wet ones, such as onions. This way it will not be necessary to stop in the middle of a recipe to wash the processor bowl.

☐ To make ten-minute rice, cook it like pasta. Place the rice in a large pot of rapidly boiling water for ten minutes, drain and add sauce, oil or butter. No need to cover it, but stir the rice once to ensure that it doesn't sit on the bottom of the pot.

☐ If you make your own salad dressing, mix it in the bottom of your salad bowl. Add salad and toss. You won't have to use extra mixing bowls.

☐ Use a few small chopping boards. They can be carried to the stove or pot with the ingredients—and you won't have to stop and wash boards while working.

☐ To speed up stir-frying, place each of the ingredients on a plate or chopping board in order of use so you'll easily know which ingredient to add next.

☐ To get a quick high- or low-heat response from electric burners when sautéing or stir-frying, keep two burners going—one on high, one on low—and move your pot back and forth.

☐ To help meat marinate quickly, poke holes in it with a skewer or knife. Use high temperatures to brown, broil or stir-fry in order to seal in the juices.

☐ To peel garlic quickly, firmly press the clove with the side of a knife and the paper skin will fall off or peel away easily.

☐ To wash watercress or fresh herbs quickly, immerse the leaves in a bowl of water for several minutes. Lift them out of the bowl. Sand and dirt will be left behind. For quick, easy chopping, cut them with scissors.

Source: Linda Gassenheimer, executive director of Gardner's Market, a chain of gourmet supermarkets in Miami. She is the author of *Dinner in Minutes: Memorable Meals for Busy Cooks*, Chapters Publishing, Ltd., Shelbourne, VT.

Wrapping a package the right way

☐ Seal a sturdy carton with six strips of two-inch-wide plastic tape (not masking or cellophane tape, which tears easily): A strip across the center of top and bottom and across each open edge on flap ends. Don't just go to the ends. Go a few inches around.

☐ Put an address label inside so that if the outside label is lost or defaced, the package can be opened and sent with the second label.

☐ Don't use brown paper or string; they only increase chance of loss if paper tears and label rips off or the string unties and gets caught in a sorting machine.

Things you never thought of doing with plastic bags

Use plastic bags:

☐ As gloves when greasing a cookie sheet, cleaning the oven or changing oil in the car.

☐ To help preserve a plant when you are going away. Spray the leaves with water, then cover the pot with a bag secured at the top with a rubber band.

☐ To protect your camera, film and lenses from moisture.

☐ As storage bags for woolens. Add a few mothballs.

☐ Put meat to be tenderized inside a bag before pounding.

Cleaning jewelry

☐ Gold and platinum. Use a soft brush with a mild, warm water/detergent solution.

☐ Turquoise, ivory, lapis and other porous gems. Mild soap and water only.

☐ Opals. Use barely cool distilled water (they're sensitive to cold).

☐ Pearls. Roll them in a soft cloth moistened with water and soap (not detergent). *To rinse:* Roll them in a cloth dipped in warm water.

☐ Most other gems. Add a tablespoonful of baking soda to a cup of warm water. Swish the jewelry through or rub it with a soft toothbrush. Rinse well.

Source: *Woman's Day*, New York.

Secrets of a great lawn

You don't have to work harder to get a grassier lawn. In fact, you can work less. Here's how:

□ Set the mower blades to a height of 2–2½ inches, and cut the grass only once a week. When the weather gets really hot, every other week is fine. Taller grass means less mowing, stronger and healthier plants that spread faster, more shade to discourage weeds.

□ Let the clippings lie. They will return nutrients to the soil.

□ Water only when there has been no significant rain for three or four weeks. Then give a one-inch soak. (Use a cup under the sprinkler pattern to measure—it takes longer than you think.) Frequent shallow watering keeps roots close to the surface, where they are vulnerable to drought and fungus disease.

□ Use herbicides and insecticides only for specific problems. Routine use weakens the grass and kills earthworms.

□ Sow bare spots with rye grass for a quick fix. Proper reseeding should be done in late August or early September, when the ground is cooler and moister.

□ Apply fertilizer twice a year, but not in the spring. September and November are the right months.

Home remedies for plant pests

□ Red spider mites. Four tablespoons of dishwashing liquid or one-half cake of yellow soap dissolved in one gallon of water. Spray weekly until mites are gone, then monthly.

□ Hardshell scale. One-fourth teaspoon olive oil, two tablespoons baking soda, one teaspoon Dove liquid soap in two gallons of water. Spray or wipe on once a week for three weeks; repeat if necessary.

□ Mold on soil. One tablespoon of vinegar in two quarts of water. Water weekly with solution until mold disappears.

□ Mealybugs. Wipe with cotton swabs dipped in alcohol. Spray larger plants weekly with a solution of one part alcohol to three parts water until bugs no longer hatch.

Source: Decora Interior Plantscapes, Greenwich, CT.

Top garden catalogs

Send for these catalogs for the best in mail-order plants and flowers.

□ *Breck's*, Peoria, IL 61632. 309-689-3850. Dutch tulips, crocus, etc. Free.

□ *Brittingham Plant Farms*, 2538 Old Ocean City Road, Salisbury, MD 21802. 410-749-5153. Twenty-seven varieties of strawberries. Free.

□ *W. Atlee Burpee Co.*, 300 Park Ave., Warminster, PA 19874. 215-674-4915. Many varieties of vegetables and flowers. Free.

□ *Henry Field's Seed & Nursery*, 415 N. Burnett, Shenandoah, IA 51602. 712-246-2011. A hundred pages of fruits and vegetables. Free.

□ *Jackson & Perkins Co.*, 2518 So. Pacific Highway, Medford, OR 97501. 503-776-2000. Bulbs, trees, wide variety of roses. Free.

□ *J. W. Jung Seed Co.*, 335 South High St., Randolf, WI 53957. 414-326-3121. Trees, flowers, vegetables. Free.

□ *Liberty Seed Co.*, 128 First Drive SE, New Philadelphia, OH 44663. 216-364-1611. All kinds of garden seeds. Free.

□ *J. E. Miller Nurseries*, 5060 West Lake Rd., Canandaigua, NY 14424. 716-396-2647. Fruit trees, vines, berries. Free.

□ *Musser Nursery*, Box 340, Indiana, PA 15701. 412-465-5685. Fine-quality tree seedlings. Free.

□ *George W. Park Seed Co.*, PO Box 31, Greenwood, SC 29648. 803-223-7333. Complete garden supplies. Free.

□ *Spring Hill Nurseries*, 6523 N. Galena Rd., Peoria, IL 61632. 309-689-3849. Widest variety of fruits, vegetables and plants. Free.

□ *Stokes' Seed Catalog*, Box 548, Buffalo, NY 14240. 716-695-6980. Everything. Free.

□ *Van Bourgondien & Sons*, PO Box 1000, Babylon, NY 11702. 516-669-3500. Finest domestic and imported bulbs and plants. Free.

□ *Vermont Bean Seed Co.*, Garden Lane, Fair Haven, VT 05743. 802-273-3400. All kinds of vegetables. Free.

□ *Wayside Gardens*, One Garden Lane, Hodges, SC 29695. 800-845-1124. Over 1,000 varieties of garden plants. Free.

□ *White Flower Farm*, Litchfield, CT 06759. 203-496-9600. Everything for the garden. Small charge.

How to make flowers last longer

□ Cut off the stems half an inch from the bottom. Make the cut at an angle so that the stem will not press against the bottom of the vase, closing off the flow of water.

☐ To slow water buildup (which makes petals droop), make a tiny incision at the base of the bloom.

☐ Fill an absolutely clean vase with fresh water.

☐ Add floral preservative. *One recipe:* Two squeezes of lemon juice, a quarter teaspoonful of sugar and a few drops of club soda.

☐ Change the water and preservative daily.

☐ Display the flowers out of the sun, and keep them cool at night.

☐ Remove leaves below the water line.

Source: T. Augello and G. Yanker, co-authors, *Shortcuts*, Bantam Books, New York.

Ten foolproof houseplants

These hardy species will survive almost anywhere and are a good choice for timid beginners without a lot of sunny windows.

☐ Aspidistra (cast-iron plant). This Victorian favorite, known as "The Spittoon Plant," survived the implied indignity in many a tavern.

☐ Rubber plant. Likes a dim, cool interior (like a hallway). If given sun, it grows like crazy.

☐ Century (Kentia) palm. A long-lived, slow-growing plant that needs uniform moisture. Give it an occasional shower.

☐ Philodendrons. They like medium to low light and even moisture, but will tolerate dryness and poor light.

☐ Dumb cane. Tolerates a dry interior and low light, but responds to better conditions. Don't let your pet chew the foliage or its tongue will swell.

☐ Bromeliads. Exotic and slow-growing, they like frequent misting, but are practically immune to neglect and will flower even in subdued light.

☐ Corn plant (dracaena). Good for hot, dry apartments.

☐ Snake plant. Will survive almost anything.

☐ Spider plant. A tough, low-light plant that makes a great trailer and endures neglect.

☐ Nephthytis. Will flourish in poor light and survive the forgetful waterer.

Source: Edmond O. Moulin, director of horticulture, Brooklyn Botanical Garden, Brooklyn, NY.

Poison plants

Plant poisoning among adults has increased alarmingly in the last decade. For children under five, plants are second only to medicines as a cause of poisoning. *Prime sources:* Common houseplants, garden flowers and shrubs, as well as wild mushrooms, weeds and berries.

Among the most common poisonous plants:

☐ Garden flowers: Bleeding heart, daffodils, delphinium, foxglove, hens and chickens, lantana, lily of the valley, lupine, sweet pea.

☐ Houseplants: Caladium, dieffenbachia, philodendron.

☐ Garden shrubs: Azalea, mountain laurel, oleander, privet, rhododendron, yew.

☐ Wildflowers: Autumn crocus, buttercups, jimson weed, mayapple, moonseed berries, poison hemlock, water hemlock, wild mushrooms.

Flowers that are good to eat

Many common flowers also make gourmet dishes. Here are some suggestions:

☐ Calendula (pot marigold): Add minced petals to rice, omelets, chicken soup, clam chowder or stew.

☐ Nasturtium: Serve leaves like watercress on sandwiches, or stuff flowers with basil-and-tarragon-seasoned rice, then simmer in chicken stock and sherry.

☐ Squash blossom: Pick blossoms as they are opening, dip in a flour-and-egg mixture seasoned with salt, pepper and tarragon, then deep-fry until golden brown.

☐ Camomile: Dry the flowers on a screen in a dark place to make tea.

☐ Borage: Toss with salad for a cucumberlike taste, or use fresh for tea.

Source: *House & Garden,* New York.

All you need to know about bird feeders

The main thing is to mix your own seed. You can create a mix that will attract a wide variety of birds. What birds like most:

☐ Niger seed (thistledown).

☐ Sunflower seeds (particularly the thin-shelled oilseed).

☐ White proso millet.

☐ Finely cracked corn.

Avoid:

☐ Milo and red millet, which are used as filler in commercial mixes and are not attractive to birds.

☐ Peanut hearts attract starlings, which you may want to avoid.

Requirements of a good feeder:

☐ It should keep the seed dry (mold by-products are toxic to birds).

☐ Be squirrel-resistant (baffles above and below are good protection.

☐ For winter feeding of insect-eating birds (woodpeckers, chickadees, titmice and nuthatches), string up chunks of beef suet.

Source: Aelred D. Geis, Patuxent Wildlife Research Center of the US Fish and Wildlife Service, Laurel, MD.

How to choose a kennel

When you need to board your pet for any length of time, visit the kennel with your dog a week or two before you leave him there. Plan to spend some real time looking for:

☐ Operators who own the kennel. They will have a real stake in your satisfaction.

☐ A staff that shows sincere concern for the pet's welfare, not willingness to do whatever you tell them.

☐ Kennels and runs that are well designed. A combination of two feet of concrete with four feet of fencing above it is desirable so that timid dogs can hide from their neighbors. *More important:* No dog can urinate into another dog's run. (Urine and feces spread disease.)

☐ A security fence around the entire establishment (in case a dog escapes from its run).

☐ Kennels that are neat and clean. Kennel helpers are picking up waste, hosing down runs, exercising the dogs, etc.

☐ Beds that will not harbor parasites. Fiberglass is good. Wood is bad. Dogs with parasites should be dip-treated before boarding.

☐ A requirement of confirmation of your dog's shots, either by a recent inoculation certificate or contact with your veterinarian.

Questions you should ask

☐ What is the kennel owner's background? Ask about his/her experience in breeding and handling. Such experience helps the kennel owner notice when an animal is not feeling or moving well.

☐ What kind of food is used? A good kennel is flexible and serves nearly anything. Some even cook to order.

☐ What will you do if my pet won't eat? If a dog does not eat for two days, the kennel should try a variety of foods until it finds one that works.

☐ What kind of medical and behavioral history is taken? A thorough history includes more than a record of shots and your vet's name and phone number. You should be asked about your pet's temperament, behavior, sociability, likes and dislikes.

☐ Who will administer my dog's medication? Only the owner or the kennel manager should administer medicine, and careful records should be kept.

☐ What happens if my dog gets sick or there's a medical emergency? The kennel owners should call your veterinarian first, then bring your dog to your vet—or, if that's not possible, to a local veterinarian. If it's an emergency, your pet should be taken immediately to the kennel's attending veterinarian. Check the professional credentials of the kennel's attending veterinarian with your own vet.

☐ How often will my dog be walked? Dogs should be walked at least twice a day, in addition to exercising in their kennel runs.

☐ Will my dog be played with, and how often? Your pet should be played with and petted at least twice a day. Some toys should be allowed.

Source: Michael and Phyllis Scharf, owners and operators of Pomona Park Kennels, Pomona, NY.

When to trade in your old furnace

If your fuel bills seem higher than they should be, it may be time to replace your old furnace with a new one.

Calculate whether your old oil furnace is costing you more than the price of a new one:

(1) Estimate your annual fuel bill.

(2) Divide your present furnace's efficiency rating by the efficiency rating of the new model you're considering. (Your local utility will rate your system for a small fee or for free.)

(3) Multiply the result by your annual fuel bill to estimate the savings. A new furnace should pay back its costs in about five to seven years.

Source: *Home*, Des Moines, IA.

Painting guidelines

Follow these simple suggestions for the effect you are looking for:

☐ To make a room look larger, use the same color on walls, floor and ceiling.

☐ Dark colors don't always make a room look smaller, though they can make a large room more intimate.

☐ Dark colors on all surrounding surfaces can highlight furniture and give an illusion of spaciousness.

☐ Cool wall colors make a room seem bigger.

☐ Warm colors make a room seem smaller.

☐ A long, narrow room can be visually widened by painting the long sides a lighter color than those at the ends.

☐ A ceiling slightly lighter in color than the walls appears higher…a darker one, lower.

Source: *Woman's Day*, New York.

Five easy ways to cut heating costs

(1) Clean furnaces. Home heating bills can be cut 10% or more by having the furnace cleaned and adjusted properly. If you have an oil burner, an annual inspection by a qualified technician is important.

(2) Replace furnace burners. Find out if your oil burner is a *conventional* or a *retention head* burner. The latter is much more efficient. These use smaller fuel nozzles and save as much as 15% on your fuel bill.

(3) Clean filters. Forced warm-air furnaces need to have their air filters cleaned and replaced at least twice each winter. A clogged filter chokes off the necessary breathing of the furnace and makes it work harder.

(4) Unblock registers. When you are rearranging furniture, be sure that radiators, warm-air registers or heating units aren't blocked from proper functioning. If you prefer an arrangement that blocks heat flow, let it wait until summer when it won't affect heating efficiency.

(5) Add humidity. A little extra humidity permits a lower thermostat setting without discomfort. Some furnaces will accept a humidifying system easily and inexpensively. If yours won't, use pans of water on radiators or heat registers to put a little moisture into the air.

Source: *547 Tips for Saving Energy in Your Home*, Storey Communications, Box 445, Schoolhouse Rd., Pownal, Vermont 05261

An automotive wish list

Car & Driver editors bravely responded to the query "If you could have any car…" by choosing their favorite cars based on the following criteria:

☐ They had to live with their choice for five years.

☐ It would be their only car.

☐ They would drive it daily, on vacations and in many climates.

☐ They would be responsible for all nonwarranty expenses.

Here are the choices they made:

☐ *Mercedes-Benz SL500* ($108,000): "The best-engineered, best-handling, best match of power to weight ever put together in one automobile."

☐ *Mercedes-Benz E500* ($87,920): "Sumptuous wood and leather-lined interior…speed and stealth make for a quick ride home…care and feeding is pricey but not exotic, and parts are available nationwide."

☐ *Acura NSX* ($78,075): "How to justify 60 months in a two-seater—with a 24-valve V-6 purr…user-friendly and efficient …with the world's most sophisticated chassis."

☐ *BMW M3* ($36,595): "This car embodies some enduring virtues— hearty torque at all engine speeds… steering mechanism that separates road feel from noise…add a chassis that responds with precision and predictability."

☐ *Porsche 911 Turbo* ($108,753): "There's no substitute for the racy rush of a powerful turbo…it has enough boosted thrust to hit 60 mph in four seconds and the 911 provides a comfortable, upright driving position with excellent visibility."

Not from the editors, but a real dream machine:

☐ *Aston Martin Lagonda Vignale* ($255,000): "Timeless elegance displayed impeccably in an art-deco design (fit for royalty, it's English, of course)…V-8 engine, front seats like thrones, rear sofa adjusts to seat three in comfort…more space than a Bentley …nickel-plated front panel…desk tables power down from front seats…and a TV on the side."

How to win the car-buying game

Car salesmen thrive on confusion. They bombard you with questions and numbers to divert your attention from simple issues.

Tactics:

☐ Go shopping armed with specific information. Remember that you're not there to fall in love with a car or to make a friend of the salesman. Get answers you can understand.

☐ Buy the latest edition of *Edmund's New Car Prices*. It lists the base costs of each car and accessories, such as air conditioning and automatic transmission.

☐ When you find the car you like, copy down all pricing information from the manufacturer's sticker on the window. Compare the sticker prices with those in *Edmund's* to determine the dealer's profit. This gives you real bargaining ammunition.

☐ Be indecisive. The salesman will think there's a car you like better down the road. That means he must give you his best shot.

☐ Best times to shop: The last day of the month, when dealers close their books and want good sales figures, and very late in the day, when the sales staff is exhausted.

☐ Beware of red tag sales. Dealers' profits are higher than at any other time. Customers mistakenly assume they will save money during special sales. Really, they are fantasies that draw you away from reality. Stay with black-and-white issues you can control.

☐ Stick with what you can afford. This is determined by two things: How much cash your trade-in gives you toward the down payment and how much you can pay each month.

☐ Tell dealers you are interested in selling your car for cash. Their figures will give you a better idea of what your car is worth than a blue book. It's best to sell your car privately.

Source: Remar Sutton, car dealer and author of *Don't Get Taken Every Time: The Insider's Guide to Buying Your Next Car,* Penguin Books, New York.

What to look for when you test-drive a car

Before you buy a new car, take full advantage of your test drive. Make sure the dealer lets you drive the vehicle where you can give it a thorough workout…on bumpy roads…in stop-and-go traffic…and on highways, especially the entrance and exit ramps. Pay special attention to how the car matches up to your expectations for comfort, drivability, interior layout and *power*.

Comfort

☐ Engineers call the science of fitting the car to the person ergonomics. You'll soon see how well they did when you climb in behind the driver's seat.

☐ You probably won't be the only one driving the new car regularly. Don't forget that the "feel" of the car should suit your co-drivers and frequent passengers.

☐ Clearance: Can you get in and out without hitting your head?

☐ Headroom: Your hair shouldn't touch the ceiling. If it does, and you love the vehicle, consider ordering it with a sunroof. This will give you another inch or two.

☐ Seat height: Does it give you good road visibility?

☐ Headrest: Will your head, neck and back be comfortable after driving for a while?

☐ Leg room: Does the seat move far enough forward and back not only for you but for all drivers?

Drivability

☐ Test-drive the car at night to make sure that the headlights are powerful enough for your comfort.

☐ Power: Does the car run smoothly and accelerate adequately? *Hint:* Make sure the car you test has the engine size, transmission type or gear ratios that you want.

☐ Rear visibility: Can you see adequately with the exterior rear-view mirrors? If they're too small, be aware that replacements don't exist.

☐ Noise: Does engine exhaust or wind noise bother you?

☐ Fuel type: Does the car need expensive high-test gas? High-performance, multi-valve, super- and turbo-charged models all do.

Interior

☐ Instrumentation: Can you read the gauges easily?

☐ Controls: Do you hit the wiper switch and put the radio on?

☐ Door handles: Can you find them in the dark?

Bottom line

☐ If you're satisfied with your test drive, don't assume the car that the dealer delivers to you will be as good.

☐ Check out the finish of the car you want to buy to make sure you haven't been sold a vehicle that already has been driven…or damaged in transit. Look for tell-tale signs of repainting… like paint traces on the rubber stripping or trim, mismatched colors and misfit panels. And take a good look at the undercoating. It should look slightly weathered—not sparkling clean and still soft.

☐ Insist on a test drive of your new car before you accept delivery. *Also:* Never take delivery at night. You want to examine your car carefully in broad daylight. You may also want to have the car looked over by a good mechanic.

Source: David Solomon, editor, *Nutz and Boltz*, Box 123, Butler, Maryland 21023.

Understanding car terms

☐ Rack-and-pinion steering: This compact system has fewer moving parts than older systems and therefore is cheaper to make. But it is not necessarily better than the standard system.

☐ Unibody construction: Everything fastens onto the body, reducing the car's weight and increasing mileage. But a minor fender-bender can create hidden damage in another part of the structure.

☐ Automatic overdrive transmission: This is a fuel-economy measure. An extra high gear slows the engine when the car is cruising at a constant speed. *Disadvantage:* The car has reduced acceleration and hill-climbing ability when in this gear.

☐ Overhead camshaft engine: This slightly improves efficiency at high speeds, which is why some race cars use it. But this difference is not significant in normal driving.

Source: Automobile Club of New York.

Making the right choice of options on a new car

The value of an optional feature depends on how, when and where most of the driving will be done.

Important for everyone: Options that make the car safer.

☐ Air bags.

☐ Steel-belted radial tires. They hold the road better, provide better fuel economy and longer life.

☐ Buy accessories that relate to the character of the automobile. A very lightweight car does not require power steering or power brakes.

Important but not essential:

☐ Cruise control. This is a great advantage for driving long distances on a regular basis. It sets the pace and helps the driver avoid speeding tickets.

☐ Air conditioning. This is very important for comfort and for the subsequent resale value of the car.

☐ Heavy-duty suspension system. It makes the car feel taut and firm and hold the road better. There is little initial cost and little value on resale. It is important for car owners who are either going to carry heavy loads or who love to drive and are extra sensitive to the performance of the car. It's not an important feature for those whose car use is limited mainly to trips to the supermarket.

☐ Power seats. Extremely useful feature for drivers who go long distances regularly. Permits moving the seat back. Allows arm position to be manipulated and fine-tuned in relation to steering wheel. In some ways a safety factor because it helps ward off driver fatigue. Power seats are quite expensive.

☐ Adjustable seat back. Some form of this is highly recommended and should be considered because it wards off driver fatigue and thus is a safety element.

☐ Tilt steering wheel. This is another aid in fine-tuning the driver's relation to the car and is therefore recommended as a safety factor. It is an important feature especially for large or short people.

☐ Electric door locks. Key unlocks all doors simultaneously. Button locks all doors at once, including the trunk lid. It is a convenience because it makes it unnecessary to open each door from the outside in bad weather. When driving through dangerous neighborhoods, the electric lock provides immediate security with the touch of a button.

Some options have disadvantages:

☐ Sunroof. Redundant if the car has air conditioning. Noise and the problem of water leakage are constant irritations.

☐ Power windows. They are recommended for drivers who use toll highways on a regular basis. Power windows can be dangerous to both small children and pets.

Fixing your present car vs. buying a new one

Most older cars can be refurbished—and in fact be made as good as new—for far less than the cost of a brand new car. *The key:* The break-even point of the deal.

To figure fix-up costs: Have a competent mechanic give you a detailed list of everything that's wrong and costs to fix it up. With that kind of renovation, a car should be good for another five years with no major repair expenses.

☐ Even if the car needed a completely new engine, it would still be cheaper to repair the old car than to buy a brand new one.

☐ Gas mileage is not a key consideration. Assume that a new car would get 50% better gas mileage than the older car. It would still take at least ten years to break even on mileage alone. *Example:* Your present car gets 15 mpg, and a new car would get 30 mpg. You buy 1,000 gallons of fuel per year (15,000 miles of driving) and it costs $1.40 per gallon. Your present gas bill is $1,400 per year. The 30 mpg car would cost you $700 per year. At that rate, disregarding all the other expenses of the new car, it would take 14 years for a payback on the improved mileage.

☐ On the other hand, if your car is worth less than $1,000 and is rusting, rebuilding is not recommended. Severe rusting can't be fixed.

Source: Tony Assenza, editor of *Motor Trend*.

Shop for a used car

Before looking for a used car, decide the exact make, model and price you want (just as you would if you were buying a new car).

☐ Determine whether you want to use the car for extensive traveling, for weekends and summer travel or just for getting to the train station and back. This helps you decide whether you want a 3- to 5-year-old car (extensive travel) or one 5 to 7 years old (suitable for weekend use and summer travel). For trips to the train station in the morning, or for equivalent use, a car that is 7 to 10 years old will do.

☐ Choose a popular make in its most successful and long-lasting model. Repair parts are also easier to find.

☐ Get the local paper with the most advertising for used merchandise. Privately owned cars are often very well maintained and are generally available at prices much lower than those being offered by dealers.

☐ Look for the deluxe model of the popular make you've chosen. Since it cost a lot more when it was new, there's a better chance it was well cared for.

☐ Establish (by shopping) the going price of your desired make and model. Then select only those cars offered at above the average price. Owners of the better-cared-for cars usually demand a premium, and it's usually worth it.

How to check out a used car

You don't have to be an expert to decide whether a used car is worth paying a mechanic to check out. The key steps:

☐ Get the name and telephone number of the previous owner if you buy the car from a dealer. If the dealer won't give you this information from the title, pass up the car. (It could be stolen.)

☐ Call the former owner and ask what the car's major problems were (not if it had any problems). Also, get the mileage on the car when it was sold. If the speedometer now reads less, it has been tampered with. Go elsewhere.

☐ Inspect the car yourself. Even a superficial look can reveal some signs that will warn you off or will be worth getting repair estimates for before you settle on a price.

☐ Check the car for signs of fresh undercoating. There is only one incentive for a dealer to undercoat an old car —to hide rust. Check this with a knife or screwdriver (with the dealer's permission). If you find rust, forget the car.

☐ Rub your finger inside the tailpipe. If it comes out oily, the car is burning oil. Your mechanic should find out why.

☐ Kneel down by each front fender and look down the length of the car. Ripples in the metal or patches of slightly mismatched paint can indicate bodywork. If a rippled or unmatched area is more than a foot square, ask the mechanic to look at the frame carefully. (Ask the former owner how bad the wreck was.)

☐ Open and close all the doors. A door that has to be forced is another sign of a possible wreck.

☐ Check for rust around moldings, under the bumper, at the bottom of doors, in the trunk, under floor mats and around windows. Lumps in vinyl tops are usually a sign of rust. Rust and corrosion on the radiator mean leaks.

☐ Check the tires. Are they all the same type? Does the spare match? If there is excessive wear on the edges of any single tire, the car is probably out of alignment.

☐ Check the brakes by applying strong pressure to the pedal and holding it for 30 seconds. If it continues to the floor, it needs work.

☐ Test-drive the car, and note anything that doesn't work, from the air conditioner to the windshield wipers. Listen for knocks in the engine and grinding or humming in the gears. Check the brakes and the steering. Drive over bumpy terrain to check the shock absorbers.

Source: Remar Sutton, author of *Don't Get Taken Every Time: The Insider's Guide to Buying Your Next Car*, Penguin Books, New York.

Buy a car at police auctions

Big-city police departments, in the course of their work, collect abandoned cars, evidence vehicles (those used in crimes) and towed-away cars that haven't been picked up. Buying a car at auctions of these vehicles can be a good deal, especially for a teenager who can do repair work.

Rules to follow:

☐ Inspect the autos the day before the auction. Each is listed by its make and year and is given an auction number that also appears on the windshield of the car. (You can make notes on the list of the cars that interest you and then check prevailing prices for such cars in the local newspaper want ads or in publications at the library.)

☐ Usually there is no ignition key, and in most cities you're not allowed to hot-wire a start, either. *What you can do:* Inspect the car by opening the doors and hood and working the windows. Inspect the engine compartment for quality of maintenance and check the wires, hoses, motor oil level, transmission and brake fluid levels. Find out the mileage and determine the condition of the interior and tires.

☐ At the auction, fill out a form with your name and address to get a bidding number. All transactions are cash. You must pay the full price, plus tax, during the auction, not afterward. All sales are final.

☐ Set limits to your bidding and stick to them. No more than one half the Blue Book value is recommended, and no more than one third is safer. This way you'll come out ahead even if major repairs prove necessary.

☐ When you pay, collect a bill of sale acceptable to the local state motor vehicle department for registering the car. If you live out of state, check with your state automotive agency to see what other documents might be necessary to register the car in your state.

☐ Arrange to have the car towed away within a day or two of the auction. Even if you replace the ignition or jump start it, the car has no license plate or insurance. It also may not run.

Auto lemonaid

If that new car you just bought has been in the shop more than on the road, don't despair. Under state "lemon laws" you may be able to get most of your money back, or at least a more reliable car…and without the risk of heavy court costs.

☐ The law: The car is usually covered for one year or the written warranty period, whichever is shorter.

☐ If a defect isn't repaired in four tries, the manufacturer must replace the car or give a refund (less depreciation). The same goes if the car is out of commission for 30 days or more for any combination of defects.

☐ If the manufacturer has a federally approved arbitration program, you must first submit your complaint to the arbitrators. But if you aren't satisfied with their decision, you can still take the company to court.

Strategy:

☐ Check the state attorney general's office for details of the law. *Key point:* Whether the manufacturer (as well as the dealer) must be given a chance to solve the problem.

☐ Submit a list of repairs to the dealer each time you bring the car in. Keep a copy for yourself.

☐ Keep a detailed record of car-repair dates and of periods when the car was unavailable to you.

☐ If the company agrees to settle but offers too little money or a car with too many miles, don't be afraid to dicker. The company doesn't want to go to court any more than you do.

Source: *Medical Economics,* Oradell, NJ.

What you must know to buy a used car

☐ Don't let your words or actions indicate what car you really want. If you say you want a Chevy, a Chevy will suddenly cost more than any Ford on the lot.

☐ Browse around at the dealership. Make the salesperson spend time with you—and use this as leverage to pay less. Only when he or she is nearly exasperated should you zero in on the car you really want and begin your serious negotiating.

☐ Negotiate a price first, then have your mechanic evaluate the car. If possible, drive the car to your mechanic. Otherwise, bring your mechanic to the dealer's lot. If there's a problem with the car, you're in a good position because the dealer is anticipating the sale. Ask to have any problems corrected at no cost to you.

□ Negotiate a warranty. Some used-car dealers don't offer warranties, but you should have one. Ask for a 100% 30-day warranty to cover all parts and labor, but be willing to accept a 50/50 warranty (under which you'll pay 50% of costs). Demand that labor costs be based on a mechanic's estimate. Request the right to buy parts yourself and supply them to the dealership. Many dealers mark up parts by 100%.

□ Don't forget to nibble. Ask for the little extras that can add up, such as filling the air conditioner with Freon (which could cost $80 to $90). If the car doesn't turn over on the first key turn, ask for a new battery ($22 to $60).

□ You can save a lot by buying directly from an owner instead of a dealership. To get negotiating leverage over the phone, ask the following questions…

□□ Is there a defect in the title? (Is this a recovered stolen car or a rebuilt car with a salvaged title?)

□□ What concerns do you have about the car?

□□ What's your bottom line price? Then, offer $100 less.

Source: Burke Leon, owner of BL Auto Enterprises, Ontario, CA, and author of *The Insider's Guide to Buying a New or Used Car*, Betterway Books, 800-289-0963.

Recreational vehicles

Design improvements have made recreational vehicles (RVs) cheaper, better built and more fuel-efficient. Miles-per-gallon have doubled. Weight has been reduced by the use of plastics, aluminum and other lightweight materials.

Motorized RVs

□ Motor homes: These provide all the conveniences of home (bathroom, air conditioning, etc.) and sleep six to ten people. They come in three types of size.

□ Van conversions: Conventional vans are turned into campers by installing beds and stoves. They sleep up to six people.

Towable RVs

□ Travel trailers: Considered mobile bunk rooms that sleep eight. The con-ventional trailer is attached to a car. The fifth-wheel trailer attaches to a pick-up truck by means of a special plate (the "fifth wheel").

□ Park trailers: Meant for long stays in one place. These little houses attach to the facilities of a trailer park for power and water. They sleep eight.

□ Folding camper trailers: Collapsible sides that fold into a boxlike shape make these small enough to be towed by compact cars. They can sleep up to eight.

□ Truck campers: Similar to van conversions in features, these units fit on the flatbed of a pick-up truck. They can sleep up to eight.

□ Maintenance: The RV is a combination home and car…and requires the maintenance of both. You have to be alert to car-related upkeep as well as the emergencies you would encounter at home, such as frozen pipes or faulty wiring. Before you start on a trip, make sure everything in both the car and the RV is in good working order. *Recommended:* A checkup by your local service center.

□ RV appliances are fueled by liquid propane. Some tunnels and urban areas do not allow RVs to enter with propane aboard. Check ahead for regulations in areas where you plan to drive.

□ Driving an RV or the car that tows one requires special skills. Upon request, the Recreation Vehicle Industry Association will send you a list of its booklets that can help you learn the new skills.

Source: Bill Garpow, vice president, Recreation Vehicle Industry Association, Chantilly, VA.

Best car burglar alarms

Most insurance companies will give you a discount if your car is equipped with a burglar-alarm system. Generally it's 10% off the premium—each year.

Don't put stickers in the car window announcing to the world what type of burglar-alarm system you have. Most experts feel that this removes the element of surprise and can even help the thief.

Cheap alarms provide little more than a false sense of security for a car owner. A good thief can foil them easily. The features of a good alarm system:

□ Passively armed. That is, it should require nothing more of the driver than shutting off the motor and removing the ignition key, without complicated setup procedures.

☐ Instant "on" at all openings. That means the alarm should trigger as soon as any door, the hood or the trunk is opened.

☐ Remotely disarmed by a code, instead of by means of a switch or a key. A lock can be picked. A code is impossible to break.

☐ Hood lock. Denying a thief access to your engine, battery and siren is a major deterrent.

☐ Back-up battery to prevent a thief from crawling under your car, cutting the car's main battery and killing the entire electrical system, and, therefore, the alarm system.

☐ Motion detector. The best kinds are the electronic motion detectors that sense a car's spatial attitude at the time the alarm is armed whether it's on a hill, on uneven ground, etc. (Also least prone to false alarms.)

☐ *Extras:* Pressure-sensitive pads in the seats and under carpeting. Glass-breakage detectors. Paging systems and air horns.

☐ Wheel locks if you own expensive optional wheels.

Make your car hard to steal

☐ Lock your car.

☐ Take your keys.

☐ Park in well-lighted areas.

☐ Park in attended lots. Leave ignition key only (not trunk key) with attendant.

☐ Install a burglar alarm.

☐ Activate burglar alarm or antitheft device when parking.

☐ Don't put the alarm decal on your car.

☐ Install a secondary ignition switch.

☐ Park with wheels turned toward the curb.

☐ Remove rotor from distributor.

☐ Install a fuel-shutoff device.

☐ Remove coil wire from distributor cap. (Especially useful for long-term parking at airports.)

☐ Close car windows when parking.

☐ Replace T-shaped window locks with straight ones.

☐ Install a steering-wheel lock, and use it.

☐ Install an armored collar around the steering column to cover the ignition.

☐ Don't hide a second set of keys in car.

☐ Never leave your car running when no one is in it.

☐ Don't let a potential buyer "test drive" alone.

☐ For front-wheel–drive cars, put on emergency brake and put in park.

☐ Back your car into your driveway. A potential thief will then be forced to tinker with ignition system in full view of neighbors.

☐ Lock your garage door.

☐ Lock your car in your garage.

☐ Be sure inspection sticker and license tag are current and were issued by the same state.

Source: Aetna Life and Casualty.

Sensible car maintenance

☐ Average life expectancy for some vital parts of your car. *Suspension system:* 15,000 miles. *Ignition wires:* 25,000 miles. *Water pump:* 30,000 miles. *Starter:* 40,000 miles. *Brake master cylinder, carburetor and steering mechanism (ball joints):* 50,000 miles. *Fuel pump:* 75,000 miles. *Clutch, timing gear chain/belt, universal joints:* Up to 100,000 miles.

☐ Replace brake fluid at least once a year. This isn't a common practice, and few owner's manuals mention it, but brake fluid attracts water (from condensation and humidity in the air), often causing corrosion in the master and wheel cylinders, shortening their lives. Replacing brake fluid regularly saves the more costly replacement of cylinders.

☐ Cold weather probably means your tires need more air. A tire which may have lost a few pounds of pressure during the summer and fall driving season could easily become 8–10 pounds underinflated on a freezing day. This is enough to cut tire life by 25%. *Rule of thumb:* For every ten-degree drop in the ambient temperature, the air pressure in a tire decreases by one-half to one pound.

☐ The oil-pressure warning light on the dashboard is not a foolproof system. By the time the light flashes, the engine has been without oil long enough to harm the machinery.

☐ Car-scratch repair. *When the scratch hasn't penetrated to the metal:* Sand with fine sandpaper (400–600 grit) until the scratch disappears. Wipe the area clean with a soft cloth. Paint it carefully, and let the paint dry for a few days. Then apply rubbing compound according to the directions in the package. *When the scratch has penetrated to the metal:* After sanding with fine paper, apply a primer. After the primer dries, sand again with 320–400 grit sandpaper. Paint and let dry. Apply rubbing compound. Buy materials at an auto-supply store.

☐ Use vinegar to clean dirt from chipped exterior car surfaces. Then, when the spot is dry, restore with touch-up paint.

☐ Essential warm-up. Idling the car doesn't warm up all the car's systems, such as lubricants, steering fluid or even all the drive train. *Better:* Keep speeds under 30 mph for the first quarter mile and not much over that for the next several miles.

☐ Replace radials whenever the tread is worn down to 1/16 inch from the bottom of the tire groove. At that point, the grooves are too shallow to take water away, and hydroplaning may occur at higher speeds.

☐ Do not "cross-switch" radials. Always exchange the left front with the left rear and right front with the right rear. Radials should never be remounted in a manner that will change the direction of rotation.

☐ If your car is shaking and vibrating, wheels may need aligning. Improper alignment causes excessive tire wear and increases fuel consumption.

☐ Wax your car at least twice a year… more often if it is exposed to salt air, road salt or industrial air or if it's parked outside. *Clue:* If water doesn't bead up on the car's surface after rain, waxing is needed.

Source: *National Association of Fleet Administrators' Bulletin* and *The Durability Factor,* edited by Roger B. Yepsen, Jr., Rodale Press, Emmaus, PA.

Auto service intervals

Average recommended service intervals (in miles) under both normal and severe driving conditions, from a survey of mechanics:

☐ Oil & oil filter change. *Normal:* 4,155. *Severe:* 2,880.

☐ Replace air filter. *Normal:* 10,363. *Severe:* 5,927.

☐ Replace fuel filter. *Normal:* 11,597. *Severe:* 8,591.

☐ Replace spark plugs. *Normal:* 14,185. *Severe:* 11,298.

☐ Tune-up. *Normal:* 14,254. *Severe:* 11,245.

☐ Replace PCV valve. *Normal:* 16,202. *Severe:* 14,288.

☐ Flush and change coolant. *Normal:* 22,848. *Severe:* 18,049.

☐ Replace V-belts. *Normal:* 24,853 or when necessary. *Severe:* 20,610 or when necessary.

☐ Replace radiator and heater hoses. *Normal:* 29,031 or when necessary. *Severe:* 24,679 or when necessary.

☐ Change auto-transmission fluid. *Normal:* 25,862. *Severe:* 18,994.

☐ Adjust auto-transmission bands. *Normal:* 26,591. *Severe:* 19,141.

☐ Chassis lubrication. *Normal:* 5,550. *Severe:* 4,701.

☐ Repack wheel bearings. *Normal:* 21,580. *Severe:* 16,414.

☐ Rotate tires. *Normal:* 9,003. *Severe:* 7,929.

☐ Replace windshield-wiper blades. *Normal:* 15,534 or when necessary. *Severe:* 11,750 or when necessary.

Source: *National Association of Fleet Administrators' Bulletin.*

Car-battery rules

Car batteries give off explosive hydrogen gas and contain sulfuric acid. When cleaning or working around a battery, take the following precautions:

☐ Never smoke or light a match.

☐ Remove rings and other jewelry. The metal could cause a spark if it touches a battery terminal.

☐ Wear goggles to prevent acid from splashing into your eyes.

☐ If acid spills on your skin or on the car, flush the area with water immediately.

☐ Work in a well-ventilated area.

Source: *The Family Handyman,* New York.

Buying the right size tire

With the exception of high-performance sports cars, the tires manufacturers install as original equipment are too narrow and too small. While they're perfectly adequate for the kind of day-to-day driving most people do, they don't offer the same performance offered by aftermarket tires. Finding the right tire depends on your needs.

☐ If you're a very aggressive driver, you'll want a wider, low-profile tire that puts more rubber on the road.

☐ If you're an average driver, who makes modest demands on his car, switching the original tires may not be a worthwhile expense. However, even an average, non-high-performance driver can gain some safety advantages in braking and wet weather adhesion by investing in uprated (wider, lower) tires.

☐ *The key to determining tire size for any car:* The ratio of the width of the tire to its height (called "aspect ratio").

☐ Most compacts these days are fitted with a 14-inch wheel and a 70 series (aspect ratio) tire.

☐ Some small cars still come equipped with a 13-inch wheel.

☐ To increase performance and traction, a driver with a 14-inch wheel and 70 series tire could move up to a 60 series tire with little or no compromise in ride.

Rule of thumb: Virtually any original equipment tire could be replaced by one size larger.

Source: Tony Assenza, editor of *Motor Trend.*

New-tire do's and don'ts

☐ First check your owner's manual for the correct tire size. It may also list an optional size, but tires must be the same size and construction on each axle.

☐ If you must mix tire constructions, the radial pair should be on the rear axle.

☐ If you're buying only a pair of replacement tires, put the new ones on the rear wheels for better handling.

☐ Buy tires according to your needs. If you are planning to sell your car soon, don't buy long-lasting radials—get a shorter-term tire, such as a bias-ply or bias-belted.

☐ Consider the new all-season tires, especially if you live in a colder climate. These radial tires combine the traction of snow tires with the quiet ride and longer tread wear of a highway tire. And twice-a-year changing is not necessary, as it is for conventional snow tires.

☐ Radial tires are expected to last for 40,000 miles, bias-belted tires for 30,000 and bias-ply tires for 20,000.

☐ Spring and fall are best for good discounts on tire prices.

☐ All tires sold in the US must meet Department of Transportation standards. You should always look for the DOT symbol on the sidewall of any tire sold in the US, whether foreign or domestic.

☐ Any tires, old or new, must be properly inflated if you expect good performance and long wear.

Source: Ed Lewis, deputy director, Tire Industry Safety Council, Washington, DC.

Cutting down on gas usage

☐ Tuning. Poor engine tuning adds 5%–20% to fuel usage.

☐ Acceleration. The best mileage is at cruising speed (usually 35–45 mph). *Recommended:* A brisk, smooth acceleration to the highest gear.

☐ Stopping. A red light ahead? Slow down. If you can avoid stopping altogether, you will save gas. Don't follow others closely, or you'll pay for their stops in your fuel bill.

☐ Luggage. Every 100 pounds of needless weight costs up to .5 mpg.

☐ Remove ski or luggage racks (which create wind drag) when not in use.

☐ Speed. Driving an eight-mile commute each day at 70 mph instead of 55 mph will add more than $100 a year to fuel costs.

☐ Tire pressure. Inflate to the maximum listed on the sidewall.

☐ Radials. Cut 3%–4% off the average gasoline bill.

☐ Hill driving. A 3% grade will add 33% to fuel usage. On the downward slope, build up momentum to carry you through the base of the next hill. Let up on the accelerator as you climb.

☐ Gas usage increases 2%–6% with automatic transmission; 1%–2% for each 10°F drop in temperature; 10% with heavy rain or head winds.

Source: California Energy Commission.

How to winterize your car

To make your winter driving easier:

☐ Put snow tires on all four wheels for maximum traction. If this isn't possible, make sure to put them on the drive wheels.

☐ Drain and flush the cooling system on any car more than two years old. On newer cars, add antifreeze if necessary.

☐ Use a concentrated windshield-washing solution: One quart rubbing alcohol, one cup water and one table-spoonful of liquid dishwashing detergent.

☐ Keep your gas tank at least half full to prevent condensation that might freeze and block the fuel line.

☐ For better traction on rear-wheel-drive cars, place sandbags in the forward part of the trunk.

☐ Keep these winter supplies where you can get at them easily: A scraper/brush, a shovel and a bag of sand or kitty litter.

Source: *Parents*, New York.

Car emergency equipment

☐ Flashlight with fresh batteries.
☐ Flares or warning reflectors.
☐ Extra washer fluid.
☐ First-aid kit.
☐ Drinking water and high-energy food.
☐ Booster cables.
☐ Extra fan belt and alternator belt.
☐ Fully inflated spare tire.
☐ Tool kit (including jack, lug wrench, screwdrivers, pliers, adjustable wrench and electrical tape).

Extras for winter driving:

☐ Tire chains and traction mats.
☐ Ice scraper.
☐ Warm clothing or blankets.
☐ Square-bladed shovel.
☐ Extra antifreeze.

A flashlight isn't enough

An old-fashioned flashlight is helpful, but it's not enough for all driving contingencies. Your car should have:

☐ A spotlight to pick out street signs and house numbers at night.

☐ A floodlight for broad illumination (under the hood, around a flat tire).

☐ A map-reading light that can be used without bothering the driver.

☐ A signal light to alert other cars to a breakdown.

☐ *Most convenient:* Two multipurpose lights—one that plugs into your cigarette lighter and one that operates on flashlight batteries.

Flat-tire do's and don'ts

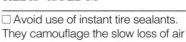

☐ Avoid use of instant tire sealants. They camouflage the slow loss of air that signals a punctured tire.

☐ Repair a tire (rather than replace it) only when the puncture in the tread area is $\frac{1}{4}$ inch in diameter or smaller. This puncture must be at least 15 inches away from a prior one, and tire tread depth must be more than $\frac{1}{16}$ inch.

☐ Remove the tire from the wheel. A permanent repair can be made only from inside the tire. An internal inspection is a must. Driving on a flat (even a short distance at low speeds) can damage the crucial inner surface.

☐ After repair, have the tire and wheel assembly rebalanced. This will more than pay for itself in a smoother ride and longer tire life.

Coping with car trouble on the highway

Unexpected breakdowns on the open road are frustrating and can be very dangerous.

How to avoid them:

☐ Practice preventive maintenance. Have your car checked before you set out on a long trip.

☐ *Likeliest sources of trouble:* Battery, tires, belts and engine hoses.

☐ Be sure you have emergency supplies, such as flashlights, flares and basic tools, and that your spare tire is inflated.

☐ At the first hint of trouble, move off the road, activate your emergency flashers and only then assess the problem.

☐ Fix the things you can yourself.

☐ If your car is overheating, you may be able to let it cool down and then proceed slowly to a gas station if you know one is nearby.

☐ If you are really stuck, wait for help. Major highways are regularly patrolled by troopers. Less traveled roads may require a Good Samaritan.

☐ Don't leave your car. An abandoned car is vulnerable to theft and vandalism. And in winter, you are vulnerable to the elements.

☐ To signal for help, raise your hood or your trunk lid as a distress signal. Hang a white handerchief or colored scarf from it. If you have flares or reflectors, set them out (in those states where they are legal).

☐ Run the motor (and heater or air conditioner) only 15 minutes out of every hour, keeping a window slightly open to guard against carbon monoxide poisoning.

☐ If you are a woman alone, keep the car doors locked and the windows rolled up while waiting. This gives you a protected vantage point for sizing up strangers who approach the car.

☐ When help arrives, describe your car problem clearly so a service station can send the proper equipment. Beware of helpful strangers who are not mechanically inclined. Using battery jump cables incorrectly can cause an explosion or ruin your alternator. Improperly hitched tows can ruin your automatic transmission.

☐ You must stay calm and be patient. If this is too upsetting a proposition for you, consider investing in a car phone or CB radio so that you can get help sooner.

Source: Francis C. Kenel, PhD, director of traffic safety, American Automobile Association, Falls Church, VA.

Your car audio system

☐ Don't turn on your car stereo during the first five minutes of your drive. Use that time to listen for noises that could signal car trouble.

☐ Organize your tapes and CDs before you leave, so you can pick them out without taking your eyes off the road. Keep them within easy reach.

☐ Don't wear headphones while you drive. A safe driver must be able to hear the traffic as well as watch it.

☐ Wait for a straight patch of road before glancing at the stereo to adjust it.

☐ Read your tape or CD titles at eye level so you can see the road at the same time.

Source: *High Fidelity,* New York.

Top-of-the-line car stereos

For the serious music lover who spends a lot of time in a car, first-rate radio and tape systems are available—at a price. Although most factory-installed stereos are mediocre, a number of audio companies make good sound systems for cars.

Like home stereo systems, car stereos are bought in components:

☐ Radio/tape deck/CD unit. Pioneer, Alpine and Sony.

☐ Speakers. Sound to rival home units… Boston Acoustics and MB Quarks.

☐ Amplifiers. High-powered units with low distortion and good reliability are made by Precision Power and Sound Stream.

☐ *Essential:* Professional installation with a warranty. Proper mounting and wiring of the components affect not only the sound but also the system's longevity.

Buying a cellular phone

Before you buy a cellular phone, be aware that:

☐ Phone bills are expensive because you're typically billed for incoming as well as outgoing calls. And—an access charge is tacked on to your monthly bill. Some cities now have an option of "calling party pays."

☐ Insurance costs may go up because few basic auto policies now cover the theft of cellular phones from cars. Check your homeowners' or renters' policy for coverage.

☐ The phone is worth the expense whenever: (1) Making calls from your car actually frees you for more productive activities at the office, (2) you can prove that the calls really result in an increase in company business or (3) you feel assured of a sense of security by always having a phone available.

☐ There is inconclusive evidence in some studies that cellular phones (only portables) may be connected to brain cancer.

What to look for today when you buy a cellular phone:

☐ A hands-free model so you can talk without holding the handset, a valuable feature because it lets you keep both hands on the wheel except when you're dialing.

☐ A system that hooks into the company switchboard. Then office calls can be forwarded directly to you by the switchboard operator.

☐ An electronic lock that lets you dial a code number to stop calls from being made to or from the phone. This should be a standard feature.

☐ A choice of analog or digital phone. Heavy users should buy a dual mode phone to talk on either network. *Note:* Soon there will be two kinds of digital phones to choose from.

☐ The ability to hook fax machines and modems to the cellular phone.

Source: Joseph Baylock, vice president of networking technologies, Gartner Group, Stamford, CT.

Driving small cars safely

In a severe crash between a large car and a small one, those in the small car are eight times more likely to be killed. Defensive strategies:

☐ Wear seat belts. A belted occupant of a small car has the same chance of surviving as the unbelted occupant of a big car in a crash between the two.

☐ Keep your lights on at low beam full time to increase visibility.

☐ Be aware that light poles and signs along the road may not break away as designed when hit by a lightweight compact car.

☐ Respect the inability of larger vehicles to maneuver or stop as quickly to escape a collision.

Dealing with trucks on a highway

To pass a truck:

☐ Blow your horn or blink the headlights to indicate your intentions.

☐ If it's raining, pass as quickly as possible to reduce road spray.

☐ After passing, speed up to avoid tailgating.

When following:

☐ Maintain a distance of 20–25 feet so the truck driver has a complete view of your vehicle.

☐ Be prepared for a possible truck shift to the left (even when it's signaling a right turn) as the driver makes sure he clears the right curb.

☐ Stay at least one or two car lengths back so as to remain in the truck driver's line of vision. This is especially important on an upgrade, where the truck may roll back a few feet.

Source: Canadian Vehicle Leasing's *Safe Driving Bulletin,* as reported in the *National Association of Fleet Administrators' Bulletin,* 295 Madison Ave., New York.

Driving in hot weather

☐ Inspect the auto radiator for leaks, and check the fluid level.

☐ Check all hoses for possible cracks or sponginess. Make sure all connections are tight and leak-free.

☐ Test the thermostat for proper operation. If it does not operate at the proper temperature, overheating could occur.

☐ Inspect the fan belt for cracks and proper tension. Belt slippage is a common cause of boilovers. It also drains electrical power.

☐ If loss of coolant has been a problem, check for water seepage on the water pump around the engine block.

☐ Don't turn off the engine when the temperature warning light goes on. If stuck in traffic, shift to neutral, and race the engine moderately for 30 seconds at two-minute intervals.

☐ Shut off the air conditioner to avoid further overtaxing of the cooling system.

☐ Turn on the heater for a few minutes. It may help.

☐ If the radiator continues to overheat, drive the car off the road, turn off the engine and raise the hood.

☐ Wait at least half an hour before removing the radiator cap. Then do it very slowly and carefully, with the help of a towel or thick rag. Keep your face turned away from the radiator.

☐ If your car has the see-through over-flow catch tank, replace any loss of coolant. Don't touch the radiator.

☐ If the fluid level is low, restart the engine while adding cool or warm water as the engine idles.

Source: Automobile Association of America.

Preparing for cold-weather driving

☐ Radiator coolant: Read the label on your antifreeze to be sure you make the right blend of water and antifreeze. The antifreeze keeps your radiator from freezing and cracking; the water, even in winter, keeps your car from overheating.

☐ Battery condition: Your car needs three to four times more starting power in winter than in summer. Have a mechanic do a complete battery draw-and-load test. If your battery fails, a recharge may save it for another year. Otherwise, invest in a new one.

☐ Windshield washer fluid: Frozen fluid in the washer tank is dangerous. Use a premixed commercial fluid. Check that the hoses are clear, and clean the washer nozzles out with a thin piece of wire.

☐ Electrical system: Make sure the distributor cap, points, condenser, ignition coil, spark plugs and spark-plug cables are in good shape. Borderline components that still function in summer will give out in cold weather.

☐ Hoses and belts: If they are cracking or fraying, replace them.

☐ Tires: If you have all-season tires, be sure the tread is still good enough to give you traction on slippery roads. Otherwise, put on snow tires. *Important:* If you have a front-wheel-drive car, the snow tires go on the front. Store summer tires on their sides, not on the tread. (Storing on the tread causes a flat spot and an unbalanced tire.) Inflate stored tires to only 50% of their operating pressure.

☐ Windshield: Apply antifogging compound to the inside.

☐ Cleaning: Clear dead bugs off the radiator by hosing it from the inside of the engine compartment. Pick out dead leaves and debris from the fresh-air intake box of the ventilation system.

☐ Stock up: Buy flares, an aerosol wire-drying agent, a scraper and brush, chains and a military-style collapsible trench tool for emergencies. Keep a lock de-icer at home and/or at the office.

How to brake on ice

☐ Start early.

☐ Squeeze the brakes with a steady pressure until just before you feel them begin to lock.

☐ Ease up, and slowly repeat the pressure.

☐ Disc brakes do not respond well to pumping (the old recommendation for drum brakes). They will lock, causing you to lose control of the car.

Source: National Safety Council, Chicago, IL.

How to get out of a snow drift

To get unstuck:

☐ Turn your wheels from side to side to push away the snow.

☐ Check to be sure that your tailpipe is clear (so carbon monoxide won't be forced into the car).

☐ Start the motor.

☐ Put the car in gear, and apply slow, steady pressure to the accelerator to allow the tires to get a grip.

☐ Don't spin the wheels (this just digs you in further).

☐ Let the car pull out straight ahead if possible.

☐ *Extra help:* Sprinkle kitty litter in front of the wheels for traction.

Source: National Safety Council, Chicago, IL.

Auto-dealer ripoff

☐ Car-purchase padding: A prep fee of $100 or more (whatever the dealership thinks it can get away with). The cost of preparing your car for delivery is already included in the manufacturer's sticker price.

Source: *Consumer Guide to Successful Car Shopping* by Peter Sessler, TAB Books, Blue Ridge Summit, PA.

Avoiding rental-car penalties

To avoid penalties and higher charges when renting a car, ask the time at which you must return the car. Some companies give a one-hour grace period, some charge an hourly rate for late returns and some charge for an additional full day even if you are only an hour late. Also, if you return a weekly rental early, you may be charged the higher day rate instead. When renting at a weekend or weekly rate, find out the earliest and latest times you can return the car.

Source: *Consumer Reports Travel Letter*, Yonkers, NY.

Accidents with aggressive drivers

Violent and aggressive drivers are dangerous when they get into an accident. If you're in an accident with one, stay calm.

☐ Don't escalate any argument.

☐ Copy down the other driver's license number immediately.

☐ If you are threatened, leave at once.

☐ Call the police so that you won't be charged with leaving the scene of an accident…but do it from a safe distance.

☐ If your car is disabled, lock the doors and wait for the police to arrive.

All about speeding tickets

The best way to avoid speeding tickets is, of course, to avoid speeding. But all of us drive over the limit occasionally.

Here are some suggestions to help you avoid tickets:

☐ Know the limits. It's no illusion that police officers generally ignore cars driving just slightly over the posted speed. In fact, many departments set threshold speeds (six miles an hour above the limit in one state, for example) at which officers are to take no action. You might be able to slip by at 65 mph in a 55 mph zone, but you're unlikely to do the same at 70 mph.

☐ Be selective. Most speeding tickets are written during the morning and evening rush hours, when there are more motorists and more police officers on the road. Late night and very early morning are not watched nearly as carefully.

☐ Drive unobtrusively. Flashy cars attract attention, something to keep in mind if you drive a red Maserati. The same applies to flashy driving styles. Don't tailgate slower cars to force them aside. Don't weave in and out of traffic.

☐ Be vigilant. The likeliest spot to get nabbed on the highway is just beyond a blind curve or the crest of a hill, the best hiding places for patrol cars. Learn to recognize likely traps, and reduce your speed whenever appropriate.

☐ Remember that police officers can nab speeders from virtually any position —the rear, the front, the side or even from aircraft. Be on the lookout at all times. An unmarked car on the side of the road with its trunk open is especially suspect. (A radar device may be inside.)

☐ Fight back. Radar guns can be foiled occasionally. *What to do:* Position your car close to other cars whenever possible. Police officers generally cannot match you with the speed indicated on their guns unless they have an unobstructed view of your car. In most states, motorists also can make use of radar detectors, devices designed to alert drivers to radar early enough to slow down before police officers can get a good reading. If you do a lot of driving, a detector is a sensible investment if it is legal in your area.

☐ Use psychology. All is not lost even if you are pulled over. Police officers feel vulnerable when stopping speeders— you could be speeding away from a murder for all they know, and consequently they are usually nervous. Put them at ease. Sit still, keep your hands in plain view (on the steering wheel is a good place). Be courteous and respectful. Above all, be honest. If you have a good excuse for going over the limit, state it. Otherwise, admit guilt and apologize. Police officers can be surprisingly lenient if you're cordial.

How to ease long-distance driving

For a safe, healthy trip when you're driving a long distance:

☐ Do most of your driving during daytime hours. Visual acuity is lessened at night.

☐ Be particularly careful to check out your car's exhaust system before leaving—a leak can send odorless but deadly gases into the car.

☐ To insure sufficient fresh air inside the car, leave both a front and a back window open. Tailgate windows should be kept closed. Use your air conditioner. It provides fresh air and quiet inside the car. Although it reduces gas mileage, the loss is not much more than the loss from open windows' drag.

☐ Use seat belts and shoulder harnesses to relieve fatigue, as well as to boost safety.

☐ Take 20- to 30-minute rest breaks after every one-and-a-half or two hours of driving.

☐ Exercise during your breaks.

☐ Eat frequent high-protein snacks for improved driving performance.

☐ Don't stare straight ahead, even if you're the only car on the road. Keep your eyes moving.

Car-jacking self-defense

If you suspect you're being followed while driving, make four right turns—essentially driving in a circle. If, after the four turns, the same car is still behind you, drive to the nearest police station or busy gas station. *Important:* Do not drive home.

Source: *Secure from Crime: How to Be Your Own Bodyguard* by bodyguard Craig Fox Huber in Richmond, Virginia. Path Finder Publications, Woodland, CA.

Driving with big trucks

One of the most stressful and frightening aspects of driving is sharing the road with big trucks.

But if you have better insight into the world as seen through truckers' eyes, you may understand more about the way they perform and can avoid tangling with them. Here's what you need to know.

Sharing the road with big trucks:

☐ Mirrors: Most trucks have a multitude of mirrors, both flat and convex. Because of their size, they can distort the picture or leave out whole sections of the lane beside the truck. For this reason, the most dangerous place to drive is beside a big rig. To get an idea of big-rig blind spots, try to see the trucker's face in his/her mirror. You'll quickly learn how limited his visibility is.

☐ Lanes: A trucker's turn signals are most important. Always watch for them. If a trucker signals to change lanes and you are in the way, move out of his way as fast as you can.

☐ Escape: Seasoned truckers know they must have an escape path if they need to get off the road quickly—in case the air pressure fails and the brakes suddenly lock up. If a trucker is in the left-hand lane, he will always be looking for a path to the right so he can get off the road before the brakes cause the truck to come to a skidding halt.

☐ Blind spot: One thing all trucks have in common is a blind spot directly behind the trailer. If you want to slip in behind a truck to save gas by being pulled along in the truck's wake, you'll find the trucker very uncooperative. Truckers hate it when a four-wheeler hangs back there. It makes them nervous. This is one of the reasons truckers like to drive in caravans, so the trucker behind can watch the "back door." They try to discourage you from slipping in between.

☐ Passing: Truckers hate passing. It is one of the most risky things they have to do. They have to plan their approach, speed, exit and re-entry back into their lane. Anytime they must change lanes, there is a risk of hitting someone hiding in the blind spot. So avoid passing, slowing down and forcing him to pass you.

Consider how much energy a truck uses to speed up and pass. The trucker typically must break the posted speed limit to gain enough momentum to pass. In a trucker's mind, there are two rules to live by—deliver the load on time and use as little fuel as possible. When you get in his way, you become the enemy.

☐ Hills: Truckers like to gain speed while going down hill so they have more momentum to go up the next hill. If you are in their way, you either force them to pass you or to ride on your tail. Sometimes it is better to give up the right-hand lane so the truckers can speed up and slow down when going up and down the hills. *Remember:* Give them room—lots of room.

☐ Wet roads: The water splash from a truck can be overwhelming. Stay away from big rigs when it is raining hard or when there are large puddles in the road. The splash can blind you, especially at night. If your vehicle, trying to pass the truck, is covered with the spray, the truck driver won't be able to see you. Also, trucks have better traction than cars in the wet weather and can stop much faster than cars. Don't follow too closely.

☐ Snow and ice: Because of their awesome weight, trucks can drive on ice and snow long after four-wheel-drive vehicles have lost traction. Don't be deceived into thinking you can continue driving in this weather just because trucks are traveling. If anything, you might become a hazard when you spin out right in front of one.

Dangerous trucks:

In the perfect world, no trucks would have faulty brakes and no trucks would be driving with more than they were designed to carry. But in the real world of everyday driving, many trucks are loaded beyond their rated capacity and many have brakes that are not functioning properly.

For example, the federal formula for bridges dictates the maximum amount of weight that trucks can carry over highway bridges (you've seen the signs along the sides of smaller bridges).

Even though there is a federal formula, some states allow trucks to legally exceed this limit by 25%.

The more axles and tires a truck has, the better its stopping ability. If you consider the actual amount of braking ability a truck has in relationship to the weight of its load, you can get an idea of how effective the truck's brakes are. Once the truck's front wheels lose traction, the truck becomes a huge, deadly projectile.

Because dump trucks (also known as "sand haulers") don't have to cross state lines, they don't have to stop at the weigh stations. They only run short distances from the rock pits to the construction sites. Because they are not closely checked for overloading, some may exceed the safe gross vehicle weight limit by as much as they can.

A majority of the single-axle dump trucks in use are designed to carry a maximum of 16.5 tons. But most states do not limit them to the manufacturer's gross weight limit, allowing them to carry in excess of 20 tons. It is estimated that 95% of all single-axle dump trucks are running over the manufacturer's specified safe-load limit.

Some container haulers fit into this category. They run from the shipyard or railroad loading docks to local warehouses, and don't go very far on the highway.

In some states, container haulers are allowed to exceed the manufacturer's safe-load limits. Some owners of container haulers use old, run-down trucks with tires that are unfit for use. Their extra-heavy loads break up streets and bridges faster than anything else on the road.

Source: David Solomon, editor of *Nutz & Boltz®*, Butler, MD.

Leaving the office at the office

It's important to learn to separate your professional from your private life. Particularly today, when the business world seems more fast-paced than ever, this can be hard to do. In the now famous quote of a hard-driving executive: "Nobody ever said on his deathbed, 'I wish I had spent more time at the office.'" Bear in mind that work has its busy seasons and its peak periods. Then, and during ambitious times such as a business start-up, it may not be appropriate to think of leaving the office behind every day. But that shouldn't always be the case. Balance is the goal to work toward.

☐ Make a conscious effort to change your mind-set when you are not at work. *Clues that your head is still at the office:* You chafe because the host is slow in moving you and other guests to the dining table…You make an agenda before going out to spend the afternoon with your child and stick to the agenda even when something more interesting intrudes. These are business mind-sets inappropriate to nonoffice activities.

☐ Give yourself a steady stream of physical cues to help you separate your office from your private world. Don't wear a watch on weekends. If you feel time pressures even when you're at home, don't use digital clocks in the car or home. They pace off the seconds and minutes too relentlessly for many people.

☐ Change your clothes as soon as you get home. And if you feel naked without your dictating machine or your briefcase with you at home, experiment with feeling naked!

☐ Use your physical setting to help you keep work in its place. Tell yourself that you can work only at a particular place at home if you must work. Don't take papers to bed with you. Don't spread them out over the couch, the dining table and the floor.

☐ Relax before plunging into housework or domestic activities. Working women especially have trouble giving themselves a ten-minute break when they get home because they're inclined to feel anxious about talking with the children or starting dinner. Take the break. It can make all the difference between experiencing the rest of the evening as a pleasure or as yet another pressure.

☐ Rituals are a useful device for making the switch. Secretaries do this by tidying up the desk or covering the typewriter. Lyndon Johnson symbolically turned off the lights in the Oval Office when he left. For managers, some useful rituals are loosening ties or other constricting clothing, turning a calendar page or making a list of things to do for the next day. They all help make the break. The to-do list also helps curb the desire to catch up on tomorrow's tasks while you're at home.

☐ Resist the growing tendency to abuse the whole winding-down process by taking up activities that create problems of their own…compulsive sex…addictive exercise…overeating or overdrinking… recreational drugs. *Better:* Use the transition time as a period of discovery. Walk or drive home along a different route. Pick up something new at the newsstand instead of the usual evening paper.

☐ The other side of leaving the office at the office is to leave home at home. It may be productive to use lunchtimes to buy paint, but that's not helpful in keeping the two worlds separate.

Source: Dr. Marilyn Machlowitz, Machlowitz Associates, a management development firm, New York.

Planning your leisure time

If you're like most people, there are lots of activities you'd like to do in your leisure time, but you never seem to get around to them. The solution is to plan—not so much that you feel like you're "on the job," but not so little that you fail to accomplish whatever is important to you, whether that means learning French or going dancing. *Recommended:*

☐ Create a "to-do" list for your spare time just as you might for your workday. You probably don't want every hour accounted for, but you should at least list what you most want to do with each leisure evening or weekend.

☐ Allot some specific times on a regular basis when you will pursue the leisure activities that are most important to you. A scheduled time will help ensure the successful fulfillment of your plan.

☐ If it's culture you're after, consider getting at least one subscription series to eliminate some of the paperwork and phone calling that often accompany even leisure-time plans. (You will also avoid wasting time in line!)

☐ Set up regular social contacts, like monthly Saturday dinner with specific friends, so you spend less time coordinating your meetings and more time enjoying them.

☐ If you use too much of your recreation time for household chores, try delegating those tasks to professional help or family members. Or do it more efficiently and less frequently.

☐ If you often work in your leisure hours, consider that you may be more efficient if you plan, and carry out, pleasurable activities that energize you (and prevent work burnout).

☐ To keep your leisure-time plans active (not reactive to other people's demands on you), make appointments with yourself. You will be less inclined to give up your plans if someone else asks you to do something, since you have a previous commitment to yourself.

☐ Just as a "quiet hour" of uninterrupted time at the office increases your work efficiency, a "quiet" leisure hour enhances your nonwork time. On a fixed schedule, if possible, take some time each evening and weekend to meditate, listen to music, reflect or just plain old "unwind."

☐ How can you find more hours for recreation? By setting your alarm clock only half an hour earlier on weekends you'll gain four hours a month. Become more efficient at work, so you can leave earlier (and not have to take work home as often). To find the time to read that mystery novel, try switching from showers to baths, and read in the tub.

Source: J. L. Barkas, PhD, author of *Creative Time Management*, Prentice-Hall, Englewood Cliffs, NJ.

47 inexpensive ways to have a good time

Having fun can't be calculated in dollars and cents. Sometimes the less money you spend, the more you enjoy yourself. Here are some inexpensive ways to have fun:

☐ Explore the beach and collect seashells.

☐ Visit the zoo and feed the monkeys.

☐ Go to a free concert in the park.

☐ Pack a picnic and drive to an attractive spot for lunch.

☐ Go skiing at your local park or a nearby mountain.

☐ Window-shop at your favorite stores.

☐ Eat early-bird-special dinners at local restaurants. Then go home and see a movie on TV.

☐ Hug each other more.

☐ Dress up with your favorite person and enjoy a formal dinner at home with fine food and wine.

☐ Go camping or backpacking.

☐ Go gallery-hopping. See the latest art exhibits.

☐ Enjoy your public library. Go to the reading room and catch up on the new magazines.

☐ Go for a drive on the back roads to just enjoy the scenery.

☐ Visit friends in a nearby city. (Arrive around lunchtime.)

☐ Eat dinner at home. Then go out for dessert and coffee.

☐ Instead of eating dinner out, eat lunch out over the weekends. It's less expensive.

☐ Seek out discount tickets and twofers for local entertainment.

☐ Take in the local museum's cultural events, including low-priced lectures and concerts.

☐ Invite friends in for drinks when a good movie is on TV.

☐ Take an afternoon walk in the park.

☐ Row a boat on the lake.

☐ Have a beer-and-pizza party for friends.

☐ Go back to the old family board games.

☐ Raise exotic plants or unusual herbs in a window box.

☐ Learn to paint or sculpt.

☐ Learn calligraphy.

☐ Take a long-distance bus ride.

☐ Go out to the airport and watch the planes.

☐ Visit the local amusement park and try the rides.

☐ Have friends over for a bring-your-own-specialty dinner.

☐ Become a do-it-yourselfer.

- [ ] Take an aerobic exercise course.
- [ ] Join a local political club.
- [ ] Go shopping for something really extravagant. Keep the sales slip and return the item the next day.
- [ ] Play cards for pennies, not dollars.
- [ ] Go to the races and place $2 bets.
- [ ] Explore your own city as a tourist would.
- [ ] Learn to be a gourmet cook.
- [ ] Treat yourself to breakfast in bed.
- [ ] Hold a family reunion.
- [ ] Attend religious services.
- [ ] Learn a foreign language.
- [ ] Join a local chorale or dramatic club.
- [ ] Watch local sports teams practice.
- [ ] Play golf or tennis at local parks or courses.
- [ ] Read everything in your area of interest at the library.
- [ ] Buy books. Get many hours of pleasure (and useful information) for still relatively few dollars.

To celebrate a really special occasion

- [ ] Take over a whole performance of a play or concert for your special guests. During the course of the event, have a prominent individual step out of character and tell the audience about you and your special day.
- [ ] Have a song written especially for the occasion.
- [ ] Run a tennis or golf party, with a name professional hired to give lessons to all.
- [ ] Hire a boat and bring along a large group for a cruise and buffet supper.
- [ ] Arrange a block party.
- [ ] Rent a hay wagon and a big barn for a square dance.
- [ ] Hire the museum or the lobby of a key office building in the downtown area for a huge buffet supper and dance.
- [ ] Hire a well-known singer to entertain at a party.
- [ ] Have a cookout on the beach, with the guests digging for related buried treasures.
- [ ] Take over a country inn for a day, and run a big house party.

- [ ] Fly a group of friends to a special place for a holiday.

The six best champagnes

- [ ] *Taittinger Comtes de Champagne*—vintage only. The blanc de blanc is a light-styled and elegant champagne. It has great finesse and subtle nuance and is the tete de cuvée of Taittinger.
- [ ] *Dom Perignon*—vintage only. Probably the most widely acclaimed champagne and deservedly so. Elegant and light, with delicate bubbles. Moet et Chandon also makes a vintage rosé champagne, a vintage champagne, a nonvintage champagne and a nonvintage brut.
- [ ] *Perrier-Jouet Fleur de Champagne*—vintage only. This house produces champagne of the highest quality in a particularly popular style. The wine is austere, yet tasteful. It is also extremely dry without being harsh or acidic. Perrier-Jouet also makes a vintage rosé champagne.
- [ ] *Louis Roederer Cristal*—vintage only. Cristal's magic lies in its plays with opposites: Elegant yet robust, rich taste without weightiness. Roederer also produces a rosé champagne, a vintage champagne and a nonvintage brut.
- [ ] *Bollinger Vieilles Vignes*—vintage only. This is the rarest of all fancy, esoteric champagnes, produced from pre-phylloxera vines. The champagne is robust and rich. Bollinger also makes a vintage champagne and a nonvintage brut.
- [ ] *Krug "Grande Cuvée"*—multivintage champagne. Fermentation occurs in old oak barrels with extended aging, making Krug unique among producers. This process creates depth and harmony of exquisite balance. Krug also produces single vintage blanc de blanc, rosé and single vineyard "clos du mesnil" vintage "blanc de blanc."

Source: Gary Fradin, Quality House Wines and Spirits, Two Park Ave., New York.

Networking: Constructive, fun get-togethers

Do you often wonder how to get to know someone you've met in passing without seeming too pushy? Would you be interested in finding out about current issues from people who are actually involved in them? It is possible to do all of the above, and in addition expand your business and social contacts and have a great time, without spending a lot of money. Here are some suggestions from three veteran networkers:

Networking dinners

☐ Have dinners for 13 to 15 people on Tuesday, Wednesday or Thursday at 6:30 so people can come straight from work and leave at a reasonable hour.

☐ Don't worry about the mix. There's a surprising commonality that develops among people of all ages and professions. Avoid inviting coworkers, couples or business partners. Candor diminishes when a guest comes with someone he sees all the time. *Guests who spark conversation especially well:* Journalists, headhunters, celebrities.

☐ Use a modest typewritten or telephoned invitation. Ask guests to call your secretary. Send the invitations at least two weeks in advance.

☐ It's up to you, as the host or hostess, to get conversation started. Give informative introductions for each guest, mentioning at least three things people can ask questions about.

☐ A cozy, circular table keeps one conversation rolling rather than several private ones.

☐ The food needn't be fancy—only good and plentiful, with lots of wine so tongues loosen. Chinese food works well because everyone seems to like it.

☐ Don't worry about inviting equal numbers of men and women. People are being matched for dinner, not for life.

Networking salons

☐ Encourage guests to drop off their business cards as they enter. This serves as a conversation-opener and theme. Since business networking is the purpose, it is socially acceptable to go up to someone and ask, "What do you do?"

☐ People should be encouraged to exchange business cards. The cards you collect may become one basis for invitation lists.

☐ Hold salons on a regular basis, from 6 PM to 9 PM on Wednesday or Thursday. For example, every week it becomes a different, exciting mini-event with new people.

☐ People, not food, are the focus. You might have a simple but beautiful vegetable spread. The wine might be donated as a promotion.

Issue discussion groups

☐ Finding people to invite is not hard. And it gets easier as time goes on.

☐ Send out a list of topics six months in advance to those who've come to previous groups, and they often recommend others. At this point, many people know about the groups and call to ask about upcoming evenings.

☐ The key to success is active participation. Encourage guests to do homework, read relevant articles and bring copies with them.

☐ To begin, each person introduces himself or herself briefly, explaining why he's interested in the topic, and then presents an interesting fact unrelated to the main topic for a 15-second presentation.

☐ The groups should be held after dinner hour. Each guest might bring something for dessert. Eat after the discussion to give people an opportunity to socialize.

☐ Get ideas for topics from articles that you file based on what you predict will be newsworthy in six months. Try to plan evenings around upcoming events. Topics tend to grow out of each other.

Source: Machlowitz, Rubin & Yaffe.

Bill Blass's favorite restaurants

Fashion designer Bill Blass has simple and very American gastronomic preferences. His top-rated restaurant choices:

New York

☐ *The Four Seasons*, 99 E. 52 St. 212-754-9494. It is a beautiful place to have a quiet business lunch.

☐ *La Grenouille*, Three E. 52 St. 212-752-1495. The food is superb, and the flowers make it really special.

☐ *Mortimer's*, 1057 Lexington Ave. 212-517-6400. A good place to see friends and enjoy good American cooking.

Boston

☐ *The Ritz Carlton Dining Room*, 15 Arlington St. 617-536-5700. Its view of the Public Garden is splendid.

Chicago

☐ *The Cape Cod Room*, Drake Hotel, N. Michigan Ave. at Lake Shore Dr. 312-787-2200. Excellent seafood.

Beverly Hills (Los Angeles)

☐ *The Bistro*, 176 N. Canon Dr. 310-550-3900. A lovely setting for fine food.

San Francisco

☐ *Trader Vic's*, 20 Cosmo Place. 415-776-2232. Excellent Polynesian, Continental and American food.

Paris

☐ *The Ritz Hotel Dining Room,* 15 Place Vendôme, 260-38-30. Extraordinaire.

London

☐ *Connaught Hotel Restaurant*, Carlos Place. 499-7070. The ambience and attentiveness are tops.

Tipping guide

Restaurant tipping guidelines from leading New York restaurateurs:

☐ Waiter: 15% of bill (excluding tax).

☐ Captain: 5%. *Note:* If you write the tip on the check, the waiter gets it all, unless you specify how it is to be split. (*Example:* Waiter $5, captain $2.)

☐ Headwaiter who seats diners: $5 or $10 or more at intervals for regular patrons. He should be tipped in cash.

☐ Sommelier: 10% of the price of the wine or 5% if the wine is expensive. $2 or $3 is a good tip.

☐ Bartender: $1 minimum or 15% of the check.

☐ Hat-check: 50 cents to $1 per couple.

☐ Restroom attendant: 50 cents.

☐ Doorman (to get taxi): 50 cents normally. $1 in bad weather or rush hour.

☐ Other staff at a restaurant that is regularly used should be tipped once or twice a year: Hosts, switchboard operators (where the restaurant provides telephone service).

☐ Nightclubs: Headwaiter should get $2 to $10 per person, depending on the impression the party host wishes to make on his guests. (Higher tip usually ensures better service.)

Other tipping

☐ Limousine service: 15% to the driver. If service charge is included in the bill, tip an additional $5.

☐ Hotels: Valet, room service, bartender should get about 50 cents, depending on amount and quality of service. Bell-boy: 50 cents per bag. Chambermaid: $1 per day.

☐ Sports arenas and racetracks: A $5 tip to an usher as you ask, "Are there better seats available?" will often give you and your guests access to reserved seats that are not being used.

How to taste a wine

Careful tasting allows you to evaluate and appreciate a wine's quality and value. It also helps you identify the components that make a wine pleasurable to you.

Proper wine tasting is performed in systematic steps that involve three senses…sight, smell and taste.

Sight

☐ Study the wine's color by tilting a glass of it away from yourself and toward a white surface. The color is your first indication of its quality. Be aware that a white wine gets darker and richer in color as it ages, while a red wine becomes lighter. So a lighter-colored red is older and presumably better than a very dark one.

Smell

☐ Swirl the wine in your glass by moving the stem while leaving the base of the glass on the table. This lets the wine's esters accumulate in your glass.

☐ As soon as you stop swirling the wine, bring the glass to your nose (actually put your nose into the glass) and inhale. What does the wine smell like? Fruity? Woody? Your sense of smell affects your taste buds, giving them a hint of what is to come.

Taste

☐ Sip the wine, being conscious of three stages in the tasting process:

The *attack* is the dominant taste in the wine, the one your taste buds respond to first. (If a wine is very sweet, for example, that will be the first taste impression.)

The *evolution* involves the other taste components that you become aware of after the attack. Notice the more subtle flavors such as bitterness and acidity.

For the *finish*, evaluate how long the flavor remains in your mouth after you swallow. What is the aftertaste? Is the wine memorable? And do you like it?

Source: Mary Ewing Mulligan, director of education, International Wine Center, New York.

Naming your poison: The hangover potential of various alcohols

Part of the reason you may feel bad after drinking stems from the congener content of the booze you consume. Congeners are toxic chemicals formed during fermentation. The higher their content in the beverages you drink, the worse you will feel.

Here's how various types of alcohol stack up:

☐ Vodka: Lowest congener content.

☐ Gin: Next lowest.

☐ Blended scotch: Four times the congener content of gin.

☐ Brandy, rum and pure malt scotch: Six times as much as blended scotch.

☐ Bourbon: Eight times as much as blended scotch.

How to reduce hangover discomfort

☐ Retard the absorption of alcohol by eating before and during drinking, especially foods containing fatty proteins, such as cheeses and milk.

☐ Use water as a mixer. Carbonation speeds the absorption of alcohol.

☐ If you get a hangover anyway, remember that the only known cure is rest, aspirin and time. The endless list of other remedies—ranging from cucumber juice and salt to a Bloody

Mary—have more to do with drinking mythology than with medical fact.

☐ Despite the preceding caveat, believe in a cure if you want to. Psychologists have found that believing something helps may actually do so.

Alternatives to alcohol

Forget Shirley Temples and Virgin Marys! Nonalcoholic beverages in the form of beer, wine and champagne have come into their own. Not only can one have an immense variety at the choicest nightspot in town, but the same can be obtained at one's neighborhood watering hole as well. Some popular brands are listed below. Check with your local liquor store for the ever-increasing new brands.

Beer

☐ (German) St. Pauli Girl, Holsten, Haaki.

☐ (American) O'Doul's, Shaarpe's, Coors Cutter.

☐ (English) Kaliber.

Wine

☐ *Ariel Wines* makes these nonalcoholic wines: Rouge, blanc, cabernet sauvignon and zinfandel.

☐ *Sutter Home* makes a sparkling wine that is sulfite-free.

Champagne

☐ *Ariel* also makes several varieties of champagne.

Lean cuisines

You can stay on your diet even while dining at your favorite restaurants. Here's how to order to avoid excess fat, sugar, cholesterol or salt:

☐ Italian: Pasta dishes with marinara (meatless) sauce. Baked or broiled chicken or veal. Pizza with mushrooms, bell peppers and tomatoes (but ask them to go light on the cheese). Minestrone.

☐ French: Grilled swordfish. Chicken breast with wild mushrooms. Steamed vegetable plate. Salade nicoise (with dressing on the side). Poached salmon. Raspberries.

☐ Mexican: Chicken taco in a steamed corn tortilla. Tostadas (light on the avocado, sour cream on the side). Red snapper Vera Cruz. Avoid fried rice or beans.

☐ Chinese: Broccoli, scallops and mushrooms sautéed with ginger and garlic. Stir-fried bean curd or chicken. Steamed fish and rice. Ask for preparation without MSG or soy sauce.

Source: Dr. Cleaves Bennett, author of *Control Your High Blood Pressure Without Drugs,* and Chris Newport, a Paris-trained nutritionist and chef, cited in *Los Angeles.*

Surviving weekend guests

Weekend guests can be a drag. They leave the lights on, show up late for breakfast and expect to be waited on. This is a checklist for the clever host or hostess who graciously but firmly takes charge and doesn't let guests become a nuisance.

☐ Be a benevolent dictator. The host or hostess has the right not to be put upon. If someone is cadging an invitation when you'd rather be alone, suggest another time. Set the dinner hour at a time that's most convenient for you.

☐ If you live without servants, tell guests what you want them to do— pack the picnic lunch, bring in firewood. You'll resent them if they're having fun and you're not.

☐ Don't let food preparation become a chore. Plan ahead to have options if you decide to spend the afternoon on the boat instead of in the kitchen. Have a dish you can pull out of the freezer, or a fish or chicken that will cook by itself in the oven or crockpot and maybe yield leftovers for other meals.

☐ Involve guests in preparation and cleanup. If guests volunteer to bring a house gift, ask for food. If guests have special diets that vary radically from your own, give them the responsibility for supplying and preparing their own food.

☐ Give guests a kitchen tour and coffee-making instructions so they can fend for themselves when they wake up.

☐ Present your own fixed responsibilities and activities. Don't be embarrassed to do something without your guests.

☐ Present optional activities for everyone. Mention anything you expect them to participate in. Discuss availability of transportation facilities and other amenities.

☐ Set up a way to communicate changes in schedules and important information (a corkboard for messages, an answering machine, etc.).

☐ Encourage independence. Supply maps, guidebooks, extra keys. And provide alarm clocks, local newspapers, extra bicycles.

Putting off unwanted guests

Favorite ploys of city dwellers who don't want to put up all the out-of-town relatives and friends who invite themselves: "We'd love to have you, but…"

☐ The apartment is being painted.

☐ We will be out of town ourselves.

☐ The house is full of flu.

☐ My mother-in-law is visiting.

☐ The elevator is out of order.

☐ The furnace is broken and we have no heat or hot water (winter version).

☐ The air conditioning is out, and you know how hot and humid it gets here (summer version).

How to make a party a work of art

☐ Serve only one kind of hors d'oeuvre on each serving tray. Guests shouldn't have to stop their conversations to make decisions about food.

☐ Don't overload hors d'oeuvres on your trays. Space them elegantly, and garnish the trays with attractive combinations of flowers, vegetables, greenery or laces and ribbons.

☐ Small bouquets of flowers and greenery tied with a satin ribbon make a convenient decoration that can easily be removed and replaced in the kitchen as trays are returned to be refilled.

☐ A layer of curly green parsley makes a good bed for hors d'oeuvres such as stuffed grape leaves, which have a hard time standing up by themselves. Parsley also makes a good bed for somewhat greasy hors d'oeuvres.

☐ Don't limit yourself to conventional equipment. Woven baskets, wood trays, colored glassware, lacquered trays, an unusual set of pudding molds—anything beautiful can be put to use for serving hors d'oeuvres.

☐ Heavy glassware is a good idea at an outdoor party. Unusual glasses (such as colored Depression glass) make drinks interesting, as do offbeat combinations of glassware and drinks (using long-stemmed wine glasses for mixed drinks, for instance).

☐ Lights should be soft but not dim. Abundant candlelight or tiny electric spots can be very effective.

Surviving the cocktail party game

You can't avoid cocktail parties? How can you survive them? Five tips:

☐ If possible, attend with someone sociable and loquacious who will stand at your side and banter with passers-by as you think about tomorrow's headlines.

☐ Pick one interesting person, someone who seems to be eyeing the clock as longingly as you, and spend the next half hour getting to know that person as though you two were alone in the world. If you choose well, time will fly.

☐ Act as you would if the party were in your honor. Introduce yourself to everyone, and ask them about themselves head-on. People will be profoundly grateful for your initiative. They don't call you overbearing—they call you charming.

☐ Tell the host you have an injured leg. Then commandeer a comfortable chair and let people come to you. (They'll be glad for an excuse to sit down.) If no one does, find an oversized art book to browse through, or indulge in a few fantasies.

☐ Help the host. You'd be amazed at how overwhelmed a party giver can be and how many small tasks need doing—even with hired help. You can pass the hors d'oeuvres, hang up coats, refresh the ice buckets and generally free the host for socializing. What's in it for you? A chance to move around (some call it "working the room"), the gratitude of your host and a nice feeling of usefulness.

Source: Letty Cottin Pogrebin, writer and editor.

Hot-tub etiquette

☐ Take a towel.

☐ If it's daytime and the tub is outdoors, you might want sunglasses.

☐ If you're ambivalent about dress (or undress), take your cue from the host or hostess. It's like avoiding the awkwardness of using the wrong fork at a dinner party. Nudity works best with everyone doing the same thing, too.

☐ Nonchalance is absolutely *de rigueur*—a combination of Japanese politeness and California cool is recommended.

☐ Sustain the mood by maintaining eye contact with members of the opposite sex, especially when they are getting in and out of the tub.

☐ If you think it's getting too hot, speak up. Better still, get out.

Great party themes

☐ A Raj ball with decor, food, music and costumes out of India.

☐ A Venetian masked ball, where the guests dress formally and vie for the best and most elaborate masks.

☐ A night in Montmartre, with red, white and French blue decorations, wine, can-can dancers and costumes from the Paris Left Bank.

☐ A Sunset Boulevard party: Decor and costumes are Hollywood, 1930s and 1940s vintage.

☐ A Kentucky Derby party around a TV set, with mint juleps and a betting pool.

☐ A speakeasy party: A password gets you in, the men wear wing collars, the liquor is drunk from cups and hoods carry violin cases.

☐ A Wild West party: Dress is cowboys and cowgirls, and the room looks like an old saloon.

☐ An Old Customs House party: The invitations are in the form of passports, and guests wear costumes from their country of origin.

☐ A patriotic party: Guests wear red, white and blue, and there must be fireworks.

☐ A Mexican party with strolling musicians, mariachis, waterfalls and Mexican food and drink.

☐ A Moroccan dinner where guests sit on low pillows, eat roast lamb and couscous with their fingers and watch belly dancers.

☐ A bal blanc with balalaikas for music, an ice-palace decor, Russian food and vodka.

☐ A New Orleans jazz party with hot music and Creole food.

☐ A Viennese waltz party: The music reflects the theme and guests dress appropriately.

☐ A physical-fitness party: Hold it in a health club, and let guests work out, then eat a healthful meal.

☐ Celebrity look-alike party: Guests dress as famous people from the past or present and try to guess each other's identities.

Source: Sheelagh Dunn, associate, Gustavus Ober Associates, New York 10021, a public relations firm that specializes in business parties.

Parties on cruise ships

If you want to impress your friends, invite them to the ship for a bon voyage party. It can be quite elegant but remain inexpensive.

☐ Make all the arrangements through the shipping company.

☐ The ship will usually supply setups, soda and hors d'oeuvres at a very modest price.

☐ Expect to bring your own liquor when the ship is in port, but you can easily buy a few bottles from a local liquor store and take them aboard.

☐ The steward can serve drinks and other items to your guests in your cabin.

☐ If your crowd is large enough, ask for a section of one of the public rooms.

☐ Play expansive host by holding nightly parties while cruising, and it won't be too costly. The ship's staff will help you with parties in your room or in a public room at a fraction of the cost of a party in a hotel ashore. You also usually get the service of waiters and bartenders at no cost (but you provide the tips).

Overcoming dinner-party jitters

☐ Define the goals of this dinner party. The main purpose may be to establish a professional connection or to bring together two people likely to be attracted to each other.

☐ Eliminate anxieties by verbalizing them. Ask your spouse or a close friend to listen while you describe your worst fears. Once verbalized, the actual possibilities will appear less of a problem than when they were vague apprehensions.

☐ Specify that the invitation is for dinner. It's not enough to say that you are having a get-together at 7:30.

☐ Let people know about dress—casual, nice but not formal, formal but not black tie.

☐ While phoning, mention one or two of the other guests, what they do and, if possible, what they are interested in. If a guest is bringing a friend, don't hesitate to ask something about the friend.

☐ Do not serve a dish you have never prepared before. Guests will enjoy what you prepare best.

☐ Have everything ready at least an hour before the party. Take a relaxing warm bath or shower. Allow extra time to dress and make up, and give yourself an additional 20 minutes to sit quietly.

☐ Arrange to be free from the kitchen when the first two or three guests arrive. They need the host's help to start up conversation.

☐ For the single host: Reduce last-minute anxieties by inviting a close friend to come over early, test the food and look over the arrangements.

Source: *Situational Anxiety* by Herbert J. Freudenberger and Gail North, co-authors, Anchor Press, Doubleday & Co., Garden City, NY.

Party size

The kind of entertaining you do depends on the length of your guest list and the dimensions of your house.

☐ For ten or fewer people, a sit-down dinner is appropriate.

☐ For 25, a buffet is usually better.

☐ An open house—usually 1–4 PM or 3–6 PM—can accommodate more people. If your rooms for entertaining hold 90 to 100 people for a party, you can invite as many as 250 to an open house. *Trick:* Stagger the hours you put on the invitations.

☐ To entertain several disparate groups —family, business associates and/or social friends—consider giving separate parties on succeeding nights. It takes stamina, but it does save effort and expense. You buy one order of flowers and greens for decorating the house. You assemble serving dishes and extra glasses (borrowed or rented) just once. You arrange furniture one time only. And you can consolidate food, ice and liquor orders, which, in bulk, can save money. Extra food from the first party can be served at the second.

☐ Remove some furniture—occasional chairs and large tables—to give you space and keep guests moving. Clear out a den or downstairs bedroom, and set up a food table or bar to attract guests to that room, too. If you have a pair of sofas facing each other in front of a fireplace, open them out so guests can easily walk around them. Use a bedroom or other out-of-the-way place for coats. (You can rent collapsible coat racks, hangers included.)

☐ Set up different foods at different parts of the party area. If you have open bars, put different drink makings at each setup. A group drinking a variety of cocktails will not be able to congregate for refills in the same place.

☐ To avoid bottlenecks: Don't put a bar or buffet table in a narrow hall, for example, or at the back of a tiny room.

☐ To make the most of a small space, have waiters to take drink orders and a bartender to fill the orders in the kitchen or pantry. Waiters can also pass the hors d'oeuvres in tight quarters, saving the clustering at a food table.

☐ Count on seven hors d'oeuvres or canapés per person. Stick to finger foods. You'll want a variety of eight to ten canapés, but pass each separately, starting with the cold foods and bringing out the hot dishes later.

☐ For long parties where a turnover of guests is likely, arrange two cycles of passing food, so the later guests get the same fresh selections as the earlier guests.

☐ Figure that a 40-pound bag of ice will provide enough cubes for 50 people. Get more if you are also chilling wine.

☐ Use a bathtub to keep the ice in. (No matter what kind of holder you devise for ice, the container will sweat and you'll have a puddle.) A bathtub full of ice and chilling champagne can be a festive sight by itself. Or, you can decant from the tub to smaller ice chests for each bar. If the nearest bathtub is too far from the party area, buy a plastic garbage can to hold the major supply.

Source: John Clancy, chef, teacher, restaurateur and author of several cookbooks.

Hiring help for a party

☐ The ideal ratio is one tray carrier for every ten guests.

☐ Two or three extra kitchen workers are sufficient.

☐ One extra person can tend bar for up to 30 to 40 guests.

☐ In the kitchen, set out a prototype of each hors d'oeuvre, and expect your helpers to make exact replicas.

☐ Servers should be neat and pleasant and should avoid conversing with guests.

☐ Serving people are responsible for maintenance—keeping the party attractive. Provide lots of ashtrays (if you permit smoking), and make sure servers are told to empty them frequently.

☐ Avoid hors d'oeuvres that lead to messy leftovers (for example, shrimp tails or skewered foods) if you don't have enough people to clean up after your guests.

☐ If you expect a caterer, empty the refrigerator and clear all kitchen surfaces. In an office, make sure all desks are cleared. Food should be prepared well in advance and, when possible, frozen.

☐ Stock wine and liquor a day or two ahead of time.

☐ Flowers and decorations should be in place two hours before the party.

Source: Martha Stewart, the co-author of *Entertaining* and author of *Quick Cook* and *Martha Stewart's Hors d'Oeuvres*, all published by Clarkson-Potter, a division of Crown Books, New York.

How to enjoy holiday entertaining

Although everyone is supposed to look forward to the holidays, they can be a season of great strain, especially for those who are entertaining. To minimize the strain:

☐ Include nonfamily in your invitations. *Reason:* Everyone is then on "party manners." Snide comments, teasing or rivalries are held back. This is not the time for letting it all hang out.

☐ Accept help. Encourage your family and friends not only to make their favorite or best dish but to be totally responsible for it—heating or freezing or unmolding and serving. Meals then become a participatory event, rather than one or two people doing all the work and the rest feeling guilty or, worse still, awkwardly attempting to help. (The one who hates to cook can supply the wine or champagne.)

☐ Let the table itself set a mood of fun, not formality. Use place cards wisely and make them amusing with motifs appropriate for each guest, rather than names. Or, let one of the younger children make them with a sketch of each guest or hand lettering. Set them out with forethought. Make sure a particularly squirmy youngster is nowhere near an aunt known for her fussy table manners. If there are to be helpers, seat them so they can get up and down with ease. Put the famous spiller where the disaster can be readily cleaned up. If the light is uneven, seat the older people in the brightest section.

☐ Put everyone around a table. It creates a warmer, more shared meal than does a buffet, and it's amazing how tables can expand. *Hint:* Use desk or rental chairs, which are much slimmer than dining chairs. (Avoid benches for older folks.)

☐ Borrowing and lending furniture, such as tables, can help you to find room for everyone. It doesn't matter if the setup is not symmetrical or everything doesn't match. A ping-pong table covered with pretty new sheets can provide plenty of room, or you can have tables jutting into hallways or living rooms.

☐ Have some after-dinner games ready. Ping-pong, backgammon, chess and cards are among the favorites. You may want to buy the latest "in" game or a new word game.

☐ Bringing out old family albums can be fun.

☐ Gift exchanging is really a potential hazard. Children, especially, can grump all day if something they expected hasn't been forthcoming. Grandparents

often ask what is wanted, but they may be unable to do the actual buying. Do it for them. A check is not a fun package to open. If you want to be sure no one overspends, set a limit. Or set a theme. Or rule out gifts altogether, except for the children.

Source: Florence Janovic, writer and marketing consultant.

Planning a big family reunion

Because a reunion brings together people of all ages, it presents special challenges. To make your party more enjoyable for everyone:

☐ Infants and toddlers. Parents will appreciate a place to change diapers and a quiet room for naps and nursing. Let them know if you can provide high chairs, cribs, safety gates or playpens. *Toys:* A box of safe kitchen equipment. *Food suggestions:* Mild cheese, bananas, crackers, fresh bread or rolls.

☐ Preschool children. Set aside a playroom. *Best toys:* Balloons, bubbles and crayons. Pay an older cousin or neighborhood teen to baby-sit.

☐ School-age children. A den or basement room and board games, felt pens and coloring books will keep them happy. Put them in charge of setting and decorating a children's dining table.

☐ Teenagers. Most teenagers find family reunions boring. For those who have to come, provide a room with a stereo, video games and radio. Teenagers may be shy around relatives they don't know. When they come out of hiding, give them tasks that encourage their involvement with others, such as helping out grandparents.

☐ Older folks. They need comfortable chairs where they can hear and see what's going on without being in the way. Some may also need easy access to a bathroom and a place to rest or go to bed early. *Food considerations:* Ask if anyone needs a low-salt, low-cholesterol or special diabetic diet. Spicy foods are probably out.

☐ Make travel arrangements for those who can't drive so they don't worry about inconveniencing others.

☐ Now that you've seen to individual needs, how do you bring everyone together? *Common denominator:* Family ties. Make an updated family tree and display it in a prominent place. If you have an instant camera, take pictures as people arrive and mount them on the appropriate branch of the tree. *Special:* Ask everyone to bring contributions to a family museum. *Suitable objects:* Old photographs, family letters, heirlooms, written family histories, old family recipes. After dinner, gather around the fire and exchange family anecdotes. You may wish to record them.

Source: *Unplug the Christmas Machine: How to Give Your Family the Simple Joys of Christmas* by Jo Robinson and Jean Staeheli, co-authors, Morrow, New York.

Self-indulgent ideas for New Year's Eve

☐ Get away to a country inn and enjoy a peaceful respite away from home with your spouse.

☐ Have a white-tie party in your home, complete with champagne, caviar, an elegant menu, your stored wedding-present silver serving dishes and crystal and your fanciest table linens.

☐ Rent a batch of old movies for good friends to share throughout the night. Serve beer, popcorn and pretzels.

☐ Plan a dinner for people you haven't seen in at least five years and catch up on old times.

☐ Charter a yacht for a lavish but intimate supper-dance.

☐ Hire an artist to document your New Year's party with sketches.

☐ Run an ethnic party—French, Italian, etc.—with appropriate food, wine, music and dress.

☐ Fly to Paris for the night on the Concorde, dine and sleep at the swank Hôtel Plaza Athénée and return home the next day.

☐ Go to a ski resort for the weekend to enjoy the bracing air, good athletic activities and grog.

☐ Run a masked ball, complete with fancy dress costumes and prizes for the best. Have plenty of room for dancing and include at least one waltz.

☐ Have a wine-tasting party for a group of appreciative friends. Or, design a meal around special vintages from your own cellar that you want to share with some fellow wine lovers.

☐ Have a country party with a caller and musicians for square-dancing.

☐ Take a group to Atlantic City or Las Vegas and gamble the evening away.

☐ Organize a literary evening; let each person recite or read from his or her favorite works. Or pick a favorite play and do a reading, with each guest taking a role.

☐ Invite close business associates for dinner to discuss the coming trends for the next 12 months—in business and in national and international politics.

Holiday shopping

Those wonderful but tiring gift-buying chores can be relatively painless with organization.

☐ Know what you're looking for. Browse through mail-order catalogs and department-store catalogs before you go out.

☐ Shop during the early morning or at dinnertime, when stores are least crowded.

☐ Shop by yourself. One person travels more efficiently than two.

☐ Wear comfortable shoes.

☐ If it will be a long tour with lengthy stops at several stores, leave your heavy winter coat in the car.

☐ Write the names of recipients on the sales slips and save them. They may come in handy for exchanges.

☐ Keep a list of what you give to whom, so you won't buy duplicate presents next year.

Guidelines for Christmas tipping

☐ Household help: The equivalent of a week's pay is standard. But much more elaborate gifts are appropriate for employees who have been in your service for a long time or to whom you are very close.

☐ Newspaper deliverer: $5 to $10.

☐ Garbage removal person: $5 to $10 each if it is legal in your community; a bottle of liquor or fancy foodstuffs are an alternative.

☐ Mail carrier: While it is technically illegal to tip the postman, many people give $5 to $10 to their regular carrier.

☐ Delivery person: $10 per person for those who come regularly to your house, like the dry cleaner, the milkman or even your United Parcel Service man, if you get a lot of packages.

☐ Baby sitter: A tape or a book for a regular teenage sitter; a bottle of perfume or $10 to $15 for an adult.

For apartment dwellers:*

☐ Superintendent: $25 to $50.

☐ Door person: $15 to $25.

☐ Elevator operator: $15 to $25.

☐ Concierge: $20 to $25.

☐ Handy person: $20.

☐ Porter: $15.

☐ Garage attendant: $15 to $20.

Outside the home:

☐ Restaurants where you are a regular customer: Maitre d', $20 to $40. Bartender, $10 to $15. Captain, waiter, bus person: Divide the average cost of a meal among the three of them.

☐ Beauty salon or barber shop: Give the owner-operator a bottle of wine or a basket of fruit. For employees who regularly attend you, $15 to $25.

☐ Butcher: $10 to $15 for regular good service.

☐ Tailor or seamstress: $10 or wine or perfume.

*If your building establishes a pool for tips that is divided among employees, you need only give an additional amount to those service people who have gone way beyond the call of duty for you this year.

What to do when you win the lottery

Many people assume that winning the lottery would automatically solve all their problems.

In fact, winning the lottery creates a whole new set of problems. Steps to take if you're ever among the lucky ones:

☐ Tell no one outside your immediate family that you've won. Your silence—and the freedom from pressure that it buys you—will allow you to think about how to invest your windfall in privacy. If you are interviewed by the media, be an uninteresting, dull and boring interviewee. In the long run, that will discourage others from bothering you.

☐ Don't assume that you've won. Some people choose to buy a "quick pick" ticket, for which the numbers are chosen for you at random. If this was the case with your winning ticket, there is the possibility—although a slim one—that you may not have won at all.

Reason: Under the rules of most state lotteries, only a certain number of quick-pick tickets can hit the jackpot in a single game. If more than the intended number of big winners are mistakenly printed, all may be disqualified—

leaving their owners with no more than a refund of the amount spent on the ticket.

☐ Secure your winning ticket. Start by signing the back of your ticket, which seals your right to the proceeds. Then photocopy both the front and back of the ticket to protect yourself. Type up a separate statement of authenticity with your signature, and, as an added precaution, have this statement notarized. You must surrender your lottery ticket to have it validated, and copying it will protect you in case the original is lost by the lottery bureaucracy. Keep the photocopies in a safe-deposit box until you are ready to turn in your ticket and claim your prize.

☐ Claim your prize correctly. If you neglect to mail in an official claim form (available from your lottery retailer) within a set number of days or fail to appear in person and have your winning ticket validated, you may be disqualified.

Deadline: Usually from 6 to 12 months after the winning drawing, depending on the state.

☐ If you have indeed won big, get an unlisted phone number. Database marketers, reporters, charities and curiosity-seekers obtain lists of lottery winners' names through the Freedom of Information Act. Though addresses and phone numbers are not so readily available, they may leak out eventually. Be prepared to change your phone number two to three times within the first nine months after you win—the period in which pressure to seek you out will be greatest.

☐ Don't assume you've won the total jackpot. Approximately one-third of the time, several winners share a prize.

☐ If you've won as part of a group, set up a partnership by drafting a simple agreement using one of the Do-It-Yourself Fill-in-the-Blank legal kits (available from TitleWaves and many bookstores). Call the IRS at 800-829-3676 and ask for the SS-4 Form to obtain a federal employer identification number. Validate your ticket under the name of the new entity. This will add another line of defense between you and the mail that is soon to come your way.

☐ Get a post-office box—preferably one from the US Postal Service instead of a mail-service company—rather than receiving mail at home. Winners often receive solicitations for business schemes, media deals, marriage proposals, etc.

☐ Buy a home-security system. It should include perimeter contacts on all doors and windows, interior infrared motion detectors, motion-sensitive lighting, audible on-site alarm plus a 24-hour monitoring service that connects your home to a central station alarm.

Consider: A drive-by armed-guard service. Request high-visibility protection for the first nine months after you win. Several lottery winners have had their homes burglarized even before they received any cash.

☐ You may have to quit your salaried job. It may not be practical for you to keep working at your company when you earn far more than your bosses. Resentment can arise, and bosses may assume that you will eventually quit, making promotions unlikely and limiting your responsibilities. In addition, many "jackpot chasers" will phone you at work, causing even further disruption of the workplace.

☐ Be a little frivolous—and then a lot cautious. Blow 10% of your first lottery check. Be mindless and irresponsible—and get it out of your system. Put the remaining 90% away for at least three months. Park it in a money-market mutual fund or a 90-day CD to avoid temptation. Few people are accustomed to dealing with large sums of money, and they need time to adjust. In either case, make sure your money is adequately insured by investing no more than $100,000 at a single bank.

☐ Get out of town. Take an inexpensive trip—and treat it like a business trip. Go where you will have the solitude you need to plan the next steps in your new life.

Source: Rob Sanford, certified financial planner based in Malibu, California. He is the author of *Infinite Financial Freedom: What to Do Before and After You Win the Lottery,* TitleWaves Publishing, Malibu, CA.

How to really appreciate movies

If you really want to appreciate movies, stray a little from the heavily beaten track. There are a number of good critics in small or specialized magazines who can alert you to fine—and unusual—new films, as well as notable revivals.

Movie buffs typically go through three stages in their appreciation of films:

☐ First, they find movies awe-inspiring magic.

☐ Second, they begin to realize those are actors up there and that all kinds of technology are involved. In this stage, which some people never leave, they become "fans." Many fans don't care about movies—they're just interested in following their favorite actors.

☐ Third, they realize movies aren't magic, that it may be a miracle they ever get made, but that they're a human achievement that also happens to be marvelous. At this stage they can start to look at movies critically.

To get the maximum enjoyment from movies:

☐ Watch a lot of them. Make a special effort to see foreign films. You'll begin to see what's original and fresh and what's stereotyped.

☐ Learn about movie forms and genres and the unique visual language of cinema.

☐ Read, follow other art forms. Read about psychology, politics, history and other branches of knowledge.

☐ Avoid the rush. Don't dash off to see the latest blockbuster. It'll be around a while. See a film more likely to close soon, even though it was well-reviewed.

☐ Watch movies on cable TV and on cassettes. Both these forms have done a lot to make film scholarship possible and good movies accessible.

☐ Go to foreign films. More than a few are worth seeing, but most people aren't interested in them anymore. In the past, the "ooh-la-la" factor drew viewers. But now that American films are no longer censored, foreign films have lost their cachet.

Source: Andrew Sarris, film critic for New York's *Village Voice,* a professor of cinema at Columbia University and author of *The American Cinema: Directors and Directions,* Octagon Press, New York, and *Politics and Cinema,* Columbia University Press, Irvington, NY.

How to enjoy a day at the races without going broke

The aim of a day at the track should be to enjoy every race while controlling your losses. Fifty dollars lost out of a hundred dollars played could be considered a highly satisfactory day.

☐ When betting, begin with the choices of the handicappers. Handicapping—the prediction of likely winners—is done by a track official who assigns odds to the horses in the morning races. Handicapping is also done by bettors in the course of the day (which causes the odds to change). One third of the favorites chosen by handicappers win their races.

☐ Decide on the amount of money you are willing to lose. Set aside one fifth of it for entertainment betting. The rest should be spent on serious betting. For about $20 you can bet on every race plus the daily double.

☐ Avoid the temptation to increase bets when losing in order to catch up. Also avoid the trap of betting more when winning to try to make a killing.

☐ To control spending, bet just 20% of your remaining capital each time you bet, whether your capital goes up or down.

☐ For fun betting, choose horse by name, jockey, appearance or any means you wish. You may get lucky and win one out of ten bets this way.

☐ For serious betting, pick the appropriate races to bet on. Always eliminate maiden races (the horse's first year of racing), two-year-old races and races where it's indicated that the horses chosen won no race but their maiden race.

☐ To pick the two or three likeliest winners in the race, check handicappers' choices in local newspapers, racing forms and tip sheets sold at the track. Look especially for handicappers who predict in great detail how the race will be run, and those who tell you the front runners and the come-from-behind horse as well as the outcome.

☐ Late scratches (the elimination of contenders) can very much change the projected script of a race. If one of the two predicted front-runners is scratched, the remaining front-runner's chance is increased.

☐ Rain. In the racing charts, "mudders" (horses that have a history of doing well in the rain) are indicated with an asterisk. As the track is progressively softened by rain, the chances of mudders improve. The horse in the most adverse position on a rain-sodden track is a speed horse—a front-runner in the post position.

☐ Shifts in odds. Lengthening (higher) odds on a horse increase your chance of a good return. Observe the physical condition of your horse during the viewing ritual, when the horses are paraded at the rear of the track before each race.

You can place several types of bets:

☐ To win: Pays only if the horse comes in first.

☐ To place: Pays only if the horse comes in first or second.

☐ To show: Pays if the horse comes in first, second or third.

Source: Peter Shaw, cultural critic, historian, college professor and occasional bettor.

Casino gambling: A matter of strategy as well as luck

Too many casino gamblers lack a good strategy for cutting the house's advantage to something reasonable—say under 2%. They don't bring enough money to ride out a losing streak. Worst of all, they don't know how to manage the money they do bring, win or lose.

To have any real chance of success in Nevada or Atlantic City, you must learn money management. Find out what your minimum bet can be, and bring at least 100 to 125 times that amount to last your total stay. With any less you won't be able to play comfortably.

☐ Divide your total stake into four parts. This leaves you $100 per gambling session—the bare minimum for survival at a five-dollar table. (*Important:* Never draw from one session's stake to replenish another.)

☐ If you lose the $100 quickly, leave the table, and the casino, to clear your head for the next session.

☐ If after 30 minutes of slow-but-steady losing, you find you're down to $50, cash in your chips and take at least a 30-minute break. Never play more than a half-hour at a losing session.

☐ If you're winning, preserve your profits. As soon as you've doubled your money (to $200), put your original $100 in your pocket, not to be touched until you see the cashier. Now you're in the ideal situation: Playing with the casino's money. If your luck sours, quit when you've lost 25% of your profits—in this case $25. If you manage to run your profits to $200, quit after losing $50, and so on. Although it's hard to leave when you're still ahead, this kind of discipline separates potential winners from inevitable losers.

Source: Lee Pantano, a professional gambler, teacher, consultant and editor of *Gamblegram*, Atlantic Highlands, NJ.

Traps in casino ✓ gambling

Casino gambling can be high-risk entertainment, if you're not careful. Avoid these common casino mistakes:

☐ Making "flat bets"—wagering the same amount each time. Since the odds are against you, your progress will soon resemble a sales chart in a recession… peaks and valleys, but down in the long run.

☐ Trying to get even by chasing losses with meal money…or the next month's rent. It's a big mistake to dig into your pocket after your stake is gone. You can't outspend the casinos.

☐ Flitting from craps to baccarat to the slots. It's better to stick with one game until you're comfortable.

☐ Taking too many long-shot bets (such as "proposition" bets in craps). They generally offer the worst odds.

☐ Staying at a "cold" table too long. If a new dealer is giving you terrible cards, or there's a loudmouth across the table, or you don't like the smell of your neighbor's cigar, move on. The problem may be purely psychological, but it can throw off your game nonetheless.

☐ Accepting complimentary alcohol. When you drink too much you start making irrational "hunch" bets, and you get frivolous with your money.

☐ Playing when tired. The casino may stay open till 4 AM, but you don't have to close the casino. Stick to your normal weekend hours.

☐ Getting caught up in the casino mentality. When everyone refers to $5 as a "nickel" and $25 as a "quarter," it's easy to treat money like plastic. Never forget that it's real money. Stick to your basic units and progressions.

☐ Viewing the dealer as a shark who's out to get you. At worst, the dealer is a mechanical device. At best, he can be your ally. *Example:* In a hot craps game, he may remind you when to take a bet down. To keep him on your side, don't forget to tip. (Dealers make two thirds of their income from tips.) *Tactic:* It's

more effective to bet $1 for the dealer (giving him a stake in your game) than to give him $10 when you leave.

☐ Celebrating prematurely. Be happy when you win, but don't brag about it. You don't want to advertise that you're carrying a lot of money. And…don't play with a huge pile of chips in front of you. If you hit it big, convert to larger denominations, and put them in your pocket. (For safety, use the casino's valet parking. With a validated ticket it will cost you only a tip, and it's far better than walking three blocks to your car.)

☐ Forgetting what you came for. Take in a floor show and enjoy a good meal. If you lose at the tables, write it off as entertainment. If you're not a professional, that's the whole point of visiting a casino…to have a good time.

Source: Lee Pantano, a professional gambler, teacher, consultant and editor of *Gamblegram*, Atlantic Highlands, NJ.

Winning at poker ✓

Not so many years ago, every poker book told you the same thing: Play tight (fold bad hands). This is still good advice, as far as it goes. But there are other tactics to keep in mind:

☐ Be selective but aggressive. Ideally, you should end a hand by either folding or raising. Avoid calling bets with vulnerable hands, such as two pair.

☐ To own the table psychologically, so that other players are glancing at you every time they make a bet, be friendly, but at the same time confusing and unpredictable.

☐ Never gloat. You want your opponents to enjoy trying to beat you.

☐ In a low-to-moderate-limit game, you can win without mathematical genius or brilliant originality. Most of your profit will come from your opponents' mistakes. *Their chief error:* Calling for too many pots with mediocre hands.

☐ Bluffing is a poor strategy in a low-stakes game. Unsophisticated opponents won't even understand your intended deception. Second, they're likely to call you anyway, a habit you want to encourage. Try a strategic bluff just once, early in the session, as an "advertisement."

☐ Discipline is especially crucial in a low-limit game, when you need more hands to make up losses.

☐ Decide in advance how you will react in each of various situations. Never play a hand out of impatience or on a "hunch." Play it for a good reason.

☐ Monitor yourself carefully. If you make a mistake, admit it to yourself and get back on track. Don't let one bad play erode your entire system.

☐ Don't look for immediate revenge after an opponent burns you on a big pot. If you force the action, you're apt to get burned again.

☐ Stay later when you're ahead and leave early when behind. When you're losing, you lose psychological control of the game, too. Opponents try to bluff you out of pots and are less likely to call your good hands.

☐ Watch for and learn to read opponents' "tells"—the mannerisms they fall into that tend to give away whether their hands are good or bad. In general, follow the rule of opposites: Players usually act weak when their hands are strong, and they commonly act strong when their hands are weak.

☐ Look for reasons to fold just as eagerly as you look for reasons to call.

Source: Mike Caro, a gambling teacher and columnist for *Gambling Times* and, according to world poker champion Doyle Brunson, the best draw-poker player alive. He is also the author of *Caro on Gambling*, published by Gambling Times, Hollywood, CA.

Successful poker: ✓ Reading your opponents

Bluffers generally:

☐ Breathe shallowly or hold their breath.

☐ Stare at their hands—or at you as you prepare to bet.

☐ Reach for chips out of turn.

☐ Bet with an authoritative pronouncement.

☐ Fling chips into the pot with an outstretched forearm.

☐ Show unusual friendliness toward opponents.

Players with powerful hands:

☐ Share a hand with a bystander (especially a spouse).

☐ Shake noticeably while making a bet. (This reflects a release of tension. Most players show obvious outward nervousness only when they feel they're in little danger.)

☐ Talk easily and naturally.

☐ Behave in an unusually gruff manner toward opponents.

☐ Lean forward in their seat.

☐ Bet with a sigh, shrug or negative tone of voice.

☐ Ask, "How much is it to me?" or request another clarification.

☐ Glance quickly at the player's chips after receiving a (good) card.

Source: Mike Caro, author of *Mike Caro's Book of Tells—The Body Language of Poker*, published by Gambling Times, Hollywood, CA.

Darts: Tips from ✓ a champ

☐ Start off with a set of three brass darts with a one-piece plastic shaft and flight. Brass darts are big and easy to handle. They're also the most durable. As you throw more, the dart will feel lighter.

☐ As your game improves, you'll want to buy tungsten darts. The darts are heavier, narrower and a little harder to control.

☐ Buy a pressed bristle board. When you remove a dart from this material, it doesn't leave an indentation. Cork or wood boards are cheaper, but they'll disintegrate with heavy play.

☐ To play well, you need eye-hand coordination, good concentration and good balance. Keep your head still so that your eyes stay on the target.

☐ When throwing darts, use your forearm, not your entire body. (It's like hammering a nail.)

☐ Stay loose and fluid on the follow-through movement after the dart leaves your hand. If you jerk your arm back, the dart won't reach the board.

☐ Most newcomers to the game overthrow to the left of the target. You can start by aiming a little to the right, but that's not a long-term cure. You must see the pattern of your throw and move accordingly on the toe line.

☐ Strategy: The two most important targets are the triple 20 and the outer double ring.

☐ Basic courtesy: Shake hands before and after play.

☐ Take your darts out of the board promptly.

☐ Be quiet when someone else is shooting.

Source: Nick Marzigliano, reigning singles champion of the Brooklyn (NY) Dart League.

Contest winners: ✓ Secrets of success

Cash, vacations, houses, cars, electronic equipment, cameras and much, much more are the dream prizes that keep millions of Americans doggedly filling out entry blanks for contests. More than $100 million worth of prize money and goods are dispensed annually through an estimated 500 promotional competitions and drawings.

Dedicated hobbyists know that there is an advantage of a planned approach to overcome the heavy odds against each entrant.

Here are some winning strategies:

☐ Use your talents. If you can write, cook or take photographs, put your energy into entering contests rather than sweepstakes. Contests take skill, so fewer people are likely to compete… improving your chances. Photography contests have the fewest average entries.

☐ Follow the rules precisely. If the instructions say to print your name, don't write it in longhand. If a three-inch by five-inch piece of paper is called for, measure your entry exactly. The slightest variation can disqualify you.

☐ Enter often. Always be on the lookout for new sweepstakes and contests to enter. *Sources:* Magazines, newspapers, radio, television, store shelves and bulletin boards, product packaging.

☐ Make multiple entries. The more entries you send in, the more you tip the odds in your favor.

☐ For large sweepstakes: Spread out your entries over the length of the contest—one a week for five weeks, for example. When the volume of entries is big enough, they will be delivered to the judges in a number of different sacks. The theory is that judges will pick from each sack, and your chances go up if you have an entry in each of several different mailbags.

☐ Keep informed. Join a local contest club or subscribe to a contest newsletter. Either source will help you to learn contest traps and problems—and solutions. They'll alert you, too, to new competitions.

☐ Be selective. You must pay taxes on items that you win, so be sure the prizes are appropriate for you. If you don't live near the water, winning an expensive boat could be a headache. (Some contests offer cash equivalents, but not all do.)

☐ If you do win, check with your CPA or tax lawyer immediately. You must report the fair market value of items that you win, whether you keep them, sell them or give them away. This can be tricky. Also, if you win, you can deduct the expenses of postage, stationery, etc., that you have used to enter this and other sweepstakes and contests in the same year. These costs are not deductible if you don't win.

☐ Most contests and sweepstakes ask you to enclose some proof of purchase or a plain piece of paper with a product name or number written on it. Many people assume that a real proof of purchase will improve their chances of winning. *Fact:* In a recent survey, more than half the winners of major prizes reported that they had not bought the sponsor's product.

Source: Roger Tyndall, co-editor with his wife, Carolyn, of the country's largest circulation newsletter, *Contest Newsletter*, Fern Beach, FL.

Reluctant vacationers

Not everyone loves to get away from it all on a vacation. Some people really prefer to work. But families need vacations, and so do workaholics occasionally.

How to take yourself away from the office successfully:

☐ Make vacations somewhat similar to your year-round life, so that they offer continuity as well as contrast. If you enjoy a daily swim at the gym, be sure to pick a vacation stop with a pool. If you never step into art museums at home, don't feel you have to drag yourself to them when you're away.

☐ Leave your calculator, beeper, dictating device and briefcase at home.

☐ Avoid finishing lots of work at the last minute. It can leave you feeling frantic.

☐ Don't drive your staff crazy by leaving lots of lists and memos or calling continually. Limit yourself to two calls the first day and one a day thereafter.

☐ Take enough time off to recharge your energy. Two weeks may feel too long, but three days is too short.

Source: Dr. Marilyn Machlowitz, a New York organizational psychologist and consultant.

Don't let your vacation home cut into your leisure time

The most desirable thing to look for in a weekend house is ease of maintenance.

☐ Get rid of rugs in the summer.

☐ Ask the landlord to remove his accumulations of dustcatching peacock feathers and other decorator touches. Keep your own importations to a minimum.

☐ Cut down on weekend cleaning chores and outdoor work with hired help.

☐ Consider expanding leisure time by commuting with the laundry. That's cumbersome, but better than hours in a laundromat on a sunny afternoon.

☐ Cultivate the fine art of list-making. Shopping and menu planning can be almost painless if the list is done right.

☐ If you're planning a Saturday dinner party, don't rely on the local supermarket for the perfect roast unless you've ordered (and confirmed) in advance. The accompanying wines might be better purchased at home, too, unless you're sure of your local supplier.

☐ Don't forget to take the same precautions as you would for a trip—extra reading glasses and copies of prescriptions might save you an unwanted journey home.

Fishing a new lake

If you know where to start looking, you can fish any lake successfully.

Where bass congregate:

☐ Near trees that have recently fallen into the water.

☐ In hot weather: Under lily pads, especially in the only shallow spots around.

☐ In consistently mild weather: In backwater ponds and coves off the main lake. *Best:* Good weed or brush cover, with a creek running in.

☐ Any time at all: In sunken moss beds near the shore.

Source: *Outdoor Life.*

Portrait photography secrets

People are the most popular subject for photography. There are ways to turn snapshots of family and friends into memorable portraits. Techniques:

☐ Get close. Too much landscape overwhelms the subject.

☐ Keep the head high in the frame as you compose the shot. Particularly from a distance, centering the head leaves too much blank background and cuts off the body arbitrarily.

☐ Avoid straight rows of heads in group shots. It's better to have some subjects stand and others sit in a two-level setting.

☐ Pose subjects in natural situations, doing what they like to do—petting the cat, playing the piano, etc.

☐ Simplify backgrounds. Try using a large aperture (small f-stop number) to throw the background out of focus and highlight the subject.

☐ Beware of harsh shadows. The human eye accommodates greater contrast of light to dark than does a photographic system. Either shadows or highlights will be lost in the picture, usually the shadowed area.

For outdoor portraits

☐ Avoid the midday sun. This light produces harsh shadows and makes people squint. Hazy sun, often found in the morning, is good. Cloudy days give a lovely, soft effect.

☐ Use fill light to cut shadows. A flash can be used outdoors, but it is hard to compute correctly. *Best fill-light method:* Ask someone to hold a large white card or white cloth near the subject to bounce the natural light into the shadowed area.

☐ Use backlight. When the sun is behind the subject (but out of the picture), the face receives a soft light. With a simple camera, the cloudy setting is correct. If your camera has a light meter, take a reading close to the subject or, from a distance, increase the exposure one or two stops from what the meter indicates.

☐ Beware of dappled shade. The effect created in the photograph will be disturbing.

For indoor portraits

☐ Use window light. A bright window out of direct sun is a good choice. However, if there is high contrast between the window light and the rest of the room, use filler-light techniques to diminish the shadow.

☐ Use flashbulbs. A unit with a tilting head lets you light the subject by bouncing the flash off the ceiling, creating a wonderful diffuse top lighting. (This won't work with high, dark or colored ceilings.)

☐ Mix direct light and bounce flash. An easy way to put twinkle in the eyes and lighten shadows when using bounce light is to add a little direct light. With the flash head pointed up, a small white card attached to the back of the flash will send light straight onto the subject.

☐ Keep a group an even distance from the flash. Otherwise, the people in the back row will be dim, while those in front may even be overexposed.

Making New Year's Eve a family or neighborhood affair

☐ Invite close relatives to spend the evening reminiscing and becoming a family again. Organize a slide show of old family photographs or show home movies to break the ice.

☐ If you are a runner, do an evening five miles with running friends and then see the new year in with a pasta feast. (New Yorkers can run in or watch a mini-marathon in Central Park, with fireworks at the finish line at midnight. Check for similar events in other cities.)

☐ Rent the local high-school auditorium and sponsor a band concert for the community. Or organize your own band with fellow musicians.

☐ Have a bake-in in your kitchen, with prizes for the best chocolate desserts.

☐ Have a multigenerational party for your whole family and friends of all ages.

☐ Spend New Year's Eve taking down holiday decorations, finishing your thank-you notes for holiday gifts and otherwise cleaning the slate for the coming year.

☐ With your mate, make a list of do's and don'ts and resolutions for the new year.

☐ Organize a neighborhood "progressive dinner" with a different course in each house. Watch the time so you get to the last stop and the champagne by midnight.

☐ Rent a skating rink—ice or roller—for a big, many-family party with an instructor or two to get the fainthearted going smoothly.

How to solve caterer problems before they arise

☐ The ideal way to select a caterer is to attend one of his or her parties.

☐ If that's not possible, ask for recommendations from your most trusted and sophisticated friends and acquaintances.

☐ Another source of information is gourmet magazines. Local publications often write articles about caterers, too.

☐ Many caterers provide pamphlets or sample menus, but these are a poor substitute for a solid personal recommendation.

☐ Try, if at all possible, to sample the food each caterer offers. Keep in mind, however, the kind of party you are planning. Someone who prepares exquisite nouvelle cuisine may not be the best person to cater a large outdoor barbecue.

☐ When you have the names of a few reputable caterers, meet with each, preferably where the party will take place. Many hosts are distressed by caterers' tendency to "take over"—to dictate all arrangements and ignore the host's concerns. Know your own feelings about this and try to gauge the caterer's willingness to accommodate you.

☐ Never hire anyone who has a specific number of parties in her repertory and simply "does" party number six at your home. Even if the caterer is to take total control, you want her to approach your party as a unique situation.

☐ Ask at the beginning of the discussion whether the caterer herself will be present at the actual function. If she plans to send an assistant, meet that person and make sure you have confidence in her abilities.

☐ Be sure also to discuss clean-up arrangements with the caterer.

☐ Although most caterers actually only prepare the food and hire the service themselves, they can certainly make arrangements (and take responsibility for them) with liquor stores, florists, musicians, etc. They can also recommend people you can contact directly (possibly helping you to cut corners economically). Or, you can come up with your own choices.

☐ Never hire independent help to serve your caterer's food. After the quality of the food itself, service is probably the most important ingredient in a successful party. Your caterer should work with people she knows and trusts.

☐ The caterer should draw up a contract that spells out every cost and makes the caterer's list of duties clear.

☐ You will probably be asked to make a down payment for up to half the total cost.

☐ The caterer's price is all-inclusive; you are free to tip the staff if you should wish to, but you need not feel obliged to do so.

☐ The caterer will expect to find the scene of the party clean and ready for her to get started. Your equipment (serving trays, etc.) should be at its sparkling best.

☐ Now you should stand back and let her do her job. Don't make any last minute additions to the menu or suddenly rearrange the floor plan.

Source: Germaine and Marcel Chandelier, owners and managers of Germaine's, Long Island City, NY.

How to make slot machines pay off

☐ Key to successful play: A basic understanding of slot mechanics. In Las Vegas, dollar slot machines return on average 88¢–98¢ per dollar invested. (At the high end, they compare favorably with the odds offered by craps, roulette or any other game.)

These are long-term returns over six hours or six months…depending on the machine. The short-term return for a given player will vary tremendously—but not randomly. Every machine has a pay cycle and a down cycle. During its pay cycle, the machine will give back far more than you put in. It might stay "hot" for a hundred pulls or more, spilling out jackpot after jackpot. (At one machine, I hit a triple-bar jackpot—a $150 to $1 payoff—three times in a row.) But during a machine's cold cycle, you can easily drop $100 in less than an hour.

Finding pay-cycle machines

☐ Observe before you play. If you see a player empty $100 or more into a machine (whether or not he hits a few small jackpots along the way) and walk away with nothing, step up and try your luck. There's a good chance the machine is near the end of a down cycle and entering a pay cycle.

☐ If you play a machine "blind," without prior observation, feel the coins in the tray after your first win. If the money is warm, it's probably been sitting in the machine for a time without a jackpot. *Point:* A down cycle may be ending. If the money is cool, move on.

☐ Ask a change clerk to steer you to a hot machine…with the unwritten understanding that you'll tip him/her 10% of your winnings on that machine. (Casinos tolerate this because it doesn't affect their overall take.)

☐ Play machines near casino entrances and exits. The house programs these slots to pay off the best, because their jackpots will attract the most attention. *Also hot:* Any machines near blackjack or other gaming tables. The casino hopes to lure to these machines wives who are watching their husbands play the other games. *Colder:* Machines isolated against the rear wall (and especially in the corners), where jackpots have less advertising value.

☐ Watch for empty coin racks—coin holders next to each machine used by players to stack coins for play or to hold winnings—and play the machine immediately to the left of one. An empty rack means the previous player busted. (When a player hits a jackpot, the rack is used to cart away the coins.) The more empty racks near a machine, the closer it is to a pay cycle.

☐ After I gave an extravagant tip, a casino mechanic once told me to look for three-reel machines with a cherry sitting in the middle reel. While worthless in itself, he said, the cherry was a sign that better times were coming. Since then, I've found that 75% of middle cherry machines return at least a small jackpot within five to six pulls. They're also good bets for a pay cycle.

☐ Your odds are best on single-line, dollar slots. Multiple-line machines offer a greater chance of hitting any jackpot, but the payoffs are much smaller. *Also:* For top value, play the maximum number of coins for each pull.

☐ "Progressive" slots, where the jackpot can build to $1 million or more, can be wildly profitable, but only if they're within their programmed payoff range.

Example: At the Sands in Las Vegas, a clerk told me (after a big tip) that one progressive machine always paid off when the jackpot reached between $48,000 and $64,000. I found it one night at $59,000 and pumped in $300 before I had to leave town. The next morning, the clerk called to tell me that the machine had been hit at 10 AM, when its jackpot reached $62,000.

☐ If you ever see a new machine being uncrated, jump on it. Play it until it bursts. Casinos program new slots to pay particularly well for the first two days so they'll draw more business later.

Source: Dick Phillips, author of *Winning Systems on Slots*, Box 12336, Beaumont, TX 77706.

Secrets of doing crossword puzzles much faster

In order to successfully complete a crossword puzzle, follow these helpful hints…

☐ Start with the fill-in-the-blank clues. These are usually the easiest and the least ambiguous.

☐ Next, try to fill in an across answer in the top row or a down answer on the left side. You can then proceed to answers that start with a known letter …and they're always easier to solve than answers where the known letter is in the middle.

☐ In a thematic puzzle, the longest blanks on the grid always relate to the theme.

☐ When the clue is expressed in the plural, the answer is probably plural. Most clues that are expressed in the past have answers ending in *-ed*. Most clues that are expressed in the superlative have answers ending in *-est*.

☐ Remember that *e* and *s* are the most popular word-ending letters. Also, puzzles use a disproportionate number of common letters and very few rare letters, such as *q, z, x, j,* etc.

☐ When you are missing one or two letters in a word, scan the alphabet. Plug in all possible letters or combinations…one is bound to work.

Source: David Feldman, author of *How to Win at Just About Everything*, Morrow Quill, William Morrow & Co., 105 Madison Ave., New York 10016.

Bingo never was a game of chance

Most people play bingo as if it were a game of sheer chance—as if any set of cards had just as good a chance of winning as any other. They are mistaken. If you correctly choose the cards you play, you can significantly improve your odds of winning any bingo game.

The following system works with *straight* bingo (where you must cover five squares in a row—vertically, horizontally or diagonally), *coverall* (a jackpot game, in which you must cover every square on your card) or any other variation.

Key strategy: To get as many of the 75 numbers as possible on a given set of cards. There are 24 numbers printed on every bingo card. (There are 25 squares, but the center square is a non-numbered free space.) If you chose three cards at random, their 72 numbered spaces would represent only 49 different numbers—the other 23 spaces would have duplicate numbers.

It is possible, however, to find sets of three cards with no duplicates—with 72 different numbers. (Time permitting, players can choose their cards freely at the beginning of any session.) If you were to play such a set, you would be 25% more likely to win a given game than a player with a random set. Depending on the size of the prizes, that edge can translate into hundreds—or even thousands—of dollars of winnings within a few weeks.

The truth about "lucky" cards:

Ironically, most players choose sets that are worse than random. They look for cards with one or two "lucky" numbers —7 or 11, for example. And they are especially drawn to cards where those lucky numbers are at the corners.

The results are devastating. In an average straight game with 1,000 cards in play, a bingo will occur after 15 numbers are called. That means that any given number—regardless of whether it is "lucky" or not—will be called in only one of five games. In those other four games, any set of cards with an uncalled "lucky" number is 25% less likely to win. (When a number is at a corner, it affects three lines—one vertical, one horizontal, one diagonal.)

Another advantage of choosing non-duplicating cards is that it makes it easier to keep track of the numbers you're covering—and harder to miss one by accident.

There are countless statistical systems favored by bingo players, but this is the only one I've found that generates consistent profits.

Where to play:

The only live variable in bingo is the proportion of money collected that is returned to the players. Most operators hold back at least 50% for overhead and revenue. (The percentage is usually posted on the bingo sheets or somewhere in the hall.)

Other games, however, return as much as 75% to the players. The more money that comes back, of course, the better your chances of coming out ahead.

Source: John "Dee" Wyrick, author of *Complete Authoritative Guide to Bingo*, Gambler's Book Club, Box 4115, Las Vegas, NV 89127.

Ex-"Jeopardy!" people picker tells how you, too, can be a game-show contestant

After years of watching game shows and knowing most of the answers, you may want to become a contestant.

More than 650,000 potential contestants audition every year, so if you want to be a winner you must master your game and develop your personality.

Select your game:

Every TV game show is different, so for the best chance target the one for which you are most suited. Spend time watching as many game shows as possible. Determine which of the four types most interests you and which game most closely fits your skills and personality.

☐ Trivia/quiz games test your knowledge of topics including people, current events, history, religion, business, sports, entertainment, products and how quickly you can recall your knowledge.

☐ Word/puzzle games test your vocabulary and language skills.

☐ Personality games test your spontaneous responses and emotional reactions to your personal experiences and real-life situations.

☐ Kids/teens game shows feature contestants who are less than 18 years old.

Focusing:

If you can't decide immediately, try playing board/computer/video games that duplicate the shows you think you might want to try for. See which you enjoy most, are quickest at and win most often.

Choose a particular game: After watching all the shows of that type, study their formats.

Zero in on your final choice by asking yourself what you want in a game show. Do you want money? Goods? A great date? Do you want to play individually or with teammates? Other contestants? Celebrities? How fast-paced is the game? How far are you willing to travel for the audition?

Know your game:

Become an expert: If you want to win or even to get through the audition, you must be thoroughly familiar with your chosen game. You need to know the playing format.

Example: On *Jeopardy!*, contestants provide a question to the host's answer.

You must know the rules cold.

Example: On *Wheel of Fortune*, after spinning the wheel, you must supply a consonant to put in the puzzle.

Learn your game's jargon and the particular phrases favored by the game show. If you don't use them at the audition, you're unlikely to get on the show.

Example: Contestants on *Wheel of Fortune* waiting for the wheel to stop always urge: "Come on $5,000!"

Practice, practice, practice until the game becomes second nature. To play along while watching it: Cover up the answers on the screen or turn your chair around while you answer, write down your answers and check your score, use the game's language and expressions and talk and act like the contestants.

Sharpen your skills with board games or videos, broaden your knowledge of a subject by reading books, magazines and newspapers and compete with family members and friends who play the game well.

Helpful: Set up a mock game-show set in your own home using your own furniture and simulate studio distractions with bright lamps and a noisy radio in the background.

Develop your personality:

Imagine you were auditioning yourself. What would you notice about your appearance and personality? What have other people told you are your five strongest points?

Examples: Winning smile and quick wit.

Those strong points will show in your audition if you have spent hours practicing the game in front of the TV so it feels natural to you.

Work on your verbal skills, enunciate clearly and loudly, speak in complete sentences using words you are comfortable with, maintain eye contact, always show enthusiasm and smile.

When you feel you have practiced enough, call or send a postcard to the show to say you want to be a contestant. Ask if you can audition in your own area. If you must travel to the show's hometown, schedule it when you have time.

When audition day arrives, make sure you look your best and let your sparkling personality shine through. Be prepared to fill in forms and take a written puzzle test.

Those who pass, go on to a second audition where the game is actually played in competition with others. If you do well enough, you will be one of the chosen few.

Important: Shows have many legal restrictions. Example: Knowing anyone who works at the studio will disqualify you.

The show:

If you are chosen, you will get about a month's notice, with instructions on where to go and what to bring.

Example: Five shows are typically taped in one day, so take five outfits in case you are a multiple winner.

How well you do depends on your skills, practice and competitors. You may win big money and/or valuable merchandise. Even if you end up with only a consolation prize, you'll have a memorable experience and lifetime recollections of your few moments of fame.

Source: Greg Muntean, a former contestant co-ordinator for *Jeopardy!* He is the coauthor of *How to Be a Game Show Contestant,* Ballantine Books, New York.

Better composting

Slice, chop or shred everything as fine as possible—large chunks take longer to turn into compost. Include a mixture of items high in carbon, such as leaves and paper egg cartons...and those rich in nitrogen, such as grass clippings and vegetable scraps. Put the compost bin in a convenient spot—so you will use it. *Rule of thumb:* If it comes from a plant, compost it. If it comes from an animal, throw it out—except for cow manure.

Source: *Beautiful Easy Lawns and Landscapes* by Laurence Sombke, host of *The Environment Show* on National Public Radio. Globe Pequot Press, Six Business Park Rd., Old Saybrook, CT 06475.

President's greeting

Did you know that President Clinton will send a greeting card to anyone over age 80—and those who have been married for 50 years? Send a postcard at least one month in advance of the birthday or anniversary to: President William J. Clinton, c/o Greeting Office, The White House, Room 39, Washington, DC 20500.

Name that squash

Personalize a squash by scratching your name or a design onto the skin of the newly formed squash. The name will grow with the squash, and it can be picked and presented once it is fully grown.

Source: *Fun Factor,* Box 3618, Peace Dale, Rhode Island 02883.

How to get more out of your travel

☐ Take along a small tape recorder when you travel. This is easier than jotting notes or trying to find the time to keep a diary.

☐ Interview people you meet along the way. Ask them all about their lives, occupations and backgrounds. This will preserve the facts and actual voices of interesting people you meet.

☐ Tape guided tours. Guides give out lots of information that is forgotten during the excitement of a tour but can be enjoyed later.

For very special occasions

Here are some very classy, exclusive hotels frequented by those who know the right places to stay when they travel. Make reservations a few months in advance.

☐ *Malliouhana Hotel in Anguilla, the Caribbean.* On a small little-known island with few tourists. This new hotel is the ultimate in luxury. Suites and private villas are available, some the size of private homes. Tennis courts, boating and all water sports, including scuba instruction, attracts a jet-set crowd of all ages.

☐ *Baden-Baden in Schwarzwald, Germany.* In the elegant style of a 19th-century spa. Extensive grounds, impeccable service, an excellent restaurant and hot springs where you can "take the waters." Attracts an old world, conservative crowd.

☐ *Hotel Los Monteros in Marbella, Spain.* On one of the Mediterranean coast's most fashionable stretches. Wide range of sports, spacious rooms and tropical gardens. Has a 1920s charm reminiscent of the Gatsby era. Ask for a room with an ocean view. Attracts all types, from young families to older couples.

☐ *Hotel San Pietro in Positano, Italy.* Picturesquely perched on top of a cliff, with all 55 double rooms overlooking rocky coast and sea. Scenic beaches. Secluded and elegant, it attracts a young to middle-aged highly sophisticated crowd. Open March 14 through November 3.

☐ *Mount Kenya Safari Club in Nairobi, Kenya.* A distinguished private retreat located halfway up Mt. Kenya. One hundred acres of rolling lawns, waterfalls, gardens, a heated pool, sauna, three dining rooms and safari excursions for both photography and hunting. Special events such as African barbecues and tribal dances. Dress is formal, with jacket and tie required for dinner. Guests tend to be families, couples and ultra-exclusive tours and groups.

☐ *Lake Palace in Udaipur, India.* Originally an 18th-century royal residence. Located on an island in the middle of Lake Pichola, it has air-conditioned rooms, exotic suites, water sports, a marble-inlaid pool and a restaurant serving Continental and Indian cuisine. Guests are all ages but tend to be very sophisticated.

☐ *Hotel de Paris in Monaco.* A superior hotel. Has an underground passage to the Casino and Le Club. Palatial rooms and facilities. Spa, sauna, two restaurants and a cabaret. Old money stays here.

☐ *Voile d'Or Hotel in St.-Jean-Cap-Ferrat, France.* Overlooks the harbor. Its spacious, French provincial–style rooms all have balconies and marble baths. A favorite honeymoon spot, the atmosphere breathes intimate elegance. Gourmet cuisine. Open February to October.

☐ *Splendido Hotel in Portofino, Italy.* A super-deluxe classic hotel on high ground overlooking the sea. Charming rooms, suites, gardens, a seawater pool, sauna and health spa. Attracts all types and ages, including many businesspeople. Open March 29 to October 29.

Source: Francesca Baldeschi, manager, Ports of Call Travel Consultants, Inc., New York.

Plan for very special trips

If you're the type who finds the sameness of Holiday Inns comforting or prefers to have dinner at McDonald's—in Paris—this checklist isn't for you. But if you love country inns, a pot of coffee brewing in your room, four-poster beds, claw-legged bathtubs, lunch beside a swan pond, discovering the best wine cellar in Vermont or the trail that isn't on a map, then you might want to plan your vacations differently.

☐ Consult the guidebooks and travel agent last.

☐ Year round, collect information on all kinds of interesting vacation possibilities.

☐ Keep geographical files labeled Caribbean, West Coast, The South, New England, Europe, Israel, Japan and Exotic Places, for example. You can make your own headings and add new folders when the catch-all category gets too full to be manageable.

☐ Subdivide your files into subject files labeled Ski Vacations, Tennis Vacations, Club Med Locations, Charming Inns/Elegant Small Hotels, Houses for Rent or Exchange and Great Restaurants in Other Places (to distinguish it from your home town restaurant file).

☐ File articles from airline magazines, newsletters and the travel section of your newspaper.

☐ Interview friends. When you agree with your friends' taste in food, furnishings, theater or painting, chances are you can trust their vacation advice.

☐ Talk with neighbors, clients, friends at work.

☐ Think of exchanging visits with friends you meet on vacation.

☐ Save picture postcards from active travellers.

☐ Eavesdrop in an airport or restaurant, on the bus or train to work. If you hear a total stranger describe a perfect meal she had in Kansas City, or a rustic lodge in the Adirondacks with a gorgeous view of the sunset, jot it down. Check out the details later. (That's where guidebooks and travel agents come in handy.)

☐ Books, movies, magazines. In vacation terms, life can imitate art. You'll want to visit Big Sur if you've read Henry Miller.

Eight grand old hotels that are still magnificent

Some great old hotels have never lost their luster, and an increasing number of formerly faded dowagers have recently had facelifts, restoring them to their original beauty. Here are a few special places:

☐ *Adolphus Hotel, Dallas.* Texans used to describe this turreted pile of stone as "early beer baron," but their laughter turned to admiration when this Gothic revival hotel reopened in 1980 after four years of careful restoration to its original 1912 magnificence.

☐ *Bürgenstock Hotel Estate, Switzerland.* A splendid aerie 1,500 feet above Lake Lucerne. It artfully mixes modern meeting facilities featuring the latest electronic gadgetry with truly baronial accommodations. The guest rooms are luxurious, and the public spaces resemble museums. Open May–October.

☐ *The Connaught, London.* This landmark in the perennially stylish Mayfair district is elegance itself, and the service is as impeccable as only the finest English establishment could make it.

☐ *Four Seasons Olympic, Seattle.* This eclectic hotel in the center of Seattle had its ups and downs between its construction in 1924 and its renovation in 1982. The World War II blackout paint is now off the ballroom windows, the lobby is grandly furnished and the rooms are modern yet luxurious.

☐ *Hotel Imperial, Vienna.* Built in 1867 on a fashionable boulevard as the home of the Duke of Wurttemburg, it has been a sumptuous hotel since 1873. Personalized service in the tradition of the Hapsburg empire still reigns supreme.

☐ *Hotel InterContinental, Paris.* Built for the 1878 World's Fair, it was taken over by InterContinental in 1968. Its public spaces gleam, and its guest rooms are sybaritic retreats with extras like hair dryers, minibars, bathroom scales and color TV with in-room movies. The Salon Imperial is a stately banquet hall, and the recently restored Garden Court is a tranquil oasis in the busy heart of Paris.

☐ *The Mandarin Oriental, Hong Kong.* Classic hotel in the center of Hong Kong's business district. All other hotels in the Orient are ultimately judged by this one. Lovely and luxurious, it sets the standard for impeccable service, superb cuisine and Oriental ambience combined with Occidental efficiency.

☐ *Hotel Seelbach, Louisville.* It was built in 1905 and hit a long, slow decline before closing in the early 1970s. The restorers (rather than the wreckers) took over, embarking on a three-year refurbishment to its original glory. This Louisville landmark reopened to rave reviews in March 1982.

Best hotels in the world

The world's premier travel accommodations, according to a poll of leading bankers, are (in order of preference):

- ☐ Bangkok, *The Oriental.*
- ☐ Hong Kong, *The Mandarin.*
- ☐ Tokyo, *Hotel Okura.*
- ☐ Zurich, *Dolder Grand Hotel.*
- ☐ Singapore, *Shangri-La Hotel.*
- ☐ Paris, *Hotel Ritz.*
- ☐ Hamburg, *Hotel Vier Jahreszeiten.*
- ☐ Hong Kong, *The Peninsula.*
- ☐ Madrid, *Ritz Hotel.*
- ☐ London, *Claridge.*
- ☐ New York, *The Hotel Carlyle.*
- ☐ Paris, *Hôtel Plaza Athénée.*
- ☐ Zurich, *Baur au Lac.*
- ☐ London, *The Connaught Hotel.*
- ☐ Rome, *Hotel Hassler Villa Medici.*
- ☐ Munich, *Hotel Vier Jahreszeiten.*
- ☐ London, *The Berkeley.*
- ☐ Washington, DC, *Four Seasons.*
- ☐ Vienna, *Hotel Imperial.*
- ☐ Washington, DC, *The Madison.*
- ☐ Manila, *The Manila Hotel.*
- ☐ Chicago, *The Ritz-Carlton.*
- ☐ Toronto, *Four Seasons Hotel.*
- ☐ Tokyo, *Imperial Hotel.*
- ☐ Paris, *Hotel Meurice.*
- ☐ Geneva, *Le Richmond.*
- ☐ New York, *The Pierre.*
- ☐ Paris, *Hotel George V.*
- ☐ London, *Four Seasons Inn on the Park.*
- ☐ Vienna, *Hotel Sacher.*
- ☐ Los Angeles, *Regent Beverly Wilshire.*
- ☐ Sydney, *Sheraton Wentworth.*
- ☐ Stockholm, *Grand Hotel.*
- ☐ New York, *The Park Lane Hotel.*
- ☐ Mexico City, *Camino Real.*
- ☐ Geneva, *Les Bergues.*
- ☐ Montreal, *Ritz-Carlton.*
- ☐ San Francisco, *The Mark Hopkins Hotel.*
- ☐ London, *The Savoy.*
- ☐ New York, *The Regency Hotel.*

Source: *Institutional Investor.*

Super executive travel

The best hotels to visit if you are on an expense account—or if money is no object:

- ☐ Amsterdam: The *Amsterdam Hilton* and the *Amstel.*
- ☐ Athens: *Athenaeum InterContinental* and the *Athens Hilton.*
- ☐ Berlin: The *Bristol Kempinski* and *Steignenberger.*
- ☐ Florence: *Excelsior, Savoy, Villa Medici* and *Rest Lorenzo de'Medici.*
- ☐ Geneva: The *Richmond* and the *Rhone.*
- ☐ London: The *Connaught* is tops, followed by the *Hyde Park, Ritz, Claridge, Churchill, Savoy, Dorchester Grosvenor House, Berkeley, Carlton Tower* and *Inn on the Park.*
- ☐ Madrid: Heading the list are the *Ritz* and the *Villa Magna.* The *Palace, Eurobuilding, Miguel Angel, Mindanao, Milia Castilla, Wellington, Princess Plaza* and *Luz Palacio* run close seconds.
- ☐ Milan: The *Excelsior Gallia* and *Principe e Savoia.*
- ☐ Paris: The *Ritz* or the *Plaza Athénée.* Next: The *Inter-Continental, Meurice, Lotti, George V, Bristol, Crillon* and *Prince de Galles.*
- ☐ Rome: The *Hassler Villa Medici* is the best. Also highly recommended: *Le Grand Hotel, Excelsior, Jolly* and *Cavalieri Hilton.*

Source: The *Michelin 20 Cities of Europe* guide.

Luxurious one-week trips

If you want to experience a magic vacation week—seven days to match your wildest fantasies—try any of these ideas:

- ☐ Travel first class by present standards and those of another age. Whip to London on the Concorde in three hours. Then settle into the new Orient Express for a leisurely trip to Venice. The legendary train (with its 1920s cars completely restored to their former polished-brass-and-crystal glory) makes the London-Paris-Milan-Venice run twice a week. Base your Venetian sightseeing at the Hotel Cipriani before returning to London and flying home.

- ☐ Lose weight in luxury with the Lancaster Farm program at Brenner's

Park Hotel in Baden-Baden, Germany. (The main building was a residence of Napoleon III.) Do water exercises in a Pompeiian pool. Have a daily massage, facial, body wrap and beautiful meals that add up to only 1,000 calories a day. Makeup, manicures and pedicures are part of the program. Baden-Baden has colonnaded shops and a famous casino.

☐ See Burgundy by balloon. View the chateaus and vineyards of southeastern France from the gondola of a hot-air balloon (between terrestrial tours of the region by car). Stay in the Hotels de la Poste in Beaune and Vezelay, sampling the local wines. The great French Balloon Adventure leaves every Sunday from Paris starting in May and is organized by the Bombard Society in San Francisco. Airfare to Paris is extra.

☐ Charter a yacht—with crew—and cruise the Caribbean. Captain, cook, hands and provisions are included. Airfare from New York to the Virgin Islands is extra.

☐ A villa or a castle for a week. Try Dromoland Castle in Ireland or an Acapulco villa.

☐ Entertain like a king (or a Comstock Lode heiress) in San Francisco by renting the penthouse suite of the Fairmont Hotel. Designed in the 1920s for Maude Flood, a gold and silver baroness, the suite has a walnut-paneled living room, a dining room that seats 50, a domed library, a mosaic-walled gameroom complete with pool table, three bedrooms and baths with gold fixtures. The kitchen is fully equipped. The bar is stocked. Dinnerware, silver and linens are included, as well as a vault, a baby-grand piano, books, artwork, a butler and a maid. Food is extra.

☐ Great hotels. Pick a city you want to explore and put yourself in the hands of a master innkeeper for a week. Some suggestions:

☐☐ California wine country, *Sonoma Mission Inn.*

☐☐ Colorado Springs, *The Broadmoor Hotel.*

☐☐ Paris, *The Plaza Athénée.*

☐☐ Beverly Hills, *The Beverly Hills Hotel.*

☐☐ New York, *The New York Palace.*

☐☐ London, *The Savoy.*

☐☐ Dallas, *The Mansion at Turtle Creek.*

☐☐ Rio de Janeiro, *The Meridien Hotel.*

Getting VIP treatment on a cruise ship

☐ Get the word to the shipping line that you rate A-1 treatment. Your travel agent can do this by writing the shipping line. Also, the more expensive your cabin, the better service you will generally get.

☐ What you can expect when you're tagged for VIP treatment: Dinner at the captain's table, an invitation to the captain's special cocktail party or perhaps flowers and assorted gifts in your cabin.

☐ Make sure to get a good seat in the dining room. Usually, that means in the center, close to the captain's table. Ask your travel agent to see if he can reserve a well-placed table for you in advance. If that can't be done, make sure that as soon as you go aboard ship, you tell the maitre d' what you want—with a tip.

☐ Have an early talk with your dining-room captain and waiter. Ask them what the chef's specialties are. Order those far in advance for your dinners later on in the cruise. The trick is to know what the kitchen is good at and to give the chef time to prepare it.

☐ Tip the dining-room captain and let him know there's more for him if the service is excellent.

☐ Also give the dining-room waiter, in advance, half the amount you would normally tip him at the end of the cruise and indicate he'll get at least as much more for top-notch service. He's the man who can get you all sorts of snacks, like fruit, cheeses, sandwiches, iced tea and ice cream—almost any time of day or night. Ask him what is available, and if there is a best time to order these items for your cabin. If you want ice cream at 11 PM every night, tell him in advance, so he can plan accordingly. Similarly, give your room steward half the tip in advance and let him know that good service will bring a reward.

☐ Book the second sitting for meals when on a cruise. That leaves you more time to get ready for dinner after a day of touring, a longer cocktail hour and less time to kill until the evening activities begin.

Best cruises

☐ Cunard Royal Viking Line, 555 Fifth Ave., New York 10017. 800-221-4770,

800-458-9000 for Sea Goddess. The Queen Elizabeth II, one of the most palatial ships afloat, makes regular trans-atlantic crossings and offers free return flights on the Concorde to its Top of the Queen class passengers. The QEII and the Sagafjord also offer round-the-world cruises, and Cunard's other ships offer itineraries in Caribbean and European waters.

□ Renaissance Cruises, 1800 Eller Drive, Suite 300, Box 350307, Fort Lauderdale, FL 33335. 305-463-0982, 800-525-2450 for info, 800-525-5350 for reservations. The eight Renaissance ships, each carrying about 100 passengers, sail everywhere from the Baltic to the Seychelles Islands. The ships are, on occasion, chartered by groups.

□ Holland America Line Westours/ Windstar Cruises, 300 Elliott Ave. West, Seattle, WA 98119. 206-281-3535. The three elegant Windstar ships are powered mainly by the wind harnessed in giant computer-controlled sails. Itineraries include Polynesia, the Caribbean and the Mediterranean.

□ Seabourne Cruise Line, 55 Francisco St., Suite 710, San Francisco, 94133. 415-391-7444, 800-929-9696. Seabourne's two ships offer luxurious 100% outside cabins, and sail in Asia, the Mexican Riviera and the Mediterranean.

□ Royal Cruise Line, One Maritime Plaza, San Francisco, CA 94111. 415-956-7200. The refurbished Royal Odyssey and Star Odyssey and the newly launched Queen Odyssey are all winners with spas, fitness centers and plenty of room. They offer cruises in the Riviera, to the Greek isles, along the coast of Turkey and through the Panama Canal.

How to get a cruise ship's best price

□ Don't rely solely on travel agents. Not all of them are knowledgeable about cruises, and some promote only one or two lines.

□ Instead, read the latest issues of *Travel Weekly*, especially the issues with a cruise guide. Then ask agents about specific cruises that interest you.

□ Get prices from several agents. Surprisingly, prices often vary because of the many promotional gimmicks of the cruise lines.

□ Ask about cash rebates, free airfare to the port of departure, flat rates for inside and outside cabins, free passage for third and fourth persons.

□ Try checking with the steamship company itself, which may give you an even better deal.

Source: Daniel A. Nesbett, travel marketing consultant, Darien, CT.

Freighter and cargo cruises

These increasingly popular cruises can be taken only by people who can be away from business for long periods of time and have flexible schedules. They're very good for retirees.

There is no assurance that a ship scheduled to depart on a particular day will indeed leave that day. The first consideration of such ships is their cargo, and they will stay in port until they are completely loaded, even if that means waiting for weeks. The same holds true all along the route. You are protected on price, however. The longer the voyage, the lower the per diem costs.

Some advantages of cargo cruises:

□ Costs are considerably lower than for other types of cruises. Everything is included in the price.

□ Most ships carry only 8–12 passengers, so you have an excellent opportunity to get to know your fellow cruisers. (However, you risk traveling with people you don't care for.)

□ You get more port time than with regular ships.

□ The quarters are usually first-rate. The food is simple and good. Larger ships sometimes have their own swimming pools.

Points to keep in mind:

□ There are certain restrictions on age and health on the smaller ships. On those with 12 or more passengers, a doctor is required, so they are more lenient about health restrictions.

□ When you make your reservation, you pay a deposit. The balance of the cost must be paid by a month before scheduled sailing time. Cancellations are refundable if the ship company is able to resell your space.

□ Book your trip through a travel agency familiar with this type of ship. A travel agency can help you with the many documents to be filed—and with refunds, if necessary.

Most popular freight and cargo lines:

☐ *Ivaran Line*, 111 Pavonia Ave., Jersey City, NJ 07310. 201-798-5656.

☐ *Blue Star North America*, 180 Howard St., Suite 560, San Francisco 94105. 415-247-5300.

☐ *Lykes Line*, 300 Poycras St., New Orleans, LA 70130. 504-523-6611.

☐ *Compagnie Polynesienne de Transport Maritime,* 595 Market St., Suite 2880, San Francisco 94104. 415-541-0677.

Best months at top overseas tourist spots

Europe

☐ *Greece*. March–May, October and November.

☐ *London*. April–June, October and November.

☐ *Paris*. April–June, October and November.

☐ *Riviera* (Monaco, France, Italy). Christmas, New Year's and Easter holidays. *Also:* June–August.

☐ *Rome*. March–May, October–December.

☐ *Scandinavia*. May–September. Winter sports: February and March.

☐ *Switzerland*. Winter sports: December–April. Summer activities: May–August.

☐ *Confederation of Independent States (former USSR)*. April–June, September and October. Summers are torrid, with no air conditioning. Winters are harsh.

☐ *Venice*. March–June.

Africa

☐ *Egypt*. Always hot and humid. *Best:* March–May, October–December.

☐ *Kenya*. Seasons are reversed. June, July and August are coolest. December, January, February and March are hot and dry.

☐ *Morocco*. The sun shines 300 days a year. In the south around Agadir and in Marrakech: December–March. Avoid visiting in August or September.

☐ *South Africa*. There are no extremes of climate. Capetown: January–March. Kruger National Park: June–September. Johannesburg: May–August.

Middle East

☐ *Israel*. Tel Aviv: April–June, October–December. Jerusalem: January–June, October and November.

☐ *Jordan*. Hot and dry all year. *Best:* March–May, November and December.

☐ *Saudi Arabia*. December–March.

Orient

☐ *China*. The country is vast, with a wide-ranging climate. The most visited cities are Beijing, Tientsin, Nankin, Hangchow, Shanghai and Canton, where summers are hot and humid and winters are relatively mild. *Best:* April–June and October.

☐ *Japan*. April–June, October and November.

Asia and the Pacific

☐ *Australia*. Seasons are reversed. Melbourne, Sydney, Canberra: October–February. Darwin: June–August.

☐ *India*. The climate varies greatly. *Best:* November, December, February and March. Monsoons: June–September.

☐ *Malaysia*. March–July and September.

☐ *Nepal* (Himalayas). September–November.

☐ *New Zealand*. The weather is always cool and temperate.

☐ *Philippines*. November–March.

☐ *Singapore*. Always hot, with little variation in rainfall.

☐ *South Korea*. March–May, October and November.

☐ *Sri Lanka*. December–March.

☐ *Tahiti*. May–October.

☐ *Thailand*. November–April.

South America

☐ *Argentina*. October–March.

☐ *Brazil*. October–March.

☐ *Chile*. October–February.

☐ *Peru*. Lima: January–March. Mountains: June–September.

☐ *Venezuela*. December–March.

Closer to Home

☐ *Bermuda*. May–October. *Also:* Easter week.

☐ *Canada*. Winter sports: November–April. Summer sports and city vacations: May–September.

☐ *Caribbean*. November–April.

☐ *Florida*. December–April.

☐ *Hawaii*. Ideal all year.

☐ *Mexico*. October–April.

☐ *Puerto Rico*. November–April.

Best places to ski

California

☐ *Squaw Valley*. Developed for the Olympics, it includes an 8,200-foot tram. 916-583-5585. *Stay at:* Squaw Valley Lodge.

Colorado

☐ *Aspen*. Ski Aspen Mountain, Ruthie's Run, Snowmass or Aspen Highlands. 303-925-9000. *Stay at:* Aspen Inn, Aspen Lodge, The Gant or Hotel Jerome.

☐ *Vail*. A wide variety of runs is available in this movie-star ski capital. *Alternate:* Beaver Creek, just 12 miles farther on Interstate 70. 303-476-5677. *Stay at:* Inn at West Vail, Sunbird Lodge, Vail Village Inn.

Idaho

☐ *Sun Valley*. An old-timer, but still going strong. Experienced skiers enjoy Mount Baldy and Dollar Mountain. 208-622-4111. *Stay at:* Sun Valley Lodge.

Utah

☐ *Alta*. Experienced skiers attempt the High Rustler Run, with 40-degree slope, no trees and frequent avalanches. 801-942-0404. *Stay at:* Alta Lodge.

☐ *Snowpine*. Known for powder skiing. Hidden Peak is 11,000 feet high. There are also runs for beginners. 801-742-2000. *Stay at:* The Lodge.

Vermont

☐ *Killington*. Highest lift-served summit in New England. 802-422-3333. *Stay at:* Mountain Inn, Summit Lodge.

☐ *Stowe*. Ski the demanding sectors of Mount Mansfield, Spruce Peak, Sterling Mountain. 802-253-7321. *Stay at:* Green Mountain Inn, Stowehof, Topnotch.

☐ *Warren*. Excellent skiing is available at Mount Allen, Mount Lincoln Peak or Sugarbush Valley. 802-583-2381. *Stay at:* Sugarbush Inn.

Western Canada

☐ *Vancouver area*. Ski the Black Comb and Whistler Mountains, with the highest vertical drop in North America. Heli-skiing is also available. 604-932-3434. Call Whistler Resort Association, 604-932-3928.

Eastern Canada

☐ *Mount Tremblant*. 90 miles north of Montreal, in the Laurentians. 819-425-2711. *Stay at:* Gray Rocks Inn, Mount Tremblant Lodge.

Austria

☐ *Innsbruck*. Twice an Olympic site, this 800-year-old city is surrounded by excellent ski areas. Austrian National Tourist Office, 500 Fifth Ave., New York 10017. 718-994-6880. *Stay at:* The Europe, Goldener Adler, Sporthotel.

☐ *Kitzbuhel*. A favored, more chic ski spot in the lofty Austrian Alps. *Stay at:* Grand, Goldener Graf, Hirzingerhof.

France

☐ *Chamonix, Courcheval, Val d'Isere*. Ski the Haute Savoie chain of mountains, including Mont Blanc. French Government Tourist Office, 610 Fifth Ave., New York 10020. 212-757-1125. *Stay at:* Carlton, Croix Blanche or Mont Blanc in Chamonix. Carlina, LeLana or Pralong 2000 in Courcheval. Christiania or Grandes Parades in Val d'Isere.

Italy

☐ *Cortina d'Ampezzo*. Downhill skiers are enthusiastic about the spectacular Dolomites, just north of Venice. Italian Government Travel Office, 630 Fifth Ave., New York 10020. 212-843-6880. *Stay at:* Hotel Cristallo, Hotel de la Poste, Miramonti Majestic.

Switzerland

☐ *Swiss Alps*. The finest downhill skiing. Swissair, 608 Fifth Ave., New York 10020. 718-995-8400. *Stay at:* Belvedere, Derby or Schweizerhof in Davos. Palace, Park or Residence Palace in Gstaad. Badrutt's Palace, Kulm or Suvretta House in St. Moritz. Monte Rosa or Mount Cervin in Zermatt.

Phone numbers in the US and Canadian sections are for area-information services that can take your reservation.

Best uncrowded resorts in Mexico

For the cheapest prices and probably the most exciting vacations, stay away from well-known, overcrowded resorts like Acapulco and Taxco.

Travelers who know Mexico well say they especially like:

☐ *Ixtapa*, 150 miles north of Acapulco on the Pacific. Warm, dry and uncrowded, the resort has one of the most luxurious hotels in Mexico, the Ixtapa Camino Real.

☐ *Merida*, the capital of Yucatan, is old, exotic and cheap. The elegant Montejo Palace costs much more than other hotels. Merida is the takeoff point for excursions to nearby Mayan ruins, where hotels are similarly priced.

☐ *Oaxaca* is near the site of some of the most beautiful pre-Columbian ruins. A 16th-century convent has been converted into El Presidente hotel.

☐ *Vera Cruz*, not touted by Mexico's tourist officials, is a picturesque old city on the Gulf of Mexico with some of the best food in the country. The six-hour drive from 7,200-foot-high Mexico City to sea-level Vera Cruz is spectacular. The beachside Mocambo Hotel is reasonably priced.

The secrets of better vacations in the Caribbean

The Caribbean is just like any other vacation destination. It is always cheaper to go in the off-season. That runs from mid-April to mid-November. Vacation prices across the board can be as much as 30% to 40% cheaper in the off-season than during the height of the season.

Prices begin to rise as the high season approaches, but in general there are deals to be had throughout the region right up to the beginning of the high season. What makes the Caribbean different from a lot of vacation spots is the consistency of the weather. There is, in fact, little difference in weather between the high season and the middle of the off-season when temperatures are, at most, 5 to 10 degrees warmer.

Even during the height of the season, there are opportunities to get a price break. There is a three-week period between January 10 and early February when demand slackens somewhat and hoteliers are willing to cut rates by as much as a third.

Watch the headlines

Another way to tap into a great vacation at an affordable price is to think about going to the Caribbean immediately following a hurricane, storm or some international crisis.

Demand always falls off at these times and hotels and resorts trim prices to encourage vacationers to return. *Catch:* Make sure that the hurricane or storm you're following hasn't disrupted your target island's infrastructure.

The best deals to the Caribbean are usually found on the larger islands with the greatest number of hotels and resorts, particularly Jamaica and the US Virgin Islands. The reason is simple. The greater number of vacation choices provides competition that helps keep prices down. Conversely, smaller, less developed islands, such as St. Barts, Grenada, the Grenadines and Anguilla, are generally more expensive.

Honeymooners forever

Ask if there are special rates for honey-mooners. They are regularly offered special deals, sometimes cutting as much as 50%—but at least 10% to 20% —off the price of a stay. Hotels and resorts do this in hopes that honey-mooners will come back repeatedly in future years.

Villas:

Some of the best deals in the Caribbean don't involve hotels or resorts—but villas. These range in size from one or two bedrooms to small mansions. Depending on the price, they include pools, maid service, cooks, private beaches, tennis courts and other amenities. The cost can be quite reasonable. A small one or two bedroom villa might rent for $1,000 a week during the high season, while the larger villas can go for $5,000 a week.

Even at the upper end of the market, the price can still be reasonable if it's split between three or four couples. Villas are available on most islands. Good source to check: Villas and Apartments

Abroad Ltd., 212-759-1025 or 800-433-3020.

Source: Larry Fox, a *Washington Post* reporter, and Barbara Radin-Fox, a social worker and photographer. They are coauthors of several books including *Romantic Island Getaways: The Caribbean, Bermuda and the Bahamas,* John Wiley & Sons, New York.

Best gambling casinos in the world

We offer here the very best places to gamble, along with their best hotels.

Rates vary according to the season. It's best to book through a travel agent, since gambling packages are usually available at lower costs than the average room rates.

United States

☐ *Atlantic City, NJ*: Bally, Caesar's Palace, Claridge, Bally's Grand, Harrah's, Resorts, Sands, TropWorld.

☐ *Las Vegas, NV*: Caesar's Palace, Desert Inn, Las Vegas Hilton, Bally's Las Vegas, Mirage.

☐ *North Lake Tahoe, NV*: Hyatt Lake Tahoe.

☐ *Reno, NV*: Bally's, Reno, Harrah's.

☐ *South Lake Tahoe, NV*: Caesar's Tahoe, Harrah's Lake Tahoe.

Caribbean

☐ *Antigua*: Curtain Bluff, Halcyon Beach Cove Resort.

☐ *Aruba*: American Aruba, Aruba Concorde.

☐ *Curaçao*: Curaçao Caribbean.

☐ *Dominican Republic*: Casa de Campo at La Romana, Hotel Santo Domingo, Plaza Dominicana, Sheraton Santo Domingo.

☐ *Guadeloupe*: Meridien St.-François.

☐ *Martinique*: Hotel Meridien Trais-Ilets, Hotel La Bataliere.

☐ *Nassau/Cable Beach*: Carnival's Crystal Palace, Nassau Beach Resort Club.

☐ *Paradise Island*: Paradise Island Hotel.

☐ *Puerto Rico*: Caribe Hilton, Hyatt Dorado Beach/Hyatt Regency Cerromar Beach, Condado Beach Hotel El Convento.

☐ *St. Kitts*: Golden Lemon.

Europe

☐ *Baden Baden, Germany*: Brenner's Park Hotel.

☐ *Cannes, France*: Carlton, Martinez.

☐ *Deauville, France*: Normandy Le Royal.

☐ *Estoril, Portugal*: Palacio, Ritz Lisbon (in Lisbon, half an hour away).

☐ *Marbella, Spain*: Marbella Club, Los Monteros.

☐ *Monte Carlo, Monaco*: Hotel de Paris, Hotel Hermitage, Loews.

☐ *Venice, Italy*: Excelsior (Lido Beach), Gritti Palace, Royal, Royal Danieli.

Elsewhere

☐ *Macao*: Hyatt Regency Macao, Lisboa, Royal. (Macao is a Portuguese territory on the tip of mainland China, 40 miles from Hong Kong by jetfoil.)

☐ *Marrakech, Morocco*: Hotel Mamounia.

The best alpine ski resorts

Christmas (when most hotels insist on a minimum two-week reservation) and February in the Alps are booked up quickly by jet-setting regulars, but other weeks are open. Here are some top spots:

☐ *Badrutt's Palace* in St. Moritz is arguably the classiest ski resort hotel in the world.

☐ *The Goldener Graf* in Kitzbuhel is charming and luxurious—and located in the center of this stellar Austrian resort.

☐ *Hotel Christiania* in Val d'Isere. Good skiers in search of powder can do no better than skiing off-piste (off the patrolled courses) in the expansive terrain of Val d'Isere and Tignes.

☐ *Hotel Cristallo* and *The Hermitage* in Cervinia. The Cristallo has a spectacular view of the Matterhorn from the Italian side, and the Hermitage is a small and lovely chalet-style hotel in the center of Cervinia.

☐ *Swissair packages*. Billing itself as the airline of the Alps, Swissair packages accommodations and land transfers in conjunction with its plane tickets. Among the luxury leaders are the *Mont Cervin* in Zermatt, the *Palace* in Gstaad, the *Schwarzer Adler* in St. Anton and the *Annapurna* in Courchevel. Probably the best bargain among deluxe ski hotels is the *Sporthotel Igls* in a village outside Innsbruck.

Fantastic learning vacations

If you've grown weary of the typical vacation activities of golfing, tennis, swimming and sunbathing, it's time to take advantage of one of many vacations that combine learning with relaxation. Your body may arrive home rested and tanned, and your mind will have received quite a workout!

Some great ones to try…

☐ Backroads: Biking trips to 64 destinations in the United States and abroad. The health and fitness trip winds through the California wine country and includes organized runs, hikes, swims and stretch classes, in addition to bicycling. The art lovers' inn trip explores the backroads of the Sonoma and Napa valleys, combining bicycling with visits to two or three of the region's finest artists each day. Other specialty trips are offered as well. Trips last 2 to 16 days.

More information: Backroads, 1516 Fifth St., Berkeley, California 94710. 510-527-1555.

☐ Canoe Country Escapes: Five- to 11-day canoe trips in the magnificent Boundary Waters Canoe Area Wilderness of northeastern Minnesota and southwestern Ontario. No prior paddling experience is needed. "Lodge-to-Lodge" itineraries combine four nights of accommodations with several nights spent at preset campsites (all of which are ready and waiting when you hit the shore). All trips are led by experienced guides, who teach the basics of the sport. You can also hike with a naturalist or fish with a fishing guide.

More information: Canoe Country Escapes, 194 S. Franklin St., Denver 80209. 303-722-6482.

☐ The Chautauqua Institution: A summer learning center with a wonderful mix of programs for all ages. The 750-acre complex borders Chautauqua Lake and encompasses a Victorian village and a 5,500-seat amphitheater. Each of the nine summer weeks focuses on a different political, economic, scientific or religious theme. *Other highlights:* Art exhibits…a symphony orchestra…theater and opera companies…and a wide array of recreational facilities.

More information: Chautauqua Institution, One Ames St., Chautauqua, New York 14722. 800-836-ARTS.

☐ Crow Canyon Archaeological Center: Links laypeople with professional archaeologists in scientific research.

Participants help reconstruct the cultural and natural environment of the Anasazi, the prehistoric people who lived in the "Four Corners Region," where Colorado, New Mexico, Utah and Arizona meet. Each August the center offers a family week in which grandparents and grandchildren (fourth grade or older) can participate in activities together.

More information: Crow Canyon Archaeological Center, 23390 County Rd. K, Cortez, Colorado 81321. 800-422-8975.

☐ Hudson River Valley Art Workshops: Offers a series of five-day workshops taught by nationally recognized artists. These workshops are held from May to October each year at the Greenville Arms, a Victorian country inn located in the northern Catskills. Artists of all levels of accomplishment come here to learn, seek inspiration and enjoy the fellowship of others who share their interest. Classes are offered in water-based media, oil, acrylics, pencil, pastel and charcoal. Recreational activities are also plentiful.

More information: Hudson River Valley Art Workshops, Box 659, Greenville, New York 12083. 518-966-5219.

☐ National Habitat Wildlife Adventures: Incredible trips that enable you to observe animals close up—in their own natural habitats. On most adventures, program leaders are joined by local guides with intimate knowledge of the region visited. North American adventures include a trip to Alaska to observe moose, caribou, Dall sheep, sea lions, whales, porpoises, sea otters, puffins—and the world's largest concentration of bald eagles. The company also operates Sealwatch, a series of 13 tours scheduled from late February through the middle of March. These tours allow people to view the quarter of a million harp seals that enter eastern Canada's Gulf of Saint Lawrence each year to bear their young on the vast floating ice fields off the Magdalen Islands of Quebec.

More information: Natural Habitat Wildlife Adventures, 2945 Center Green St. S., Suite H, Boulder, Colorado 80301. 800-543-8917.

☐ The Omega Institute for Holistic Studies: Offers more than 250 summer workshops focusing on many aspects of music, dance, theater, the fine arts, writing, environmental and social concerns, spiritual understanding, business and work issues and gender, relationship and family subjects. The Omega campus occupies 80 acres of rolling woodlands and lawns in the Hudson River Valley. Its Wellness

Center offers massage and body work, nutritional counseling, wellness evaluations, holistic health therapies, sauna and flotation tanks. The institute offers programs year-round as well.

More information: Omega Institute, 260 Lake Dr., Rhinebeck, New York 12572. 914-266-4301.

☐ Van Der Meer Tennis Center: Daily, weekend and week-long clinics year-round for players at all skill levels. Dennis Van Der Meer personally conducts the adult programs and the advanced adult clinics. Students work on mastering a variety of strokes, building stroke consistency and developing mental skills for tennis. Senior citizen programs are also offered.

More information: Van Der Meer Tennis Center, Box 5902, Hilton Head, South Carolina 29938. 800-845-6138.

☐ Vermont Off Beat: Wonderful workshops at lovely country inns throughout Vermont. Topics change from year to year, but typical sessions focus on building techniques, gardening, painting, crafts, music and businesses.

More information: Vermont Off Beat, Box 4366, South Burlington, Vermont 05406. 802-863-2535.

☐ Walking The World: Year-round outdoor adventures in the United States and abroad for those 50 and older. Trips balance activity, rest and personal time. They appeal to a diverse group of people. Programs provide instruction in map and compass/route finding, backpacking, hiking, expedition planning, back-country cooking, hazard evaluation and back-country first aid/emergency procedures. Group gear and meals are supplied.

More information: Walking The World, Inc., Box 1186, Fort Collins, Colorado 80522. 303-225-0500.

Source: Harriet Webster, author of *Great American Learning Adventures,* HarperPerennial, New York.

Offbeat three-day weekends

For an extra-long weekend you will never forget:

☐ Ballooning. A great way to see the countryside. In most of the US, ballooning trips are available within 100 miles of major cities. You can also take a trip that includes gourmet picnics in France and Austria or wild-game-watching in Kenya.

☐ Spas. Most spa resorts include massage, aerobics, swimming and succulent diet cuisine, and many feature beauty facilities for facials, pedicures, etc. Spas can be found in Florida, California, Arizona, Texas, New York, New Jersey and Illinois. *A favorite:* World of Palmaire, Pompano Beach, Florida.

☐ Iceland. Not too far a flight from most northeastern cities, Iceland offers swimming in naturally heated bubbling springs and quick flights to the smaller islands (which the US astronauts used to simulate the lunar surface). Reykjavik, the capital, features great Scandinavian restaurants and shops.

☐ Tennis ranches. Besides excellent tennis facilities, these ranches usually provide horseback riding and swimming.

☐ Snowmobiling. Many national parks have snowmobile trails and rental arrangements and lodging is available in cabins or lodges at low, off-season rates.

☐ Cruise to nowhere. Going (or actually not going) from various East and West Coast cities on a cruise ship can be great fun. All normal shipboard cruise facilities are available for a luxurious weekend.

☐ Paris weekend. For those who will spend a dollar to save a dollar, bargain hunting or Christmas shopping in Paris is the answer. *Typical package deal:* Airfare from an East Coast city, lodging at a *pension* on the Left Bank, breakfasts and a list of recommended shops in the area. Major American credit cards are accepted in Europe, so you can charge away.

☐ Dude ranches. Most prevalent in the West and Southwest. Smaller private ranches and farms that take in guests are homier than the bigger ones. Families are especially welcome. An inexpensive get-away-from-it-all including riding lessons and home cooking.

☐ Biking tours. You can travel in the Berkshires, the Smokies or any beautiful countryside.

Source: Carole M. Phillips, CTC, of Certified Travel Consultants, New York.

Unusual and adventuresome vacations

☐ Backpack in the West.
☐ Visit Australia's haunting Great Barrier Reef Islands.

- [ ] Take an air safari to East Africa.
- [ ] Heli-ski in the Canadian Rockies.
- [ ] Visit native villages in New Guinea.
- [ ] Canoe down the Amazon River.
- [ ] Balloon in California.
- [ ] Cruise the Mississippi.
- [ ] Ride the Colorado River on a raft.
- [ ] Barge through the rivers of Europe.
- [ ] See the unspoiled wildlife on the Galapagos Islands.
- [ ] Study-tour in Mexico.
- [ ] Go on a religious retreat.
- [ ] Work on a kibbutz in Israel.
- [ ] Explore Australia's outback regions.
- [ ] Visit the ancient city of Machu Picchu in Peru.
- [ ] Join an archaeological dig in China or Tunisia.
- [ ] Climb the Himalayas and visit Nepal.
- [ ] Go deep-sea fishing off the coast of Baja California.
- [ ] Visit Bali and learn about its ancient music.
- [ ] Learn a foreign language by living with natives.
- [ ] Explore the coral reefs of the West Indies.
- [ ] Visit Alaska's national parks.

America's best museums

California

☐ *J. Paul Getty Museum*, 17985 Pacific Coast Highway, Malibu. 310-458-2003. Extraordinary private art collection from Greek and Roman to 20th century.

☐ *Huntington Library, Art Gallery and Botanical Gardens*, 1151 Oxford Rd., San Marino. 818-405-2100. Gainsborough's Blue Boy, 18th-century British and European art.

☐ *Los Angeles County Museum of Art*, 5905 Wilshire Blvd., Los Angeles. 213-857-6111. Outstanding collection from antiquities to 20th-century art.

☐ *San Francisco Museum of Modern Art*, 151 Third Street, San Francisco. 415-357-4000. Fine collection of 20th-century European and American art, and a museum dedicated to ethnic art.

☐ *Asian Art Museum of San Francisco*, Golden Gate Park, San Francisco. Finest collection of Oriental art in the Western world. Exhibition hotline: 415-668-7855.

Colorado

☐ *Denver Art Museum*, 100 West 14th Ave. Parkway, Denver. 303-575-2793. North and South American Indian collections.

Connecticut

☐ *Wadsworth Atheneum*, 600 Main St., Hartford. 203-247-9111. The oldest art museum in the United States and one of the best.

☐ *Yale University Art Gallery*, 1111 Chapel St., New Haven. 203-436-0574. John Trumbull's paintings of the American Revolution and much more.

District of Columbia

☐ *Corcoran Gallery of Art*, 17 St. and New York Ave. NW, Washington. 202-638-3211. Historic American paintings, European art.

☐ *Freer Gallery of Art*, 12 St. and Jefferson Drive SW, Washington. 202-357-2104. Far and Near Eastern art; Whistler's works.

☐ *Hirshhorn Museum and Sculpture Garden*, Independence Ave. at Seventh St. SW, Washington. 202-357-3091. The entire collection—sculpture and modern art—of millionaire Joseph Hirshhorn.

☐ *National Gallery of Art*, Fourth St. and Constitution Ave. NW, Washington. 202-737-4215. A jewel of a museum with a brilliant new wing by I.M. Pei. General European and American art collection.

☐ *National Portrait Gallery*, Eighth St. at F St., Washington. 202-357-1300. Portraits of all the American presidents displayed in an 1840 Greek Revival building, the former US Patent Office.

Georgia

☐ *The High Museum of Art*, 1280 Peachtree NE, Atlanta. 404-733-4400. Renaissance of 20th-century American and European paintings, sculpture and decorative arts.

Illinois

☐ *Art Institute of Chicago*, Michigan Ave. at Adams St., Chicago. 312-443-3600. Outstanding Impressionists and post-Impressionists in a first-rate collection.

Maryland

☐ *Baltimore Museum of Fine Arts*, Art Museum Drive (near N. Charles and 31 St.), Baltimore. 410-396-7101. Fine

French post-Impressionist works; mosaics from Antioch.

Massachusetts

☐ *Boston Museum of Fine Arts*, 465 Huntington Ave., Boston. 617-267-4300. The new I.M. Pei wing is impressive.

☐ *Fogg Museum*, 32 Quincy St., Cambridge. 617-495-7768. Harvard's extensive art collection.

☐ *Norman Rockwell Museum at Stockbridge,* 9 Glendale Rd., Stockbridge. 413-298-4100.

Michigan

☐ *Detroit Institute of Art*, 5200 Woodward Ave., Detroit. 313-833-7900. Great masters and moderns.

Minnesota

☐ *Walker Art Center*, Vineland Place, Minneapolis. 612-375-7622. Post-Impressionist and contemporary art.

New York

☐ *Albright-Knox Art Gallery*, 1285 Elmwood Ave., Buffalo. 716-882-8700. Splendid modern collection, as well as general collection.

☐ *Brooklyn Museum*, 188 Eastern Parkway, Brooklyn. 718-638-5000. Fine general collection with strong Egyptian art and American paintings.

☐ *The Frick Collection*, Fifth Ave. at 70 St., New York. 212-288-0700. One of the best private collections.

☐ *The Solomon R. Guggenheim Museum*, 1701 Fifth Ave. at 88 St., New York. 212-360-3500. Modern art and sculpture in a circular building designed by Frank Lloyd Wright.

☐ *Metropolitan Museum of Art*, Fifth Ave. at 82 St., New York. 212-879-5500. Probably the finest general collection in the US.

☐ *Museum of Modern Art*, 11 W. 53 St., New York. 212-708-9400. First US museum devoted to 20th century art—from paintings and sculpture to design and film.

☐ *The Pierpont Morgan Library*, 29 E. 36 St., New York. 212-685-0610. Illuminated Bibles, Rembrandts and other superb art.

☐ *Whitney Museum of American Art*, 945 Madison Ave. at 75 St., New York. 212-570-3676. 20th-century US art.

Ohio

☐ *Cleveland Museum of Art* , 11150 East Blvd. at University Circle, Cleveland.

216-421-7340. All cultures. Strong in medieval and Oriental art.

Oregon

☐ *Portland Art Museum,* 1219 SW Park Ave., Portland. 503-226-2811. Appealing outdoor sculpture, mall, general collection.

Pennsylvania

☐ *The Frick Art Museum*, 7227 Reynolds St., Pittsburgh. 412-371-0600. Eclectic collection of Russian, Chinese, Flemish and French art and artifacts.

☐ *Philadelphia Museum of Art*, 26 St. and Benjamin Franklin Parkway, Philadelphia. 215-763-8100. Magnificent general collection.

☐ *Rodin Museum*, 22 St. and Benjamin Franklin Parkway, Philadelphia. 215-763-8100. Sculpture, sketches and drawings by this famous French artist.

Texas

☐ *Amon Carter Museum of Western Art*, 3501 Camp Bowie Blvd., Fort Worth. 817-738-1933. Extensive collection of Frederic Remington's and Charles Russell's work.

☐ *Houston Museum of Fine Arts*, 1001 Bissonnet, Houston. 713-526-1361. Fine general collection.

Offbeat museums around the US

☐ Ketchikan, Alaska: Totem Pole Heritage Center.

☐ Vermont: Two maple sugar museums.

☐ Baraboo, Wisconsin: The Circus World Museum recreates the glitter and razzmatazz of The Greatest Show on Earth with antique carousels, costumes and other memorabilia. Visitors can view a sideshow, participate in a Big Top performance and ride an elephant.

☐ New York City: The Songwriters' Hall of Fame.

☐ Sacramento, California: The California State Railroad Museum traces railroad history from early steam engines to modern diesel locomotives.

☐ Las Vegas, Nevada: The Liberace Museum houses some of the prized possessions of "Mr. Showmanship" himself—a fleet of customized cars, his flashy wardrobe and several rare pianos.

☐ Eureka Springs, Arkansas: The Hammond Museum of Bells.

☐ Nashville, Tennessee: The Country Music Hall of Fame.

How to stay healthy while traveling

No matter what your destination or reason for traveling, staying healthy is a prime concern whenever you're far from home.

Fatigue, stress, an upset stomach or worse can spell disaster for your vacation—or sap your business productivity. Fortunately, the wear and tear of travel can be kept to a minimum with some simple advance planning.

Here are some easy ways to make your travel more comfortable—and healthful.

Self-care checklist

Your chief consideration when packing for a trip will be where you're going, how long you'll be away and what the climate is like at your destination. But no matter what sort of trip you're planning, bring along a well-stocked self-care kit. It should be easily reachable in your carry-on luggage and should contain...

☐ Antacid. Familiar store-bought remedies such as Maalox, Mylanta, Gelusil, Tums or Rolaids combat stomach upset, heartburn and abdominal cramping sometimes caused by unfamiliar food or drink—or overindulgence in either.

☐ Diarrhea remedy. Over-the-counter preparations like Imodium AD, Kaopectate or Pepto-Bismol are all effective at stopping diarrhea. Tablets are easier to take along on a trip, although the liquid forms of these medications usually offer faster relief.

☐ Laxative. On the road, constipation is often more of a problem than diarrhea.

Reason: Your diet while traveling is apt to lack high-fiber foods. Also, it may be difficult while traveling to maintain a regular exercise routine. Take along some Metamucil or Senokot just in case.

☐ Antihistamine. The over-the-counter medication Benadryl is effective against a host of potential allergens and irritants and is well-tolerated by most people. If you have to stay alert, ask your doctor to prescribe Seldane. It causes little or no drowsiness.

☐ Antibiotic. For tooth abscesses, severe bronchitis, festering skin wounds or other stubborn bacterial infections, ask your doctor to prescribe an antibiotic in advance.

Caution: Antibiotics should be used only under a doctor's supervision. Call your doctor at home for instructions.

☐ Motion-sickness remedy. Dramamine or Bonine tablets and scopolamine skin patches (Transderm Scop) are all effective. The patches are especially useful if you'll be spending long periods of time at sea, although they can cause dry mouth and, in the elderly, confusion.

Caution: Dramamine and Bonine can cause drowsiness. Avoid them if you have to stay alert.

☐ Athlete's foot remedy. Include antifungal foot powder or solutions like Lotrimin, Micatin or Tinactin in your travel kit since showers in hotel rooms and fitness centers aren't always fungus-free. Also helpful: Rubber thongs to wear in the shower.

☐ Sunscreen, sunglasses and hat. These are a must for travel to sunny places or if you intend to be outdoors for extended periods of time. Your sunscreen should have an SPF of at least 15 and should guard against both UVB and UVA rays.

☐ Insect repellent. Look for one that contains 20% to 30% DEET.

☐ Aspirin, acetaminophen or ibuprofen.

☐ Decongestant and facial tissues.

You might also want to bring along a basic first-aid kit containing an antibacterial cream or ointment, bandages, gauze, thermometer, scissors, tweezers and a pocketknife.

If you wear corrective lenses, pack a spare pair of contacts or eyeglasses—plus your prescription.

If you intend to swim in unchlorinated water, take along a remedy for swimmer's ear, an infection marked by redness, itching and pain of the outer ear canal. I recommend an over-the-counter preparation called Vosol.

Fighting jet lag

Anytime you fly across several different time zones, you disrupt the body's circadian rhythms. The resulting jet lag should be thought of not as a special problem, but as another form of manageable stress. Ways to control it:

☐ Avoid alcohol during your flight. Alcohol, a depressant, can aggravate lethargy and fatigue, two classic symptoms of jet lag. It can also cause restlessness, which can disturb your sleep or keep you from sleeping altogether. And because it acts as a diuretic, alcohol can leave you feeling dehydrated.

☐ Limit your consumption of caffeine. Like alcohol, caffeine is a diuretic that can leave you feeling dehydrated and out of sorts. Too much caffeine can also cause nervousness, anxiety, tremors and insomnia.

☐ Drink plenty of water. Recent studies have shown that even slight dehydration can cause listlessness and fatigue and can even make you more prone to mental errors—symptoms similar to those of jet lag.

Bear in mind that you may be dehydrated even before departure. *Reason:* Your eating and drinking patterns may be erratic in the hours before your flight. Breathing dry cabin air only increases this dehydration and all its enervating effects.

To stay hydrated, drink plenty of water or other nonalcoholic beverages before and during your flight—one eight-ounce glass every two to three hours. Don't wait until you feel thirsty—by then you may already be dehydrated.

☐ Adapt to local time as quickly as possible. Example: If you land in Paris the morning after an all-night flight, have no more than a brief 90-minute nap—then stay awake until it's 9 or 10 pm in Paris.

Schedule nonstressful activities and eat light, refreshing meals on your arrival day. Pack a swimsuit and use the hotel's pool or hot tub to help you relax.

Safe food and drink

Regions of the world fall into three "tiers":

☐ Europe, North America, Australia.

☐ Israel and the Caribbean.

☐ The rest of the Middle East, most of Africa, the Far East and other developing regions.

Anytime you travel to the second or third tier, you must be especially vigilant about what you eat and drink. *Self-defense:*

☐ Eat cooked food while it is still hot. Make sure meats are well-done. Throughout developing countries, undercooked beef and pork are major sources of tapeworms and other parasites. Likewise, all poultry, seafood and vegetables should be fresh and thoroughly cooked.

☐ Avoid peeled fruits (and those with broken skin). Watch out for raw vegetable salads, too. They can be contaminated with bacteria from food preparer's hands or from the water used to rinse the vegetables.

☐ Avoid custards, pastries and other baked desserts. These foods are often contaminated with microbes that trigger gastric distress, especially if improperly refrigerated. *Exception:* Served still hot from the oven, these foods are generally safe. If you want dessert, stick to wrapped candy or fresh fruit that you peel yourself.

☐ Stick to bottled or canned beverages. And watch out for ice cubes, which might be contaminated. Avoid milk, milk products and foods prepared with them unless you're sure they have been properly pasteurized.

☐ Avoid bread left lying in open baskets. It may have been exposed to flies and other disease-bearing insects. If you're not certain whether bread has been properly stored, remove the crust and eat only the interior of the loaf.

Watching out for infectious diseases

If you're planning a trip to the tropics, ask your doctor about protecting yourself against malaria, yellow fever, schistosomiasis and other potential threats. If you'll need immunizations, get them at least a month before your departure. Frantic, last-minute efforts to obtain "shots" only compound the ordinary stress occasioned by an overseas journey. And multiple immunizations require several shots over a period of days or weeks.

A 24-hour hotline run by the Centers for Disease Control and Prevention (CDC) provides recorded messages outlining immunization requirements and recommendations for international travel. Call 404-332-4559.

Health information for overseas travelers is also available from some medical schools and teaching hospitals. For a list of regions where war or political strife might jeopardize travelers, contact the US State Department at 202-647-5225.

Malaria—probably the most serious of all the infectious diseases found in the tropics—used to be easily controlled with medications. *Now:* In many parts of the world, there are drug-resistant strains of malaria. Chloroquine and other antimalarial drugs are virtually useless against them.

A new drug called mefloquine (Lariam) is often effective against drug-resistant malaria, but even this medication is losing strength in Southeast Asia and parts of Africa. Doxycycline can combat stubborn strains but should not be taken by children or pregnant women.

To avoid malaria, ask your doctor about taking prophylactic drugs. These must be taken one week before you travel to ensure that adequate blood levels of the drug are reached before you arrive —and that any adverse reactions occur while you're still at home. For more information, contact the CDC's 24-hour malaria hotline at 404-332-4555.

Ultimately, no matter where you travel, common sense should prevail. Medications and inoculations are no substitute for adequate rest during a trip, for avoiding excesses in eating and drinking or for following basic hygiene. With these precautions in mind, you should always be able to travel in comfort— and good health.

Source: Karl Neumann, MD, editor and publisher of *Traveling Healthy,* 108-48 70 Rd., Forest Hills, New York 11375. He is also coeditor of *The Business Traveler's Guide to Good Health While Traveling,* Chronimed Publishing, Minnetonka, MN.

How to make the most of your time in unfamiliar towns

☐ Be a part-time tourist. An hour or two between appointments gives you enough time to check out the local aquarium, museum, library, antique district, park or waterfront. Major tourist attractions are often located near enough to a city's business district for you to mix meetings with pleasure conveniently.

☐ Have a great meal. Do some advance research, and equip yourself with a list of the best restaurants in each city on your itinerary. Then, when your free time coincides with a mealtime, invest instead in a delightful hour of gourmet adventure.

☐ Look up old friends. Perhaps you can share that gourmet meal with a college friend you haven't seen in years, or surprise an uncle or cousin with a call or visit.

☐ Take pictures. If you're into photography, you know that a new environment frequently yields new visions and special scenes and subjects. Keep your eyes open and your camera ready.

☐ Go gift shopping. On autumn trips, carry a list of holiday gift ideas for friends and family. Use even a spare 15 minutes to pop in on the local boutiques and specialty shops. Charge and send your purchases, and when you get home they'll be there, all ready for your December giving.

☐ Bring busywork. When you're too tired to kill time on the move—or it's raining or the neighborhood is threatening or everything is closed—you should have something to do in your hotel room other than watch TV and order room service. Try catching up on a pile of periodicals or going through seed catalogues.

Source: Letty Cottin Pogrebin, an editor at *Ms.* magazine and author of five books, most recently *Family Politics,* McGraw-Hill, New York.

Making the most of travel time

Some people claim that they can work on airplanes, trains or boats, but you may not be one of them. If you, too, are unable to concentrate while traveling:

☐ Go to sleep. Traveling is a natural soporific. Catching up on your sleep will give you an edge when you arrive.

☐ Find someone to talk with. Walk around and see if anyone who looks interesting has a copy of the *Official Airlines Guide* (which frequent travelers carry) or other travel guides. Start talking about travel, and you'll learn a few things.

☐ Clean out your wallet or briefcase. This is something you always mean to do but never get around to.

☐ Write letters. They don't take much concentration.

Killing time creatively at airports

☐ Make phone calls. Check into your office, pick up a dozen phone messages and return eight calls before being driven from the public phone by the furious stares of others waiting to use it.

☐ Write letters or pay bills. Bring notepaper, envelopes, bills and your checkbook. Use your briefcase as a desk.

☐ Shop for the unexpected. Airport gift shops are notoriously glitzy. And at first glance, the merchandise in every gift shop looks alike except for the city etched into the beer mugs. But you may well find a Pierre Cardin belt at a bargain price in Cleveland, live lobsters in Boston and sourdough bread in San Francisco.

☐ Read indulgently. Buy a spy novel if you usually lean toward business books. Pick up a foreign magazine and test your French. Indulge in a crossword puzzle magazine or cartoon book. Read the local papers.

☐ Get a haircut or shoeshine. Men have the edge here. Although airport barber shops sometimes advertise "unisex," I've never seen a woman in any of them. Bootblacks will gladly shine a woman's shoes.

☐ Jog. With throngs of people running to catch their planes, no one will know you are just jogging along the concourses to kill time. Leave your coat and carry-on bag under someone's watchful eye while you run.

☐ People-watch. This is a surprisingly diverting pastime, especially for hyperactive types who don't often stop to observe the world around them.

☐ Eavesdrop. Airports are great places to tune in on some fascinating conversations—one as melodramatic as a soap opera dialogue, another as funny as a Mel Brooks sketch.

☐ Think. If you're uninspired by the above alternatives, you can simply stare out at the landing field, letting your mind go blank. Or you can give yourself a specific problem to mull over. Sometimes the brain does a better job of thinking at rest than it does under pressure.

Source: Letty Cottin Pogrebin, an editor at Ms. *magazine and author of five books, most recently* Family Politics, *McGraw-Hill, New York.*

Saving time and money at hotels

☐ When you arrive at a hotel, check your bags. Then go to the pay telephone in the lobby and call the hotel. Ask to have your reservation confirmed, give them your charge card number and go on your way. You'll sidestep convention check-in lines.

☐ To avoid the long check-out line after the convention, go down to the desk very early in the morning, before official check-out time, and check out. You won't have to turn in your room key, and

you can still use your room until official check-out time (usually around 1 PM).

☐ Don't stay glued to your hotel room if you're waiting for a call. If you ask, the hotel operator will transfer your calls to another room, interrupt the call you're on for a more important one or hold any calls while you run out for a soda.

☐ Save money by not paying for things you didn't order. Don't charge anything to your hotel room. It's too confusing when you're checking out to verify the list of room charges. And it's only too easy for the hotel to make a mistake. If you don't charge anything at all, you'll know that extra items on your bill can't be yours. *How to do it:* Use your telephone credit card for calls, and pay cash for room service, laundry, etc. Use your credit card for food.

☐ Don't depend only on the hotel for services such as typing, film developing, etc. Call the local convention bureau. It's specifically set up to help out-of-town businesspeople, and every city has one.

Source: Dr. Barbara A. Pletcher, executive director of the National Association for Professional Saleswomen, is author of Travel Sense, *ACE Books, New York.*

Loss-proof luggage

List items contained in each bag…and your home address inside…carry a photo of your luggage for easy identification…check bags at least 30 minutes before domestic and an hour before international flights…never leave bags unattended…always put valuables and a spare set of clothing in a carry-on. Extra theft protection: Use a security belt or wallet…when waiting, stand with your back against the wall to discourage pickpockets.

Source: The Senior Citizens' Guide to Budget Travel in Europe *by Paige Palmer, Pilot Books, Babylon, NY.*

Don't be a victim of hotel overbooking

It's not always the hotel's fault. Sometimes guests overstay. (Hawaii is the only state that allows hotels to compel guests to leave on time.) But hotels generally accept more reservations than they have rooms, betting that some reservation-holders won't show. Sometimes they bet wrong.

To keep from being a loser:

☐ Plan trips sufficiently in advance to get written confirmation of reservations. That gives you something extra to argue with should you need it. If there's no time for a written confirmation, try to get a confirmation number when the reservation is made.

☐ Get "guaranteed" reservations with a credit card. This does obligate you to pay for the room even if you can't make it. However, it reduces the incentive a hotel clerk has to sell your room to somebody else. American Express has an "assured reservations" program. Under it, the hotel that "walks" you has to pay for the first night's lodging in a comparable hotel room nearby, for a long-distance call to inform the office or family where you will be and for transportation to the substitute hotel. Several chains have a similar policy.

☐ Arrive early in the afternoon, when last night's guests have checked out, but before the bulk of new arrivals.

☐ Take your case to a higher-up—probably the assistant manager on duty—since it's unlikely that the desk clerk will find a room after telling you he has none. The assistant manager might be persuaded to "find" one of the rooms that inevitably are set aside by luxury hotels for emergencies such as the arrival of a VIP. Make a loud fuss, some people suggest. This often works, since hotels try to avoid drawing public attention to their overbooking practices.

☐ If neither raving and ranting nor quiet persuasion moves the assistant manager, insist that he call other comparable hotels to get you a room, and at the same or lower price. The better hotels will usually do their best.

How to save on air travel

☐ Fly between 9 PM and 7 AM. Most airlines have cheaper night flights, especially on long distances.

☐ Plan business trips so that the schedule qualifies the business traveler for vacation excursion fares (discounts up to 50%).

☐ Fly out-of-the-way carriers looking for new business.

☐ Make sales or service trips, or tours of branch offices, using the unlimited mileage tickets offered by some airlines.

☐ Before making flight and car-rental arrangements, find out if a small commuter airline will make the hop to the traveler's final destination. It may actually cost less.

Recommendation: Use only travel agents that have developed, purchased or contracted for a low-fare search program used in conjunction with the reservations process. These electronic search capabilities continue to probe the airline inventory to determine if a lower-priced seat has become available. These systems work tirelessly, 24 hours a day. Whenever there is an adjustment to the pricing of available inventory or a cancellation releases a lower-priced seat, the computer takes it and rebooks your higher-priced trip at the newer lower cost.

Source: Harold Seligman, president, Management Alternatives, Stamford, CT.

Getting a good airplane seat

Getting the seat you prefer on an airplane has become an increasing problem.

☐ If you're assigned to a seat you don't like, go back to the desk when all the prereserved seats are released (usually about 15 minutes before flight time). Prime seats for passengers who didn't show up are available then.

☐ If you discover on the plane that you don't like your seat, don't wait until the plane takes off to find a better one. Look around the plane, and the second before they close the door, head for the empty seat of your choice. Don't wait until the seat-belt sign goes on.

☐ Prereserve a single seat on a non-jumbo where the seats are three across and you'll increase the odds of getting an empty seat next to you.

☐ Ask for a window or aisle seat in a row where the window or aisle is already reserved by a single. The middle seat between two singles is least likely to fill up.

What the airlines don't tell you

☐ Never accept the first fare quoted. Half the time, some other airline's flight within hours of the one you booked has a special, less expensive deal.

☐ Take advantage of "illegal" connections. These are connecting flights usually less than 45 minutes apart—that usually do not even show up on the computer when your trip is being routed. *Solution:* Have your agent write up your flight in two separate tickets. The second is for the illegal connection that originates at your transfer point. To make fast transfers, travel with carry-on luggage.

☐ Use do-it-yourself searches with your computer. Plug into the *Official Airlines Guide* data base and search out the flights available at the desired time. Using another code, find out what fares are available on each airline for the time period. If no asterisk is shown, it's possible to book the flight right up to the last minute. If there is an asterisk next to the airline flight number, ask the system what the restrictions are.

Source: Harold Seligman, president, Management Alternatives, Stamford, CT.

How to have a more comfortable flight

If you have flown extensively, you already know the advantages of arriving early at the airport, drinking lots of water during the flight, removing your shoes and bringing a fabulous book to read. What flight attendants know that you may not know…

☐ Bring your own big coffee mug. You'll get more coffee from the flight attendant the first time he/she passes by…and it will stay warmer longer.

☐ Accept headsets or bring your own. When you want to get a great deal of work or reading done on a flight—or even if you just want to think undisturbed —headsets politely say "do not disturb" to a chatty neighbor.

☐ Count your carry-ons before boarding. Then recount them as you leave the plane. Passengers often must use two or three overhead compartments when storing carry-ons, making it easy to forget one of these bags when leaving the plane.

☐ Wear wrinkle-free or fashionably wrinkled clothes. Then you won't have to worry about seat-belt marks, and you'll look fresh when you deplane.

☐ Bring an inflatable pillow. This will allow your head to rest firmly in place. You'll snooze more easily and won't wake up with your head on your neighbor's shoulder.

☐ Don't overclothe a baby. Nine times out of ten, babies cry on a plane because they are too hot. *Also:* Be sure to use clothes that can be put on and taken off quickly and easily.

☐ Carry your driving glasses with you. If they go into the suitcase that goes into the baggage compartment, you won't be able to see the movie clearly…or even the flight attendant at the head of the plane. And if your luggage is lost or misplaced for a time, you won't be able to drive yourself from the airport.

Source: Barbara McCain and her daughter, Kelly McCain, flight attendants for Northwest Airlines and Delta Air Lines, respectively.

Know when not to fly

Avoid flying if you have had:

☐ A heart attack within four weeks of takeoff.

☐ Surgery within two weeks.

☐ A deep-diving session within 24 hours.

Don't fly at all if you have:

☐ Severe lung problems.

☐ Uncontrolled hypertension.

☐ Epilepsy not well controlled.

☐ Severe anemia.

☐ A pregnancy beyond 240 days or threatened by miscarriage.

Source: *Pocket Flight Guide/Frequent Flyer Package.*

Nonrefundable tickets can be avoided

Problem: "Super Saver" tickets cost as little as 30% of regular airfares, but airlines say you can't get a refund if you change travel plans.

Solution: A cooperative travel agent. When you buy a ticket from an agent, the agent makes your reservation immediately. But it doesn't forward your money to the airline for a few days—in some cases not until a week later. That's because agents pay airlines only once a week. During the time gap a friendly travel agent will let you cancel the reservation and get your money back.

☐ *Caution:* Travel agents don't have to accommodate you. But if you're a good customer and the agent wants to keep your business, chances are good that you can get a refund.

☐ *Helpful:* Check with your agent to see if two round-trip, noncancelable discount fares cost less than one full round-trip ticket. Even if you use only half of each of the discount tickets, the cost for both may be less than a full-fare ticket.

☐ If your plans change too late for the agency to cancel your ticket, another option is to use the value of the ticket for future travel. Although nonrefundable, the ticket still has a value with the same airline. For a small reissuance fee, the airline can apply the amount of your canceled ticket to a new itinerary.

Source: Harold Seligman, president of Management Alternatives, travel management consultants, Stamford, CT.

Your ears and air travel

☐ Avoid flying with a cold or other respiratory infection. A cold greatly increases the chances of your suffering discomfort, additional fluid buildup, severe pain or even rupture.

☐ Take decongestants. If you must fly with a cold, or if you regularly suffer discomfort or pain on descent, decongestants can give real relief. For maximum effect, time them to coincide with the descent (which begins half an hour to an hour before landing). Use both oral decongestants and a spray for best results. *Suggested timing:* Take quick-acting oral decongestants two to three hours before landing or slow-release tablets six to eight hours in advance. Use nasal spray one hour before landing. *Caution:* If you have hypertension or a heart condition, check with your cardiologist about taking decongestants.

☐ Don't smoke or drink. Smoking irritates the nasal area, and alcohol dilates the blood vessels, causing the tissues to swell.

☐ Try the Valsalva maneuver. While holding your nose closed, try to blow through it as though you were blowing your nose. This will blow air through the ears. Do this gently and repeatedly as the plane descends. *Warning:* Don't use this method if you have a cold, as you'll be blowing infection back into the middle ear. Use the tried-and-true routines of yawning and swallowing instead. They can be quite effective if the problem is not too severe. Chew gum and suck candy. *Aim:* To activate the swallowing mechanism in order to open the eustachian tubes.

☐ If your ears are stuffed after landing, follow the same routine. Keep on with decongestants and gentle Valsalvas. Temporary hearing loss and stuffiness may persist for three to four weeks. If the symptoms are really annoying, a doctor can lance the drum to drain the fluid. If pain persists for more than a day, see a doctor.

☐ See a doctor before flying if you have a bad cold, especially if you have a history of ear pain when flying. If you absolutely must fly, the doctor can open the eardrum and insert a small ventilation tube that will allow the pressure to equalize. The tube should eject by itself in a few weeks…or you can go back to your doctor.

Source: Neville W. Carmical, MD, attending otolaryngologist, St.Luke's–Roosevelt Hospital Center, New York.

Coping with high altitudes

One out of three travelers at altitudes of 7,000 feet above sea level (Vail, Colorado, for example) experiences some symptoms of altitude sickness. By 10,000 feet (Breckenridge, Colorado), everyone is affected. *Common complaints:* Headaches, nausea, weakness, lack of coordination and insomnia.

To minimize the effects:

☐ Take it easy the first two or three days. Get plenty of rest and don't schedule vigorous activities.

☐ Eat a little less than usual. Avoid hard-to-digest foods such as red meat and fats. Carbohydrates are good.

☐ Drink more liquids than usual. (Breathing harder in dry air causes you to lose water vapor.)

☐ Avoid alcohol, smoking and tranquilizers. Their effects are compounded at high altitudes.

Flyer's health secrets

☐ Taking your mind off the motion can help your body restore equilibrium without drugs. *How to do it:* Close your eyes, or concentrate on a spot in front of you, and hold your head as steady as possible. Then focus your attention on your breathing or on alternately tensing and relaxing your muscles. Continue to concentrate until the nausea has vanished.

□ The low air pressure in an airplane's interior can aggravate some medical problems unless precautions are taken. Gas trapped in the colon can expand, causing severe discomfort or cramps. People with heart or lung diseases should check with their doctor in advance to discuss requesting supplemental oxygen.

□ Don't fly with a serious sinus problem. If a sinus is blocked, the trapped air inside expands and can lead to serious infection. Improve drainage prior to ascent and descent with decongestants or nose drops.

□ The arid atmosphere of pressurized cabins encourages evaporation from the skin's surface, drying the skin. *Remedies:* Avoid beverages that contain alcohol or caffeine (they both have a diuretic action). Drink plenty of water during the trip and afterward.

Getting to and from the airport:

□ Arrive early to avoid stress.

□ Schedule an appointment at the airport. If you're in a strange city, try to get your last appointment of the day to meet you there a few hours before your plane leaves. Why should you be the one to do all the running?

□ Join an airport club. Most airlines have them. Choose the one that belongs to the principal carrier flying from your city. Then you can relax in comfort while you wait for your flight. *Benefits:* Special services to members, such as a separate check-in desk.

Source: *Healthwise* and Commission on Emergency Medical Services, American Medical Association, Chicago.

When renting a car

□ Give a rented car the once-over before driving away in it. Check the headlights, turn signals and brakes. Squirt the windshield washer to be sure that there is fluid. Check the oil level. Drive it around the block before taking it on the expressway.

□ Don't pay for more insurance than you need on a rented car. Rental agencies routinely encourage customers to pay around $5 a day for optional collision coverage. Chances are, however, that your own personal-car policy may extend coverage to a rented car. Check the insurance policy before signing up for unnecessary coverage.

Automatic drop-off can be a rip-off on late-night rented-car returns. Unlike normal rental-car check-in, where the clerk totals up the costs and gives you a copy of the bill, automatic drop-offs require you to return all copies. You often don't get a copy until your credit-card company has billed you.

Protective alternatives:

□ Return your rental car during business hours.

□ Make a copy of the rental form before returning it, noting your entry of the final mileage.

□ Don't pay your credit-card bill until you get the car-rental bill and make sure their figures agree with yours.

□ If they have overcharged you, dispute the bill and let the credit-card company know about the problem.

Source: *Travel Smart for Business.*

How to avoid vacation time-sharing traps

Some owners of time-shares in beach- and ski-area condominiums are becoming disenchanted. *Reasons:* They find that committing themselves to the same dates at the same resort every year is too restricting. Or they find they overpaid.

To avoid problems:

□ Locate one of the companies that act as brokers for swapping time-shares for owners of resort properties in different areas.

□ Don't pay more than ten times the going rate for a good hotel or apartment rental in the same area at the same time of year.

□ Get in early on a new complex. Builders usually sell the first few apartments for less.

□ Choose a one- or two-bedroom unit. Smaller or larger ones are harder to swap or sell.

□ Deal with experienced developers who have already worked out maintenance and management problems.

□ Pick a time in the peak season. It will be more negotiable.

□ Look for properties that are protected by zoning or geography. Vail, Colorado, for example, has a moratorium on further time-share development.

□ Beware of resorts that are hard to reach or are too far off the beaten track.

Your time-shares will be harder to rent, swap or sell.

If your tour is a disappointment

To get your money back:

☐ Go back to the travel agency or sponsor who promoted it with your evidence of a breach of contract.

☐ Keep all brochures or a detailed itinerary that constitutes your contract.

☐ Keep evidence that the promises were not kept. *Example:* Out-of-pocket receipts, pictures you took of your hotel or room, etc.

☐ If you come to an impasse on the terms of the tour agreement, check with the American Society of Travel Agents in New York, for an explanation of standardized industry terms (first class, deluxe, etc.).

☐ *Last resort:* File a complaint with either small claims court or civil court. *Advantage with either:* You don't have to retain a lawyer. Judgments are made quickly.

☐ *Final action:* Class-action suits have been successful in cases where it's unclear who is at fault. Sometimes it's your only hope for recovering anything from wholesalers and suppliers that are hard to reach.

☐ *Warning:* If your complaint is with a travel agency that went out of business while you were on tour (such things do happen), your recovery chances are virtually nil against that business, no matter how far you take your case.

Source: Patricia Simko, Assistant Attorney General, New York State Bureau of Consumer Frauds, New York.

Essentials *before* you leave for overseas

☐ Check your health and accident insurance to see if you're covered for illness or injury abroad.

☐ Does your policy pay for transportation home if you're on a litter and need more than one airplane seat?

Although a number of companies will pay for treatment, transportation is rarely covered. *Recommended:* Check with your travel agent for a company that provides this kind of coverage.

☐ Leave a detailed itinerary with someone close to you—the more detailed, the better. If you fail to get in touch, this might be the only clue to your whereabouts.

☐ Be sure to fill in the section provided in your passport for a contact in case of emergency. Keep it accurate and up to date for each trip. Don't list your spouse if he/she is going with you. It can delay notification of your next of kin by the Department of State.

☐ Carry a copy of the prescriptions for any medications you're carrying. Don't carry large amounts of any prescription drug, as you might come under suspicion by foreign customs.

How to get a passport faster

If you seek a passport at the height of the tourist season, you'll inevitably face a long wait. But whenever you go for your passport, you can ease the delay by doing the following:

☐ Go to the passport office in person.

☐ *Bring:* Your airline ticket, two passport pictures, proof of citizenship (an old passport, voter registration or birth certificate), a piece of identification with your photo on it and the fee.

☐ Give the passport office a good reason why you are rushed.

If your passport is lost or stolen when you're traveling abroad, here's what to do:

☐ Immediately notify the local police and the US embassy or consulate. An overnight replacement is sometimes possible in an emergency.

☐ To hasten this process, know your passport number.

☐ *Next best:* Have a valid identification document with you. A photostat of your passport is best.

Source: *Travel Smart.*

How to have a safer vacation

One of the best ways to avoid travel problems—or at least be prepared for their possibility—is to know as much as you can about your destination before you leave.

Be aware of the political climate and whether Americans are likely to be targets of angry nationals if political disruptions turn violent. Key questions:

☐ What is the level of street crime— and are Americans prime targets?

☐ Are there any major religious, political or social events planned during your visit? Is the country, for example, hosting the usually tumultuous World Cup soccer finals?

☐ Is your host country in the midst of any medical emergencies such as flu epidemics, water problems or shortages of certain medicines or medical services?

Your best and most reliable sources for this information are friends and business associates who have recently visited your planned destination. Other sources:

☐ The Regional Security Officer (RSO) in the US Embassy where you are going. Get the US Embassy number and name of the RSO from the State Department Country Desk Officer. 202-647-4000 (expect delays and misdirected calls).

☐ Bureau of Consular Affairs, Citizens Emergency Center. 202-647-5225 or 202-647-0900. Know details of your trip so you can respond to touch-tone instructions.

☐ A knowledgeable travel agent—ask someone who travels to your destination who he or she uses to book flights or call a travel manager of a US company that does business where you are going.

If you are arrested, call your embassy immediately and explain that it is an emergency. If you are permitted to call home in the US, ask a friend or relative to call the Citizens Emergency Line at the State Department (202-647-5225) so someone in the US is following up on your distress. If there are complications, call the International Legal Defense Council (215-977-9982) during business hours. Lawyers there specialize in getting Americans out of jail.

Source: Peter Savage, crisis management planner, The Parvus Company, Silver Spring, MD, and author of *The Safe Travel Book*, Lexington Books, New York.

Currency-exchange strategies

A sudden drop in the dollar could leave you vulnerable while overseas. To protect yourself:

☐ Take about 40% of your travelers' checks in commission-free foreign currency and the rest in dollars.

☐ Prepay your foreign hotel in its own currency to lock in the current rate.

☐ If you fly first class, business class or on the Concorde, find out if you can pay for the return trip in foreign currency.

☐ Shop carefully before buying foreign currency. Even major US banks' conversion rates vary.

☐ Avoid changing dollars into foreign currency at overseas hotels and restaurants. Stick to banks.

☐ When shopping overseas, ask for prices in the local currency. Then request a discount if you intend to pay that way.

Customs rates on what you buy abroad

As a tourist returning to the US, your first $400 of purchases is duty-free. The next $1000 is taxable at 5%–10% (depending on the country). Beyond this, rates vary by category as follows:

☐ Alcohol (per liter): $.23–$4.00.

☐ Antiques over 100 years old: Duty-free.

☐ Automobiles: 2.5%.

☐ Cameras: 3%–6.6%.

☐ Crystal: 6%–20%.

☐ Furs that are not illegal to bring in: 3.4%–5.8%.

☐ Jewelry, silver: 27.5%.

☐ Jewelry, other: 6.5%.

☐ Leather: Free.

☐ Paintings: Free.

☐ Perfume: 5.6% plus $3.56/liter.

☐ Tape recorders: 3.7%–4.9%.

☐ Watches, depending on jewels: 3.9%–14%.

For details send for the free booklet *Know Before You Go*, US Customs Service, 1301 Constitution Ave. NW, Room 246, Washington, DC 20229.

Source: *Travel Smart*, Dobbs Ferry, NY.

Clearing customs

Declare more expensive items first if you expect to go over the duty limit in customs. The lower the value of an item, the less extra duty you will have to pay.

Personal exemption: $400 ($1200 from Guam, American Samoa or the Virgin Islands). *The next $1000:* A flat rate of 10% duty (5% from the US islands). *Above this:* Individual assessments are made on goods.

□ *Sending gifts:* Duty-free, if marked unsolicited gift, value under $50. Gifts cannot be sent to yourself or to a traveling companion.

□ *Sending goods home:* Duty must be paid on major items. They do not count as part of a personal exemption.

□ Liquor and tobacco: You are allowed one liter of alcohol, 100 cigars and 200 cigarettes. (State laws take precedence over federal regulations.)

□ Drugs: Medications obtained abroad could be seized.

What to do if you're arrested overseas

In a sample year, 3,000 Americans were arrested in 97 foreign countries for offenses ranging from narcotics and disorderly conduct to murder. If arrested, here's what you should do:

□ Don't panic. Keep your wits about you.

□ Ask to contact the US embassy. Be polite but persistent in making this request. (Normally, the local authorities will notify the US embassy anyway.)

When a consular officer comes to see you in jail, here's what he or she can do for you:

□ Provide you with a list of local attorneys, including their specialties.

□ Call an attorney for you if you are unable to make a call.

□ Notify relatives or friends at home.

□ Help you wire for funds.

□ Make sure your basic health and safety needs are being met.

□ Make sure you're not being discriminated against because you're an American.

□ Do not expect the embassy to get you out of jail. You are subject to the laws of the country you're visiting.

Source: John P. Caulfield, Bureau of Consular Affairs, US Department of State, Washington, DC.

Offenses most likely to get you arrested abroad

When traveling, these are the major dangers that can land you in a foreign jail:

□ Auto accidents. In many foreign countries, you can be arrested or imprisoned for driving while intoxicated or held criminally liable for an accident in which someone is injured.

□ Narcotics. Those convicted of possession or trafficking in drugs usually spend from two to ten years in jail, often with long waits in jail for a trial. Bail is generally not possible for narcotics offenses or other serious offenses in most foreign countries.

□ Black marketeering. Selling unauthorized goods is a very serious offense in many countries and is often punished by a prison term. *Also:* Beware of black-market currency transactions. You could be robbed or wind up with counterfeit currency.

Source: John P. Caulfield, Bureau of Consular Affairs, US Department of State, Washington, DC.

Tipping while traveling

Deluxe restaurants

□ Maitre d', $1–$15 every few visits (if you get special treatment).

□ Waiter, 15%.

□ Captain, 5%.

□ Sommelier, 7% of the liquor bill or $2 for each bottle.

□ Cloakroom, 50¢–$1 per coat.

□ Doorman, $1 if he hails a cab.

Other restaurants

□ Waiter, 10%–15%.

□ Coat check, 25¢–50¢.

Hotels

□ Chambermaid, $1–$1.25 per room per night, or $7 a week.

□ Dining room (American Plan), waiter gets 15% of the food bill for the total stay and the maitre d' a flat $10 for a stay of five to seven days.

□ Room service, if service charge is not added, 10%–15%, depending on the amount of service given.

□ Pool attendant, $1 per day.

☐ Waiter (snack bar, golf club, beach or tennis club), 15% of the bill.

☐ Locker attendant, 50¢–$1 a day.

☐ Bartender, 15% of bill.

☐ Doorman, 25¢–$1 unless baggage is handled, then 50¢–$1.

☐ Baggage handler, 50¢ per bag.

☐ Bellman, 50¢–$1 per errand.

☐ Taxi driver, 15% of bill, 25¢ minimum for small bill.

☐ In Europe and the Orient, tips are usually included in the form of a service charge of 10% to 15% of the bill. Be sure to check your bill before leaving additional money.

Cruises (two in a cabin)

☐ Cabin steward or stewardess, $3–$4 per day.

☐ Dining-room steward, $3–$3.50 per day.

☐ Shoe cleaner, $5 at end of trip.

☐ Cabin boys, $1 per errand.

☐ Wine steward, 15% of total bill.

☐ Night steward, $2 per night if services are used.

☐ Deck steward, $10–$15 for the whole cruise.

☐ Bar steward, 15% of the total tab.

Personal services

☐ Hairdresser, 15%–20% of his or her services (but do not tip the owner of a salon).

☐ Shampooer, $2.

☐ Manicurist, $2.

☐ Pedicurist, $4.

☐ Coat check, $1.

Caterers

☐ Party supervisor, $20.

☐ Headwaiter, $10.

☐ Head cook, $10–$15.

☐ Others, $5 each.

Miscellaneous

☐ Garage attendant, 50¢–$1.

☐ Valet parking, $1.

☐ Redcap, 50¢ per bag.

☐ Washroom attendant, 25¢–$1.

☐ Strolling musicians, $1–$2/single, $5/group.

Taking really good vacation photographs

The new fully automated cameras have taken technical burdens off the backs of amateur photographers.

Here are some practical suggestions:

☐ Get up close. A sure way to take boring pictures is to make all your shots "overalls." The details in a scene are what make it interesting and expressive. Don't hide behind your telephoto lens for close-ups. Move in close with a wide-angle lens, which gives a greater sense of intimacy, involvement and graphic drama.

☐ Make value judgments. Many amateurs take too many photos of boring things, especially boring landscapes. They walk into a market and miss the one gnarled vendor in fantastic ethnic clothing.

☐ Ask yourself…What does this subject symbolize? Is it the best evocation of this environment? *Helpful:* Pick out a symbol or idea that represents the country and come home with 15 or 20 photos as a treatment of that theme. Working on a theme keeps you intellectually alert, too.

☐ Study good photographs. Go to gallery shows and museum exhibitions. Buy books, and subscribe to publications that feature the works of leading photo artists. Try to understand the intent of other photographers even if you don't like their photographic effects. Take a photo workshop. Find a teacher whose style is different from your own—someone who will shake you up.

☐ Be flexible. Seek out opportunities to become photographically involved with people who may seem strange to you. Cities always have a place where people congregate on Sunday afternoons. Learn to relate to these people and to become quickly at ease with strangers. Then neither you nor they will feel threatened when you photograph them.

☐ Be physically flexible. Many travel photos are boring because they're taken from a standing position. Try climbing, stooping or lying flat on the ground to get a fresh angle.

☐ Practice at home. Don't expect to take great photos on vacations if that's the only time you use your camera. Take photos in your spare time and on weekends. Pretend you're a foreigner visiting from abroad, and be a travel photographer in your own backyard.

☐ Criticize your own work. Be as objective as possible about your failures and successes. Don't be afraid to be hard on yourself. A discouraging moment of dissatisfaction with your own work can be the first step toward style.

Source: Lisl Dennis, author, *Travel Photography: Developing a Personal Style,* Curtin & London, Somerville, MA.

Collecting seashells overseas

The most colorful shells are found near coral reefs in tropical waters. Many areas offer special arrangements for shell collectors, from boat trips to uncombed beaches to guided snorkeling or scuba diving.

Sanibel Island, Florida, is the best-known shelling spot in the US.

The best spots overseas:

☐ Costa Rica offers both Atlantic and Pacific varieties.

☐ The Philippines are known for their many local dealers and good values.

☐ Cabo San Lucas, Mexico, on the southern tip of the Baja Penninsula.

☐ The Portuguese Cape Verde Islands off Senegal.

☐ Keep in mind that much of Southern California and Australia's Great Barrier Reef are closed or limited for environmental reasons.

What you should put in your traveling gear box

A practical travel kit should include:

☐ Swiss army knife (complete with scissors, small screwdriver, nail file and clippers).

☐ Safety pins.

☐ Large bandages.

☐ Styptic pencil.

☐ Small tin of aspirin.

☐ Two packets of antacid tablets.

☐ Dental floss.

☐ Two pairs of shoelaces.

☐ Small sewing kit.

☐ Sample bar of soap.

☐ Two packets of cold-water laundry detergent.

☐ Envelope of talc.

☐ Four feet of cord to tie your suitcase together if it has been damaged in transit.

Source: *Medical Economics.*

Advice for solo travelers

Traveling alone can have its advantages. But what if the traveler next to you won't stop talking? What if your wallet or purse disappears? For trouble-free trips…

☐ Don't travel without telling someone. Contact a friend or family member, and give that person your itinerary so someone knows how to find you.

☐ Streamline your wallet or purse. Avoid having to replace everything—if it's lost or stolen—by only carrying identification and those cards that you may actually use.

☐ Don't wear fine jewelry. It's risky to put it in your luggage so—leave it home.

☐ Travel light. An overloaded traveler is a vulnerable traveler. Ship bulky items in advance.

☐ Keep an inventory of items—and put a copy of it and your personal identification inside your suitcase, and keep a copy, too. You'll know by checking the inventory if something's missing and you will increase the odds that you'll see it again if it's lost.

☐ Wear a wedding ring. You'll discourage unwanted advances.

☐ Have single bills handy. You won't have to get change and attract the wrong kind of attention, and you'll speed your progress through the airport if you need to give a tip.

Source: Natalie Windsor, author of *How to Fly— Relaxed and Happy From Takeoff to Touchdown,* CorkScrew Press, Box 833, Old Saybrook, CT 06475.

Preventing hotel burglaries

☐ Don't talk to strangers about gambling winnings, family finances or other money matters.

☐ Avoid disclosing your personal itinerary for the day.

☐ Make sure that sliding doors to balconies or patios are locked.

☐ When out of the room, leave a light on and the drapes slightly open.

☐ Never leave valuables in the room.

Source: *Travel Expenses Management.*

Traveling with a computer

Avoid mistakes that many people make. Be sure you:

☐ Carry a long extension cord…many hotel rooms have only one outlet.

☐ Use a padded carrying bag to protect the computer and its peripherals. Avoid models with name-brand advertising…they're targets for thieves.

☐ Carry your computer on the plane… checking it is begging for trouble.

Phoning from Europe

Four ways to cut down on often excessively high Europe-to-US hotel phone charges:

☐ Where high surcharges apply, make a brief call home just to leave your phone and room numbers—and have your party call you back.

☐ Use your phone credit card in countries where it is honored. Although there could be a surcharge, it is usually much less than a call charged to your hotel bill.

☐ Always check your hotel's surcharge policy. *Countries notorious for rip-offs:* Germany, Switzerland, Austria and Italy.

☐ Use telephone centers (usually in the post office or railway station) to skip middlemen and surcharges.

Source: AT&T, as reported in the *Journal of Commerce,* New York.

Taxi tips for you

☐ *London.* The famous black cabs can be hailed from the street. *Tip:* 15%.

☐ *Paris.* Taxis are hard to flag, except at hotels. *Best bet:* A taxi stand.

☐ *Rome.* Look for taxi stands at train stations, hotels and shopping areas. *Tip:* 10%–15%.

☐ *Tokyo.* Get help from your hotel in writing your destination in Japanese. *Tip:* Not expected.

☐ *Hong Kong.* Cabs are easily hailed on the street, but the driver's command of English will vary. *Tip:* Small.

Source: *Travel & Leisure,* New York.

The best zoos

☐ *Philadelphia Zoological Gardens.* The nation's oldest zoo (in Fairmount Park) now features the Tree House, where children can see the world from animals' perspectives.

☐ *International Wildlife Conservation Park,* formerly Bronx Zoo (*New York*). Outstanding natural habitat exhibits in Jungle World and Wild Asia.

☐ *Miami Metrozoo.* Monorail tours of more than 200 acres of plains, jungles and forests. Wings of Asia features more than 300 species of birds.

☐ *San Diego Zoo.* Wild Animal Park (30 miles north of the city) offers day or night safaris through a land of 2,200 uncaged animals.

☐ *Woodland Park Zoo (Seattle).* New bioclimatic zone replaces cages with a contoured, tall-grass terrain.

☐ *Cincinnati Zoo.* Attractions include the Cat House and a children's zoo for preschoolers.

☐ *Brookfield Zoo (Chicago).* Three daily tropical rainstorms, dolphin acts and a black rhinoceros.

☐ *St. Louis Zoo.* A grand legacy of the World's Fair of 1904, now moved to Forest Park.

Source: *TWA Ambassador.*

The most walkable cities

☐ *San Francisco.* Climbing the hills can be arduous, but the summit views are unsurpassed.

☐ *New York.* Manhattan is a never-ending street show, ranging from the elegant to the tawdry or hilarious. You'll find every possible ethnic snack along the way.

☐ *Venice.* The car-free streets are perfect for walking, the light and water enchanting. *Pedestrian high spots:* Piazza San Marco, Ponte di Rialto, Santa Maria della Salute.

☐ *Copenhagen.* You'll enjoy its seaside streets, flower-filled parks and story-book palaces. Shop along the famous Stroget (pedestrians only).

☐ *New Orleans.* The French Quarter is compact, historic and lively. Go to

Bourbon Street for jazz and to the Mississippi River for port-town bustle.

Source: *The Washington Post.*

Travelers' medical kit...nonprescription items

☐ Spenco 2nd Skin Blister Kit. New, and the best treatment for minor burns of all kinds. Soothes and heals at the same time. Adhesive knot bandage (included) keeps troubled areas sterile. The salve relieves the itch of healing burns. Also recommended for the home medicine cabinet.

☐ Hibiclens Surgical Scrub. An antiseptic cleaner for scrapes and open wounds. More effective than pHiso-Hex or Betadine—and also more expensive —this product is now in use at many hospitals.

For illness

☐ Meclizine (Bonine). Sold as a motion-sickness preventive, but also effective for nausea and vomiting. Best taken an hour before boarding vehicle...lasts 24 hours.

☐ Antacid tablets. Any brand will do, but be sure to get one marked "high potency."

☐ Diasorb. As effective as Imodium for diarrhea, and can be used safely over a longer period of time. Comes in tablets for adults and liquid for children. *Problem:* Not available everywhere.

Allergies

☐ Benadryl antihistamine. For allergy conditions of the skin, but also relieves viral-induced congestion and acts as a powerful cough suppressant. *Caution:* Produces drowsiness...if you are driving, substitute Claritin, Seldane or Hismanal...antihistamines available over the counter in Canada—and by prescription in the United States.

Source: William W. Forgey, MD, a member of the Medical Advisory Board, International Association for Medical Assistance to Travelers (IAMAT), and a practicing physician in Merrillville, Indiana. He is the author of the *Travelers' Self-Care Manual*, ICS Books, 1370 E. 86 Pl., Merrillville, Indiana 46410.

Ways to travel free

Become a tour escort for a travel agency especially if you are fluent in one or more foreign languages. Organize your own tour—if you put enough people together, your own travel can be free.

Become an air courier, accompanying small parcels and documents on overseas flights. Courier companies give couriers free or deeply discounted tickets—70% off or more. Couriers must be very flexible and travel light.

Source: Lynne Scanlon, travel writer and author of *Overcoming Jet Lag*, Berkley Publishing, 200 Madison Ave., New York 10016.

Cruise dining

Ask for a table for at least six when traveling on a cruise. Dining usually takes at least two hours every night—a long time to spend with people you find you dislike. It is easier to leave a table with two other couples than to leave one with only one other couple. If you find on the first night that you do not like your assigned dinner companions, request another table immediately—do not wait until the second or third night.

Source: Douglas Ward, veteran of more than 700 cruises and president of International Cruise Passengers Association, 1521 Alton Rd., Suite 350, Miami Beach 33139.

Weekend travel bargains

Weekend car-rental rates usually start at noon on Thursdays. Rates can be up to 50% less than weekday rates.

Self-defense: If traveling on a Thursday, arrange to pick up a car after noon. If arriving earlier in the week but staying into the weekend, ask about returning the car you rented at weekday rates at noon on Thursday—exchanging it for a car at the lower rate.

Source: Herbert J. Teison, editor, *Travel Smart*, 40 Beechdale Rd., Dobbs Ferry, New York 10522.

Best ways to make better first impressions

First impressions aren't formed in the first ten minutes of a conversation—or in the first half hour. They are formed in the first few seconds.

Of course, a one-hour meeting with someone you've never met before gives you ample time to refine and embellish the first impression you make. But what occurs in the last few minutes of a first encounter is deeply influenced by the experience of the first few seconds.

The lesson for businesspeople is that you can prepare beautifully for a favorable first impression and blow it by paying too little attention to the instantaneous perception people get based on your posture, your eye contact, the way you hold your head and your general expression and demeanor.

Polishing the first impression

Your attitude has a great deal to do with your expression and demeanor. To make a positive impression, you must be sincere and sensitive to what makes others feel comfortable. There's a kind of natural graciousness that some people have. But anyone can learn to think of the other person first.

When you are going to an important meeting with strangers, concentrate on putting others around you at ease, instead of focusing only on driving home your agenda. *Helpful:* Pretend you are the host of the meeting, and treat everyone accordingly.

Self-restraint is a virtue today. The time is long gone when Americans could get away with arrogant or overbearing behavior around the world. Projecting self-esteem does not mean projecting arrogance.

Much better: Exhibit the strength to be considerate of others, the deference to hold a door open or write a note to thank someone who has helped you and the generosity of spirit that leaves others with something after your meetings with them.

Proper attire

Dress as if you are always on stage—because you are. While the dress code varies widely from company to company, depending on climate and other factors, there are certain wardrobe guidelines that will stand you in good stead anywhere in the world…

☐ Strive for a well-groomed, coordinated look. This means conservative suits or dresses of simple lines and solid colors, such as navy, gray, beige or black. Women can branch out to brighter shades, such as yellow, green and red, as long as the outfits have a conservative cut. Because good tailoring is expensive, many women are now turning to softer clothes and knits. These allow them to look professional without having to pay for costly alterations.

Men should have at least a few custom-tailored shirts for important first-impression occasions. They fit better and look much neater than traditional button-downs. Choose fabrics that breathe, but at the same time look crisp and unwrinkled. Choose a straight or spread collar. They are appropriate anywhere in the world.

Most executives will always feel right in a conservative tie with small or repeat prints. If you want to stand out, shop for patterns from Hermes, Ferragamo or Gucci. A sassy Nicole Miller tie makes a creative statement. (*Caution:* Not for everyone.)

Important: Be sure that your tie does not have spots or stains around the edges of the knot. And put away ties that have a width that has gone out of fashion. Width styles change every few years.

☐ Wear the outfit that is appropriate to the role you are in or that you aspire to. Influential decision-makers really do look different. Pattern your wardrobe after those in the company or social circle you admire and hope to emulate.

Creative entrepreneurs do not have to follow tradition as much as corporate managers do, and they often want to signal that by dressing less convention-ally. Even they, however, are wise to suit up—or at least wear a blazer and gray slacks—when they are meeting with influential bankers, lawyers or shareholders.

☐ Concentrate on your head because that's your power center. It's the place where much of the other person's attention will focus first. *Note:* Women with long hair are too often not taken seriously in business. For men, it's essential to be clean shaven, especially for those who travel internationally. In Asia and certain other countries, facial hair indicates lower class or servitude.

Women should wear some makeup, but not too much. The same goes for jewelry, where a simple gold necklace or pearls (real or not) and nondangling earrings effectively frame the face. A colorful silk scarf tied around your neck is also flattering.

Avoid wearing anything that jingles, such as a charm bracelet or too many bangles. One piece of good gold jewelry is much more impressive than a lot of costume jewelry.

☐ Avoid exposing the skin on your legs. Women should always wear stockings, and men's hosiery must be of a length so as to avoid showing skin if they cross their legs.

Don't ever show the soles of your shoes. In Middle Eastern countries that is a terrible insult. When you do cross your legs, do it in such a way that the soles are not facing another person.

☐ Invest in accessories. Shoes are perhaps the most important accessory. People around the world size you up by your shoes. Ferragamos are so well made that they will keep their shape even after a thorough soaking. Moreover, they are recognized everywhere as a standard of good taste and quality.

Be sure to carry your papers and laptop computer in a handsome tote or briefcase. A briefcase does not have to be brand new, but it should be in good shape. It should not look like a leftover from school days. That marks you as a worker bee rather than a decision-maker.

Don't think people don't notice these details of your bearing. Conclusions are drawn quickly.

By the same token, wear a quality watch and carry a distinguishing pen. Never put your Montblanc in your shirt pocket. That signifies an order-taker, rather than an order-giver. Do, however, use the pen for personal messages to capture attention.

A captivating voice

Gain and hold someone's attention by speaking clearly and slowly. If a dialogue goes off track, try not to ever interrupt, disagree or offend the other person. At times it may help to add a little humor to relieve the tension.

Top off all of these tips with a warm smile and a gracious farewell. If you want to walk away knowing that you've made a great first impression, plan ahead. It doesn't mean that you are trying to be someone other than yourself. It just means that you are willing to discipline yourself to make someone with certain expectations more comfortable in your presence. This gives you the edge when you are trying to land—or keep—a job or influence a client.

Source: Camille Lavington, international communications consultant, 160 E. 38 St., New York 10016.

How to buy clothes that make you look good

☐ Choosing color to "go with" your hair and eyes is a mistake. It's your skin tone that determines how a particular color looks on you.

☐ The more intense and dark your clothing, the larger you'll appear and the less likely to blend into the environment.

☐ White tends to wash out the face and yellow the teeth. Soft ivory tones are somewhat better.

☐ Don't rule out whole color groups—all blues or all greens. Most people can wear certain shades of most color groups. *Exceptions:* A few colors, such as orange and purple, are really not good for many people in any shade.

☐ Pay attention to pattern or weave. People who are short or small-boned should not wear big prints or checks. They can wear small true tweeds. Slender, smallish men and women are overwhelmed by heavy fabrics. Light wools are better for them than heavy worsteds.

☐ Consider aging skin in choosing colors. Wrinkled skin is minimized by softer shades. Hard, dark, intense colors maximize the evidence of aging.

☐ The colors surrounding you in your home or office determine the way in which the eye perceives your skin and even your features. Some colors will produce deep shadows, enlarge certain features or produce deep facial lines because of the way they interact with your skin tone.

☐ Don't change makeup to "go with" clothes. Makeup should be chosen according to skin tone only. Using the wrong color makeup is worse than wearing the wrong color clothing.

☐ Most men can't wear madras or bold plaids. When men choose sports clothes, they go wild in the other direction from the conservative clothes they wear to work. Most have had little practice in choosing dramatic colors that are suitable.

☐ A tan does make you look healthier, but it doesn't change the basic effect of certain colors on your skin. With a tan, wearing colors you normally look good in is important, because that's when those colors look better than ever.

Source: Adrienne Gold and Anne Herman, partners in Colorconscious, Inc., Larchmont, NY.

Dressing for special occasions

Unusual circumstances may call for a thoughtful adaptation of basic dress rules. Learn as much as possible about the geographical, educational and socioeconomic background of the people you'll be dealing with and tailor your wardrobe to their expectations. *Examples:*

☐ Appearing in court. The main problem here is establishing credibility, and the best way to appear credible is to surprise no one. For maximum effectiveness, look just as others expect you to look.

If you are appearing as a high-ranking financial officer, you'll dress differently than if you're appearing as a technical expert—even though you may be both. The higher up the management pyramid you wish to represent yourself, the more quietly opulent your dress should be.

☐ Keep regional/local considerations in mind. A New Yorker, for example, testifying in Texas would be well advised to tone down his dress, keeping it low-key.

☐ Appearing at an IRS audit. The right image for this situation combines authority with humility—respectable and respectful, but not too prosperous. Keep it simple and conservative. Wear one of your older suits (a well-worn Brooks Brothers would be excellent), preferably two-piece, with a plain white shirt and a conservative striped tie. Avoid jewelry and other signs of affluence.

☐ Television appearances. The dress standards of a TV-show host are a reasonable guide. Dress less conservatively. Wear lighter colors. Leave the

three-piece suit and other power symbols at home. Keep accessories simple and understated. Wear solid colors. Avoid small patterns.

☐ Public speaking. If you know in advance what color the background will be (or if you can choose it), wear a suit (preferably dark) that will stand out. Wear a contrasting shirt (preferably light-colored) and a solid tie.

☐ Job interviews. Dress for the interview, not for the job. Even if you will be a field engineer, come to the interview in a three-piece suit.

Tailor the quality of your dress to the level of the position you seek. A recent college graduate will be forgiven a $200 suit. A candidate for an $80,000 management position will not.

Source: John T. Molloy, author of *Dress for Success* and *The Woman's Dress for Success*, Warner Books, New York.

What women hate about what men wear

No matter how differently women dress from one another, they are surprisingly unanimous about what looks bad on men. Results of an informal survey is a ten-point program:

☐ Socks are by far the most frequently mentioned item of annoyance. They must be long enough to cover the calf or "it's death to a woman's libido." Also "out" are socks with clogs, black socks with tennis sneakers, white cotton socks with business shoes and socks with holes in the heels.

☐ Comb-overs. Letting hair grow long at the side and combing it over a bald head was high on women's list of loathing. "Who does he think he's kidding?" they asked. Women don't dislike baldness per se. They do dislike comb-overs and other compensatory acts of denial and bravado. They like men who like themselves.

☐ Miami Beach macho. Even women who think men are nifty in manicures and pinky rings hate the men who expose five buttons' worth of chest and a gold medallion.

☐ Misfits. Women say clothes that don't fit advertise a guy who doesn't really see himself, which means he is probably oblivious to all his other flaws, too, or one who doesn't like himself enough to care how he looks, which means a woman will spend her life shoring up his self-image.

☐ Textures. Men shouldn't shine. Anything synthetic that glistens is too glitzy and anything naturally shiny is "pseudo-regal." As one woman put it, "Men need a matte finish."

☐ Affectations. Women opt for simplicity. They like their men unadorned, not gimmicky. "Playboy rabbit insignia drive me wiggo," said a normally subdued woman. "Full-dress fully-grown cowboys look ludicrous on Lake Shore Drive," said another. *Also contemptible:* Men wearing one earring (not to mention two); initials on shirts, tie clips or lapel pins promoting a lodge, Lions Club, PT-109, the American flag or God; sweaters with reindeer; leprechaun hats; and anything Tyrolean.

☐ Shoes. This is an easy one. Whether women were partial to men in Guccis or Adidas, cordovans or bucks, glove-leather wing tips or crepe-sole Hush Puppies, nobody loves tassel loafers.

☐ Color. Anything goes—except the too-bright tones. If it stops traffic…don't wear it.

☐ Gestures. Certain items of clothing inspire annoying gestures in men. The worst: "Shooting cuffs" (pushing arms out so that his sleeves show more of his shirt cuffs and ostentatious cuff links). "The mirror sneak"—checking and re-arranging his tie in every looking glass. "The hoist"— the vaguely obscene lifting of the waistband of loose trousers.

☐ Underwear. The issue is settled by body type. The man with a "good bottom" and tight belly should wear jockeys. The well-muscled-shoulder man should wear sleeveless undershirts.

Source: Letty Cottin Pogrebin, writer and *Ms.* magazine editor.

How to prolong the life of your clothes

☐ Hang jackets on wooden or plastic hangers that are curved to the approximate shape of the human back.

☐ Remove all objects from pockets.

☐ Leave jackets unbuttoned.

☐ Keep some space between garments to avoid wrinkling.

☐ Allow at least 24 hours between wearings.

☐ Use pants hangers that clamp onto trouser bottoms.

☐ Remove belt before hanging up pants.

Hair-care hints

☐ Baby shampoos are not as mild as special-formula shampoos for dry or damaged hair. Detergents and pH levels put baby shampoos into the middle range of hair cleansers, which makes them right for normal hair.

☐ People with oily hair need a stronger shampoo especially made for that condition.

☐ Wet hair should be combed, not brushed. Hair is weakest when wet and can be easily damaged then. Use a wide-tooth comb to reduce the chance of breaking your hair.

☐ Twenty-five brush strokes a day is optimal for best distribution of natural oils in the hair. More brushing can cause damage.

Looking good for less

☐ Get a home manicure kit. Save $8 a week on costly salon manicures and pedicures.

☐ Rent exercise videos instead of re-joining the expensive health club that you rarely visit.

☐ Buy inexpensive home exercise equipment. Get a free catalog from Better Health, which sells brand-name exercise equipment for up to 50% off. 718-436-4693.

☐ Book court time at off-hours for tennis and racquetball and save up to 50% off peak time.

☐ Buy your workouts in quantity. You may get ten aerobics classes for the price of eight, for example.

☐ Join a community swimming pool.

☐ Have a makeup swap party. Everyone throws their cosmetic "giveaways" on a table—for switching.

☐ Take advantage of free makeovers offered by cosmeticians in department stores. And…be sure to ask for samples.

☐ Always get a gift with cosmetic purchases. Remember to ask, since stores don't always tell customers about gifts.

☐ Buy generic-brand cosmetics. They're made of the same stuff as brand names, but they can cost up to 70% less.

☐ Buy name-brand cosmetics by mail. For a free catalog, call Beauty Boutique at 216-826-3008.

☐ Use stick or roll-on deodorant. It lasts much longer than aerosol.

☐ Stay away from pump toothpastes. Tubes last longer.

☐ Buy combination shampoo-conditioners rather than buying them separately. To make the bottle last longer, cut it with tap water when it's half-empty.

☐ Take showers instead of baths. If you don't linger, this can save up to half the cost of heating hot water for a bath.

Source: Ellen Kunes, lifestyle director for *McCall's*, and author of *Living Well on Less*, Putnam Publishing Group, New York.

The secrets of a great shave

Treat your face to the most up-to-date equipment. It is false economy to buy anything less than the best, since the entire annual cost of shaving seldom exceeds $100. Also, blades and shaving creams are constantly being improved.

☐ Shaving cream. All types of cream (lather, brushless and aerosol in either lather or gel form) are equally efficient. Brushless shaving cream is recommended for dry skin. Buy three or four different kinds of shaving cream. Use different ones for different moods.

☐ Blades. Modern technology makes the current stainless-steel blades a real pleasure to use. *The best type:* The double-track blade.

☐ Proper preparation. Wash your face with soap at least twice before shaving. This helps soften the skin, saturate the beard and remove facial oils. *Best:* Shave after a warm shower.

☐ Shaving cream is more effective if left on the face for a few minutes prior to actual shaving. This saturation causes the facial hairs to expand by about one-third, which enhances the cutting ability of the blade.

☐ Except on the warmest days, preheat lather in the can or tube by immersion in hot water.

☐ The manufacturing process leaves a slight oil residue on the edge of the new blade. This can catch and pull the tender facial skin during the first couple of strokes. So start by trimming the sideburns, a painless way of breaking in the new blade. Always shave the upper lip and chin last. *Why:* The coarsest hairs grow here. Your skin will benefit from the extra minutes of saturation and wetness.

☐ When you have finished shaving, rinse the blade and shake the razor dry. Never wipe-dry a blade; this dulls the edge. When rinsing the blade, hold it low in the water stream for quicker results.

☐ After shaving. Save money by skipping the highly advertised after-shave lotions. Use witch hazel instead. It is odorless, less astringent, leaves no residue and is better for your skin than most of the after-shave lotions.

How to be happy with a less-than-perfect body

It has become "normal" for people to be dissatisfied with their bodies. To varying degrees, most of us are unhappy with what we see in the mirror. We're too fat, our feet are too big, our hair the wrong color, our noses misshapen, our muscles too small. The list of complaints is endless.

Each day, we're barraged by messages from the media, advertisements and even friends and family—all suggesting that we are physically inadequate, that unless we have the "perfect" weight, height, hair, facial features, etc., we are somehow freaks.

But there are many more "normal" people than fashion models—so maybe it's them and not us who are freakish.

I believe that "perfection" has far more to do with being comfortable with who and what we are than with having the "ideal" body.

Is "imperfection" unhealthy?

Not at all. A receding hairline certainly isn't a sign of poor health, nor is a long nose, wrinkles around the eyes or being a bit shorter than friends and coworkers.

Again, let's look at fat. Studies have repeatedly shown that as we reach middle age, our bodies naturally gain weight. A man who weighs 160 pounds at age 25 can reasonably expect to gain at least 20 pounds by age 50. This weight gain is not unseemly or dangerous, although popular culture would suggest otherwise.

Result: To keep the weight off, middle-aged people diet continually and engage in overly strenuous exercise programs. Ironically, these diets and exercise programs can pose greater threats to their health than a few extra pounds.

Lesson: Bodies change over time, and the slow, gradual accumulation of weight is not inherently bad.

In fact, being slightly overweight may be healthier than being thin. A recent study by the Metropolitan Life Insurance Company found that underweight people have considerably higher mortality rates than people who are overweight.

This is not to suggest that it's okay to "let yourself go." Eating indiscriminately and without regard to nutrition inevitably leads to health problems—as does a lack of exercise. And the fear of falling victim to such problems only heightens the stress.

If you have crossed the line to unhealthy weight gain, you should take steps to shed a few pounds. But if your feelings are based only upon what you fear others think about your weight, there may be no need to lose weight.

Caution: Excessive weight gain that occurs despite a sensible diet and regular exercise suggests a glandular problem. See a doctor.

Perception versus reality

Like most people in our society, I once had a very negative impression of people who are overweight—including my wife. This was especially true because I am quite lean and thought everyone should be like I was.

But about 15 years ago my attitude began to crumble. I started to see my wife not as "fat," but as "pleasingly plump." I stopped criticizing her weight and started to accept her the way she was. I've been happier ever since—and so has she.

What changed me? I began to realize that the people I knew came in all different shapes and sizes, and most were capable, ambitious, intelligent and warm-hearted. With some embarrassment, I realized that it was wrong to criticize these people just because their bodies failed to conform to an artificial image of perfection.

What you can do:

☐ Focus on how you feel—not on what you look like. Most of us feel better when we eat a low-fat, high-fiber diet, drink alcohol in moderation or not at all, avoid smoking and get regular exercise. But even if you follow this familiar wisdom, there's no assurance that you will look like a model—even if your parents did.

If your ancestors were bald, or had big jowls or protruding ears, it's pointless to blame yourself if you share the same traits. More problems are caused than resolved when people try to repudiate their bodies. Try to accept the natural shape of your family tree.

☐ Avoid fad diets. Many of the diets advocated today deprive people of wholesome, necessary foods and don't take into account an individual's natural body composition. Instead of picking a diet from a magazine or a bestseller, follow the guidelines of the Department of Agriculture's Food Guide Pyramid. Vary the size of the portions according to your desire to lose or gain weight.

Never diet solely to change your body shape. And you absolutely must avoid yo-yo dieting, in which large quantities of weight are repeatedly lost and regained. Recent studies have found this to be dangerous to your health.

Think: Do you feel comfortable with your body? If you feel no lack of energy, if you feel attractive, if you enjoy sex (studies have shown that so-called fat women have sexual relations more often and enjoy them more than underweight women) and if you feel that you can accomplish personal or career goals, then why attempt to change things?

Source: Charles Roy Schroeder, PhD, professor of exercise physiology, biomechanics, fitness and wellness, Memphis State University, Memphis, Tennessee. He is the author of *Fat Is Not a Four-Letter Word,* Chronimed Publishing, Minneapolis. •

Secrets of happy couples

The high rate of divorce, combined with the skyrocketing number of dysfunctional families, suggests that there is no such thing as a truly happy marriage…but my interviews with couples across the country show otherwise.

The couples I talked to had been married between 7 and 55 years. More than half described themselves as very happily married. Only two or three were actually miserable.

The remaining 35 couples are hanging in there and doing all right.

The happiest couples share a number of characteristics—qualities from which we can learn. And they dispelled several popular misconceptions…

☐ Myth: Be realistic, not idealistic.

Reality: In fact, the most happily married people idealize their spouses. Many of them say they think their husbands or wives are the greatest people in the world. That belief certainly helps bring out the best in their partners. Research has shown that people live up—or down —to our expectations.

Even after the "crazy-in-love" phase has long passed, the happy partners continue to see each other through rose-colored glasses—often more positively than others might see them.

☐ Myth: Happy couples rarely fight.

Reality: Of course, happy couples fight—some more often than others. But happy couples fight by the rules and are able to keep conflicts from escalating.

The rules differ depending on the temperaments of the people involved. Some couples say, "We never go to bed angry." They insist on resolving issues rather than walking away from them.

Happy couples have impulse control. They are willing and able to censor themselves, even in the midst of rage, so as not to say or do the thing that would be "fatal" to the relationship.

☐ Myth: There's no such thing as love at first sight.

Reality: Some romances blossomed slowly. But there were also many who remembered feeling a powerful attraction at their first meeting…and who are still in love with each other years later. There were also cases in which one partner fell in love immediately, while the other partner took longer to come around.

☐ Myth: Friendship, not sex, is the key to a long-lasting relationship.

Reality: Both sex and friendship are important.

While the happiest husbands and wives say they are each other's best friends, they also have very strong sexual bonds. True, the intense infatuation—being ready to jump into bed at any opportunity—fades after a few years. But the sexual chemistry remains, even during periods when a couple isn't making love.

Example: One wife was so exhausted after having a baby that she temporarily lost interest in sex. Nevertheless, she continued to have vivid sexual dreams about her husband.

☐ Myth: Happy couples have independent lives.

Reality: Even if they don't share all the same interests, happy couples spend a lot of time together.

This is another characteristic that has to do with temperament—some couples require less togetherness than others. But the idea that separate identities are essential is completely untrue. These couples have definitely found a shared identity. Over time, they stopped feeling single at heart and came to be married at heart. If that process doesn't happen, the marriage is in trouble.

☐ Myth: The happiest couples raise children together.

Reality: The few childless couples I interviewed are quite happy. What seemed to be important is not whether a couple has children, but whether they agree that children should or should not be part of their lives together.

In fact, children are the subject couples fight about most often—more than sex, money or in-laws. Children can disrupt the unity of a couple, introducing an element of separation and continuous potential conflict.

That doesn't mean that children damage a relationship—far from it. But raising children is very difficult, with a lot to disagree about. Happy couples who are parents face and grapple with these conflicts and learn from each other.

Example: One husband was a severe disciplinarian, while his wife was very gentle with the children. This difference caused an ongoing disagreement between them. Eventually, he realized that she was able to get exactly the response she wanted from the children without screaming or yelling…and he began to temper his own approach.

Why couples get along:

For a marriage to be happy, the partners need to be identical in background but opposite in personality—one woman said.

I saw this truth borne out over and over again. If a couple shares the same background (age, religion, ethnicity, economic status), they are more likely to agree on many of the day-to-day decisions, such as how to raise the children, what vacations to take, what colors to use when decorating the house, etc.

Having opposite personalities is what provides the spark. I saw many couples in which one partner was somewhat depressive and pessimistic and the other was optimistic. They seemed to balance or compensate for each other.

I'm not suggesting that people with different backgrounds can't have good marriages. But shared reference points do make marriages work better.

Source: Catherine Johnson, PhD, author of *Lucky in Love: The Secrets of Happy Couples and How Their Marriages* Thrive, Viking Penguin, New York.

Family and career: The right mix

Professionally successful men and women are often failures in their personal lives. Just as common are the underachievers in the office who have rewarding family and love lives. Successful businesspeople who can balance their two lives are rare. Many traits useful in the office are counterproductive at home.

Here are some key differences:

☐ Business is goal-oriented in the sense that expectations are put on a schedule with emphasis on such end-products as promotion and money. By contrast, love, despite efforts to direct it, basically exists in the present for the sake of pleasure and well-being.

☐ Business requires efficient use of time. It is often difficult to quantify the value of time spent watching children play or caressing a lover.

☐ Business puts a premium on organization. Life outside the office, however, usually works best when it is disorderly. For example, in order to grow, teenagers need an environment of change and expansion where they can assemble the pieces of their own personalities.

☐ Business thrives on aggression and concentration. Love, on the other hand, is protective and spontaneous. In most cases, it just happens.

Many people caught in the conflict between their professional and personal lives try to minimize it by emphasizing one over the other. There are no magic formulas for recognizing the problem, and solving it is even more difficult. The best approaches are to:

☐ Monitor your motivation. Ask yourself if you need to put in 15 hours a day at the office. Are you doing it to get away from your spouse or because you fear failing as a parent?

☐ Confront problems head-on. If you are angry at a coworker or child, do not work off the anger by jogging. Instead, put your energies where they count—into finding a solution.

☐ Consider professional counseling. Even though you may have just recognized the full impact of the office-versus-home conflict, it is a familiar problem to most counselors.

☐ See yourself in perspective. There is probably no ideal balance between professional and private lives. But constantly striving for it can be one of the most rewarding aspects of both.

Source: Jay B. Rohrlick, MD, author of *Work and Love: The Crucial Balance,* Summit Books, New York.

How to be prepared when your spouse retires

One of the greatest mistakes a couple can make is to assume that retirement will simply be a continuation of married life as they have known it.

Retirement has its own rhythm, just as the honeymoon years, child-rearing years and empty-nest years had theirs.

Most likely change: You will spend much more time together. *Result:* Trouble spots may arise in the smallest areas of daily life. Many newly retired couples, even those who agree on the major issues of their retirement—where to live, how to handle the finances—are surprised by how infuriating they may suddenly find their comfortable, cherished mate.

Most common trouble spots:

☐ **Lack of retirement planning.** Many a husband has been shocked to learn that his wife has no desire to move to the fishing village he always pictured as a retirement home. Failure to communicate expectations about retirement, or to do the preplanning necessary to make your plans a reality, can cause terrible conflict in retiring couples.

To offset clashes over major issues: Attend a retirement-planning workshop at your local Chamber of Commerce, community college or senior center. Workshop leaders say that no session is conducted without each person making at least one amazing discovery about their spouse's retirement goals.

☐ **Failure to appreciate the psychological impact of retirement.** Couples must realize that retirement can be a traumatic passage, particularly for men. Even men who look forward to retirement may feel fearful and "lost" when they no longer have a routine and the familiar identity of their working selves. Concerns with mortality and self-worth may loom large for the first time.

Best course for women: Respect the grieving period. Don't crowd or smother your husband with suggestions, opinions, questions or demands or push him into a full schedule before he is ready. But do let him know that you are there. This is a good time for extra cuddling, affection and reassurance. Let him percolate a bit, and shift the focus to your own feelings.

Many women feel that they have spent their entire lives deferring to the needs of their husbands and families. They expect retirement to be "their turn" and fear being trapped again by their husbands' needs.

Best course: Have compassion for your husband's feelings, but be very firm regarding your own needs.

Once the transitional period passes, women can help their husbands back into active life. Men are badly needed as community volunteers. Some may just want to "play" awhile, others may enjoy part-time work or a second career.

☐ **Alcoholism/clinical depression.** Alcoholism is under-recognized and badly under-treated in seniors, even though treatment has a high likelihood of success in this age group.

Depression, with or without alcohol, can afflict either sex, but is especially common among those forced to take "early retirement." Depression can also be triggered by many medications. If you suspect either problem in your family, don't hesitate to seek professional help.

Small stuff—but major gripes

☐ **Grocery shopping.** It sounds hilarious —but this is a top area of conflict cited by retired couples. Often the wife has been shopping for years, and finds it insulting when her husband suddenly questions every choice and examines every tomato.

I have met many couples who have had bitter arguments over who gets to push the cart!

Solution: Decide that one of you will do all the shopping. Or shop with two lists. He can select the produce, while she does the rest.

☐ **Territorial strife.** With two people in one house, problems often arise over rooms and routines.

Examples: She wants the spare room as a sewing room, he wants a den. He used to leave for work, so she could drink coffee and watch *Good Morning, America* before starting her chores. Now he wants to watch CNN and complains when she starts the housework.

Solution: Communication, compassion and compromise. It's your retirement as well as your spouse's. Wives must be willing to cede some domestic territory —it's his kitchen, too. Husbands must face the necessity to "get a life," and not expect their wives to provide one.

☐ **Comings and goings.** Insecurity often manifests as controlling behavior …*Where are you going? When will you be home? Who's on the phone?*

Solution: Stay calm and considerate. Reassure your mate, but don't be bullied. *Essential:* Keep your sense of humor.

☐ **Division of labor.** He expects her to perform the same chores she always has, even if she's still working part-time.

She expects that now that he's retired, he'll take on some household chores.

Solution: It's time to be fair.

Men: You may have retired from work, but not from the partnership of a marriage. Offer to take on the vacuuming. Don't force her to ask.

Women: Acknowledge the work he does do—caring for the yard, garbage, car, etc. Then ask for the help you need from your spouse. But if you ask him to vacuum, let him do it his way.
Helpful: List chores you each hate, and negotiate for the other to take them on. Hire help for chores you both hate.

☐ Sex. Many men find sex a means of self-proof as well as pleasure. So a pleasant side effect of the anxieties retirement can produce is that many men discover a renewed enthusiasm for sex. Older men often have a stronger sex drive in the morning—so don't be too quick to leap out of bed. You don't have to—you're retired!

Wives: Enjoy it, buy some new lingerie and be willing to try new things.

Caution: Some couples experience the opposite, and shy away from intimacy after retirement. If your sex life is unhealthy, this is a problem that needs to be resolved through frank discussion or counseling.

☐ Television. Get two!

Source: Gloria Bledsoe Goodman, author of *Keys to Living With a Retired Husband*, Barron's Educational Series, Inc., Hauppauge, NY.

Sex therapy

It isn't easy for couples who have sexual problems to seek professional help. *The most common problems:* Lack of interest. Trouble with erections and orgasms. Pain, real or imaginary.

When to consider therapy:

☐ When the problem becomes so great it jeopardizes the relationship.

☐ When preoccupation with the problem becomes so overwhelming that work suffers and enjoyment of life wanes.

☐ *Especially dangerous:* Trying to avoid the problem by drinking, abstaining from sex or turning to extramarital partners.

To find a reputable therapist:

☐ Ask your physician or county medical society for a recommendation.

☐ Review the directory of The American Association of Sex Educators, Coun-

selors and Therapists. It sets education and training standards.

☐ Look for a therapist with degrees in a behavioral science (psychology, psychiatry) as well as training in sex therapy. Although sex therapy focuses primarily on sexual problems, a knowledge of psychology is essential because sexuality is so connected with total personality and life events.

☐ If a sex therapist doesn't ask at the first visit if you've had a medical exam, or refer you for one, find another therapist.

When you have to refuse a family member

This is the hardest kind of refusal to deal with. You not only need the interpersonal skills to say no gracefully but you also have to rethink your real obligations to your family, so you can say no without guilt. Suggestions:

☐ Resist the hidden-bargain syndrome. Parents often operate under the assumption that since they've done all these wonderful things for their children to bring them up, the offspring owe them everything. Both young and grown children can be manipulated by this assumption. *Remedy:* Recognize that parents do nice things at least as much for their own benefit as for their children's sake.

☐ Recognize that a family member who acts hurt at a turndown—when it's for a legitimate reason—is torturing himself. You're not responsible for other people's reactions.

☐ Don't sit on guilt. As soon as you feel it, share it. Guilt pushers know better than anyone how awful it is to feel guilty. Frequently, just pointing out a guilt manipulation makes the other person back off. Once that's done, you're free to sit down and honestly discuss how making another person feel guilty hurts a relationship.

☐ Learn to say no to your children. Parents, more than anything, want their children to like them. But children need structure and limits in order to learn self-discipline and independence. Remind yourself that you are teaching your child how to grow up rather than remain a perennial emotional infant.

Source: Barry Lubetkin, PhD, Institute for Behavior Therapy, New York.

Rules for family fights

Essential: Fighting fair. Every couple must develop its own rules of combat, but the following are generally sound:

☐ Never go for the jugular. Everyone has at least one soft, defenseless spot. A fair spouse attacks elsewhere.

☐ Focus on a specific topic. Don't destroy your spouse with a scorched-earth campaign. *Fair:* "I'm angry because you don't make breakfast before I go to the office." *Unfair:* "I'm angry because you're useless, and my mother was right—you're not tall enough, either."

☐ Don't criticize things that probably can't be changed. A physical blemish or a spouse's limited earning power is not a fair target. On the other hand, it's dangerous to stew in silence if your partner drops dirty socks on the floor or chews with mouth agape. Minor irritations fester.

☐ Don't leave the house during a fight. You'll be talking to yourself—your own best supporter. *Result:* A self-serving reconstruction of what happened, rather than an objective view of the situation.

☐ Argue only when sober. Alcohol is fuel for the irrational. Disagreements are beneficial only if you use reason.

☐ Keep your fights strictly verbal. A fight that turns physical intimidates rather than resolves.

☐ Don't discuss volatile subjects late at night. It's tempting to sum up your day at 11 o'clock. But everything seems worse when you are tired. And if you start arguing at 11, you'll be still more exhausted the next morning. *Better:* Make a date to go at it when both sides are fresh.

☐ Always sleep in the same room, no matter how bitter the fight. The bed is a symbol of the marital bond, and it's more difficult to stay angry with a spouse there.

☐ If you're getting nowhere after a long stretch of quarreling, simply stop. Don't say a word. Your spouse will have great difficulty arguing solo. You can

always resume the next day.

☐ Don't sulk after the real fighting is over. Pride has no place here. The winner of the fight should be the one to initiate the reconciliation.

☐ Consider outside help. If you never seem to resolve an issue despite both parties' best efforts, use other resources…not necessarily a ten-week course or a formal session with a counselor. You might simply cultivate a couple whose marriage you admire and try to profit by their example.

☐ Don't give up too easily on either the fight or the relationship. A strong marriage demands risk-taking, including the risk of feeling and showing extreme anger. The intimacy of marriage is won through pain and friction as well as through pleasure.

Source: Kevin and Marilyn Ryan, co-authors of *Making a Marriage,* St. Martin's Press, New York.

Cooling down family fights

Dealing with emotionally violent situations within your family is one of the hardest things you will ever have to do, since the peacemaker must try to stay emotionally uninvolved.

In a confrontation between a teenager and parents:

☐ One parent must step out of the fight and act as a negotiator. This involves sitting the other two down and listening to both sides.

☐ Stop your spouse from cutting off the child.

☐ Restate what each one tells you, and always give each a chance to add comments.

☐ Recognize that it will be difficult to convince the teen you are unbiased.

☐ To end the fight, suggest a compromise solution. Phrase it carefully.

☐ Make sure both the child and the other parent agree to accept the compromise, a date to start it and the length of time the compromise solution will be tried.

When intervening in a fight between children:

☐ Avoid making one right and the other wrong.

☐ Involve both. Say, "I think it's better if John does not do this, and I think it would help if Jim does not do that."

Source: Peter Martin Commanday, consultant and security expert, New York City school system.

Day-care center criteria

A decent day-care facility offers clean quarters, good food, reasonable safety precautions and regular naps. Beyond that, parents should look for:

☐ A stable staff, with relatively little turnover…specialized training in child development or psychology…staff members assigned to specific children.

☐ A staff-to-child ratio of no less than one to three for infants, one to four for two-year-olds and one to eight for children age three to six.

☐ Ambitious activities (trips to a zoo, a tour of the firehouse) but no heavy academic instruction.

☐ A welcoming attitude toward parental involvement, including unannounced visits.

Source: *Newsweek.*

How to be a much better long-distance grandparent

You may be one of the many grandparents today who live far from their grandchildren. So—it's important to know that there are ways to produce and preserve emotional closeness between grandchildren and grandparents despite geographical distance …and both the older and the younger partners in the relationship can reap rich rewards over the years.

Benefits

By keeping a close connection with your grandchildren, you can experience once again the joys of watching beloved children grow up …this time without having to take on the disciplinary role and 24-hour-a-day responsibility of parenthood.

Your grandchildren will gain a sense of love and belonging to a bigger family… and learn to identify with traditions handed down from their forebears. Realizing they are part of a continuing heritage will protect them from the alienation that emotionally cripples so many individuals in today's disconnected world.

Even large distances need not be a barrier to transmitting the warmth you feel for your grandchildren if you take advantage of the different means of communication we possess today.

On the spur of the moment, you can convey your feelings by telephone…at minimal expense, you can send long or short messages by mail…photographs, audio- or videotape can provide a partial substitute for your physical presence…and even relatively infrequent personal visits can provide lifelong memories of happy moments.

Telephone connections

You can begin to have meaningful communication with your grandchildren over the telephone when they are very young.

Example: I began talking to my grandson Arlo over the phone when he was only about six months. I asked my daughter to put the receiver to the baby's ear, and began speaking the same way I would have if I had been right there…"Where is your nose, Arlo?" …"Where are your eyes?"…"Where are your toes?" My daughter reported his excited reactions to my voice…and within a few months I enjoyed them myself, when he began giggling and repeating words back to me.

Now, Arlo and his brother have learned to expect my regular calls and run to answer the phone and engage in simple conversation.

What do you talk about?

With preschoolers, express your feelings of love for them openly…"I wish I could put my arms around you and give you a big hug!" They will not be embarrassed to reply in kind. When you ask questions to keep the conversation going, be specific. Don't ask "What are you going to do today?"… but "What toy are you playing with?" When you find a question they like to talk about, use it every time you talk… young children love repetition.

As the children grow up, their conversation will become more sophisticated. They may become less comfortable with effusive displays of affection…but they probably will welcome your willingness to hear their interests and concerns.

One important part of your role as a grandparent is to be a good sounding board to help your grandchildren work things out in their own minds when they feel their parents are unsympathetic or narrow-minded.

Dos and don'ts for good listeners

☐ Do listen patiently, attentively and with respect…express your understanding of their point of view.

☐ Don't insist they talk to you if they don't want to.

☐ When they want to talk, don't interrupt or interrogate.

☐ Don't make light of feelings.

☐ Don't be judgmental.

☐ Don't offer advice.

☐ Never criticize either parent.

Save money on long-distance bills by calling when rates are lowest, for example, before 8 am. *Important:* Make sure your call doesn't interfere with young children's regular schedules… or disturb their parents' sleep.

Communication by mail

As soon as your grandchildren are old enough to realize that a piece of paper with words on it is a means of communication…not just a potential foodstuff or plaything…they will appreciate receiving their own mail. It shows them someone else thinks they are important.

Postcards: A two-year-old will appreciate a picture postcard with a short personal message.

Example: "Dear Arlo: Can you see this cable car? It runs up and down the big hills here in San Francisco. It has a big, loud bell that goes 'Clang! Clang!' I love you. Grandma."

You don't have to travel to send postcards…every drugstore has a collection with hometown attractions. As your grandchildren grow up, you can make your messages more informative.

Letters: To capture their interest, simply discuss experiences you find interesting…your own, recently or from childhood…or your reaction to their experiences, appropriate for their age.

Example: "Dear Christopher: Your mommy told me you have a new tooth. How many do you have now? You are getting so big I wonder if I will recognize you when I see you. Love, Grandma."

If narrative writing is not for you, send letters with riddles, puzzles, rhymes, pictures…and your grandchildren will respond in kind. Magazines for children have a good selection.

Gifts: Your grandchildren will feel the love communicated by frequent small, inexpensive, but imaginative, gifts.

Young children: Balloons, magnets, flower seeds, old hats for dressing up.

Older children: Stamps, recipes, card or magic tricks.

Photographs: Your grandchildren will probably love old family photos…especially of their parents or grandparents as children. Hint: If you don't want to part with your old photos, you can make acceptable copies cheaply on many photocopiers.

Dos and don'ts when visiting

When parents come to visit grown children with their own families for more than a day or two, some strain is inevitable. To minimize it…

☐ Don't try to take charge of your children's household.

☐ Don't give unsolicited advice.

☐ Don't interfere with disciplinary rules.

☐ Don't agree to help around the house beyond your capabilities or patience.

☐ Respect your children's privacy.

☐ Try to fit into the family routine.

☐ Respect your grandchildren's feelings.

☐ Make clear your special needs—in advance.

☐ Try to be a very good guest.

Source: Selma Wassermann, an educator and writer who lives in Vancouver, British Columbia. She is the author of *The Long Distance Grandmother,* Hartley and Marks, Point Roberts, WA.

How to pick the right school for your young child

☐ Visit each school you're considering. Be wary of schools that try to sell themselves to you over the phone. The good ones will insist you judge their curriculum firsthand.

☐ Talk with the director and the staff members who will be involved with your child.

☐ Ask to see the school's license, insurance contract and health- and fire-department inspection forms.

☐ Be sure the school allows only approved persons to pick up your child at the end of the school day. The school should have a strict rule that if someone who is not on the list comes for the child, the parent should be called immediately. Also, see if the school has a code system whereby the only people who can pick up a child are those who know the code. Of course the child also knows the code.

□ Check cleanliness and hygiene.

□ Review the school's educational goals. The program should be designed to develop social, emotional, intellectual and physical skills. See the teacher's lesson plans.

□ Ask how students are disciplined.

□ Observe the other children. Will they be compatible with yours?

□ Ask yourself: "Could I spend a few years of my life here?"

□ If possible, make surprise visits to the school at different times of the day after your child has been enrolled. If you're denied admission to areas you wish to see, be suspicious.

Questions to ask when choosing a summer camp for your child

□ Is your child really ready for sleepaway camp? Knowing your child's and your family's needs is the first step to finding the right camp. If your child can't handle being away from home overnight, a day camp is probably a better choice. You may want to have your child sleep overnight at a friend's home to make this determination.

□ Is the camp accredited? The American Camping Association is the only organization in the US that has a voluntary standards-and-accreditation program for all kinds of camps. These standards cover health and safety, camp management, personnel, programming facilities and transportation. If a camp you're considering is not accredited, ask the camp director why not and then make your decision.

□ What is the camp's philosophy? Does the camp have a religious background? Is the camp's philosophy one of sports and competition? Sports and instruction? Arts? How does the camp director describe the camp's philosophy? Is that what you want for your child?

□ Who is directly responsible for your child's supervision at the camp? Find out the counselor/child ratio to determine whether supervision is adequate. This ratio differs by age group and between day and sleepaway camps.

Some offer smaller ratios among younger children.

Ages six to eight: Day camp/one counselor to eight children…sleepaway camp/one to six children.

Ages nine to 14: Day camp/one counselor to 10 children…sleepaway camp/one to eight children.

Ages 15 to 17: Day camp/one counselor to 12 children…sleepaway camp/one to 10 children.

□ Who else besides the counselor can children go to with problems? Make sure the camp offers a good support system (group or division leaders, counselors in charge of particular activities, head counselors, the director) so your child has more than one person to talk with if he/she is upset about something. Also find out what the camp's policy is on telephone calls home.

□ How are the counselors screened and trained? If the camp is accredited, you can be assured that the staff is screened and trained. But get specifics on how the counselors are chosen… what the screening process involves… and what the training covers. Most important is that you feel comfortable that the camp director knows his/her business and is concerned enough to provide the best possible care and supervision.

□ How much instruction is provided during each activity period…and how long do activity periods last? This will give you a good idea of whether the camp will suit your child's attention span and level of independence. Also find out which activities are required and how many electives your child can choose.

□ Are any trips offered as part of the camp…and what transportation arrangements are made for trips? Accredited camps will have specific requirements for drivers, vehicles and on-board safety equipment. If you choose a nonaccredited camp, make sure you're comfortable with these arrangements.

□ How does the camp integrate new campers into the group? If your child is thrown into a group without being properly introduced and made to feel welcome, he won't enjoy himself, no matter how many exciting activities are offered.

□ What medical facilities are available on-site? Nearby? Any time you have several children together in an active setting, you're bound to have a few injuries here and there. While the majority of these are minor scrapes and bruises, broken bones are not unheard-of.

Most camps have registered nurses or the equivalent on-site and doctors either on-site or nearby. You will want to know what the camp's policies are on medical insurance and notification of parents in the event of illness or injury. You should feel comfortable that the camp is prepared to deal with—and has the ability and experience to deal with—any eventuality.

☐ What references can you give me? Talking to the parents of children who have recently attended the camp can prove invaluable in your decision. Find out what the child and the parents liked best and least about the camp. Also find out whether the reference's child's temperament is similar to that of your child.

Source: Laurie Edelman, executive director of the New York section of The American Camping Association, New York.

Your child could be in a TV commercial

TV commercials feature some 40,000 to 50,000 lucrative parts for youngsters. A child who appears in commercials may gross $25,000 to $30,000 a year. Stars make $100,000 or more. No previous experience is required. Prospective young commercial actors should meet the following criteria:

☐ Age: Child commercial actors range from three months to 17 years, but most parts go to kids from ages 7 to 12. Babies are always in demand unless they're teething.

☐ Personality: Poise, self-confidence and intelligence are essential.

☐ Location: It helps to be in New York City, where 60% of commercial work is generated, or Los Angeles. Most other work is in Chicago, Philadelphia and New Orleans.

☐ Appearance: Send clear, close-up photos of the child to 10 or 12 agents. Also include a personal cover letter and sheet supplying vital statistics (height, weight, clothes size, hair and eye color). The photo should depict the child naturally. Do not pose or costume the child.

Parents must devote:

☐ Time: Agents quickly stop calling parents who have to "play bridge" or "don't feel like" showing up with the child for auditions.

☐ Energy: As a rule, it takes 25 one-hour auditions to get one assignment. Assignments require at least a day of shooting.

☐ Love: Parental support helps children withstand the pressure, jealousy and rejection commercial work entails. Because 20 to 50 children audition for each part, self-esteem should never be linked to making it.

Source: James Peacock and Graham Chambers, co-authors of *How to Get Your Children into Television Commercials,* Beaufort Books, New York.

Understanding sibling rivalry

There are patterns in families that may help parents better understand how sibling rivalry is triggered.

☐ Where there is an intense, close relationship between the mother and a first-born daughter, the girl is usually hostile to a new baby. A year later, the children are likely to be hostile to each other.

☐ First-born boys are more likely than girls to become withdrawn after a new baby's birth. Children who withdraw (both boys and girls) are less likely to show positive interest in, and affection for, the baby.

☐ In families where there is a high level of confrontation between the mother and the first child before the birth of a sibling, the first child is more likely to behave in an irritating or interfering way toward the new baby.

☐ Where the first child has a close relationship with the father, there seems to be less hostility toward the new baby.

☐ A child whose parents prepare him for the birth of a new baby with explanations and reassurances does not necessarily react any better than a child who wasn't prepared. *More important:* How the parents act after the new baby is born.

☐ Inside the family, girls are just as physically aggressive as boys.

☐ Physical punishment of children by parents leads to an increase in violence between children.

☐ Breastfeeding the new baby can have a beneficial effect on first-borns. *Reason:* Mothers who breastfeed tend to find distractions for the older child during feeding. This turns a potentially provocative time into a loving situation where the first child is also cuddled up with the mother, getting special attention while the baby is being fed.

Source: Judy Dunn, author, *Siblings: Love, Envy & Understanding,* Harvard University Press, Cambridge, MA.

Dealing with sibling rivalry

☐ Don't blame yourself. Much sibling rivalry is unavoidable. There's no way you can blame a mother for an intense relationship with her first-born child.

☐ Try to minimize a drop in attention to the first child. This change in attention is dramatic—not just because the mother is occupied with the new baby, but because she is often too tired to give the older child the kind of sensitive, playful focus he or she received in the past. (A month after a new baby was born, half the mothers in a recent study were still getting less than five hours' sleep a night.) *Recommended:* Get as much help as possible from the father, grandparents and other relatives and friends.

☐ Quarreling between siblings increases when the parents are under stress. Anything that alleviates marital stress will also quiet sibling rivalries.

☐ Keep things stable. A child's life is turned upside down when a new baby arrives. Toddlers of around two and three appreciate a stable, predictable world in which the daily schedule of events—meals, naps, outings—can be counted on. In families where the mother tries to keep the older child's life as unchanged as possible, there is less disturbance.

☐ Involve the older child in caring for the baby. In families where the mother draws the older child in as a helper for the new baby, there is less hostility a year later.

☐ Offer distractions to the older child. An older child gets demanding the moment the mother starts caring exclusively for the baby. Mothers who are prepared with projects and helping tasks head off confrontations.

☐ Recognize and avoid favoritism. Studies show that mothers intervene three times as much on behalf of a second child, although the second is equally likely to have been the cause of the quarrel. The first child's feeling that parents favor the second is often well-founded. Older siblings tend to hold back because they know their aggression is disapproved of, while younger ones often physically attack brothers and sisters because they feel they can get away with it.

☐ Be firm in consistently prohibiting physical violence. In the context of a warm, affectionate relationship, this is the most effective way to minimize sibling rivalry and to keep jealousies in check.

☐ Try to keep your sense of humor and your perspective when a new baby is born. Things will get better sooner than you think.

Source: Judy Dunn, author, *Siblings: Love, Envy & Understanding,* Harvard University Press, Cambridge, MA.

When you are invading your child's privacy

How much should parents know about their children's lives? The answer really depends more on maturity than on age. Children's lives become more and more their own business as they move away from parental supervision. It's part of growing up to have an increasingly greater private life and to feel you don't have to tell your parents everything.

☐ During the years when children are living under your roof, the key to keeping track is dialogue. If the relationship is sound and there are matters they don't want to share, they may have a good reason. Respect their privacy.

☐ It's an invitation to open up if parents talk about their own lives—especially if they admit that they, too, sometimes feel worried or embarrassed—or about feelings on something that is happening with the child. This helps create an atmosphere in which the child can talk about subjects he finds embarrassing.

☐ When you have something difficult to discuss with your children, do it in the car. No one can get up and walk out. You don't have to look at each other, if that is a problem. Pick a trip that will last at least half an hour. Try not to ask questions.

☐ Sometimes it is enough to give your opinion on a subject, even if you elicit no information. *Example:* A divorced father with custody of a 16-year-old daughter had this conversation with her about her relationship with a boyfriend: "You and David are getting very close, and I think that's fine. I don't know how active a sex life you're having, but I hope you will delay a full sex life. I think you're too young for that. But whether in six weeks or six years you do go all the way, the one experience I don't want you to have is getting pregnant. I want you to feel free to come to me to ask for the name of a doctor."

Her response: "We're not doing anything like that now." A month or two later, she said she was having problems with menstrual bleeding and asked for the name of a gynecologist. The father had expressed what he wanted to say and had opened the door. The child had not invited him in, but she had certainly received the message.

☐ Whether invasion of privacy is justified depends on the stakes. For parents to read a child's diary because they're curious about his or her sex life is indefensible. If the problem is something damaging to a child living under your roof, even if the child is 18, 19 or 20, you should intervene. *Example:* A parent who suspects a child is getting into drugs should search the child's room thoroughly.

☐ Movies: Some parents might be concerned about sexuality or violence in films. They wouldn't want a 12- or 14-year-old seeing a frightening or perverted horror film. They might, though, be more lenient about sex that isn't X-rated. *For this age group:* Strongly advise against an unsuitable film. Refuse to pay for it. If necessary, prohibit seeing it.

☐ Friends: If you're going to press a negative opinion, have a good reason. Check yourself: "Do I object because this is not my preference for a friend? Do I think no one's good enough for my child? Am I afraid of competition?" If the association is dangerous, you can refuse to allow the friend in your house, but it is impossible to police who your child sees outside the house.

☐ You can exercise more control about what goes on in the house than what takes place outside. If you don't know that your child is getting drunk at parties, there's not much you can do. If your 15-year-old comes home drunk, you can say, "You're grounded. This

has got to stop." If you pass a prohibition ("You're not to get high any place at any time"), obviously you have no way of enforcing it.

☐ In general, keep the lines of communication open by expressing your own feelings and values. It may not always yield information, but at least it creates a receptive climate for exploring important issues.

Source: Howard M. Halpern, author of *Cutting Loose: An Adult Guide to Coming to Terms with Your Parents,* Bantam Books, New York.

Temper tantrums

Realize that tantrums are part of the process by which toddlers declare their individuality. They usually occur when the child is tired.

☐ A child's temper tantrum is best handled by simply walking away. This usually stops the display, as the child grows bored without the attention.

☐ Don't rush to the child and try to smother it with affection. This may make you feel better in front of onlookers, but it doesn't help.

☐ Don't automatically accept the blame for the problem.

☐ Don't berate the youngster.

☐ *Best:* Let the storm pass. Allow the child to have a nap, and don't mention the incident later.

Source: Dr. Dennis Allendorf, pediatrician, Columbia Presbyterian Medical Center, New York.

When a child needs a therapist

Children don't come to parents and say they need a therapist. They don't perceive the locus of the problem as themselves. They'll blame it on parents or school. Treatment revolves around helping children to see what it does have to do with them.

Most children get into therapy because a teacher or school psychologist suggests it to a parent. Parents often do not recognize deviant behavior until the child goes to school. But many problems can be corrected if they are caught early.

Major tip-off: A child is stuck in development and is not doing what one would expect of a child in his or her age group.

Signs of poor emotional development:

☐ A four-year-old in nursery school cries and misses his or her mother.

☐ An eight-year-old with no friends comes home after school and watches television.

☐ Rigid rituals: The child's bedroom has to be a certain way. Particular foods must be served on certain nights.

☐ Major sleep disturbances: Frequent nightmares, waking in the middle of the night.

☐ Lack of learning progress: The child is not performing at grade level in school.

☐ Psychosomatic illnesses: Whatever the root cause, ailments are exacerbated by stress (ulcerative colitis, asthma, etc.)

☐ When in doubt, ask the school psychologist or pediatrician to recommend a therapist. Don't bring the child in for the first visit. Request a consultation. In some cases, there may not be anything wrong with the child. The parents may be the ones who need help.

Source: Pearl-Ellen Gordon, PhD, child psychologist, New York.

How to talk with your child about sex

Parents who want to give their children mastery of the facts about sexuality have to start early in the child's life. That's when to begin, too, to build the attitudes they will need to enjoy themselves as sexual beings and to respect the sexuality of others.

A child is born sexual, just as he or she is born with the capacities for walking and for talking. Once you understand and accept your children's sexuality as normal and beautiful—the same as their other human endowments—you will be free to help them in their sexual socialization.

A child needs guidance and support in developing sexual behavior that fits in with his parents' value system. A proven approach:

☐ Establish a sense of intimacy and trust with a newborn by touching and holding. Do not stop the cuddling, kissing and hugging when the child reaches three, by which time some parents feel awkward with physical demonstrations of affection, especially with boys.

☐ When you start the game of naming parts of the body, include the sex organs. Avoidance of the area between the waist and the knees causes confusion and lays the groundwork for problems in adult life.

☐ Don't interfere with a child's natural discovery and enjoyment of self-pleasuring. At six or eight months, a child learns to put its hand where it feels good. Don't slap on a diaper, pull the hand away or look upset or disapproving. Leave the child alone.

☐ As the child gets older, teach what you consider appropriate sexual behavior. You don't want your child masturbating in the supermarket or living room even at 15 to 18 months, so you pick up the child and, smiling, carry him/her to its bedroom. Explain that the place to pleasure yourself is in your own room with the door closed— that sex is good but should be private.

☐ Parents need privacy, too. Tell children: "When our door is closed, you don't come in without knocking and being invited. When we see your door closed, we'll do the same for you. Everyone likes privacy during sex games." This is when you can introduce the idea that sex games are something people who love and respect each other can play together.

☐ Sex play between children is usual. If parents banish the play, it will only drive the child underground. It's better to keep the lines of communication open and to reinforce socially appropriate sexual play.

☐ Make sure your child knows that sex play with someone older is inappropriate. Child molestation is more commonly practiced by someone in the family or known to a child than by a stranger. The message: "You don't have to let anyone touch your body against your will. You are in charge and you can say 'no.'"

☐ Be aware that much sex education is transmitted before nursery school by attitudes and body language—how you react to scenes on TV, your tone of voice or facial expression in sexual conversations or situations and significant silences.

☐ Children delight in affection openly expressed between their parents. Withholding such demonstrations can indicate sexual hang-ups.

☐ Don't avoid opportunities to discuss sex or to answer questions. Always speak only the truth. You may wish to withhold some of the details until later. Explain appropriate behavior outside the home. "In our family we are open with each other about sex. But most other families don't talk about it the way we do. So we keep what we do private. It's a good thing to respect what other people believe."

☐ A child who doesn't ask questions by the age of four or five has gotten the idea that the parent is uncomfortable about sex or that sex is not an open topic, or was not given straight answers. Initiate a discussion. *One idea:* Tell your child about your own questions when you were the same age. If there is no response, try again another day to prove you're available. Choose a time when you (or both parents) are alone with the child and have plenty of time. Be encouraging about behavior that is appropriate or shows maturation.

☐ Don't associate sexual parts of the body with dirt, ugliness or sin. Guilt and shame so transmitted will never be erased.

☐ Don't lie. You may have to tailor the truth to the level of the child. *Example:* To a three-year-old who asks, "Do you have to be married to have a baby?" the correct answer is, "No, you don't, but…." Then you go into your own value system about why marriage is important—on a level that a three-year-old can understand.

☐ You and your spouse should be clear on attitudes toward standards and rules and on what you agree and disagree. If there are differences of opinion, call them that, but try not to confuse the child.

☐ If you have laid the groundwork between birth and six or seven, you can take advantage of the major learning years until 12. Before puberty is when to pour in reliable information about sexually transmittable diseases, reproduction, etc.

☐ Keep the lines of communication open. Give opinions when they're asked for. Avoid judgments—they tend to close off discussions. Express your own values frankly and give sound reasons.

Source: Mary Steichen Calderone, MD, former medical director of the Planned Parenthood Federation of America and co-founder and president of SIECUS (Sex Information and Education Council of the US).

Child sexual abuse: How to recognize the signs

Sexual abuse occurs when a child is forced or tricked into sexual contact with an older person. *What constitutes sexual contact:* Touching of the child's genitals. Requests that the child touch or look at the genitals of an older person…participate in oral-genital contact with an adult…undress and/or be photographed in sexual positions with other children or adults…witness the sexual activities of adults. Sexual abuse may or may not include actual penetration.

Parents have an important responsibility to educate their children about sexual abuse as part of their general sex education. This responsibility cannot be left to the schools or the child's peers.

What parents should communicate

☐ There is "good" touch and "bad" touch. If the child feels uncomfortable about any kind of touching by anyone, including family members, he or she has the right to say, "No. I don't want to." The child should be told that not all adults care about children's feelings.

☐ If the child feels that something that just doesn't seem right is going on with an older person, whether it's a friend, family member or stranger, he or she should feel free to discuss it with you. No matter what kind of threats or promises have been made, you won't get angry or blame the child.

☐ Make it very clear that if by any chance the child doesn't feel free to tell you about a disturbing situation, he or she should talk to some other trusted adult. You might suggest a teacher, clergyman, friend or parent of a friend.

Reading your child's signals

☐ *Danger signs:* Change in appetite, nightmares, acting out or hyperactivity.

☐ The child avoids or reacts fearfully or abnormally to a person he or she has usually felt comfortable with.

☐ If you suspect sexual abuse, you will have to approach the child very carefully to get an honest answer. Questions such as "Is something wrong?" or "What's bothering you?" are likely to elicit simple denials. *Better:* "I know you're involved in something that's hurting, something you want to discuss, but maybe you're afraid I won't understand."

Be positive in your questioning. Show empathy, compassion and understanding. If you come on like gangbusters, aggressively asking who, when, what and where, you'll frighten the child and get no answers.

If your child has been sexually abused

☐ React calmly. If you get hysterical or visibly angry, you'll frighten your child.

☐ Talk about specific details, but don't push the child to reveal more than he or she feels comfortable with at any one time.

☐ Reassure the child that he or she is not to blame, that you don't doubt his/her word and that you will protect him/her against any repercussions from the accused person.

☐ Report any case of child sexual abuse to your local social services or law enforcement agency. If the abuser is a family member, contact the local chapter of Parents Anonymous or Parents United.

Source: Dr. Vincent S. Fontana.

Helping a preadolescent

The transition to adolescence is a difficult time both for children and for parents. But parents can create an environment that will make it easier for everyone involved to weather this stressful preadolescent passage.

Entry into adolescence begins between the ages of 10 and 13. The process is earlier than it used to be and is much more condensed.

The parent is heading toward middle age at the same time the child is heading toward adulthood. That's often painful.

☐ Look for the physical changes, such as body growth, hormonal functioning and appearance. But right before that, changes usually show up in feelings and moods, an increase in sexual drive and aggressiveness. Children eat a lot more and are more self-centered. They regress. *Example:* Boys tell toilet jokes.

☐ Schools are often sensitive to dips in students' performances in the seventh and eighth grades. Parents need to be supportive but also must set limits so that the child doesn't go under completely. Be aware that there will be some slippage. That doesn't mean the youngster has suddenly become stupid or will never work again.

☐ In the uneasy transition to adolescence, youngsters are no longer involved in the simpler tasks of childhood. In fact, sometimes it looks as though it's all been lost. It hasn't been. The tasks of early adolescence are different.

☐ The major task for the child is disengagement from parents. He experiences a conflict between the upsurge of drive and the pullback to the early parental relationship. He acts older and then younger. He progresses and then regresses.

☐ The parent must disengage from the dependent child of the earlier period. Parents too often pull the child back into the nurturing, dependent status. The child may go along because it's hard to give that up.

☐ Resist "re-entering" adolescence with the child…by dressing like him, getting involved with his friends, becoming a participant. This does not help the child, although he may enjoy it at the moment. It keeps the child with the parent at a time when he needs support in disengaging.

☐ Expect stress and conflict. No one disengages easily.

☐ Let children know what you expect, but be reasonably tolerant. They are still not up to assessing the reality of the dangers of drugs, alcohol or sexually transmitted diseases. Rules and regulations for social life are important.

☐ Try to work on a rational level first. *But remember:* You are the parent. You have a certain awareness of the child's needs. Ask yourself: "Why do I need to keep the child as a baby (which is not going to help him)? What do I need to be a parent who knows what's safe and what's reasonable?" It's the ability to recognize one's own motivation that distinguishes parents who can handle their child's adolescence from those who can't.

☐ During this transition, parents must shift. They have to find new sources of gratification away from their children and accept limitations. They can't control as closely as they did earlier. The child will no longer tell you everything, which is actually positive. He won't be as responsive or as responsible.

Source: Pearl-Ellen Gordon, PhD, child psychologist, New York.

Managing teenagers

The trap for many parents of teenagers is not realizing that they can no longer communicate with their children as they did when the kids were younger. While teenagers might not show it, they're at the age when self-esteem is usually at a low point…as they prepare to move into the adult world. As youngsters they didn't mind having parents help run their lives. But now they resent obvious efforts to help them.

☐ Just listen. That's the big thing a teenager wants—to be listened to. And this gives parents an overlooked opportunity to find out more about their children and boost their egos at the same time, simply by asking questions.

☐ Don't be afraid to ask their opinion: "Why do you think kids take drugs?" But never say: "I bet the kids you hang out with take drugs."

☐ You can help make teenagers feel more like winners by helping them set goals.

☐ First ask them to list the things they're good at. You'll probably get a list of two or three activities. Remind them of other things they're good at.
As the list grows, your child's self-esteem will be boosted—and so will the communication between you.

☐ If you can't catch your teenager doing anything right, catch him or her doing something approximately right.

☐ If you can't display affection, you're going to have real hassles. This is when a kid needs a hug the most. Kids who aren't touched feel they're not touchable—that they're not lovable. It's that simple. Parents are the only ones who can give total acceptance to their teenage children. The kids themselves tend to beat up on their peers, and their peers on them, because they're all so insecure.

☐ Don't be afraid to put your foot down about misbehavior. You can be intolerant of intolerable behavior. Make it very unpleasant for the first 30 seconds. But the last half of the reprimand is the most powerful. Say: "You don't need this in your life. You're a great kid, and you deserve a great life." The message that he or she is a good kid is one that's not being gotten from peers.

☐ Too many parents tend to pay most attention when their kid is fouling up. That's the trap. The kid figures it out, and then it's worth fouling up to get that attention. That's why it's so important to look for opportunities to praise. Because if kids like themselves, they'll cause you few, if any, problems.

Source: Dr. Spencer Johnson, author of *The One Minute Father* and *The One Minute Mother* and co-author of *The One Minute Manager,* William Morrow & Co., New York.

How to deal with a defiant teenager

Adolescence is a period when children must separate from the family. At the same time, they still need guidance. Parents need to know how to exercise the right proportions of flexibility and supervision. How parents set limits will influence their success in maintaining them. Some suggestions:

☐ Parents should have their own standards, but it's a good idea to check with other parents, and perhaps the school, about the prevailing views on curfews, use of alcohol and allowances. You can't always trust children to report accurately about regulations in other families.

☐ Parents should agree on a course of action and support each other. Kids will use every opportunity to take advantage of differences between parents.

☐ Discuss the rules with children. Explain your position calmly, and be prepared to back up your ideas. *Remember:* Things have changed a great deal since you were the age of your child. Listen carefully to your children, particularly to the oldest one, who usually has the toughest time because he or she is a trailblazer for those who follow.

☐ Rules must be geared to the ability of the child to handle responsibility.

Development in adolescence is uneven not only physically but emotionally. One child of 16 may be able to manage a flexible curfew, but another may not be mature enough.

☐ If rules are being flouted, parents must first examine their own roles, expectations and motivations. Are they contributing to the problem? Are their demands arbitrary and unreasonable? Do they set the kind of example they wish their children to follow?

☐ What is the dinner-table ambience? Is it one a child would want to get away from?

☐ School grades: Are parental expectations realistic?

☐ Avoid hostile confrontation and open warfare. Create an atmosphere where attitudes are expressed, where there is a positive feeling about learning, the intellectual spirit and the arts. The child should feel home is a comfortable place to be, where friends are welcome.

☐ Praise the child for what he is doing right before you tell him what he is doing wrong. If a child is told he is bad, he begins to live up to that reputation and is more likely to get into trouble.

☐ Defiant behavior is most often used to get attention or to test limits.

☐ It's all right to be angry if your anger is motivated by your concern for your child's safety. It is your job to protect him.

☐ Don't impose restrictions you can't enforce.

☐ Always give a warning before you punish.

☐ Don't make any threats for punishment you're not able or willing to carry out. Effective punishment requires the cooperation of both parents. What kind of punishment? Withholding part of the allowance or a planned trip or other treat is better than corporal punishment.

Let the punishment fit the crime. Lesser matters (untidy rooms) may not call for the same approach as more urgent ones (drugs, alcohol).

☐ *Important:* Do not discipline your child in front of other people, including siblings—and especially not in front of his friends.

Source: Clifford J. Sager, MD, director of family psychiatry, Jewish Board of Family and Children's Services, New York.

Father/daughter talks: Men, dating and sex

When a daughter comes of age, it is often only the mother who has heart-to-heart talks with her concerning "life." But there is a role here for the father, too, since he can supply the male point of view on these vital topics.

These father/daughter discussions not only help the young woman in her understanding of life but initiate a healthy exchange of ideas and opinions that benefits both parties for the rest of their lives.

Important prerequisites

☐ The tenor of a talk between a father and a 12- to 14-year-old daughter depends on their existing relationship. It is usually difficult for the father to take a young woman into his study and blithely talk about sex any better than he might with a son unless there is a feeling of trust and mutual understanding.

☐ The father must know what the mother has been telling the daughter about the facts of life.

☐ Begin the conversation along these lines: "You're getting to an age now where your mother and I notice your growing interest in boys and the facts of life and sexuality. Your mother has spoken to you about these things from the woman's point of view. I wonder if there are any questions you have about men, life, sex or anything else that you would like me to answer from the male view."

From here the discussion could include a range of subjects. *Example:* If the father worries about the type of people his daughter is socializing with, this is the time to air those misgivings.

☐ Reiterate the family attitudes toward sexuality. *Background:* Talk with other parents to explore their rules and regulations concerning dating and sex. This will help provide back-up facts in case the daughter says, "Mary's parents let her go out any night she wants." Although the attitudes of other parents help in setting guidelines, the father still makes clear his views as to what is proper and healthy.

☐ Always level with your daughter and don't hide behind excuses. If she has been going out with older boys who drive cars, explain why this is a worry to you—the fear that she will be drawn into premature sexual relationships, drinking and dangerous driving.

□ Make clear that she need not feel pressured to go along with the crowd.

□ Always welcome your daughter's male friends into your house. At times you may have to swallow hard before being polite. But if you turn them away, most likely she will see them outside your house—and you'll lose contact with your daughter.

□ Guard against putting down her boyfriends. The jealousy of a father is often revealed in the disparaging remarks he makes about his daughter's male friends. *Another sign of this jealousy:* Overprotectiveness.

□ Realize that it is not uncommon today for girls around the age of 16 to engage in sexual activity. Make sure that your daughter knows the truth about sex. Certain myths still persist. *Example:* In one survey made not too long ago, 30% of the youngsters age 14 to 16 believed that if you have sex standing up, the girl won't get pregnant.

□ Explain that men, when sexually excited, have an imperative desire for an orgasm. *Contrast:* Young girls are usually satisfied with holding, kissing and some petting. Make sure she understands that a girl has a right to say that she is not ready for sex. The male will always want to go further because of his crushing need for orgasm.

□ Be sure your daughter knows it is all right to enjoy sexual feelings. The pleasures of her limited sexual experiences are nothing to feel guilty about. If sex takes on a blind negativity, the daughter will not be able to enjoy the riches of conjugal love after she is married.

□ A father can be surprisingly helpful to a daughter when she is breaking up with a steady boyfriend, especially if she feels she is hurting a decent person with whom she has shared a lot. The father can point out that since his daughter is a warm and giving person, her friend should be honored that he had the privilege of her exclusive company. Through this relationship, the daughter has learned more about love, men and sex. *Message:* The love that lasts for a few months or a year or two is the love with

which the daughter tests herself. It's part of learning about life.

□ A formidable obstacle in a father/daughter relationship is the daughter's sexuality. The daughter he once kissed in greeting he now shies away from. Be aware of this sexuality, and don't be alarmed by it. If you kissed your daughter when you greeted her as a little girl, continue to do so when she becomes a young woman.

□ The father is the first intimate male model the daughter has for the adult world. This is important in developing her sense of the opposite sex. *Note:* Although the father is a model, he must not fear showing his human frailty. At all costs, avoid hypocrisy. Be honest, even if it hurts—or makes you look like less than a god.

Source: Clifford J. Sager, MD, director of family psychiatry, New York Hospital–Cornell Medical Center.

Building a good credit history for your child

The sooner your child starts to establish a good credit history, the easier it will be for him or her to have access to bank loans in the future.

State regulations on giving credit to minors vary, but even if your state is one of the more restrictive ones, you may still be able to get your child a credit card. Many bank credit-card firms and department stores skirt the issue by authorizing the use of cards to children of any age when parents are willing to assume responsibility for their debts.

Set guidelines at the time you authorize the credit card for a minor:

□ Let the card be used only for purchases agreed upon in advance. Give permission purchase by purchase.

□ Set monthly limits to the amount your teenager can charge.

□ Insist that teenagers save receipts of purchases.

□ Act as a co-signer on any charge card your teenager assumes, even if your signature isn't required for a purchase, so that you can monitor the child's spending.

□ Require teens to pay for credit purchases with earned income and to use their allowances for daily expenses. This builds in an incentive for a teenager to supplement income for major purchases.

Source: Meredith Fernstrom, senior vice president, Office of Public Responsibility, American Express Co., New York.

Children and money

An allowance is an excellent means by which to teach children to manage money. But for it to work, parents, as well as children, must take responsibility.

☐ Be clear about what you expect an allowance to cover. If the child blows his allowance two days after getting it, he should have to do without until the next allowance day rolls around. Be flexible, however. If a special event comes up that your child wasn't planning for but really wants to attend, feel free to be generous.

☐ Don't use money to manipulate your youngster. Some parents are overly free with gifts and dollars to pacify a child they don't spend enough time with.

☐ Keep in mind that youngsters will learn their major lessons about money management by example. *Suggested:* Share your family's budgeting procedures with your child, showing in practical terms how the family's money is allotted. When he reaches adolescence, teach him how to balance a checkbook.

☐ When a youngster gets a job, it's time to discontinue his allowance and ask him to take on some responsibility for his own expenses. Suggest he start paying for his own school supplies, save for a trip, buy some clothing or put money away for college.

☐ If you are divorced, make sure the children don't start using money to play one parent against the other. *To avoid it:* The custodial parent gives the allowance, which should be part of the child-support agreement. The noncustodial parent shouldn't undermine the arrangement by showering the child with money during visits. If there's joint custody, one parent should give the allowance.

☐ If you want a child to learn to save, give incentives. *Example:* Offer to add to her savings account if she saves an agreed-upon amount by Christmas.

Allowances: Resolving potential conflicts

An allowance often becomes the center of a power struggle between parents and children. Parental ambivalence about letting go often expresses itself in the allowance arena. Here's how to handle allowances without turning them into a battlefield.

☐ Allowances are for extras—junk food, records, entertainment with friends, small gifts for the family. Parents should provide the necessities—transportation to and from school, lunch at school, clothing, etc. When there's a conflict, use common sense.

Example: Your child says he hates school lunches and wants to eat with his friends at the local pizza place. If you agree that the school lunches are inedible, you might want to pay for the pizza. But if the school serves healthful, reasonably appetizing food, you might insist he spend his own money on lunch at the pizza place.

☐ Since part of giving an allowance is to impart a sense of values, parents have a responsibility to take a stand when a child spends allowance money on things you disapprove of, such as cigarettes and liquor. You can and should take money off the allowance if it's being spent on such items.

☐ Deduct money only if your youngster is doing something extremely self-destructive with it. Don't deduct for every minor expenditure that you disapprove of, or for non-money-related misbehavior.

☐ Recognize that there are certain cultural pressures on your youngster. For example, the family that eats only health foods shouldn't punish a child for buying candy.

☐ Before you do any deducting, negotiate. Talk over the issue with your child and find out why she's doing something you disapprove of. If you can convince her of your concern for her well-being and acknowledge her need for independence, you may reach an agreement.

□ You can use money to encourage a child to display behavior you want to see. But such "tokens" should not be connected to the allowance. A certain amount should be considered as "base pay." Over and above this you can use the barter system, paying a child extra for doing extra chores, getting higher grades, etc.

□ It's better to use money as a positive reinforcement than as a negative one.

Example: You want your teenager to stop smoking. Instead of deducting cigarette money from his allowance, it's more effective to pay him extra to stop smoking.

□ Start a youngster's allowance early—seven is a good age—with a small amount, like $3 a week. Increase it annually by a dollar or so. Take into account teenagers' need for extra money for dating. Since dutch treat is a standard operating procedure these days, a teenage girl should get as much as a boy.

□ Always give the same amount on the same day every week. An allowance should be like a paycheck—something your child expects, not something he has to beg for.

□ If your child complains that all the other kids are getting more money, talk with a few parents to check it out. If you can afford to, do give your child the amount customary among his or her schoolmates. Any less will be seen as punishment and deprivation. If you really can't afford the local average, don't give more than you can afford. Explain your financial situation to your child so he or she doesn't take it personally.

Source: Robert F. Scherma, PhD, a school psychologist who has counseled teenagers and their families in the New York City area for the last 18 years.

Teaching children the value of money

An appropriate timetable for allowances and money management:

□ Age 5. Start with a weekly or twice-weekly allowance of 50¢. (Regular expenses, such as school lunches or bus fare, would be in addition.)

□ Age 10. Increase to $2.50 to $3.00 weekly, allowing a small surplus that can be saved for future purchases.

□ Age 13. Change to a monthly allowance and encourage the child to pre-pare a simple budget.

□ Age 15. Children are ready to participate in family budget discussions. (But don't burden them with severe financial problems.) Handle their big expenditures (motorbikes, stereos, etc.) with loans. Don't set a schedule of steep payments that leaves the child with virtually no pocket money.

Basic guidelines:

□ Keep the allowance in line with what other children receive. Too much money can make the child wasteful and guilty. Too little creates resentment.

□ Hold fast to the agreed sum. Exceptions should be rare and clearly identified.

□ Encourage earnings. They are better than allowances and gifts. Don't pay for routine home chores. But do hire the kids for special work, instead of outside workers, as often as possible.

□ Withhold or cut the allowance as a punishment only when the offense is directly related to misusing the money.

□ Use money as a reward on a matching basis. For example, an improved report card earns a bonus equal to after-school earnings.

□ Give praise when the child does well and keep criticism low-key and constructive. Expect mistakes, anger and tears. This is a learning-by-doing process.

Source: *Your Money & Your Life,* AMACOM, New York.

Computerized children: Warning signs... and solutions

Computers are now being pushed on kids for many of the same reasons parents used TV—as a convenient, cheap baby sitter. Dual-career couples and single parents find they can have a bit of peace at home (or time to do the work they brought from the office) if Johnnie is off working on the terminal. But TV is now considered "bad"...and computer work "good." *Reality:* Children are being encouraged to relate to a machine rather than to other human beings, just as they were with the TV screen. They're learning a narrow set of skills—and retreating from the more complex set of social skills that they need for healthy growth.

Symptoms of overuse of the computer:

☐ Edginess and crankiness—the result of mental fatigue.

☐ On and off communication patterns with parents and siblings…yes…no…yes.

☐ Impatience because parents take too long to get to the point…the book has too many descriptive words…the situation is too ambiguous.

☐ Few friends, little time spent outdoors, limited physical activity.

But as youngsters develop their computer skills and focus their attention on the computer during more and more of their "leisure" time, they're also increasing the negative impact of such work:

☐ Youngsters don't learn to deal with the inevitable negative feedback they'll get in real-life human relationships. As adults they may wind up being immobilized by criticism. The computer does not give negative feedback, but it does keep encouraging the computer worker to become more perfect, to stop making errors in the program, to work in a logical, deductive way.

☐ Young children (4–6 years) begin matching their thinking style to that of the computer—which is logical and deductive. Computer thinking is really quite simplistic and "dumber" than the natural thinking of children of this age, which is metaphorical. Metaphorical thinking is at the base of true genius and creativity.

Managing kids and computers

☐ Put limits on computer use—just as limits should be put on TV watching. It's natural to lose a sense of time when working on the computer, so put a clock beside the terminal—and set an alarm to ring when the child must leave computer work.

☐ Train the child to recognize the signs of mental fatigue such as taking deeper breaths or making more mistakes. Explain that when he feels those symptoms—or when the alarm rings—he must stop working on the problem. Teach children to state the problem they're working on—either by logging it on the computer or writing it in a notebook that they keep near the computer. *Goal:* Write the problem down so that the child doesn't have to keep it in his short-term memory and continue to worry about it.

☐ Allow for a 20-minute (at least) transition time between computer work and dinner or time for other family relationships. If this isn't done, the child will spend half the time at the dinner table thinking about what he just left on the computer instead of conversing with those around him. By the time he's ready to talk, dinner is over and everyone scatters again. Left alone, the child, looking for companionship, turns back to the computer—and still hasn't communicated with other members of the family.

☐ Don't let the computer substitute for time spent with your children. Though it seems silly to have to say it, spend nontechnological time with your children every day—not time spent watching TV, working on the computer terminal, working on the car, talking about new gadgets. Don't underestimate the value of simple playfulness and horsing around. And with older children, sit and talk for a few minutes each day.

☐ Don't insist that your child work on a computer if he seems uninterested. Despite all the media publicity (much of it stirred by manufacturers of computers), not all children take to computers automatically. At least one child in three resists learning to use them—even for playing games. There's no reason to worry that such a child is scarred for life.

Source: Dr. Craig Brod, author of *Technostress,* Addison-Wesley, Reading, MA.

Common problems in stepfamilies

Both partners in a remarriage usually have unrealistic expectations about their new roles. As parents, they are not prepared for the problems they will face when all their children are thrown together through various custody and visitation arrangements. The children, of course, are not prepared either.

Problems that frequently develop:

☐ Children, especially young ones, fantasize that the new parent will replace a deceased parent or provide something their custodial parent doesn't.

☐ A stepparent who has never had children anticipates becoming an ideal mother or father with an instant family. Being rejected by the children can be a real shock.

☐ Parents who have failed with their

own children think they have a second chance. But they may not really understand why they failed, and they often end up making a similar mistake.

☐ Children vie for seniority. A child who has been the oldest in one family may now be number two or three. The usual results are rivalry, jealousy and hurt feelings.

☐ The new stepparent is sought after by all the children, which causes conflict between that parent's loyalty to his or her own children and the need to relate to the stepchild.

☐ Blood ties tend to be pitted against nonblood ties. It is always more difficult to love, or even to get along with, someone else's children. A parent tolerates more inconvenience and conflict from a natural child than from a stepchild, and consequently suffers from feelings of guilt and hostility.

☐ Differences in parenting style. Watching one's spouse cope with a child in a way that you do not approve of can lead to marital problems. *Example:* A man who had long-standing problems with his adolescent son married a woman he thought would take care of these problems. She didn't consider it her role to be the disciplinarian. As she watched her husband tolerate abuse from his son, she began to lose respect for him.

How to be a better stepparent

Marriage and parenting are skills you learn from your own parents. You blunder along, imitating or rejecting their behavior. But most people never had any role models for stepparenting. Useful guidelines:

☐ Establish new rules. Some have to be negotiated between the parents. It is helpful to set times when the family gets together to work on those decisions the children can be included in.

☐ Realize that love is not instant. Someday you may learn to love stepchildren, and they may learn to love you—but not necessarily.

☐ Respect old ties. A new stepfamily has many complicated connections with relatives. A natural parent and child have a unique relationship. Allow children time to be alone with natural parents, grandparents or other relatives. Do not feel that a new family has to do everything as a group.

☐ The basis for any successful remarriage is for ex-spouses to be as considerate of the children as possible. Conflicts between parents should be dealt with by them. Children should not feel they are included in these problems.

☐ Realize that even the best stepparent can experience hostility from a stepchild for reasons that have nothing to do with the stepparent. For example, the child may feel that the natural parent won't approve if he likes the new stepparent.

☐ Children can love more than two adults as parents. It's an enriching experience for a child to have more than two parents, two sets of grandparents, etc. The natural family should understand that it may be better for the child to develop a close relationship with someone in the stepfamily.

☐ The couple relationship is primary. This is the core of the new family unit, in spite of the fact that each partner has strong loyalties to his or her family of origin. Children have to know that the new couple is an unshakable combination and cannot be broken up (which they often try to do in order to get their own parents back together again).

☐ Discipline. You cannot discipline even your blood children without a good relationship. It may take a year or two before this happens with stepchildren. In the meantime, the natural parent should be the disciplinarian for his or her children. The authority of an absent natural parent should be vested in the stepparent. This must be made clear to the children.

☐ Ironing out discipline policy. Parents should discuss priorities and compromises. If they can't work out their differences, they should look into getting professional help.

Source: Barbara C. Freedman, CSW, director of the Divorce and Remarriage Counseling Center, New York.

Adopting a foreign child

It is difficult to adopt within the US, and especially to adopt a newborn. It is not impossible if people are serious about adoption and work with it. People are able to adopt independently, privately and legally. One of the most important factors to keep in mind is to ask questions; never view those whom you are paying—such as an attorney or a social worker—as someone who is doing you a favor. Remember, they are paid for their professional performance.

Because of changes related to the Hague Treaty on International Adoption, today it is more practical to work with a reputable agency. It is important to choose a social worker who may have an agency affiliation if need be. Paying for an agency home study up front may not be necessary and will be more costly. An alternative to an agency would be to work directly with an orphanage or a private facilitator with a good reputation and references. Before starting, it is best to check with the local INS office for the requirements. New INS regulations require all family members living in the household to be interviewed during the home study. Child-abuse clearance for the adoptive parents is an additional requirement.

It is vitally important to speak with large adoptive parent groups, but equally important to seek out local adoptive parent groups to inquire about the agencies or facilitator you may be thinking of using.

Always involve yourself in the adoption process; never leave questions unanswered. Be wary of agencies or facilitators who ask for a large sum of money up front. Try to work with people who are represented within the US. Also, find out how many people in your area have adopted using the people to whom you are talking.

Ask parent groups for country references. Many countries in South America and Latin America place children. Many people adopt from Mexico. Central America is good but bears close scrutiny. China, India and Korea now place on a regular basis. Eastern European countries do also, but get references and investigate with the INS and parent groups. Contact Adoptive Families of America (AFA) in Minnesota for a list of countries from which Americans have adopted in recent years. AFA also has an Adoption Resource Kit available at no cost (612-535-4829).

Source: Felix Fornino, Adoptive Parents Committee, 1762 64th St., Brooklyn, NY 11204. 718-259-7921.

Re-establishing your marriage when the kids leave home

Initially, most parents are pleased when children leave home for college or an out-of-town job. But after the pleasure subsides, the new reality needs to be dealt with.

Some commonsense steps to take:

☐ Realize that the parting is a signal that one chapter of your life is closed. The next chapter depends on how well you handle the transition.

☐ Say good-bye to the past without fear of grieving or of airing feelings of remorse, guilt and anger.

☐ Discuss with your spouse where you want to go in life.

☐ Congratulate each other on how well you have done with the children.

☐ Discuss resentments that have built up and start negotiating for changes.

☐ Set aside time to share activities and intimate conversation. Recognize that some interests are best pursued individually. Give each other leeway to do so.

☐ Ask yourselves, "How are we really different from the way we were at the beginning of our marriage? What are the implications of those differences?" To answer, take inventory of the bonds that connect you and your spouse— activities and interests, degree of intellectual closeness, physical attraction to one another and the like.

☐ Assess the degree to which you have been nurturing or neglecting intimacy. One test of adequate intimacy is to find out how willing you are to share both good and bad feelings.

☐ If you and your spouse cannot reestablish a satisfying relationship, recognize the possibility that the presence of children may have masked a hollow marriage that is not worth salvaging. When this situation becomes apparent after children leave home, couples should discuss terminating the relationship. If this happens to you, seek the services of a therapist or counselor. Remember that the more valuable a relationship is, the more it is worth saving and the more useful counseling is likely to be.

Source: Gisele Richardson, president, Richardson Management Associates, Montreal.

Helping older children gain independence

Having the family all together for the holiday season may be cheerful. But togetherness can pall if it is overdone. And low starting salaries, high rents and a scarcity of apartments are keeping many young people at home and economically dependent on their parents well beyond graduation from college.

To encourage independence, parents should:

☐ Supplement their children's income at the outset so that they can live in their own quarters. There is no substitute for the experience of having to manage a household.

☐ Charge for room and board if children must live home. Some parents put this money aside as a stake for the child's marriage or business.

☐ Put a time limit on living at home: Six months, a year or until the first salary raise. Whatever the arrangement, make it clear that independence is the goal.

☐ If you are not comfortable when your children bring sex partners home, say so. Making feelings clear before a guest arrives avoids unpleasantness later.

☐ Ask grown children under your roof to help with chores and with family obligations, such as visiting relatives.

☐ After children mature, some parents want to simplify their lives by moving into a smaller house or apartment or nearer to work. Do not be deterred by sentimental arguments of the children. Independent parents foster independent children.

Source: Dr. Clifford J. Sager, director of family psychiatry for the Jewish Board of Family & Children's Services, New York.

Parents' guide to corporate training programs

What can you do to help your child land the right job offer? A corporate training program may be the answer, especially for liberal arts students.

☐ Recent graduates can earn while they learn. Most corporate training programs pay well. Starting annual salaries for trainees range from $15,000 to more than $30,000.

☐ Such programs give in-depth training in a specific industry while also offering a practical view of the corporate world. This hands-on training is useful in whatever field the student finally picks.

☐ Let your graduate know you understand that competition for corporate training programs is fierce. Most applicants face a number of rejections before landing the perfect job.

How to prepare

There is no such thing as too much preparation for a job interview. Encourage your graduate to first learn about the industry that interests him. Once he understands the industry and the key players, he can zero in on particular companies. He should study annual reports, recruitment materials and magazine articles. (Articles can be obtained by telephoning a company's public relations department to request a press kit.)

☐ Information interviews in advance of a job interview can also be helpful. Alumni from your son's or daughter's alma mater who are already working for that company or industry are often willing to take a few minutes—either over the phone or in person—to offer insights into what it's like to work there. Your own business contacts and friends may also be able to serve as informal career advisers.

☐ Questions the job hunter should ask contacts: "What are the most satisfying aspects of your job? What are your priorities in an average work week? What do you wish you had known about this career field before you entered it? What about this employer?"

Source: Marion Salzman, co-author of *Inside Management Training: The Career Guide to Training Programs for College Graduates,* New American Library, New York.

Living better with adult children

We have entered the era of the nesters: Adult offspring (past age 18) who are living in the parental home. Largely because of economics, at least 25% more young adults today live with their parents than 15 years ago. Living with adult children can be stressful. But if you play your cards right, it can be rewarding for parents as well as children.

☐ Release your parental authority. When children reach adulthood, it's time to reshape old roles. This adjustment can be toughest for fathers, who often deal with their children as authoritarians.

☐ Don't be too generous with advice or financial aid. For many parents, excessive giving may be an unconscious attempt to gain control. Don't offer, but don't refuse. Try to find a solution that preserves the nester's responsibility. Co-sign a bank note.

☐ Communicate. The issue may be trivial—breakfast dishes that don't get cleared, ice-cube trays that are never refilled. But if resentment is allowed to build, the entire family suffers. Speak up about what's bothering you.

☐ Don't perform an adult child's personal business. As adults, they are responsible for walking their dog, getting up in time for work and paying their taxes. There will come a day when you won't be around to bail them out.

☐ Share household chores equitably. Make a written list. A 23-year-old bachelor's standard of cleanliness may not mesh with your own.

☐ Ask that they contribute something toward room and board. One survey found that nesters with full-time jobs pay an average of $75 a month. (One third pay nothing at all.) *Fair formula:* Propose that your nester pay 15% of take-home pay. Don't feel guilty about this. You're teaching a key survival skill: How to handle money and live within one's means. (If you really don't need the money, you can put it aside for a nest egg for when your nester leaves.)

☐ Remember that it's your roof and mortgage. If your adult children want to live in your home, they must abide by your rules and value system. If you feel uncomfortable with certain behaviors in your home, it's your right to forbid them. (Flexibility helps. Much as you might despise cigarettes, for example, you might let a nester smoke in his or her bedroom.)

☐ House rules stop at the front door. What nesters do outside is their own choice, unless they bring their problems home (no drunk driving or drug dealing condoned). Curfews are unrealistic. Like it or not, much of a young adult's social life happens after midnight.

☐ Reject the notion (quite popular in this culture) that nesters are failures.

☐ Set a target departure date before your adult child moves back home. This could be three months after college graduation or six months after a divorce. The date can be modified later on. Affirming that your nester's stay is temporary relieves much anxiety on both sides.

Source: Monica Lauen O'Kane, author of *Living with Adult Children,* Diction Books, St. Paul, MN.

Troubled parent and adult-child relationships

Parent and adult-child relationships that depend too much on rewards and punishments make both sides unhappy. If two or more of the following statements are true about how you think of your parents, problems are brewing.

☐ I let my parents have their way even though I know this is wrong.

☐ When I do something of which my parents disapprove, I feel very guilty.

☐ No matter what I do, I cannot get my parents to see what my problems are.

☐ I try to anticipate their every need.

☐ I am always fighting with my parents, but I know we love each other.

☐ I wish they would think about me sometimes instead of only themselves.

☐ I know they order me around, but that is really very good for me.

Source: Carol Flax and Earl Ubell, co-authors of *Mother, Father, You: The Adult's Guide for Getting Along Great with Parents and In-Laws,* Wyden Books, Ridgefield, CT.

Helping parents with money problems

Your parents are faced with inflation and rising home maintenance bills. They refuse to sell their house and are too proud to take outright gifts. What can you do?

One solution might be to consider a nonamortized bank loan for your parents, using the house as collateral.

How it works:

☐ You negotiate a loan from a bank where you keep a minimum balance equal to the principal of the loan.

☐ Your parents pay interest on the loan and you arrange for the principal to be paid back after they die and the house is sold.

☐ With the loan, you buy annuities to supplement your parents' income.

For example, a mother is 65 and has a $120,000 house with no mortgage. She gets a loan from her son's bank for 80% of the house's net value ($96,000), at 15% interest. With the money, the son buys her a 20-year annuity that pays 15% interest. The annuity covers her interest payments and provides her with $1,000 a month. And by borrowing on the house, rather than selling it, the woman and her family hold onto its appreciation value.

Coping with elderly parents

Getting along better with elderly parents isn't easy. But it can be done. Here's how:

☐ Avoid criticizing, making demands or challenging their ideas. Instead, try to demonstrate support and concern.

☐ Do not bombard them with direct questions. Instead, search gently for their true feelings. Parents listen to you only if they are heard in return.

☐ Tell parents directly when they hurt your feelings.

☐ Give your parents a choice if you want their help as a baby sitter, house sitter or whatever. Don't expect them to be at your beck and call.

Source: Carol Flax and Earl Ubell, co-authors, *Mother, Father, You: The Adult's Guide for Getting Along Great with Parents and In-Laws,* Wyden Books, Ridgefield, CT.

Coping with visits to elderly parents

Many adult children are reluctant to visit their elderly parents, particularly when the family relationship has been ridden with conflicts. *Reasons:*

☐ Problem parents are likely to become more so as they age. One who has always been a guilt provoker, excessively demanding or inclined to play the martyr's role will likely be more demanding and guilt-provoking in old age.

☐ Seeing parents aged and infirm threatens adult children by reminding them of the approach of their own old age and of their own mortality.

☐ Parents' aging usually reverses the parent-child role. The dependency and frailty of old parents, whether physical or psychological, may make them assume childlike roles. Adult children, in turn, experience a sharp loss because they recognize that they can no longer turn to their parents.

To deal with the reluctance you may feel about visiting your parents:

☐ Remember that a mature, parental response on your part is now in order. However enraged or frustrated you are by a parent's behavior, accept that a role reversal has taken place. Your parent now is actually dependent and helpless in some way and is not the same antagonist you remember from early-childhood conflicts.

☐ Visit regularly, so your parents can plan and look forward to your arrival. Remember, though, some parents lead busy, extremely independent lives and may not want too many visits from children.

☐ When going away for an extended period, inform your parents of your return date, when they can expect to hear from you and how often you'll be in touch.

☐ Don't visit parents at the expense of your own adult priorities. Excessive guilt often pushes children into running themselves ragged visiting parents too often.

☐ Be aware that too much indulgence of a parent's wishes, or treating a parent as an infant, can impair the parent's will to continue assuming responsibility for his or her own life. Avoid placating behavior, which is a hangover from the childhood relationship. A realistic and caring attitude is better.

☐ During the visit, listen to your parents' problems, but also try sharing concerns of your own (if they are not overwhelming). Many parents would like to feel themselves still capable of giving advice and of having authority.

Source: Dr. Howard Halpern, author of *Cutting Loose: An Adult Guide to Coming to Terms with Your Parents,* Simon & Schuster, New York.

Helping aging parents care for themselves

Elderly people suffer emotionally and physically when facing dramatic changes. Ideally, preserve their daily routines and environment as long as possible, even in the face of growing infirmities.

Steps to take before considering a nursing home:

☐ Hire a cleaning person to come in once a week.

☐ Arrange with another elderly but healthier neighbor to share meals or visit daily.

☐ Sign up for Meals-on-Wheels delivery of hot meals daily.

☐ Register at a neighborhood senior citizens' center.

☐ Schedule frequent visits from individual grandchildren.

☐ Find a smaller apartment with fewer stairs in the same building.

☐ List local stores that deliver phone orders.

☐ Familiarize parents with local public transportation routes.

☐ Purchase a pet as a present that provides company and diversion. The pet should require minimal care.

☐ Set definite limits on your own direct involvement in your parents' lives. Assume the role of creative coordinator. Involve a variety of others who can perform the jobs as well, and perhaps more cheerfully.

Source: Stephen Z. Cohen, MD, and Bruce Michael Gans, MD, authors of *The Other Generation Gap: The Middle Aged and Their Aging Parents,* Follett Publishing Co., Chicago.

Some alternatives to nursing homes

To keep parents functioning in their own homes as long as possible, consider:

☐ Adult day-care centers. They offer one meal a day, transportation to and from medical appointments and various programs to keep people healthy and alert. Get more information from your state's department of social services.

☐ Congregate homes. Apartment buildings or clusters of detached homes provide low-cost rental housing and essential services for elderly people who need minimal day-to-day help. Eligibility is based on income. For more information, contact your local area office of the US Department of Housing and Urban Development.

☐ Home care. Services include convalescent care, nursing, household maintenance and Meals-on-Wheels. Most programs are run by the state or the community.

Source: Joseph Michaels, author of *Prime of Your Life,* Quarto Marketing, New York.

How to select a nursing home

Selecting a nursing home is one of the most important and difficult decisions you may need to make—either for yourself or a family member. So it's important to base your decision on the most complete and timely information available.

The selection process should include:

☐ Visiting and examining facilities.

☐ Talking to nursing-home residents and their families.

☐ Finding out about the costs involved.

☐ Making financial plans to cover the costs.

☐ Determining the level of care needed.

By planning ahead and doing a thorough investigation, you can alleviate much of the stress that often accompanies choosing a nursing home.

Planning ahead

Involve the person as much as possible in the decision-making process. It is essential that the person's wishes be considered and that he or she takes part in the selection process.

Discuss the subject well in advance of such a move. Educate the family about the realities of nursing-home care.

Make preferences and needs known early on, so that if the time comes when others must make difficult decisions, you will feel assured that your wishes will be respected. Planning ahead gives you and your loved ones more control.

Know your options

Nursing homes are only one of a range of long-term, comprehensive medical, personal and social services designed to meet the needs of chronically ill and disabled persons. Before considering such placement, explore other alternatives.

Discuss your needs and plans with your physician or caregiver and your family. Then decide on the most appropriate place to receive care. Your financial ability will also affect your decision.

Home- and community-based care facilities are becoming more available. They provide health care, support services and specialized living arrangements. Here are the options available in various communities:

☐ Home health care.

☐ Respite care.

☐ Adult day-care centers.

☐ Foster care.

☐ Residential care in a board-and-care home.

☐ Retirement communities.

☐ Hospice care.

If a person needs 24-hour nursing care and supervision, however, a nursing home may be the best answer.

Know the law

Important nursing-home reforms took effect in October 1990. They were designed to strengthen both the quality of life and quality of care for residents. The reforms enforce the provision of certain rights of residents to dignity, choice, self-determination and quality services and activities.

Knowing details of the law will allow you to make a better decision about selecting a nursing home. It will also enable you to better prepare the resident, to know what to expect and to know what to ask for if the resident is not receiving the care and services to which he or she is entitled.

Ask questions and observe.

☐ Are administrators and staff courteous, helpful and frank?

☐ Are the nurses' aides trained?

☐ Is a comprehensive assessment of resident needs done within two weeks of admission?

☐ Do residents have a right to choose activities, schedules and health care consistent with their interests and needs?

☐ Does the facility provide a safe, clean, comfortable homelike environment?

Remember: Residents must receive the necessary care and services that enable them to reach and maintain their highest practicable level of physical, mental and social well-being.

Example: Married residents should be assured privacy for visits from spouses. If both partners live in a home, they should be able to share a room, if possible.

Essential ingredient: Warm, professional relationships between staff and residents equal quality care.

Caution: Residents should not be transferred or discharged arbitrarily and should be given reasonable advance notice if they must be moved.

Consult resources

1. Seek referrals. Get information from professionals in the long-term care field, your medical community, friends or acquaintances who've been in a similar situation. Don't rely on any one source in making your decision.

2. Talk to your local ombudsmen. Federal law requires each State Agency on Aging to have an Office of the Long-Term Care Ombudsman. These offices provide help and information to the general public. Ombudsmen visit nursing homes on a regular basis and have a lot of knowledge of what goes on in various facilities. They also receive and investigate complaints.

3. Talk to hospital discharge planners or social workers.

4. Call local religious organizations and volunteer organizations, such as Meals-on-Wheels or pet therapy programs.

5. Get information from state nursing-home associations.

6. Call local advocacy groups or support groups for the aged and their families, if any exist in your area.

During this research stage, ask about:

☐ The facility's reputation in the community.

☐ The latest survey report.

☐ Any complaints against the homes someone might be considering.

☐ The number and nature of complaints in the past year, and the results and conclusions.

Key questions

☐ Is the nursing home certified to participate in Medicare or Medicaid programs?

☐ What are admissions requirements?

☐ Is there a "typical profile" of a resident in the facility?

☐ Are residents required to sign over personal property or real estate in exchange for care?

☐ Are there vacancies, or is there a waiting list?

☐ What kind of daily activities are offered to residents? Ask to see the monthly activities calendar.

☐ Does the facility have a list of references—especially family members of current residents?

The search

☐ Consider the location. How easy is it to visit?

☐ Is religious or ethnic emphasis important?

☐ Visit a nursing home more than once, and at different times of the day.

☐ Ask residents what they like about the home and what they do when they need something to be different.

☐ Inquire about the volunteer program. If you see no volunteers, ask why.

☐ Ask residents, visitors and volunteers what they like about the staff.

☐ Ask staff what they like about working there.

☐ Talk to residents and observe conditions by yourself, without staff or administrators assisting you.

☐ Determine if the building is clean, free from overwhelming odors and well maintained.

☐ Evaluate the quality of care and concern for residents. For example, do nursing assistants speak slowly and clearly so the residents can see and hear them?

☐ Overall, form your own impressions.

☐ Consider the staff-to-resident ratio. How many residents is each nurses' aide or direct-care nurse assigned to care for?

☐ Sit in on activities. How large is the activity staff and how varied is the monthly program?

☐ Inquire about the nursing home's philosophy on restraints. Remember, the law strictly limits circumstances for physical or chemical restraint of residents. And any restraint must be ordered by a physician.

☐ Evaluate the quality and variety of meals. Ask the dietitian for a list of menus for the month.

Signs of a good home

☐ Staff members respond quickly to calls for assistance and treat residents with courtesy, respect and affection.

☐ The Residents' Bill of Rights is posted prominently and there are lively meetings of the Residents' Council.

☐ The physical condition of the facility is good; the buildings are clean and odor-free.

☐ All residents have freedom and opportunity to make friends and socialize. There is a competent, creative activities director who organizes a varied, lively schedule of events, classes, visits and day trips that include music, art, cooking and literary activities.

☐ In general, residents are up and dressed for the season and time of day.

☐ Activities are tailored to individual needs and interests, and fit with each resident's short- and long-term goals.

☐ Meals are served efficiently and attractively, and residents seem to enjoy their food.

☐ Care is used in selecting roommates. Personal and social considerations are taken into account, as well as ethnic and religious interests.

☐ The facility has a pet therapy program, as well as the involvement of a variety of volunteer and community organizations.

☐ There is a comprehensive offering of services: Physical therapy, occupational therapy, speech and language therapy.

☐ There are adequate handrails in hallways and grab bars in bathrooms. And it is easy for residents in wheelchairs to move around the home.

Contract tips

Before you sign any contract with a nursing home, stop and carefully review the document.

A good contract should:

☐ State the resident's rights and obligations.

☐ Specify daily or monthly rates.

☐ Detail prices for items not included in the basic fee.

☐ State the policy on holding a bed temporarily if the resident leaves for hospitalization or vacation.

☐ State whether the facility is Medicaid and/or Medicare certified. *Note:* If so, and if the resident desires and qualifies, the facility must accept Medicaid or Medicare payments. Private-pay admissions contracts are illegal and cannot be enforced. *Remember:* Discrimination against Medicaid recipients is illegal.

Always talk to a lawyer before signing any contract. And don't forget that you can change terms of the contract by negotiating specific items and then both you and an authorized nursing-home representative must initial the changes.

It's important to remember that when people enter nursing homes, they don't leave their personalities at the door. Nor do they lose their basic human rights and needs for respect, encouragement and friendliness. A nursing home can be a wonderful new phase of life!

Source: *Guide to Choosing a Nursing Home* (Publication No. HCFA-02174), US Department of Health and Human Services, Health Care Financing Administration, 6325 Security Blvd., Baltimore, MD 21207.

When the money runs out

When the nursing-home patient's assets run out, Medicaid should take over. It is illegal for a home to evict a patient who can no longer pay privately, although some homes use devious tactics to do just this. *Example:* A patient gets a high fever in the middle of the night, is dropped off at the local hospital and is then refused readmittance to the home when the fever subsides.

☐ Except for the very rich, it is unlikely that any family can support for many years an annual nursing-home bill of $30,000. Since almost all nursing-home patients eventually wind up on Medicaid, it is imperative to protect your assets (and your children's inheritance) by making sure Medicaid takes over as soon as possible.

☐ *Problem:* Almost all states have laws that forbid the transfer of assets during a time (anywhere from three to five years) prior to nursing-home admission. Since it is impossible to

predict when nursing-home care will be needed, advance planning is crucial.

☐ A trust fund is one good way to move assets of $50,000 or more out of an elderly person's direct ownership. It can also help with taxes and the problem of children who cannot be trusted with a lot of money.

Essential: Set up the trust in a way that minimizes the potential of its being attached as an evasion of Medicaid rules, a federal crime. This difficult and complicated matter is best handled by a lawyer experienced in the field.

Lost relatives

The Salvation Army, known for saving souls, has an impressive record of finding them as well. Its little-known missing-persons service is devoted to reuniting scattered families. Four regional offices coordinate cases for the United States. The New York bureau has processed 10,000 inquiries in the past ten years and concluded 4,000 of them successfully.

Working through local chapters throughout the US and in 85 other countries, the Salvation Army carries on a heavy correspondence with government agencies such as the Social Security Administration and the IRS, checks local phone books and places ads in its own publications.

"We don't help wives track down missing husbands to collect alimony, nor do we do much work with runaway children," says Major Mary Jane Shaw, director of the New York bureau. "And if someone doesn't want to be found, we respect that."

Many requests come from overseas families trying to locate relatives who emigrated and lost touch. "People who move to a foreign country get busy and neglect to keep up with their families until their lives are more established," says Major Shaw. Her proudest moment was the reconciliation of a patriarch with his surviving heirs after 50 years of separation.

Easing the impact of relocation on employees

Be cognizant of the fact that transfers may create serious problems, especially in these situations:

□ Midlife crisis. A relocation that coincides with a period of personal transition adds to emotional confusion if you are already trying to cope with changes in life goals and lifestyle.

□ Career-oriented spouse. There is a good chance your working spouse will greatly resent the career interruption and show it. One solution is to ask your employer to help your spouse find rewarding work at the new location or help pay for more education.

□ Adolescent offspring. Children of other ages cope better with a move than do teenagers.

□ Repeated relocations. Even an adaptable family resents moves that occur every few years.

Your company can alleviate the problems by:

□ Encouraging your family to discuss their reactions to the transfer openly.

□ Helping them make a clean break.

□ Bidding fond farewells to you and your family, perhaps throwing an informal send-off party.

□ Providing extensive information to your family on their new area.

□ Checking back after the move for a progress report.

Source: *The Effective Manager,* Warren, Gorham & Lamont, Boston.

How your company can help you buy/sell a house when you're transferred

Companies are increasingly under-writing housing costs to encourage their executives to relocate when they have to give up a low-interest fixed-rate mortgage.

Three ways your employer can help:

□ Cover the loss you suffer from trading the old mortgage for a new one.

For example, you sell a house with a $50,000 balance on a 7% mortgage. You then buy a new house with a 15% mortgage. The company reimburses you for the extra interest, usually for the next three years. *Calculation:* $50,000 (old mortgage balance) times 8% (difference in interest rates) equals $4,000 a year. *Total payout:* $12,000.

□ Company financing. It can offer interest rates below market levels but high enough to minimize losses.

□ Purchase the new home jointly with you and share the profits from its future appreciation. This is similar to a bank's share appreciation mortgage.

Source: Patricia E. Matteson, marketing director, Merrill Lynch Relocation Management, Inc., White Plains, NY.

Choosing the right breed of dog for your family

When contemplating buying a puppy, your first consideration should be the type of dog, rather than size. Many large dogs actually need less room than smaller ones. The original function for which the breed was developed often dictates the animal's need for space and influences his temperament.

□ Scent hounds (beagle, basset, dachshund, bloodhound). Well-suited to city living and children.

□ Sight or gaze hounds (saluki, Afghan, Irish wolfhound, Scottish deerhound, greyhound). Originally bred for running down prey and killing it, they still need lots of room to be happy.

□ Sporting dogs (spaniels, setters, pointers, retrievers). Originally bred to locate game and retrieve it. Need a little less room than sight hounds. But with the exception of Labrador and Newfoundland retrievers, sporting dogs are not especially protective or good with children.

□ Working dogs (German shepherds, malamutes, huskies, collies, sheep-dogs). Probably the most intelligent and protective of all groups. Large (60–150 pounds) and used to outdoor work, but they adapt nicely to city life if exercised twice a day. Actually require less space than smaller, more active dogs like terriers.

□ Terriers (Airedale, Scottish, Welsh, West Highland white, fox, schnauzers). The most alert and active dogs. Also tenacious, extremely protective and often aggressive. Need space. Good with children and older people, as long as they can cope with the terrier's high level of activity.

☐ Toy dogs (Pekinese, toy poodle, Yorkshire terrier, Maltese, Italian greyhound, Pomeranian). Charming companions for adults. But strongly not recommended for small children. No matter how adorable these dogs may look, they're much too fragile.

☐ Nonsporting dogs is a catch-all group with no special characteristics. Includes unrelated breeds, such as the poodle, French and English bulldogs, Boston terrier, chow chow and dalmatian.

Most dog owners strongly prefer one sex over the other. General pros and cons:

☐ Males (called dogs by breeders) tend to fight, wander, chase cars and display aggressive dominant behavior toward people.

☐ Females (bitches) are more protective and gentle. They neither wander nor fight but if they're not spayed, they can become pregnant. Even if they're kept locked up, living through their semiannual heat periods is difficult because of all the unwanted attention from neighboring dogs.

How to select a puppy

The main thing is to buy from a breeder rather than a pet shop. Don't buy a puppy on impulse. Consider the following points:

☐ It's best to see both the pup's parents or their photographs at the breeder (chief reason to buy there rather than at pet store). Not only will you see what the puppy will look like as an adult, you will also be able to judge its genetic inheritance by the health of its parents.

☐ Buy a puppy at 6 to 12 weeks of age. That's when they make the best adjustment to a new home.

Try these quick and easy visual tests:

☐ Shine a pocket flashlight at the pup.

☐ Show it a mirror.

☐ Roll a ball toward it.

☐ Wave a sheet of white paper.

☐ Drag an object along on a string.

Similarly, here are some hearing tests (to be done out of the puppy's sight):

☐ Blow a police whistle.

☐ Honk a car horn.

☐ Clap hands.

☐ Blow a kazoo or noisemaker.

☐ Body sensitivity is important in training. Gently pinch the puppy's ear between the ball of the thumb and the forefinger. Then push down its hindquarters, forcing it to sit. A puppy that doesn't react has little body sensitivity and won't feel corrections. A puppy that whines, cowers or runs away is so sensitive that it will fear corrections and be difficult to train.

☐ Temperament can be tested by seeing the puppy's attitude toward strangers. Jump right in front of the puppy. It should show neither fear nor anger. Surprise followed by friendliness is a good reaction.

Training your puppy

Some suggestions:

☐ Don't encourage a puppy to chew on facsimiles of valued objects. You can't expect it to tell an old shoe from a new one.

☐ Never place your hand or finger in a puppy's mouth when playing. That biting might seem cute today, but you won't enjoy it a year from now.

☐ Allow the puppy to climb and jump on you only when you're seated on the floor. If you let it jump on you when you're in a chair, you're teaching it to sit on furniture.

☐ Never encourage a puppy to bark on command. This can lead to excessive barking and a dog that "talks back."

☐ Puppies become bored and anxious easily. If you leave your puppy alone too long and too often, you must expect destructive behavior.

☐ Praise the puppy when it's good. Treat bad behavior with a stern "no" and a shaking or a harsh noisemaker. Physical abuse will teach a dog only fear.

What to feed your dog

A dog's healthy condition can best be maintained by a good diet. Falling into sloppy habits may ultimately hurt your dog. Feed the dog what it needs, not what *you* think it needs!

☐ Dry kibble should be your dog's basic food. Kibble should contain at least 22% protein, preferably more.

☐ Supplement the kibble with raw meat, preferably tripe or meat fresh frozen specifically for dogs. Meat should not be more than 25% of the dog's diet.

☐ Canned meats or table scraps, although readily available and convenient, are not advised.

☐ Two smaller meals are healthier than one larger meal. Puppies up to age four months require three meals a day, with feeding times adhered to strictly—morning, noon and early evening.

☐ Give puppies twice-weekly servings of yogurt to restore intestinal flora, and wheat germ for B vitamins.

☐ Fresh water—in sufficient quantity—is a must. Change it daily. Water may be taken up at night, especially during house training.

☐ Never cancel a feeding as punishment to your dog.

Source: The Monks of New Skete, authors of *How to Be Your Dog's Best Friend*, Little, Brown & Company, New York.

Getting your pet into TV commercials

☐ Get your animal an agent. Like any other model, he needs an agent to get jobs. In bigger cities, there are animal talent agencies. In smaller cities, animal trainers are usually the contact for commercial producers.

☐ *What agents look for:* Trained animals that photograph well. At a minimum, dogs should respond to basic obedience commands—*sit, down* and, most important, *stay.*

☐ Prepare your pet with a test many agents use. Make him stay in a busy corridor where there are many distractions. (The set for a commercial shoot is a noisy, bustling place.)

☐ *Other important tricks:* Fetching and carrying a product gently by mouth, "speaking" on command.

☐ For pet-food commercials, a healthy, indiscriminate appetite is essential. Few ads are completed on the first take, so the animal may have to eat several times.

☐ If you have a cat that does tricks, you may have an advantage because trained cats are rare.

☐ To audition your pet, make an appointment for an interview. Take along pictures. Color snapshots are fine if they are clear and show the animal close up, at eye level. Bring a résumé that includes the pet's vital statistics, its training and special tricks, and your phone number.

☐ Payment. There is no union for animals, so fees vary widely. In general, TV pays more than print work.

Norman Vincent Peale's ten rules for getting along with people

☐ Remember their names.

☐ Be comfortable to be with. Don t cause strain in others.

☐ Try not to let things bother you. Be easygoing.

☐ Don't be egotistical or a know-it-all.

☐ Learn to be interesting so that people will get something stimulating from being with you.

☐ Eliminate the "scratchy" elements in your personality, traits that can irritate others.

☐ Never miss a chance to offer support or say "Congratulations."

☐ Work at liking people. Eventually you'll like them naturally.

☐ Honestly try to heal any misunderstandings and drain off grievances.

☐ Develop spiritual depth in yourself and share this strength with others.

Source: *Time Talk*, Time Management Center, Grandville, MI.

How to build a personal support system

Individuals need not only a few intimate friends but also a network of friendly relationships that make anyone more effective. To build a support system:

☐ Join groups. Participate in self-help groups—not so much for the help as for the support, to get a sense of community and belonging.

☐ Pursue with other people some of the activities you like. A runner can join a running club; a photographer can take a photography course. This way, you weave your interests into a friendship network.

☐ Reciprocate acts of friendship. If someone waters your plants, you'd better be prepared to do the same for him. Reciprocity—both giving and accepting—is part of keeping any kind of friendship. People who have problems with accepting favors should remember that other people feel good doing things for them.

☐ Mentor friends. The younger person ordinarily seeks out the older one. However, the older person might do well to encourage such a relationship because there's something in it for him or her, too—a revitalization that comes from dealing with a younger person with ambition, enthusiasm and a fresh education.

What nourishes and what poisons friendship

Key nourishing qualities:

☐ Authenticity. Inauthentic behavior is contrived and false. Authentic behavior is spontaneous and unpremeditated. Being freely and deeply oneself is important to friendship.

☐ Acceptance. A sound friendship permits the expression of anger, childishness and silliness. It allows us to express the various facets of our personality without fear of harsh judgment. A feeling of being valued promotes our fullest functioning with other people.

☐ Direct expression. Coaxing, cajoling, dropping "cute" hints, manipulating and beating around the bush are all barriers to clear communications. When people know what they want from each other, they establish clear communication and contact. They're in a position to attempt an agreement regarding their desires. They may also realize they're too different to get along and that they may be less frustrated if their relationship is more casual.

☐ Empathy. This involves an effort to understand another's beliefs, practices and feelings (not necessarily agreeing with them). Empathy means listening, trying to understand and communicating this understanding to the speaker.

What poisons friendships:

☐ Blame. Blame shifts responsibility and also can be a way of avoiding self-examination. The antithesis of blame and defensiveness is to assume responsibility for one's own feelings. If a person is honest enough to admit his mistakes and finds he's forgiven, he can then be tolerant of his friends' foibles.

☐ Excess dependency. Some people have lost touch with their values and their strength and need other people to lean on. This kind of person feels unable to be alone. In the dependent friendship, growth and development are stifled rather than enhanced.

Source: Dr. Joel D. Block, clinical psychologist and author of *Friendship: How to Give It, How to Get It*, Macmillan, New York.

All about nerds

Nerds get attention by being obnoxious. They don't pay attention to the signals other people send them.

How not to be a nerd:

☐ Let people finish what they are saying.

☐ Don't always insist that you know more than other people about the subject under discussion.

☐ Slow down on advice-giving.

☐ Open up to new ideas.

☐ Let yourself change your mind once in a while.

When a nerd starts to realize that much of his behavior stems from anxiety about being accepted and loved, he is well on his way to being a nerd no longer.

Source: Doe Lang, author of *The Secret of Charisma*, Wideview Books, New York.

Making friendships stronger

Even the best of friendships can have their ups and downs. How to minimize this type of stress:

☐ To move closer to a friend, take him or her into your confidence. Share your thoughts and feelings. There's no guarantee that this approach will produce positive results, but the probabilities increase dramatically when you give what you want to get.

☐ Use compromise to resolve differences. The only other alternatives are domination by one and the consequent resentment on the part of the other or withdrawal. Compromise restores the reciprocity needed in friendship.

☐ Avoid a mismatch. It's foolish to pursue a friendship with someone who isn't interested in you. Friendship involves mutual feelings.

☐ Observe the Golden Rule. Most of us want the same things in our friendships—honesty, a sharing of good feelings and thoughts, empathy, support, fun. If you're not getting these, ask:

"Do I offer the same things to others that I want for myself?"

Source: Dr. Joel D. Block, a clinical psychologist, and author of *Friendship: How to Give It, How to Get It*, Macmillan, New York.

Changing an enemy into an ally

If there's someone in your business with whom you're always at odds:

☐ Think of this person as someone you like, someone who can work with you.

☐ Create in your mind an image of the relationship restored.

☐ Treat this person as a valued friend and associate.

☐ You won't see immediate results, but over time, you'll find that this person is responding to you in a more positive way.

☐ *The lesson:* Be aware of your expectations of others. People are likely to deliver what you expect them to deliver.

Source: The late Dr. Norman Vincent Peale, author and lecturer.

How to say "no" to anyone

Many of us say "yes" more often than we'd like. Whatever the reason, if you find yourself saying "yes" because you feel too guilty about saying "no," here are some practical measures to help you protect yourself.

☐ Stall. This gives you precious time to work up an honest rationale for a total refusal. Simply say: "I don't know. I need time to think about it—give me an hour (or a day, or whatever seems reasonable)."

☐ Use humor.

☐ Try flattery.

☐ Tell white lies, if necessary.

Source: Barry Lubetkin, PhD, Institute for Behavior Therapy, New York.

How to forgive and forget

To forgive another is the greatest favor you can do—for yourself. It's the only way to release yourself from the clutches of an unfair past. Beyond that, it opens the possibility of reconciliation, often a gift in itself.

What to do:

☐ Take the initiative. Don't wait for the other person to apologize. (That cedes control to the one who hurt you in the first place.)

☐ If the forgiven person wants to re-enter your life, it is fair to demand truthfulness. He or she should be made to understand, to feel the hurt you've felt. Then you should expect a sincere promise that you won't be hurt that way again.

☐ Be patient. If the hurt is deep, you can't forgive in a single instant.

☐ Forgive "retail," not "wholesale." It is almost impossible to forgive someone for being a bad person. Instead, focus on the particular act that hurt you. (It might help to write it down.)

☐ Don't expect too much. To forgive doesn't mean you must renew a once-close relationship.

☐ Discard your self-righteousness. A victim is not a saint. You, too, will need forgiveness some day.

☐ Separate anger from hate. *To dissolve your hate:* Face your emotion and accept it as natural. Then discuss it, either with the object of your hatred (if you can do so without escalating the hatred) or with a trusted third party.

☐ Forgive yourself. This may be the hardest act of all. Candor is critical. Admit your fault. Relax your struggle to be perfect. Then be concrete and specific about what is bothering you. Your deed was evil. You are not.

☐ *To make self-forgiveness easier:* Prime the pump of self-love. Do something unexpected (possibly unappreciated) for a person you care about. By acting freely, you'll find it easier to think freely.

Source: Lewis B. Smedes, author of *Forgive & Forget*, Harper & Row, New York.

How to read people

Much of people-reading involves making elementary, common-sense observations and then acting on them.

Observation tips:

☐ Don't generalize. Conventional wisdom says that if someone slumps in his chair, he's not very commanding, or if he leans forward, he's ready to make a deal. However, I've seen a lot of erect, attentive types who hung on my every word but never made a move.

Any useful observation must be considered in the context of the particular situation.

☐ Learn the difference between posture and posturing. Look out for people who lean in toward you, who push things back on the desk at you, who sit back and strike poses, who dress pretentiously, who do strange things with lighting or who have your chair placed lower than theirs. All those things are keys that you're dealing with a phony, someone who's more concerned with appearance than with accomplishment.

☐ Look at the eyes. People communicate with their eyes in situations where silence is called for. The next time you're in a meeting with people you don't know, notice the eye contact of the participants. It will tell you who's allied with whom, who is most influential and, if you're the speaker, whether you're boring everyone to death.

☐ Use ego to your advantage. Most successful people are one giant ego with a couple of arms and legs attached. But a giant ego isn't necessarily a strong ego. It may be compensating for low self-esteem. Or someone who seems to have a weak ego may simply be low-key. When you know these things, you can work with them or around them.

☐ Make inferences from coworkers and subordinates. For example, if someone seems unwilling to commit himself to even minor details, it may be that his boss is a person whose ego demands that he make all the decisions.

☐ Take the fish out of water. People tend to reveal themselves in unexpected ways when outside their usual settings. For this reason I favor breakfast, lunch and dinner meetings. Even the way someone treats a waiter can be very revealing.

Source: Mark H. McCormack, author of *What They Don't Teach You at Harvard Business School: Notes From a Street-Smart Executive.*

How to spot a liar

Less than 5% of the population are natural liars…performers who lie flawlessly and make no mistakes. But research shows that the majority of people are fooled by liars. Clues to look for:

☐ The single biggest giveaway is a series of inconsistencies in the lie.

☐ Watch for changes in patterns of speech, especially when a person has to pause and think more often than usual to answer a simple question.

□ Look for signs that the person is deviating from a usual pattern of behavior. Liars may use a monotonous tone of voice or change inflection less frequently when they lie. They may also use fewer hand and body motions than usual.

□ A smile is the most common mask of a person's true feelings.

□ Liars sometimes lie just for the thrill of telling a successful lie. *Giveaways:* Widening of the eyes and a trace of a smile.

□ Ask questions when inconsistencies start to pop up in a story. Most people become willing prey to liars because they don't want to act suspicious or don't think they have the right to ask questions.

Source: Dr. Paul Ekman, professor of psychology, University of California, San Francisco, and author of *Telling Lies*, W. W. Norton & Co., New York.

More on lying

When we lie, we feel varying degrees of discomfort. Some people feel actual fear—others, the mildest tension. But at least to some degree, our feelings are expressed in our behavior. We may control our words, our voice, our face or our posture. But we cannot control everything. Here's how we give ourselves away to an astute observer:

□ Sometimes the giveaway is only a "micromovement"—a brief, minimal change in facial expression.

□ The voice is a rich source of information. People who are lying tend to talk slowly. (By definition, they're not spontaneous.) They speak in shorter sentences than usual. They realize that the more they talk, the more likely they are to slip up.

□ Liars cut back on gestures and eye contact. The less exposure, the better. They sit sideways, rather than face to face. They rarely lean forward toward their listeners.

□ Liars are more self-conscious. They shift in their seats, adjust their clothing and scratch themselves. Often, they bring a hand to the face—another way to reduce exposure.

□ A very reliable sign is body stiffness. Look for a rigid posture (whether the person is standing or seated), with strict symmetry of limbs.

It should be noted that these signals can appear in someone who is not lying. The person may simply be uncomfortable—either about saying something or about saying it to a particular individual.

Source: Albert Mehrabian, PhD, professor of psychology, UCLA, and author of *Silent Messages*, Wadsworth Publishing Co., Belmont, CA.

Disarming difficult people

To deal with infuriating people, what counts is your response, not what they do. If you don't confront them, you end up making a negative judgment on yourself. Familiar types:

□ The person who keeps repeating negative remarks about you made by others.

□ The person who keeps referring to everything he has done for you.

□ Those who insist you act in a certain way: "Isn't my daughter Frannie wonderful?" (demanding applause). Or, those who tell a joke or story and wait for you to laugh on cue.

How to handle such people:

□ Avoid recriminations.

□ Don't attribute bad motives or bad character.

□ Make the point that you have as much right to your response—or lack of response—as the speaker does to his. You'll put a stop to the annoyance, and in most cases you'll also improve the friendship.

□ Understand that if this doesn't work and you lose a friend, that's better than to be in a state of constant, impotent fury.

Source: Dr. George Weinberg, author of *Self-Creation*, Avon Books, New York.

Better one-to-one conversations

It's been said before, but the surest way to improve your one-to-one conversations is...to become a better listener. Listening skills may seem simple enough, but many people (particularly men) need to work on them.

□ Live in the present moment. Resist distractions. Don't let your mind wander to your bank balance or to after-dinner plans.

☐ Stay alert and concentrate on what your "partner" is saying—not only the words, but the emotions behind them. Rephrase what you've heard in your own words (mentally or verbally).

☐ Maintain consistent eye contact.

☐ Lean toward the person if seated.

☐ Nod or smile in response.

☐ *To handle a long-winded anecdote or complaint:* Steer the conversation to a mutually interesting subject. Or…approach the old subject from a new angle.

☐ When it's your turn to talk, think about the point you want to make before you start speaking.

☐ Get to the point in as few steps as possible.

☐ Consider your audience. Make what you're saying relevant to the particular person you're addressing.

☐ Don't be afraid to ask a "dumb" question about a subject that's new to you.

☐ If your conversations seem bland, maybe you're suppressing honest disagreements. A dispute shouldn't hurt an exchange (or a friendship), as long as a certain etiquette is respected.

☐ Give the other person credit for something before you disagree. Never say, "How can you think something like that?" *Better:* "That's a good point, but I see it differently…." Or, first point out areas of similarity: "We agree that world peace is vital—therefore…."

Sources: Mark Sherman, associate professor of psychology, and Adelaide Haas, associate professor of communications, State University of New York, New Paltz.

To rescue yourself from embarrassing situations

What to do:

☐ Simply and quickly apologize. That gives you time to think, if nothing else. But don't overdo it. Apologizing profusely just makes the other person uncomfortable.

☐ Don't put yourself down by saying "I'm so clumsy" or "I can't seem to do anything right." If you go overboard, you might wind up convincing the other person that there really *is* something wrong with you.

☐ If you're habitually tactless, ask yourself if you felt enmity or anger toward the person you insulted…if something about him made you uncomfortable or envious.

☐ *How to apologize:* Don't play innocent by insisting your remark was unintentional. The other person knows you meant to hurt because that was the result. If you apologize honestly, telling the other person about your angry feelings, you're much more likely to be forgiven.

☐ Make a joke about your mistake. It relieves the tension of the moment and shows you're a good sport. The other person also feels less embarrassed. Sharing a good laugh about something that could have created a rift can even improve rapport.

When you get in a tough, embarrassing spot:

☐ If you have personality traits that make you feel awkward in certain situations, ask a friend for feedback about how you're really coming across. You might be very self-conscious about some traits, such as your shyness or a tendency to talk too much. But others most likely won't even notice.

☐ Change the subject when it seems that you've put your foot in your mouth.

☐ Agree to disagree. One of the most awkward moments for people is disagreement, especially about personal matters. Acknowledge that you have differences, but make it clear that you still like and respect that person.

☐ Don't relive the embarrassing moment, wishing you'd done it differently. Forget it. Don't spend the rest of the day telling everyone what a fool you made of yourself, and don't keep bringing up the incident whenever you see the person it happened with.

Source: Dr. Judith Meyerowitz, PhD, a psychotherapist in private practice in New York.

Dating for mature and successful singles

When you meet someone you might like to know better:

☐ Avoid talking too much about a former spouse.

☐ Re-examine your priorities, and try to be more flexible.

☐ Don't judge another person in the first ten minutes of a date. Stay open.

☐ Keep a sense of humor.

☐ Listen to what the other person is saying. Be interested, not only interesting.

☐ Be realistic and learn from your past experience.

How to start a conversation with a stranger

☐ Pay attention to the person's name when introduced. Repeat it. If it's unusual, ask about its origins.

☐ Look directly at the person. Lean forward a bit.

☐ Ask the person something about her/himself in a flattering way.

☐ Ask encouraging questions as the person talks about himself.

☐ Don't interrupt. If you have an interest in keeping the conversation going, let the other person talk about himself and his interests. Don't immediately begin talking about yourself. Be patient.

Source: James Van Fleet, author of *A Lifetime Guide to Conversation*, Prentice-Hall, Inc., Englewood Cliffs, NJ.

Tactful flirting

Matchmaking is a thing of the past, so if you hope to find that special someone, you have to know how to go about it. Luckily the art of flirting can be learned.

To initiate contact with a stranger you think you would like to know better:

☐ Don't come on with obvious lines or a standard act. You'll be seen as crude or a phony.

☐ Don't get too personal. Make your conversational opener about something neutral, or you may be seen as pushy.

☐ Do pick up on an innocuous topic and comment on it. *Good:* That's a lovely ring you're wearing. Is it Art Deco? *Poor:* You have the most beautiful hair.

☐ Do make eye contact—but not for too long. According to a psychological study, three seconds is optimal to indicate interest without seeming to stare.

☐ Don't touch the person right away. Women especially are very put off by men they consider "grabby." You might even move away to create allure.

☐ Do show vulnerability. People love it when you're not Mr. or Ms. Self-Confidence. If you're nervous, say so. Your candor will be appealing. *Also:* Your admission will allow the other person to admit that he or she is nervous, too. This breaks the ice, and then you both can relax.

☐ Do ask for help as a good conversation opener. *Example:* I don't know this area well. Could you recommend a good restaurant around here?

☐ Don't feel you have to be extraordinarily good-looking. If you have confidence in yourself as a person, the rest will follow. Whatever your type may be, it is certain to appeal to someone.

☐ Do be flexible. The same approach won't work with everyone. If you're sensitive and alert, you can pick up verbal and nonverbal cues and respond appropriately.

☐ Don't oversell yourself or feel compelled to give all your credits. Make the other person feel like the most important person in the world to you at that moment. Being interested is just as important as being interesting (if not more so). Really listen. Don't just wait until the other person finishes a sentence so you can jump in with your own opinion.

☐ Don't let your confidence be shattered by a rejection. It may not have anything to do with you. You may have approached someone who is married, neurotic, recovering from a devastating love affair, in a bad mood or averse to your eye color. *The best remedy:* Try again as soon as possible.

Source: Wendy Leigh, author of *What Makes a Woman Good in Bed*, *What Makes a Man Good in Bed* and *Infidelity: An American Epidemic*, William Morrow, New York.

What men like in women

☐ Brunettes come in first with 36% of the men surveyed.

☐ Blondes come in second at 29%.

☐ Hair color is unimportant to 32% of the men surveyed.

☐ *Favorite eye color:* 44% select blue, 21% like brown and 20% prefer green.

☐ By two to one, men choose curly hair over straight.

☐ *The trait men first associate with a beautiful woman:* 42% say personality, 23% think of the smile, 13% say eyes and only 6% zero in on the body.

☐ *Favorite look:* Striking and sophisticated is first, with 32%.

☐ *Biggest turnoffs:* Heavy makeup, 26%; excess weight, 15%; arrogance, 14%.

Source: *Glamour*.

Talking to women

A survey of 1,000 women revealed that they most liked to talk about (in this order):

☐ Family and home, including children and grandchildren.

☐ Good health.

☐ Work or job (if a working woman).

☐ Promotion and advancement (if employed).

☐ Personal growth.

☐ Clothes and shopping.

☐ Recreation.

☐ Travel.

☐ Men (especially single women).

Subjects that were liked least:

☐ Sports such as baseball, football and boxing.

☐ Politics.

☐ Religion.

Source: James Van Fleet, author of *A Lifetime Guide to Conversation*, Prentice-Hall, Inc., Englewood Cliffs, NJ.

How to talk with men if you're a woman

The topics men most like to talk about are strikingly similar to those women like:

☐ Family and home, including children and grandchildren.

☐ Good health.

☐ Work or job.

☐ Promotion and advancement.

☐ Personal growth.

☐ Recreation.

☐ Travel.

☐ The opposite sex (especially young single men).

☐ Sports.

☐ Politics.

Men generally dislike talking about:

☐ Religion.

☐ Clothes, fashion or shopping.

Source: James Van Fleet, author of *A Lifetime Guide to Conversation*, Prentice-Hall, Inc., Englewood Cliffs, NJ.

Personal ads that get the job done

The personal classified ads in the major print media, as well as in the local community papers and online, have become an increasingly useful social avenue for meeting people.

Here are some tips on answering and placing ads:

☐ Be safe. If you don't feel comfortable leaving your personal phone numbers with a stranger on the ad's voice mail, use an answering service. It's very inexpensive and discreet, and helps you maintain your privacy until you choose otherwise.

☐ Don't lie. Even white lies do damage. Don't say you're a college professor if you really teach occasional courses in night school at several local colleges. Stretching the truth sets up unrealistic expectations, and your "date" is certain to be disappointed. Important omissions also count. If you weigh 300 pounds, it's better to say so.

☐ Look in the mirror. Don't say you're handsome, beautiful or very attractive if you're not. You have a better chance being honest because different people want different things.

☐ Exchanging photos can be disappointing. When it comes to wallet-size portraits, they lie at worst. At best, they say nothing. When you like someone, that person becomes better looking to you. And when you don't like someone, it doesn't matter how good-looking a person is. Besides, some very attractive people photograph badly…and vice versa. You'll get the best sense of a person from communicating with him or her directly.

☐ Try humor. It always gets a better response.

☐ You may be tempted to include age restrictions. If you choose to do so, be certain that you are not placing undue limitations on your possibilities.

☐ Don't brag. This unpleasant trait breeds skepticism and distaste in the reader.

☐ Be sincere. Nothing catches a person's attention more surely than a sincere, straightforward, informative conversation. When you answer an ad that looks inviting, let the person know why. Respond to the particulars in the ad in a warm and personal way. Talk honestly about yourself, your likes and dislikes, favorite vacations, funny anecdotes, etc. And never, never, never send a photocopy response.

☐ If you really liked an ad but didn't receive a response, try again. Persistence is a virtue.

□ Don't be discouraged. Chances are you won't be attracted to 99.9% of the people you meet this way. But that will also be true of singles you meet other ways. This is more efficient, however, since people are already preselected. They're singles who want to meet someone—just like you.

How to enjoy relationships

□ Accept people as they are. Nothing kills a relationship faster than the expectation that you can change someone. It's impossible. The best you can do is to become more tolerant and flexible yourself, encourage an atmosphere for change and then hope for the best.

□ When you give, give freely. If you expect people to give the same back, measured by the cup, you'll always be disappointed. If they respond, that's great. And if they don't, that's all right, too.

□ Be honest with the people you care about. Get rid of petty irritants. Don't suffer in silence until you finally explode.

□ Honesty needn't be cruel. *Good rule:* Be as tactful with your spouse and children as you are with friends and distant relatives. Most people are wonderful in courtship but later get careless. Love is not a license for rudeness.

□ Don't use your family as an alibi when you fall short of goals. Stop underestimating these people. They're much more flexible than most people assume. You can make your dreams real if you want them enough—and share them with the people you love. But if you never say, "Let's go to Nepal!" you'll never get there.

□ It's a gamble to be vulnerable. But you never really lose because the risk itself reminds you how richly you are living.

Source: Leo Buscaglia, author of *Loving Each Other*, Holt, Rinehart and Winston, New York.

Terminating a relationship

In terminating either a business or personal relationship, those who initiate the termination have the upper hand. They also have the bulk of the responsibility.

To walk away from the termination with a sense of moral clarity, it is essential to have made a genuine attempt to come to some degree of accommodation with the other party, whether employee or spouse. Terminators should meet with those terminated to share their dissatisfaction when they are still open to finding a solution.

Terminators should answer these questions:

□ What do they need from the other party to continue the relationship?

□ What support are they prepared to give the other party?

□ What is an acceptable time frame for the changes to be made? A reasonable period should be allowed for making changes and adjustments. Announcing requirements for change on Friday, and then deciding on Monday that the relationship won't work, is unfair.

□ What don't the terminators want?

□ What aren't they prepared to give?

□ How would they describe the consequences if satisfactory changes aren't made? People often resist making major changes not because they fear what's ahead but because they are unwilling to give up what they have. The same fear hinders organizational change as well as change in personal life.

Source: Gisele Richardson, president, Richardson Management Associates, management consultants, Montreal.

Are you ready for love?

Love résumé

Here is a way to consider—and maybe rethink—what you really want in a loving relationship and what you respond to. Think of this as a love résumé. Sometimes just the act of writing can change your thinking. Like a work résumé, it may show a tendency toward instability. Or it may show a logical progression from one "job" to the next. You can discover your own patterns in relationships.

Write a detailed report* about your three (or more) most serious relationships, including:

□ A description of the person and what you did and didn't like.

□ What worked and what didn't work.

*Do this before going on to read the scoring section that follows.

☐ How it ended and how you got over it.

☐ What you think you should have done differently.

☐ What your partner would say worked or didn't work, and why it ended.

☐ Would you be attracted to such a person today?

Write a description* of the person you would like to meet now, including:

☐ Is this person like the ones in past relationships? If not, why not?

☐ What sort of relationship you want (marriage, a companion for weekends, an escort, etc.)

☐ Characteristics you would avoid.

☐ Your three highest priorities.

Scoring

Use a red pencil to underline the times you have written *I* or *me*. Count them, and put the score in a box.

Use a blue pencil to underline the times you have written *he, she, we, us* or *both*. Count them. Put this score in another box.

Add the numbers in both boxes. Divide the total into the number of red underlines. If the percentage is anywhere up to 35%, you're available for a relationship. From 36% to 50% means you are borderline (okay on short-term dating but unable to sustain long-term relationships). Over 50% indicates a counterfeit lover. Your concern for yourself and lack of empathy for others almost guarantee that nothing will work, no matter who the partner is.

*Do this before going on to read the scoring section that follows.

Source: Abby Hirsch, founder and director of The Godmothers, a dating service.

Being single...again

Being involuntarily single after years of marriage can deal a serious blow to the ego. Essential to cushioning it is to start leading the single life immediately.

☐ Force yourself to make a date at least once a week, even if it is only having dinner with someone from work.

☐ Do not expect too much from yourself too soon. Scars of a broken marriage take at least a year, usually two, to heal. You are probably deluding yourself if you believe you are ready for a permanent relationship before that time.

☐ Brief sexual encounters are normal during this period, and they can be useful in rebuilding the ego. Do not be alarmed if periods of celibacy follow periods of sexual activity. These are also normal and useful in the healing process.

☐ Older people are often surprised to discover that achievement makes them attractive to the opposite sex. Not only is prestige an aphrodisiac, age itself is frequently attractive. But although younger people often have affairs with those older than themselves, usually they want permanent partners closer to their own age.

☐ Transitional partners, with whom you form a nurturing though transitory relationship, often occur during the first year of being single. This type of partner is also part of the healing process. You may feel guilty about breaking off the relationship, but do not. You may well be someone else's transitional partner.

☐ Your best chance for meeting new partners is in the normal course of business and social events. However difficult it may be at first, ask your friends to introduce you to eligible acquaintances.

☐ Once you have been introduced to a new person, avoid harping on your ex-spouse and introducing your new friend too quickly to your children. Many dates will discourage you from talking about your former spouse but may enjoy hearing about children.

☐ Although they may remind you of pain you would like to forget, it is essential to continue being a good parent to your children, maybe even a better one. Remember, the divorce or separation may have been harder on the children than on you.

☐ Expect your children to take a keen interest in your new life and be curious to know about your new day-to-day routine. After meeting some of your new friends, children may even suggest that one of them seems marriageable. Sometimes they are right.

Source: Richard Schickel, author of *Singled Out*, Viking Press, New York.

Successful marrying and remarrying

Today, with the statistical probability that two out of every three marriages will end in divorce, couples who marry or remarry need all the help they can get.

Here is some advice for a good start:

☐ Choose the right person for the right reasons. Too often, people make the wrong choice because they have needs they don't admit even to themselves. They know what they want, but even though the person they plan to marry doesn't fill the bill, they think he/she will change.

☐ Have realistic expectations about the marriage. Another person can do only so much for you. No one person can fill every need. It is important for both partners to develop their own lives and interests and not depend solely on each other.

☐ Learn to communicate. Get issues out on the table and talk about them. Try to reach conclusions regarding conflicts rather than letting them stay unresolved.

☐ Respect the other person's style of communication. People express affection in different ways. Instead of expecting a spouse to react as you do, try to be sensitive to what he or she is telling you in his/her own way.

☐ Respect the other person's feelings about space and distance. Many people have difficulty understanding someone else's needs for privacy and time alone. Conflicts about space needs can be resolved by trial and error—and patience.

☐ Create a new lifestyle. Each partner comes with different concepts about customs, handling money, vacations, etc. One may be used to making a big thing about celebrating holidays and birthdays, the other, not. Combine the best elements to get a richer blend that is distinctly your own.

Source: Barbara C. Freedman, CSW, director of the Divorce and Remarriage Counseling Center, New York.

How to disagree with your spouse

By observing their parents, children learn how to cope with life—including how to deal with conflict. To be successful parents, fathers and mothers must learn to conduct their disagreements effectively.

If this is done correctly, their children will learn a valuable lesson—that people who love each other can solve their problems in ways that satisfy both sides.

How parental arguments affect children:

No conscientious parent deliberately sets out to argue in front of his/her children…but in a family setting, it is virtually impossible to keep every disagreement hidden from them.

Even when they are too young to understand words, children are remarkably sensitive to the emotional signals of disagreement—such as facial expressions, body language and tone of voice.

Children of all ages are distressed if their parents lose control when disagreeing. The distress is reflected in different behaviors as they develop.

Toddlers who witness shouting matches between their fathers and mothers may become fearful and agitated. Some begin to copy their parents' shouting and table pounding…others suddenly burst into tears. They feel their own security is threatened when their parents show disunity.

Preschoolers understand more of the details of the argument. They may try to stop the fight by diverting their parents' attention to other matters…perhaps even by directing the anger toward themselves.

Example: Jane and her husband were in the front seat of the car bickering about the shortest route to the beach. Five-year-old Suzie started to hug her mother from behind while pointing out the beautiful flowers on the roadside. Meanwhile, three-year-old Sam began calling out in a loud voice, kicking the back of the front seat…and then punching himself.

School-age children are not only worried about their family security…they also feel socially embarrassed. They take sides in arguments.

Example: Martha was angrily accusing her husband of being stingy when eight-year-old Tom joined the fray, telling his father, "…and the last time I asked you for money for a new video game, you turned me down, too."

As Tom's case points out, sometimes children try to manipulate parental disagreements to their own advantage …and feel guilty later. More often, they blame themselves for the argument, inventing fanciful theories to explain how their actions caused their parents to quarrel.

It doesn't take an all-out screaming match to upset children. Hostility between parents that is expressed indirectly through sniping and sarcasm is also disturbing…and lays the foundation for children to develop the same style of behavior when they grow up.

How to handle disagreements:

☐ Don't deny that an argument occurred. You can't fool children by pretending that you and your spouse are in agreement when obvious discord has upset the emotional atmosphere. They will figure out on their own that something is wrong and likely think it is worse than it actually is.

If parents deny their anger, children learn that anger is unacceptable and begin to bury their own feelings rather than learn how to deal with them in positive ways.

What you should do: Acknowledge the argument and encourage your children to express their feelings about it. No matter how large or small the argument, tell the children who saw it that they can talk to you about it.

What to say: Tell your four-year-old child, "I know you just saw Mommy and Daddy yelling at each other. It was very upsetting for all of us. We're sorry… sometimes grown-ups lose their tempers. It wasn't your fault, and, of course, we still love you as much as ever."

☐ Don't plead your case to the children or expect them to take sides. It's not your child's job to be judge and jury over your disputes. And if you enlist a child to take your side, it threatens his relationship with your spouse.

What you should do: Explain the content of the disagreement in simple, neutral terms…give just enough information to reassure the child.

Example: Sara and Jeff had a heated argument over accepting Jeff's mother's invitation to dinner. The psychological origin of the dispute is Sara's resentment of Jeff's inability to refuse his mother's requests. Sara should tell the children, "You know how much Grandma likes us to come for dinner, but I would prefer not to go there tomorrow. I'd rather go next week instead."

☐ Don't trivialize your spouse's anger— or try to humiliate him/her. A child who sees that one parent repeatedly discounts the other's feelings and attitudes will conclude that the second parent need not be taken seriously. But children want two parents they can look up to… and they need to learn that adults take other people's concerns seriously.

What you should do: Find out why your spouse feels the way he/she does, and try to improve the situation with respect, not with ridicule.

☐ Don't walk out of the house in anger. A child who sees you leave may imagine that you will never come back…and think that if you can leave your spouse, one day you might leave him, too.

What you should do: If you feel so angry that you really can't take it any more, tell the child before you leave… reassure him you'll be back soon. Tell him, "I really must go out for a while, but don't worry. I'll be back to tuck you into bed."

☐ Don't resort to violence. Dishes should stay in the cupboard…books on the shelves. Violence immediately destroys trust between people…makes it impossible to resolve disputes sensibly… threatens the physical safety of children caught in the middle…and teaches them to react to their own problems in the same way.

Important: Don't use profanity either… unless you want to hear your children imitating your performance.

What you should do: Learn to recognize the real source of your anger and tell your children about it.

Two basic rules for parents:

☐ Rule 1: Learn to stop a developing argument in its tracks. Plan a strategy with your spouse when you feel a discussion is about to escalate into an angry exchange. One of you might say, "This isn't the place for us to argue. Let's stop now, and we'll discuss it later." Keep in mind, though, that despite your sincere efforts, you probably won't always succeed in avoiding arguments.

☐ Rule 2: If you do have a major argument in front of your children—let them see when you make up. Show them that grown-ups aren't perfect…but when they make mistakes they own up to them and apologize. You want your children to learn these two rules of adult life.

Source: Lawrence Balter, PhD, professor of applied psychology at New York University. He is coauthor of *Not in Front of the Children: How to Talk to Your Child About Tough Family Matters,* Viking, New York.

Misconceptions about sex after fifty

Middle age can be an opportunity to make sex better and more satisfying than ever before. People of mature years have had more experience in lovemaking. The pressures of career building are less frantic, leaving couples with more time to share. The children have grown up and left home, giving adults more privacy and fewer demands on their time. And as men age, they lose the pressure to get right to intercourse and a quick climax. They can concentrate on a fuller sensual and sexual experience in lovemaking.

Most common myths about age and sex:

☐ That your sex life is essentially over by the time you're in your fifties. Society tends to reinforce this notion with its emphasis on youth. People behave according to the expectations that the culture sets for them and begin to give up on their sexual lives at middle age. This is, in many ways, the equivalent of giving up on life itself.

☐ That the physiological changes affecting sexual function spell the end of your sex life. This is particularly damaging, because most changes can be readily accommodated. For example, many men age 55–60 or over, worry when they don't get a spontaneous erection seeing their partner undress as they did when they were 20 or 30. But this does not mean sexual function is over for them. It means only that they now require more direct stimulation. Many men put off having intercourse until they get a spontaneous erection for fear their wives will think they have some sexual problem. Sex in these circumstances becomes less and less frequent, and this is what causes wives to fear that their husbands are no longer interested in them.

☐ That sex requires a climax every time. As men get older, they need longer and longer periods between ejaculations. A man in his sixties may require a full day or even several days between ejaculations. This does not mean that he cannot enjoy intercourse and lovemaking in between. Sex partners get into serious trouble when they think climaxes are essential and that the male, particularly, must have one. (The man feels he must because his partner expects it. The woman feels that if he doesn't, he no longer cares for her.) You can enjoy all the sensations of sexual arousal without climax.

Source: Saul H. Rosenthal, MD, editor of *Sex Over Forty*.

What to expect from sex therapy

☐ If you're married, it's more effective to undergo therapy as a couple. *Reasons:* Since successful therapy may mean a change in sexual practices, your spouse will inevitably be involved. Moreover, many sex difficulties, such as lack of interest and failure to be aroused, are often the result of a breakdown in communication between partners.

☐ In some states, therapists use a surrogate partner (a paid partner) during treatment. A person with sexual difficulty is taught how to overcome it during supervised foreplay and other sexual activities with the surrogate. But many therapists consider the use of a surrogate inappropriate.

☐ A typical session lasts one hour, and therapists usually recommend one session per week. Most difficulties can be successfully treated in three to six months. Some people are helped significantly in a single session because they only think they have a problem. *Example:* A woman who fails to have an orgasm during sexual intercourse. Or a man who feels guilty when his partner fails to have an orgasm during intercourse. *The fact:* Most women *do not* have orgasms during intercourse.

☐ Lack of sexual interest, the most common problem, takes longer to treat. Therapists now recognize that although some declining interest is normal during a relationship, it's often aggravated by depression, stress or emotions that build up at home.

☐ The most common mistake couples make is assuming that sex must always be spontaneous. Few things in life really are. Most couples wince at the idea of scheduling sex. It works, say the therapists. And it's one of the simplest and most effective ways out of the problem.

☐ The therapist may recommend that a couple experiment at home with activities designed to heighten sexual interest. *Examples:* Different kinds of foreplay, verbal excitement, different positions during intercourse. Lack of interest often develops because a couple haven't been communicating their preferences in sexual activity to each other.

Source: Dr. Shirley Zussman, president, American Association of Sex Educators, Counselors and Therapists, Washington, DC.

Intimate relations

☐ Couples rate talking to each other about their own relationship as the #1 topic to avoid…especially couples in the "romantic potential" stage (in between a platonic friendship and an intimate relationship).

☐ Most couples are afraid of revealing their differing levels of involvement. The partner who is more committed fears scaring the other away, while the less committed may fear hurting the other person.

Source: Study by Leslie Baxter, Lewis and Clark College, and William Wilmot, University of Montana.

☐ Affection expressed physically but not necessarily sexually is important to a love relationship. Nonsexual physical affection nurtures feelings of caring and tenderness and opens new avenues of communication. The new-found closeness can give your sex life, as well as your relationship, new vigor.

Source: Dr. Bernard Zilbergeld, clinical psychologist and co-author of *Male Sexuality,* Bantam Books, New York.

☐ Men today welcome a woman's sexual initiative, contrary to the macho myths of the past that have put men in charge of initiating sex. Most men prefer to take turns taking the lead because they enjoy feeling desirable and giving sexual decision-making power over to their partners at least some of the time.

Source: Donald L. Mosher, PhD, professor of psychology, University of Connecticut, Hartford.

☐ Foreplay works best if a woman takes more responsibility for her own arousal. *Problem:* Many women believe it's the man's duty to arouse them. *What works:* Being honest about needs and desires …not worrying about the kids, jobs, etc. …being specific about technique.

Source: Judith E. Steinhart, sex therapist, in *Medical Aspects of Human Sexuality,* Secaucus, NJ.

How to find a missing person

When a private investigator is hired to trace a missing person, he/she doesn't immediately put on his trench coat and head for the closest seedy waterfront bar.

The first move is to do some simple research into easily accessible public records. If you want to find your long-lost uncle…old college roommate… someone who owes you money… runaway spouse…childhood sweetheart…or anyone else, you can do the same. Here are the most useful sources of information…

Motor vehicle records:

Write to the Commissioner of Motor Vehicles of the state where the missing person last lived and ask for his/her driving record. First call the driving record division to ask the fee for this service—it's usually about $3 to $7.

In your letter, give the subject's date of birth…or the year you guess is closest to it. If the Department of Motor Vehicles (DMV) informs you that many people in their file share that name and age, write back specifying which part of the state the subject lived in.

If you still get back driving records for a number of individuals, don't give up… these records list valuable information that may help you pin down your target, including some or all of the following:

☐ Address

☐ Social Security number

☐ Height

☐ Date of birth

☐ Weight

☐ Dates and locations of accidents

☐ Eye color

☐ Dates and locations of traffic tickets

☐ Hair color

☐ Restrictions (eyeglasses, etc.)

Disadvantage: Driver's licenses may be renewed as infrequently as once in eight years, so you may find that the address on the record is outdated. If that happens, write again for the motor vehicle registrations on file for your subject's name and date of birth. The address will be more current, because registrations must be renewed annually. Don't forget to enclose a check for the service.

If you still don't track down a current address, you may find more clues by writing to the tag department of the DMV. Quote the title number and vehicle identification number from the registration of a vehicle he previously owned, and request the vehicle history (sometimes called "body file").

This is a packet of up to 30 pages that includes paperwork with the subject's signature, as well as previous addresses listed on yearly registrations. The people who live at those addresses now…and/or the current owner of the subject's old car…may be able to give you more current information about your missing person.

Records of vital statistics:

State departments of vital statistics will provide records of birth, death, marriage and divorce. In some states, divorce records must be obtained from the clerk of the court in the jurisdiction that granted the divorce.

Birth records contain much valuable information, including:

☐ Complete name
☐ Exact date of birth
☐ Parents' names
☐ Place of birth
☐ Parents' ages
☐ Parents' occupations
☐ Parents' address
☐ Mother's maiden name
☐ Parents' places of birth

Using your knowledge of the family names of both parents of the missing person, you can try to contact relatives who may be in touch with him. Start looking for relatives near the subject's place of birth.

Master death file: This file kept by the Social Security Administration lists all deaths since 1962…including Social Security number, first and last names, dates of birth and death and place of death (by zip code).

How to use it: From the death record of the missing person's parent, find the place of death and write there for a copy of the death certificate.

Contact the funeral home listed on the certificate and ask for the next-of-kin of the deceased, who will be your subject or a close relative. You can obtain access to information on the Master Death File from private companies. The one I use is Research Is Company, 7907 NW 53 St., Suite 420, Miami 33166.

Running someone's Social Security number: The Research Is Company will put through their computers any Social Security number you provide to give you addresses that someone has used for the past several years. If they do not give you at least one address from that Social Security number your money will be refunded.

Federal Parent Locator Service: If you have a child-support order against a missing person, this government agency will search through government records to find him/her at no cost to you.

Important: You must first approach your state's Child Support Enforcement Division to contact the state's Parent Locator Service. Other sources:

☐ Abandoned property files
☐ Bankruptcy records
☐ College records
☐ Military records
☐ Corporation records
☐ Small claims court
☐ Boat registrations
☐ National cemeteries
☐ Bar associations
☐ Medical boards
☐ Foreign embassies
☐ Passport records
☐ Workers' compensation records
☐ US Postal Service

Good hunting!

Source: Joseph J. Culligan, licensed private investigator. He is the author of *You, Too, Can Find Anybody: A Reference Manual,* available in book or video from the author at Miami.

How to stay fit while you sit

Exercises to do at your desk to keep mentally alert, tone sagging muscles and relieve muscle strain:

☐ Tummy slimmer. Sit erect, hands on knees. Exhale, pulling abdominal muscles in as far as possible. Relax. Inhale. Exhale as you draw in stomach again. Repeat 10 to 20 times.

☐ Head circles. Drop head forward, chin on chest, shoulders relaxed. Slowly move head in large circle. Reverse direction. Do five to six times each side.

☐ Torso twist. Raise elbows to shoulder level. Slowly twist around as far right as possible, then reverse. Do 10 to 12 turns each way.

☐ Heel and toe lift. Lean forward, hands on knees. Lift both heels off floor, strongly contracting calf muscles. Lower heels, lift toes high toward shins. Do 10 to 15 complete movements.

Source: Doug MacLennon, The Fitness Institute, Willowdale, Ontario.

Real cause of flabby muscles

Lack of exercise—not aging. Muscle mass does decline between ages 30 and 70. But isotonic—strength-building—exercises can reverse the decline. Half an hour of isotonics two or three times a week can increase strength within two weeks and double it in 12 weeks—by changing the ratio of muscle to fat. Bonus: Increased bone density—helping prevent fractures caused by osteoporosis.

Source: William J. Evans, PhD, Director of Noll Laboratories of Human Performance Research, Pennsylvania State University, University Park. He is coauthor of *Biomarkers: The Ten Determinants of Aging You Can Control*, Simon & Schuster, Inc., New York.

Fitness vs. health— they are two different things

Exercise will make you physically fit— fitness being defined as the capacity to do physical activity comfortably. But, contrary to popular misconception, fitness and health are two separate things. Don't fool yourself into thinking that exercise is an all-benefit, no-risk proposition.

The main myths about exercise and coronary health:

☐ *Myth:* Exercise makes your heart healthier. Exercise *does* make your heart mechanically more efficient—it makes it possible to do more physical activity more comfortably. But your heart isn't healthier just because it's beating more slowly. This would be true only if each of us were allotted a certain number of heartbeats per lifetime. There is no such allotment. There are people in their nineties who have had fast heartbeats all their lives.

☐ *Myth:* Exercise improves your coronary circulation. Exercise does not stimulate your body to grow collateral blood vessels around the heart. The only thing that does this is the clogging of your original arteries. The original idea that exercise improved coronary circulation was based on an early-1950s study done with dogs under highly artificial conditions. The tests had nothing to do with anything resembling human life.

☐ *Myth:* Exercise reduces your coronary-risk factors. Most hypertension specialists would agree that the likelihood of reducing blood pressure to a significant degree via an exercise program is very small. A California study of trained distance runners found that they had the same range of blood pressure as nonrunners.

Common misconception: That lower heart rate means lower blood pressure. One has nothing to do with the other. So far, a low-fat, low-cholesterol diet is the only reliable way to lower cholesterol levels. It's been claimed that there are several types of cholesterol: HDL (high-density lipoprotein), the "good" cholesterol…and the "bad" ones, LDL (low-density lipoprotein) and triglycerides. The latest evidence suggests that even when your HDL goes up after exercise, it may be the wrong kind of HDL. Some studies show that HDL doesn't go up with exercise and that triglycerides and LDL don't go down. There's even an important study that shows the opposite actually occurs.

☐ *Myth:* Exercise makes you live longer. No one really knows why some people live longer than others. Innumerable factors contribute to it, including genes, marital status, number of social contacts, resistance to stress and educational level. There's never been an unflawed study showing that exercise prolongs life. An interesting book called *Living to Be 100* analyzed 1,200 centegenarians. Avoidance of stress was a common denominator.

☐ *Myth:* Exercise makes you feel better. Although many claims have been made that exercise alleviates depression and anxiety, the data are contradictory. Some studies claim benefits, others don't. Some studies comparing the benefits of exercise with those of meditation and relaxation have found no difference.

Source: Henry A. Solomon, MD, author of *The Exercise Myth*, Harcourt Brace Jovanovich, San Diego.

Shape-up cycle for special fitness needs

☐ Precor M8.2E/L. This heavy-duty recumbent cycle trainer has an ergonomically designed seat for a comfortable workout that is easy on the lower back. Also good for people with high blood pressure, seniors, pregnant women or anyone who is out of shape and is just beginning an exercise program. *Features:* Built-in heart-rate monitor, programmable computer, frictionless, magnetic-resistance mechanism, adjustable seat, padded handlebars and wheels for easy portability. *Dimensions:* 63" x 27" x 43".

Available from: Precor Inc., Box 3004, Bothell, Washington 98041. 800-477-3267, ext. 105.

Working up to rigorous exercise

It takes middle-aged men and women six months of regular exercise (fast walking, light jogging, weight training, etc.) to work up to rigorous exercise. Even then, they should move gradually into each workout. The steps to follow:

☐ Walk or jog in place for two or three minutes.

☐ Do ten minutes of stretching.

☐ When you move into your sport, take the first five minutes at a slow pace (a relaxed volley in tennis, for example) until you break into a light sweat.

☐ For the first few months, aim for 40% to 60% of your maximum heart rate. After six months, go for 70%. After nine months, shoot for 85%.*

☐ Take ten minutes to cool down with slow jogging and more stretching.

☐ Recognize when you've done too much (if it aches to take a step the next day).

*To calculate these goals, subtract your resting heart rate from your maximum rate—220 minus your age—and multiply by the desired percentage. Then add your resting rate to get your goal. Example: A 45-year-old man has a maximum heart rate of 175 and a resting rate of 60. To perform at 70% of maximum, he should reach a rate of 140.

Source: Everett L. Smith, director of the Bio-gerontology Laboratory, Department of Preventive Medicine, University of Wisconsin, Madison.

Health-club secrets

More than ten million Americans work out in 15,000 health clubs and spas across the country. They pay substantial amounts for the privilege—but things don't always turn out as planned.

Health-club members face three common pitfalls—insolvency, incompetence and injuries. *To protect yourself:*

☐ Check with consumer watchdog groups. Call your state or local consumer protection agency and the Better Business Bureau. Ask whether any negative reports have been filed against the club you have in mind. At least 36 states have enacted legislation designed specifically to protect the interests of health-club members.

For additional information, contact the Association of Physical Fitness Centers, 600 E. Jefferson St., Rockville, MD 20852 (301-424-7744). This trade group monitors member clubs to ensure that they meet minimum standards.

Caution: Never join a health club before it opens, no matter how sterling its prospects or how luxurious its facilities. Look for a club with at least three years of continuous operation—or a new branch of an established chain.

☐ Conduct a thorough inspection of the club. Go at peak time—at lunch, for example, or after work. If the place is wall-to-wall with people, there is probably a lack of equipment or instructors. If it's empty, something else is wrong. What else to look for: The pool, bathrooms, locker rooms and weight rooms all should be clean and well-maintained. Equipment should be in good repair. Faulty or worn equipment can cause injuries. As you walk around the club, find out what members like most about the club—and what they like least.

☐ Make sure the club is bonded. Some states require health clubs to post a minimum bond of $500,000. While that's hardly enough for a large club, it suggests at least some financial security on the part of the owner. Request evidence of bonding from the club or from the consumer protection agency.

☐ Insist upon qualified instructors. Though many fine trainers lack formal credentials, competent ones often will be certified by one of three sanctioning bodies…

☐ American Council on Exercise, 800-825-3636.

☐ American College of Sports Medicine, 317-637-9200.

☐ Aerobics and Fitness Association of America, 800-445-5950.

☐ Resist hard-sell tactics. An eager salesperson may offer you a special membership contract that expires "at midnight tonight." Don't take the bait—no matter how interested you are in the club. Instead, request a one-day trial membership. *Cost:* No more than a few dollars—perhaps free. If possible, try a sample session with a personal trainer.

☐ Negotiate your membership fee. Annual fees range from several hundred dollars for a family all the way up to $3,500 for an individual. Some clubs tack on a nonrefundable initiation fee of several hundred dollars. But no matter what the initial quote, membership fees and conditions are almost always negotiable.

☐ Insist on a short-term contract. Sad but true—90% of health-club members stop coming after three months. To avoid paying for workouts you never get, arrange to pay on a monthly basis …or sign up for a 90-day trial member-ship. *Important:* Don't sign on the spot. Take the contract home and review it with a friend or family member.

☐ Read the fine print. A typical contract is two pages. Each portion must be scrutinized not only for what it includes, but also for what it omits. Make sure you will have full access to all facilities that interest you…swimming pool,

squash courts, etc. Avoid contracts that limit the hours you can use the club—unless that fits your schedule.

If the contract does not include an "escape" clause, insert one. It should stipulate that you will get a prorated refund if you move or become disabled before the term is up. *Caution:* Watch out for the club's escape clause—a waiver of liability in case you are injured. Such clauses are illegal in many states, but cross it off and initial it before signing just to be sure. If possible, get the club to guarantee that it won't move.

Finally, make sure the contract covers everything that you've discussed with club employees. Never rely on verbal agreements.

If you have second thoughts about joining a health club, ask for a full refund. Most states mandate a three-day "cooling-off" period, during which consumers can back out of contracts and major purchases.

Source: Stephen L. Isaacs, JD, professor of public health at Columbia University and a practicing attorney in New York City. He is coauthor of The Consumer's Legal Guide to Today's Health Care: Your Medical Rights and How to Assert Them, *Houghton Mifflin, NY.*

Jogging and Achilles tendinitis

The repetitive impact of running often causes inflammation, degeneration and small tears in tendons. Orthopedists from Boston University Medical School suggest these preventive steps:

☐ Decrease weekly mileage.

☐ Cut down on uphill workouts.

☐ Prepare for running by stretching the tendons. With heels flat and knees straight, lean forward against a wall and hold for 30 seconds.

☐ Warm heels and tendons with a heating pad before running. After running, apply ice for 10–12 minutes.

☐ Elevate heels by placing small felt pads inside running shoes. They relieve tension on the Achilles tendon and contiguous structures.

☐ Monitor wear on outer sides of shoes. Tendons are stressed when shoe sides give no support.

☐ If these measures fail, consult a physician about immobilization and anti-inflammatory drugs.

Source: American Journal of Sports Medicine.

Easy exercises to strengthen your back

Strengthening the back and stomach muscles is the best protection against a back injury. If you have back trouble, consult your doctor before starting this, or any, exercise program.

☐ Flexed-knee sit-ups. Lie on your back, with knees bent and arms at your side. Sit up slowly by rolling forward, starting with the head.

☐ Bent-knee leg lifts. In the same position as the sit-ups, bring one knee as close as you can to your chest, while extending the other leg. Alternate the legs.

☐ Knee-chest leg lifts. Work from the bent-knee sit-up position, but put a small pillow under your head. Use your hands to bring both knees up to the chest, tighten the stomach muscles and hold that position for a count of ten.

☐ Back flattening. Lie on your back, flex the knees and put your arms above your head. Tighten your stomach and buttock muscles and press the lower back hard against the floor. Hold this position for a count of ten, relax and repeat.

☐ Don't overdo the exercises. Soreness is a sign to cut back.

☐ Never do these exercises with the legs straight.

Source: *American Journal of Nursing,* New York.

Indoor exercise machines

Indoor exercise machines can provide excellent exercise. Certain types of machines are best suited to particular muscle groups and fitness regimens. Here's a rundown of the main types:

☐ Multipurpose gyms. To develop major muscle groups, not cardiorespiratory fitness. *Check for:* Smoothly tracking weights. A sturdy, level bench. Padded levers. Steel pulleys. Coated cables.

☐ Stationary cycles. For cardiovascular fitness, injury rehabilitation and lower-body strength. *Check for:* A rigid frame. A heavy flywheel. A seat post that can be locked into position.

☐ Treadmills. For cardiovascular fitness through running or walking. *Check for:* Comfortable, secure footing.

☐ Rowing machines. For cardiovascular fitness, all major muscle groups and injury rehabilitation. *Check for:* A smoothly sliding seat. A track that allows full leg extension. Oars with equal resistance. A covered flywheel.

☐ Skiing machines. For cardiovascular fitness, major muscle development.

Source: *Changing Times,* Washington, DC.

Realities of exercise equipment

The sophisticated machinery that has turned old-fashioned gyms into today's fitness centers is designed to offer continuous resistance during each of the movement exercises you use it for.

☐ Using machines is a much faster, more efficient way to build muscle strength than using weights.

☐ Doing all the exercises for all the muscle groups on a regular basis does not make you perfectly fit.

Strength and fitness are not equivalent. Although muscle strength is a component of fitness, you also need flexibility and heart-lung capacity. Stretching exercises make you flexible, and aerobic exercises such as running and bike riding build up your heart muscle and your lung capacity.

☐ Strengthening exercises do not turn fat into muscle. It doesn't work that way. People who are overweight need to follow a calorie-restricted diet and do aerobic exercises, which trigger the body to use up fat. Working out on machines only builds up muscle under the fat layer. However, combining a weight-loss program with strengthening exercises can improve body tone as the weight comes off.

☐ The machines are safe if you learn the proper technique for using each machine, including proper breathing, before you are allowed on the equipment alone. On the Nautilus, for example, all the straps must be secured before you start. If one is broken or missing, don't use the machine. Poor form on the machines can lead to serious injuries. So can using the wrong weight settings.

☐ *Good rule of thumb:* Use a weight setting that lets you do 8–12 repetitions comfortably. If you must struggle to get beyond five, the setting is too heavy. If you complete ten without feeling any fatigue at all, it is too light. You will have to experiment with each machine to get the right setting. Then, from time to time, you can adjust the weights upward. But be cautious. Pushing yourself too hard not only invites injury, it also discourages you from sticking to the program on a regular basis.

How to pick a stationary bicycle

A good in-home stationary bicycle should be made from sturdy steel (not lightweight aluminum).

Check that it has:

☐ A comfortable, adjustable-height seat.

☐ Smoothly rotating pedals.

☐ A selector for several degrees of pedal speed and resistance (simulated "uphill" pedaling that makes your heart work harder).

☐ A heavyweight flywheel, which creates a smoother and more durable drive system.

Sophisticated electronic gadgets, such as "calories-burned" or "workload" meters are frills.

To choose the right cycle: Visit a large sporting-goods store and try a variety of models. The one that works you hard and still feels comfortable is right for you.

Source: Eastside Sportsmedicine Center, New York.

How to stick to an exercise program

☐ *First:* Find an exercise program you enjoy. If you enjoy it, the chances are you're going to want to stick with it.

☐ *Second:* Find something that fits your lifestyle. For example, something that doesn't require you to go to the mountains to hike, or require special equipment that you don't have or can't afford.

☐ *Third:* Make an appointment with yourself to exercise so there's always time that's scheduled in. Without that reminder, it's easy to run out of time.

☐ *Fourth:* Psych yourself up. You have to recognize the benefits of exercise. By doing something you like to do and getting into some consistency, if you're

on a program for a while, you'll start to feel the results. You'll feel better, have some pride when you finish your workout, maybe reduce some stress. And you may notice you've gotten a little stronger or lost some weight. You can use these things and really dwell on them to help reinforce your positive mental attitude for exercise.

☐ *Fifth:* Morning is a good time to exercise. It helps get your day started and you get it done and out of the way.

☐ *Sixth:* Exercise at least three times a week. And try to incorporate activity that exercises the cardiovascular system as well as strengthens your muscles. Things like taking a brisk walk for 20 or 30 minutes, cycling, playing recreational sports or exercise classes are all valuable workouts for the cardiovascular system.

☐ *Seventh:* Exercise in moderation. Some people, when they get on a program, get fanatical for a few weeks, then they stop. The key is consistency, not how intense you are per session. It's much more important to have a moderate session and do it consistently over a long period of time.

Source: Jake Steinfeld, personal trainer to Hollywood stars and author of *Don't Quit*, Warner Books, New York.

To get into shape for skiing

Being physically fit makes skiing more fun and helps prevent soreness and injuries. What to focus on:

☐ Muscle tone and flexibility. Stretching exercises keep your muscles long and pliable. They also warm muscles up for strenuous sports and help relax them afterward. Always stretch slowly. Hold the extended position for 20 to 30 seconds. Don't bounce.

☐ Do sit-ups with your knees bent to strengthen abdominal muscles (this can take stress off the back).

☐ Practice any active sport, from swimming to tennis, for three one-hour sessions a week.

☐ Jogging builds up the muscles of the lower torso and legs. Running downhill strengthens the front thigh muscles, essential to skiing. Running on uneven terrain promotes strong and flexible ankles. Biking builds strong legs and improves balance.

How to improve your tennis

Here are some secrets that help tennis pros on the court:

☐ Psych yourself up for a big point by triggering the adrenaline response. *Here's how:* Open your eyes wide and fix them on a nearby object. Breathe deeply and forcefully. Think of yourself as a powerful, aggressive individual. Exhort yourself with phrases like "Fight!" Try to raise goose bumps on your skin—they signal a high point.

☐ To switch from one type of playing surface to another, practice easing the transition. If you're moving to fast cement from slow clay, for example, practice charging the net before the switch. If it's the other way around, spend extra time on your groundstrokes.

To play well against a superior player:

☐ Suspend all expectations. Avoid thinking about the situation. Watch the ball, not the opponent.

☐ Play your game. Don't try to impress your opponent with difficult shots you normally never try.

☐ Hit the ball deep and down the middle. The more chances for your opponent to return your shot, the more chances for him to err.

☐ Concentrate on your serve. No matter how outgunned you may be, you can stay in the match if you hold your serve.

Source: *Tennis* and *World Tennis.*

How to play good singles tennis after 40

Older tennis players can win and avoid injuries by using the right strategies and techniques. Pancho Gonzales, the former champion who is now a leading Seniors player, advises playing a "thinking man's" game:

☐ When hitting, watch the ball right up to the point where it hits the strings of the racket.

☐ Aim for consistency rather than winners. Older players often hit too hard.

☐ For power and pace, shift your body weight forward on every stroke. At impact, the weight should be completely on the front foot.

☐ Anticipate your opponent. *Example:* If you hit a shot to your right, it will probably be returned to your left. Be ready to move left, but don't commit yourself until the ball has been hit.

☐ Get the racket back quickly and all the way before each shot.

☐ Try to swing the same way on every shot, both for consistency and for deception. Your opponent shouldn't be able to tell from the swing if the shot is hard or soft.

☐ Try to hit flat shots deep to the corners, rather than underspin slices, which provide more time for your opponent to reach the ball.

☐ Always change a losing game. Lob frequently against opponents who are dominating plays, especially if they have a winning net game. Against winning base-line players, hit drop shots to force them to come in and play the net.

☐ Save energy. Take plenty of time between points and before serving.

☐ Work on a consistent second serve. The resulting gain of confidence will lead to improvement of the first serve.

☐ When practicing the serve, spend time on the toss. Practice with a bucket placed where a perfect toss should fall.

☐ Beware of the topspin serve. Though effective, it is hard on the back muscles.

☐ Return serves as early as possible, and keep them low.

☐ Adopt sound health and conditioning practices.

☐ Do some weekly running and exercises. Squeeze an old tennis ball a few minutes a day to build up arm muscles, and jump rope to improve footwork.

☐ Rest before and after playing.

☐ Use a warmup jacket to speed the loosening of the muscles before play.

☐ During play, run with bent knees to reduce shock to knees.

☐ After play, apply lotion to the palm of your racket hand to keep it from scaling and blistering.

☐ Use the right equipment for your changed style of play. Choose a flexible wood racket, which jars the arm less than a metal racket.

☐ Try a lighter-weight racket more loosely strung.

Source: Pancho Gonzales, author of *Tennis Begins at Forty,* Dial Press, New York.

How to play better tennis doubles after 40

Here are some more hints from Pancho Gonzales:

☐ Agree on strategy and signals with your partner before playing. *Most important signal:* Net players must let their partners know when they plan to cross over to intercept the return of a serve. (A clenched fist behind the back is often used.) During this move and all other moves, remember you both should be in motion…one to make the shot and the other to cover the exposed part of the court.

☐ Agree that the weaker player should take the forehand court. This player should be assigned to serve when the wind and sun are behind the server.

☐ Make sure the weaker player plays closer to the net. *Reason:* It is easier to volley in this position.

☐ Keep in mind that one player normally concentrates on setting up shots. This person hits the ball low to force the opponents at the net to hit up on the ball.

☐ The second player has the job of making the put-aways.

Source: Pancho Gonzales, author of *Tennis Begins at Forty,* Dial Press, New York.

Martial arts schools teach more than martial arts

The martial arts offer more than a simple exercise program. They build both physical and mental strengths. Students learn the skills to extricate themselves from dangerous situations and, if necessary, to defend themselves.

Styles and systems

☐ Tai Chi Chuan uses slow, graceful movements.

☐ Karate employs powerful, focused techniques.

☐ Judo and Aikido make use of joint locks and throws.

Finding the right school

☐ To get a list of schools, talk with friends and check out the ads in your local *Yellow Pages.*

☐ Visit the schools to observe a few classes before you sign up.

☐ Clarify your goals before you make a choice—do you want mainly a physical fitness and self-defense program, or are you interested in the mental/spiritual aspects?

What to consider

☐ A balanced approach to both the mental aspects (such as concentration and focus) and the physical aspects of the particular martial art.

☐ The temper of the fighting classes, if the school has them. Make certain that care is taken to minimize injuries. Fighting is a part of most martial arts, and you should be comfortable with the school's fighting program.

☐ Thoughtful answers to your questions. If the school is evasive in its explanations, it is probably not a good bet.

☐ Instructors create the training environment of the school. Make certain they suit you. Some people like a "marine sergeant," while others might prefer a more temperate teacher.

☐ Students should be brought into the regimen slowly in a progressive process. Only as a student gets used to one style should new techniques be added to his repertory.

☐ Make sure the school accommodates different levels of athletic ability and different ages. Inflexible standards may only frustrate you.

☐ Attitudes of students. Do they encourage and help each other? Or are they bullying? The attitude of the instructor is passed on to his students.

☐ Facilities. Is there room to practice in between classes? Does the school have exercise equipment such as weights and jump ropes? Are the locker rooms big enough for the number of students? Are there showers?

☐ Schedule. If you will have a hard time getting to the workouts, you probably won't go often enough.

Source: Ken Glickman, self-defense expert and coordinator, Educational Services, Greenwich Institute For American Education, Greenwich, CT.

How to get back in shape after 40

Americans over 40 are not very physically fit. Recent Gallup polls indicate that people are more interested in exercise than ever before…and that about 40% of adults exercise aerobically three times a week. I'd say the real number is probably closer to 15%–20% —and that's too few people exercising regularly.

The physiological benefits of regular exercise—weight loss, improved HDL (good) cholesterol, lower blood pressure, decreased coronary risk, etc.—are well-known. Many people, however, are not aware of the psychological benefits of exercise. Since 1977, we've done psychological testing of all patients coming to the Cooper Aerobics Center. We've found that those who are physically fit are less depressed, have a better self-image and a more positive attitude toward life. These people are just plain happier than their non-exercising counterparts.

Yet despite all the good reasons to do aerobic exercise, many people over 40 believe it's too tough, too risky or too late to start.

Nothing could be further from the truth. Surprisingly, even a modest increase in your present activity level can make a world of difference in your health and the overall quality of your life.

Whether you're beginning a fitness program for the first time or want to get back into shape, there are some important steps to follow—and pitfalls to avoid…

☐ Get your doctor's okay. Make sure your doctor endorses your plan. Ideally, you should first be given both a resting and a stress cardiogram. These tests should be repeated every three years or as often as your doctor recommends.

☐ Go slow. Don't rush into exercise. It may have taken you 20 years to get out of shape, and if you try to get back into shape in 20 days, it can be dangerous …and potentially fatal.

☐ Aim for just 30 minutes of sustained activity, three times a week. Even an exercise program that modest will greatly enhance your level of health and fitness.

The program

I've created a six-week starter program, which is ideal for men and women over 40. I have found that even people with advanced heart disease or who have had bypass surgery can follow this routine with medical supervision.

☐ Weeks 1 to 3: Walk for 15 minutes. Don't worry about how far you get, even if it's just a couple of blocks. It's best to do this the first thing in the morning— exercise tends to be most consistent when it's done before breakfast. If that's not feasible, take a brisk walk an hour or two after dinner with your spouse, a friend or your dog. Do this three times a week, more if possible.

☐ Week 4: Walk for five more minutes, totaling 20 minutes each time.

☐ Week 5: Walk for 25 minutes each time.

☐ Week 6: Walk for 30 minutes each time. Alternatively, instead of walking for longer and longer periods, you may find it more challenging—and fun—to work on decreasing the time it takes you to cover two miles. Take it slow—at first it might require 45 minutes to complete the two miles. Gradually decrease your time to 30 minutes, three times a week, over a six-week period.

Caution: Walk, don't run or jog during this phase.

If, after the end of the six weeks, you don't develop any symptoms or problems—chest pains, musculo-skeletal problems—you may then want to move on to a more vigorous program of slow jogging. Aim to reduce the time it takes you to cover two miles from 30 minutes to 20 minutes. Again, do it gradually, over a six-week period.

Caution: Make sure you get your doctor's okay before increasing the intensity of your exercise program.

Walking and slow jogging are the easiest and least expensive exercises. They can be done anywhere.

But you may prefer to try something else, and there are three activities—cross-country skiing, swimming and cycling— that will produce equal, or even better, aerobic benefits.

The more varied your exercise program, the more likely you'll stick with it. It takes much more discipline to maintain the same routine month after month, year after year.

Exercise is important, but it's no panacea. I endorse a program of total wellness, including a low-fat/low-calorie diet, the elimination of smoking and stress management.

If you do just 30 minutes of sustained activity three times a week, you'll substantially reduce most major causes of death—heart attack, stroke, diabetes and even cancer. What's more, you'll look better, feel better and dramatically improve the quality of your life.

Source: Leading fitness and health expert Kenneth H. Cooper, MD, director, Cooper Aerobics Center in Dallas.

Exercises that can harm you

The most important benefit of exercise is that, properly done, it increases longevity. But exercises that promote a single aspect of the body, such as form, stamina, coordination, speed or strength, generally have a negative impact. Especially dangerous are:

☐ Muscle-building exercises. They can harm joints and connective tissues. Weight lifters are not known for longevity.

☐ Skill-producing activities. Ballet, handball and squash require arduous training and stop-start patterns. Both are negatives for long life.

☐ Marathon sports. Jogging, swimming, cycling and strenuous walking can work the body to the point of exhaustion. This is dangerous because stress and injury occur more easily during body fatigue.

☐ Speed-oriented activities. Those that require lots of oxygen, such as sprinting or speed swimming, can be fatal, especially for those who have not trained extensively for them.

Source: Dan Georgakas, author of *The Methuselah Factors: The Secrets of the World's Longest-Lived Peoples,* Simon & Schuster, New York.

Regular exercise makes a difference

Exercise helps provide the energy necessary for personal wellness…and even moderate levels of exertion bolster the immune system. In fact, new studies show that a small increase in physical activity—climbing five flights of stairs instead of taking the elevator, for example—lowers your risk of heart disease, high blood pressure, diabetes, osteoporosis, obesity, breast cancer and colon cancer.

Exercise also fights the destructive thought patterns associated with depression, anxiety, stress, worry, panic and anger. These negative patterns contribute significantly to our physiological illnesses.

Each day of your wellness week, do some form of exercise for at least 20 minutes. Even a brisk walk will do.

Maximum weight

Bench pressing builds muscles on the negative phase of the exercise—that is when the weight is being returned to the starting position. *For maximum benefit:* Concentrate on lowering the bar to your chest slowly and steadily. *Careful:* Don't drop the weight or bounce it off your chest.

Source: Cardell Hairrill, personal trainer, Wichita Falls, TX.

Exercise tips

☐ Aerobic exercise can lower mildly high blood pressure to normal within two months.

Source: Research by John E. Martin, a behavioral psychologist with the Veterans Administration Medical Center, Jackson, MS.

☐ For post-workout showers, keep the water at about body temperature. A hot shower is relaxing, but it slows circulation and leaves you sluggish. A cold shower, although bracing, can strain the heart.

Source: John Cantwell, MD, a team physician for the Atlanta Braves in *Esquire.*

☐ After a heavy workout, drink two to four glasses of water to replace lost fluids. Follow the water with a chaser of orange, apricot, pineapple or grapefruit juice for electrolytes, potassium and added energy. If you really want a beer, drink it after a few glasses of water. Otherwise the alcohol can interrupt the release of hormones that hold water in the body. This leads to excessive urination, which can leave your body more dehydrated.

Source: *Women's Sports and Fitness.*

☐ Stationary bicycling burns off almost as many calories per hour as running. *Example:* 700 calories per hour for a 150-pound runner at an eight-minute-mile rate vs. 655 calories per hour for a stationary cyclist pedaling 15 miles per hour.

Source: *Maximum Personal Energy* by Charles Kuntzleman, quoted in *The Runner.*

Body building after 40

Weight training offers just as much body building, fitness and sense of well-being to the middle aged as it does to the young. It will change the shape of your body faster than any other sport, with visible results in just six to eight weeks.

Common myths

☐ "I can't build muscle at my age." You can still "bulk up," although not as quickly.

☐ "I'll hurt myself." Exercising incorrectly can lead to physical injury at any age. At midlife you do need to think more about your back, knees and shoulders. But if you start out slowly and learn the proper techniques, weight lifting will actually help cure orthopedic problems. (It is often used for rehabilitation.)

☐ "The muscle that I build will turn to fat if I stop training." Muscle doesn't turn to fat. When you stop training you expend less energy and have to adjust your diet to take in fewer calories.

Equipment

☐ Free weights (barbells and dumb-bells). These give the quickest results but they take some time to learn properly.

☐ Universal gyms. Weights and pulleys are arranged around a single large machine in "stations." Each station works a different set of muscles.

☐ Nautilus machines. These operate with a unique mechanical action geared to the natural strength curve of each working muscle group. Each machine works a single muscle group.

The best weight-training programs include all three types of apparatus.

Source: Bill Reynolds, editor-in-chief of *Muscle and Fitness* magazine.

Unexpected health-club hazard

Number and motility of sperm cells are decreased for up to six weeks after a dip in a hot tub.

☐ *Shocking:* Only one hour of soaking in water 102.4 degrees or hotter (most health clubs keep tubs at 104 degrees) causes immediate harm to sperm.

☐ *Fertility low point:* Four weeks after bath, when sperm that were immature upon bathing mature.

☐ *Remedy:* Patience…sperm life span is 75 days, so all damaged sperm are replaced within that time frame.

Source: Dr. Richard Paulson of the University of Southern California School of Medicine.

Winter sports pointers

☐ Ice skating is an underrated exercise that works all your muscles. It's also easy to learn…most people can glide around the rink after three or four sessions.

☐ *Skier's hazard:* Sunburned corneas, caused by the sun's ultraviolet rays. (Snow reflects 85% of those rays, compared with 10% from water and 5% from grass.) *Recommended:* Goggles or wraparound glasses made of impact-resistant polycarbonate.

Source: Dr. Paul Vinger, a Boston ophthalmologist and eye/medical consultant to the US Olympic Committee, in *Executive Fitness Newsletter.*

Bicycle seat danger

Bicycle seats can cause numbness, temporary impotence or even a painful permanent erection (priapism) in men who ride often or for long distances. *Reason:* The traditional narrow, one-piece design puts too much pressure on the internal erectile chambers of the penis. *Self-defense:* Pedal as smoothly as possible to avoid bouncing…or fit your bike with a newer split seat that has one side to support the right buttock and another to support the left. Stationary exercise bicycles do not seem to pose a threat.

Source: E. Douglas Whitehead, MD, director, Association for Male Sexual Dysfunction, New York.

The healthy gourmet

☐ Cut fat in your favorite recipes by 25% to 50%. *Example:* If the recipe suggests one cup of oil, try ¾ cup. If that works, try ⅔ cup the next time. In many casseroles and soups try eliminating butter or margarine completely.

☐ Instead of sautéing vegetables in oil or butter, add several tablespoonfuls of water or broth and steam them in a covered pot.

☐ Compensate for lost fat flavor by adding spices and herbs.

☐ Use skim or low-fat milk instead of whole milk…evaporated skim milk instead of cream.

☐ In sauces that call for cheese, stick to grated Parmesan or Romano (about 25 calories per tablespoonful).

☐ Rather than starting sauces with a fatty "roux," add cold milk or fruit juice to the flour or cornstarch.

☐ Substitute veal, skinless poultry or flank or round steak for fat-marbled cuts of beef.

☐ Slice meats thinly and add more vegetables to the meal.

Source: *Tufts University Diet & Nutrition Letter*, New York.

How to reduce the fat in your food

☐ Sauté vegetables in a few tablespoonfuls of soup stock rather than in fat.

☐ Sauté and fry foods less often. Steam, broil, bake and poach instead.

☐ For salads and cooking, use corn, safflower or olive oil—sparingly.

☐ Substitute egg whites or tofu for egg yolks.

☐ Use low-fat yogurt instead of sour cream or mayonnaise.

☐ Try low-fat cheeses such as part-skim mozzarella in recipes.

☐ Use ground turkey or crumbled tofu in place of ground beef.

☐ Thicken cream-style corn with a mashed potato or uncooked oatmeal.

☐ Replace nut butters with bean spread for sandwiches and snack dips.

Source: *Medical Self-Care*, Inverness, CA.

To protect your immune system

Your immune system is made up of white blood cells. To give optimal protection, these cells should be working 24 hours a day. They're directly affected by the quality of food you eat,* the way you behave and the nature of your thoughts.

Dangers to the immune system:

☐ Excessive sugar.

☐ Inadequate protein.

☐ Inadequate zinc, iron or manganese.

☐ Inadequate Vitamin C, Vitamin E, Vitamin B_6, folic acid or beta-carotene.

☐ Diet and psychology are intimately related. Be especially cautious during times of stress, bereavement, sorrow and trauma. They often translate into suppression of the immune function.

☐ Monitor magnesium intake. Most people don't get enough magnesium in their diets. And a magnesium deficiency can create anxiety symptoms. The minimum amount necessary is usually 300 to 500 milligrams a day. Under conditions of high stress, you would need more magnesium (since it's utilized very rapidly at such times). *Best sources:* Sea vegetables, whole grains, nuts, blackstrap molasses and green leafy vegetables.

☐ Exercise enhances the function of your immune system by reducing stress.

☐ Examine your expectations about health. Do you expect, and accept, a couple of bouts with colds or flu each year? Instead, focus on strengthening your immune system. Sickness a couple of times a year is inevitable only if your immune system has been compromised.

*The amount of nutrients you need is best determined on an individual basis. To find out how much you need, consult a physician who specializes in disease prevention. *Also useful: Nutrition Against Disease* by Dr. Roger Williams, Bantam Books, New York.

Source: Jeffrey Bland, chief executive officer, Health Community International, Inc., Gig Harbor, WA.

All calories aren't equal

Dieters myth: A calorie is a calorie is a calorie. *Reality:* Fat calories are more fattening than carbohydrate calories. A single fat calorie has a greater chance of being converted into body fat than a single carbohydrate calorie.

☐ *Reason:* The body burns up 25 of every 100 carbohydrate calories converting them into fat—net gain, 75 calories. But it burns up only 3 calories of every 100 fat calories—net gain, 97 calories.

Source: Dr. Jean-Pierre Flatt, University of Massachusetts Medical School.

Dr. Dean Ornish clears up the confusion over cholesterol

Despite all that's been said and written about cholesterol in recent years, many Americans remain understandably confused on the topic. While most of us know that too much cholesterol in the bloodstream can cause heart disease, many people remain unclear on certain subtle but very important issues…

What's a healthy cholesterol level? For years, the American Heart Association and the National Institutes of Health have recommended an optimal total serum cholesterol level of less than 200 milligrams per deciliter.

But we now know that roughly one-third of all heart attacks occur in individuals with cholesterol readings between 150 and 200. In fact, only when cholesterol falls to 150 or lower does heart disease cease to be a meaningful risk.

Unfortunate: The average American has a cholesterol level around 220…and the average American develops heart disease.

What about "good" and "bad" cholesterol? Total serum cholesterol is made up of two different compounds—low-density lipoprotein (LDL) cholesterol …and high-density lipoprotein (HDL) cholesterol.

☐ LDL (bad) cholesterol forms fatty plaques inside your coronary arteries, which can lead to heart attack.

☐ HDL (good) cholesterol is what the body uses to remove excess LDL from the bloodstream.

Doctors sometimes use the ratio of total cholesterol to HDL as another means of gauging heart-disease risk.

Example: Someone with a total cholesterol count of 200 and an HDL level of 50 has a ratio of 200/50 or 4:1. In general, a ratio of 3.5 (200/57 is 3.5:1) or lower puts you at minimal risk for heart disease. The lower the ratio, the lower the risk—at least for people eating a traditional fatty, cholesterol-rich diet.

Exception: Vegetarians and others on a very low-fat, low-cholesterol diet with less than 10% fat and virtually no cholesterol. Because they consume less fat and cholesterol and thus have less LDL in their blood, their bodies don't need to make as much HDL. Consequently, they may have high ratios yet they have a reduced risk of heart disease.

What causes high cholesterol? The single biggest factor is simply eating too much saturated fat and cholesterol. In fact, in the traditional American diet, roughly 40% of calories come from fat… and foods rich in fat are often rich in cholesterol. In countries where people eat much less cholesterol and less fat and where cholesterol averages around 130, heart disease is very rare.

Eating too much fat causes not only heart disease, but also has been linked with cancers of the breast, prostate and colon, as well as stroke, diabetes, osteoporosis and, of course, obesity.

There is a genetic variability in how efficiently or inefficiently your body can metabolize, or get rid of, dietary saturated fat and cholesterol. On one end of the spectrum, some people are so efficient that they can eat almost anything and not get heart disease. On the other end of the spectrum are people who may get heart disease no matter what they eat. Ninety-five percent of people are somewhere in the middle. If your cholesterol level is less than 150, then either you're not eating very much fat and cholesterol or your body is very efficient at getting rid of it. Either way, your risk is low.

If it's above 150, begin by moderately reducing the amount of fat and cholesterol in your diet. If that's enough to bring it down below 150, that may be all you need to do, at least as far as your heart is concerned. If not, then continue to reduce the fat and cholesterol in your diet until your cholesterol stays below 150…or you are following a low-fat vegetarian reversal diet.

Which foods contain cholesterol? All foods derived from animals, including meats, poultry, fish and dairy products. Meat is also high in iron, which oxidizes cholesterol into a form that more quickly clogs arteries. Skim milk has almost no fat and virtually no cholesterol. "Low-fat" milk is not really very low in fat. Foods derived solely from plants contain no cholesterol.

Caution: Some plant foods, including avocados, nuts, seeds and oils, are rich in saturated fat.

Just because a food is "cholesterol-free" doesn't mean it's good for your heart. All oils are 100% fat, and all oils contain at least some saturated fat, which your liver converts into cholesterol.

How often should I have my cholesterol checked? About once every two years, starting as early as age two. *To insure a reliable reading:* Find a testing lab certified by the Lipid Research Clinics. Use the same laboratory each time. Be sure to fast* for at least 12 hours prior to your test.

How can I get my cholesterol under control? Exercise—it raises HDL cholesterol.

Stress raises LDL cholesterol, as does eating a high-fat, cholesterol-rich diet.

So the best way to raise HDL and lower LDL is to get regular exercise, avoid smoking, practice meditation or other stress-management techniques and eat a healthful diet.

If you have heart disease: Eliminate all animal products except egg whites and nonfat dairy products…and all high-fat vegetable products, including oils, nuts, seeds, avocados, chocolate and other cocoa products, olives and coconut. In most cases this "reversal" diet not only keeps heart disease from progressing, but also reverses its course.

Eat more vegetables, fish and skinless chicken. Use skim milk instead of whole milk. Use as little cooking oil as possible. Avoid oil-based salad dressing. If after eight weeks your cholesterol remains high, go on the "reversal" diet.

What about cholesterol-lowering drugs? I prescribe cholesterol-lowering drugs for people with heart disease who make only moderate changes in diet and lifestyle. Why? Several studies have shown that people with heart disease who only follow the American Heart Association guidelines tend to show worsening of their disease. People who follow the

*Drinking water is OK.

reversal diet—or who take cholesterol-lowering drugs—often can stop or reverse heart disease. Diet is preferable, because you avoid the high costs and side effects (both known and unknown) of drugs.

Source: Dean Ornish, MD, assistant clinical professor of medicine and an attending physician at the School of Medicine, University of California, San Francisco, and at California Pacific Medical Center. He is the author of *Dr. Dean Ornish's Program for Reversing Heart Disease,* Ballantine Books, 201 E. 50 St., New York 10022.

How to read nutrition labels

Cutting down on cholesterol, sugar and salt requires a close reading of nutritional labels.

A simplified guide to understanding the fine print:

☐ Ingredients. They are listed in descending order, according to their weight.

☐ Sugar. Whether it's called sugar, dextrose, sucrose, corn sweetener, corn syrup, invert sugar, honey or molasses, the food has little nutritive value if it's among the first three ingredients. When listed as a minor ingredient, a combination of two or more sugars may mean a hefty sugar count.

☐ Cholesterol. Avoid coconut and palm oil. They are more saturated than animal fats. Nonspecified vegetable oils frequently mean palm or coconut. When purchasing margarine, choose the brand with liquid vegetable oil as the primary ingredient. It contains less saturated fat.

☐ Salt. While sodium levels are not shown on many ingredient lists, look for brands that list sodium by milligrams. *Rule of thumb:* No one should consume much over 4,000 milligrams of sodium daily. Those on restricted diets should have considerably less than that amount.

Cholesterol basics

Results of an exhaustive, ten-year National Heart, Lung and Blood Institute study have put to rest any doubts about the links between high blood cholesterol levels and heart disease.

For most Americans, careful diet can keep cholesterol in control, particularly the dangerous low-density lipoprotein (LDL) cholesterol. *Keys:* Cut cholesterol consumption to 300 milligrams or less per day. Keep the percentage of calories from fats to 30% or less of the daily intake. Substitute polyunsaturated fats for saturated fats in the diet.*

□ No foods that come from plant sources contain cholesterol.

□ The most concentrated sources of edible cholesterol are egg yolks (one yolk from a large egg has 252 mg) and organ meats (three ounces of calf's liver has 372 mg).

Bacon (2 slices)	15
Beef (3 oz. lean)	77
Beef kidney (3 oz.)	315
Butter (1 tbsp.)	35
Cheese (1 oz. cheddar)	30
Chicken (3 oz. light meat, no skin)	65
Cottage cheese (½ cup 4% fat)	24
Cottage cheese (½ cup 1% fat)	12
Cream (1 tbsp. heavy)	21
Flounder (3 oz.)	69
Haddock (3 oz.)	42
Ice cream (½ cup)	27
Milk (1 cup skim)	5
Milk (1 cup whole)	34
Pork (3 oz. lean)	75
Salmon (4 oz. canned)	40
Sardines (3 oz.)	119
Turkey (3 oz. light meat, no skin)	65
Yogurt (1 cup low-fat)	17

While many fats have no cholesterol content *per se*, certain types of fats actually raise the cholesterol levels in the blood even if the rest of the diet contains very little cholesterol.

□ Saturated fats. You can recognize these by their tendency to harden at room temperature. They contribute most to a buildup of LDL cholesterol. They include meat fats, butter, chicken fat, coconut and palm oils, vegetable shortening and even some margarines (read the label).

□ Monounsaturated fats. These play a more neutral role in cholesterol chemistry, although, like all fats, they should be eaten in moderation. These are the fats found in avocados, cashews, olives and olive oil, peanuts and peanut oil.

□ Polyunsaturated fats. When kept to a limited part of the total diet, these actually lower the amount of LDL cholesterol in the blood. *Good fats:* Corn oil, cottonseed oil, safflower oil, soybean oil, sunflower oil and fats from nuts such as almonds, pecans and walnuts.

□ If you are overweight, reducing will lower your cholesterol level.

□ Certain fiber foods such as carrots, apples, oats and soybeans also help reduce cholesterol.

*Recommendations of the American Heart Association.

□ Aerobic exercise can cut down the percentage of LDL cholesterol in the blood.

The right middle-age diet

It's not too late to change the eating habits of a lifetime when you reach middle age. As a matter of fact, it's probably a necessity because of the changes the body is going through at that time. *Most obvious change:* Slowing of the metabolic rate. Individuals who don't reduce their caloric intake after age 45 commonly gain ten pounds a year, regardless of the amount of exercise they do. It takes 12 hours of tennis to burn off 3,500 calories, roughly equivalent to one pound.

□ Steak is highly caloric, and its fat content has been linked to coronary disease and colon cancer, two potentially fatal disorders that plague older people. Chicken and fish are more healthful alternative sources of proteins.

□ Because bones begin to grow progressively brittle after age 30, the body needs more calcium. But this important mineral can be absorbed effectively only by reducing the intake of protein (from meats) and phosphorous (from carbonated soft drinks). To prevent the brittle-bone problem, a calcium supplement with magnesium once a day is recommended by most nutritionists.

□ Because many older people secrete less hydrochloric acid, they have difficulty absorbing iron and, therefore, are more vulnerable to pernicious anemia. The best source of iron is meat, especially liver. But to avoid eating too much meat, you should turn to iron-fortified foods, especially cereals. Absorption of iron is helped by intakes of vitamin C, which is abundant in citrus fruits, broccoli, kale, red peppers and Brussels sprouts. For some older people, taking an iron supplement may be necessary.

□ The bodies of older people often have trouble absorbing vitamin B_{12}, which can actually be destroyed in the body by large doses of vitamin C. B_{12} deficiency can lead to anemia, particularly among vegetarians, because the vitamin is found exclusively in animal products (especially liver) and shellfish. Multivitamin supplements may be needed to insure that you are getting the right amount of each vitamin.

☐ Digestive problems associated with aging make fiber especially important to persons over 45. *Sources:* Whole grains, fruits, vegetables.

☐ Although all the evidence is not yet in, most nutritionists advise against taking vitamin megadoses. In the case of vitamins A and D, megadoses are highly dangerous. *Exception:* Vitamin E, large doses of which may help with colon cancer and the painful blood-vessel spasms in the legs that older people often experience. Even with this vitamin, consult a physician before considering taking megadoses.

Source: Dr. Brian Morgan, Institute of Human Nutrition, Columbia University College of Physicians & Surgeons.

Better bone-loss prevention

Although it's well-known that hormone therapy prevents loss of bone mass following menopause, only one in ten women chooses this therapy. *Reasons:* Undesirable side effects such as menstrual bleeding…unanswered questions about hormone therapy's relationship to cancer. *Safer alternative:* Calcium supplements. Studies show that women who took 1,700 mg of calcium along with 400 IU of vitamin D experienced a significant slowing in skeletal bone loss. However, those who took calcium, vitamin D and hormone replacement lost even less bone mass.

Source: John F. Aloia, MD, chairman, department of medicine, Winthrop–University Hospital, Mineola, NY.

How to get along without cream and mayonnaise

Fat is the enemy of both the heart and the waistline. Learn to substitute yogurt and other low-fat milk products. They are tasty as well as healthy.

Yogurt

☐ Thicken commercial yogurt. Line a sieve with a paper coffee filter and place it over a bowl. Pour in the yogurt and let it drain until it is the consistency you want…that of light, heavy or sour cream.

☐ Use the drained yogurt as a base for any dip that originally called for sour cream. (If the yogurt seems too thick, beat a little of the drained whey back into it.)

☐ In cooking or baking, replace each cup of cream or sour cream with ¾ cup of drained yogurt mixed with 1 table-spoonful of cornstarch. The yogurt should be at room temperature.

☐ In dishes such as beef Stroganoff, where the yogurt-cornstarch mixture replaces sour cream, fold it gently into the beef at the last minute…and let it just heat through.

Basic recipes

☐ Light mayonnaise: Mix ⅓ cup thickened yogurt into ⅔ cup mayonnaise.

☐ Light salad dressing: Mix ⅔ cup slightly thickened yogurt into ⅓ cup mayonnaise.

☐ Mock sour cream dressing:* Mix 1 cup drained low-fat yogurt with 2 table-spoonfuls of wine vinegar. Add a dash of sugar (or substitute), a bit of garlic powder and ¼ cup vegetable oil. Mix and chill.

Other good substitutions

☐ Replace the cream in cream soups with buttermilk, which is satisfyingly rich, yet low in calories. To eliminate any hint of buttermilk's slightly acidic taste, add a liberal amount of mild curry powder.

☐ Mix 1 cup skim milk with ½ cup dry skim milk. Add to soup to thicken it. This works with all cream soups, including vichyssoise.

*The Low-Cholesterol Food Processor Cookbook by Suzanne S. Jones, Doubleday, Garden City, NY.

Just when you thought it was safe to eat salt…

The vast majority of foods sold in stores are laden with salt. Since we've eaten these foods for most of our lives, we're conditioned to expect the taste of heavily salted foods.

To cut down on salt intake:

☐ Reduce salt gradually. When people are abruptly placed on a very low-sodium diet, they develop cravings for salt that cause them to revert to their former eating habits. But a gradual reduction of salt will change your taste for salt…so much so that food salted to its previous level will taste unpleasant. *Time:* Allow up to three months to adjust to a salt-free diet.

☐ Keep daily records of the amount of sodium you eat. This is now relatively easy because federal law requires most grocery-store foods to be labeled for sodium content. A pocket calculator is sometimes useful as you shop, but don't think you'll have to keep count for the rest of your life. After a couple of months, separating high from low-sodium foods will be almost automatic.

☐ Substitute other flavor enhancers, especially herbs and spices.

☐ If you have children, start now to condition their taste by not feeding them salty foods. For the first time, low-sodium baby food is now on the market.

Source: Dr. Cleaves M. Bennett, clinical professor, University of California at Los Angeles, and author of Control Your High Blood Pressure Without Drugs, Doubleday, New York.

Tasty, low-salt, low-fat cooking

If your doctor puts you on a no-salt, modified fat, cholesterol and sugar diet, with limited alcohol consumption, you might feel as though you're in a gastronomic straitjacket. However, the benefits are enormous—no more edema, a reduction in blood pressure, considerable weight loss and a feeling of well-being—and you can increase your food intake without increasing your weight.

Basics of the diet

Do use:

☐ Low-sodium cheeses.

☐ Seltzer.

☐ Trimmed meat.

☐ Stews and pan drippings skimmed of all fat.

☐ Fish, poultry without skin, veal and lamb.

Don't use:

☐ Eggs, except those used in food preparation.

☐ Sugar. Drinks made with sweet liqueurs. Soft drinks.

☐ Canned or packaged foods.

☐ Sodas with high salt content.

☐ Rich and/or salty products—bacon, gravies, shellfish, organ meats, most desserts except fruit and fruit ices.

Tricks to fool the taste

☐ The sweet-and-sour principle. A touch (sometimes as little as half a teaspoonful) of sugar and a dash of vinegar can add the sweet-and-sour flavor needed to fool the palate.

☐ Garlic. Essential in salad dressings and tomato sauces. Use it with rosemary to transform broiled chicken, broiled fish or roast lamb.

☐ Fine or coarse black pepper. When broiling and roasting meats and chicken, use as much as a tablespoonful for a welcome flavor. Use a moderate amount in soups, stews and casseroles (the pungent nature of pepper will not diminish in these as it will with broiling and roasting).

☐ Crushed hot red pepper flakes. A good flavor distraction or flavor addition. Not for every palate.

☐ Curry powder. Use judiciously and without a large number of other spices. Combine it only with a bay leaf, green pepper, garlic or black pepper. Add smaller amounts for rice, more for poultry or meat.

☐ Chili powder. Similar to curry, but you might want to add more cumin, oregano or garlic. Also try paprika, ground coriander, ground hot chilis. They're good with almost any dish made with tomatoes.

☐ Homemade hot-mustard paste. Dry mustard and water does wonders for salad dressing and grilled foods.

☐ Freshly grated horseradish. Goes well with fish or plain yogurt.

☐ Bottled green peppercorns. A welcome touch for bland foods.

☐ Plain boiled or steamed rice, cold yogurt relish, chutneys and other sweet relishes are a good foil for spicy dishes.

Cooking techniques

☐ Charcoal broiling helps compensate for lack of salt.

☐ Steaming is preferable for fish and better than boiling for vegetables.

☐ No-salt soups are difficult to make palatable. *Solution:* A stockpot going on the back of the stove, to which you add bones, cooking liquid, vegetables. The more concentrated the broth, the greater the depth of flavor. Use only the freshest, ripest vegetables.

Source: Craig Claiborne, food critic.

"Good" foods that can be bad for you

☐ Blood-sugar–sensitive types who experience a temporary lift from sugar followed by fatigue should be cautious about fruit juice intake. Six ounces of apple juice contain the equivalent of more than five teaspoonfuls of sugar—

40% more sugar than a chocolate bar. *Recommended:* Eat a whole apple or orange instead of drinking juice. The fiber dilutes the sugar impact. *Alternative:* Eat cheese, nuts or other protein with juice.

☐ Nondairy cream substitutes, often used by those on low-fat diets, usually contain coconut oil, which has a higher fat content than most dairy products.

☐ Decaffeinated coffee can lead to significant stomach acid secretion, causing heartburn and indigestion in many persons. Caffeine was assumed to be the culprit. A new study shows that decaffeinated coffee is even worse. The effect is seen in doses as small as a half cup of decaffeinated coffee. People experiencing ulcer symptoms, heartburn and dyspepsia should avoid decaffeinated as well as regular coffee.

☐ Most commercial products billed as alternatives to salt are based on potassium chloride. *Problem:* Although potassium chloride does enhance flavor, it leaves a slightly bitter or metallic taste. And excessive potassium may be as bad for your health as too much salt. *Alternatives to the alternatives:* Mrs. Dash, a commercial blend of 14 herbs and spices; Lite Salt, a half-sodium, half-potassium blend. Or try adding parsley.

☐ One of the few proven substances that can bring on flare-ups of acne is iodine. Excessive, long-term intake of iodine (a natural ingredient of many foods) can bring on acne in anyone, but for people who are already prone to the condition, iodine is especially damaging. Excess is excreted through the oil glands of the skin, a process that irritates the pores and causes eruptions and inflammation. *Major sources of iodine in the diet:* Iodized table salt, kelp, beef liver, asparagus, turkey and vitamin and mineral supplements.

☐ Chronic diarrhea, gas and other stomach complaints are often linked to lactose intolerance, the inability to digest milk. One of every four adults suffers from this problem. Their bodies don't make enough lactase, the enzyme that breaks down milk sugar in the intestinal tract. *Among the offending foods:* Milk, ice cream, chocolate, soft cheese, some yogurts and sherbet. Lactose is also used as a filler in gum, candies and many canned goods.

☐ People on low-sodium diets should check out tap water as a source of salt intake. Some local water systems have eight times the amount of sodium (20 milligrams per quart) than people with heart problems or hypertension should use.

☐ Health-food candy is really no better for you than traditional sweets. *Comparison:* Health-food candy often contains about the same number of calories. The fat content is often as high or higher. Bars made of carob are caffeine-free, but the amount of caffeine in chocolate is negligible. And the natural sugars in health bars have no nutritional advantage over refined sugars.

Source: *Journal of the American Medical Association,* Chicago; *Dr. Fulton's Step-By-Step Program for Clearing Acne* by J. E. Fulton, Jr., MD, and E. Black, Harper & Row, New York; *The Sodium Content of Your Food,* Consumer Information Center, Colorado.

Best whole-grain breakfast cereals

Whole-grain breakfast cereals are a rich source of protein, vitamins, minerals and fiber. *Bonus:* They have relatively low percentages of cholesterol, fat and calories. *Added bonus:* Often the cheapest cereals are the best nutritionally.

What to look for:

☐ Cereals in which the first listed ingredient is a whole grain—whole-grain wheat, oats (rolled or flour), whole corn kernels or bran.

☐ Cereals with three or more grams of protein per serving.

☐ Avoid cereals with sugar or other sweeteners (honey, corn syrup, fructose) as a main ingredient. *Guide:* Four grams of sugar equals one teaspoonful.

☐ *Also avoid:* Cereals with dried fruits. They are concentrated sources of sugar. *Best:* Add your own fruits.

Caffeine facts

☐ Low doses of caffeine can increase alertness and motor ability, reduce drowsiness and lessen fatigue. Small to moderate amounts of caffeine pose no health danger, according to the Clinical Nutrition Section of Boston's University Hospital. Heavy doses produce ill effects —nervousness, anxiety, irritability, headache, muscle twitch and insomnia.

☐ Tolerance to caffeine varies widely from person to person. Two cups of caffeine-rich coffee make some people nervous. Others cannot survive the day without several cups. *Most sensitive to caffeine's effects:* Children and the elderly.

□ The caffeine quantity in coffee depends on how it is brewed. The drip method produces a higher caffeine content than the percolator. Instant coffee contains much less caffeine than brewed coffee. Tea contains half as much caffeine as coffee, and cola drinks have even less.

How much is too much: Four cups of coffee a day (500 milligrams of caffeine) is a heavy dose for most people.

□ There is no evidence that caffeine is a causal factor in either arteriosclerosis or heart attacks.

□ Caffeine does not increase the blood pressure of regular users.

□ Caffeine does not seem to be a cancer hazard, but other compounds (found in negligible amounts) in beverage coffee are known carcinogens in animals.

□ Caffeine is a much less important factor than cigarette smoking in heart disease, hypertension, bladder cancer, peptic ulcers and cystic breast disease.

□ Caffeine stimulates the central nervous system and can help reduce boredom from repetitive tasks. It increases the body's muscle strength.

□ Caffeine can relieve certain types of headaches by dilating blood vessels and reducing muscle tension.

Source: American Council of Science and Health, Summit, NJ.

Caffeine count

□ A five-ounce cup of drip-brewed coffee contains 146 milligrams of caffeine.

□ Regular instant coffee has 53.

□ Decaffeinated coffee has 2.

□ Most soft drinks range between 33 and 44. (Diet citrus drinks, root beer, ginger ale and tonic water contain little or no caffeine.)

□ A one-minute brew of tea has half the caffeine of a five-minute brew. (Steeping for five minutes can take a cup to 50 mg, depending on the leaf used.)

□ *Exceptionally high in caffeine:* Non-prescriptive stimulants. The average dose is 200 mg. Even higher, diuretics and weight-control drugs.

It's never too late to lower your cholesterol

Despite all the information we've been seeing in the media about the health benefits of a low-fat diet and regular exercise, not enough of us are translating this information into action.

Current estimate: Even now, almost one out of every two Americans will die of a heart attack or stroke.

Those who are lucky enough to survive a heart attack can attest that the experience is painful and incapacitating. But most heart attacks don't kill people—at least not right away. They just cause pain and incapacitation for a time.

A heart attack requires a long stay in a hospital's intensive-care unit…bypass surgery or angioplasty, neither of which are pleasant or comfortable…and may be accompanied by angina, the repeated, intermittent lesser pains that can be very frightening when they strike in the midst of normal activity. In short, if a bad heart doesn't kill you, it can drastically interfere with your enjoyment of life.

Given the frightening odds—and the dramatic potential of proper diet and exercise to improve them in our favor—why aren't more people switching to healthier habits?

Common excuses

Excuse: It's too late for me to change. In fact, much of the damage to arteries from years of poor diet is reversible. Studies conducted by Dr. David Blankenhorn, Dr. Dean Ornish and others have shown that strictly controlling the intake of saturated fat and cholesterol can start to open up arteries that were clogged by years of plaque buildup. This reversal process may take several years…but it's never too late to change your habits and improve the health of your heart.

Excuse: I avoid foods that contain cholesterol—so I don't have anything to worry about. Cholesterol is only one dietary contributor to poor heart health. Saturated fat is worse. Even if you shun cholesterol, your body will manufacture it if you eat saturated fat. Labels can be misleading—a bag of potato chips may be correctly labeled "cholesterol-free," but the chips are loaded with heart-damaging saturated fat.

My experience: I thought I was doing all I needed to do by eating more fish and less red meat…and then I experienced angina while jogging. Tests showed that my coronary arteries were 98% blocked. I was a heart attack waiting to happen, and was scheduled for bypass surgery. I'd given up hamburgers and ice cream—but the fish and chips I was eating instead were soaked in fat and continued to contribute to plaque buildup.

Excuse: I'm a busy person—I don't have time to look up everything I eat in an index and count grams and percentages all day. This is certainly a frequent complaint. The recommended guidelines seem so complicated that most people don't bother to use them— at least not after the first week or two.

That's why I teamed up with the renowned Dr. William P. Castelli, who directed the famous Framingham Heart Study sponsored by the National Institutes of Health, to develop a formula for heart-healthy eating that's easy to use and won't occupy a person's entire waking hours.

I also wanted to find out how to make changes in eating habits that didn't result in diets that were so boring no one could stick to them. I discovered that you can switch to low-fat eating without feeling tortured or deprived.

Simplified guidelines

Most reports recommend that people cut fat intake to a percent of total calories. But who has time to figure daily calorie intake, total fat grams and what percentage that represents? At first, I facetiously thought I'd have to hire a full-time dietitian and accountant to follow me around if I were to meet these standards.

Dr. Castelli and I worked out the math and arrived at a general formula that applies to a very broad number of people. Originally, we developed daily limits for cholesterol, saturated fat and total fat…but we found that this was too much for most people to keep track of.

Our solution: Cut back on all fats—but count only the grams of saturated fat you eat each day. Not calories, not cholesterol…just saturated fat. Limit saturated fat to 20 to 22 grams per day.

For someone who routinely takes in 2,000 calories a day, 20 to 22 grams of fat represent about 10% of calories from saturated fat.

We think those at greater risk for heart disease should limit saturated fat intake to 10 to 12 grams, or a little less than the usually recommended 7% of total calories. Risk factors include:

☐ Previous heart attack.

☐ Bypass surgery.

☐ High blood pressure.

☐ Smoking.

☐ Strong family history of heart attack.

☐ High cholesterol.

Although the official guidelines consider a blood cholesterol level of 200 to 240 to be "borderline," half of heart attacks occur in that range. More meaningful is the ratio of total cholesterol to HDL (the so-called "good cholesterol"). To find this figure, just take your total cholesterol count and divide by your HDL count. Even if your total cholesterol count is not in the high range, you are at a high risk for a heart attack.

Even if you aren't considered at risk for heart disease, it's still a good idea to cut the amount of fat—especially saturated fat—in your diet.

Watching fat intake is also a good way to lose weight without going hungry… and it will improve your overall energy level—and many people on a low-fat diet just feel better.

How to do it

How do you go about reducing dietary fat in general…and saturated fat in particular?

There's no mystery to it. As new labeling regulations take effect, more and more packaged foods are listing detailed nutritional information—including grams of saturated and other kinds of fat per serving—on their labels.

For foods without such labels, you can use tables found in many books on nutrition available at your bookstore or library.

Think about eating a variety of wholesome, minimally processed foods— such as grains, fruits, vegetables and legumes. Cut back on meats and animal-derived products (such as butter), which are high in saturated fat. Fortunately, there are good substitutes for butter and ice cream.

This doesn't mean you have to go without meat forever—that prospect is what keeps many people from improving their diets. Just eat less of it, and choose your cuts more carefully.

Instead of buying US choice grades of beef, which are heavily marbled with streaks of fat, choose the very lean cuts called "select grade."

Look for the leaner cuts of pork now on the market.

Trim the fat and skin from chicken.

You don't have to give up your favorite recipes, either—just learn to substitute low-fat ingredients. There's hardly any recipe for which that can't be done. (I'm still working on a really good pie crust without much saturated fat, and I'm almost there. I haven't found the secret yet, but I'm convinced I will.)

Example: Mushroom and beef on pasta, using only one teaspoon of canola oil and three ounces of thinly sliced extra-lean beef. Stir in eight ounces sliced mushrooms. Don't overcook. Salt and pepper to taste and serve on angel hair pasta for a gourmet meal for two.

If you enjoy a hearty breakfast, try making French toast using Eggbeaters or Simply Eggs in the batter in place of eggs…and frying the toast in a non-stick pan lightly coated with canola oil rather than butter.

Oatmeal is another satisfying breakfast dish. Pour nonfat milk over it…or if, like me, you're not a fan of nonfat milk, just top the cereal with jam or maple syrup and skip the milk.

(Commercial granola is not a low-fat breakfast choice—it tends to be high in coconut and palm oils, which are loaded with saturated fat.)

You don't even have to give up dessert. One of my favorite treats is an orange freezie. Peel and section three oranges and place them in a heavy-duty blender with ¼ cup water and ¼ cup sugar. Gradually add crushed ice and puree until smooth. Turn off the blender periodically and mash the ice in with the rest of the ingredients. Keep adding ice until the texture is the way you like it —thick enough to eat with a spoon or thin enough to drink. I used to think a day wasn't over without a milk shake or ice cream sundae…but since I discovered orange freezies, I don't miss those high-fat desserts.

What about exercise?

Diet is only part of the healthy-heart lifestyle—exercise is also important in improving the total-cholesterol-to-HDL ratio. Like diet, exercise has been treated as far more complicated than it needs to be…causing people to get discouraged and give up.

Some guidelines will tell you that you need to work out until you achieve a certain pulse rate, which must then be maintained for a certain period of time, for a given number of sessions a week.

But you don't need fancy measurements or an elaborate regimen to benefit from exercise. I think it's more practical—

and equally effective—to make sure you get some form of moderate to vigorous physical exercise every day. That exercise can be walking, hiking, jogging, swimming, bicycling—anything that gets your heart pumping.

How long and intense should each session be? Common sense is the best guideline. Start at a pace you can handle…keep going until you're challenged but not completely exhausted… and gradually increase the challenge. If you haven't been on an exercise program recently, check with your doctor before beginning a workout regimen.

Don't discount "natural" forms of exercise that are already a part of your life— walking a reasonable way to work, digging vigorously in the garden and so on. Do more of the physically demanding activities you already enjoy—even if they aren't officially designated as "exercise."

Source: Glen C. Griffin, MD, who was a practicing primary-care physician for 29 years before becoming editorial director of McGraw-Hill Healthcare Publications. He is editor in chief of the medical journal Postgraduate Medicine, writes a newsletter column on healthful gourmet cooking and is the coauthor (with Dr. William P. Castelli) of *Good Fat, Bad Fat: How to Lower Your Cholesterol & Beat the Odds of a Heart Attack,* Fisher Books, Tucson, AZ.

Choosing the right sweeteners

☐ It is a myth that brown sugar and raw sugar (unrefined sugar) are more healthful than white (refined) sugar. Nor is turbinado, a partially refined sugar, any more nutritious than the others.

☐ The corn sweeteners—dextrose, corn syrup and high-fructose corn sweetener (HFCS)—are all refined from corn starch and are as nutritiously bankrupt as cane and beet sugars.

☐ Maple sap straight from the tree is only 3% sucrose (and quite delicious), but the syrup made from boiling down the sap is 65% sucrose. Imitation maple syrup is 97% sucrose. Although pure maple syrup contains some calcium and potassium, it is not a prime source of either.

☐ Blackstrap molasses (made from sugar cane) and sorghum (made from the sorghum plant) have varying amounts of iron, calcium, potassium and B vitamins. The darker the color, the better the nutrition.

☐ Honey has small amounts of minerals and vitamins.

Better choices

☐ Vegetables such as parsnips, carrots, winter squash and beets have 4%–9% sucrose plus fiber, vitamins and minerals.

☐ Fresh fruits have 10% to 25% fructose and glucose, plus fiber, vitamins and minerals. Dried fruits are much sweeter, but they do contain iron.

☐ Date sugar (dried and crushed date particles) can be substituted for other sugars in baking. Use half as much date sugar as the recipe calls for in regular sugar. Grind it in a coffee mill or food processor to get a smooth consistency. You can buy date sugar at natural-food stores.

☐ Complex carbohydrates—whole grains, whole-grain flours and seeds such as sunflower and sesame—are a good source of glucose plus other important nutrients. Grain-based syrups such as barley malt, rice syrup, wheat syrup and amasake (made from fermented brown rice) are somewhat more nutritious than other sweeteners and can be used in baking.

Source: Leslie Cerier, a personal-fitness specialist, Charlemont, MA.

To avoid food poisoning

☐ Never let food cool to room temperature before putting it in the refrigerator. Slow cooling encourages the growth of bacteria.

☐ Do not thaw frozen foods for hours at room temperature. Allow them to thaw slowly in the refrigerator or wrap them in plastic and soak in cold water.

☐ Bacteria in raw poultry, fish or meat could contaminate your cutting board. Scrub the board after each use.

☐ Do not use cans that bulge or that contain off-color or unusual-smelling food. *Dangerous:* Tasting the contents to see whether they are bad.

☐ Lead poisoning can result from storing food in open cans. The solder that seals the tinned-steel can leaches into the contents. *Most hazardous:* Acidic foods, especially juices. They interact quickly with metal.

☐ Although cooking spoiled food destroys bacteria, it does not remove the poisons the bacteria produced.

Source: *Modern Maturity.*

Lemons beat morning sickness

Fresh lemons are an old cure for seasickness. They often prevent morning sickness, too. *Alternatives:* Sniff fresh lemons…suck wedges plain or sprinkled with salt…drink lemonade. Experiment to find the most effective approach. *Other natural aids:* Anise… ginger or ginger ale.

Source: *No More Morning Sickness: A Survival Guide for Pregnant Women* by Miriam Erick, RN, affiliated with Brigham & Women's Hospital, Boston. Plume, New York.

Hot flashes

Hot flashes and other symptoms of menopause may be minimized by eating a diet rich in soybeans. Eating a soy-rich diet may also reduce the risk of breast cancer. Soy and other legumes (beans, yams, etc.) contain phytoestrogens, compounds that may mimic estrogens in older women and act as a natural estrogen-replacement therapy for menopausal symptoms. Phytoestrogens may also lower younger women's risk of breast cancer.

Source: Barry R. Goldin, PhD, associate professor of community health, Tufts University School of Medicine, Boston.

What vitamin manufacturers don't tell you

While vitamins can have beneficial effects on your health, they can be dangerous if used improperly. You should know that:

☐ Vitamin B$_6$ can poison you. Those one-gram B$_6$ tablets sold in health stores far exceed the body's need of one or two milligrams a day. Overdoses may lead to loss of sensory and motor control.

☐ Vitamin E should be used with restraint. High doses can cause blood clots, phlebitis, hypertension, severe fatigue, breast tumors and reproductive disturbances. A daily intake of more than 100 to 300 units of "active tocopherol" is excessive.

☐ Vitamins A and D are not passed out of the body through the kidneys when taken in excess. They are stored in fat and in the liver, where they can cause cirrhosis, dry, itchy skin, fatigue, painful muscles and loss of body hair. Limit supplementary intake of these vitamins to the recommended daily dietary allowances.

☐ Consumers are frequently short-changed when they purchase vitamins. Many compounds both off the shelf or through mail-order houses are far less potent than their labels claim. Buy vitamins with expiration dates on the labels and avoid vitamins that contain a long list of stabilizers and preservatives. Return vitamins that have a strong, rancid odor or that crumble easily.

☐ Niacin is not a tranquilizer, despite the stories about its calming effects. Taking niacin tablets in search of tranquility can cause niacin toxicity. *Symptoms:* Flushed face and blotchy skin on arms.

Source: *New England Journal of Medicine, Journal of the American Medical Association, The Health Letter* and Dr. Jeffrey Blanc, professor of nutritional biochemistry, University of Puget Sound, Tacoma, WA.

Maybe it's yeast that's causing your aches and fatigue

New evidence suggests that many puzzling, chronic health problems resistant to treatment—from infections and allergies to the aches and exhaustion of chronic fatigue syndrome—are yeast-related.

One type of yeast is regularly found on the body's mucous membranes, especially the intestinal tract and vagina. When we talk about this kind of yeast, we usually mean Candida albicans, by far the predominant type found in the body.

In a healthy man or woman, candida (pronounced "can-did-a") is kept under control by so-called friendly bacteria living in the intestinal tract. But several factors can upset the yeast-to-bacteria balance—especially long-term use of broad-spectrum antibiotics. When this happens, yeasts grow out of control—leading to unpleasant symptoms.

Based on my critical review of continuing research, I believe there are three possible mechanisms for yeast's troublesome effects...

☐ Just as some people are allergic to pollens or mildew, some may be allergic to candida.

☐ Candida may produce certain toxins that are harmless in small amounts, but that in larger quantities weaken the immune system...leaving the body vulnerable to disease.

☐ Yeast overgrowth in the intestinal tract (candidiasis) may lead to changes in the intestine. In turn, these changes can cause the body to absorb and react to allergens in food.

The connection between yeast and health problems is highly controversial. Beginning with Dr. C. Orian Truss's article in the late '70s, a number of reports have linked yeast to illness, but the mainstream medical community remains skeptical.

Yet, my experience in treating hundreds of chronically ill patients, as well as similar experiences of a number of colleagues, suggests that a diet designed to curb yeast growth—along with certain antifungal medications—helps alleviate many symptoms that have proven resistant to other forms of treatment.

Do you have a yeast problem?

There is no simple diagnostic test for a yeast-related problem. For this reason, patients must undergo a thorough physical exam to rule out other possible causes of their symptoms. *Next step:* A complete medical history.

You may have a yeast problem if you...

...have used antibiotics repeatedly over a long period of time, such as for control of acne or recurrent infections.

...have taken corticosteroids. One known side effect of nasal cortisone spray is candidiasis of the nose.

...have used birth-control pills. Women on the Pill are far more prone than others to vaginal yeast infection.

...eat a high-sugar diet. A recent study at St. Jude Research Hospital in Memphis found that mice eating large quantities of the sugar glucose had 200 times as much candida in their intestinal tracts as did other mice.

...experience frequent digestive problems, such as abdominal pain, bloating, constipation or diarrhea.

...have a history of vaginal or urinary infections. Women develop yeast-related health problems far more often than men for a number of reasons. These include anatomical differences and hormonal changes associated with the menstrual cycle that promote yeast growth.

…have symptoms involving many parts of the body—for which usual examinations have not found a cause.

Treating a suspected yeast problem

The cornerstone of treatment is a sugar-free diet. Yeasts in the digestive tract feed on sugar—and multiply. Some patients show remarkable improvement from dietary changes alone. Others need additional help—in the form of over-the-counter anti-yeast preparations sold in health-food stores…and, for more serious cases, from prescription antifungal medications.

The yeast-control diet:

☐ Eliminate sugar and other simple carbohydrates, such as honey and corn syrup.

☐ Avoid foods containing yeast or molds, such as cheese, vinegar, wine, beer and other fermented beverages and pickled or smoked meats. Although breads are probably safe, try eliminating yeast-leavened breads for a few weeks.

Note: Yeast-containing foods should be avoided not because intestinal yeast feeds on food yeast—it doesn't. But most people with candida-related problems are sensitive to yeast in foods and can have negative physical reactions. As the candida problem improves, the sensitivity may subside…and yeast can again be included in your diet.

☐ Strengthen your immune system by boosting your intake of vegetables, minimally processed whole grains and other wholesome foods. Eat lean rather than fatty meats, and cut back on other sources of fat. Avoid potentially harmful additives, including artificial colors and flavors.

Some physicians recommend eliminating fruits from the diet, because fruits are quickly converted to simple sugars inside the body. I believe fruits are safe —unless your yeast-related symptoms are severe. However, I do recommend avoiding commercially prepared fruit juices, which may be contaminated with mold.

Follow this recommended diet for at least three weeks. If your symptoms subside, resume eating forbidden foods one by one. If your symptoms flare up again after you add one of the forbidden foods, stop eating that food for good.

Good news: After they show significant improvement, most people find that they can follow a less rigid diet—and can occasionally consume a bit of sugar.

Over-the-counter remedies

Many preparations sold in health-food stores can be a useful adjunct to the yeast-control diet…

☐ Citrus-seed extract, an antimicrobial substance made from tropical plants. Because the extract can irritate mucous membranes, it should be generously diluted with water before drinking.

☐ Caprylic acid, a saturated fatty acid available in tablet form. It helps keep yeast from reproducing.

Note: Some patients develop digestive problems or notice a slight worsening of yeast-related symptoms during the first week on this medication. If these don't go away within a few days, stop the medication and check with your doctor.

☐ Lactobacillus acidophilus, a friendly bacterium that helps restore the normal balance of intestinal flora. It is present in yogurt, especially homemade varieties. Store-bought yogurt that contains active cultures will be labeled to that effect. Be sure to buy only unsweetened varieties. Acidophilus is also available as a nutritional supplement.

☐ Garlic. This herb is known to stimulate the immune system…and at an international medical conference several years ago, researchers reported that garlic also seems to fight candida. Persons wary of the taste of cooked garlic—or its effect on the breath—should consider aged garlic extract (Kyolic), a deodorized supplement. It is widely available in local health-food stores.

Antifungal medications

When a yeast-related symptom fails to respond to diet or supplements, prescription medication often helps—although the drug may take up to a year to have any effect in severe cases. Drug options:

☐ Nystatin (Mycostatin or Nilstat). In more than 30 years of use, this oral medication has demonstrated no toxic side effects. It knocks out candida in the intestines. It is not absorbed by the bloodstream, however, so it is ineffective against particularly severe cases of candidiasis.

☐ Fluconazole (Diflucan). This safe, highly effective antiyeast medication has been available in the US for about three years. Unlike nystatin, fluconazole is absorbed into the bloodstream.

☐ Itraconazole (Sporanox). This medication, a chemical "cousin" of fluconazole, was recently approved for use in the US. Although it appears to be quite safe, a related drug, ketoconazole (Nizoral) has been linked to liver damage.

Source: William G. Crook, MD, a fellow of the American College of Allergy and Immunology, the American Academy of Environmental Medicine and the American Academy of Pediatrics. He is the author of *The Yeast Connection and Chronic Fatigue Syndrome and the Yeast Connection,* both published by Professional Books, Inc., Jackson, TN.

Aspirin miracle

Research suggests that one aspirin tablet, taken every other day, helps reduce risk of heart attack, certain kinds of stroke, cancer of the gastrointestinal tract and possibly Alzheimer's disease, among other serious ailments. All this for $1.83 per year—less than a penny a day.

Aspirin and heart attack

Data on aspirin's preventive value comes from the Physicians' Health Study, a five-year study of more than 22,000 male doctors between the ages of 40 and 84.

Half of the subjects took a standard five-grain aspirin tablet every other day. Result: Subjects older than 50 who took aspirin were 44% less likely to suffer a heart attack than were similar men given a placebo (sugar pill).

Aspirin and stroke

Most strokes occur as a result of atherosclerosis. When arteries are narrowed, even a tiny blood clot can block blood flow to the brain, thereby depriving the tissue of oxygen.

Aspirin apparently fights stroke by preventing atherosclerosis and thinning the blood, which helps prevent blood clots.

Aspirin and colon cancer

In 1991, the Journal of the National Cancer Institute reported that people who took aspirin or other nonsteroidal anti-inflammatory drugs at least four days a week for three months halved their risk of colorectal cancer. The results held for men and women across a broad range of ages.

A recent Emory University study suggested that taking one aspirin a week significantly reduces the risk of these cancers. Another study found a 50% reduction in the colon-cancer death rate among daily aspirin takers.

But another study of older subjects (average age 73) showed that frequent aspirin users face a heightened risk of kidney and colon cancer, as well as of heart attack. More research is needed. But—at least for younger patients, the preliminary findings are promising.

Aspirin precautions

Caution: Aspirin should generally be avoided by anyone with asthma… ulcers or other chronic stomach problems…or an allergy to aspirin.

☐ If you're pregnant or nursing an infant, take aspirin only with a doctor's consent. *Danger:* Aspirin taken during the last three months of pregnancy can injure the fetus or cause birth complications.

Source: Robert S. Persky, coauthor of *Penny Wonder Drug: What the Label on Your Aspirin Bottle Doesn't Tell You,* The Consultant Press, Ltd., New York.

Herbs and spices

Blending herbs and spices is a wonderful way to give foods an international flair. You can also use them to enliven dishes that have become boring over time. Here are my favorite combinations.

☐ *Italian blend.* Two tablespoons basil, two tablespoons marjoram, one tablespoon garlic powder, one tablespoon oregano, one-half tablespoon thyme, one-half tablespoon rosemary, one-half tablespoon crushed red pepper.

Sprinkle one-fourth teaspoon over each serving of chicken before baking or grilling…or add one-fourth teaspoon to four servings of your favorite pasta sauce.

☐ *Vegetable blend.* One tablespoon marjoram, one tablespoon basil, one tablespoon chervil, one-half tablespoon tarragon, one-half tablespoon celery seed. It adds a garden-fresh flavor when sprinkled on steamed vegetables. Use one-quarter teaspoon per four servings.

Source: Judy Gilliard, a food columnist, instructor and radio talk-show host in Palm Springs, California. She is co-author of *The Flavor Secret: Using Herbs and Spices to Put Flavor Back into Low-Fat, Low-Calorie, Low-Cholesterol Cooking,* Chronimed Publishing, Inc., Box 59032, Minneapolis 55459.

Simple secrets of being healthier and happier

Did you know that loosening your necktie or collar will improve your vision?

Indeed, according to Cornell University researchers, tightly knotted ties interfere with blood flow to the brain and eyes. So, computer operators, pilots, surgeons and other professionals who must pay close attention to visual detail should avoid confining neckwear. If you must wear a tie, make sure your shirt has plenty of neck room and leave the top button on your collar unfastened. Make the knot loose enough that you can slip a finger between your collar and neck.

Other ways to feel healthier, smarter and safer…

☐ Exercise in the morning. A recent study showed that 75% of morning exercisers were likely to still be at it one year later, compared to 50% of those who worked out at midday and 25% of the evening exercisers.

Explanation: As the day progresses, people are more apt to think of excuses for avoiding exercise.

☐ If you eat bacon, cook it in a microwave. Bacon cooked in a microwave contains lower levels of cancer-causing compounds called nitrites than bacon that is pan-fried or baked. Drain away as much fat as possible—bacon drippings contain twice the level of nitrites as the meat itself.

Vitamin C helps counter the cancer-causing effect of nitrosamines (which are formed when nitrites combine with amino acids in the stomach). People who eat bacon, ham, pepperoni, bologna or other nitrite-preserved meats should be sure to include oranges, tomatoes and other vitamin C-rich foods in their diet.

☐ Cure hiccups with sugar. Swallowing a teaspoon of sugar almost always does the trick. In a recent study published in the *New England Journal of Medicine,* sugar worked in 19 out of 20 people—some of whom had been hiccuping for as long as six weeks!

Other effective remedies: Grasping your tongue with your thumb and index finger and gently pulling it forward…swallowing a small amount of cracked ice…massaging the back of the roof of the mouth with a cotton swab…and eating dry bread slowly.

Caution: Hiccups that recur frequently or persist for more than a few minutes may be a tip-off to other health problems, including heart disease. Consult a doctor for such hiccups.

☐ Don't suppress a cough. Coughing is the body's way of clearing mucus and other debris from the lungs.

☐ To avoid motion sickness, close your eyes. Motion sickness occurs when your eyes and the motion-sensing system of the inner ear receive conflicting signals—the inner ear says you're moving in one direction while your eyes say you're going in another. Keeping eyes closed helps reduce the conflict.

If you're prone to motion sickness in cars, offer to drive. Like closing your eyes, keeping your eyes focused straight ahead on the road helps reduce queasiness. Also helpful: Air from the air conditioner or an open window directed toward your face.

☐ Don't aggravate a strained back. Many people use heat immediately after a minor back injury. But heat increases circulation to the area, causing increased swelling and inflammation. Better: To reduce swelling and pain in the first few days following a back strain, use cold compresses made of crushed ice wrapped in a towel. Keep the pack on for 20 minutes, then leave it off for 20. Repeat this cycle for two to three hours a day for three to four days. Only after this interval should heat be applied.

Caution: For severe or persistent back pain, consult a doctor.

☐ Eat fresh fruit. Fruit juice doesn't give you as much fiber—or vitamins and minerals—as whole fruit. Dietary fiber promotes regularity and helps regulate digestion of carbohydrates. The sugar in fruit is absorbed more slowly than the same sugar in fruit juice. The longer absorption time makes fruit more filling, a boon if you're watching your weight. This keeps your blood sugar levels stable, leaving you feeling more energetic.

☐ Don't drink tea if your blood is iron-poor. Tea contains tannins, compounds that inhibit iron absorption. (Herbal tea is okay.) To raise iron levels: Eat more green, leafy vegetables, lean red meat, poultry, fish, wheat germ, oysters, fruit and iron-fortified cereal. Foods rich in vitamin C help your body absorb iron from other foods.

☐ Stop snoring—with a tennis ball. Sewn into the back of the snorer's pajama top, it discourages sleeping on the back, a major trigger of snoring. Also helpful: Using blocks to raise the head of your bed…or using pillows to elevate the snorer's head.

☐ Use a cookie jar to lose weight. But—instead of cookies, fill the jar with slips of paper reminding you to do some calorie-burning activity, like going for a walk or gardening.

☐ Make exercise a game. If you're a swimmer, for example, see how long it takes you to "swim the English Channel." If you swim in a standard 75-foot pool, you'll have to do 1,478 laps to go the 21 miles from Dover to Calais. For stair-climbers, reaching the 29,028-foot summit of Mt. Everest takes 49,762 stairs. Be creative in whatever form of exercise you pursue, and you'll be more apt to stick with it.

☐ Be careful when shoveling snow. To avoid back injury or heart attack, keep knees bent and both feet firmly planted…push the snow aside instead of lifting it up…protect head and hands from the cold and avoid caffeine or alcohol before going outdoors.

☐ Develop a "cancer-resistant" personality. Although this finding remains controversial, cancer seems to be more prevalent among people who take a hopeless, helpless view of life, suppress their feelings, allow anger to build and have long-standing unresolved conflicts with loved ones.

Source: Don R. Powell, PhD, president and founder of the American Institute for Preventive Medicine, Farmington Hills, Michigan. He is the author of *365 Health Hints,* Simon & Schuster, New York.

How to reduce the risk of heart disease

Designed to uncover the leading risk factors for heart disease in a typical American community, the Framingham Heart Study has been tracking the daily living and eating habits of thousands of residents of Framingham, Massachusetts since 1948.

Dr. William Castelli, director of the study for 15 years and a popular lecturer on heart disease, discusses the study's most recent findings.

How does the current generation of Americans compare with the original subjects of the Framingham Heart Study? Are we becoming healthier—or are we at greater risk? While many of us are benefiting from lower-fat diets and the greater emphasis that is put on fitness, children today may actually be in worse shape than those of previous generations.

One surprise is that teenage boys and young men in Framingham today weigh more than their fathers did at the same ages and they are not as physically active. Therefore, they may be at higher risk for heart disease and diabetes.

The combination of TV and computer technology has made children more sedentary, and their diets are unacceptably high in saturated fat and cholesterol.

Girls in grammar and high school are now smoking at a much higher rate than ever before. If the present pattern continues, the rate of women's deaths from heart disease and diabetes will match or even exceed that of men. From other studies, we have learned that arterial disease can begin as early as the grade-school years.

What are the most recent findings regarding the links between diet and heart disease? One of the latest discoveries in cardiology is that the newest fat deposit in your arteries—for example, the one that was placed there by the cheeseburger you ate yesterday—may be more likely to break loose, clog your arteries and kill you than the older deposits that have been partially blocking your arteries for years.

These "young" deposits from your most recent high-fat meal don't impede blood flow while attached to artery walls. But they are unstable and can easily snap off and block a coronary vessel.

An estimated 65% to 70% of acute heart attacks are now believed to come from these newer, barely detectable lesions, which are covered by only a thin layer of cells. The older, larger obstructions are covered by thick scar tissue and are rather resistant and stable.

But don't discount big blockages. They are, of course, still undesirable and an indication of widespread disease. In fact, if you have a coronary artery that is at least 50% blocked, the smaller arteries of your heart cannot possibly be free of disease. That would make you a "walking time bomb"—and especially vulnerable to the effects of one fatty meal.

We have all heard that saturated fat is the chief culprit in heart disease. Where does cholesterol fit in? How much of each can we safely consume? While fat is the primary villain in heart disease, cholesterol is definitely an accomplice.

As a nation, we would be better off if every day we each ate no more than 300 milligrams of cholesterol and 35 to 40 grams of total fat—of which 20 grams or less were in the form of saturated fat. This is the "bad" fat that contributes to heart disease.

Once you reach this goal, you can see whether making these changes gets your serum cholesterol down to a level of 200 or less. The closer you get to the 150-to-160 range, the less likely you are to have a heart attack.

If these adjustments don't "straighten out" your cholesterol, then you should aim for a daily quota of no more than 17 grams of saturated fat, 30 grams of total fat and 200 milligrams of cholesterol.

Example: A lunch of a four-ounce steak, coffee with low-fat milk and a pat of butter on a roll is about 150 milligrams of cholesterol and 30 grams of fat—of which 18 grams are saturated.

Are triglycerides the same as "bad" cholesterol? How critical are they as risk factors for heart disease? One of the by-products of the fatty foods we digest are substances called triglycerides. They are formed in the liver and are known as Very Low Density Lipoproteins (VLDLs). The familiar LDL, or "bad," cholesterol is not formed directly—it comes from VLDL.

We are now learning that there are four different types of triglycerides, two of which are damaging to arteries and two of which are not. The most dangerous ones are small and dense and associated with diets high in saturated fats. These VLDLs have been linked with very early heart attacks—striking victims in their 20s, 30s and 40s.

Recently, we have discovered that these VLDLs enter the white blood cells in our artery walls even faster than LDLs. This makes them particularly destructive.

Genetic predispositions and unwise eating habits play roles in the formation of these dangerous fats, but the dangers can be curbed by maintaining a healthy lifestyle.

Other types of triglycerides can be raised by eating diets high in whole grains, vegetables and fruits, but these are not the kind that are harmful to our hearts or artery walls.

What are the best ways to raise levels of HDL, or "good," cholesterol? When our Framingham data showed that the relative amount of HDL in our blood is even more important than total cholesterol and that exercise can have a favorable impact on HDL, I began jogging regularly. This raised my HDL level from 49 to 63. A regular routine of brisk walking or any other exercise is fine for most people—but talk with your doctor before beginning a new exercise regimen.

Losing weight also elevates HDLs, and certain foods and nutrients, such as brewer's yeast, garlic, onions, ginseng and chromium, have been credited with boosting them as well.

My advice is to have a test done after eating such wholesome, harmless foods for about a month—as part of a low-fat diet—to see whether they have any measurable effect on your HDLs.

Aim: The ratio of your total cholesterol to HDL should be under 3.5.

How does the risk of heart attack in men compare with that of women? One of the most shocking findings to emerge from the Framingham Heart Study is that one out of every five men has had a heart attack by the time he reaches age 60. The heart attack rate for women is only one in 17 by the same age.

Unless they have diabetes, smoke or have familial hypercholesterolemia (inherited abnormally high serum cholesterol), women are relatively immune to heart disease before menopause because they produce high levels of estrogen, which apparently plays a protective role.

However, within six to 10 years after menopause—when estrogen levels drop off sharply—women's risk becomes similar to that of men. Unfortunately, women tend to have more advanced heart disease by the time they are treated, since physicians still consider them to be less susceptible to coronary problems and often don't diagnose the condition early enough.

How many people survive heart attacks today? Can any of them ever return to "normal"? As the Framingham data have shown, when people get heart attacks, about 85% of them survive.

With the new thrombolytic therapy, in which people having a heart attack are injected with a clot-dissolving drug, we

*HDL is high-density lipoprotein, one of the breakdowns of cholesterol that can be measured in the bloodstream.

193

can increase the percentage of survivors to about 93%. Even in the oldest age groups, 75% of first-time heart attack victims survive.

Of those who survive, about half lose the normal pumping ability of their hearts—when we put them on a treadmill, they "flunk." If we subsequently inject them with a radioisotope such as thallium, which allows us to scan the heart, we find that the heart muscle tissue in 30% of these people is "hibernating" but still very much alive—which means it can eventually be restored to normal function.

In the short run, we can't lower the cholesterol levels of these patients sufficiently or fast enough—either through dietary changes or drugs—to shrink the deposits inside their coronary arteries and get their hearts pumping at full capacity again.

Today's "high-tech" treatments, such as coronary bypass surgery, balloon angioplasty or atherectomy, can help restore cardiac function and allow these people to return to work. But in the long run, the only treatment that works is aggressively lowering blood cholesterol through diet and lifestyle changes. If blood cholesterol is lowered within three to five years of the first heart attack, we can markedly reduce the risk of a second heart attack.

What are your latest recommendations for a "healthy heart" diet? When it comes to protecting yourself from heart disease, the best strategy is to become a vegetarian—eating primarily fresh vegetables, legumes, whole grains, fruits and nonfat dairy products.

Vegetarians not only outlive the rest of us, they also aren't prey to other degenerative diseases, such as diabetes, strokes, etc., that slow us down and make us chronically ill.

If you can't be a vegetarian, the next best thing is to eat a vegetarian from the sea. One type of shellfish fits this description—mollusks (clams and oysters). They loll around on the ocean floor and are filter feeders, sucking in the phytoplankton (the vegetables of the sea). Mollusks have the lowest cholesterol levels of all seafood.

The second best choices are moving shellfish such as shrimp and lobster. While they contain more cholesterol than most meats and cheeses, they are so low in saturated fat that they are a much better bargain nutritionally—more desirable even than skinless white-meat chicken. Also good, of course, is to eat any fish—even fatty fishes. They are very low in saturated fat and contain fish oils, which also benefit your heart.

If you prefer a more standard American diet, recent changes at your supermarket allow you to have some beef, too. The newest grade of beef available—select—contains only 10% saturated fat by weight, or approximately four grams of fat in four ounces of precooked meat. And ConAgra now puts out a product called "Healthy Choice Extra Lean Ground Beef" that contains only 1.5 grams of saturated fat per four-ounce serving. That means you could have burgers for breakfast, lunch and dinner and still have plenty of saturated fat to "spend" that day. Similarly, everything from ham to ice cream comes in a low-fat and delicious version at your local market today.

Does heart disease follow a predictable course—and is it ever too late to stop it? Once it begins, atherosclerosis—the hardening and thickening of arteries because of fatty deposits—follows a fairly predictable course.

It starts in the abdominal aorta, spreads to the coronary arteries, the big artery in the chest, then down into the leg, up into the neck and finally inside the head. This is why strokes generally occur later in life than heart attacks do.

Now that we have such diagnostic tools as echocardiography, which uses ultrasound, we can look inside the neck arteries of our Framingham subjects. By the time they are in their 60s, 76% of them have deposits or lesions in that area. This means that the disease is already well advanced elsewhere in their bodies and has been in their coronary arteries for at least ten years.

If these people continue on their present course, about half of them will end up dying from this arterial clogging.

While we can intervene and make a difference even at this point, the earlier one starts the better, so I don't want to exclude children or premenopausal women from good preventive programs.

Twenty-five years from now, when these children are adults and the women are past menopause, they and their families will have already acquired healthy eating habits to keep them well protected from heart disease.

I've yet to meet anyone whose genes are so good that they have license to eat whatever they want—or who can get away with being too sedentary. It's only by altering diet and exercise habits that I can change the destiny of 75% of the people who are headed for heart attacks. The remaining 25% will need lipid-lowering drugs in order to achieve the same result.

At age 62 and as the first man in my family to reach the age of 45 without any coronary symptoms, I'm living proof that a healthful change of lifestyle can definitely work.

Source: William Castelli, MD, director of the Framingham Heart Study, Five Thurber St., Framingham, Massachusetts. Dr. Castelli is credited with coining the terms "good" cholesterol and "bad" cholesterol and is among the nation's preeminent experts on the heart and heart disease prevention.

Turn around tiredness

One of the best tools for boosting your energy is a fatigue diary—a daily journal in which you jot down all your daily activities and your level of fatigue.

Your fatigue diary should include everything that you believe might be contributing to your fatigue. Most common culprits:

☐ Sleep problems. The leading source of fatigue is sleep deprivation—a condition that now affects about 30% of the adult population.

Self-protection: Refuse to let work and family commitments get in the way of a good night's sleep. Make your bedroom a cozy haven, free of drafts—and of reminders of work.

Avoid all sources of caffeine, especially after 5 pm.

☐ Stress. Psychological stress is enormously draining. While it's not always possible to eliminate the sources of stress in your life, meditation, biofeedback and talking with a therapist or friend can help.

☐ Medications. In many cases, aches and pains will intensify feelings of fatigue. So, one quick way to cut fatigue is to take an occasional aspirin.

On the other hand, many prescription and nonprescription drugs induce fatigue—especially antidepressants, antihistamines and blood-pressure drugs. While you may not be able to stop taking a particular drug, you might be able to find a substitute that does not cause fatigue. Ask your doctor about switching…or about tapering off a drug temporarily to see if that reduces your fatigue.

Fatigue can also be caused by interactions between drugs. To avoid trouble: Buy all your prescriptions at the same place. Pharmacists are expert at spotting potentially dangerous drug combinations—but they have to know all the drugs you're taking before they can help.

Review your diary for clues:

After a month, review your fatigue diary. Look for potential causes of fatigue and take steps to eliminate these causes. If you cannot find evidence linking specific behaviors to your fatigue, or if the changes you make don't help, use the diary instead as a guide for interacting with your doctor.

Severe, life-threatening diseases such as cancer and AIDS can cause fatigue. But so can several other easily treatable conditions. Most widely known: Anemia, arthritis, Lyme disease, heart disease, thyroid disorders, diabetes, breathing disorders, obesity, anorexia or bulimia.

Chronic infection is another common cause of fatigue. An overtaxed immune system drains energy meant for other endeavors.

If you suspect you have a fatigue-causing illness, have a thorough physical exam. The examination should last at least 90 minutes and should include a complete blood count (to check for infection or anemia), an erythrocyte sedimentation rate (to check for infection or inflammation), routine chemistry assays (to screen for diseases of the thyroid and other organs) and a chest X ray (to check for tumors.)

Source: David S. Bell, MD, a pediatrician with a special interest in chronic fatigue. Affiliated with Harvard Medical School and Cambridge (Massachusetts) Hospital, Dr. Bell is coauthor of Curing Fatigue: A Step-by-Step Plan to Uncover and Eliminate the Causes of Chronic Fatigue, Rodale Press, Emmaus, PA, and author of A Physician's Handbook of Chronic Fatigue Syndrome, Addison-Wesley.

How we can slow our aging processes

Today, people are living longer, but enjoying it less. Many of us fear old age as a period of declining powers and failing health. But if we learn to replace that fear with a positive attitude, an enhanced physical and spiritual awareness of our bodies and a sensible pattern of activity, we can expect to enjoy the blessings of a vigorous and healthy old age.

A century ago, less than one person in ten reached the age of 65. Most of those who did live that long had been worn out by a lifetime of inadequate nutrition…widespread disease …backbreaking physical labor. Their remaining years were difficult not because they were old, but because their bodies were in a state of breakdown.

Today, relieved of those harsh external pressures, most of us will live well into our 60s and 70s…and the physical disease and mental breakdown we fear in old age is largely a result of internal stress we can learn to avoid.

People age differently:

Your well-being depends far less on your chronological age—how old you are according to the calendar—than on two other indicators…

☐ Biological age tells how old your body is in terms of critical life signs and cellular processes.

Every individual is affected differently by time…in fact, every cell and organ in your body ages on its own timetable.

☐ Psychological age indicates how old you feel. Depending on what is happening in your life and your attitude to it, your psychological age can change dramatically within a very short period.

Aging is reversible:

It is not news that psychological age can decrease. We all know the old proverb: "You are as old as you feel." And—now scientists have learned that biological aging can be reversed.

That's not all the good news for aging bodies. The Tufts team found that regular physical exercise also reverses nine other typical effects of biological age…

☐ Reduced strength.
☐ Lower metabolic rate.
☐ Excess body fat.
☐ Reduced aerobic capacity.
☐ Higher blood pressure.
☐ Lower blood-sugar tolerance.
☐ Higher cholesterol/HDL ratio.
☐ Reduced bone density.
☐ Poorer body temperature regulation.

To get optimum benefits from exercise, the type and amount have to be expertly tailored to your individual constitution. You don't have to be a fitness freak to gain from exercise…just 20 minutes of walking three times a week improves the cholesterol/HDL ratio. No expert advice is needed to benefit from another important route to longevity…a balanced lifestyle.

A study of 7,000 Southern Californians found that the longest-lived followed seven simple rules:

☐ Sleep seven to eight hours a night.
☐ Eat breakfast.
☐ Don't eat between meals.
☐ Don't be significantly over- or underweight.
☐ Engage in regular physical activity… sports…gardening…long walks.
☐ Drink moderately…not more than two alcoholic drinks a day.
☐ Don't smoke.

The study found that a 45-year-old man who followed these rules could expect to live another 33 years…but if he followed only three of them or less, he would probably die within 22 years.

Role of stress:

The human body reacts to stress by pumping adrenaline and other powerful hormones into the bloodstream. This "fight or flight" response provides energy for taking rapid action and is vital when you are actually faced with pressing external danger.

But it makes your metabolism work in the direction of breaking your body down instead of building it up.

If it occurs too often or continues too long it produces lasting harmful effects including muscle wasting…diabetes… fatigue…osteoporosis…hypertension… effects typical of aging.

That is why a major contribution to the aging process in modern life comes from situations that do not present real physical dangers but produce dangerous levels of stress.

Example: Our cities are full of unavoidable noise, a serious source of stress. Studies have shown increased levels of mental disorder in people who live under the flight paths near airports…elevated blood pressure in children who live near the Los Angeles airport…more violent behavior in noisy work environments.

Fortunately, we have discovered a number of measures that can reduce the aging effects of stress and other hazards of modern life.

To reduce stress and slow the aging process:

☐ Experience silence. Research has shown that people who meditate have higher levels of DHEA, a hormone that protects against stress and decreases with age. Spending 20 minutes twice a day in calm silence pays great benefits in detaching you from the mad bustle of the world and finding your true self.

☐ Avoid toxics…not only foods and drinks that stress your system, but relationships that produce anger and tension.

☐ Shed the need for approval by others…it's a sign of fear, another stress factor that promotes aging.

☐ Use relationships with others to learn your own self. People we love provide something we need…those we hate have something we need to get rid of.

☐ Change your inner dialogue. Change from "What's in it for me?" to "How can I help others?" Selfishness is bad for you. Psychologist Larry Scherwitz found that people who used the words "I," "me," "mine" most often in their conversations had the highest risk of heart disease.

☐ Be aware of your body's needs. The body only recognizes two signals… comfort and discomfort. You will be healthier if you learn to respond to its signals.

Source: Deepak Chopra, MD, executive director for the Institute for Mind/Body Medicine, San Diego, California. He is the author of *Ageless Body, Timeless Mind: The Quantum Alternative to Growing Old,* Harmony Books, New York.

Skin wrinkles

Skin wrinkles can be removed safely and painlessly via a short burst of laser light. The new "ultra-pulse" laser is also effective against acne…brown spots…blotchy, sun-damaged skin…and scar tissue. The laser vaporizes the sun-damaged top layer of skin and "realigns" the underlying layers. Cost: $500 to $3,000, depending on the extent of treatment.

Source: Sand S. Milgraum, MD, clinical assistant professor of dermatology, University of Medicine and Dentistry of New Jersey–Robert Wood Johnson Medical School, New Brunswick.

Improve the quality of your sleep

☐ Researchers cannot easily determine how much sleep is optimum for a specific person. They have determined that, on average, people need seven or eight hours of sleep a day.

☐ Establish a regular bedtime and wakeup schedule. Stick to it, even on weekends and holidays.

☐ Avoid trying to make up for loss of sleep one night by sleeping more the next. Sleep deprivation of two to four hours does not severely affect performance. Having the normal amount of sleep the next night compensates for the loss without changing the regular sleep pattern. And that has long-term benefits.

☐ Relax before bedtime. *Good ways to unwind:* Take a bath, read, have a weak nightcap or snack (milk is ideal for many people), engage in sex. Avoid late-night exercise, work, arguments and activities that cause tension.

☐ Knowing the reason for insomnia is the only way to start overcoming it. If the cause is not quickly obvious, see a doctor. Many emotional and physical disorders express themselves as sleep disturbances.

☐ Avoid sleeping pills. On a long-term basis, they are useless and sometimes dangerous. And when taken infrequently, they may produce a drug hangover the next day.

☐ Don't attempt to reduce the total amount of sleep you need. Carefully researched evidence from monitoring subjects in sleep laboratories indicates these schemes are not only ineffective but unhealthful. The daily biological cycle cannot be changed by gradually cutting back sleep over a period of months. Older persons apparently need slightly less sleep, but even here the exact difference is not yet known.

Source: Dr. Charles P. Pollak, codirector, of Sleep-Wake Disorders Center, Montefiore Hospital, New York.

Avoiding Sunday afternoon blues

Worries about Sunday night insomnia may also be one of the major causes of the widespread Sunday afternoon blues.

The cause: Going to bed late Friday and Saturday nights and sleeping late Saturday and Sunday mornings—or napping Sunday afternoon—can put your internal clock two, three or four hours behind the actual time you try to go to sleep Sunday night at your "regular" 11 pm bedtime. That's why you can't fall asleep. And because it's Sunday night, you begin to worry about work on Monday as you toss and turn. So you think work stress is causing your insomnia.

The cure: Get up at your regular weekday wake-up time on Saturday and Sunday mornings. If you absolutely must sleep later—make it no more than one hour later than your usual wakeup time. And expose yourself to daylight as soon as you wake up. Don't nap—especially not on Sunday afternoon. Get into the habit of exercising Sunday afternoon or early evening.

Source: James Perl, PhD, a clinical psychologist in private practice, 4761 McKinley Dr., Boulder, Colorado 80303. Dr. Perl is author of *Sleep Right in Five Nights,* William Morrow, New York.

The straight story on sleep

☐ Both drowsiness and fatigue during the daytime hours are usually the result of sleep disorders of which sufferers often aren't aware. There are also chronic sleep disturbances of which the sleeper may not be aware. *Example:* Loud noises from aircraft or a nearby highway that disturb sleep regularly even though people don't always waken.

☐ Contrary to common notions, the inability to get a refreshing night's sleep is rarely caused by stress or anxiety. For people younger than 15 or older than 50, the main cause is usually a physical one. In older people, the most common problem is apnea, a disorder that causes them to stop breathing periodically during sleep. *Other frequent problems:* Asthma and chronic disease.

☐ A cool bedroom is not necessarily better for sleeping than a warm one. No temperature (within a normal range) has been proved better than another for sleep.

☐ Some people who have insomnia do sleep, and much more than they think they do. *The real test of sleeping well:* Whether you feel fully alert the next day, not the number of hours you've slept. If you sleep just five hours and you don't feel tired the next day, you don't have a sleep disorder.

☐ Heavy snoring followed by daytime sleepiness is virtually a sure sign of apnea. In this condition, episodes of impaired breathing or failure to breathe at all causes the apnea sufferer to wake up many times a night. *Most vulnerable to sleep apnea:* Middle-aged males (particularly those who are overweight) and people with large adenoids, a deviated septum or polyps. Some apnea sufferers are so used to their condition that they're not aware of their wakening, only of their daytime fatigue.

☐ Drink a glass of milk and eat a light snack before going to bed. *Reason:* Hunger can disturb sleep. Avoid rich or spicy foods or stimulants such as coffee, tea, cola drinks or sweets. (Sugar is a stimulant.) Eating the wrong foods before bedtime may not actually keep you from falling asleep, but it will often wake you within a few hours.

☐ Check to see if there are noises that may be disturbing your sleep without your being aware of them. Mute the sounds by putting up heavy curtains or by using earplugs.

☐ Avoid too much mental stimulation in the period before you go to sleep. Don't discuss family problems or finances, and don't take up unfinished work problems before bedtime. *Instead:* Do some light reading or watch a television show that relaxes you.

☐ If you wake up in the middle of the night and can't get back to sleep right away, don't lie there. Get up, put the light on and use the time, perhaps to read. Lying in bed and trying to sleep without success only makes you more tense.

☐ Avoid strenuous physical exercise within a few hours of bedtime. It can cause excessive stimulation and stress, which can disturb sleep. Exercise can benefit sleep if taken in the afternoon or early evening. Morning exercise is of no great help in inducing a good night's sleep.

Source: Dr. William C. Dement, director, Sleep Disorders Center, Stanford University School of Medicine.

How to stop snoring

☐ Put a brick or two under the legs at the head of your bed. Elevating your head will keep the airway open.

☐ Don't use extra pillows. They'll only kink the airway.

☐ Avoid all depressants a few hours before bed. Take no alcohol, tranquilizers, sleeping pills or antihistamines late in the day.

☐ Lose weight. Three of four snorers are at least 20% over their ideal weight.

☐ Wear a cervical collar. It keeps the chin up and the windpipe open.

☐ Wear a "snore ball." Cut a small, solid-rubber ball in half. Using two patches of Velcro, attach the flat side of the half-sphere to the back of your pajama top. If done right, it should keep you off your back—the position for virtually all snoring.

Source: *Prevention,* Emmaus, PA.

How not to be an air pollution victim

Air pollution is more than a nuisance. It's a threat to life. According to recent research, long-term exposure to soot, haze, dust and smoke raises the risk of early death by as much as 26%, translating into thousands of premature deaths a year.

Even when it doesn't kill, air pollution compromises health and wellness, especially for people with asthma, bronchitis, emphysema, heart disease or other chronic illnesses. At special risk: Elderly people, because their lungs aren't as healthy as they once were…and young people, because their lung tissue is just forming.

Airborne enemies:

Particulate matter is just one of the many types of dangerous pollutants in the air we breathe. Other dangerous pollutants include…

☐ Ozone. It causes coughing, shortness of breath and chest pain. It also boosts susceptibility to infection. At high concentrations, ozone can scar the lungs.

☐ Sulfur dioxide. It irritates the airways, causes asthma attacks and sets the stage for permanent lung damage.

☐ Nitrogen dioxide. It causes bronchitis and, like ozone, increases susceptibility to infection.

☐ Carbon monoxide. This odorless, colorless gas reduces oxygen levels in the blood, starving the body's cells. It's especially dangerous for people with heart disease.

☐ Lead. This heavy metal causes permanent brain, kidney and cardiovascular damage.

Indoor air pollution

The average American spends 90% of his/ her time indoors—65% of that time at home. So if your home is polluted, you could have big trouble.

Self-defense:

☐ Clean air conditioners, humidifiers, dehumidifiers and heat exchangers on a regular basis. Follow manufacturers' instructions. Fill humidifiers with distilled or demineralized water only.

☐ Test your home for radon. This colorless, odorless gas—a powerful carcinogen—percolates up into the home from soil beneath the foundation. Pick up from your local hardware store a radon test kit bearing the label, "Meets EPA Requirements."

☐ Check furnaces once a year before heating season. Be sure the air intake is adequate and that the exhaust system is operating properly. And check flues and chimneys for blockage by debris and for cracks that could allow fumes to enter the house.

☐ Choose the right appliances. If you're considering replacing old gas appliances, select models with spark ignition rather than a pilot light. Or choose electric appliances instead. They're "cleaner" than gas appliances.

☐ Watch out for household products—cleaning agents, pesticides, paints, hobby products, solvents and other potentially dangerous products. Follow label instructions carefully regarding both use and disposal.

Better: Buy nontoxic alternatives and products in a nonaerosol form. Example: Use soap instead of phosphate detergents.

If there are no nontoxic alternatives to a particular product, buy only as much as is needed —no matter how good the price for bulk quantities.

☐ Ban cigarettes, cigars and pipes. Secondhand smoke more than doubles a person's indoor exposure to cancer-causing particles.

At greatest risk: Babies. Those living with a parent or parents who smoke are more likely than other children to have serious lung disease during the first two years of life. And children exposed to secondhand smoke are more likely to cough and wheeze and to have middle ear problems.

☐ Sweep and vacuum regularly—especially if you have rugs or wall-to-wall carpet. Use a vacuum cleaner with revolving brushes and disposable vacuum bags. Reusable bags tend to collect—and disperse—lots of dust.

If you have new carpet installed, keep your house well-ventilated for at least 48 hours afterward. Reason: New carpet releases into the air potentially harmful chemicals called volatile organic compounds (VOCs).

These chemical vapors irritate the eyes, nose and throat and trigger rashes and allergies. Recent animal studies have linked them to cancer.

Sick-building checkup:

Because of the materials used in modern construction, new or recently renovated office buildings are likely to contain VOCs.

To cut heating and cooling costs, some employers set their heating/air conditioning systems to use stale, "recirculated" air. In addition, many modern offices have sealed windows.

Danger: Stale air can cause headaches, nausea and fatigue. These symptoms could signify harmful indoor air pollution.

Self-defense: If you experience eye or throat irritation or coughing while at work, tell your building manager. If the system is using recirculated air, ask that more fresh air be pumped into the system.

Any office with sealed windows should have both a supply vent (usually on a windowsill) and an exhaust vent (usually on the ceiling). If your office does not have a ventilation system, call the department of health or speak to the landlord to find out why.

Make sure that air circulation is unimpeded. Walls, partitions, file cabinets and even temporary stacks of cartons can block air flow. If the air in your office is stagnant, talk to your office manager about ways to improve the air circulation.

If you begin to feel tired or dizzy or have headaches, there may be an air-circulation problem. Check with other employees to see if they are experiencing the same symptoms. If they are and the symptoms persist, it may be time to complain to your office manager.

Whatever kind of ventilation system is used in your workplace, your office or building manager should see that it's properly maintained. Every part of the system—including humidifiers and dehumidifiers, air filters, air-circulation pumps and blowers—must be cleaned and disinfected regularly.

The building's mechanical staff should follow the manufacturers' recommendations for maintenance and cleaning of the ventilation system. The building manager should know how often it needs to be cleaned and make sure that this schedule is being followed.

Make sure computer printers and copying machines have adequate space for free circulation of air. Ideal location: A large room with an open window.

Source: Alfred Munzer, MD, president of the American Lung Association, New York. He is also codirector of pulmonary medicine at Washington Adventist Hospital in Takoma Park, Maryland.

What to do if you're mugged

☐ Cooperate. Assume the mugger is armed. No matter how strong or fit you are, you are no match for a gun or knife. Remember that your personal safety is far more important than your valuables or your pride.

☐ Follow the mugger's instructions to the letter. Try not to move too quickly or too slowly—either could upset him.

☐ Stay as calm as possible, and encourage companions to do the same.

☐ Give the mugger whatever he asks for. Don't argue. But if something is of great sentimental value to you, give it to him, and only then say, "This watch was given to me by my grandfather. It means a lot to me. I'd be very grateful if you'd let me keep it."

☐ When he has all he wants of your valuables, ask him what he wants you to do while he gets away—stay where you are, lie face down, whatever. If he dismisses you, leave the scene immediately, and don't look back. Don't call the police until you are in a safe place.

Some important don'ts:

☐ Don't reach for your wallet in a back pocket without explaining first what you plan to do. The mugger might think you are reaching for a gun.

☐ Don't give him dirty looks or make judgmental remarks.

☐ Don't threaten him with hostile comments.

☐ Don't be a wiseguy or a joker. Even smiling is a dangerous idea. He may think you are laughing at him.

☐ Don't try any tricks like carrying a second empty wallet to give to a mugger. This could make him angry. Some experts even recommend that you carry at least $50 with you at all times to keep from upsetting a mugger.

Source: Ken Glickman, chief instructor, American Self-Defense Institute, New York.

Winter wellness

To help you get through winter as healthily as possible, three experts in the treatment of colds and flu give their advice…

☐ Dr. Jack Gwaltney—virus self-defense:

Every year when cold and flu season rolls around, we get some new information about the common cold to wonder about, take hope from or fret over.

There are two distinct phases to the process of catching a cold. The first is becoming infected, and the second is becoming sick. Instead of coming out in a full-blown cold, some people may develop a symptomless or subclinical infection, which is common in many infectious diseases.

About 25% of natural rhinovirus (the "common cold" virus) infections are of the "silent," symptomless type.

Why this is good news: If you get one of these subclinical infections, you may then acquire immunity and not develop the symptoms of a cold in response to subsequent exposure to that virus.

The most effective way to avoid catching a cold is to prevent the virus from getting into your eyes, nose or, in some cases, your mouth. Ideally, you should avoid all contact with infected individuals.

But if you are unwilling or unable to become a hermit for several months of the year, simply keep your hands clean…don't touch your face, especially your eyes, and don't put your fingers near your nose when you're around someone who obviously has a cold. No one knows exactly how cold viruses are spread, but the prevailing theories favor skin-to-skin contact or an airborne route via coughs and sneezes.

Uncertainty remains over whether viruses spread through the air are transmitted in small particles (droplets of about one to two microns in diameter) that can float and remain suspended for a time, or in larger particles that are heavier and would therefore drop more quickly. Currently, the best evidence about the transmission of rhinovirus is that it's probably spread via large particles. So turning away from an uncovered cough or sneeze is useful, because those large particles will drop from the air around you.

The whole phenomenon of a "winter cold season" is intrinsically contradictory, because rhinovirus, which thrives in high humidity, is much more prevalent from mid-spring through summer and into early fall.

When the humidity begins to drop (about the beginning of October), the rhinovirus population tends to fall off significantly, and the viruses that do better in low humidity—parainfluenza virus, respiratory syncytial virus, influenza virus and corona virus—become more prevalent.

Bottom line: Whatever the weather conditions, there's a virus out there that's waiting to infect you.

☐ Dr. Bruce Yaffe—on colds and flu:

The simple truth about cold and flu season: The more people you're exposed to, the more likely you are to get a cold. And certain factors can increase your risk of becoming infected—for example, crowded classroom or office settings, indoor environments that are very dry and closed spaces, such as airplanes, in which the air-filtration systems constantly recirculate viruses (as well as lung irritants and indoor pollutants).

Cold and flu viruses may be transmitted through the air by coughs and sneezes, but about 50% of the time, viruses travel via hand-to-hand contact. Shaking hands with someone or sharing a telephone can transfer a dose of live cold virus to your hand.

Stop giving bugs a free ride: Wash your hands frequently, wipe a shared phone with alcohol before using it, and—most important—don't touch your face. (The mucous membranes that line the eyes, nose and mouth transmit viruses efficiently.)

The use of a hot-steam vaporizer at night may help prevent colds. People tend to breathe through their mouths when they sleep, which dries out mucous membranes and makes a person more susceptible to infection. When someone coughs on you in the elevator the next morning, those dry membranes will be more permeable to infecting organisms.

It may be helpful to change toothbrushes periodically during cold season. You may be harboring a stockpile of viruses and bacteria in your brush.

Flu self-defense:

You can help to prevent influenza infection, of course, with an annual flu shot. Influenza is a type of virus usually prevalent between December and March. An influenza infection is characterized by high fever and a dry cough…it is much more severe than a "common cold." A flu shot can prevent the flu, although a small percentage of people will react to the shot by developing a sore arm and a low-grade viral syndrome that lasts for a day or two.

Helpful: Elderly people and people with chronic medical conditions (including diabetes or chronic respiratory diseases) should strongly consider flu shots.

☐ Dr. Robban A. Sica-Cohen—self-defense:

It's important to take steps to increase your resistance to colds and flu when you know that cold season is coming.

I recommend decreasing your intake of sugar and refined carbohydrates, and increasing your intake of garlic, onions and cruciferous vegetables like broccoli and cauliflower. These vegetables contain natural antibiotics, as well as high amounts of vitamins A and C—both of which are important to immune system functioning.

Vitamin and mineral supplements may also be useful additions to your diet during cold and flu season. Suggested daily dosages: Vitamin C—2,000 to 4,000 mg/day…zinc, picolinate form (the most absorbable form)—25 mg/day… vitamin A in the form of beta-carotene—do not exceed 50,000 units/day. You should also take a multivitamin tablet with minerals added.

All your mother used to tell you about not getting chilled or overheated turns out to have significant implications for immune-system functioning. There is a close correlation between temperature and immune-system effectiveness — cold temperatures suppress the immune system. This is why you develop a fever when you get an infection—the body switches into high gear to fight off the invading organisms.

Caution: The benefits of these higher body temperatures level off after about 102.5° F.

I believe that the individual immune response, rather than the strength of the infecting organism, is the key factor in determining why some people get sick after exposure to a virus and some don't. I recommend the use of herbal remedies like echinacea and Golden Seal to strengthen the immune system. These preparations can be found in most health-food stores, and they apparently make you less susceptible to infection and may even be able to boost immune-system functioning after the symptoms of a cold appear. They should be taken in a "pulsed" manner.

The stress connection:

In view of recent evidence that stress may make you more susceptible to infection, I suggest that if you know you have a problem dealing with stress, you consider taking a course on relaxation exercises, meditation or another stress-management technique to control your body's physiological response to stress.

Flu season:

The duration and severity of the symptoms of influenza can be markedly decreased by a homeopathic remedy, oscillococcinum. Take one to three doses at the onset of symptoms. Available in health-food stores.

Sources: Jack Gwaltney, MD, professor, department of internal medicine, University of Virginia School of Medicine, Charlottesville, VA. Bruce Yaffe, MD, internist in private practice in New York. Robban A. Sica-Cohen, MD, private practitioner at the Center for the Healing Arts, Orange, CT.

Checkups pay off

☐ Get your money's worth. Show up as prepared for each doctor's visit as you would for an important business meeting. Bring notes about your medical history, symptoms, medications and questions that you want the doctor to answer. Have your doctor explain what he is writing in your file.

Once you pay the bill, you're entitled to a copy of the lab report—free. Ask your doctor to explain it to you.

The more you know, the better able you will be to gauge what treatments are appropriate—and which expenses are worth questioning.

☐ Phone it in. Take advantage of a doctor's phone hours, which will save you time and money. A Dartmouth Medical School study found that this saved each patient an average of $1,656 over a two-year period.

☐ Avoid the annual physical. Symptom-free adults under age 65 can save $200 to $500 a year by reconsidering whether they really need an annual physical. The American Medical Association's guidelines suggest a full checkup every five years for adults ages 21 to 40.

☐ Ask your doctor to prescribe generic drugs when appropriate.

☐ Ask your doctor for free samples of prescribed medicines.

☐ Cut back on over-the-counter (OTC) medicines. Most OTC remedies for colds, pains and minor problems don't really do any good. In fact, only 30% of all OTC medications can prove their claims.

Source: Frederick Ruof, president, National Emergency Medicine Alliance, 524 Branch Dr., Salem, VA.

Headache relief without drugs

Relief from incapacitating tension, vascular and migraine headaches is possible without drugs, using a self-administered form of acupuncture know as acupressure.

The technique:

☐ Exert very heavy thumbnail pressure (painful pressure) successively on nerves lying just below the surface of the skin at key points in the hands and wrists. As with acupuncture, no one's sure why it works.

Pressure points to try:

☐ The triangle of flesh between the thumb and index finger on the back of your hands (thumb side of bone, near middle of the second metacarpal in the index finger).

☐ Just above the protruding bone on the thumb side of your wrist.

Operations that are often unnecessary

Major surgery is too often thought of as an easy way to deal with certain ailments. But as medicine becomes more sophisticated, some operations that were once routine have been replaced by less radical treatments or should be performed only when there is clear cause.

Examples:

☐ Tonsillectomy. Now prescribed only for recurring ear infections that cause loss of hearing, after a series of strep throat infections or when enlarged tonsils substantially impair breathing.

☐ Hysterectomy. To relieve profuse bleeding or back pain ostensibly caused by a large or displaced uterus. Be certain that the uterus is indeed to blame and that the problem cannot be stopped by other means.

☐ Ruptured-disc surgery. Symptoms can often be relieved completely with bed rest, painkillers, muscle relaxants and traction. Before an operation, make certain that X rays prove that the disc is indeed ruptured.

☐ Exploratory surgery prompted by chronic abdominal pain. Modern X-ray and other diagnostic testing has made this operation virtually obsolete.

Source: George D. LeMaitre, MD, author of How to Choose a Good Doctor, Andover Publishing, Andover, MA.

Questions to ask a surgeon

To protect yourself against unnecessary surgery, get a second opinion. Then, ask the physician these important questions before you have an operation:

☐ What are the risks?

☐ What is the mortality rate for this operation?

☐ What is the likelihood of complications?

☐ How long will it take to recover?

☐ Are there ways to treat this condition medically (that is, nonsurgically)?

☐ How many people have you seen with similar symptoms who have chosen not to have surgery? What happened to them?

☐ How many of these operations have you done in the past year?

How to cut your family's medical bills...now

Hospitals:

☐ Make sure your hospital stay is necessary. Studies show that only one of every eight hospital admissions is medically necessary and only one of every five operations really makes sense. So when you're told you should have a certain procedure or test, be appropriately skeptical.

☐ Ask the right questions. The right questions concern both health and money. Often the answer that is best for your health is also best for your wallet. Ask your doctor the following questions about any recommended procedure…

☐ What are the risks of the procedure?

☐ Which hospital do you suggest—and why? Some are safer than others… some are cheaper…some are both.

☐ Are there any less-invasive alternatives to this type of surgery? Examples: Clot-dissolving drugs instead of heart bypass surgery… lumpectomy instead of total breast removal for a breast tumor.

☐ Can I have this procedure done as an outpatient?

☐ Always get a second opinion. An eight-year study by the Cornell Medical Center found that one out of four second opinions recommends against an operation. The long-term survival rate of people who take such advice is excellent. So even if your insurance company doesn't require a second opinion, get one. And be sure to ask a lot of questions of all doctors, since you must make the final decision regarding your treatment.

Studies show that the operations most often considered unnecessary are tonsillectomies, coronary bypasses, gall-bladder removals, cesarean sections, pacemaker surgeries and joint surgeries. Be particularly diligent about getting a second opinion in such cases.

☐ Pick your hospital. Don't let it pick you. Years ago, no one "shopped" for a hospital. Today, 35% of patients do. Clearly,

this is the best option only if you have time before the surgery is necessary.

Opportunity: Community hospitals may be up to 25% cheaper than for-profit hospitals, which order more tests and have bigger markups on procedures and services.

Most doctors are affiliated with more than one hospital, so discuss your options, balancing cost against the success rate for your type of surgery.

☐ Look for the least-expensive option. Many procedures that traditionally required overnight hospital stays can now be done on an outpatient basis, which can be up to 50% cheaper than a regular hospital procedure. When you discuss outpatient alternatives with your doctor, ask about new "minimally invasive" surgical techniques, which can be considerably less expensive and less traumatic.

Trap: Never assume that your doctor or surgeon will automatically recommend the cheapest way of treating your medical problem. Ideally, you should go prepared to ask him/her about a variety of options that you've already researched.

☐ Resist unnecessary tests. Always ask your doctor why a hospital test must be given. The tests most frequently over-ordered are urinalyses, chest X rays and two types of blood tests—one that measures white blood cell count and another that measures the amount of time it takes blood to clot. Once in the hospital, insist on advance approval of tests and procedures.

☐ Save on "incidentals." Check to see what the hospital charges for various services before you check in. The most frequently hidden hospital costs are the $50-to-$100 fees for providing routine information when filling out forms. These charges are levied by 25% to 30% of hospitals. If yours is one of them, ask to fill out the papers yourself—assuming, of course, that you are well enough to do so.

Another example: Fees for health and beauty aids. In some cases, you can save more than $100 by bringing your own toiletries and pills, if you are already on the appropriate medications before being admitted. You may also be able to fill new prescriptions outside the hospital when you are a patient.

☐ Assume there is a problem with your bill. A new General Accounting Office study found overcharges in 99% of all hospital bills. Why does this matter to someone who has health insurance? Because more and more plans are requiring patients to share hospital costs.

Strategy: Request a fully itemized bill. Then review it carefully. Look for:

☐ Duplicate billings (often for tests).

☐ Shoddy testing (don't pay for unreadable X rays).

☐ Unauthorized tests (if you previously specified that you wanted advance approval).

☐ "Phantom" charges (often for sedatives and other medications that may never have been given to you).

☐ Bulk charges. If you see a broad heading such as "radiology" or "pharmacy," you can't possibly know if the total is accurate. Ask for a more detailed breakdown of the charges incurred.

Doctors:

☐ Get your money's worth. Show up as prepared for each doctor's visit as you would for an important business meeting. Bring notes about your medical history, symptoms, medications and questions that you want the doctor to answer. Have your doctor explain what he is writing in your file.

Once you pay the bill, you're entitled to a copy of the lab report—free. Ask your doctor to explain it to you.

The more you know, the better able you will be to gauge what treatments are appropriate—and which expenses are worth questioning.

☐ Phone it in. Take advantage of a doctor's phone hours, which will save you time and money. A Dartmouth Medical School study found that this saved each patient an average of $1,656 over a two-year period.

Warning: There's a difference between avoiding unnecessary visits to specialists and forgoing important preventive measures. People who save money by avoiding flu shots or treatment for high blood pressure are making serious mistakes.

☐ Avoid the annual physical. Symptom-free adults under age 65 can save $200 to $500 a year by reconsidering whether they really need an annual physical. The American Medical Association's guidelines suggest a full checkup every five years for adults ages 21 to 40—and every few years thereafter, depending on your health. Doctors themselves get physicals much less often than do other professionals of the same age.

Insurance:

☐ Increase your deductible. Talk with your insurance agent or with the benefits person at your company. The amount you save each year may be substantial, particularly if you are a healthy adult.

☐ Avoid being overinsured. Be prepared to absorb some occasional minor expenses rather than seeking a policy that covers every penny of your expenses all the time. This kind of insurance policy is never a bargain.

☐ If your benefits are ever denied—fight back. Some surveys show that policyholders who contest denials get partial or complete satisfaction 50% of the time.

Drugs:

☐ Ask your doctor to prescribe generic drugs when appropriate.

☐ Ask your doctor for free samples of prescribed medicines.

☐ Cut back on over-the-counter (OTC) medicines. Most OTC remedies for colds, pains and minor problems don't really do any good. In fact, only 30% of all OTC medications can prove their claims.

Source: Frederick Ruof, president of the National Emergency Medicine Alliance (NEMA), an organization that specializes in providing consumers with ways to reduce medical costs. NEMA publishes a booklet called *How to Cut Your Family's Medical Bills by $1,000,* Salem, VA.

How to use imagery and inner wisdom to conquer illness

Though it would be overly simplistic to say that the mind causes—or cures—illness, it's clear that our emotions, attitudes and beliefs can influence our health…and that altering those thoughts and emotions can have a powerful effect on health as well.

Surprisingly, the most health-supporting emotional state seems not to be enthusiasm or even optimism, but serenity and peacefulness.

Body, mind and spirit:

In addition to exploring the role of the mind in promoting health, I believe it's equally important to consider the role of the spirit. When we're aware of the spiritual dimension of life, we have access to many powerful resources that aren't available when we limit our focus to mind and body.

It isn't necessary to practice a particular religion—or to hold any special theological views—in order to embrace the concept of spirituality. The dictionary refers to spirit as life principle…the force that gives us vitality, drives and motivates us and supports our survival.

I don't view work with the mind and spirit as a substitute for established Western medical practices. Humans are physical, as well as mental and spiritual, beings. All three aspects need to be addressed.

Your innate healing capacity:

At the Simonton Cancer Center, we have developed an effective group of techniques that can help patients mobilize their innate healing capacities. Essential elements of the program…

☐ Social support and communication. Your support system could be a formal group made up of people with problems similar to yours. Or it could be an individual, such as a friend or spouse, who is committed to encouraging your efforts toward healing.

The idea of support can be broadened to include your entire environment— physical surroundings, the people with whom you spend time, your own commitments. How do they make you feel?

When Person X is around, do you tend to feel more hopeful, confident, moving in the direction of better health? Or are you fearful, anxious, depressed?

Evaluate your environment and make a point of spending more time with people and situations that enhance health-promoting feelings… and avoiding those that do the opposite.

There are some people you won't want to banish from your life—and shouldn't. If your spouse is anxious about illness and unable to provide the support you need, don't feel you have to avoid him/her—but do look for other sources of support. And encourage your spouse to get support as well, perhaps through counseling or a group geared to partners' needs.

Caution: Evaluate a support group the same way you do the rest of your environment—by how it makes you feel. If it leaves you more fearful or depressed than before, find another group.

Much stress between loved ones can be avoided through straightforward communication. People tend to assume they know what the ill person needs and attempt to provide it, without checking first.

This leads to frustration—the unwilling recipient may feel manipulated or intruded upon, while the would-be helper feels punished for his efforts. This scenario can be avoided by a simple discussion during which the helper agrees to ask beforehand, "Would it be helpful if I did X?"…and to accept the honest answer.

☐ Imagery:

Imagery, broadly defined as the way we think about things, can have a powerful effect on the body. Healthy images lead to healthy emotional responses, which stimulate the body to produce chemicals important to the healing process.

Conversely, unhealthy images and emotions can stimulate the production of stress hormones and other chemicals that divert the body's resources away from healing and make it more vulnerable to illness.

We can help ourselves toward health by searching for words and mental pictures that allow us to think about illness and its treatment in ways that promote health.

Example: A patient going in for chemotherapy may be thinking about the procedure with dread, seeing it as a hurtful poison and dwelling on the unpleasant side effects…or, conversely, he may view it as a powerful tool that can help him get well—a healthier image.

There are many kinds of healthy imagery, and patients need to find the images with which they feel comfortable.

Some people like to visualize the body's immune system attacking the disease, picturing the white blood cells as soldiers attacking the hostile invader.

Others prefer less aggressive imagery—such as vividly imagining an arthritic joint with white blood cells exploring joint surfaces, removing debris and soothing any areas of irritation until the joint is imagined as smooth with glistening surfaces.

☐ Meditation—tapping our inner wisdom. Years ago Albert Schweitzer observed that each person has a wise physician within him. We already possess many of the keys to health and healing, and we can learn to gain greater access to that deep center of wisdom within each of us.

One of the most effective tools for doing so is meditation. There are many forms of meditation, and many excellent books have been written on the subject.

The main element tying these various meditation approaches together is the act of quieting oneself in a ritualized manner, whether through rhythmic breathing, physical movement (as in yoga or tai chi) or contemplation of an image or a sound pattern. Once in this quiet state, we can learn a great deal by asking ourselves for guidance.

Often when we step outside of our usual way of thinking, the mind rebels and stirs up a great deal of mental noise. It can sometimes be difficult to tell whether we've tapped a fount of inspiration or just a new way of kidding ourselves.

Useful guideline: If an inner message produces distressing emotions such as guilt, fear or depression, it's not arising out of inner wisdom. A truly inspiring message creates a feeling of rightness, a sense of peace. (The mental static tends to decrease with practice.)

☐ Setting goals. Goal-setting skills are useful no matter what the state of your health, but they're especially important for those dealing with serious illness. Since lifestyle changes can be such important healing tools, people are often tempted to make too many drastic changes all at once. Result: Stress and discouragement, which are definitely not health-producing emotions.

I suggest making goals for the long term. Look at where you'd like to be in two years and set goals that will help you get there. This will give you a structure for change, but with very little pressure. Major areas for goal-setting:

☐ Diet   ☐ Play
☐ Exercise   ☐ Life purpose
☐ Social support ☐ Meditation
☐ Creative thinking

Play and life purpose are often neglected, but they're vital to maintaining a healthy emotional state. It might seem frivolous to set aside more time for fun when you're sick—but that's when you need it most. As for life purpose, that's what mobilizes us to reach for other goals. Ask yourself: "What gives me deep fulfillment? Why am I on the planet today?" Keep answers specific, not global: "I'm here to make sure my kids get fed and loved" is more motivating

than "I hope to contribute to world peace"—though that's a worthy desire.

After you assess what you'd like to achieve in these seven areas, prioritize them. Don't try to tackle them all at once. Pick one area to focus on first…then, in two or three months, add the next priority…then the next. Not only will you find it easier to reach more of your goals…you'll have the energy to appreciate them.

Source: Radiation oncologist O. Carl Simonton, MD, medical director of the Simonton Cancer Center in Pacific Palisades, California, and pioneer in the study of mind-body techniques for treating cancer. His most recent book is The Healing Journey: The Simonton Center Program for Achieving Physical, Mental and Spiritual Health, *Bantam Books, New York.*

How to diagnose ✓ yourself—when your doctor can't

Few experiences are as frustrating as having a chronic health problem that your doctor can't identify.

If the doctor cannot diagnose the problem, you must either learn to live with the symptoms…or go on to another doctor.

Trap: The more doctors a patient consults with, the less seriously each new doctor is likely to take the patient's complaints.

Eventually, even the patient begins to doubt the reality of the symptoms… while remaining debilitated by them. The fear that he/she may be neurotic adds to the problem.

I know about this phenomenon first-hand. I came down with a mysterious and incapacitating illness that turned out—after six years and nearly 30 doctors—to be Lyme disease.

In consulting with a seemingly endless procession of specialists, I learned how important it is to take an active role in the search for a diagnosis. I also found out what to do to get respect and cooperation from doctors—many of whom were skeptical of my symptoms.

The lessons I learned during my search for a diagnosis should be helpful to anyone who is sick but doesn't know why—people in what I call the pre-diagnosis period of a long illness.

Trust your instincts:

Our society has a need to categorize. We tend to doubt the reality of anything we can't label.

This is certainly true of most doctors. It's also true of friends and relatives, who may have difficulty being supportive of someone whose condition has no name. It helps to know that you're not alone. Many, many illnesses can take months or years to diagnose.

Recently, I surveyed 180 patients in support groups for five different chronic illnesses. What I found: The average time between the onset of symptoms and diagnosis was five years.

Lyme disease isn't the only disease that's often misdiagnosed. Others include lupus, colon cancer, ovarian cancer and Parkinson's disease.

Several things changed once I learned to believe in myself—to accept that I had a real illness even though no one knew what it was. I began to feel less desperate. I learned to cope with my mysterious symptoms. And because I no longer had anything to prove, I stopped acting defensive with doctors.

Example: When a doctor suggested that my illness might be psychogenic (originating in the mind), I no longer jumped to deny it. Instead, I calmly said, "I've had psychological problems at certain times in my life, but I can't believe that is what's causing all of these symptoms." The doctor considered my symptoms and my attitude, then replied, "You're right. This is not a psychological problem."

Find the right doctor:

Even if he/she can't diagnose your illness, the right doctor can help you sort out what's wrong.

Your doctor can refer you to specialists, analyze medical opinions and test results and help you manage your symptoms as you await a correct diagnosis and appropriate treatment.

To find the right doctor, get referrals from friends and acquaintances—especially people who work in the medical profession.

Tell them you're looking for a doctor who is compassionate, understanding and willing to take time with patients. Say you want someone who will encourage you to ask questions and be involved in decision-making about your own care.

You're also looking for someone who enjoys being a medical detective. Not every doctor does. You may have to interview several before you find one who takes you seriously and with whom you have a good rapport.

During your first meeting with a prospective doctor, make it clear that you don't expect him/her to have all the answers. Doctors get frustrated, too. If the doctor knows you're looking for someone to help manage your symptoms and guide your search, he/she will be less likely to feel put on the spot—or to brush you off as neurotic.

Examine your records:

Don't assume that you know what's in your medical file. Reviewing your test results and doctors' notes may reveal startling discrepancies…or new avenues to explore.

Problem: Specialists reviewing your file may not always see the big picture—how their findings fit in with those of other specialists. Doctors may record information that's different from what they told you…or from what you meant to relay. Test results may be ambiguous or incomplete.

Example: Three years before my diagnosis, my blood was tested for several illnesses, including Lyme disease. I was told at the time that all the tests came back normal. So, for the next three years I told doctors that I'd tested negative for Lyme. Later, I learned that the Lyme test had never been performed—the state lab had sent a note saying that no such test was available in Minnesota. If I had examined the file, I would have given doctors the correct information and I might have been diagnosed years earlier.

Medical records are usually easy to obtain. Simply request them from the doctor's office or the medical records department of your hospital or clinic. A simple medical dictionary will help you interpret jargon. Some places may ask you to sign a release form and/or pay a small copying fee.

Learn about medications:

Be sure you understand the possible side effects of all drugs prescribed for you. Understand, too, their potential interactions with other medications.

The pamphlets that drug companies put out about their medications are extremely thorough. Ask your pharmacist for copies.

Use the library:

You may discover valuable clues about your illness by doing your own research.

Many hospital and university medical libraries are open to the public. Some general libraries have medical collections. Ask the librarian to steer you toward relevant reference books, journals and databases. Phone the library ahead to find out what times are least busy. Look up your symptoms and their possible causes in diagnostic textbooks.

If your doctor has mentioned possible diagnoses, read about those conditions. Journals frequently include case histories of people with specific diseases or symptoms—the articles are often listed by subject in databases.

Provide your doctor with any scientific article that you think might help him/her with the diagnosis.

For more information on library research, read *Ask Your Doctor, Ask Yourself* by Annette Thornhill Schiffer (Publishing Ltd., 77 Lower Valley Rd., Atglen, Pennsylvania 19310).

Another good source of medical information is the Health Resource (209 Katherine Dr., Conway, Arkansas 72032. 501-329-5272). This service will research the relevant medical literature for you, then send you a report of up to 150 pages in length.

Learn to live with uncertainty:

Learn to accept your illness without giving up your search for answers. Acknowledge that your symptoms are real. Don't worry about the future— focus on one day at a time. Try to experience joy even in the midst of uncertainty.

This attitude fosters the relaxed open-mindedness that makes a good detective. It also helps you cope more effectively with your symptoms.

Important: If you stay reasonably relaxed rather than tensing up when symptoms flare up, the discomfort is likely to be of shorter duration and less intense.

Acceptance also helps you notice your body's signals and enables you to respond to them appropriately— whether by eating more nutritiously or taking a nap in the afternoon. You'll be a more effective partner with your body as it works toward healing.

Source: Linda Hanner, coauthor of *When You're Sick and Don't Know Why,* Chronimed Publishing, Minneapolis. For information on a national support network now being set up for people with undiagnosed illnesses, write to the author at Box 307, Delano, Minnesota 55328.

What you may not know about high blood pressure

More than 40 million Americans—about 75% of whom are adults over age 30— have high blood pressure (hypertension). Yet too few understand what they can do to possibly prevent or treat it.

Many people with mild hypertension ignore the problem or fail to spot it soon enough through medical checkups.

Danger: By the time hypertension causes medical complications, heart health has already been put at risk.

What's normal, what's not:

An initial blood-pressure reading should be taken at about age three and again during adolescence. If your blood pressure is normal during this period, it should be rechecked every two or three years throughout your adult life.

If your blood pressure rises above 140/90, more frequent readings may be needed. Mild high blood pressure or Stage I—from 140/90 to 160/100— usually requires lifestyle changes. Medication may also be necessary.

Here's what you may or may not know about high blood pressure and how to control it…

☐ Being tense or nervous will not give you high blood pressure. The term hypertension refers to elevated pressure in the arteries, not to someone's personality. Many calm, cool-headed people have hypertension…many anxious, jittery people have perfectly normal blood pressures.

Nervousness may cause a short-term rise in blood pressure because of the adrenaline response. But there's no evidence that a nervous personality or even a stress-filled life causes hypertension.

☐ Blood pressure is variable. Your blood pressure does not remain constant. It can fluctuate by as much as 20 to 30 points a day.

Your blood pressure is at its highest during the early morning hours—just before and as you awaken—and when extra blood is needed, such as when you exercise.

It is at its lowest during sleep and restful times, dropping to the lowest point from about 1 AM to 4 AM.

☐ Blood pressure can change with the weather. Generally, your blood pressure drops during hot weather or when you're perspiring a lot. Warm weather causes blood vessels to dilate—and that lowers blood pressure.

In cold weather, blood-pressure readings may rise because blood vessels constrict. Unless weather conditions are extreme, the change isn't enough to be medically significant.

☐ Excessive alcohol consumption can increase risk. Moderate to heavy drinking (about three to five drinks daily) can raise blood pressure over the long term.

Reason: Though large amounts of alcohol may dilate blood vessels, which can lower blood pressure, drinking also increases the heart rate, which raises blood pressure and cancels the dilation effect. Alcohol can also affect certain hormone systems that regulate blood pressure.

Cutting back on alcohol can bring levels to within normal range in some individuals. One or two drinks daily generally does not affect blood pressure, and some researchers have found that small quantities of alcohol can protect against cardiovascular disease.

Treatment:

☐ Exercise is good—but not all kinds. For some people, mild, repetitive exercise over time helps reduce blood pressure slightly. For others, it reduces levels significantly. It is not necessary to take up jogging or join an exercise club unless you need or prefer a structured plan. Walking or other leisure activities are satisfactory.

Warning: Isometric (pushing) exercises, like weightlifting (free weights or weight machines), should be avoided by anyone with high blood pressure or heart disease. The tightened muscles constrict blood vessels and can raise blood pressure. Avoid inversion bars and "antigravity boots," from which you hang upside down and do sit-ups. This increases blood-pressure levels.

☐ Losing weight is the most effective nondrug method to reduce high blood pressure. Excess weight increases the volume of blood in the body, constricting blood vessels and putting extra demands on the heart, which elevates blood pressure. In some cases, losing as little as ten pounds can return blood-pressure levels to normal. If you plan to lose a significant amount of weight (more than 30 pounds), ask your doctor to monitor cardiovascular effects.

☐ Sex will not dramatically affect hypertension. Though sex can raise blood pressure temporarily—particularly with a new or unfamiliar partner—just minutes after the peak at orgasm, it will drop back to levels equivalent to or lower than before.

☐ Good nutrition can help keep levels in line. Lowering sodium intake helps some people with high blood pressure—about 20% or 30% of all cases. Others are hardly affected at all.

Best way: Be aware of salt in cooking and on the table, as well as hidden sources of sodium. Many processed foods that don't taste salty—soft drinks, ice cream, breakfast cereals—are high in sodium.

Other dietary factors: Potassium—found in fresh fruits and vegetables, unprocessed meats and fish—and calcium are thought to have protective effects. Adequate calcium—800 to 1,000 mg a day for adults—rather than high doses is best. The minimum daily intake of potassium is 2,000 mg, but 4,000 mg is optimal. Daily sodium intake should be about half that of potassium.

Source: Marvin Moser, MD, clinical professor of medicine, Yale University School of Medicine. He is the author of *Lower Your Blood Pressure and Live Longer,* Berkley, New York.

Cough medicines that don't do what they advertise

The Federal Drug Administration is beginning to agree with an increasing number of doctors who say commercial cough remedies interfere with the body's natural way of clearing the respiratory tract, which is coughing. Doctors are especially concerned with:

☐ Antihistamines, which they say work by thickening, not thinning, lung secretions. Good only for allergies.

☐ Decongestants, which might be good for extreme stuffiness but are otherwise of doubtful effectiveness.

☐ Expectorants, which drug companies say loosen mucus and phlegm, although the evidence is scanty.

☐ Suppressants, which suppress the brain's cough reflex. They are especially hazardous for people with asthma or bronchitis who rely on coughing to breathe when their lungs are not clear.

Source: *Executive Fitness Newsletter,* Emmaus, PA.

First aid mistakes

One of the most frustrating aspects of working in emergency medicine is coping with people's botched attempts at administering first aid. Often they simply make the situation worse. Yet it's easy to give first aid properly if you learn a few basic rules. Most common errors:

☐ Mistake: Smearing butter or lard on a burn. Applying fat only intensifies the injury. Instead, run cold water over the burned area for 10 to 15 seconds. Then wrap it with a handkerchief or other clean, dry dressing. Seek medical care for any burn that is blistered…or in which decreased sensation exists…or which occurs around the mouth, nose, fingers or toes.

☐ Mistake: Moving someone's head after a neck injury. This can cause permanent paralysis. Sad: Most cases of paralysis result not from the initial injury, but from moving the injured person. Never move an injured person's head from side to side to "see if they're okay." Instead, tell the victim to lie still while you call an ambulance.

☐ Mistake: Insisting that "it couldn't be a heart attack." Anyone experiencing chest pain, nausea, excessive perspiration or shortness of breath needs immediate medical attention. Delaying treatment to see if symptoms "go away" can turn a survivable heart attack into a fatal one. Don't drive yourself to the hospital. Call an ambulance or have someone else drive you.

☐ Mistake: Holding down someone who can't breathe. Encourage the person to sit up. The intestines and diaphragm will descend, giving the lungs more room to expand.

☐ Mistake: Touching an electric shock victim. Always turn off the current before touching the victim—or you risk getting shocked yourself. If you cannot turn the current off, use a book, a dry wooden stick or some other nonconducting object (not metallic or wet) to push away the source of the current.

Examples: Hook the heel of a shoe over the wire and pull it off…separate the victim from the wire using a wooden-handled broom or a rolled-up newspaper or magazine.

Drag or gently push the person away from the source of the current. Call for help.

☐ Mistake: Applying a tourniquet to a minor cut. In most cases, bleeding can be controlled simply by applying pressure to the site, then applying a cold compress to help blood vessels constrict.

Tourniquets are appropriate only for life-threatening blood loss, as happens with a complete or partial amputation…or for bad cuts sustained in a remote area where help is not nearby.

To apply a tourniquet: Place a clean strip of cloth at least two inches wide between the wound and the rest of the body. Wrap it around the limb twice and tie a knot. Place a stick, pen or other straight, rigid object atop the knot and tie it in place. Twist the stick to tighten the tourniquet until the bleeding stops. Tie the loose ends of cloth around the stick to hold it in the tightened position. Do not loosen or remove the tourniquet while waiting for medical help.

Important: If you use a tourniquet, make sure you have cut off circulation only in the veins—not the arteries. Briefly press on a toenail or fingernail or indent a quarter-inch patch of skin on the "far" side of the tourniquet. If you've applied the tourniquet properly, the skin should turn white, then return to its normal color within a couple of seconds. If it doesn't, loosen the tourniquet slightly.

If a body part has been severed, seal it in a plastic bag and put the bag on ice. Never put the part directly on ice.

☐ Mistake: Overheating frostbitten fingers, toes or ears. Immersing the injured part in hot water only causes additional tissue damage. Instead, thaw it rapidly in water that's between 98°F (normal body temperature) and 110°F. Water that feels uncomfortably hot is too hot.

☐ Mistake: Overtreating a snakebite. A snakebite itself usually poses less of a risk than amateurs' efforts to treat it. They typically cut too deeply into the skin, severing arteries, tendons or nerves. And when they try to suck out the venom, they often contaminate the wound.

Instead: Keep the victim calm and as motionless as possible while he/she is transported to an emergency room. If you suspect the snake was poisonous, use a tourniquet to restrict venous circulation (and venom flow) between the bite and the victim's heart or main part of the body.

☐ Mistake: Hesitating to perform CPR. People often shy away from doing cardiopulmonary resuscitation because they can't remember the technique precisely—especially the ratio of chest compressions to breaths. (For two rescuers, it's five compressions for every "ventilation." For one rescuer, it's fifteen compressions for every two ventilations.)

Good news: Even imperfect CPR will help the person breathe and keep some of his/her blood circulating. Before you start, however, call for help.

☐ Mistake: Squeezing too hard or too long when performing the Heimlich maneuver. Squeezing the chest from the sides can break the person's ribs. Correct procedure: Stand behind the choking victim. Shove your fist up and in just above the navel. This will push the diaphragm upward. Then release. Repeat if necessary—but don't stand there squeezing.

Source: Stanley M. Zydlo, Jr., MD, director, department of emergency medicine, Northwest Community Hospital, Arlington Heights, Illinois. He is coauthor of *The American Medical Association Handbook of First Aid and Emergency Care: A Comprehensive Step-by-Step Guide to Dealing with Injuries, Illnesses and Medical Emergencies,* Random House, New York.

X-rated videos ✔

X-rated videos help men with fertility problems produce better sperm for use in artificial insemination. In a recent study, those who masturbated while watching the videos produced semen with more than double the sperm counts—and with higher proportions of healthy sperm. Theory: Sperm quality and fertilizing potential improve with increased sexual excitement.

Source: Nikolaos Sofikitis, MD, PhD, assistant lecturer in urology, Tottori University School of Medicine, Yonago, Japan.

Bicycle seats 〰

Bicycle seats can cause numbness, temporary impotence or even a painful permanent erection (priapism) in men who ride often or for long distances. Reason: The traditional narrow, one-piece design puts too much pressure on the internal erectile chambers of the penis. Self-defense: Pedal as smoothly

as possible to avoid bouncing…or fit your bike with a newer split seat that has one side to support the right buttock and another to support the left. Stationary exercise bicycles do not seem to pose a threat.

Source: E. Douglas Whitehead, MD, director, Association for Male Sexual Dysfunction, New York.

If you've become dependent on prescription drugs

☐ Cut drug dependency gradually, under a doctor's supervision. Stopping the pills immediately is sometimes possible. But it is often accompanied by insomnia, muscle twitches, a burning sensation of the skin or even seizures.

☐ Expect withdrawal symptoms to occur days after you stop taking the drug. When they occur, don't fall into the trap of believing you're overstressed and resume taking the drug that caused the problem in the first place.

☐ Sign up for a detoxification program. There are many throughout the country, from low-cost therapy offered through most state and local health departments to luxury "spas." To find out about detox programs, contact Center for Substance Abuse Treatment Hotline, 11428 Rockville Pike, Rockville, MD 20852. (800) 662-4357.

☐ At various points in your withdrawal from drugs, you may decide it is not worth the effort. Except for those people with chronic, incurable physiological (not psychological) pain, it is worth it. If you have any doubts, ask a former addict.

Source: Josette Mondanaro, MD, Santa Cruz, CA.

Sexual side effects of high blood pressure medicines

Many illnesses can themselves cause lack of libido and impotence, but in other cases, it is the medication used to treat the illness that brings on changes in sexual desire and capability. Research in this area is scanty, and the sexual side effects of many drugs are not universal. Discuss your own situation with your doctor. The following drugs are known to have affected the sex lives of many who take them regularly:

☐ Esimil and Ismelin (guanethidine) may cause impaired ejaculation and lack of potency in men.

□ Aldomet, Aldoclor and Aldoril (methyl-dopa) can decrease sexual desire and make holding an erection difficult for men. In rare cases, they cause a man's breasts to develop.

□ Diupres, Exna-R, Rau-Sed, Regroton, Salutensin, Ser-Ap-Es and Serpasil (reserpine) can cause reduced libido and potency, delayed ejaculation and enlarged breasts.

□ Catapres (clonidine) may produce impotence in men and failure to achieve orgasm in women.

□ Eutonyl and Eutron (pargyline) may bring on impotence, delayed ejaculation or delayed orgasm.

□ Inderal and Inderide (propranolol) rarely cause side effects, although difficulty with erections has been reported.

Source: Joe Graedon, pharmacologist and author of *The People's Pharmacy* and *The People's Pharmacy–2*, Avon Books, New York.

Sexual side effects ✓ of mood-altering drugs

□ Librium and Valium have quite opposite effects on different individuals. For some, these drugs reduce inhibitions and increase sexual desire. In other cases, they decrease libido.

□ Depression itself often causes a lack of interest in sex. Antidepressant drugs sometimes increase libido and sometimes decrease it. Other sexual side effects vary widely and are not well recorded. Possible problems include impotence, testicular swelling, breast enlargement and milk secretion, impaired ejaculation in men and delayed orgasm in women.

□ Many medications used to treat psychosis have adverse sexual side effects that have not been fully documented. Among the symptoms are impotence, difficulty in ejaculation, irregular menstruation, abnormal lactation, increased and decreased sexual desire and even false-positive pregnancy tests.

□ Sleeping pills reduce the desire for sex. As administered in therapy, barbiturates often diminish sexual inhibitions, which raises sexual enjoyment. But chronic use of sleeping pills causes difficulty in reaching orgasm. *More dangers:* Men can become impotent, and women may suffer menstrual problems.

Source: Joe Graedon, pharmacologist and author of *The People's Pharmacy* and *The People's Pharmacy–2*, Avon Books, New York, and Dorothy DeMoya, RN, and Dr. Armando DeMoya, MD, both of Georgetown University, writing in *RN*, Oradell, NJ.

Precautions when you need blood

There are certain steps individuals can take to insure against getting contaminated blood in hospitals:

□ Prior to surgery, make a specific request of your physician to use only volunteer-donor blood. Volunteer blood does not cost any more than commercial blood. And commercial (paid-donor) blood has a much higher incidence of contamination.

□ Better still, arrange beforehand to donate your own blood to be used during your surgery.

□ If your blood type is rare, join the National Rare Blood Club*, which has 16,000 volunteer donors throughout the US who will supply blood without charge in an emergency.

□ Despite your precautions, you may still get commercial blood. Hospitals cannot be held liable if they have no volunteer-donor blood and must, in an emergency, give paid-donor blood to a patient who requested volunteer-donor blood only. Several states, including California, Illinois and Oklahoma, have outlawed the use of commercial blood.

All about receding gums

If you're worried about your gums receding —relax. While gum recession can be a cosmetic problem, it does not cause tooth loss, it tends to be self-limiting and it rarely requires treatment.

Gum recession occurs when the gum shrinks from the neck of a tooth, exposing some of the root and giving the appearance of being "long in the tooth." Recession can occur with a single tooth or with many.

Causes of gum recession:

Gum recession can be part of the normal aging process. But age isn't the only thing that causes receding gums.

Other possible causes:

□ Heredity. Some people are simply destined to have receding gums. They may have inherited thin, delicate gums...or may have teeth that are "too big" for their jaw—like inheriting grandma's large teeth with grandpa's narrow jaw. If the gums are stretched beyond their limits, recession can occur.

*The rare blood types are B+, O, A, AB+, B, AB.

In some cases, recession occurs when the frenum—the band of muscle fibers attaching the upper and lower lips to the gums—attaches too close to the gum line.

☐ Improper brushing. Scrubbing your teeth with a harsh side-to-side motion damages delicate gum tissue, which can result in recession. Using a toothbrush with hard bristles can make it even worse, so be sure to use one that's labeled "soft."

Hard brushing can also cause the exposed portion of the roots to become notched. This situation can lead to tooth decay…and the need for fillings.

☐ Braces. As crooked teeth are straightened, they may be moved beyond the edge of the jaw. Result: Exposed roots. A skilled orthodontist may be able to avoid this problem in some cases. In others, it's simply the price you pay for having straight teeth.

☐ Chronic irritation. Anything that irritates the gums—whether it's a poorly placed filling, improper flossing or chronic "picking" with a fingernail, hairpin, paper clip, etc.—can cause recession.

Treatment

Can gum recession be minimized? Yes. Brush properly (have your dentist or dental hygienist check your technique)…ask your dentist about replacing irritating fillings…and be sure not to pick at your teeth.

Source: Alan A. Winter, DDS, associate clinical professor of dentistry, New York University School of Dentistry, New York City. A board-certified periodontist, he also maintains a private practice in New York.

Arthritis can be controlled

Myths about arthritis abound. Many people assume that arthritis is inevitable with age… that it's invariably crippling…that it can't be treated.

Yet in my 20 years as a rheumatologist, I've rarely seen an arthritic patient who didn't feel much better after following a comprehensive course of treatment. Arthritis refers to inflammation in the joint. There are more than 100 different kinds of arthritis, which fall under two general categories:

☐ Inflammatory—including rheumatoid arthritis, which afflicts 2.5 million people in this country. This type starts in the membrane that lines the capsule surrounding a joint. Rheumatoid arthritis tends to affect many joints, as well as muscles, nerves or other parts of the body. Inflammatory conditions are systemic in nature and influence other parts of the body. Fatigue and flu-like symptoms are common. It most often has its onset in women between the ages of 30 and 50.

☐ Degenerative—or osteoarthritis, afflicting 36 million Americans. It is thought to result from natural wear and tear on joints and is more common in older adults…as well as younger people who have suffered sports injuries, accidents or other severe trauma to the joints.

Although we don't know the cause or cure for either type of arthritis, we have many, many resources for controlling it by relieving pain, restoring motion, slowing degeneration and helping patients lead normal and active lives.

Diagnosis and treatment:

Because there is so much prejudice about arthritis in the medical community, the disease is often incorrectly diagnosed. Just because a patient is older and has joint pain doesn't mean he/she has arthritis—and even if arthritis is present, it may not be what's causing the symptoms.

Bursitis (inflammation of the protective sac near a joint) and tendinitis (inflamed tendons) are treatable conditions that are frequently confused with arthritis.

Example: A patient complains that his right hip aches. Because the patient is 65, his doctor assumes he has arthritis. An X ray shows some wear on the hip joint, confirming the doctor's assumption. The physician says, "What do you expect at 65?" and puts him on anti-inflammatory drugs, which don't help him. In fact, the arthritis isn't causing the pain—this patient is actually suffering from bursitis, which could be easily treated with physical therapy or steroid injections.

I urge patients who are diagnosed with arthritis not to accept the attitude that nothing can be done for them. If a primary-care physician isn't sure about the diagnosis, or if treatment isn't successful in relieving symptoms, I recommend consulting a rheumatologist— a specialist in arthritic diseases.

The best approach to treating arthritis is a multi-modal one.

Medications help, but they are far more effective when used in conjunction with other factors, including physical therapy, exercise, adequate sleep, diet and stress management.

Mechanical devices such as splints and canes can also provide relief by resting the affected area.

Many of these elements are surprisingly simple—but often ignored. Common sense remedies the medical establishment once scorned as old wives' tales are now gaining scientific support.

Though new drugs are coming onto the market all the time, I believe the real news in treatment is validation of the old treatments.

Medication:

Physicians have a whole arsenal of drugs to draw from. Mild cases of osteoarthritis may respond to over-the-counter painkillers such as acetaminophen.

More severe cases of degenerative joint diseases and cases of rheumatoid arthritis are usually helped by anti-inflammatory drugs. Most of these can have side effects, such as stomach irritation, but so many varieties are available that doctor and patient can usually find one the patient can tolerate.

Nonprescription anti-inflammatories aren't usually strong enough in recommended doses to be effective against arthritis…and increasing the dose can lead to unpleasant side effects. Talk to your doctor before taking—or increasing—any medication.

New: Capsaicin, a topical cream originally developed to treat shingles. Capsaicin is rubbed into the skin around the joint. Unlike other topical products, which provide only temporary relief, this cream appears to reduce concentrations of chemicals which lead to the pain response.

It must be used diligently—three to four times a day. Side effects can include a mild burning sensation. Capsaicin is available over the counter, but like any drug it should be used under a doctor's supervision.

For rheumatoid arthritis, gold compounds—taken orally or injected—have long been a mainstay of treatment. But these compounds have been associated with problems including rashes and kidney dysfunction—and must be closely monitored.

Other medications are also helpful for treating rheumatoid arthritis, chiefly antimalarial drugs and immuno-suppressive agents—the kind used to treat cancer.

Physical therapy:

Physical therapists are vastly under-utilized by physicians in general, and certainly where arthritis is concerned.

A physical therapist will often manipulate the affected area and prescribe therapeutic exercises for the patient to do at home—in order to restore use of the joints and the muscles and tendons supporting them.

Other techniques used by these health-care professionals include massage, application of heat or cold and electrical stimulation of surrounding nerves.

Exercise:

In addition to specific exercises prescribed by a physical therapist, people with arthritis can benefit dramatically from recreational exercise, such as walking, swimming or tennis. The typical patient might respond, "I can't even move without pain—how can I exercise?" But inactivity is likely to make arthritis worse, not better.

When you don't move a painful joint, the muscles around it begin to weaken and atrophy. Scar tissue may form, and you lose mobility.

Everyone—arthritic or not—should exercise 25 to 30 minutes, three or four times a week. The key is to find the right window—enough exercise to be beneficial, but not so much as to cause great pain. It's a good idea to start very slowly—with ten minutes of walking, for example—and note how your body responds. If your joints hurt severely while you're working out, or you feel very uncomfortable afterward or the next morning, don't give up…just cut back to five minutes for a while. Then gradually increase the length of your workout to 30 minutes. To guard against overuse, consult with a doctor and physical therapist before you begin your program.

Diet:

Changes in diet have not generally been shown to help arthritis. Exceptions:

☐ In rare cases, eliminating certain foods from the diet, especially dairy products, provides relief for sufferers.

☐ Dark-meat fish—tuna, salmon, mackerel, bluefish, swordfish—are rich in oils that may have a positive anti-inflammatory effect on joints. This, though, hasn't been proven. Eating more fish can't hurt you (though I wouldn't recommend nothing but fish)…and might help.

Sleep:

The value of sleep in controlling pain is often overlooked. Arthritis patients often find themselves in a vicious cycle. Their joint pain makes sleeping difficult, and poor sleep in turn leads to more stiffness and pain.

I have found that very low doses of antidepressant medication can break this cycle by reducing chronic pain enough to ensure sound sleep.

Stress management:

Though there's no evidence that stress causes arthritis, it may make symptoms more noticeable or bothersome. Therefore, learning to deal effectively with stress is an essential part of a comprehensive treatment program.

Meditation, deep breathing or other relaxation techniques can be helpful. Yoga is gaining popularity as a relaxation method that's also good exercise.

Can arthritis be prevented?

Theoretically, no—but there are steps we can take to reduce risk and slow progression of the disease…

☐ Maintain ideal weight. Obesity is a risk factor for osteoarthritis, possibly because greater weight causes more wear on the joints.

☐ Exercise regularly—to keep supporting muscles strong and joints moving smoothly.

☐ Seek medical attention early. If you notice recurring stiffness in a joint, or if it appears swollen, warm to the touch or red, see your physician. The sooner the problem is identified and treatment begun, the better the prognosis.

Source: Fred G. Kantrowitz, MD, who is on the faculty of the Harvard Medical School and the author of *Taking Control of Arthritis*, Harper-Perennial, New York.

Maybe it's yeast ✓ that's causing your aches and fatigue

New evidence suggests that many puzzling, chronic health problems resistant to treatment —from infections and allergies to the aches and exhaustion of chronic fatigue syndrome—are yeast-related.

One type of yeast is regularly found on the body's mucous membranes, especially the intestinal tract and vagina. When we talk about this kind of yeast, we usually mean Candida albicans, by far the predominant type found in the body.

In a healthy man or woman, candida (pronounced "can-did-a") is kept under control by so-called friendly bacteria living in the intestinal tract. But several factors can upset the yeast-to-bacteria balance—especially long-term use of broad-spectrum antibiotics. When this happens, yeasts grow out of control—leading to unpleasant symptoms.

Based on my critical review of continuing research, I believe there are three possible mechanisms for yeast's troublesome effects…

☐ Just as some people are allergic to pollens or mildew, some may be allergic to candida.

☐ Candida may produce certain toxins that are harmless in small amounts, but that in larger quantities weaken the immune system…leaving the body vulnerable to disease.

☐ Yeast overgrowth in the intestinal tract (candidiasis) may lead to changes in the intestine. In turn, these changes can cause the body to absorb and react to allergens in food.

The connection between yeast and health problems is highly controversial. Beginning with Dr. C. Orian Truss's article in the late '70s, a number of reports have linked yeast to illness, but the mainstream medical community remains skeptical.

Yet, my experience in treating hundreds of chronically ill patients, as well as similar experiences of a number of colleagues, suggests that a diet designed to curb yeast growth—along with certain antifungal medications— helps alleviate many symptoms that have proven resistant to other forms of treatment.

Do you have a yeast problem?

There is no simple diagnostic test for a yeast-related problem. For this reason, patients must undergo a thorough physical exam to rule out other possible causes of their symptoms. Next step: A complete medical history.

You may have a yeast problem if you…

…have used antibiotics repeatedly over a long period of time, such as for control of acne or recurrent infections.

…have taken corticosteroids. One

216

known side effect of nasal cortisone spray is candidiasis of the nose.

…have used birth-control pills. Women on the Pill are far more prone than others to vaginal yeast infection.

…eat a high-sugar diet. A recent study at St. Jude Research Hospital in Memphis found that mice eating large quantities of the sugar glucose had 200 times as much candida in their intestinal tracts as did other mice.

…experience frequent digestive problems, such as abdominal pain, bloating, constipation or diarrhea.

…have a history of vaginal or urinary infections. Women develop yeast-related health problems far more often than men for a number of reasons. These include anatomical differences and hormonal changes associated with the menstrual cycle that promote yeast growth.

…have symptoms involving many parts of the body—for which usual examinations have not found a cause.

Treating a suspected yeast problem:

The cornerstone of treatment is a sugar-free diet. Yeasts in the digestive tract feed on sugar—and multiply. Some patients show remarkable improvement from dietary changes alone. Others need additional help—in the form of over-the-counter anti-yeast preparations sold in health-food stores…and, for more serious cases, from prescription antifungal medications.

The yeast-control diet:

☐ Eliminate sugar and other simple carbohydrates, such as honey and corn syrup.

☐ Avoid foods containing yeast or molds, such as cheese, vinegar, wine, beer and other fermented beverages and pickled or smoked meats. Although breads are probably safe, try eliminating yeast-leavened breads for a few weeks.

Note: Yeast-containing foods should be avoided not because intestinal yeast feeds on food yeast—it doesn't. But most people with candida-related problems are sensitive to yeast in foods and can have negative physical reactions. As the candida problem improves, the sensitivity may subside…and yeast can again be included in your diet.

☐ Strengthen your immune system by boosting your intake of vegetables, minimally processed whole grains and other wholesome foods. Eat lean rather than fatty meats, and cut back on other sources of fat. Avoid potentially harmful additives, including artificial colors and flavors.

Some physicians recommend eliminating fruits from the diet, because fruits are quickly converted to simple sugars inside the body. I believe fruits are safe—unless your yeast-related symptoms are severe. However, I do recommend avoiding commercially prepared fruit juices, which may be contaminated with mold.

Follow this recommended diet for at least three weeks. If your symptoms subside, resume eating forbidden foods one by one. If your symptoms flare up again after you add one of the forbidden foods, stop eating that food for good.

Good news: After they show significant improvement, most people find that they can follow a less rigid diet—and can occasionally consume a bit of sugar.

Over-the-counter remedies:

Many preparations sold in health-food stores can be a useful adjunct to the yeast-control diet…

☐ Citrus-seed extract, an antimicrobial substance made from tropical plants. Because the extract can irritate mucous membranes, it should be generously diluted with water before drinking.

☐ Caprylic acid, a saturated fatty acid available in tablet form. It helps keep yeast from reproducing.

Note: Some patients develop digestive problems or notice a slight worsening of yeast-related symptoms during the first week on this medication. If these don't go away within a few days, stop the medication and check with your doctor.

☐ Lactobacillus acidophilus, a friendly bacterium that helps restore the normal balance of intestinal flora. It is present in yogurt, especially homemade varieties. Store-bought yogurt that contains active cultures will be labeled to that effect. Be sure to buy only unsweetened varieties. Acidophilus is also available as a nutritional supplement.

☐ Garlic. This herb is known to stimulate the immune system…and at an international medical conference several years ago, researchers reported that garlic also seems to fight candida. Persons wary of the taste of cooked garlic—or its effect on the breath—should consider aged garlic extract (Kyolic), a deodorized supplement. It is widely available in local health-food stores.

Antifungal medications:

When a yeast-related symptom fails to respond to diet or supplements, prescription medication often helps— although the drug may take up to a year to have any effect in severe cases. Drug options:

☐ Nystatin (Mycostatin or Nilstat). In more than 30 years of use, this oral medication has demonstrated no toxic side effects. It knocks out candida in the intestines. It is not absorbed by the bloodstream, however, so it is ineffective against particularly severe cases of candidiasis.

☐ Fluconazole (Diflucan). This safe, highly effective antiyeast medication has been available in the US for about three years. Unlike nystatin, fluconazole is absorbed into the bloodstream.

☐ Itraconazole (Sporanox). This medication, a chemical "cousin" of fluconazole, was recently approved for use in the US. Although it appears to be quite safe, a related drug, keto-conazole (Nizoral) has been linked to liver damage.

Source: William G. Crook, MD, a fellow of the American College of Allergy and Immunology, the American Academy of Environmental Medicine and the American Academy of Pediatrics. He is the author of *The Yeast Connection and Chronic Fatigue Syndrome and the Yeast Connection,* both published by Professional Books, Inc., Jackson, TN.

Problems that ✓ respond to acupuncture

Acupuncture has gained in respectability in this country in recent years. You may wish to consider this treatment for a variety of conditions.

The sensation of the needles varies among patients. Some feel only the slightest prick and others find them painful. The more pain a patient feels, the more resistance and stress there are in the related part of the body. As in deep massage, where the patient must "work through" the pain to get real relief, patients are asked to get through the painful part of acupuncture until they get some positive effect.

☐ Back pain. First acupuncturists ease the discomfort by working on the circu-lation in the spinal area. Then, they try to analyze the cause of the problem— posture, weight or a poor mattress. Or, the patient may need a better diet and more exercise. The object is to keep the pain from recurring. *Success rate:* 95%.

☐ Insomnia. Acupuncturists try to relax the natural functions of the body through the nerve system to get the patient into a natural rhythm of feeling energetic when he wakes up and sleepy at night. *Success rate:* 90%.

☐ Addictions. Whether the substance is cocaine or nicotine, the user must want to shake the habit. Acupuncture can help people get into a healthier, more energetic cycle. *Success rate with patients who want to quit:* 80%.

☐ Excess weight. Business people do a lot of nervous eating. Acupuncture relaxes them and strengthens their sense of well-being. They can then better burn off fat and control eating. *Success rate:* 80%.

☐ Depression. Many people tire and get nervous too easily. Acupuncturists attempt to give them more energy with acupuncture and a combination of herbs and vitamins. *Success rate:* 80%.

☐ Hearing loss. Acupuncture can help if the problem is the result of some (but not all) kinds of nerve damage. *Success rate for hearing improvement:* 80%.

☐ Impotence. Sometimes people lose sensitivity and desire because they are tired. Acupuncture can contribute to general well-being and appetite and can specifically stimulate the nerves of the sex areas. *Success rate:* 70%.

☐ Hair loss. Acupuncture can increase circulation to the scalp and may be helpful to men under 50.

☐ Look for an acupuncturist who is certified by your state's licensing board. If you find a practitioner by word of mouth, be sure he has the proper credentials.

Source: Zion Yu, a 20th-generation acupuncturist who came to the US from Taipei in 1970 and now directs a private clinic in Beverly Hills, CA.

Before you have any teeth extracted

Eye teeth (canines), the large, pointed teeth on either side of the upper jaw, are strong teeth, the cornerstone of the mouth's arch and are essential to maintaining the ridge of the mouth. *Other important teeth:* Front teeth. When they are removed, they cause a collapsed-looking mouth, particularly in areas of the lips and nose.

☐ When any teeth are removed, the bony structure around them shrinks up and inward.

☐ Before allowing teeth to be removed, get two other dentists' opinions. It is important to try to keep teeth even if it is obvious they can last only a few years more.

☐ *The only reason to consider teeth hopeless:* When the bone around them has been lost to the degree that it cannot hold the teeth.

☐ *Nonvalid reasons for extracting teeth:* Abscesses, decay, pain. These conditions can be corrected with treatment.

About dentures

One third of all Americans end up losing all their teeth in an arch requiring a full denture. This is a horrible statistic since people need not lose all their teeth.

☐ Upper dentures can usually be worn satisfactorily and comfortably.

☐ Lower dentures always pose much more severe and continuous problems than do uppers. *Why:* Uppers hold much better because they rest on a palate and a wide ridge. Lowers have only a very thin ridge to adhere to, and the tongue tends to displace the dentures. (Lowers cost more because of the additional problems with fitting.)

☐ An immediate denture is a prosthesis inserted at the same time the teeth are extracted. This is done to avoid going without teeth for any period of time. *Usual effects:* Swelling and discomfort for a few days.

☐ Within the first six weeks to three months of the time teeth have been pulled, shrinkage of bone and gums in that area accelerates rapidly. *Significance:* The original denture no longer fits and must be relined with acrylic to fill in areas that have shrunk.

☐ At the end of the first year, an entirely new denture (or dentures) should be made. This second denture has a better fit and appearance than the original, which had to be molded while real teeth were still in the mouth.

☐ Denture wearers should be checked by a dentist at least once a year, and their dentures regularly relined, even if the denture does not feel loose. *Why this is important:* The better the denture fits, the less the bone around it will shrink away.

☐ Denture teeth should look as natural and individual as possible, not perfectly symmetrical. It is a mistake to insist on completely even picket-fence or piano-key teeth.

☐ Look for a dentist who stresses natural and individual-looking teeth and who gives detailed attention to planning an aesthetic appearance and proper balance of dentures.

☐ The materials used in dentures do not vary much or cost much. What does vary from dentist to dentist is expertise, time and attention to aesthetic considerations.

Source: Arthur S. Brisman, DDS, dentist, New York.

Dentures may not be for you

People prone to problems with dentures:

☐ Diabetics or people with poor general health. They tend to have more bone disappearance after their teeth have been pulled.

☐ People with a very high palate (tapered arch), a result of thumb-sucking in childhood or of genetic inheritance. They tend to have trouble retaining even an upper denture.

☐ People whose psychological approach or sensitivity to the feel of dentures is negative. They will probably never adjust to them properly.

☐ People with bony projections sticking out from the palate. Most people who have them are not aware of them. They can be removed surgically, before the denture is fitted.

How to protect yourself from your doctor

The best doctors are sometimes the ones with the poorest personalities. Bedside manner is not necessarily a relevant criterion. The prime do's and don'ts:

☐ Do ask questions. Many patients are intimidated by the doctor's professional status. Don't be. Ask your prospective doctor about his medical philosophy. Pose specific questions—for example, does he believe in taking heroic measures in terminal cases? Look for a doctor who is attuned to the patient/ doctor relationship. Be wary of a doctor who puts you off, who takes a question as a personal affront or who says things like, "Don't worry, I'll take care of it."

☐ Don't be impressed by the diplomas on the wall. Many are probably from organizations that the doctor joined for a fee. *What you should know:* Is the doctor board-certified in his specialty?

☐ Do find out about the doctor's hospital affiliation. Is he on the medical staff of a hospital? Is it a local hospital of good reputation?

☐ Don't go straight to a specialist when you're having a problem. Specialists can be blind to any ailment that doesn't fall into their specialty. Have a generalist or internist assess your problem and send you to the appropriate specialist.

Source: Leonard C. Arnold, MD, JD, Chicago.

Very, very, very aesthetic dentistry

Until recently, there wasn't much a dentist could do to create teeth that were beautiful as well as healthy. Now dentists can close the spaces between teeth, cover stains, repair chips and create caps and dentures that look real. *Choices:*

☐ Bonding. *How it works:* The tooth is roughened with a mild acid. Next, a liquid material (the best is porcelain laminate) is painted on in layers and set by an intense white light. Then a tooth-colored bonding material of a puttylike consistency is sculpted onto the tooth. This material will not set until an intense white light is applied to it.

☐ Porcelain over gold is considered the ideal crown or bridge replacement today. *Leading edge:* Cast ceramic. The process, developed by Corning Glass, uses ceramic material cast the same way as gold. It's almost as strong as metal and looks much better.

☐ The newest thing in bridges is the Maryland bridge. Instead of grinding down and ruining the teeth on either side of a space in order to attach a bridge, dentists can now bond metal to the backs of the adjoining teeth so that it doesn't show and attach a porcelain tooth in between. This prevents the destruction of good teeth. *Problem:* For people who have strong bites or large spans of missing teeth the Maryland bridge is not advisable.

Source: Irwin Smigel, DDS, the founder and president of the American Society for Dental Aesthetics, author of *Dental Health, Dental Beauty*, M. Evans & Co., Inc., New York.

Drug interaction dangers

There is a real danger in this age of multiple drug therapy: Drug interactions. Some of them are potentially life-threatening. Always ask your doctor or pharmacist about interaction hazards whenever you begin a new medication …and before you take any over-the-counter medication.

The most-likely-to-be-encountered drug interactions and what to do to prevent them…

Add-on interactions

"Add-on" interactions are the most common type and can be the most dangerous. These occur between drugs that have similar effects, either depressant + depressant or stimulant + stimulant. Some of these combinations have proven fatal.

Depressants include: Alcohol, anti-anxiety agents, tranquilizers, anticonvulsants, antihistamines, certain high blood pressure drugs, muscle relaxants, narcotics and the popular pain-reliever propoxyphene (e.g., Darvon).

Stimulants include: Antidepressants (MAO* inhibitor type), appetite suppressants, some asthma drugs, caffeine, nasal decongestants, methylphenidate (Ritalin) and pemoline (Cylert).

Always ask your doctor or pharmacist about this type of interaction before you take a new medication.

Antihistamine interactions

☐ Seldane + Antibiotics. Seldane, one of the new nonsedating antihistamines (prescription-only), has become very popular for relief of allergies. Recently, a dangerous drug interaction was identified between Seldane (terfenadine) and antibiotics—ketoconazole (an antifungal agent with the brand name of Nizoral), erythromycin and troleandomycin. The newer erythromycin-like antibiotics—clarithromycin (Biaxin) and azithromycin (Zithromax)—may cause the same problems.

These antibiotics can increase the amount of Seldane in the blood. Seldane is broken down for elimination in the liver. Antibiotics interfere with this process. That has led to life-threatening, abnormal heart rhythms. Also at risk are individuals with liver disease (whose bodies may not

*Monoamine oxidase.

eliminate Seldane properly)—and those who take excessive doses of the drug.

On the heels of the Seldane revelation came reports of a similar risk with Hismanal (astemizole), another non-sedating antihistamine. In this case, no interactions with other drugs have been reported, but taking more than the recommended dose of 10 mg (one tablet) daily has caused heart-function abnormalities.

Self-defense: Do not take Seldane (terfenadine) or Hismanal (astemizole) with other drugs that prolong the heart's QT interval, such as Quinidine, Disopryamide, Procainamide, most antidepressants and most neuroleptics. Do not take terfenadine or astemizole if you have significant liver dysfunction.

Avoid taking either drug with grapefruit juice. Early findings suggest the juice may block the drug's breakdown.

If you experience fainting, dizziness, palpitations or any other unusual symptoms while taking Seldane or Hismanal, the Food and Drug Administration (FDA) advises you to contact your physician immediately.

Interactions involving food

☐ Fruit juices + Antibiotics. Penicillin and erythromycin, the interacting antibiotics, are used for microbial infections such as strep throat. The effect of the antibiotic may be decreased by the acidity of the fruit juice—and the infection may not be eradicated.

Self-defense: Avoid taking antibiotics with fruit juices.

☐ Salt + Lithium. Lithium is prescribed for manic-depressive illness. A diet too low in salt may cause lithium toxicity. Be alert for symptoms such as dizziness, nausea, dry mouth, weakness, confusion, appetite loss, abdominal pain, loss of coordination.

A diet too high in salt may reduce the effect of lithium so that the condition treated may not be properly controlled.

Self-defense: Avoid extremes in salt intake. Table salt (sodium chloride) is found in numerous foods.

☐ Milk/dairy products + Tetracycline. Tetracycline is an antibiotic used for microbial infections such as urinary-tract infections. Milk may decrease the effect of the antibiotic—and the infection may not be eradicated.

Self-defense: Take tetracycline antibiotics one hour before or two hours after ingesting milk or other dairy products.

☐ Carbohydrate-rich foods + Acetaminophen. Foods such as bread, crackers, jelly and pasta may blunt the pain-relieving and fever-reducing effects of the widely used over-the-counter drug acetaminophen (e.g., Tylenol, Tempra, Datril).

Self-defense: Limit servings of high-carbohydrate foods while taking acetaminophen.

☐ Monosodium glutamate + Phenytoin. Phenytoin (brand name Dilantin) is used for seizure disorders such as epilepsy.

The adverse effects of monosodium glutamate (MSG)—a flavor enhancer often found in Chinese food and other foods—may be increased. Watch for symptoms such as weakness, numbness at back of the neck, heart palpitations.

Self-defense: Avoid foods high in MSG.

☐ Amine-containing foods + MAO inhibitors. MAO inhibitors are used in some cases of clinical depression. This can be a life-threatening combination that may result in a dangerous rise in blood pressure with severe headache, fever, visual disturbances and confusion, possibly followed by brain hemorrhage/stroke.

Self-defense: Avoid amine-containing foods, even for several weeks after stopping an MAO inhibitor-type antidepressant.

Amine-containing foods: Avocados, baked potatoes, bananas, bean pods, beer, bologna, broad beans, caviar, cheese, chicken liver, canned figs, instant soup mixes, meat tenderizers, nuts, pepperoni, pickled herring, raspberries, salami, sauerkraut, summer sausage, sour cream, soy sauce, wines, yeast and yogurt.

Over-the-counter drug interactions

☐ Antacids + Quinidine. Quinidine is used for heartbeat irregularities. Brand names include Cardioquin and Quinidex Extentabs. Antacids (e.g., Maalox, Mylanta, etc.) are used for indigestion or stomach ulcers.

The adverse effects of quinidine may be increased. *Result:* Possible fall in blood pressure, vertigo, heart block and a serious heart irregularity called ventricular fibrillation.

Self-defense: Your physician should monitor quinidine blood levels and symptoms, and lower the quinidine dose as needed. (An aluminum-only antacid may not interact—e.g., Alterna-GEL, Amphojel.)

☐ Antacids + Iron. Iron is an essential mineral found in many over-the-counter vitamin/mineral products. Antacids can decrease the effect of iron so those taking iron supplementation may not receive its full benefits.

Self-defense: Take the two at separate times, as far apart as feasible.

☐ Antacids + Aspirin. Aspirin is used for pain, fever and inflammation. Antacids may hamper the effect of aspirin. *Result:* The condition treated may not respond properly.

Self-defense: Use a higher dose of aspirin as needed.

Source: Richard Harkness, PharmD, a consultant pharmacist in Ocean Springs, Mississippi, and the author of several books on drug topics, including *Drug Interactions Guide Book,* Prentice-Hall Business and Professional Books, Rt. 9W, Englewood Cliffs, NJ.

Beware of mixing

Don't mix aspirin or acetaminophen (Tylenol) with cold medications.

Trap: If the cold medication also contains aspirin or a similar analgesic, you could overdose—suffering stomach irritation, ringing in the ears or liver damage.

Also: Avoid decongestants and nasal sprays while taking diet pills. Both can contain similar or identical ingredients that can result in overdose. Always read labels carefully before taking any over-the-counter medication.

Source: Lisa Tuomi, PharmD, drug information coordinator, Stanford University Medical Center, Stanford, CA.

Expand your thinking power

Over the past few years, there have been important developments in our understanding of effective thinking and how to teach it.

You can improve your reasoning skills by:

☐ Using analogies and metaphors. Deliberately ask yourself, "What am I assuming? If art is creative, for example, does that mean business is noncreative?" This will lead you to think about the real meaning of creativity.

☐ Not getting bogged down in a particular line of reasoning. Deliberately step outside it. *Suggestion:* Take ten minutes to think of the problem in a completely different way. If that doesn't work, you've lost only a little time.

☐ Paying more attention to the aesthetic aspects of the problem than to the pragmatic ones. If you're designing an inventory system, for example, it shouldn't only be functional but should also solve certain difficulties in keeping track of things in an easy, elegant way.

☐ Looking at how you're being conventional. Break that conventional set. Watch out for clichés. Avoid timeworn and obvious answers.

☐ Being self-conscious. It's a myth that self-consciousness is a barrier to effective thinking. Be aware of the way you do things. Do you brush aside problems, or do you take them seriously? Do you look for opportunities to think about something a little longer, or do you pass them by?

☐ Opening up to ideas. Don't dismiss suggestions with "That's just common sense" or "I already do that." Common sense isn't always common practice, and if you think you already do it, you probably don't. Research on actual behavior tells us that people don't accurately perceive whether or not they follow their own advice. Typically, they don't.

☐ Taking a course in thinking. Look for one that requires a lot of small-group work over a 6-to-20-week period. Investigate the course carefully, including the teacher's credentials, before taking it.

Source: David N. Perkins, PhD, senior research associate in education, Graduate School of Education, Harvard University, author of *The Mind's Best Work,* Harvard University Press, Cambridge, MA.

Relaxation: The key to concentration

Ironically, when people know they must concentrate on a task, they often fail because they make the mistake of concentrating on concentration. They focus on the mechanism of getting the job done rather than the objective itself. The result is anxiety over the task, which only leads to further distractions.

Ways to help concentration:

☐ Recognize what type of thinker you are—one who focuses broadly and can juggle many ideas or one who does best by focusing narrowly on one aspect of a problem. Try to take on only those tasks that match your abilities. If this isn't possible, ask for support in troublesome areas.

☐ Don't be afraid to take a little longer than usual to finish a job. Good concentration doesn't necessarily mean you will work faster.

☐ If concentration slips during a project, boost your adrenaline level by taking a short rest, exercising, meditating or bringing in others who wouldn't ordinarily be involved in the job.

☐ Avoid thinking about the consequences of not getting a job done or how the result will be viewed by others. Just focus on the work at hand.

Source: Dr. Ari Kiev, a psychiatrist and founder of Life Strategy Workshops, New York.

Scheduling time to concentrate

☐ Your time budget should include "quiet hours" when you have a chance to think without interruptions. Best time in the office is early morning before official hours begin.

☐ If possible, work during noon hour when interruptions are rare because most others have gone to lunch. Go out to eat at 1 PM or later.

☐ When scheduling your day, schedule the interruptions as well. Try to restrict all calls on routine matters to a certain time of the day. If calls come in at other hours, have your secretary say you'll call them back. (Even VIPs will accept this if you establish a reputation for returning calls when promised.)

☐ Spend a few "office hours" at home. Use an answering machine to cover telephone calls so you won't be interrupted.

Use your intuition to improve your thinking

Intuition, the spontaneous generation of fresh ideas for solving problems, can help you in your work and personal life. Here are some ways to use intuition and evaluate its effectiveness relative to other methods of making decisions:

Keeping a journal will enable you to discover successful intuitions. For each intuition, record at the moment it happens:

☐ The date and time.

☐ Content.

☐ Type (future prediction, creative insight, problem solution, etc.).

☐ Description (verbal, visual, a faint idea, etc.).

☐ Vividness.

☐ What you were doing and how you felt immediately before and after having it.

☐ Your initial reaction (skepticism, belief, etc.).

Later, add the following to your journal:

☐ Was the intuition a departure from custom, authority or logic?

☐ Was it something you wanted or didn't want to hear?

☐ Did it return at various times?

☐ Did you analyze it, try to verify it, seek other opinions?

☐ Were you under pressure to come up with a decision?

☐ Did it represent a high risk?

☐ How did it work out in the end?

☐ If you went with an intuition that was wrong, do you understand why?

☐ Leave room in your journal for random thoughts and observations.

☐ Note any patterns that you may come across.

Source: Philip Goldberg, author of *The Intuitive Edge,* Jeremy P. Tarcher, Inc., Los Angeles.

Real problem solving

Management's job isn't simply to predict the problems—many of them can't be predicted, no matter how well the project is planned. *What is critical:* The way managers respond to inevitable problems.

☐ Seeking a victim and assigning blame is the most common response to a problem—and the least effective way to solve it. *Inevitable result:* Everyone avoids blame and argues that if others had done what they should have, the problem wouldn't have come up.

☐ Not putting the emphasis on blame creates the atmosphere for making rolling adjustments and changes in plans and specifications in any new venture. This will not take place if individuals feel that concessions will be held against them or are an admission of guilt for originating the problem.

☐ Don't gloss over problems and figure mistakes can be fixed up later. Solve problems when they first surface.

Source: Dr. Leonard R. Sayles, Center for Creative Leadership, Greensboro, NC.

Memory magic

Forgetting names as fast as you hear them is a common problem. Yet, putting names and faces together correctly only takes a little practice…if you know the Mnemonic Method of Memorization.

The Mnemonic Method is simple. All you have to do is take the time to link a person's name to a mental picture you create in your own mind. Here's how to do it…

☐ Listen very carefully to the name. Does the name or part of the name conjure up an image?

Example: If you hear the name Gene Mapley, associate the name with…blue jeans and…a map. (Jeans for Gene… map for Mapley.)

☐ Coordinate. Search Mapley's head and face for unique features that you can link to the image of blue jeans and a map.

Example: If Gene Mapley has a deeply furrowed brow, you could pretend that the furrows are the roads found on a map.

☐ Visualize. See Gene Mapley's face as a caricaturist might, drawn in exaggerated and ludicrous form—with the blue jeans dancing frantically along the lines of the map on Mapley's face. The more absurd the link and the mental picture you associate with the person, the more impossible it is to forget his or her name.

If you push yourself to use this technique every time you meet a new person over the next few days, you'll be amazed at how quickly you get good at it. By the time you attend your next gathering, you'll be able to put on a dazzling display of memory—whether you're shaking hands with just one new person or 100.

Source: Tony Buzan, The Buzan Center USA, 415 Federal Highway, Lake Park, Florida 33403. 800-964-6362.

Problem solving: Some traits that get in the way

Would-be problem solvers often run into trouble because they:

☐ Cannot tolerate the ambiguity associated with a complex problem and believe all problems must be clear-cut.

☐ Stick to a preconceived belief and reinterpret inconsistent data to fit it.

☐ Hesitate to ask questions for fear of appearing ignorant.

☐ Give in to unrealistic anxiety about failing without systematically doing worst-case scenarios.

Roadblocks to creativity

☐ Assuming that creative means new. Borrowing and modifying the ideas of others is just as useful.

☐ Relying too heavily on experts or self-styled creative types, who often are blinded by traditional approaches.

☐ Believing that only a few gifted people can be creative.

☐ Confusing creativity with emotional instability. What is needed instead is the ability to let the mind wander without fear of losing control.

☐ Failing to promote ideas voluntarily. Not pointing out achievements to superiors (a common failing of fired executives).

☐ Waiting for inspiration. Concentration and fact-finding are the most solid bases for innovation.

☐ Getting bogged down in technology. Look for solutions that can be accomplished with existing hardware and systems.

Source: M. LeBoeuf, Imagineering: How to Profit from Your Creative Powers, McGraw-Hill, New York.

Fears that stifle creativity

☐ Making mistakes.
☐ Being seen as a fool.
☐ Being criticized.
☐ Being misused.
☐ Standing alone.
☐ Disturbing traditions.
☐ Breaking taboos.
☐ Not having the security of habit.
☐ Losing the love of the group.
☐ Truly being an individual.

Learning how to remember

Contrary to the conventional wisdom, memory doesn't work like a muscle. You can't exercise your way to a perfect memory. But you can learn tricks and techniques that can give you a far better memory than you'd believe. Here are the best ones:

☐ Chunking. That's the basic technique for short-term memory improvement. How it works: Grouping apparently isolated facts, numbers, letters, etc., into chunks. Thus, the series 255789356892365 turns into 255 789 356 892 365.

☐ Sleep and remembering. There is some evidence to indicate that things learned just before sleep are retained better.

☐ Spacing. Don't try to memorize by swallowing the whole thing down in one gulp. Instead of a three-hour study marathon, try two 1½-hour spans. Experiment to see what time period is best for you.

☐ Reciting. Vocalizing provides a kind of feedback as you literally hear (in addition to seeing) the words. It also forces you to organize the material in a way that is natural for memory improvement.

☐ Story system. A very effective way to remember some obviously unrelated objects. Just make up a silly story, using each of the objects in the story. Thus, if you want to remember the words *paper*, *tire*, *doctor*, *rose*, *ball*, try this story:

The paper rolled a tire down the sidewalk, and it hit the doctor, knocking him into a rose bush, where he found a ball.

Source: Kenneth L. Higbee, author of *Your Memory: How It Works and How to Improve It*, Prentice-Hall, Englewood Cliffs, NJ.

Improving your short-term memory

Memory exercises are most useful for those who face special short-term tasks such as the memorization of facts for a presentation. These tasks can be accomplished through the application of a few simple techniques.

Basic steps:

☐ Before resorting to memorization, use such aids as shopping lists, memos or charts.

☐ When you do need to memorize, do so in the kind of environment in which you function best. Learn whether you concentrate better in total silence, with background music, etc.

☐ Arrange for short, frequent periods of study. Memory flags during long sessions.

☐ Outline what you need to learn, and carry your notes with you in a small notebook.

☐ Refer to your notes at every empty interval during the day—waiting in line, riding the bus, etc.

How to remember people's names

To remember the names of people to whom you have just been introduced, the classic system is best:

☐ Take an interest in the person.

☐ Concentrate by looking directly at him or her. Notice appearance and dress.

☐ If you forget the name right after hearing it, ask immediately for it to be repeated.

☐ Repeat the name to yourself every few minutes. Over the next few days, keep calling the name to mind.

☐ Gradually decrease the frequency of repetition.

Source: Alan Baddeley, author of *Your Memory: A User's Guide*, Macmillan, New York.

Remembering faces and names better

There are no special gimmicks to remembering important names and faces. You need only apply a few simple techniques:

☐ Take every opportunity to study lists of names that are important to you. It takes time, but it's worth it.

☐ Look through the names carefully, taking time to study each one and recollect when, and if, you ever met the person.

☐ If a name looks familiar, try to recall something about the person.

☐ Jot a friendly note to the person thanking him for the donation or order. The act of writing the note reinforces your memory of the person.

Source: Joseph F. Anderson, vice president for communications and development, Hamilton College, Clinton, NY.

How to develop intuition

To develop intuition, the first step is to accept that it isn't a gimmick. Intuition is spontaneous. It can't be contrived or programmed. However, you can create the conditions under which it's most likely to occur:

☐ Promote inner calm. An agitated, tense mind creates too much mental noise for intuition to operate. Stress-management techniques help people to be more intuitive, though this isn't their stated aim.

☐ Relax your mind by allowing it to wander. Take a walk on the beach, watch fish swim in a fishtank, take long baths, go away for the weekend. Some people have had their best intuitions while shaving or washing the dishes.

☐ Don't keep working harder and harder, struggling desperately for an answer to a problem. Like having a word on the tip of your tongue, the answer will come of its own accord when you're thinking of something else. The old saw, "sleep on it," really works.

☐ Approach problems in a flexible way. Many people acquire such rigid thought patterns that they effectively inhibit intuition. Loosen up. Be prepared to go with your feelings. Improvise. Get started before you know where an idea is going.

Source: Philip Goldberg, author of *The Intuitive Edge,* Jeremy P. Tarcher, Inc., Los Angeles.

How to use fantasy as a creative tool

Fantasy has many useful functions in our lives. Here are some of them:

☐ Fantasy lets us "try out" new roles. For example, anyone who contemplates a job or career change first fantasizes what it would be like to do other kinds of work.

☐ Fantasy is a way of testing concepts and ideas, from new products to financial systems.

☐ Fantasy helps us master negative emotions and events. If we're very depressed over a loss or other unhappy event, we can allow ourselves to feel better by imagining something that makes us feel good.

☐ Fantasy can relieve boredom or an unpleasant experience. We've all fantasized through a traffic jam.

☐ Fantasizing can mean the difference between life and death in truly traumatic situations—war, solitary confinement, etc. Diaries of concentration camp survivors and prisoners of war attest to this.

☐ In sex, fantasy has been touted as an enhancer of pleasure, and shared sexual fantasies can indeed do this. But unshared fantasy during sex can be one way of tuning out and avoiding intimacy with the other person.

☐ Love relationships are predicated on fantasy. We project onto the loved one our fantasy of the ideal lover. This is an obstruction in one way because it keeps us from seeing the real person, but if we didn't do it, we wouldn't fall in love at all.

☐ Fantasy displaces fear. We displace frightening things through fantasy as adults, just as we did as children. Thus, we imagine that harmful things will happen elsewhere—that someone else will have a car accident or get cancer.

While fantasy has many benefits, it's important to temper fantasy with reality. When we retreat into a fantasy world untempered by reality, there is the real danger of becoming nonfunctional— not getting out of bed in the morning or not taking care of the routine matters that ensure our daily existence.

Source: Dr. Simone F. Sternberg, a psychotherapist and psychoanalyst in private practice in New York.

Depression

Many Americans share a tragic misconception about depression—that people who are depressed could "snap out of it," if they wanted to. As a result, more than 30 million Americans troubled by emotional illness never get the help they need.

The result is devastating. Sufferers feel hopeless, inadequate and unable to cope with daily life. Their self-esteem is shattered—and so are their ties with family and friends. What's more, depression is often lethal. Up to 30% of people with serious mood disorders kill themselves.

Warning signs of depression

☐ Poor appetite or overeating.

☐ Insomnia.

☐ Sleeping more than usual.

☐ Chronic low energy or fatigue.

☐ Restlessness, feeling less active or talkative than usual, feeling "slowed down."

☐ Avoidance of other people.

☐ Reduced interest in sex and other pleasurable activities.

☐ Inability to derive pleasure from presents, praise, job promotions, etc.

☐ Feelings of inadequacy, low self-esteem or an increased level of self-criticism.

☐ Reduced levels of accomplishment at work, school or home.

☐ Feeling less able to cope with routine responsibilities.

☐ Poor concentration, having trouble making decisions.

If you're experiencing four or more of these, consult a doctor immediately.

Kinds of emotional illness:

The most common type of depression is unipolar illness, in which the person's mood is either normal or depressed. Other common types:

☐ Dysthymia. This condition is marked by a chronic mild state of depression. Sufferers of dysthymia experience little pleasure and are chronically fatigued and unresponsive. Sadly, many people suffering from dysthymia mistake their illness for a low-key personality…and never get the help they need.

☐ Manic depression. Patients whose periods of depression alternate with periods of euphoria are suffering from manic depression (bipolar disorder).

During the "high" periods, manic-depressives may also have an inflated sense of self-esteem…a decreased need to sleep…a tendency to monopolize conversations…the feeling that their thoughts are racing…increased activity…impulsive behavior (including buying sprees, promiscuity, rash business decisions).

Though manic episodes sometimes occur when a person has never been depressed, they are frequently followed by severe depression. *Danger:* Manic-depressives often do not realize that they're ill, even though the problem may be obvious to family and friends. As with all forms of biological depression, manic depression calls for immediate treatment.

☐ Cyclothymia. A variant of manic depression, this disorder is characterized by less pronounced ups and downs. Like manic-depressives, cyclothymics are often unaware of their problem and must be encouraged to seek help.

Diagnosis and treatment

First, have a complete physical exam to rule out any medical disorders. Certain ailments including thyroid disease and anemia can produce various symptoms that mimic depression.

If the exam suggests no underlying medical problem, ask for a referral to a psychopharmacologist—a psychiatrist who is trained in biological psychiatry. Caution: Nonphysician therapists, such as psychologists and social workers, lack medical training and cannot prescribe medication…and may be less adept at distinguishing between biological and psychological forms of depression.

When a biological form of depression is diagnosed, antidepressants should almost always be used as the first line of treatment. They completely relieve or lessen symptoms in more than 80% of people with severe emotional illness… and they are not addictive, nor do they make people "high." Once medications have brought the depression under control, however, psychotherapy often proves helpful—especially to patients embarrassed or demoralized by their illness.

Antidepressants:

Among the oldest and most effective antidepressants are the so-called tri-cyclics and monoamine oxidase inhibitors (MAOIs). These drugs are often very effective, but they must be used with caution.

Tricyclics have a wide range of side effects, including dry mouth, constipation, blurred vision and sexual difficulties. MAOIs must never be taken in combination with foods containing high levels of tyramine—such as aged cheese. Doing so causes a potentially dangerous rise in blood pressure. Other side effects include low blood pressure, sleep disturbances, weight gain and sexual difficulties.

Although these medications are still valuable in the treatment of depression, newer classes of drugs, including fluoxetine (Prozac), sertraline (Zoloft) and paroxetine (Paxil), are often superior. These new medications have few side effects, although some people who take the drugs complain of drowsiness or anxiety. *Note:* Despite one recent report claiming that Prozac caused some patients to attempt suicide, follow-up studies have not confirmed this finding.

For manic depression, the clear treatment of choice is lithium. Common minor side effects include diarrhea, a metallic taste in the mouth, increased frequency of urination, hand tremor and weight gain.

For seriously depressed or suicidal patients who do not respond to antidepressants, electroconvulsive therapy (ECT) is often a lifesaver. In this procedure, electrical current is applied to the brain via electrodes.

How to find the right help

If your family doctor cannot recommend a good psychiatrist, contact the nearest medical school or teaching hospital. Many have a special treatment clinic for depression. Local branches of the American Psychiatric Association will provide names of psychiatrists in your area, but they cannot evaluate the psychiatrist's training in biological psychiatry.

Source: Donald F. Klein, MD, professor of psychiatry at the Columbia University College of Physicians and Surgeons and director of research at the New York State Psychiatric Institute, both in New York City. Dr. Klein is coauthor of *Understanding Depression: A Complete Guide to Its Diagnosis and Treatment,* Oxford University Press, New York.

All about happiness

Sometimes happiness seems like a terribly elusive goal. We tend to forget that it doesn't come as a result of getting something we don't have, but rather of recognizing and appreciating what we do have. Some steps on the pathway to happiness:

☐ When you think about time, keep to the present. Those who are excessively future-oriented often score very high in despair, anxiety, helplessness and unhappiness. As much as practical, focus on the here and now.

☐ Don't dwell on past injustices. You'll be unpopular company. No one wants to hear about how you got a raw deal in your divorce or how your boss doesn't appreciate you.

☐ Develop the habit of noticing things. An active mind is never bored. Make a resolution to notice new things each day—about nature, people or anything else that interests you. Ask questions. Don't assume you know all the answers or that showing curiosity will be considered prying. Most people love to talk about themselves or their interests.

☐ Don't wear too many hats. Focus on one thing at a time. Set time aside for your family, yourself, your golf game, etc.—for having fun.

☐ Drop your bucket where you are. Take advantage of what you already have. There are already interesting, stimulating adventures waiting in your own backyard. Get to know your own children, for example.

Source: Dr. Frederick Koenig, professor of social psychology, Tulane University, New Orleans.

Words of wisdom

Here are the mottoes and proverbs that helped the following celebrities get to—and stay at—the top:

Isaac Asimov, writer:

"Laugh, and the world laughs with you; weep, and you weep alone. For the sad old earth must borrow its mirth, but has trouble enough of its own."

Helen Gurley Brown, editor, *Cosmopolitan:*

"I don't remember any motto or saying that was valuable to me when I was 'getting there,' but there is one I like now (not that it helps, but it just happens to be true.) 'There is no free lunch.'"

Midge Decter, former director, Committee for the Free World:

"The perfect is the enemy of the good."

Jean Louis Dumas-Hermes, chairman, Hermes:

"Patience and time do more than force and anger."

The late Rose Kennedy, matriarch of the Kennedy clan:

"To whom much is given, much will be required." (St. Jude)

Edward Koch, former mayor of New York City:

"Be not afraid."

Jack La Lanne, pioneer physical-fitness expert:

"*Pride* and *discipline.* If you use those two words, you can't fail."

Leonard A. Lauder, president, Estee Lauder, Inc.:

"Anything can be done as long as everybody gets the credit."

Willard Scott, weatherman on NBC's *Today* show:

"If a job is once begun, do not leave 'til it is done. Be it great or be it small, do it well or not at all."

Carl Spielvogel, chairman, Backer Spielvogel Bates Worldwide:

"Do unto others as you would have others do unto you."

Gloria Steinem, founder of *Ms.* magazine and author of *Outrageous Acts and Everyday Rebellions:*

"If there's no dancing, it's not my revolution!"

How to make it in the needy, numbing 1990s

Almost 20 years ago, I wrote that anyone who wanted to succeed could do so. That remains true today but it is both more difficult and more important to succeed now than it was then.

Today, management at all levels is less tolerant of those who fail to produce and less generous to those who are merely competent. Corporations are eager to trim workers who do not excel, and company loyalty is not enough to ensure survival.

Even if you do your job well, success is not an automatic consequence. It results from a systematic approach that makes sure you get things done and that others see you as successful. To achieve these two results, you must cultivate a number of specific qualities—energy, competitiveness, realism, memory and communication.

Energy

Success requires a great deal of energy. This does not mean a capacity for long hours of hard work. It means enthusiasm to get things done—combined with the ability to do them right.

☐ Structuring your time. If you are not a hard worker by nature, structure your time to encourage achievement by following two rules:

☐ Break up your workload into small, manageable parts.

☐ Reward yourself as you complete each task.

As you reach each goal, you will develop a sense of accomplishment that will encourage you to continue.

Example: My energy level used to dissipate within two hours of my arrival at the office each morning. I found myself trying to deal with a deluge of phone calls, letters to answer and people waiting to see me.

Solution: I decided to spend my first hour each morning doing nothing but answering mail. By completing this limited but essential chore, I was able to start my day with an "achieving" frame of mind. Then, I rewarded myself with a short coffee break and was ready to go on to successfully tackle the more ambitious tasks of the day.

☐ Focus on the important tasks. You won't get very far if you stick to small tasks, but it is tempting to put off an important job that will take a few hours or days of hard work.

A simple trick to tackling large projects: Promise yourself a period of relaxation after you complete the necessary hard work. That will help you put in the extra effort to finish the job as quickly as possible and show how much you can accomplish when you work at a high level of efficiency.

☐ Eat and sleep well. You won't have much energy in the afternoon if you have a heavy midday meal, so stick to a light lunch. If you get drowsy in the middle of the afternoon, don't be embarrassed to take a short nap as long as everyone is aware of how busy you were in the morning and how energetic you are after your nap.

☐ Look energetic. Promote an image of success, both to others and yourself, by always appearing energetic. Always move briskly, don't slouch—stand straight, with head up, stomach in, chest out, and never keep your hands in your pockets.

Competitiveness

To get ahead, you must be willing to compete with others and eager to accept responsibility.

Sometimes, competition leads to direct confrontation. Make sure that it is no more brutal than it has to be and that you keep the advantage. Rules of direct confrontation:

☐ Don't sit opposite your opponent—it sharpens the conflict. Try to sit side-by-side. To keep your resolve, look at his/her mouth, not eyes.

☐ Strike the first blow. Capture the advantage by stating your case rapidly and terminate the initial confrontation as soon as possible.

☐ Take responsibility for your position. Otherwise, you will get bogged down in a pointless discussion of your personal opinion. Successful people carry out decisions after they have been made, they don't agonize after the fact.

You also must accept responsibility without being asked. This means taking on vital tasks that others avoid because the tasks are perceived to be too trivial or tedious. Within a short time, you will acquire knowledge and skills that nobody else has, and more important responsibilities will begin flowing to you.

Hint: Pay careful attention to routine memos that everyone else ignores. You will find many problems as you search for solutions. If you suggest and volunteer to implement improvements, your reputation for success will grow.

Realism

To succeed, you must see the world as it is, not as you think it should be. Some important examples:

☐ Be realistic about other people. You can't trust everyone, and those whom you can trust may not always perform the way you want them to.

☐ Be realistic about yourself. Recognize your good points but be aware of your faults.

☐ Study your past failures. You may find a way to transform them into successes.

Important: Realism must be balanced by an ability to fantasize. Dreams of success will motivate you to achieve them in reality.

Memory

You are unlikely to succeed unless you can remember what you have to do and whom you should know.

☐ Use the best memory aid: Lists. Don't try to memorize every fact you need to know—simply write them down.

☐ Remember people's names. Get them correct from the start. When you are introduced to someone, repeat his name several times during the first conversation and make sure of the spelling. At the earliest opportunity, write down the name together with other useful memory-jogging information, such as the person's occupation and where you met.

Hint: If you run into someone whose name escapes you, a graceful solution is to announce your own name. The other person will usually reciprocate.

Communication

Successful people know how to let others know who they are and what they want. Good verbal communication requires you to speak and write clearly in positive terms.

Hint: Try to postpone areas of disagreement until you have demonstrated how much agreement you share.

☐ Use body language to get attention.

Example: At meetings, don't sit forward with your elbows on the table. Sit back to listen. When ready to speak, straighten out, move forward and put your arms on the table. You will get everyone's attention.

☐ Speak in public successfully. Speak in short sentences, touch on a variety of points, be unambiguous and summarize at the end. And always finish sooner than the audience expects.

Source: Michael Korda, editor-in-chief of Simon & Schuster. He is the author of four nonfiction best-sellers, including *Success! How Every Man and Woman Can Achieve It,* Ballantine, New York.

How to take charge of life problems you thought you couldn't change

Most people have difficulty coping with change. But in today's world, change is inevitable—and if you do not take charge of your own life, change will take charge of you. Even if you are content with things as they are, you have to prepare for change since situations shift frequently today.

Performing your job well is not really a defense. If your company decides to downsize or is put up for sale—no matter how well you have mastered your current position—you may need a different set of skills to meet the needs of the future. In the 1990s, life planning is a survival skill.

Avoiding change

People who cannot face change are in a state that I call Inner Kill. Prime symptoms include:

☐ Always taking the safe way.

☐ Reacting instead of taking risks.

☐ Avoiding decisions.

☐ Daydreaming and talking rather than taking action.

Inner Kill is closely related to fatigue, which may result from overwork and a pressure-filled life or underwork and too little engagement in life.

Examples:

☐ Middle-aged people are often under intense pressure. They must juggle overwhelming work schedules and personal and financial responsibilities that may include aging parents and growing children.

Result: Some middle-aged people just go through the motions of their daily activities—fatigued and unable to think about where they are headed.

☐ Early retirees who have unexpectedly and involuntarily been removed from the workforce may find themselves bewildered and unable to respond to life meaningfully—especially if they never took time during their careers to define themselves in ways other than their occupation.

Result: Many of these early retirees become ill within two years of their retirement.

☐ Young adults graduating from college and beginning their careers rarely think through what their talents and interests are best suited for. Many allow events to control them.

Result: Five, 10 or 20 years down the road, they find themselves in a rut and wonder how they ever got into it.

How to face change

☐ Take the initiative. To engage life, you must take the initiative when facing change. That requires overcoming a number of very common fears—of criticism, rejection, betrayal, failure, even success. You must rescript yourself to trust both your own judgment and that of other people who can help you.

☐ Accept that change is inevitable and impossible to avoid. Decide to change, instead of escape—use change for personal and professional growth.

☐ Be prepared to take risks. It is better to choose the calculated risk of a positive decision for change than to let outside events force other less-welcome risks on you. Prudent risk-taking requires excellent information, so the first step is to acquire the information you need.

☐ Take stock. Before creating a vision of where you want to go in life and how you can get there, you must know yourself. Answer the questions "Who am I? Why am I here? Where am I going?" Finding the truth about yourself requires courage. You must think seriously and answer a series of questions to assess your quality of life in ten fundamental areas.

☐ Time. What is your daily schedule? Do you have time for your real priorities? What is your most important need now?

Suggestion: Keep a journal of your activities, and review it at least quarterly. If your schedule is not consistent with your priorities, be prepared to change it.

☐ Values. What are your top three values now? Can you describe one risk you have taken recently because of your values?

Suggestion: Ask yourself why you do the things you do. Consider what values your actions express and whether you agree with them.

☐ Vitality. How do you spend your leisure time? Do you have fun? If you are tied to a routine and never enjoy spontaneous fun, you are suppressing an important part of yourself.

☐ Purpose. Why do you get up in the morning? Do you have a sense of purpose?

Suggestions: Consider what you would like your epitaph to say. If you learned that you had only two years to live, how would you spend your time?

☐ Career. How did you get where you are? Did you choose your career—or did it choose you? At what point did you come to love what you are doing, and why? If your current job does not match your needs and wants, the mental and physical costs can be high. True career progress requires not continual promotion but continual growth.

☐ Talents. What natural talents do others see in you? Which talents do you most enjoy using?

Suggestions: Consider your ability to handle facts, figures and concepts, deal with people, manipulate objects, etc. Consider keeping a talents inventory.

☐ Spirituality. Do you set aside time for contemplation? What principles govern your actions? You will live a more satisfying and fulfilling life if you know you are here for a higher purpose—not just to satisfy your material wants and compete in a rat race.

☐ Health. How is your health and your energy level? Do you exercise enough, relax, smoke, drink? If you take care of your health, you can expect a longer, better life.

☐ Relationships. Do you have friends? To whom do you talk? Do you talk about what is important to you? The single most important source of meaning in our lives is our connection with the people we love—spouse, family and friends. Reflect on how well you are able to communicate with those closest to you.

☐ Money. What annual income do you need to support your lifestyle? How is your financial health? Do you have written financial goals and plans? If your current situation is unsatisfactory, decide whether the appropriate change is to make more money or to need less.

Important: You cannot take stock by yourself. Discuss the questions with the people who know you best.

Taking charge

After taking stock of your current activities and setting your priorities, you are equipped to decide the changes you want to make for a better future.

☐ Write a master dream list of all the things you would like to do throughout your life.

☐ Talk with your partner—or your family—and make a joint list.

☐ Choose four major goals to pursue for the next 12 months—one each for your personal life, your work, your relationships and your finances. Key questions to ask yourself:

☐ Do the people who matter to me support me?

☐ Do I have enough time and enough money?

☐ Am I willing to sacrifice any lower-priority items that conflict with a more important one?

If you can answer each question with a "yes," tell others about your plan to increase your motivation.

☐ Develop an action plan for each goal—with deadlines. Break the plan down into small, measurable steps. Put a date on each step to track your progress. Your action plan will put you on the road to meaningful change.

Source: Richard J. Leider, a partner in The Inventure Group, a personal growth and team-effectiveness consulting firm, Minneapolis, MN. He is the author of *Life Skills: Taking Charge of Your Personal and Professional Growth,* Pfeiffer and Company, San Diego.

Lessons in leadership

Becoming a leader does not require super intelligence or an important-sounding title. It does, however, require the ability to make others respect you and believe in your vision. Leadership is an attitude and a state of mind.

Leadership characteristics

Here are leadership characteristics that anyone can incorporate into his/her life—qualities you can use to unlock the doors that keep you from achieving your leadership potential:

☐ Leaders have the authority of knowledge. Every leader develops a business skill at which he is better than anyone else—a demonstrated talent that colleagues admire.

To be a leader, you can't just be a talker. You need to demonstrate that you are deeply involved in whatever you do. You must also bring something special to the party—something that will make other people's jobs easier.

☐ Leaders are visionaries. They are able to see facts and ideas that others view as ordinary and rearrange them so that they become extraordinary.

Leaders form visions that draw simplicity out of complexity and clarity out of obscurity. By simplifying what is complex, leaders make patterns emerge that become the inspiration for their visions.

How can you become a visionary? By developing the ability to step back from your immediate context. Visionaries can elevate themselves above the minutiae and rearrange all the available facts into a larger whole.

Example: When you're in a crowd, all you can see is what is immediately around you—one person's shoulder and another person's back. But from a helicopter high above the crowd, you can see all the people and buildings. You can see everything from a new perspective.

☐ Leaders produce change. They are not disoriented by change and don't run from change. They see change not as a threat but as an opportunity and a challenge.

Leaders are able to master change because they have already experienced and managed painful change within their own lives. In fact, they are what I call twice-born.

This sounds spiritual—even metaphysical—but it isn't. I am referring to episodes of great stress and trauma. We have all experienced such events. They range from universal episodes, like passing through adolescence, to tragic episodes, like losing a sibling at a young age or surviving a serious illness.

Leaders emerge from these events with a sense of clarity, a feeling of renewal and a need to ask, "Why do things work the way they do?" A leader—as long as he is healthy enough emotionally to master his own tragedies—has the ability to emerge from trauma with the capacity to cope creatively.

While everyone has had twice-born experiences, it is how we handle these experiences—how we integrate them within ourselves—that differentiates leaders from followers.

☐ Leaders give their all. They are willing to commit themselves to their visions and their success. Leaders do not hold back. They do not conditionally dedicate themselves to the success of their visions and let themselves become sidetracked, they completely dedicate themselves. Tapping their reservoirs of passion gives leaders the energy to transform the present into a more successful and promising future.

Sometimes giving your all is expensive—to your family and your own personal well-being. Leaders understand this expense but still are willing to pay the price for pursuing their visions.

☐ Leaders are good listeners. They are able to hear what others are saying about the problems that accompany change. They accommodate the difficulty others experience in the pursuit of that vision. It is one thing to have a vision and another to empower other people to follow your vision. That doesn't mean the road toward the vision will be smooth.

☐ Leaders are good communicators. They are clear, concise, complete and consistent. Good leaders are able to deliver the messages they want to deliver—and deliver them with enthusiasm and sincerity.

☐ Leaders are students. They never stop learning and growing. They study the process and are willing to learn from their mistakes. Most people say they learn from their mistakes, but most repeat the same mistakes their entire lives.

Leaders are always thirsty for knowledge, and they seek it from the wisdom of today as well as from the wisdom of the past. Today's problems are so complex that solving them requires as many points of view as possible integrated into the solution. How can you gain this knowledge? You read…and read…and read. You listen to great people. You take time to think. You attend concerts. You visit museums. You read biographies of great people.

☐ Leaders take risks. They create change, which requires risks. They are willing to take risks because they can visualize how things can be done better.

The most important risk is the willingness to expose yourself to the possibility of a negative outcome in order to carry out your vision. Risk does not mean betting on long shots. In order to be a risk-taker, one needs some record of success. People will not take risks if they fail repeatedly.

☐ Leaders are ethical. People will not follow you if they don't trust you. It's not a matter of morals. It is a matter of mechanics. People may follow you because you con them into doing so. But in the long run, you will get caught.

☐ Leaders are optimists. They have hope. They trust their gut feelings and other people. That trust and hope are the basis on which leaders empower others.

Believe in yourself as a winner. No one will trust you unless you believe in yourself and demonstrate that you have confidence in your vision of the future.

Source: Howard G. Haas, senior lecturer at the University of Chicago's business school, chairman of Howard Haas & Associates, management consultants, 208 S. LaSalle St., Suite 1275, Chicago 60604, and former chief executive of Sealy Inc. He is coauthor of *The Leader Within: An Empowering Path of Self-Discovery,* HarperBusiness, New York.

Get more out of your dreams—skills for unlocking dreams' secrets

Dreams can be a rich resource for creativity, decision-making, problem-solving and self-understanding.

We actually do much of our information processing at night. Dreaming helps us integrate emotional and intellectual material from the day —without the defensiveness that characterizes our waking thoughts. Because we're more honest with ourselves when we are asleep, we're often more insightful as well.

Recalling dreams

You may not remember your dreams, but that doesn't mean you didn't have any. Everyone dreams at least four times a night. You can learn to recall your dreams by trying to "catch" them first thing in the morning.

Opportunity: Keep a pencil and pad by your bed. Jot down the date each night before you go to sleep. Immediately after waking up in the morning, write down a few lines about whatever is on your mind—even if all you write is, "There is nothing on my mind." Within a week or two, you'll find that you're remembering plenty of your dreams.

Using dreams to solve problems

Everyone has had the experience of "sleeping on a problem"—and waking up with the solution. We can make this process more deliberate by practicing what I call dream incubation. Here's how you can do it:

Before you go to bed, write down a one-line phrase that clearly states an issue you want to understand better, a problem you'd like to resolve or the kind of idea you need.

Don't try to solve the problem at this time. Turn out the light and repeat the phrase over and over—as calmly as though you were counting sheep—until you fall asleep. *Bonus:* This will also help you fall asleep more quickly.

As usual, when you wake up, write down what's on your mind. Sometimes the answer will be straightforward—in the form of a simple idea rather than a dream.

People have used dream incubation to find ways of resolving conflicts with a friend or colleague, streamlining office paperwork, turning around a marketing campaign and coming up with ideas for a presentation.

Other answers may require more interpretation. You might have a dream that helps you understand the situation better, even if you don't have the information to solve it completely. Or your dream may reframe the question. In rare cases, the dream incubation may not work—if another pressing problem comes up at the same time.

With my clients, I have found that dream incubation leads to helpful insights as much as 95% of the time. It sounds hard to believe, but it's true.

Interpreting your dreams

Many people think of dream interpretation as a system of rigid Freudian symbols. Sigmund Freud and Carl Jung were on the right track in taking dreams seriously, but they drew on their cultural prejudices and attached specific meanings to various dream images.

Actually, each individual's dream metaphors are very private and personal. I encourage people to dismiss their preconceptions about dream symbols and discover for themselves what they think about the images in their dreams. It's not necessary to analyze every detail of a dream in order to understand it. Record the main ideas and themes.

Then set up a dream interview with a friend, a therapist—or even yourself as interviewer—to clarify the dream's meaning. The dream interview has three major steps:

☐ Description. Describe each of the major elements—people, animals, objects, setting, action and feelings—in the dream as if you were describing them to someone who comes from another planet and has never heard of

them. If you are doing a self-interview, you might find it helpful to write down the descriptions the first few times.

☐ Bridge. For each element, ask yourself, "Is there anything in my life—or anything about myself—that's like this figure or action in my dream, which I describe as…?"

☐ Summary. Tie together what you've learned by reviewing each description and its bridge. Think about how the dream as a whole could be a parable about your life.

To use the insights you've gained, consider taking a fourth step:

☐ Action. Reread your dream several times, and keep it in mind during the day. Your dream may give you the insight and courage to make important changes.

Caution: Never act based on a dream without first evaluating the option in your conscious mind. Dreams aren't commands from the supernatural—at best, they're new ways of viewing issues. Any action you take based on a dream insight should also make perfect sense in waking life and should seem so obvious that you can't believe you didn't think of it before.

Common dream themes

Though each person's dream symbolism is highly individual, certain themes often have connotations that are common to many people. *Examples:*

☐ The examination. In the dream, you're about to take an important test and you haven't studied all semester or you can't find the examination room. In waking life, you may be facing a challenge for which you don't feel prepared.

If you are prepared, the dream may reflect simple anxiety. But it could also be a warning that you need to take steps to meet the challenge. Another possibility is that you're living under such pressure that you never feel quite ready for anything. You may need to reevaluate whether you want to keep functioning that way.

☐ Falling. Dreams in which you are falling often have to do with loss of control. Are there areas in which you're out of control? Does this present a danger to your career or a personal relationship?

☐ Having sex with a surprising partner. This doesn't usually mean that you harbor a secret attraction for the person you dreamed of making love with. More often, when you describe your dream partner, you'll find you're describing some aspect of yourself or of your real-life partner.

Source: Gayle Delaney, PhD, codirector of the Delaney & Flowers Center for the Study of Dreams, 337 Spruce St., San Francisco 94118. She is the author of *Breakthrough Dreaming,* Bantam Books, New York, and *Sexual Dreams,* Fawcett Columbine, New York.

The art and the science of making a complaint

When Martha Crawley, a financial analyst, was studying at the Yale School of Organization and Management in 1992, she purchased a Northgate personal computer that turned out to be a lemon. She did what was logical—she called the company's technical support line… and called…and called again.

Instead of giving up, Ms. Crawley got smart. "It suddenly occurred to me, 'Who has the most interest in keeping me happy?' The company's salespeople, of course. I got through immediately to the sales staff, and the replacement part I needed was in my hands within three days."

A creative approach like Ms. Crawley's goes a long way toward getting help from a company that has sold you a problem. The following are some more guidelines for successful complaining, and a list of whom to call when things go wrong.

Begin at the beginning

If you are complaining about a product, start by contacting the company. To complain about a service or a nonresponsive company in your state, contact the state's consumer protection agency (look in the government listings in the telephone book). As for the state's attorney's office and the local Better Business Bureau, they will want a record of your complaint to pursue the problem for the public good, but they will not act as your personal problem-solver. Any complaint about a merchant or service provider that requires a city license (for example, taxi drivers, dry cleaners) should be reported to your mayor's office.

Resources:

The Consumer's Resource Handbook lists the addresses of several hundred consumer representatives and federal and state agencies that handle consumer complaints. It is available in most libraries, or you can get a free copy by

writing to the Consumer Information Center, Dept. 592Z, Pueblo, Colorado 81009.

Another valuable resource is AT&T's directory of toll-free numbers for virtually every business that has any dealings with consumers. To purchase it, call 800-426-8686. A call to your library's reference section can yield a company's phone number and address from *Standard & Poor's Register of Corporations, Directors and Executives.*

Be prepared:

Before you make any calls or write any letters, gather all the necessary documentation. Know the model number of any appliance and dig the warranty out of the kitchen drawer, along with the sales receipt. When you call the company, record the name of the person you talk with and keep careful notes on what was said and how many calls you made before your call was returned.

Knowledge is power

Know your rights as a consumer before you begin the complaint process. Ralph Charell, author of *Satisfaction Guaranteed* (Linden Press, 1985), offers the following advice: "Call the state or federal agency that handles your type of complaint, and explain to the receptionist that your problem is extremely legalistic and you'd prefer to speak directly with their on-staff counsel. Most of the time, you'll be referred directly to the person most able to help you.

"Ask the attorney if he/she could copy for you any laws that directly outline your rights in this case. Also ask whether you can add his name to the list of people who will receive copies of all correspondence about this complaint. You may get faster results from a company when they see that you've already gotten an attorney from the state's Consumer Protection Agency involved."

Keep cool

"State simply and reasonably what has happened and how you'd like it resolved," says Barry Reid, director of the Georgia Governor's Office of Consumer Affairs.

Escalating:

Be prepared to escalate. "If it's clear you're being stonewalled, announce where you plan to go next in your hunt for satisfaction," Mr. Charell says. "Reporting the problem to state or federal agencies or even contacting the local news media may well be enough to make sure your claim receives attention."

Special help:

☐ Credit cards. Bankcard Holders of America, 703-481-1110, provides pamphlets that outline your rights as a credit-card consumer and that help guide the complaint process.

☐ Travel-agent trauma. The American Society of Travel Agents, 703-739-2782, or the United States Tour Operators Association, 212-944-5727, will mediate if the troublesome agent is a member. If not, your state's consumer protection agency can help.

☐ Car trouble. The Center for Auto Safety (2001 S St. NW, Suite 410, Washington, DC 20009) can help direct your complaint in the right direction. The National Automobile Dealers Association, 703-821-7000, and the Better Business Bureau's Auto Line (check with your local chapter) provide referrals for mediation for consumers with complaints about cars. Each group handles complaints about a different group of car makers—call for details.

☐ Mail order. Contact the Direct Marketing Association's Mail Order Action Line, 212-768-7277.

☐ Stockbrokers. Complaints about a stockbroker should be made to his/her brokerage house, the National Association of Securities Dealers, 212-858-4000, and the Securities and Exchange Commission, 212-748-8053.

Register your gripe about a financial planner with the following trade group: International Board of Standards and Practices for Certified Financial Planners, Inc., 303-830-7543.

Pension or mutual-fund managers must be registered with the Securities and Exchange Commission, 212-748-8053, which handles complaints related to them.

Your state's Board of Accountancy (check state listings in the phone book) should hear about any troublesome certified public accountant.

☐ Home improvement. Contractors should be licensed by the state. Call your state's consumer protection agency with complaints.

☐ Insurance. Your state insurance commission will hear your complaint. The National Insurance Consumer Organization, 703-549-8050, can provide you with phone numbers for your state commission.

☐ Real estate. Problems should be referred to your state's regulatory body.

☐ Medical mess-ups. Direct complaints to your state's medical licensing board. You can also consult the Medicare Telephone Hotline, 800-638-6833, which can refer you to your state Medicare agency.

And…

Consumer advocacy groups like the Consumer Federation of America, 202-387-6121, and the National Consumers League, 202-639-8140, may not handle your complaint directly, but they'll tell you whom to turn to.

Some government offices that handle complaints are the Consumer Product Safety Commission, 800-638-2772, the Food and Drug Administration, 301-443-4166, and the Federal Trade Commission, 202-326-2222, which deals with unfair and deceptive trade practices or advertisements and complaints about funerary services or used cars.

Source: *The New York Times.*

How to teach yourself anything— how to do well on any test

A super-high IQ is not essential to learn rapidly and efficiently. Whether you're in graduate school, taking continuing education courses or trying to assist a child in high school or college, there are studying techniques that will result in improved understanding, higher test scores and better grades.

Key: Take an active role right from the start. Don't approach the assigned reading passively and assume that if you simply pass your eyes over your textbook and notes enough times, you'll absorb it. Engage in an ongoing dialogue with the reading material.

Key questions to ask yourself:

☐ Why I am reading this? Before you begin reading, ask yourself if you are reading for general ideas or specific facts. And—how deeply you have to probe the material.

You can cut your reading time dramatically if you realize that you can skim much of the book—even skip parts that you will never need to know.

☐ What do I already know about the topic? Before you begin, spend a few minutes jotting down what you know already, what you think about it and what you would like to know.

This will prime you to ask yourself relevant questions as soon as you begin to read the material and you will probably be surprised when you realize how many ideas come from your background knowledge.

Further, thinking for yourself before you give the author a chance to influence you will improve your ability to form original insights and opinions.

Bonus: This exercise gives you practice at quick responses to new material, a valuable skill when you are faced with unexpected test questions or sudden real-life problems that you haven't studied.

After these preparations, skim the whole book. Pay particular attention, though, to the introduction, table of contents and chapter summaries and glance at the author's biography. All this information will help you answer the next question.

☐ What's the big picture? Once you begin reading, find out the main points and ideas conveyed by the book so that you don't get bogged down in details during the next stage, when you actually read the book in depth.

Your aim is to sustain an active dialogue that helps you learn as you read. Learning new material is often hard work that stretches your mind. The process becomes more enjoyable when you approach it like a game.

☐ What is the author going to say next? Try to anticipate the next step in the discussion. Even if you are learning something completely new, you can probably make a reasonable guess.

Example: If you are studying chemistry —a subject about which you know nothing—and you come to a section on "strong acid reactions," you can anticipate that the next topic will be something like "weak acid reactions"—even if it isn't, you will be more interested in following the discussion than you would if you were just reading passively.

Absorbing new material will become even easier when you answer the next question.

☐ What are the expert questions? These are the questions that are typically asked about the subject you are currently studying.

Example: Geology books repeatedly answer questions like "What is this made of?"; "What are its properties?"; "Where is it found?"; "By what process was it formed?" History textbooks deal with other questions like "When did it happen?"; "Who was involved?"; "What were the causes?"; "What were the effects?"

When you know the pattern of these questions, you can anticipate a lot of what will appear in tests.

☐ What are my own questions? To study more effectively, exercise your curiosity by asking general subject-related questions that interest you. Try to answer the questions; don't be afraid to guess.

Example: If you are studying financial planning and read that the amount available to a person in a case study for investment is the difference between earnings and expenditures, ask yourself when is it appropriate to increase earnings and when is it appropriate to reduce spending.

As you go further into the subject, you will find some of your answers are right, some are close and some are way off. Whatever the case, thinking inquisitively and comparing your ideas with the facts will help you master the material as it becomes more familiar and personally meaningful. As you read on, the next three questions will help you take notes that are useful to review the subject and study for tests.

☐ What information is important? That will, in large measure, depend on why you are reading the book. Don't waste time and effort compiling notes that are irrelevant to your real aim. In general, about 20% of the book contains 80% of the useful information.

☐ How can I summarize this information? The shorter you can make your notes, the more useful they will be, especially if you are preparing for a test.

Important: Use your own words. If you are just copying phrases from the text, there's a good chance you don't really understand it.

☐ How can I organize the information? Try grouping it in ways different from those of the text. See what connections you can find, play with the material, summarize with diagrams and sketches, acronyms, rhymes and anything that makes sense to you and helps you remember it. The more you exercise your brain to organize the material, the better you will be able to understand and recall it. Aim to condense the whole subject you are studying until it fits on one page, then study that page until you can reproduce it from memory.

You are now ready for the big test. All the thinking and questioning you did while reading has prepared you to handle any question you are likely to get. Looking beyond the immediate payoff of passing the test, active learning stimulates your continuing intellectual growth.

Source: Adam Robinson, cofounder of the Princeton Review, a program that helps students do well on standardized tests, 2315 Broadway, Third Floor, New York 10024. He is the author of seven books on education, most recently *What Smart Students Know: Maximum Grades, Optimum Learning, Minimum Time,* Crown Publishers Inc., New York.

Conquering forgetfulness

Aging and memory loss do not go hand in hand, contrary to popular belief. The chronic confusion, disorientation and loss of self-sufficiency often associated with growing older are in most cases the result of some specific neurological or psychological disorder.

Memory is not a "something" that we have. It's a skill that can be preserved and developed—no matter what your age.

The first step is to avoid—as much as possible—the things that weaken our memory.

☐ B-vitamin deficiency. Memory can be impaired by deficiencies in...

☐ B1 (thiamine)—found in whole-grain products and salmon steak.

☐ B3 (niacin)—found in meat, peanuts, tuna and turkey.

☐ B12 (cobalamins)—found in beef, milk products, eggs and flounder.

Although vitamin deficiencies are rare in this country—where most people overeat—certain people are at risk...

☐ Heavy drinkers (two or more drinks a day) are at risk of Wernicke-Korsakoff syndrome, a neurological disorder marked by partial or total loss of short-term memory—and associated with inadequate consumption of thiamine. If you drink heavily, it's a good idea to cut back or stop. Otherwise, ask your doctor about thiamine supplements.

☐ Elderly people who consume fewer than 1,800 calories a day. They, too, can have deficiencies and should ask their doctor about supplements.

☐ Strict vegetarians. Vitamin B12 is found only in meat, fish, eggs and dairy products. People who consume no animal products of any kind should ask their doctor about B12 supplements.

☐ Prescription drugs. Sleeping pills, tranquilizers, some antidepressants, antianxiety drugs and even some prescription painkillers can cause memory loss.

At greatest risk: People 55 years old or older.

If your doctor prescribes one or more of these drugs for you, ask if they are absolutely necessary. In many cases, nondrug approaches are equally effective—psychotherapy, regular exercise, dietary modification, etc.

If drug therapy is essential, ask your doctor if your dosage can be reduced —or if you can switch to another drug that might have less of an effect on your memory.

Example I: Some types of blood-pressure medications—including beta blockers—can reduce the flow of blood to the brain, resulting in temporary or perhaps even permanent memory loss. Other types of antihypertensive medication might pose less of a problem.

Example II: Certain types of antidepressants can exacerbate memory problems in persons already suffering from memory loss. Some of the newer antidepressant medications, including Prozac, might be safer.

Finally, avoid overmedication. Some doctors are in such a hurry to "process" their patients that they may fail to get an accurate picture of their patients' overall health. And, they sometimes prescribe drugs when no drugs are needed—or prescribe higher than necessary doses. This is a special problem for elderly people.

☐ Bypass surgery. One possible side effect of coronary artery bypass surgery is memory impairment. This impairment seems to be a consequence of reduced blood flow to the brain during surgery, although this remains a matter to be fully investigated.

While a recent study showed that bypass patients had slight memory impairment for up to six months after surgery on neurological testing, some of my patients who underwent bypass surgery experienced memory trouble for even longer periods of time.

Self-defense: Be careful of bypass surgery or any other long, complex operation requiring general anesthesia.

(This is especially important for people older than 55.) In some cases, non-surgical alternatives to bypass are worth trying—for example, adopting an extremely low-fat diet or taking cholesterol-lowering drugs. Or you might have your arteries cleared via balloon angioplasty, which poses less of a threat to your memory. Ask your doctor.

Alzheimer's—or not?

Doctors used to blame memory problems in older people on "hardening of the arteries"—or simply on "aging." Now some doctors blame the problem on Alzheimer's disease—even though there's no clear way to diagnose Alzheimer's. In such cases, the real problem might be something far less serious and possibly reversible.

Memory loss might be caused by depression or by numerous tiny strokes, a condition known as Binswanger's disease. Unlike Alzheimer's, depression is treatable—as is the high blood pressure that can lead to Binswanger's.

Self-defense: If you or a loved one is diagnosed with Alzheimer's, insist on a reexamination to rule out other possibilities.

Challenge your brain

A lazy brain is more apt to forget things than a brain that gets regular "exercise." No matter what your age, certain exercises can help keep your memory keen:

☐ Balance your checkbook in your head. Adding and subtracting helps boost powers of concentration and attention—and prevents the loss of mathematical abilities.

☐ Test your power of recall. While stuck in traffic or waiting on line, try conjugating verbs from a foreign language or mentally reciting the titles of Beatles songs.

☐ Occasionally use your nondominant hand. If you doodle, for example, try using your nondominant hand to reproduce a drawing done with your dominant hand. This exercise helps "transfer" functions and information from one hemisphere of the brain to the other. This is an excellent way to keep your mind "revved up."

☐ Do brain-relaxing exercises. The more relaxed your mind, the better your powers of concentration—and the stronger your ability both to memorize and to recall information.

Forms of relaxation: Transcendental meditation, self-hypnosis or the simple but effective program developed by Dr. Herbert Benson in his book, *The Relaxation Response.*

☐ Eat right and exercise. Regular exercise not only promotes physical health, but also helps prevent depression. Excessive consumption of dietary fat and other poor dietary habits can lead to stroke, which of course can cause memory loss.

☐ Work. Retirement is often viewed as a time to do little or nothing. But the less you do, the less you and your mind will be able to do. If you retire, find something to keep yourself occupied and your mind engaged. *Possibilities:* Explore a new occupation or volunteer work. The only reason to stop working is serious illness.

Source: Vernon H. Mark, MD, former professor of surgery at Harvard Medical School, Boston, and retired director of neurosurgery, Boston City Hospital. He is the author of *Reversing Memory Loss,* Houghton Mifflin Co., New York.

Recovering from a disappointment

Some steps that will help you to recover from disappointment:

☐ Acknowledge the pain and allow yourself feelings of loss and dispossession.

☐ Take a step back to gain perspective. No single hoped-for event is necessary to your survival. Remember some of your past disappointments and realize that life went on—that you achieved satisfaction without fulfillment of those particular expectations.

☐ See the positive side. Disappointment is a lesson in reality. It tells us what's possible and what isn't. It may tell you to give up a certain set of expectations or to change your behavior in order to make what you expect actually happen.

Coping with a major loss

The death of a loved one, the loss of a job, separation or divorce, all involve change and loss. A sense of loss accompanies all major changes in life, even when the change is positive, such as a job promotion, marriage or a job transfer.

Stages by which people respond to a major loss:

- ☐ Shock or denial.
- ☐ Fear and paralysis.
- ☐ Anger, at others or at oneself.
- ☐ Sadness and depression.
- ☐ Acceptance and reformulation of goals.

All the stages are important to the process of adaptation:

☐ The omission of any single stage can result in depression or incomplete adjustment because the energy needed to cope with the present remains bound up in the past.

☐ The longer people have to rehearse a new situation and work through feelings about it, the less stress there will be and the less time it will take to adapt. For example, research among widows shows that those whose husbands died after a long illness, such as cancer, had a much less difficult time making the transition to widowhood than those whose husbands died unexpectedly, in a car crash, for example.

Learning from failure

Sooner or later, everyone who is ambitious will experience a failure. Many don't recognize, however, that failure is necessary. You can't succeed without struggle. But if you're able to learn from what went wrong, you can do it right the next time.

☐ Evaluate honestly what stands between you and success, both in the outside world and within yourself.

☐ Find a mentor who will be open with you about his or her own struggles with such blind spots.

☐ Read biographies of people who overcame their own fears to become successful.

Taking criticism

☐ Don't read more into the criticism than the speaker intends.

☐ Don't be deaf to positive comments.

☐ Separate legitimate from inaccurate criticism.

☐ Don't argue about the critic's feelings rather than the facts of the situation.

☐ Delay a direct response until you have figured out whether the critic is trying to come off better by putting you down.

☐ Make sure the critic knows enough to make an intelligent observation about the subject. Then, pick your response to fit the circumstances.

Source: Dr. Jack E. Hulbert, North Carolina Agricultural and Technical State University, Greensboro, NC, and Dr. Barbara Pletcher, director, National Association for Professional Saleswomen.

How to save face while encouraging criticism

While most people agree that dissent and discussion are vital, many bristle when their own ideas are challenged or criticized. How to be open and avoid ego damage:

☐ Ask for specific ways to strengthen or improve an idea rather than for a general opinion.

☐ Meet in individual sessions rather than in a group. Opposition is easier in private.

☐ Solicit reactions to only one part of the proposal at a time.

☐ Ask for written criticism. It can be less traumatic and can be put aside for a calmer moment.

Source: Personal Report for the Executive, Research Institute of America, New York.

How to profit from criticism

You can improve yourself by encouraging friends to criticize you, and learning how to take criticism. Your critics may not always be right. But if you don't get the truth from others, you may never find out.

☐ Let your critic finish what he has to say before you answer.

☐ Don't go into the reasons for your actions or behavior. This is really just a way of excusing them.

☐ Don't jest. It is insulting to the critic.

☐ Show that you have understood (whether or not you agree) by briefly repeating the criticism in your own words.

☐ Let your critic know that you understand how your behavior has caused inconvenience or made him feel.

☐ Don't open yourself to criticism for what you are—only for what you do. You are not responsible for anything but your actions. It is by changing these that you can change yourself.

Source: Dr. George Weinberg, author of *Self-Creation*, Avon Books, New York.

Dangers in perfectionism

Emotional perfectionists believe they should always be happy and in control of their feelings.

They believe they should never:

☐ Feel insecure…so they worry about shyness, thus adding to their anxiety.

☐ Feel ambivalent about a commitment …so they're unable to make a decision in the first place and then feel miserable about their vacillation.

More reasonable goal: To have general control of emotions and accept emotional flaws as part of our humanity.

Source: Dr. David D. Burns, cognitive therapist, Presbyterian–University of Pennsylvania Medical Center, Philadelphia.

How to change Type A behavior

Here are some ways to modify dangerous Type A behavior:

☐ Walk and talk more slowly.

☐ Reduce deadline pressure by pacing your days more evenly.

☐ Stop trying to do more than one thing at a time.

☐ Don't interrupt other people in midspeech.

☐ Begin driving in the slow lane.

☐ Simply sit and listen to music you like while doing nothing else.

Big drains on personal energy

Unwillingness to face up to emotions leads to fatigue. Normal energies are expended in the effort to repress sadness or anger. Some common instances:

☐ Grieving that hasn't been attended to. Surprising, but typical, examples are getting a new job and moving to a new city. The event can be exhilarating. But, the new situation still implies some loss. This holds true for promotions or getting married—which mean saying goodbye to certain freedoms, contacts, options. People who don't deal with the negative aspects of even the most positive changes are vulnerable to psychological fatigue. Some of their energies remain bound up in the past.

☐ Situations of acknowledged loss, i.e., the death of a loved one or the fact that the children have grown up and left home, or having to face the fact of limited potential (executive's sudden realization that he'll never fulfill career objectives).

Recognizing fatigue for what it is

Fighting fatigue is a concept of success-oriented people that actually makes them fatigue-prone. Fatigue is a symptom the purpose of which is to get your attention—to tell you there's something wrong with the way you live. The main cause of fatigue is a monolithic lifestyle, in which the rational sense is used to the exclusion of the other senses, movement and the emotions. To beat fatigue, you have to get your life back in balance.

What is fatigue?

The tiredness we feel after jogging, for instance, is not fatigue. Fatigue is an absence of energy, *joie de vivre*, interest…It's a blunting of sensation, a shutting out of stimuli.

Behavioral clues:

☐ Difficulty in getting going or persevering.

☐ Not having the energy to do things you know you enjoy.

☐ Having trouble waking up or getting to sleep.

☐ Taking too many naps.

Most vulnerable

People who:

☐ Do virtually the same thing all day, every day. The classic case is the executive who spends his work hours hunched over a desk, grabs a sandwich at lunch, takes a break only to talk to coworkers about business and goes home to a set routine with his family each evening.

☐ Have lifestyles contrary to their natural inclinations. Each of us has a rhythm of activity with which we are most comfortable. If a natural doer is forced to lie on a beach in the Bahamas for two weeks, he'll come back exhausted.

Source: Mary E. Wheat, MD, an internist and counselor on fatigue at Mt. Zion Hospital and Medical Center, San Francisco.

Are you a workaholic?

People who love their work passionately and spend long hours at it are not necessarily work-addicted. True workaholics cannot stop working even in non-work situations. They make all other activities and relationships secondary to work. While the reasons differ widely, almost all work addicts share these traits:

☐ Oriented to activities involving skills and skill development. Averse to activities where skill is not a factor.

☐ Strongly analytic. Focus on precise definitions, goals, policies, facts, lists, measurements and strategies.

☐ Aggressive and unable to leave things alone. An urge to manipulate and control their environment to gain a sense of satisfaction.

☐ Goal-oriented, product-oriented. Uninterested in the sensations of the present unless they yield products or contribute to their creation.

☐ Concerned with efficiency and effectiveness. Severely upset by waste and loss. Ironically, many work addicts are inefficient because they are perfectionists and refuse to delegate authority.

Source: Jay B. Rohrlick, MD, *Work and Love: The Crucial Balance*, Summit Books, New York.

Recognizing psychological fatigue

As a rule, if a person has been overworking for some time and then takes three or four days off and sleeps adequately, he should be refreshed.

But often rest is not the answer. People whose tiredness is psychological need stimulation. The more rest such a person gets, the more tired he becomes.

Who's prone to psychological fatigue:

☐ People who are unwilling to ask for what they want or who keep waiting for people to guess.

☐ People who refuse to say what they don't want. Nothing saps energy and produces fatigue as much as unacknowledged resentment.

☐ If chronic tiredness persists and the doctor says there's no physical cause, acknowledge the problem is a psychological one.

☐ Explore the feelings engendered by work or by important relationships.

☐ Figure out what unmet needs and wants you have in these areas.

☐ Determine which expectations are realistic and which aren't, and how to go about resolving that draining aspect of your life.

Source: Gisele Richardson, management consultant, Richardson Management Associates, Montreal.

Tension-reducing techniques

Basic rules for tense individuals:

☐ Wake up early to avoid hurrying and getting keyed up before leaving the house.

☐ Take a short walk after lunch. Do it any time that tension is high. (Just say, "I'll be back in five minutes," and go.)

☐ Have a daily quiet hour. No phone calls or visitors.

☐ Plan social engagements to allow for a short relaxation period between the end of the business day and the start of the evening's activities.

☐ Always be prepared for those tense moments during the day and, when they come, concentrate on breathing slowly and deeply.

Source: *Personal Health.*

Reducing pain-producing jaw tension

Five exercises to ease discomfort:

☐ Start by opening the mouth wide, then closing it. Do this repeatedly and as rapidly as possible.

☐ Continue the same motions, but now place the palm of your hand beneath the chin when opening the mouth, and above it when closing. This offers a slight resistance.

☐ Repeat the same two steps with a sideways motion of the lower jaw, first doing it freely and then doing it against the resistance of the palm of the hand.

☐ Go through the same steps with a motion that protrudes the jaw.

☐ Chew a piece of gum alternately on each side of the mouth, then in the center of the mouth. Do each exercise for three to five minutes.

Source: Patricia Brown, RN, *American Journal of Nursing*, New York.

How nine celebrities handle anxiety

Many successful people have developed their own special ways of dealing with anxiety with a significant emphasis on physical activity. Their approaches may be worth a try for you.

☐ Yogi Berra, baseball great:

"I spend lots of time on the golf course, often with my son, who is also a ball player. And I like to play racquetball."

☐ Jane Brody, *New York Times* science writer and author of the bestselling *Jane Brody's Nutrition Book* and *New York Times Guide to Personal Health:*

"I find the best way to avoid anxiety is to exercise. I drop everything and do something physical—jog, swim, whatever. I clear the slate and calm down. When I come back, things don't seem so bad. Another thing—I keep a continuing calendar and try not to let too many things pile up at once. And I have also learned the fine art of saying 'no.'"

☐ Joyce Brothers, psychologist and TV personality:

"Whenever I get anxious, I swim. (Studies indicate that 15 minutes of strenuous exercise have a more tranquilizing effect than strong drugs). Another good way to fight stress and anxiety is take a long, brisk walk."

☐ Dr. Frank Field, science editor:

"The key word, for me, is 'awareness.' Once I am aware of my anxiety, I stand back and look at it. If someone tells me that I am shouting, I try to do something about it—not just deny it. I get swept up with so many things that often I am unaware that I am becoming anxious. So then I take control of myself."

☐ Eileen Ford, Ford Model agency:

"I do yoga deep breathing. The tension just flows from my body."

☐ Roger Horchow, founder of The Horchow Collection:

"I don't have much anxiety in my life. When I do, I guess it is when I eat too much. But mostly, I try to work harder to eliminate what is bothering me…try to accomplish more and deal with the source."

☐ Reggie Jackson, baseball great:

"My best cure for anxiety is working on my collection of old cars. I also enjoy building cars, and I find that doing physical work can relieve stress for me. Reading the Bible also puts my mind at ease and gives me spiritual comfort."

☐ Ann Landers, syndicated columnist:

"My work is not anxiety-producing, but occasionally, if there is a hitch, I get into a hot bath, take the phone off the hook and count my blessings. I have a great deal to be thankful for, and I know it."

☐ Dr. Ruth Westheimer, prominent sexologist:

"When I get anxious, I say, 'Ruth Westheimer, get hold of yourself.' The important thing is to recognize your anxiety. Sometimes this makes it go away. If it were a really serious anxiety, I would go for professional help."

Depression myths and realities

Common as it is, depression is shrouded in popular misconceptions. Whether short-term and mild or more serious and longer-lasting, those feelings of low self-esteem, aimlessness and purposelessness afflict many people periodically. You'll be able to cope with depression better if you understand the major fallacies about it.

☐ If you're feeling depressed, the cause must be psychological. *Fact:* Not necessarily. Many psychiatrists consider much emotional distress to be caused by genetically inherited body chemistry. Also, a variety of physical illnesses, such as viral infections, can cause low psychological moods.

☐ People who lack ego strength and character are more likely to get depressed than those with strong personalities. *Fact:* If anything, it's the strongest characters who are most subject to feelings of depression and low periods. Strong personalities have very high standards of success and morality and suffer most from a loss of self-esteem.

☐ Men and women are equally susceptible to depression. *Fact:* Women are more likely, by a ratio of two to one, to develop feelings of depression. On the other hand, men tend to have more serious depressions and a higher rate of suicide.

☐ Depression will affect you psychologically but not physically. *Fact:* Prolonged and serious periods of depression can result in weight loss, sleeplessness and other stress that can make the sufferer vulnerable to serious physical problems, such as heart attack and multiple sclerosis.

☐ Falling in love will lift you out of depression. *Fact:* People who are feeling low and emotionally distressed are too internally preoccupied to be either very interested or successful in handling relationships. Feelings of depression also cause a decrease in the sexual impulse.

☐ Help for depression can come only from long-term psychotherapy. *Fact:* There are ways of combating depression effectively that don't require long-term therapy. Antidepressant drug therapy may help in several weeks. People who are having a mild, short-term depression may profit from seeing a therapist or a counselor several times. However, serious and disabling depression that lasts for months does call for continuing professional treatment.

☐ Tranquilizers will help you combat feelings of depression. *Fact:* Valium and alcohol are both depressants themselves, as are all tranquilizers. The only medications that work are antidepressant drugs, which must be carefully prescribed.

☐ The cause of your depression is usually obvious. *Fact:* The cause that seems most obvious is most often not the real one. *Reason:* Depression has to do with unconscious conflict. For example, one of the frequent causes of depression is repressed hostility. When that hostility is acknowledged, the depression usually lifts.

☐ You always know when you are depressed. *Fact:* There are common forms of depression in which people do not know how they feel. Such people express their depression in other ways. Obese people and alcoholics often may not feel depressed, but their obesity or drinking are the equivalent. People who feel their depression have an advantage because they, at least, have a chance to do something about it.

☐ There are usually some aftereffects from depression. *Fact:* It's possible,

after a period of feeling depressed, to jump right back to where you were with no residuals. Depression does not change the psyche.

Source: Michael Levy, MD, psychiatrist, New York.

How to cope with depression

☐ Avoid isolation. Talk with someone who can provide counsel.

☐ If a period of depression lasts for more than a few weeks, or if your ability to function is impaired, more professional help is needed.

☐ Recognize that your outlook during a low period is going to be pessimistic and distorted. In such a period, your judgments of yourself, of your situation and of other people are not based on reality.

☐ Difficult as it may be, try to be active, do things and see people. People who are most successful at coping with feelings of depression are those who fight them.

Source: Michael Levy, MD, psychiatrist, New York.

Rules of thumb

Rules of thumb are useful because they cut down on the time needed to get information and figure things out ourselves. Some especially helpful and little-known ones:

☐ Extracurricular. Don't expect any more than one third of any professional-club members to attend a meeting. Build up a large membership so enough members are around to make up for those away.

☐ Horses. To get the best price on a riding horse, the best time of year to buy is fall.

☐ Walking. Without a pack, you should be able to walk 25 miles a day without serious strain. With a pack one fourth your weight or less, 15 miles a day is reasonable on an average trail.

☐ Dieting. Most overeating happens at night. If you can't diet all the time, diet after dark.

☐ Most for your money. You can mail five sheets of average paper for the price of a first-class stamp.

☐ Holiday time. To find out how many lights a Christmas tree needs, first multiply the tree height by the tree width measured in feet. Then multiply this figure by three.

☐ Determining your frame size. You can determine your body frame by wrapping your thumb and index finger around your wrist. *Small frame:* Thumb extends past the index finger. *Average frame:* Thumb and index finger just meet. *Large frame:* Thumb and index finger don't meet.

☐ Fixing up. It takes the average person one hour to paint 1,000 square feet plus one hour for each window or door.

☐ Bad weather. Second gear is best for driving on ice and snow.

Source: *Rules of Thumb* by Tom Parker, Houghton Mifflin Co., Boston.

How to let go of a grudge

Practically everyone has held a grudge at one time or another in their life. Some people hold on to grudges for their entire lives.

But stubbornly clinging to a grudge is counterproductive. It wastes valuable mental energy and prevents us from addressing the issues that originally led to our resentment.

Why we hold on to grudges

☐ The belief that resentment will keep us from ever being taken advantage of again. The irony is that a grudge maintains the illusion of power without the reality. As a result, our resentment can actually make us more vulnerable.

Example: A manager refused to read material suggested by an executive against whom he held a grudge. As it turned out, by not reading the material, he was ill-prepared for several key meetings.

☐ The fear that letting go of the grudge will prevent us from getting the revenge we deserve. In reality, revenge is rarely satisfying because:

☐ Being poisoned by hatred or paralyzed with rage results in a hollow victory.

☐ Grudges actually provide convenient excuses for not moving on in our lives. This is what psychologists call secondary gain.

Example: A man held a grudge against his employer, barely talking to him for eight months because of a relatively minor slight. In fact, this employee was ill-suited to his job and knew it. Instead of looking for a different job, he used his grudge as justification for not progressing in his career.

How grudges hurt us

We may have imagined the supposed slight that left us feeling betrayed, it may have been only a misunderstanding or past experience may cause us to see innocent comments as malicious. In some cases, someone really may have meant to do harm.

But whether or not it's based on an accurate perception of another person's motives, holding a grudge often hurts the grudge-holder more than it hurts the perpetrator. *Reasons:*

☐ Preoccupation with how badly we've been treated causes a tremendous amount of distracting mental activity that keeps us from productive work. It's extraordinary how much time we can spend plotting revenge, worrying ourselves sick about being cheated and feeling angry or sad—all emotions and thoughts that interfere with reaching goals in both our professional and personal lives.

☐ Anger—induced by your grudge—can cause tremendous physiological stress, potentially contributing to heart disease, ulcers and other health problems.

☐ An obsession with revenge can lead to vengeful actions that rarely relieve the anger and may create unbearable guilt if these obsessions are acted out.

☐ Nursing a grudge blocks us from engineering a real solution to the problem—such as expressing our hurt and asking for an apology— and keeps us from practicing good assertive skills that are more likely to protect us from future pain.

How to get rid of a grudge

We can get over our grudges and get back to the business of living. *Steps:*

☐ Determine whether the slight was real or imagined. Review the situation carefully. Generate alternative explanations for what happened to see if there's any room to interpret the experience as a misunderstanding. Was the other person really trying to hurt you? Or did he/she unwittingly touch upon an issue about which you are overly sensitive?

☐ Challenge all of your irrational and magical ideas. The offense itself is usually not nearly as bad as the exaggerated feelings of hurt and anger that arise in reaction to it. Identifying those automatic reactions can rob them of their power. *Examples:*

☐ Irrational belief: If I'm nice to others, they'll always be nice to me.

Challenge: It would be great if the world worked that way, but it doesn't. It's unrealistic to expect life always to be fair to me, no matter how decent I am.

☐ Irrational belief: I can't stand that this happened.

Challenge: Of course I can stand it. Who needs this resentment?

☐ Irrational belief: This person is evil and horrible and deserves my hatred.

Challenge: This person is human, with all the faults that come with that, and hating him is hurting me more than it hurts him.

☐ Take any necessary action. Assert yourself if you didn't before. Many people with long-standing grudges suffer in silence—they never even tell the perpetrator that they were hurt. Take responsibility for your feelings, and be authentic in expressing them.

☐ Perform a ritual to release your grudge. Because grudges involve such powerful feelings, a simple ceremony can help you let go by evoking equally powerful symbolism.

Strategy: Write out the grudge and all your feelings about it on a piece of paper. Bury the paper—literally—in the backyard or in the soil around a potted plant. Resolve not to raise the matter at all for three months. This is more realistic than trying to dismiss it from your mind forever. Whenever it crosses your mind, remind yourself that you've buried it. At the end of three months, dig up the piece of paper and reconsider your grudge. Are you finished with it? If not, what would it take for you to be finished? Is there an irrational belief you haven't effectively challenged? Do you need to take more assertive action? Repeat the ritual if you need to.

This is an amazingly powerful technique. I've seen it work for countless people, from business partners to spouses. It has worked on issues that have festered for years. It allows you to recognize your power to let go of the grudge. Holding on to a grudge feels powerful but it isn't; letting go is real power.

Source: Barry Lubetkin, PhD, director of the Institute for Behavior Therapy, 137 E. 36 St., New York 10016. He is the author of *Why Do I Need You to Love Me in Order to Like Myself?*, Longmeadow Press, Stamford, CT.

Dealing with details

When your mind is cluttered with details, use one of these techniques to redirect energy and improve organization:

☐ Take a mini-break. A short walk or a minute of relaxation and a drink of water. Or, simply breathe deeply for 30 seconds with your eyes closed (this can help concentration when you shift from one subject to another).

☐ Keep your schedule on paper. Resist the temptation to keep it in your head.

☐ Avoid interruptions. Work away from the office and keep your distance from the telephone.

☐ Delegate details. Rely more heavily on your secretary. Let subordinates handle routine jobs. Let them attend most of the less important meetings.

☐ Set time limits. If a task isn't completed within an allotted time limit, come back to it later.

Source: *International Management*, New York.

While standing in line

☐ Do isometric exercises.
☐ Listen to instructional tapes.
☐ Read a paperback.
☐ Watch your miniature TV set.
☐ Meditate.
☐ Meet your neighbors in line.
☐ Plan the week's schedule.
☐ Plan an upcoming trip.
☐ Bring along a dictionary to expand your vocabulary.
☐ Make a list of people you want to meet to improve your business or social life.

The basics of speed-reading

Speed-reading is not a miracle. It is a skill that takes commitment, concentration and practice. Nor is it appropriate for all kinds of reading. Poetry, for example, was never meant to be whizzed through.

Good speed-reading courses employ a variety of techniques designed to make your reading more efficient and effective. The more you train yourself to use these techniques, the faster—and more productive—your reading will become. The basics:

☐ Skim material from which you want only the main ideas.

☐ Go slowly when you need to take in all the details.

☐ Concentrate. Reading is a mental process. If you are distracted while reading, you will proceed slowly and not remember what you have read.

☐ Use typographical clues to get the general content. Headlines, boldfaced lead-ins, bullets, etc., guide you through the material, indicating what you can skip and what you need to concentrate on most.

Source: Robert de Vight, adjunct associate professor of communications at New York University.

Speed-reading: Fact vs. fiction

What to be wary of

☐ Any system that *guarantees* increased reading speed. The most deceptive thing about a guarantee is the false sense of confidence it gives to the individual with low verbal skills. If you don't start out with basic skills, you will not learn them in speed-reading.

☐ Anyone who suggests that you can read 900 or 1,000 words a minute. Impossible, except when reading extremely easy material. Average reading speed is around 250 to 300 words per minute. Some reading specialists claim 600 to 800 is the maximum for good reading comprehension.

How reading can be speeded up

☐ Preview material. Skim for key words and phrases. Then decide which memos, reports, surveys, business and professional journals you should keep to read.

☐ Read flexibly. Most experts believe learning to read flexibly is the real key to speed-reading. A fast look is valuable when you need to get through repetitious material that doesn't require

you to take in every word. It is also helpful when you're trying to locate a specific fact or phrase. Adjust to a slower reading tempo when the information on the subject is unfamiliar.

☐ Read a lot. It's necessary to keep good reading habits sharp by practicing.

Source: Dr. Charles Shearin, president, Vicore, Inc., Arlington, VA.

Beating procrastination

☐ *Problem:* You have more to do than you can handle.

Solution: Prioritize responsibilities—put the most important ones first.

☐ *Problem:* You put off a difficult task until you're "in the mood."

Solution: Remind yourself that the sooner you begin, the sooner it will be over.

☐ *Problem:* You think you work best under pressure and put off projects until the last minute.

Solution: Set an earlier deadline, and challenge yourself to meet it.

☐ *Problem:* You're a perfectionist.

Solution: Realize we make mistakes. Demanding perfection adds undue stress.

☐ *Problem:* You convince yourself that if you put off doing something long enough, somebody else will do it.

Solution: Remind yourself that the one who does it receives the credit.

☐ *Problem:* You feel so overwhelmed that you don't know where to begin.

Solution: Do something. Finishing one task could snowball into getting even more accomplished.

Source: Warren Huberman, PhD, clinical psychologist, Institute for Behavior Therapy, 137 E. 36 St., New York 10016.

Conversation basics

Here are some ways to keep good conversation flowing:

☐ When talking with someone from a field you either don't know or don't care anything about, steer the conversation toward feelings rather than facts or details. By focusing on emotions that everyone shares, you can feel secure discussing anything.

☐ Make sure both people have equal power to bring up topics, change the subject and demand attention. Avoid common conversational mistakes:

☐☐ Bombarding the other person with questions.

☐☐ Being too quick to give advice.

☐☐ Giving too many personal details.

Sources: *Better Communication* and Gerald Goodman, associate professor of psychology, UCLA, quoted in *US News and World Report.*

Conversation killers

Intimate talks will be more pleasant and productive if you avoid the following:

☐ Sentences that start with the accusatory "you" or the inclusive "let's" or "we." (Instead, try to begin more sentences with "I," to make your honest feelings known.)

☐ Absolute statements. *Example:* "That was a stupid movie."

☐ "I don't know." (You probably have some inkling of an answer, even if it's only to add, "Let me think about it.")

☐ "I don't care." (Even a weak preference should be voiced.)

☐ "Ought," "should," "must," "have to." Instead, try "I might," "I would like to" or "I want to."

☐ Questions beginning with "why," such as "Why are you feeling that way?" *Better:* Begin with a "what," as in "What is bothering you?"

☐ "Always" and "never." More flexible phrases are "up to now" and "in the past."

Source: Dr. Theresa Larsen Crenshaw, author of *Bedside Manners,* Pinnacle Books, New York.

How to be a better conversationalist

☐ Don't start with your name. A name exchange gives a conversation nowhere to go. Instead, mention something in the environment that you can both talk about, such as "How's the cheesecake in this restaurant?" Then pay attention to the cues to find out whether the other person wants to talk with you. Consider tone of voice, facial expression and body language.

☐ Develop your descriptive power. The well-told anecdote or story will express your personality and convey warmth and charm. Many people are afraid to express their feelings when it comes to description. They stick to a dry recitation of facts instead.

☐ Be sensitive to the other person. Pick up on messages about how that person is feeling. Watch body language as well as listening to what's being said. Don't be one of those insensitive, endless talkers who fear that if they stop, their partner will get bored and want to leave.

☐ Don't use boredom as a defense. People who always claim to be bored are usually just erecting a defense against rejection. If you're at a party and don't talk to anyone because you tell yourself they're all boring, you've just insulated yourself against failure. If you feel you're boring to others, that's just another excuse for not trying and therefore not failing.

☐ Don't keep asking questions. Constant queries to keep a conversation going can be a crutch. The other person will finally realize that you're not really listening but are thinking up the next question. People dislike feeling interrogated and resent answering questions under those circumstances. Ask a question only when something genuinely sparks your curiosity.

Source: Arthur Reel, who teaches the art of conversation at New York City's Learning Annex and at Corporate Communications Skills, Inc., an executive training center in New York.

Learning to listen

Here are some simple techniques to help you improve your listening ability:

☐ Relax and help the speaker relax, too. Give your full attention to what's being said. Stop everything else you're doing. Maintain eye contact.

☐ Don't let the speaker's tone of voice or manner turn you off. Nervousness or misplaced emotions often cloud the message the speaker is trying to get across.

☐ Prepare beforehand for the conversation. Take a few minutes to read or consult information pertinent to the discussion. That also helps you to quickly evaluate the speaker and the subject.

☐ Allow for unusual circumstances (extreme pressure or disturbing interruptions). Judge only what the speaker says, given the conditions he's faced with.

☐ Avoid getting sidetracked.

☐ Listen very closely to points you disagree with. (Poor listeners shut out or distort them.)

☐ Mentally collect the main points of the conversation. Occasionally, ask for clarification of one of the speaker's statements.

Bad listening habits

If you want to be a better listener, try to avoid:

☐ Thinking about something else while waiting for the speaker's next word or sentence. The mind races ahead four times faster than the normal rate of conversation.

☐ Listening primarily for facts rather than ideas.

☐ Tuning out when the talk seems to be getting too difficult.

☐ Prejudging, from appearance or speaking manner, that the person has nothing interesting to say.

☐ Paying attention to outside sights and sounds when talking with someone.

☐ Interrupting with a question whenever a speaker says something puzzling or unclear.

Source: John T. Samaras, University of Oklahoma.

How to listen to a complaint

Many people don't hear anything that doesn't fit their own assumptions. If someone comes to you with a complaint or claim, listen—just listen.

☐ Don't answer or explain.

☐ Take notes on exactly what's said.

☐ Try to imagine that the person is right, or at least justified.

☐ Put yourself in the other's place and imagine how you would feel in the same situation.

☐ Give yourself time to think the matter over before making any decision.

☐ Nobody can see all sides of an issue immediately. New facts or ideas take time to sink in.

Source: Levinson Letter, Cambridge, MA.

How to get information from others

☐ Speak softly. This encourages others to take center stage where they should be if you want to learn something from them.

☐ Look responsive. Most people don't use nearly enough facial expression. Raising one eyebrow a little and smiling slightly makes you seem receptive. Eye contact and a calculated pause will invite the person you're talking with to elaborate.

☐ Give reinforcement. Comments such as "Very impressive!" or "Excellent!" can be dropped into the discussion without interrupting the flow.

☐ Follow up and probe. If someone fails to explain the reasons for an action that you're curious about, try a casual follow-up question.

Source: Richard A. Fear, author of *The Evaluation Interview,* published by McGraw-Hill, New York.

Hidden meanings in what people say

Key words tell what people are really trying to communicate. These words and phrases may be spoken repeatedly or hidden in the middle of complex sentences. But they relay the true message being delivered through all the chatter of conversations, negotiations and interviews.

What to watch out for:

☐ Words that jump out at you. The speaker may be mumbling, but suddenly a word (or proper name) is emphasized or spoken loudly.

☐ Slips of the tongue, especially when denied by the person who made them. *Example:* "We won't leave this room until we have reached a derision" (instead of decision). The speaker is mocking either you or the subject under discussion.

☐ Embedding. The repetitive use of words or slogans manipulated to reshape your thinking. Embedding can be insidious. *Example:* At a meeting of parties with irreconcilable differences, one side keeps repeating the word *consensus.* "After we reach a consensus, we'll break for lunch." This one concept is repeated relentlessly by the speakers and members of their team until it dominates the meeting. This is a mini-version of the Big Lie.

☐ Hostile words and phrases. Any statement that hurts or sounds hostile is an affront, even when pawned off as a joke.

☐ Unstated words. These key words are those not spoken. *Prime example:* The husband or wife who can never say "I love you" to the mate.

☐ Metaphors. The turns of expression people choose often signal their inner thoughts. *Example:* A metaphor such as "We'll cut the opposition up into little pieces" takes healthy competition into the realm of aggression.

Source: Martin G. Groder, MD, psychiatrist and business consultant, Durham, NC.

How people say "yes" but mean "no"

Here are some apparently acquiescent verbal expressions that really mean "no":

☐ "Yes, but…"

☐ "I don't know why, but…"

☐ "I tried that, and it doesn't help."

☐ "Well, to be perfectly honest with you…"

☐ "But it's not easy…"

☐ "I know, but…"

☐ "I don't remember."

Spot the unspoken thought behind the poker face

Watching people's actions can bring you a lot closer to the truth than merely listening to what they say.

Here are some typical feelings and mental machinations—and their common outward expressions:

☐ Openness: Open hands, unbuttoned coat.

☐ Defensiveness: Arms crossed on chest, crossing legs, fistlike gestures, pointing index finger, "karate" chops.

☐ Evaluations: Hand to face, head tilted, stroking chin, peering over or playing with glasses, cleaning glasses, cleaning or filling a pipe, hand to nose.

☐ Suspicion: Arms crossed, sideways glance, touching/rubbing nose, rubbing eyes, buttoned coat, drawing away.

☐ Insecurity: Pinching flesh, chewing pen, thumb over thumb, biting fingernail, hands in pockets.

☐ Cooperation: Upper body in sprinter's position, open hands, sitting on edge of chair, hand-to-face gestures, unbuttoning coat.

☐ Confidence: Steepled hands, hands behind back, back stiffened, hands in coat pockets with thumbs out, hands on lapels of coat.

☐ Nervousness: Clearing throat, "whew" sound, whistling, smoking, pinching flesh, fidgeting, covering mouth, jiggling money or keys, tugging ears, wringing hands.

☐ Frustration: Short breaths, "tsk" sound, tightly clenched hands, wringing hands, fistlike gestures, pointing index finger, rubbing hand through hair, rubbing back of neck.

☐ SOS: Uneven intonation of voice, wringing of hands, poor body posture or failure to make eye contact.

How not to be put on the defensive

Criticism from fellow workers or superiors on the job can escalate if you react defensively. How to avoid this instinctive reaction:

☐ Paraphrase an accusation as a way of slowing down reaction time and giving the accuser a chance to retreat. Accuser: "How come that report isn't ready? Can't you ever get your work done on time?" Response: "Do you really think that I never get my work done on time?"

☐ Describe in a tentative fashion what appears to be the other person's psychological state. In response to a scowling superior, say: "I'm uncomfortable. I don't understand what your frown means."

☐ Ask for clarification. Accuser: "This proposal isn't what I asked you to design at all." Response: "Is nothing in the proposal acceptable?"

☐ Use a personal response to assume responsibility. Accuser: "This is entirely wrong." Response: "I guess I didn't understand. Can I review the instructions again?"

Source: Gary P. Cross, management consultant, Cross Names & Beck, Eugene, OR.

Arguments: Keeping your cool

☐ Don't fear to negotiate, even when the difference with the other person is so huge that agreement seems impossible.

☐ If the issue is important, you probably cannot accurately predict when and how a resolution will finally be made. The outcome may become apparent only after extensive discussions.

☐ Avoid the temptation to start off in a hostile manner out of anger at the other person's extreme stance.

Source: Dr. Chester L. Karrass, Karrass Seminars, Santa Monica, CA.

When to offer a solution to a dispute

Let the two sides clear the air by exchanging accusations and expressing pent-up resentments over extraneous issues, not just the one now on the table. Any trained mediator waits for this venting of feelings and buildup of frustrations before exercising influence.

☐ The best (often the only) time to recommend an innovative solution comes when desperation peaks. Both sides know they have a problem. And both know they can't settle it without third-party help.

☐ To be a hero, deliver a solution where mutual goals are not being met and where all parties already recognize that there is a gap between expectations and performance.

Build trust during a discussion

☐ Begin with a positive statement, for example, "I have been looking forward to talking with you. Joe Smith said if anyone could help us, it's you."

☐ Avoid pulling rank.

☐ Don't make veiled threats.

☐ Don't offer a reward.

☐ Show yourself to be an expert.

☐ Associate yourself with someone the other person respects.

☐ Restate the other person's opinions or feelings periodically. But do not preface the restatement with "you said" or "you think." The other person may quibble over what is attributed directly.

☐ Share something personal about yourself if the other person is wary.

☐ Point out ways the information you need will help you.

☐ Indicate ways you can help the other person.

☐ Make a commitment to action, and then ask for a commitment in return.

Source: Pamela Cumming, author of *The Power Handbook,* CBI Publishing, Boston.

Choose your words carefully

Avoid:

☐ Using popular but vague modifiers, such as "exceptional" or "efficient," without defining precisely what is meant. For example, an exceptional record can be either exceptionally good or bad. Describing something as efficiently designed does not say enough. It's better to use facts, numbers, details.

☐ Exaggerating. Overstating a fact is acceptable (and common) in conversation, but it destroys credibility in writing because readers take it literally.

☐ Generalizing. Do not use absolutes, such as: "All," "right," "wrong," "true," "false," "always," "never." Instead, say this is true under such-and-such conditions.

Source: William C. Paxson, author of *The Business Writing Handbook,* Bantam Books, New York.

Write as clearly as you think

Concentrate on simplifying your sentence structure. It's the easiest way to say what is meant and to make sure the message gets across. Three basic rules:

☐ Keep sentences short. They should be no more than 17 to 20 words. If an idea has multiple parts, use multiple sentences.

☐ Vary the length of sentences. The 17–20 word rule is the average. When sentences drone on at unvarying lengths, the reader's attention begins to wander.

☐ Vary the punctuation. Include plenty of commas, as well as a sprinkling of semicolons, to go with the necessary periods. Well-placed punctuation is a road map, leading the reader comfortably and accurately through the message.

Source: Paul Richards, author of *Sentence Control: Solving an Old Problem,* Supervisory Management, New York.

How to measure the clarity of your writing

Use the "Fog Index" to measure how clearly you write letters, memos and reports.

☐ Count off a 100-word section.

☐ Count the number of sentences and divide 100 by that number, which gives average words per sentence.

☐ Count the words with more than two syllables. Add this figure to the average words per sentence.

☐ Multiply the total by 0.4 to get the Fog Index (indicating minimum school grade level a reader needs to comprehend it).

The lower the index, the better. A score of 11 to 12 is passable for most business writing. (The Fog Index for this item: 7.6)

Source: *Time Talk*, Grandville, MI.

How to write a persuasive letter

☐ Grab your reader's attention by fitting in with his interests, either personal or in business. Tell him how he is going to benefit by doing as you ask.

☐ Give proof of what you say. The best proof is to suggest that the reader get in touch with others who have benefited from your suggestion. (Of course, you must make sure that you have people who will back you up.)

☐ In the next-to-last paragraph, tell the reader exactly what he must do to take advantage of the benefits you're offering.

☐ Close with a hook. Encourage the reader to take action by telling him about a loss of money, prestige or opportunity if he does not act at once. (A time penalty is one of the best ways to get the action you want.)

Source: James Van Fleet, author of *A Lifetime Guide to Conversation*, Prentice Hall, Inc., Englewood Cliffs, NJ.

Help readers understand your report

Readers understand a report better when they are carefully led through it. Use the right words or phrases to signal a shift of subject or emphasis:

☐ To get your reader to stop and consider alternatives. *Use:* However, but, by contrast, nevertheless, on the other hand, still, despite, notwithstanding.

☐ To expand the idea. *Use:* Actually, realistically, at the same time, unexpectedly, perhaps.

☐ To concede to a limitation. *Use:* Sometimes, to be sure, possibly, to some extent, conceivably.

☐ To make an aside. *Use:* Incidentally, digressing for a moment.

☐ To move ahead in the same direction. *Use:* Additionally, also, besides, moreover, furthermore.

☐ To make a comparison. *Use:* Similarly, in the same way.

☐ To strengthen an assertion. *Use:* Indeed, in fact, certainly.

☐ To signal importance. *Use:* Significantly, notably, remarkably.

Source: A. Weiss, author of *Write What You Mean*, AMACOM, New York.

Speeches with impact

Only rarely is it possible to change your audience's deep-seated attitudes or beliefs. Aim no higher than getting the listeners to question their attitudes.

☐ Avoid alienating an audience by pressing points too hard.

☐ State conclusions.

☐ Call for action.

☐ When you have to speak extemporaneously, develop a theme early and stick to it.

☐ Use silence to underline a point.

☐ End a speech with a short, emotional, conviction-filled summary of the main points.

Source: Michael Klezaras, Jr., director of research and planning, Roger Ailes & Associates, Inc., New York.

Delivering an important speech

☐ Find out what common bonds unite the audience so that the speech can be directed to meaningful subjects.

☐ Remember that your audience is interested first in people, then in things, finally in ideas.

☐ Start by tape-recording a spontaneous flow of ideas. Don't attempt to be logical or to follow an outline. This initial tape is the raw material to prepare the final speech.

☐ Avoid opening with a joke. Most jokes backfire. The best grabbers are a question, personal story, famous quote, vital statistic, comparison or contrast.

☐ Use questions throughout.

☐ Avoid unnecessary phrases such as "Now let me explain…." Or: "The point I want to make is…."

Audience attention drops off sharply after 20 to 30 minutes, so no presentation should run beyond that. If it's necessary to fill more time:

☐ Use slides when appropriate.

☐ Have a question-and-answer session after the speech.

Public speaking: Secrets of success

Contrary to a lot of advice about making a speech, there is no need to memorize, rehearse, rely on extensive notes or spend weeks getting ready. The key is to keep the presentation spontaneous.

The only requirements for spontaneous speaking:

☐ Thorough knowledge of the subject.

☐ Self-confidence.

☐ An assured manner of delivery.

To make sure the speech does not sound overrehearsed or canned:

☐ Don't use notes because you'll have no more than two seconds to look down, find the place in the notes and speak to the audience. You'll end up looking, reading, memorizing and reciting, but not communicating.

☐ Instead of notes, use one- to three-word "triggers." Triggers are facts or concepts designed to spark off the next train of thought. Using triggers allows you to deal easily with what is to be said. The result is that you'll gesture more, be more animated and vary your tone of voice.

☐ As a structure for the speech, adopt the same format that people use to communicate every day: State the purpose, support it with details, then recommend what should be done.

☐ Start with a 15- to 30-second grabber. The grabber explains the purpose and stimulates the audience. Work through the details by using the triggers. About five of these should suffice.

☐ End by telling the group something specific to do. If questions follow the talk, restate the recommended action at the conclusion.

☐ Stand in front of the lectern and as close to the audience as possible. This makes the talk seem more like a conversation. In a big auditorium, use a lapel microphone to avoid getting stuck at the lectern. Establish eye contact with people one at a time. Don't look at the wall.

Talking effectively to small groups

☐ Meet personally as many people as possible beforehand.

☐ Get right to the point. The first 15 seconds is what grabs the listener. Don't start with "Thank you" and "I'm very happy to be here."

☐ Make eye contact with everyone in the audience at some time very early in the presentation.

☐ Support main points with factual information and examples.

☐ Repeat the main points to be sure the listeners have gotten them.

☐ Look for a creative conclusion—a provocative thought or action-suggesting statement.

☐ Never let a talk end with an answer to a question from the audience. After answering questions, always return to the main point of the presentation. The last word is important. It shouldn't be yielded to a questioner.

☐ Never ask the audience, "Any questions?" If there aren't any, the silence will be embarrassing. Instead, suggest, "There may be some questions." It makes a difference.

☐ Limit use of notes because it inhibits spontaneity. Write out key words or short phrases to jog thoughts. Alternate lines with different color ink to facilitate quick focusing on material.

☐ Rehearsing is usually not recommended. Unrehearsed presentations have the advantage of freshness and spontaneity which only come from thoughts uttered for the first time.

Source: Dr. Roger Flax, communications training consultant, Motivational Systems, South Orange, NJ.

Using humor successfully

☐ Avoid humor when speaking out-of-doors. The laugh tends to get lost, leaving people with the feeling it wasn't funny at all.

☐ Avoid puns, even though they may go over well in a parlor. They almost always cause the audience to groan more than laugh.

☐ Leave enough time for the laugh before proceeding. Audiences sometimes react slowly, especially if the humor was unexpected. To a nervous speaker, a second's delay seems like an hour.

☐ Be prepared to carry on smoothly and self-confidently if the audience doesn't laugh. The audience will quickly forget that the speaker laid an egg if he remains calm.

Source: Paul Preston, *Communication for Managers,* Prentice-Hall, Englewood Cliffs, NJ.

How to tell jokes like a pro

Henny Youngman, the well-known master comedian and king of the one-liners, offers the following advice:

☐ Genuinely like the jokes you tell. If you don't, you'll nearly always have trouble telling them, not to mention remembering them.

☐ Practice. Memorize your jokes thoroughly. If you fumble for words in the middle of a joke, it will always fall flat.

☐ Always give your audience time to laugh. Then just as the laughter starts to die down, start another joke or resume the conversation. Timing is easier than you might think.

☐ Avoid off-color jokes. There are plenty of funny stories around that aren't dirty.

☐ Be wary of very long jokes. The longer they are, the greater the risk of failure.

☐ Stick to simple, short jokes on subjects we normally like to laugh about.

Source: Henny Youngman, renowned comedian.

How to testify before Congress

Congress holds thousands of hearings a year on subjects vital to your community and business. Can a company or civic or non-profit organization hope to influence legislation by testifying? Chances are against it.

But testimony can sometimes make a difference, particularly on a subject with which legislators are unfamiliar. And an organization or company can raise its profile if an appearance before a Congressional committee is covered by the news media.

If you wish to testify, follow these steps:

☐ Write a letter asking to appear to the committee chairman, whose name appears in the *Congressional Directory.* (You can find this book at your local public library.)

☐ In your letter, focus on your organization's expertise. Point out that its views differ from those already presented. (To protect themselves, committees look for a cross section of views.)

☐ Submit a detailed summary of testimony for committee members to review before the hearing. (Some committees require it 24 hours in advance.)

☐ At the hearing, limit testimony to two or three major points, then open it up to questions. The impact of testifying lies in the face-to-face exchange with committee members. Brief testimony is more likely to be covered by the press.

☐ To improve your chances of being asked to testify, keep in touch with committee staff members, also listed in the *Congressional Directory,* and the representatives from states where your organization is active.

Also useful is the *Congressional Record,* which gives advance notice of hearings.

Source: The *Directory* and the *Daily Record,* available from the Superintendent of Documents, US Government Printing Office, Washington, DC 20402.

How to come across well on radio or TV

If you're asked to be a guest on a radio or TV program, perhaps to promote a charity or civic group with which you're associated or to talk about the local business scene, don't say "no" for fear of doing poorly. Follow these five simple rules, and you'll do fine:

☐ Set the tone right away. Explain at the outset why the subject is important.

☐ Don't stray from the subject.

☐ Keep answers tight. Allow time for more questions and answers, and thus more information.

☐ On television, don't look at the cameras. Look directly at the show host.

☐ On radio, sit close to the microphone. The audience will lose much of what you're saying if you're too far away.

Source: Richard Goldberg, president, *You're On*, Visual Communications Consulting, Brighton, MA.

How to make an effective presentation

Presentations don't have to be speeches. Other possibilities:

☐ An interview format, with one person questioning another.

☐ A discussion among several people, one acting as leader and outlining a project, one strongly in favor, another doubtful, another opposed—thus presenting every point of view.

☐ You might even try a skit, if your people can make the time to learn the lines.

☐ Don't conduct a meeting with nothing but speech after speech. Creative presentations are much better remembered.

Source: *Successful Meetings.*

Public speaking success

Preparation is the key to successful public speaking. *Steps:* Practice a speech out loud three to six times before giving it. Know your subject inside out so you'll feel free to improvise in response to audience reactions. Arrive at the meeting site early to check the podium, seating arrangements and any visual aids you will use. Mix with the audience beforehand to establish a rapport. Speak frequently—it is a skill just like any other. You improve with practice.

Source: Marjorie Brody, president, Brody Communications, Melrose Park, Pennsylvania, quoted in *Sales and Marketing Strategies & News*, 211 W. State St., Box 197 Rockford, Illinois 61105.

Make your point

If it takes you more than 20 seconds to make a point, you're losing your listeners' attention. Most listeners drift off after 20 seconds because they are either formulating a response, focusing on something else or just bored.

Source: Kim Baldez, president, CEO International, training consultants, Austin, Texas.

About speakers

One noted public speaker states that in his 10 years of giving keynote addresses, 80% of those who hired him never called to check the content of his presentation. *Important:* Be sure any speaker hired by the company will make a presentation that fits the company's theme for the specific occasion.

Source: Joan Mather, editor, *Meeting & Conference Executives Alert*, Box 990024, Prudential Station, Boston 02199.

Write the way you speak

Use clear, straightforward language so the reader immediately understands what you have written. If you feel yourself becoming too formal when writing, try dictating the letter and transcribing it. After writing, read over the letter with particular attention to how it *sounds*.

Source: *Complete Business Etiquette Handbook*, by Barbara Pachter, business consultant based in Cherry Hill, New Jersey. Prentice Hall, Rte. 9W, Englewood Cliffs, New Jersey 07632.

Planning ahead for summer jobs, internships and study programs

It's not too soon for your college youngster to make plans for the summer. A variety of good resources to start with is listed below.

Publications

☐ *Federal Jobs*, Box 1438, Leesburg, VA 22075. A listing of federal job opportunities, state by state.

☐ *Summer Jobs in Federal Agencies*, Office of Personnel Management, 1900 E St. NW, Washington, DC 20415. 202-606-2424. Government internships, paying and nonpaying.

☐ *Vacation Study Abroad*, Institute of International Education, 809 UN Plaza, New York 10017. 212-883-8200. Nearly 1,000 summer programs sponsored by US and foreign organizations.

☐ *Work, Study, Travel Abroad: The Whole World Handbook*, Council on International Educational Exchange, 205 E. 42 St., New York 10017. 212- 661-1414. Summer and whole-year jobs and academic programs.

Agencies

☐ College career-placement offices have information and applications for competitive summer internships in government and industry.

☐ State information offices will provide lists of state government internship programs.

☐ The National Society for Internships and Experiential Education, 3509 Haworth Dr., Suite 207, Raleigh, NC 27609. Gives students information on programs in particular areas of business.

Source: Dr. Peter Shaw, author.

Tuition tactics— it pays to be a resident

Students who attend a state college or university outside their home state pay much higher tuition than do residents of that state. In addition, nonresidents do not have access to statewide scholarship and student-aid programs.

However, the Supreme Court has ruled that although state colleges and universities can charge nonresidents higher tuition, those students must be allowed to earn residency status during the period of their enrollment.

Although requirements for residency vary from state to state, most follow similar patterns. All states require continuous residence for a period of time immediately preceding application —usually one year, but as little as six months in a few states.

Basic questions a residency applicant is asked:

☐ Have you filed an income-tax return in the state?

☐ Are you dependent on your parents for support, or are you financially independent?

☐ Have you registered and voted in the state?

☐ Do you have a driver's license or car registration in the state?

☐ Do you have a record of employment in the state? (Students who are seeking financial aid are expected to earn some money through summer and part-time employment.)

State universities that welcome out-of-staters

State universities and colleges were founded primarily to provide low-cost higher education for residents of the state. However, a number of top-flight state universities and colleges welcome students from all over the country. Out-of-state students are charged higher tuition than residents of the state, but frequently, the total still represents a higher-education bargain.

Some first-class institutions that welcome out-of-state students:

☐ *College of William and Mary*, Williamsburg, VA. This is the second-oldest institution of higher learning in the country. Located in historic Williamsburg, the college admits about 30% of its student body from out of state.

☐ *Indiana University*, Bloomington, IN. Founded in 1820, the university draws 20% of its students from out of state.

☐ *New College of the University of South Florida*, Sarasota, FL. Founded in 1960 as a private liberal arts college, it is now an honors-type campus of the university. Nearly half of its students are from outside the South.

☐ *University of Michigan*, Ann Arbor, MI. One of the most prestigious state universities, it has long been popular with students from around the country.

☐ *University of North Carolina at Chapel Hill*, Chapel Hill, NC. This is the nation's first state university. Most of its students come from the South, but it is also popular with students from other parts of the country, particularly the Northeast.

☐ *University of Virginia*, Charlottesville, VA. Thomas Jefferson founded this school and designed its beautiful campus. UVA has considerable social prestige—admirers claim that Princeton is the UVA of the North.

☐ *University of Wisconsin*, Madison, WI. Long popular with students from the Eastern seaboard, it has always been generous, too, in accepting students from the Midwest.

☐ *Virginia Polytechnic Institute and State University*, Blacksburg, VA. This is a rarity—a land-grant university that seeks a national student body. Although the majority of its students come from the South, substantial numbers are from the Northeast, especially at its school of engineering.

☐ The *University of California at Berkeley* and the *University of California at Santa Cruz* do not actively recruit a national student body, but both schools admit substantial numbers of out-of-state students.

A selection of fine Canadian colleges

If your child is college or graduate-school hunting, don't overlook Canada, which has 58 universities offering quality education at relatively low cost for Americans, especially at times when the Canadian dollar is weak. Here are some of the best Canadian schools (designated "E" or "F," according to whether curriculum is conducted in English or French):

☐ *University of British Columbia*, Vancouver, BC (E).

☐ *University of Alberta*, Edmonton, AL (E).

☐ *University of Calgary*, Calgary, AL (E).

☐ *University of Regina*, Regina, SK (E).

☐ *University of Manitoba*, Fort Garry Campus, Winnipeg, MB (E).

☐ *Laurentian University of Sudbury*, Sudbury, ON (E).

☐ *University of Ottawa*, Ottawa, ON (E, F).

☐ *University of Toronto*, Toronto, ON (E).

☐ *University of Waterloo*, West Waterloo, ON (E) (Canada's M.I.T.).

☐ *University of Western Ontario*, London, ON (E) (Excellent business school).

☐ *Université Laval*, Quebec, PQ (F).

☐ *McGill University*, Montreal, PQ (E).

☐ *University of New Brunswick*, Fredericton, NB (E).

☐ *Nova Scotia Agricultural College*, Truro, NS (E).

☐ *Nova Scotia College of Art & Design*, Halifax, NS (E).

☐ *University of Prince Edward Island*, Charlottetown, PE (E).

☐ *Memorial University of Newfoundland*, St. Johns, NF (E).

Bargains in private colleges

Skyrocketing tuition costs have caused many parents and students to turn away from private institutions and opt for publicly supported schools. But state colleges and universities do not provide the only bargains in higher education.

Most of the colleges listed below are small liberal arts institutions founded by religious denominations. The large majority have become independent of church control. All of these colleges rank in the top 10% of the nearly 1,500 four-year, regionally accredited institutions in the US. They are grouped by tuition costs.

For the first group of schools, the percentage of students receiving financial aid ranges from 50% to 80%. The average amount of aid ranges from 60% to 120% of tuition costs.

☐ *Creighton University*, Omaha, NE 68178. Founded by Jesuits, now independent. Requires six hours of theology.

☐ *University of Dallas*, Irving, TX 75060. Conducted by the diocese of Dallas/Ft. Worth. No religious requirements.

☐ *Furman University*, Greenville, SC 29613. Southern Baptist. Requires one course in religion.

☐ *Hofstra University*, Hempstead, NY 11550. Founded as a commuter school for Long Island students. Now has residence halls for half its students. Seeks students from other parts of the country.

☐ *LeMoyne College*, Syracuse, NY 13214. Jesuit. Requires two semesters of nondenominational religious studies.

☐ *Marquette University*, Milwaukee, WI 53233. Jesuit. Theology courses are required of all students; the number varies with the particular college attended.

☐ *Stetson University*, De Land, FL 32720. Southern Baptist. Requires one course in religion, plus another course in religion or philosophy.

For the next group of schools, the percentage of students receiving financial aid ranges from 60% to 90%. The average amount of aid covers 60% to 90% of tuition costs.

☐ *Coe College*, Cedar Rapids, IA 52402. Independent, though historically related to the United Presbyterian Church.

☐ *Fordham University*, Bronx, NY 10458. Founded by Jesuits, now independent. Two or three courses in religious studies are part of core requirements.

☐ *Hamline University*, St. Paul, MN 55104. United Methodist. No religious studies are required.

☐ *Illinois Wesleyan University*, Bloomington, IL 61701. Independent, though maintains ties with its founding United Methodist Church. Requires one course in religion.

☐ *Luther College*, Decorah, IA 52101. American Lutheran. Requires two courses in religion.

☐ *Rose-Hulman Institute of Technology*, Terre Haute, IN 47803. Independent school of science and technology.

☐ *University of Santa Clara*, Santa Clara, CA 95053. Founded by the Jesuits, now independent. Choice of any three courses in religion required.

☐ *Rhodes College*, Memphis, TN 38112. Presbyterian. Two courses in religion and humanities required.

☐ *Ursinus College*, Collegeville, PA 19426. Independent, though maintains ties with United Church of Christ. No religious requirements.

☐ *Wabash College*, Crawfordsville, IN 47933. Independent, no religious requirements.

For this final group of schools, the percentage of students receiving financial aid ranges from 54% to 75%. The average amount of aid ranges from 58% to 101% of the costs of tuition.

☐ *Albright College*, Reading, PA 19604. United Methodist. Requires nine credits in philosophy and religion.

☐ *Allegheny College*, Meadville, PA 16335. Independent (historic ties with United Methodist Church). No religious requirements.

☐ *Cornell College*, Mount Vernon, IA 52314. Independent (historic ties to United Methodist Church). No religious requirements.

☐ *Earlham College*, Richmond, IN 47374. Church-related (Friends). Requires two courses in philosophy and/or religion.

☐ *Gustavus Adolphus College*, St. Peter, MN 56082. Lutheran. Requires one course in religion.

☐ *College of the Holy Cross*, Worcester, MA 01610. Jesuit. No formal religious requirements.

☐ *Illinois Institute of Technology*, Chicago, IL 60616. Independent school of engineering. No religious demands.

☐ *Kalamazoo College*, Kalamazoo, MI 49001. Founded by American Baptists, now independent (maintains ties with the church). Requires two quarter courses in philosophy and/or religion.

☐ *Macalester College*, St. Paul, MN 55105. United Presbyterian. Although church-related, Macalester makes no religious demands on students, and from a religious standpoint its student body is remarkably diverse. Substantial grants from the Reader's Digest Foundation in recent years have helped the college to raise and maintain academic standards.

☐ *University of Notre Dame*, Notre Dame, IN 46556. Founded by Congregation of the Holy Cross, now independent. Requires six hours of theology.

☐ *Ripon College*, Ripon, WI 54971. Independent. No religious demands.

☐ *St. Olaf College*, Northfield, MN 55057. American Lutheran. Requires three courses in religion.

☐ *Syracuse University*, Syracuse, NY 13210. Founded by Methodists, now independent. No religious demands.

☐ *Whitman College*, Walla Walla, WA 99362. Independent. No religious demands on students.

Source: James Cass and Max Birnbaum, co-authors, *The Comparative Guide to American Colleges*, Harper & Row, New York.

Lesser-known colleges that merit attention

The institutions listed below are far above the national average in quality of academic program. They are small (500–2,000 students). Most are liberal arts colleges. A substantial percentage of their graduates go on to graduate and professional schools.

☐ *Allegheny College*, Meadville, PA 16335. Emphasis on preparation for professional school. Maintains historic relationship with United Methodist Church but is nonsectarian and makes no religious demands on students.

☐ *Beloit College*, Beloit, WI 53511. Retains ties with United Church of Christ but has always been nonsectarian. Strongly committed to liberal arts, along with an emphasis on preprofessional and career-oriented studies.

☐ *Clarkson University*, Potsdam, NY 13676. Two thirds of students major in engineering, business and management. Three fourths of graduates go into business and industry.

☐ *Coe College*, Cedar Rapids, IA 52402. A liberal arts college where one quarter of graduates go into business and industry. College maintains a relationship with its founder, United Presbyterian Church.

☐ *Cornell College*, Mount Vernon, IA 52314. Students choose a traditional liberal arts course of study or a nontraditional combination of standard courses, independent study, workservice and travel. College retains some ties to the United Methodist Church.

☐ *Earlham College*, Richmond, IN 47374. A Quaker college that places primary emphasis on a "living fellowship" and individual development. Earlham has become increasingly popular with Eastern students in recent years. Two courses in religion and/or philosophy are required of all students.

☐ *Goucher College*, Towson, MD 21204. A sturdy survivor of the vanishing breed of women's colleges. Goucher has a strong cooperative program with Johns Hopkins.

☐ *Hamilton College*, Clinton, NY 13323. A reputation for high-quality academics and professors who know how to teach. More than 40% of its graduates go on for higher degrees.

☐ *Hamline University*, St. Paul, MN 55104. Founded by the United Methodist Church, Hamline maintains ties to the church. Essentially a liberal arts college, the university also includes a school of law. Cooperative programs with neighboring colleges.

☐ *Haverford College*, Haverford, PA 19041. Founded by Quakers and one of the top academic colleges in the country. The Quaker influence is felt in a student-monitored honor code that governs campus life.

☐ *Knox College*, Galesburg, IL 61401. A venerable liberal arts college. One of the most productive institutions for its size in developing corporate executives.

☐ *Macalester College*, St. Paul, MN 55105.

☐ *Manhattanville College*, Purchase, NY 10577. Founded as a Roman Catholic college for women but now coeducational and independent. Its location (25 miles north of New York City) attracts students who prefer to live in a rural environment with easy access to a major cultural center.

☐ *Mills College*, Oakland, CA 94613. A women's college that says it will stay that way. Attracts a geographically diverse student body. Half of its graduates pursue careers in business and industry.

☐ *Millsaps College*, Jackson, MS 39210. Church-related (United Methodist), Millsaps requires three hours of religious studies for graduation. Notable for its strong liberal arts program, combined with considerable emphasis on preprofessional studies.

☐ *Ohio Wesleyan University*, Delaware, OH 43015. In recent years the college has deliberately reduced the size of the student body while making admissions more selective. Top entering students and leading upperclassmen get preference in financial assistance awards.

☐ *Pitzer College*, Claremont, CA 91711. Youngest of the Claremont College Group, now coed. Advantages of a small college environment with access to the facilities of a large university.

☐ *Rollins College*, Winter Park, FL 32789. Florida's first institution of higher learning. A liberal arts college where nearly half the graduates major in business and management.

☐ *St. Lawrence University*, Canton, NY 13617. One of the largest institutions listed here. The nearest major city is

Ottawa, Canada. Attracts students from many parts of the country.

☐ *Scripps College*, Claremont, CA 91711. One of only two women's colleges on the West Coast. Scripps students enjoy the advantages of membership in the Claremont Group.

☐ *Simon's Rock Early College*, Great Barrington, MA 01230. Simon's Rock assumes that many high-school juniors and seniors are capable of doing college work. It admits qualified students after the 10th and 11th grades (as well as after grade 12).

☐ *Skidmore College*, Saratoga Springs, NY 12866. Skidmore went coed in 1971 and offers a broad liberal arts program with special emphasis on fine and applied arts and preprofessional studies.

☐ *Wabash College*, Crawfordsville, IN 47933. One of the few remaining men's colleges in the Midwest. A strong liberal arts program and notable for ranking among the top schools of comparable size whose graduates become corporate executives.

☐ *Wells College*, Aurora, NY 13026. Still a women's college, Wells sends about one third of its graduates on to graduate and professional school.

☐ *College of Wooster,* Wooster, OH 44691. A liberal arts college founded by the United Presbyterian Church, Wooster is now independent. Sends its graduates on to a wide range of professional and business careers.

How to get better test scores

☐ Most people do better on tests if they do not cram. Keep current during the semester. Prepare for tests as if they occurred without prior notice. Instead of memorizing the subject matter, paraphrase it and integrate it into your total store of knowledge.

☐ Bring several pens and pencils to the test.

☐ Arrive a few minutes early. A little excitement may improve your performance, but do not let anxiety interfere with clear thinking.

☐ Quickly scan the entire test. Ask the instructor immediately about any unclear phrasing.

☐ Be sure to follow all instructions exactly. *Example:* If a list is requested, do not compose an essay.

☐ Ask if wrong answers will be penalized. If not, guessing may improve your score slightly.

☐ Mentally schedule your answers. Set priorities. For example, if the test lasts two hours, answer at the rate of 1% each minute. This pace gives you a little reserve time for the more difficult questions and for the all-important review.

☐ Study each question carefully and plan your answer. Conserve time by avoiding repetitions. *Examples:* Label (do not write out) each question. Give as much detail as is requested, but no more. Omit side issues, especially if they encroach on other questions. Do not write out the same answer to more than one question. Cross out wrong answers (instead of taking time to erase them). *Exception:* Computer-scored tests require complete erasures of mistakes.

☐ Avoid dogmatic presentations. In an essay on a controversial issue, give all sides before justifying your view.

☐ *Short-cuts:* In an objective test, choices are usually wrong if they contain such words as "always" or "never." A statement is false if any part of it is wrong.

☐ Don't belabor the obvious. For example, don't write that a company should set goals. *Instead:* Specify what goals are appropriate. Try to cover all bases, but briefly. Most teachers disdain padding.

☐ Use clear expressions. Define technical terms so that a person who is not familiar with them would understand. *Example:* "A computer's byte equals eight bits" conveys nothing at all to someone who knows little about computers.

☐ Allow time for review.

☐ Use the test as a springboard for further learning. Don't blame the teacher or test if your grade is lower than you hoped. Pinpoint and remedy the weakness.

Source: Dr. Harold W. Fox, professor at Ball State University, and George A. Ball, business consultant, Muncie, IN.

Getting into a top college with ordinary grades

Perfect grades and board scores are no guarantee of admission to top schools. A student with board scores in the 500s and a B average can get in anywhere, if he promotes himself correctly.

Specific things a student can do to improve his chances.

☐ Give the admissions office a reason to vote for you. On a typical day, the admissions office reviews all the applications from the same high school or geographic area. Use the essay, interview and recommendations to distinguish yourself from the mob. Emphasize work or volunteer experience, interesting sports or hobbies, unusual interests, anything you're really good at.

☐ Don't feel you have to be the well-rounded kid. Most good colleges are looking for the well-rounded class. It's much better to do really well at one thing than to be mediocre at a dozen things.

☐ Go prepared to the interview. Use it as an opportunity to distinguish yourself.

☐ Don't waste the essay. It's your one real opportunity to set yourself apart, to give the admissions committee a reason to remember you. If your essay is dull or it contains misspellings or grammatical errors, you've killed your chances.

☐ Ask only teachers and employers for recommendations. Parents often think it's important to get a recommendation from an influential neighbor or politician. This can hurt your chances. Recommendations from anyone who hasn't taught or supervised you will be considered padding.

☐ Take the right courses in high school. Grades are more important than board scores, but the quality and level of courses count more than grades. It's better to get a B in an advanced placement or honors course than an A in a regular course.

☐ Don't take the college boards more than twice. More than that shows you're a little bit too neurotic and pushy. Do read the review books and take review courses. If you show improvement on your second score, that helps.

☐ Take advantage of colleges' desire for diversity. A good student from a small Midwestern town has a better chance of getting into Harvard than one from a big city. All the schools look for geographic diversity.

☐ Apply to unlikely schools. One Catholic school looked very favorably on Jewish students because so few applied. It's easier for a Catholic to get into Brandeis and a Jew into Fordham than vice versa.

☐ Don't dismiss a school just because your parents went there. It helps

admission chances considerably to have an alumnus parent. Harvard's freshman class averages 22% children of alumni.

Source: Steve Cohen, author of *Getting In! The First Comprehensive Step-by-Step Strategy Guide to Acceptance at the College of Your Choice,* Workman Publishing, New York.

College applications: Easing the anxiety

The pressures and anxieties of finding the right colleges and then filling out application forms make a child's senior year in high school a difficult time for the whole family. Parents can offer support and assistance without adding to the turmoil if they are discreet.

☐ Learn from your friends. People who have gone through the application process recently have valuable information and first-hand experience. Find out what books they found most helpful (for example, *Comparative Guide to American Colleges* by James Cass and Max Birnbaum or *Selective Guide to Colleges* by Edward B. Fiske), and provide them for your child. Filter out your friends' personal biases about particular schools. Relay only factual information about the housing crunch for freshmen at an urban college or the attitudes toward women at a formerly all-male campus.

☐ Encourage an early deadline for finishing applications. Thanksgiving is a good target date. Then, the child can concentrate on his schoolwork before the end of the semester and keep his grades up. First semester senior-year grades are important to colleges.

☐ Make copies of all the finished applications and correspondence. Most colleges acknowledge the receipt of completed papers with a postcard, so you will know if anything is missing. If too much time passes without such an acknowledgement, call and check. Having a copy on hand saves time and trauma.

☐ Consider early-action applications or at least one or two schools with rolling admissions to get early decisions. Neither admissions policy commits your child to a particular campus, but knowing before April 15 that at least one school wants a student can take the pressure off.

☐ Talk to the high-school guidance counselor. Be sure your child is applying to schools where he has a better than average chance of being accepted. One or two long shots are reasonable, but young egos are badly damaged by a series of rejections. Find out what the counselor can and will do if the worst happens and your child is not accepted anywhere. (It does occur—even to good students.)

☐ Subscribe to the newspaper published by the students at the colleges in which your child may be interested. Tune in to both the problems and the good points.

☐ Budget for campus visits to potential colleges. If time and money are a consideration, save the visits for after the acceptances come in and real choices have to be made. Be sure your youngster sees the college while it is in session. Admissions offices will arrange for dormitory stays and opportunities for going to class if your child doesn't know anyone at the school.

☐ Let your child know now that he can transfer from one college to another with no loss of face if the first choice doesn't work out. In fact, some colleges are easier to get into as a transfer student than as a freshman.

Source: Florence Janovic, writer and partner in Sensible Solutions, Inc., book marketing consultants.

Making the most of a college visit

☐ Talk to an alumnus before you tour the campus. If you know someone who graduated from the college you plan to visit, call him or her. Ask what that person would advise you to see.

If you don't know any graduates, ask the admissions department for the names of alumni who live in your area and who might be willing to chat with you.

☐ Speak with the department head. When making an appointment for an interview with an admissions officer, also set up an interview with the head of the department in which you're most interested. This will give you a chance to evaluate the quality of the education that you would be receiving.

Be prepared to discuss the curriculum …or, in the case of the arts, to be asked to audition.

☐ Tour during the summer. Life is more relaxed on campuses in the summer… but you can still get a feel for the college's student life without having to compete with the crowds of touring high-school students.

The summer is also ideal because you'll have more quality time with the college's admissions staff. In the fall, half the college's admissions staff is on the road interviewing students while the other half is interviewing one candidate every 45 minutes.

☐ Dress neatly. Do not wear jeans, cut-offs, tank tops or sweatshirts—you will look irresponsible in such attire. Instead, boys should wear chinos and collared shirts…girls should wear skirts and blouses. *Important:* Wear comfortable shoes. You do a lot of walking when you visit a college campus.

☐ Ask for directions—frequently. This will give you a chance to find out how receptive and friendly the students are. Do they go out of their way to help? Give accurate directions? Offer to show you around or answer other questions? The more you talk to the other students on campus, the better you will get to know the school.

☐ Scan the school newspaper. Ask in the admissions office for copies of the past year's issues. The more, the better. The stories will give you a sense of what was important to students last year and how the university responded. They will also tell you which arts are strong on campus—and what types of entertainment and speakers the school attracts.

☐ Check the bulletin boards around campus. Bulletin boards show what is really happening on campus on a daily basis. Everything will be there—plays, parties, where to buy used textbooks, etc. They'll also indicate what the students do on weekends.

☐ Eat in the cafeteria. At most colleges, visitors can pay to enter the dining hall. Sometimes the admissions department provides passes. This is important because it gives you a chance to sample a food plan that you would have to pay for later. It also lets you see whether students feel comfortable enough to linger or study there.

☐ Look for signs of crime prevention. Regardless of where they are located, most colleges in the US today are experiencing higher crime rates than in the past. Alarm boxes on poles and numbers to call to request police escorts show that the college is taking this matter seriously. Ask the admissions officer what other steps are being taken.

☐ Make sure you get the interviewer's name and send him a thank-you note. Few candidates do this. In addition to just being good manners, it will leave the administrator with a better impression of you.

☐ Keep a diary. Since you'll probably be seeing anywhere from three to ten campuses, it's easy to forget the good and bad points of each. This diary will give you a clear idea of what you saw and will be particularly helpful if it comes down to a choice between two alternatives.

Source: Arthur Mullaney, director, College Impressions, Box 507, Randolph, MA 02368.

How to turn the college interview to your advantage

☐ Do research. In particular, find out as much as you can about the college.

☐ Prepare questions to ask the interviewer.

☐ Be ready for two inevitable questions: Why do you want to come here? What can I tell you about our school?

☐ Give them a reason to want you. Link who you are with what the school is.

☐ Practice the interview beforehand with a friend or parent.

☐ Ask for an on-campus interview (as opposed to one in your hometown with an alumnus), especially if you live less than 200 miles from the campus.

Source: Steve Cohen, author of *Getting In! The First Comprehensive Step-by-Step Strategy Guide to Acceptance at the College of Your Choice*, Workman Publishing, New York.

College housing: New investment opportunity

On many college campuses where housing is in short supply, parents find they can save money by spending money—investing in a condominium for their student children. For middle-class families who can afford the down payment, the tax advantages and appreciation pay off even in the short term of a four-year education.

How it works:

☐ Tax break. Initially, all the mortgage interest and part of the maintenance fee are deductible.

☐ *Bonus:* The child finds a roommate to share the apartment which brings down the monthly cost.

☐ If several students share your child's condominium, the rental income may be high enough for the apartment to be treated as ordinary investment rental property, with big deductions for depreciation. The test is whether income from the other students represents fair market value for rent. *Caution:* The Tax Reform Act of 1986 classifies all property rentals as "passive" activities and limits the deductibility of losses. Check with your tax advisor.

☐ After four years of school, the apartment is sold at (or above) the original price, and the initial investment is recouped—usually with a profit. Moreover, if you had losses in previous years and were unable to deduct them because of the passive-loss rules, these losses become fully deductible in the year of the sale.

Considerations:

☐ Dormitory costs. The average cost of college housing runs upward of $1,500 a year. Obviously, the higher the cost, the more incentive there is to find an alternative.

☐ Campus restrictions. Some colleges have sufficient housing for their students, so the need for off-campus housing is minimal, making the condominium investment riskier.

☐ Responsibility. Investment real estate must be maintained to keep its value. Your child's willingness and ability to take care of an apartment full of other students should be a factor in your decision. The responsibility might be more appropriate for graduate school than for the undergraduate years, when campus social life is more important.

Send your children to college without sending yourself to the poorhouse

By the year 2004, the cost of a full college education will range from $100,000 at a state school to more than $240,000 at an elite private college.

Payment plans

☐ To help families cope with college costs, many schools now have programs to enable parents to start paying while future students are still infants. Others have loan and aid plans to make education possible for those who otherwise couldn't attend.

☐ *The tuition future:* Parents make a one-time investment with a school in the expectation that when the child is

16 KIDS AND COLLEGE

18, that's where he'll go to school. That one-time investment, compounded over time, pays for all four years of college. The younger the child when you make the investment, the less you'll have to pay.

☐ *Traps:* No one has examined the tax implications…How will the investment—and earnings on the investment—be taxed?…Who's liable for taxes, the donor or the college?…What happens if, 18 years after the investment is made, the child decides not to attend that school? …What if the child wants to attend, but doesn't meet the school's academic requirements?…And from the college's point of view, does accepting the investment mean that the student's been accepted "sight unseen?"

Other innovations:

☐ Private colleges that make up the difference between the costs of attending the private college and the cost of a state school.

☐ Tuition prepayment, where freshmen lock in prices by paying for their second, third and fourth years at the beginning of freshman year.

Prior planning

Recommended:

☐ Estimate college costs for each of your children. What type of school—public or private—will they probably attend? (College costs will probably increase about 6%–7% per year.)

☐ Project your income and expenses to estimate eligibility for financial aid. To these calculations figure in an annual income increase of about 4%.

☐ Calculate the gap between what you've saved, your current earning capacity, your probable financial aid and projected college costs. The gap will be the amount you'll need to borrow in order to pay for college.

Strategies

☐ *The ideal scenario for a family with a newborn baby and a good income:* Set aside as large a sum as possible—say, $10,000—and add to that about $500/month for the next 18 years. You'll wind up with about $250,000 (assuming 7% annually compounded interest after taxes).

☐ *Alternative:* Put $50,000 in a zero coupon bond now yielding about 8%. When it matures in 18 years, you'll have set aside about $210,000.

More modest advice:

☐ If your child is academically qualified for one of the elite schools, don't let insufficient income discourage him/her from applying. The top schools have larger endowment funds—and, hence, better financial-aid offerings—than more modest schools.

☐ Overall, qualified students now can attend the college of their choice by putting together a package of loans, grants, student aid and campus jobs that will finance four years of education.

Source: R. Jerrold Gibson, president, and Gayle Speck, vice president, Pacesetter, an educational financial-planning service, 73 Trapelo Rd., Box 78, Belmont, MA 02178.

Refinance your home to pay for your child's education

Interest on student loans is no longer a tax deduction for you and your child.

☐ Convert this nondeductible interest into a deduction. *How:* Take out an equity loan on your home and use this money instead of a student loan to pay for college. It's permitted under a special exemption that allows an interest deduction for home-equity loans up to $100,000.

Deductible school costs

☐ Courses to maintain or improve your skills on the job are deductible. But the deduction for transportation is limited to travel between your place of employment and the school. Transportation between home and school is not deductible. *Exception:* If the school is located beyond the general area of your business location (for instance, 50 miles out of town), you can deduct the cost of all transportation between that general area and the school.

☐ If you attend school away from home, you can deduct all travel expenses, including board and lodging. The rules are the same as for business trips.

☐ Since travel for education is a form of business travel, you can deduct all actual car expenses or take the regular IRS mileage allowance for business travel.

Caution: You can never deduct the costs of education to prepare you for a new or different occupation. For example, you couldn't deduct the cost of attending law or medical school.

What colleges offer in financial aid

When you contact the admissions office of a school that you're considering, ask these questions:

☐ Is there a per-student limit on aid? Some schools set ceilings, such as $2,000 a year per student.

☐ Must financial need be shown to earn assistance? Some schools won't provide aid unless the student's family demonstrates a need for $500–$800 or more to meet education costs.

☐ Does the school have an application cutoff date for assistance?

What's usually available:

☐ Low-interest loans.

☐ Installment tuition-payment plans allow parents to avoid writing out a single large check each semester. Tuition costs are paid in installments.

☐ Academic scholarships, based on scholastic achievement, not on financial need, are awarded by almost 1,000 colleges in the US. Awards amount to as much as $20,000 per year. They're based on such criteria as admission-test scores, grade point averages and class standings.

☐ Part-time employment can be found for many students through college placement offices.

☐ Middle-income assistance in the form of loans, tuition breaks and rebates are offered by many schools when the student's family can demonstrate financial need. Special consideration is often given when another family member has already attended the school.

☐ Federally backed student loans are sometimes still available, even to upper-income families, when the school attended has tuition costs that are more than the family can pay. But these loans do not cover the student's spending money. Interest rates and eligibility are subject to change at any time.

For more information about student assistance, including material on the aid programs provided by various institutions:

☐ *The As & Bs of Academic Scholarships*, Octameron Press, Alexandria, VA. Also, *The Ambitious Student's Guide to Financial Aid*, same publisher.

☐ *Scholarships, Fellowships and Loans*, Bellman Publishing, Arlington, VA.

Source: Anna Leider, education-aid consultant and president of Octameron Association, PO Box 2748, Alexandria, VA 22301.

How to look for college scholarships

Grants for students with quirky talents or particular names are numerous. They make up a sizable portion of the $15 billion in grant money identified by scholarship search services.

Exciting as they may sound, these scholarships should not be a student's first priority in the search for college.

After the family has studied the college's financial-aid package, it might want to try tracking down additional help through scholarships.

☐ Your local community can be helpful.

☐ A parent's employer or social organization often sponsors scholarships, and more and more grant dollars are being awarded through high schools to college-bound seniors.

☐ Look at the financial-aid section of college catalogs in your local library.

☐ Check the library's scholarship listings (a collection of notices, pamphlets and other materials) and how-to-find-financial-aid manuals such as *Don't Miss Out.*

☐ High-school guidance counselors should be able to provide materials on scholarships.

☐ Another useful tool is a scholarship search service. Most require a detailed application. Going on the information you provide, they send you a relevant listing of which scholarships you may qualify for. Scholarship listings are constantly updated, and the good services provide counseling and tips for applying. The best services do your research for you, but they make no guarantees of success. The worst ones can be just a waste of your money. The two that are by far the biggest, most trusted and best-known are the National Scholarship Research Service and the Scholarship Search Service.

☐ Private and business sectors are becoming the best sources of untapped scholarship aid. With diligence and research, almost any college freshman can get some private-sector scholarship help.

Source: Mary Armbruster, director of financial aid, Sarah Lawrence College, Bronxville, NY; Joseph D. Gargiulo, National Scholarship Research Service, Box 2516, Santa Rosa, CA 94901; Mary Ann Maxin, Scholarship Search Service, 407 State St., Santa Barbara, CA 93101.

Financial help for military families

☐ Army Emergency Relief Assistance Program. Loans and scholarships for needy, unmarried independent children of current or former members of the Army. Department of the Army, 200 Stovall St., Alexandria, VA 22332. 703-960-3982.

☐ The Navy Relief Society. Loans for unmarried, dependent children of present or former Navy or Marine personnel. 801 N. Randolph St., Suite 1228, Arlington, VA 22203. 703-696-4904.

☐ Retired Officers Association, for children and wards of present or former officers in any of the uniformed services. Funds are awarded only after the applicant has shown that all other sources have been investigated. 201 N. Washington St., Alexandria, VA 22314. 703-549-2311.

Helpful financial services for everyone

☐ College Student Financial Aid Services, 600 S. Frederick Ave., Second Floor, Gaithersburg, MD 20877. 301-258-0717.

☐ College Quest, c/o Peterson's Guides, Box 2123, Princeton, NJ 08543. 609-243-9111.

☐ National Scholarship Research Service, 2280 Airport Blvd., Santa Rosa, CA 94901. 707-546-6777. Local calls, 546-6781.

Each of these services charges a price for reports or print-outs that attempt to match you with useful funding sources.

How to beat the SATs

SAT scores don't really measure aptitude, intelligence or academic potential. They show only how good you are at taking the test. *Keys to doing well:* Good preparation and a thorough knowledge of how the test works.

Where to begin

Determine whether the colleges you're interested in require SAT scores. If so, take two months before your test date to:

☐ Study an SAT preparation book such as *Ten SATs*. This contains tests given over the past couple of years.

☐ Take a course on preparing for the SAT that offers good feedback. This will give you an idea of what areas you need to work on most.

☐ Don't depend solely on math and English teachers for help. They teach only academic math and English…not "SAT math" and "SAT English."

Taking the test

☐ Eliminate the wrong answers first—leaving only the right answer.

☐ Guess if you have to. Once you've eliminated one or more of the wrong answers, guessing works in your favor.

☐ Take the test slowly. Rushing results in careless mistakes that can hurt your score.

☐ Questions are usually in order of difficulty. But skip topics in which you're weak to get to those in which you excel. *Reason:* All questions are weighted equally.

☐ Use the scrap paper provided—especially for math questions—to avoid careless errors. *Also:* Don't waste time erasing mistakes in calculations.

☐ If you don't know the answer to a question, leave it and move on to the next one. Don't waste time pondering.

☐ Give the answer you feel the test authors are looking for, even if you think it's incorrect.

□ Look out for deceptively easy questions that can cause you to make mistakes. *Hint:* Each section of the test is divided into thirds—easy, medium-hard and hard, in that order. Questions that seem easy but have a twist appear on the boundary between the easy and medium-hard thirds.

□ Save the reading section for last. *Reason:* It is a time-inefficient section because it involves reading long passages. *Hint:* The passages are based on fact, so you can eliminate answers based on your knowledge or common sense.

Source: John Katzman, director of the Princeton Review (an intensive eight-week course in preparation for the SAT) and author of *Cracking the System: The SAT*, Villard Books, 201 E. 50 St., New York 10022.

College visits

When visiting a college with your child, remember to meet with the financial-aid counselor, too. Call ahead for an appointment to get personal answers to your questions and start building rapport. After returning home, have your child send the counselor a thank-you note. If your child is accepted at the college and applies for financial aid, call the counselor when you send in your aid application to say that it will be coming. Few students do this. In a close decision, it can make a difference.

Source: *USA Today Financial Aid for College: A Quick Guide to Everything You Need to Know* by Pat Ordovensky, education writer for *USA Today* and director of the newspaper's financial aid hotline. Peterson's, 202 Carnegie Center, Princeton, New Jersey 08543.

College success strategy

Plot the coming semester on a calendar. Using the syllabus for each class, enter each test, paper and assignment date so you can prepare in time. *Helpful:* Note in particular those deadlines that fall within a day or two of each other so you'll know when to plan for extra working time.

Source: *College Survival* by Greg Gottesman, a recent graduate of Stanford University. Prentice Hall, 15 Columbus Circle, New York 10023.

Safety first

Check a college's safety record by asking to see the annual security report required by federal law. Each college must report all crimes on its campus, from sex offenses to murders. In 1993, robbery, assault and motor-vehicle thefts increased at colleges. Burglaries and murders declined. *Caution:* Critics say some schools deliberately under-report campus crime.

Source: Survey of more than 750 schools by *The Chronicle of Higher Education*, 1255 23 St. NW, Washington, DC 20037.

College financing mistake

College financing mistake: Putting college savings in a child's name. *Reason:* Standard college tuition aid formulas consider 35% of a child's total assets to be available to pay tuition… compared with only 6% of a parent's total assets. So putting assets in a child's name can reduce—or eliminate—his/her eligibility for tuition aid. *Better:* Keep tuition savings in your own name. If you've already put money in a child's name, consider transferring it back to yourself or to another trusted family member—through a gift—before applying for tuition aid. Annual gifts of up to $10,000 each to as many separate recipients as desired can be made free of gift tax.

Source: David Jaffe, founder of the New York consulting firm College Pursuit and Associates and author of *The New College Financial Aid System: Making It Work for You*, Council Oak Books, 1350 E. 15 St., Tulsa 74120.

Developing your own image of success

☐ Recognize that you have talents and skills that are ingredients of success. Focus on these and forget your bad points entirely.

☐ Concentrate your energy. *One way to focus energy:* Split up your day into the smallest possible segments of time. Treat each segment as independent and get each task done one at a time. This will give you the feeling of accomplishment and will fuel your energy.

☐ Take responsibility. Be willing to accept personal responsibility for the success of your assignments, for the actions of people who work for you and for the goals you have accepted. Seize responsibility if it is not handed over easily. There are always company problems that are difficult to solve and that nobody has been assigned to— take them for starters.

☐ Take action instead of waiting to be told. Listen to other people's problems and link their ambitions to your goals. Then deliver what you promise.

☐ Nurture self-control. Don't speak or move hastily. Don't let personal emotions color decisions that must be hard and analytical. Before taking a major action, ask yourself, "What's the worst that can happen?" Let that guide your next step.

☐ Display loyalty. No matter how disloyal you feel, never show it. Show loyalty to your boss, your company, your employees. Be positive about yourself and about others. Never run anybody down.

☐ Convey a successful image. Move decisively—walk fast and purposefully, with good posture. Look as if you are on the way to something rather than moping along.

☐ When you sit, don't slump. Sit upright and convey alertness. Choose a chair of modest dimensions. A large chair makes you look small and trapped. The chair should have a neutral color and be of a material that doesn't squeak or stick to your body.

☐ Avoid large lunches—they deprive you of energy. Successful people tend to eat rather sparingly.

Source: Michael Korda, author of *Success! How Every Man and Woman Can Achieve It,* Random House, New York.

Are you really as ambitious as you think you are?

To test your ambition quotient, rate the following statements on a scale of one to five to indicate how much the statement applies to you. A rating of one means it doesn't apply at all, and five means it applies very much.

☐ I truly enjoy working.

☐ Given free time, I would rather be out socializing with people than sitting home watching television.

☐ My first response to a problem is to attempt to figure out the most practical solution.

☐ One of the things I like best about work is the challenge of it.

☐ I believe very strongly in the work ethic.

☐ I have a strong desire to get things done.

☐ When there's a difficult situation, I enjoy assuming the responsibility for correcting it.

☐ I frequently come up with ideas— day and night.

☐ I'm not satisfied with the success I already enjoy.

☐ I rarely miss a day of work because of illness.

☐ I enjoy vacations, but after four to five days I look forward to getting back to work.

☐ I can usually get along with six hours of sleep.

☐ I'm interested in meeting people and developing contacts.

☐ I set high standards for myself in almost everything I do.

☐ All in all, I consider myself a lucky person.

☐ I'm not afraid to rely on my instincts when I have to make an important decision.

☐ I can think of very few situations in which I don't have a great deal of control.

☐ I recover from setbacks pretty quickly. I don't dwell on them.

☐ I'm not afraid to admit it when I make a big mistake.

☐ Achieving success is very important to me.

Scoring: 85–100 indicates very high ambition. With the right skills, you're almost certain to achieve your goals.

70–84 means higher-than-average ambition, and chances of achieving goals are very good. 55–69 is about an average score. If you achieve your goal, it won't be on ambition alone. A score below 55 indicates that success isn't an important goal for you.

Source: Robert Half, author of *Success Guide for Accountants,* McGraw-Hill, New York.

Setting goals for success

The lack of a clear goal is the most common obstacle to success, even for people with large amounts of drive and ambition. Typically, they focus on the rewards of success, not on the route they must take to achieve it. Remedy:

☐ Whenever possible, write down your goals, forcing yourself to be specific.

☐ Periodically make a self-assessment. Take into account your education, age, appearance, background, skills, talents, weaknesses, preferences, willingness to take risks and languages spoken.

☐ Ask for feedback from others.

☐ Don't try to succeed at something for which you have no talent.

☐ Try out your goal part-time. If you dream of owning a restaurant, work in one for a while.

Targeting success

☐ Visualize the results you intend to achieve and write them down. *Example:* I will increase output 10%.

☐ List the personal benefits that reaching the goal will confer.

☐ Jot down at least ten obstacles and try to find three possible solutions for each.

☐ Set a target date.

☐ Start tackling the problems, beginning with the easiest.

Source: Audrey Cripps, Cripps Institute for the Development of Human Relations, Toronto.

Climbing to success without stumbling

The behavior our parents reinforce in us when we are children always encourages us to strive for bigger and better things. We gain approval for achievement and disapproval for failure. As adults, we keep striving because our developmental makeup says "You've got to have more."

To avoid rising to your level of incompetence:

☐ Take your life and your job seriously. But don't take yourself seriously.

☐ Don't spend your life climbing and acquiring. Instead, combine accomplishment and satisfaction.

☐ Climb to a level that you find fulfilling, stay there for a long period and then move forward.

☐ Approach promotion avoidance indirectly. One successful ploy is to display some charming eccentricities that in no way effect your work performance, but which might discourage a promotion.

Source: Dr. Laurence J. Peter, whose latest book is *Why Things Go Wrong, or The Peter Principle Revisited,* William Morrow & Co., New York.

Overcoming obstacles to success

Personality traits can be a straightaway or a dead end—on the road to success.

Don't be caught in the following common traps:

☐ Inability to let go. People often stick with a dead-end job out of pride, stubbornness or unwillingness to admit that they made a mistake. Sometimes the comfort of the familiar is just too seductive. *To start letting go:* Take small, safe steps at first. Start talking to friends and associates about possible new jobs. See what's available during your vacation. Shake things up at the office by suggesting some changes in your current job. Take some courses and learn new skills.

☐ Lack of self-esteem. This is an enormous stumbling block. But, in fact, you may be judging yourself by excessively high standards.

☐ Procrastination. Like alcoholism, procrastination is a subtle, insidious disease that numbs the consciousness and destroys self-esteem. *Remedy:* Catch it early, but not in a harsh, punitive, self-blaming way. Look at what you're afraid of, and examine your motives.

☐ Shyness. If you're shy, the obvious remedy is to choose an occupation that doesn't require a lot of public contact. But even shy salespeople have been known to succeed. As long as they're talking about product lines and business, a familiar spiel can see them through. Concentrate on getting ahead by doing a terrific job rather than by being Mr. or Ms. Charming. Or take a Dale Carnegie course. They are helpful.

☐ Unwillingness to look at yourself. If you're not willing to assess yourself honestly, success will probably forever elude you. People tend to avoid self-assessment because they feel they must be really hard on themselves. Realize you've probably taken the enemy into your own head—you've internalized that harsh, critical parent or teacher from your childhood. Instead, evaluate yourself as you would someone you love, like a good friend whom you'd be inclined to forgive almost anything.

Source: Tom Greening, PhD, clinical supervisor of psychology at the University of California at Los Angeles and a partner in Psychological Service Associates, Los Angeles.

Commonsense business and social manners

A common error today is the failure to realize that there are at least two sets of manners—one for the business world and another for the social world. In the business world, it is not vulgar to talk about money or to brag. But the social world is just the opposite.

☐ In business, manners are based on rank and position, not on gender. The business lunch or dinner check, for instance, belongs to the person who initiated the invitation or the superior in the office. The gender of the person does not alter this tradition.

☐ Never worry about what service people (waiters, maitre d's, hotel clerks) think of you. If you use the wrong fork, it is up to the waiter or bus boy to supply you with another.

☐ If you are critical of someone while at a dinner party, only to discover that the person you are belittling is the father (or close relative or friend) of the person with whom you are speaking, make a quick and complete U-turn. Add to the defamatory statement, "Of course, that's the basis of my admiration for him." Remember dinner-table conversation doesn't have to be logical.

☐ The notion that it is unhealthy to disguise your feelings has helped lead to a decline in manners and social health. *One advantage of a little disguise:* You will have more feelings to share with intimates.

Source: Judith Martin, otherwise known as Miss Manners.

Power lunching

Power-lunching tactics can turn a restaurant meal into an occasion to impress your lunch partner.

Power lunching aims to impress without letting the luncheon become a tasteless display of ego and one-up-manship.

Here are some tips:

☐ Patronize restaurants that have a reputation for business lunches and where you're known. Select restaurants with excellent service and plenty of space between tables. Eat in restaurants that important people frequent.

☐ Avoid luncheon invitations to other people's private dining rooms. You lose power on their turf.

☐ Call the maitre d' personally to make reservations. Tell him where you want to sit and how long you expect to stay. The more details you give the maitre d', the more his staff will be in tune with your needs.

☐ Don't order drinks served with a paper umbrella or a lot of vegetables or fruit. Draft beer is appropriate, but bottles look tacky. The "fancy waters" are wimpy now…club soda is a power drink.

☐ Order food that's easy to handle. *Example:* Steak instead of lobster so that you can do a lot of talking without fumbling. *Power foods:* Black bean soup, fresh oysters and clams, brook trout, calves' liver, London broil, paella, venison and gumbo. *Wimp foods:* French onion soup, fried oysters and clams, corned beef, coquilles St. Jacques, chicken a la king, lasagna, shrimp de jonghe.

☐ Pay the bill with cash, if possible. Next best is a house charge. You don't have to wait for a credit card to be processed. You can quickly sign the check and leave before your guest becomes anxious to get back to the office.

☐ Tip 20%.

Source: *Power Lunching* by E. Melvin Pinsel and Ligita Dienhart, Turnbull & Willoughby, Chicago.

Good business communication

☐ "What happened?" is the question to ask when something's gone wrong. Don't try to blame someone for the mistake right at the start. Asking "What happened?" focuses on the mistake itself, not on the person who did it, and is much more likely to lead to useful information. *Contrast:* "Who did it?" is a phrase that can turn off information flow.

☐ Oral orders are usually all that's needed to correct a basic mistake. If the oral order changes an existing policy, though, confirm it in writing as soon as possible to prevent future confusion.

☐ Tuesday is the best day for having a serious heart-to-heart discussion with an employee concerning job performance. *Friday risk:* Person broods all weekend about the conversation and comes back embittered on Monday. After the Tuesday talk, find a way by Wednesday to indicate that there's no ill will.

☐ Discuss serious problems with a subordinate in *your* office where your authority is evident. Minor matters can be handled in the subordinate's office as long as there's privacy and quiet.

☐ Value of a dumb question or a simple and honest "I don't know" is that you'll probably learn something you don't know now…and that you couldn't find out any other way. "It's what you learn after you know it all that really counts," said President Harry S. Truman, an expert at turning seeming modesty into great strength.

Source: James Van Fleet, former US Army officer, manager with Sears, Roebuck & Co. and US Gypsum and consultant on the psychology of management, writing in *Lifetime Conversation Guide,* Prentice-Hall, Inc., Englewood Cliffs, NJ.

Secrets of success

Top performers in all fields have these qualities in common:

☐ They transcend their previous performances.

☐ They never get too comfortable.

☐ They enjoy their work as an art.

☐ They rehearse things mentally beforehand.

☐ They don't bother too much about placing blame.

☐ They are able to withstand uncertainty.

Source: David A. Thomas, Dean of Cornell University Graduate School of Business.

What successful men think makes them successful

☐ Bill Blass: "I guess it is my ability to concentrate and a dedication to the best in design—first fashion, and then the best in design for other things."

☐ David Klein, Dav-El Limousines, New York: "Even when I was a kid in New Rochelle, New York, I had more paper routes than the rest of the kids. Then I began to run parking lots at the local country club, graduated to being a chauffeur and continued to work, work and work more. I really do love to work."

☐ Tom Margittai, co-owner, Four Seasons restaurant, New York: "Determined professionalism combined with high standards of quality. Also, a lot of hard work. We try to understand the psychology of our market and to be first in everything."

☐ Mickey Rooney: "Through the years, it has been my great faith in God, and lots and lots of energy. At last I have it all together. I guess my good health is also a factor. I've been luckier than a lot, and I have always taken a positive outlook."

☐ Carl Spielvogel, Backer Spielvogel Bates Worldwide: "I think getting in early and staying late and not taking the 5:15 to Greenwich is one reason [for my success]. Also, being where the business is. As Lyndon Johnson once said, you have to press the flesh. People you do business with want to know you and to be with you socially."

☐ Ted Turner, head of Cable News Network and sportsman: "Every day I try to do my very best. When you wish upon a star, your dreams really do come true."

How to be known as an expert

Improve your chances for promotion and attract outside job offers by displaying expertise and calling attention to yourself.

Some ways to do it:

☐ Write an article for a key trade journal.

☐ Join an association of peer professionals. Get to know your counterparts and their superiors in other companies. Run for office in the association.

☐ Develop a speech about your work and offer to talk to local groups and service clubs.

☐ Teach a course at a community college.

☐ Write letters to the editors of trade journals, commenting on or criticizing articles that they publish in your field.

☐ Have lunch with your company's public relations people. Let them know what your department is doing, and see if they know of some good speaking platforms for you.

☐ Use vacation time to attend conferences and seminars.

☐ Write to experts, complimenting them (when appropriate) on their work and their articles. Whether or not they reply, they'll be flattered and they'll probably remember your name.

Source: Errol D. Alexander, president, Profiles, Inc., Vernon, CT.

Putting yourself on TV

Public access (PA), a noncommercial form of cable television established expressly for amateur programming, is now available in hundreds of communities nationwide. And if your community has cable, chances are it also has PA facilities just waiting to be used.

☐ Contact the local PA coordinator first. Although most PA programs are administered by the cable company that will cablecast them, in some cities the public library, school district or some municipal-government office coordinates things.

☐ Ask around to find out exactly how PA works in your community. Don't get started with specific plans until you have let the appropriate people know exactly what you would like to do.

☐ Plan carefully in advance. Deciding upon a suitable topic is the first step toward creating a successful PA program. *Other issues that need settling:* How long will the program be? Will it be an ongoing series, or merely a one-shot deal? Who's going to operate the camera and the editing equipment? Will you need to film on location, or can all the necessary footage be shot in the studio? Will you need furniture and props for a set?

☐ Keep in mind that it takes much longer to produce a program than you've probably anticipated. You'll probably need to devote a couple of weeks, at least, to learning the television ropes before even beginning to produce your program. Usually, however, it takes much longer.

☐ Set specific goals. Decide if you simply want to convey information, to educate or to entertain. Don't try to do too much in a single show.

☐ Polish your program. Decide before you go into the studio exactly what you hope to accomplish. Rehearse your program carefully and then time it.

☐ Learn production techniques. Most PA organizations require that you demonstrate proficiency in the use of equipment before they turn you loose in the studio. Don't try to get around this requirement. Technical knowledge is crucial, even if you plan on leaving the nuts-and-bolts end of things to someone else. You can't be an effective director or producer if you're not sure what the equipment can and cannot do. Besides, the instruction is usually free.

☐ Secure sponsorship. Most of your expenses will be assumed by the cable operator—but not all. Particularly for more ambitious projects, you may want to secure outside funding from a local business or philanthropic group to help with production costs and publicity. Although PA guidelines prohibit advertising per se, there's a good chance you'll be able to list sponsors on the air. Before approaching potential sponsors, find out exactly what you can promise them.

☐ Get the message out. Many PA users concentrate so single-mindedly on getting their programs finished that they neglect one of the most important things: Getting people to tune in. So tell your friends to watch and have them tell their friends. Ask the cable operator to include your program, along with its air date and time, in the monthly schedule it distributes to its viewers. Call your local newspaper and radio stations, and even take out ads if you want to reach as many people as possible. (Of course, you'll have to foot the bill for this yourself.)

Source: Sue Buske, Executive Director, National Federation of Local Cable Programmers, Washington, DC, and James McElveen, Director of Public Affairs, National Cable Television Association, Washington, DC.

Who gets promoted first

The four most important factors in determining how fast you are promoted:

☐ How top management feels about the person who recommended your promotion.

☐ Your exposure and visibility to those in higher management.

☐ Your background, education, work experience.

☐ How well you perform in your present job.

Capitalizing on early success

Early career success can be followed up by even further success if you:

☐ Stay ambitious.

☐ Are willing to make sacrifices on the way up.

☐ Acknowledge mistakes. Avoid covering up or passing the buck.

☐ React to a setback by honestly identifying what went wrong.

☐ Behave consistently during a crisis.

☐ Don't become abusive under stress—or refuse to negotiate.

☐ Regularly reassess personal career strategies.

☐ Broaden skills—and learn new ones when necessary.

☐ Resist the temptation to become arrogant with success.

Source: Morgan W. McCall, Jr., and Michael M. Lombardo, authors of *Off the Track: Why and How Successful Executives Derail,* The Center for Creative Leadership, Greensboro, NC.

How to negotiate a big raise

The best way to get a sizable raise:

☐ Start campaigning for it on the day you're hired. Don't talk dollars then, of course, but set up standards of performance that will be the basis for future wage negotiations with your new boss.

☐ Find out if there are ways you can influence company standards so that your strongest qualities are rewarded.

Gauge the company's raise-granting profile by finding out:

☐ Pattern of raises for your type of job.

☐ Extent to which pay is part of a fixed budget process.

☐ How much autonomy your boss has in granting raises.

☐ Business conditions in the company and in the industry.

When the time comes to request a raise:

☐ Don't let your request be treated in an offhand manner. Make a date with your boss to talk just about money. If he puts it off, persist.

☐ *To negotiate successfully:* Narrow down obstacles until the supervisor is holding back because of one major factor ("Things are tough this year"). Let him cling to that, but in the process make sure he assures you that your performance has been excellent. Then attack the main obstacle ("Are things really that bad?"), pointing out that your capabilities should be rewarded in any case.

☐ Unless you're quite sure of your ground, don't threaten to quit. Even if you are a ball of fire, the boss may welcome your departure because he's scared of you.

Source: John J. Tarrant, author of *How to Negotiate a Raise,* Pocket Books, New York.

How to work at home much more effectively

More than 34 million Americans now work in their own kitchens, basements, spare rooms and garages—doing work that used to be done in high-rise office buildings.

Computers, fax machines, new phone systems and personal organizers are making it possible to do almost anything that can be done in a corporate office from your home—or your car.

But running a home office is not like running a corporate office—or like running a home. It has its own unique challenges that you must recognize and address.

Picking your space

Wherever possible, it's best to set up your office in a separate space, whether it's as small as a closet or as spacious as a spare room. While some people can work in the corner of their kitchens, there's no other place in the home that has more distractions.

Better: Carve out a space in the basement—or even the garage—that is away from household traffic.

When you go to your newly created office, you'll be ready for business. Keep all your supplies there…and keep track of them so that you won't run out of critical items while you're working.

Self-defense: Buy a second set of office supplies for the family (to be kept elsewhere) so they won't raid yours.

If children or pets will be coming into your office, arrange a comfortable area for them with their own playthings.

Trap: Nothing sounds more unprofessional while you're on the phone than a dog barking or a child crying in the background. Try to be alone when you make important calls. And never assume that because you're working at home you won't need child care. Until children are in school all day, you will almost certainly need backup during business hours.

Separating your two worlds

As a general rule, your business will be much more successful and your tax filing easier if you separate your business life from your personal life. That means having separate phone lines for home and office…using separate credit cards for business expenses… and keeping personal and business papers and records in two different places.

Exception: It's okay to have a column for personal activities in your daily or weekly planner. After all, one of the objectives of working at home is to see your family more often and to be able to fit in your kids' school activities, etc.

It's even a good idea to have your business mail sent to a post office box. This will protect your home address from unwanted commercial contacts. Also, you can leaf through your mail at the post office and discard material that doesn't need to come home.

Taking control

When you work for a company, you get a day's pay, whether or not you accomplish a day's worth of work.

At home, however, your income is directly related to how productive you are. If you spend 30 minutes on the phone with a friend or 20 minutes looking for a misplaced piece of paper, that's time spent not earning money.

At home, you probably won't have a secretary or staff to help you with typing, filing, phone calls and paperwork. You're on your own. Therefore, it is imperative to take control and get your office organized so that you can work efficiently.

Time management

Good time management is crucial for the home-office professional. Since no one is imposing a schedule on you, you need to discipline yourself. If you can't resist chatty neighbors, working at home may not be for you. Learn to ignore household tasks that need to be done. They can be done later.

☐ Prioritize. Determine your best time of day …and schedule important tasks for then.

Throughout the day (about every three hours), ask yourself if what you're doing at that moment is the best use of your time. I call this structured flexibility. You've made your to-do list and set your priorities, yet you're aware that your priorities could change at any moment.

Bonus: When you work at home, you have the freedom to work odd hours, nights, weekends or early mornings, when there are fewer interruptions.

☐ Be willing to change your schedule and focus on what seems more important. The word "focus" is key—because you don't want to keep skipping from one thing to another. Then nothing gets finished.

Helpful: Make appointments with yourself to work on certain tasks. Block out time on your calendar to write a report, develop a marketing plan, etc. Turn on the answering machine during that time.

☐ Set aside some time each week to read. Even spending a half hour or an hour every morning makes a big difference when trying to get through all the newspapers, magazines, professional journals, sales brochures and other material you need to review. Put those articles and brochures that you'll need to refer to again in a reference file (distinct from your current file).

☐ Spend at least one full day a week in your office to catch up on paperwork, make phone calls, etc. Choose a day that's most likely to be slow, and try to keep your schedule clear. This will make the rest of your week go more smoothly.

☐ Learn to say "no"—not only to non-business demands on your time but also to new business that you really can't handle. Clients are more understanding about being turned down than they are about missed deadlines. When you don't set limits on what you can accomplish, the quality of your work will suffer and you will lose business.

☐ Hire outside help when necessary. One of my clients had a beautifully organized home office but nearly failed because he couldn't type. We solved his problem with an outside secretarial service that picked up and typed drafts. Face the fact that you can't do everything yourself.

Example: If your time can be spent more profitably with a client, perhaps you should hire a high-school student to do some oft-postponed but necessary chore like entering 1,500 names into your computer.

☐ Group similar tasks together. Make all of your phone calls at once so you don't keep interrupting your work time all day. Write all of your letters during another block of time. Schedule all appointments on the same afternoon. Run several errands in one trip… perhaps at lunchtime when people are not likely to call you back.

☐ Put everything in its place. It's important to file related paperwork together so that you'll have fewer places to look for something. There are many different filing techniques. You can choose whichever one works for you.

I strongly recommend having at least one high-quality filing cabinet in which you can place hanging files. It is much more efficient to file papers rather than having them in piles that collect dust and are hard to sort through.

Telephone messages: If you're the only one taking messages from your answering machine, use either a telephone log or a plain spiral notebook to keep track of messages. You can write down the date, time, caller's name, company and message. This will provide you with an orderly record instead of dozens of loose scraps of paper. It's also useful to keep a fax-activity logbook for tax and billing purposes.

Another key tool is your Rolodex. File things under the names by which you will refer to them in the future, and keep phone numbers up to date.

Invest in tomorrow

Just as it takes money to make money, it takes time to save time. Be willing to take a few minutes at the end of every day to clean up your desk, file important papers and set up your schedule for the next day. This maintenance time will save you valuable hours in the long run. Think of it like laundry—if you do a little bit every day, it will never pile up and become a problem.

If your papers are already out of hand and your office mess has become embarrassing, resolve to take several interruption-free afternoons to straighten it out. You'll be much more productive afterward. Important: Every improvement will go right to your bottom line, so it's well worth the effort.

Source: Lisa Kanarek, president of Everything's Organized, a consulting firm specializing in paper management, office organization and productivity improvement, 660 Preston Forest Center, Suite 120, Dallas 75230. She is author of *Organizing Your Home Office for Success,* Plume, New York.

Negotiating salary in a job interview

Negotiating salary is often the hardest part in a job interview.

Here are some suggestions:

☐ Avoid discussing salary in detail until you're close to getting an offer. If the first interviewer asks what salary you want, respond, "Salary is important, but it's not the most important thing. Why don't we develop an interest in each other and then we'll see."

☐ If the interviewer insists, mention your current salary and suggest using that as a guideline.

☐ When you are actually offered the job, you are in a much stronger bargaining position. That is the time to negotiate.

☐ Do not demand more than the market will bear. It's a mistake to lie about what you have been earning, especially if you're unemployed. The higher the salary, the fewer the jobs.

Source: Robert Half, president, Robert Half International, Inc., executive recruiters, San Francisco.

How to evaluate a job offer

Questions you must ask (yourself and the recruiter) to increase the chance that you land in a job that offers opportunity for promotion, mobility, power, personal growth:

☐ Who's in the job now?

☐ What is the average length of time people have stayed in the job?

☐ Where do they go?

☐ How old do people get to be in that job?

☐ Ask to talk to people holding the same or similar jobs. Find out what other people in the company think about the job. If they think the job is dead-end, don't consider taking it. You may think you can overcome and be the "pleasant surprise." But chances are excellent that you will fail.

☐ Will the job give me a chance to know other people in the organization doing lots of different jobs?

☐ Will I represent the department (or group or section, etc.) at meetings with people from other parts of the organization?

☐ If the job is in the field, do I get much chance to meet with managers from headquarters? Does the job have too much autonomy? (Working on your own too much can be the kiss of death for upward movement if no one else gets to know you and your abilities.)

☐ Is this job in an area that solves problems for the company? The best jobs for getting power (and promotions) fast always have a sense of danger. Jobs in safe areas where everything is going well offer a slower track to promotion.

Best days to job hunt

Most job seekers think Monday is the best day to look for a job because there are more jobs advertised in the papers on Sunday. But jobs advertised on Sunday actually become available the previous Wednesday.

Recommendations:

☐ Look every day of the week.

☐ If you have to skip one day, Monday is the best choice. You will not be slowed down by the same hordes of competition on other days.

☐ The best job hunting may be when the weather is bad. Again, there are fewer competitors. Management may well believe that the bad-weather candidate is more interested in employment and will work harder with less absenteeism. However, interviewers may be depressed and executives busy filling in for absent staff when the weather is poor.

Source: Robert Half, president, Robert Half International, Inc., executive recruiters, San Francisco.

The art of getting fired

☐ Restrain your anger. Don't scream at your boss (he'll be your first reference) or threaten to sue the company.

☐ Apply for unemployment compensation immediately. It's nothing to be ashamed of, and the money will buy time to plan your next move.

☐ Find out precisely why you were fired. It may help to reevaluate your personal style for your job hunt and beyond.

☐ Don't withdraw out of self-pity. Share your feelings with your family and friends. They can sustain you in this difficult time.

☐ Reassess your career goals. It may be time for a modification—if not an outright switch.

Source: Frank Louchheim, Chairman of Right Associates, a re-employment counseling firm, Philadelphia.

What to expect from an outplacement service

If you are dismissed from your job and your company provides you with outplacement counseling, you are several steps ahead of the game in finding your next job.

What you can expect:

☐ Counseling to help with personal problems, such as how to handle family and neighbors.

☐ Assessment of your skills and achievements, including psychological and aptitude tests.

☐ Help in staying focused on the future, rather than dwelling on the past.

☐ Instruction in how to re-enter the job market.

☐ Guidance on how to handle job interviews, write an effective résumé and letters, negotiate salary and, most of all, respond to the question, "Why were you fired?"

Source: T.B. Hubbard, chairman, and E. Donald Davis, president, THinc Consulting Group International, Inc., New York.

Assess your chances of being a successful entrepreneur

Your chances of being a successful entrepreneur are best if:

☐ Both your parents were self-employed.

☐ You were fired more than once in your career.

☐ You began operating small businesses before you were 20 years old.

☐ You have spent most of your career to date in firms with less than 100 employees.

☐ You are the eldest child in your family.

☐ You are married.

☐ You have a BA degree but no advanced degrees.

☐ Your relationship with the parent who provided most of the family income was strained rather than comfortable.

☐ You are easily excited by new ideas, new employees, new financial plans.

☐ You enjoy being with people even when you have nothing planned.

Source: Joseph R. Mancuso, founder and president of The Center for Entrepreneurial Management, New York.

What it takes to have an entrepreneurial edge

The traits of successful entrepreneurs:

☐ Work for results, not praise. Don't fall into the trap of expending energy to please people who have nothing to do with your success.

☐ Continue to set higher performance goals for yourself than your boss does.

☐ Don't be afraid to take on more responsibility and the control that goes with it.

☐ Stand back occasionally from day-to-day work so you can plan strategically.

☐ Hone your ability at communications and selling.

☐ Rehearse in your mind a successful process and a successful outcome. The process helps supply the mental and physical reserves needed to get through tough situations.

☐ Learn to overcome occasional loss and rejection.

☐ Think of failure as a lesson rather than as a blow to your self-esteem. Then quickly get back on the right track.

☐ Be forthright in claiming ownership for your ideas.

☐ Assess risks by setting up a worst-case scenario. If you can cope with a negative outcome, consider taking the risk.

Source: Dr. Charles A. Garfield, professor of psychology, University of California Medical School in San Francisco.

Deciding if a blue-sky idea is worth pursuing

☐ What are the assumptions on which the idea is based?

☐ What tests can be applied to these assumptions?

☐ If the project goes ahead, what are the likely financial results? (For maximum success, for partial failure, for total failure?) What criteria will be used to make these forecasts?

☐ Is the tradeoff between the maximum gain and the maximum loss acceptable?

☐ How will this project be managed?

☐ What are the likely weak points at which difficulty could be experienced?

☐ At what point should we abandon the project?

Source: Robert Heller, author of The Supermanagers, Truman Talley Books (E.P. Dutton, Inc.), New York.

Entrepreneurial burnout

The mistakes that can bring a budding entrepreneur's career to a halt are seldom unique. And the big ones can be avoided with a minimum of effort if you know what to look for.

Common traps to avoid:

☐ Spreading yourself too thin. Entrepreneurs often think they can be all things to all people. They convert a real asset

—their flexibility—into a liability by pursuing too many directions at once. Narrowing your focus and becoming the best in a small area is the key to success.

☐ Substituting business contacts for a social life. People who work alone often forget to make the effort to develop a social/recreational world outside work. They then confuse fleeting business contacts with recreational friendships. This diffuses their business concentration and judgments. *Remedy:* Planned social encounters such as regular lunches or dinners with friends. Take the initiative to meet new people.

☐ Enjoying only the anticipation of the next accomplishment. Don't motivate yourself by putting down your past achievements and concentrating only on the next big project. After a while, you forget what you have accomplished and lose any sense of yourself. *To prevent this form of burnout:* Savor your accomplishments as they occur.

Source: Dr. Srully Blotnick, author of *The Corporate Steeplechase: Predictable Crises in a Business Career,* Facts on File Publications, New York.

Setting yourself up as a consultant

☐ Take on assignments after-hours while still with the company. Accumulate so many clients that the only way to handle them is to leave your employer.

☐ Volunteer for a sophisticated task with a prestigious nonprofit organization. Make it clear you are doing it for a reference and on a limited basis. Tell your employer, if possible.

☐ Cultivate contacts. Do favors. Pass along helpful information to people who may be in a position to help you later on.

☐ Discreetly mention finders' fees for leads that actually result in business.

How to get others to support your position

☐ Give them your cooperation and support first.

☐ Be ready to accept blame when you are wrong.

☐ Use witnesses and objective outsiders to prove your points.

☐ Ask for their ideas on how to get the job done.

☐ Be a buffer between those whose support you need and others who might threaten them.

☐ Say, "I need you."

Source: James K. Van Fleet, author of *Lifetime Conversation Guide,* published by Prentice-Hall, Inc., Englewood Cliffs, NJ.

Career crisis points

A study of executives on the fast track revealed they tended to fail when they were:

☐ Moved up during a corporate reorganization but were not evaluated until the reorganization was complete.

☐ Lost a boss who compensated for missing skills or gaps in personality.

☐ Promoted into a job for which they were not prepared.

☐ Shifted to a new boss with an unfamiliar style of management.

☐ Moved into a new area where composure and control under pressure and stress were essential.

Source: Morgan W. McCall, Jr., and Michael M. Lombardo, co-authors, *Off the Track: Why and How Successful Executives Derail,* The Center for Creative Leadership, Greensboro, NC.

If a rival beats you to a promotion by a hair

Assuming that you and your rival are very much alike in experience, education and service with the firm, you need to find out why you lost. The reasons can affect your future with the company. Areas to explore:

☐ Your rival appeared more committed to the company. Management judged you ready to bolt for a better opportunity.

☐ Your rival had a sponsor higher up in the company of whom you were unaware.

□ Your boss personally prefers your rival's company.

□ Your boss saw your rival as less of a threat to his job.

□ You are being saved for something bigger down the road, but no one thought to tell you.

□ You failed at an assignment that you thought was insignificant, but your boss judged you likely to fail again.

□ You have been too active politically within the company outside your department.

□ You are perceived as untrustworthy by some, or they question your loyalty to your boss.

Source: Marilyn Moats Kennedy, author of *Career Knockouts: How to Battle Back*, Follett Publishing Co.

Mid-career work problems

The most important problems mid-career executives face on the job can produce stress-related illnesses:

□ Overload. Putting in too many long hours because of taking on too much work.

□ Confusion about work role. This ambiguity exists when managers are unclear about job objectives.

□ Job conflict. Employees find themselves doing what they don't want to do. And performing work they feel is not part of the job specification. The greater the authority of the people sending the conflicting role messages, the more the job dissatisfaction among the managers.

□ People pressure. Those who are responsible for people suffer more stress than those in charge of things, such as equipment or budgets.

□ Boss's attitude. Those who work for a considerate boss feel less pressure than those under the command of managers who pull rank, play favorites, and take advantage of their employees.

□ Executive neurosis. This occurs when managers are promoted beyond their abilities and overwork in a desperate attempt to hold on to the top job.

Source: Cary L. Cooper, University of Manchester, Manchester, England, in *Mid-Life*, Brunner/Mazel, Inc., New York.

Dealing with political infighting

□ Don't decide that one of the infighters is "right" and the other is "wrong." That encourages the winner to pick more political fights in the future, while it leaves the loser spoiling for revenge. On the other hand, deciding that neither is right and that they must compromise leaves both parties unhappy and convinced that the boss wasn't fair.

□ Look for a third choice that both parties can live with, without each one feeling that he's lost or that the other one has won. The ideal "third way" incorporates all the important points of both sides. Only the irritants are omitted.

□ The person who leads the way to a solution comes out stronger.

Source: *The Effective Manager*, Warren, Gorham & Lamont, Boston.

High-level incompetence

High-level incompetence has many faces and lurks in some heretofore unsuspected areas:

□ Physical incompetence. A person who is professionally or technically competent may develop such anxiety over his work that he gets ulcers or high blood pressure. And that results in a poor attendance record. His boss and coworkers assume he's really very competent but just has health problems. In reality, he is physically incompetent to handle the strain of the job.

□ Mental incompetence. This occurs when a person is moved to a level where he can no longer deal with the intellectual requirements of the job.

□ Social incompetence. A person who is technically competent may be unable to get along with others. Or, problems may arise if he is promoted in an organization where a different class of social behavior is required when moving up the ladder.

□ Emotional incompetence. A technically competent person may be too unstable emotionally to deal with a particular job. Creative types, who tend to be insecure, are particularly prone to this type of incompetence when promoted to administrative positions.

☐ Ethical incompetence. Richard Nixon is a good example. Only when the White House tapes revealed his dishonesty beyond a doubt was it clear that, in office, he had reached his level of ethical incompetence. His brand of manipulative persuasiveness, an asset in local politics, became a liability in the highest office in the land.

Source: Dr. Lawrence J. Peter, author of *The Peter Principle.*

Sexual harassment on the job

Sexual harassment on the job is unlawful and a violation of fair employment practices. Supervisors who allow it to occur in their offices, even though they themselves don't commit any offensive acts, can be charged.

If you think someone is sexually harassing you at work:

☐ Keep a diary and write a brief description of each event right after it happens. Note the time and the place, the people involved, the names of any witnesses.

☐ Confront the offender. Tell the person that you think the remark or action is harassment.

☐ Write a letter to the offender, describing the event and noting that you consider it sexual harassment. Send the letter "personal receipt requested," which means the Post Office will only deliver it to the person to whom it is addressed and give you a receipt that the person signs. Or, hand the letter to the person in the presence of a witness you can trust.

☐ Report the event to management and explain the actions you have taken.

As a supervisor:

☐ Take every complaint about sexual harassment seriously. Document the actions taken in response to a complaint.

☐ Write a policy statement against sexual harassment which defines it, condemns it and provides a way in which employees can bring events to management's attention.

☐ Don't condone a regular practice of sexually-oriented conversations and jokes in the work place. And certainly don't make such remarks to the people you supervise.

☐ Don't permit employees to post sexually-oriented pictures or cartoons in the work place.

☐ Never tie sexual favors to job performance—not even in jest.

☐ Never touch an employee in a sexually-oriented manner.

Source: Howard Pardue, director of human resources, Summit Communications, Inc.

How to keep from burning out on the job

Burnout is a clear loss of interest in work. It's the feeling that work no longer has purpose. Those most vulnerable to burnout are:

☐ The workaholic, whose life is consumed by the job.

☐ The person who quickly tires of routine and can't maintain enthusiasm without constant challenge.

☐ The individual trying conscientiously to master a job that runs counter to temperament and talent.

To rekindle the joys of work:

☐ Get more rest, since stress plays a big role in burnout.

☐ Exercise regularly to get into better physical shape.

☐ Introduce as much variety as possible into your daily routine. One method is to trade some duties with colleagues.

☐ In extreme cases, consider changing your job or career. Make the decision to quit during an emotional high, rather than a low, when everything seems hopeless.

Source: *Working Woman,* New York.

The ten best companies to work for

Based on employee evaluations of pay, benefits, job security, opportunity for advancement and ambience:

☐ Beth Israel Hospital (Boston).

☐ Delta Air Lines.

☐ Donnelley.

☐ Federal Express.

☐ Fel-Pro.

☐ Hallmark Cards.

☐ Publix Super Markets.

☐ Rosenbluth International.

☐ Southwest Airlines.

☐ USAA.

Source: *The 100 Best Companies to Work for in America,* Doubleday, New York.

Avoid unnecessary overtime

Many experts feel that regular late hours at work signal inefficient, disorganized work habits, not ambition. Ways to accomplish your work during office hours:

☐ Do not linger over an office breakfast or a long lunch.

☐ Keep visits and phone calls to a minimum.

☐ Establish times when your door is shut so that you can concentrate on your work without interruptions.

☐ Before a late afternoon meeting, make it clear that you have to leave at a specified time. Most meetings will proceed more quickly.

☐ Before taking on a new job, find out if any overtime is required, aside from normal emergencies. Weigh this against the rewards of the job.

Executive stress profile

Try to change the way you operate at work if you:

☐ Plan the day unrealistically.

☐ Are the first to arrive, and last to leave.

☐ Are always in a hurry.

☐ Make no plans for relaxation.

☐ Feel guilty about doing anything else but work.

☐ Treat any unforeseen problem or setback as a disaster.

☐ Are "polyphasic" in your thinking, involved in one activity when thinking of several others. You talk fast and interrupt often.

☐ Have an overwhelming need to be recognized. Winning is the end-all. But there's no prize in winning or enjoyment of it. As a result, you seldom enjoy recognition, money and possessions.

Source: Rosalind Forbes, author of *Corporate Stress,* Doubleday, Garden City, NY.

How to reduce work-related stress

☐ Recognize the aggravating aspects of your job. Stop fighting them.

☐ Identify your emotional needs and accept them. Most executives are competitive, need to be liked, need to vent anger. They should have outlets for each of these needs.

☐ Practice listening. Listening is more relaxing than talking, and it can help you know what's really going on in the organization.

☐ Be sensitive to change. Recognize when it's occurring on the job and figure out what adjustments are necessary. By consciously recognizing change, you make it manageable.

☐ Keep alcohol consumption under control. Excessive drinking creates the illusion of dealing with stress, while in fact adding to it.

Source: Rosalind Forbes, author of *Corporate Stress,* Doubleday, Garden City, NY.

Secrets of getting a new job

After almost 20 years of testing and perfecting, I have developed an amazingly effective process for getting a job. What makes this process so effective is that it is based on the principles of good communication with potential employers.

In these highly competitive and economically strapped times, employers are looking for people with the skills to deliver more—more profit…more customers…more productivity. Here are six steps and why they should work to get you a job offer within 60 days…

☐ Create a word bank. This is a written account of an important achievement in your career. In 200 words or more, describe the task and how you went about it. What problems did you overcome? How? What were the results, in terms of percentage of improvement, dollars saved, etc.?

This is called the word bank because you will borrow from it for each of the following steps. This account of an important achievement is the key to a successful job hunt.

Take your time on your word bank. Go into detail. Include as many of your skills as you can. But stick to just one achievement. If you have a number of notable achievements, you can create other word banks using this one as the model. The more word banks, the more skills. The more skills, the more job opportunities.

What if your work is largely routine? Routine jobs are historically subject to errors and poor performance brought on by boredom and repetition. Write 200 words about your ability to avoid errors and ensure reliability, accuracy and high productivity. These are qualities that are currently in low supply and that employers value highly.

What if you have just finished school and are looking for your first job? Write about the skills you developed in school. Did you get an "A" in a French course after memorizing 500 irregular verbs in just two days? This shows you can learn quickly and handle crash projects—the criteria for many positions. Focusing on how you work, rather than on job titles and descriptions, lets you expand from your current position into new fields that make use of your skills.

☐ Write a contact letter. As the name implies, the contact letter is written to people who work in your target industry and who you have targeted because they may know of opportunities for someone with your skills. You can find these people by consulting trade directories and publications.

Your contact letter should not include a résumé and should make it clear that you are in search of information—not employment. The heart of your letter is a paragraph of the best ideas from your word bank. The letter informs the contact when you will call for an appointment, during which you will ask just one question and make some notes.

There are three reasons why a contact will probably agree to see you:

1. He/She is a nice person.

2. You're asking for something that this nice person can give you easily.

3. Your word bank convinced your contact that you are worth talking to.

☐ Begin the contact conversation by asking just one question: "What criteria do you use to hire people in this field?" This is an honest question and one that your contact is qualified to answer. Pay careful attention to the reply. Make a note of each criterion on a legal-sized pad with a black, felt-tipped pen, so that your notes are clear when you review them later.

As the answer unfolds, you will learn a great deal about what your target industry is looking for. When you have learned enough, thank your contact and ask for the names of other helpful industry contacts. Send your contact letter to any new names, mentioning your first contact as a reference.

☐ Create a competitive résumé. Now, instead of just listing your jobs and titles, focus your résumé on the specific criteria by which people are hired in your target industry. Borrow from your word bank to show how you meet those criteria. The more focused your résumé, the more competitive it is and the better your chances of landing a job interview.

Hints: Don't include any information that does not focus on the criteria. Do send a copy of your competitive résumé and a thank you letter to the contact who helped you write it. It's more than just polite—it could be productive.

☐ Prepare for the job interview. It will be really anticlimactic when you've done such good homework. Though most decision-makers know their own jobs well, they often have little time to prepare for interviews. Because of your preparation, you'll be in a position to help the interviewer keep the discussion on target. A single question will do it: "By what criteria will you select the person for this job?" This time you're not talking about the industry in general, but about a specific job.

Feel free to suggest the addition of any

criteria you have learned during your research. The more criteria, the more chances to draw on your word bank for the necessary skills. After you've shown how you meet a particular criterion, be sure to check it out with the interviewer by asking, "How does that compare with what you had in mind?"

Hints: Before the interview, practice presenting skills from your word bank so that you feel comfortable with what you're going to say. Bring along documentation of your achievements whenever possible.

☐ Follow up after the interview. Periodically asking how your presentation compared with what the decision-maker had in mind might well result in a decision during the interview.

But if not, write a letter enclosing a summary of your qualifications. If you don't get a job offer, ask for ideas on how to improve your presentation.

Source: Irv Zuckerman, a New York-based communications consultant who has more than 40 years' experience in the field and has taught thousands of people his job-seeking techniques. He is the author of *Hire Power: The 6-Step Process to Get the Job You Need in 60 Days—Guaranteed!*, Perigee Books, NY.

Eleven most common reasons job applicants aren't hired

☐ Too many jobs. Employers are suspicious of changes without career advancement.

☐ Reluctance of applicant or spouse to relocate if necessary.

☐ Wrong personality for the employer.

☐ Unrealistic salary requirements.

☐ Inadequate background.

☐ Poor employment record.

☐ Unresponsive, uninterested or unprepared during the interview. (Being "too aggressive" is not a serious handicap.)

☐ Negotiations with employer handled improperly.

☐ Little apparent growth potential.

☐ Long period of unemployment.

☐ Judged to be an ineffective supervisor.

Source: National Personnel Associates.

When to change jobs

It's time for you to leave the company when you:

☐ Realize management is neglecting its basic business.

☐ Your company has had a sensational run for several years. (A downturn is inevitable. It's best to leave a winner.)

☐ You're being excluded from sharing in the company's success.

☐ Your firm isn't keeping up with the competition.

☐ You've run out of interest.

☐ You've run out of ideas.

☐ You start aiming at a position a relative of management might want.

☐ You don't know why you're there.

(Sketch out a career plan and find the job that will be your next step up.)

Source: Tom Hopkins, author of *The Official Guide to Success*, Warner Books, New York.

Characteristics of a good boss

- [ ] Directs and communicates clearly.
- [ ] Rewards good performance.
- [ ] Is encouraging.
- [ ] Keeps a finger on all important areas of work.
- [ ] Is responsive to requests for aid.
- [ ] Is predictable.
- [ ] Is fair.

Key skills for managers

- [ ] Interest in improving the way things are done.
- [ ] Continuing desire to initiate.
- [ ] Confidence in abilities and goals.
- [ ] Ability to develop, counsel and help others improve.
- [ ] Concern with the impact managerial actions have on the activities of others.
- [ ] Capacity to get others to follow the manager's lead.
- [ ] Knowledge of how to inspire teamwork.
- [ ] Faith in others.
- [ ] Skill in oral and written communication.
- [ ] Spontaneity of expression.
- [ ] Tendency to put organization needs before personal needs.
- [ ] Objectivity in a dispute.
- [ ] Knowledge of own strengths and weaknesses.
- [ ] Adaptability to change.
- [ ] Stamina to put in long hours.
- [ ] Logical thought.

Source: *International Management,* New York.

Behaving like a top professional

You can reap a great deal of self-esteem and a wide variety of other rewards by learning how to behave like a real professional.

Essentials:

- [ ] Sense of responsibility for clients (or customers). People who are cynical about their work, who despise the people they have to deal with, demoralize themselves and generally perform badly in the long run.
- [ ] Avoid rules of thumb, quick answers and rigid thinking. Be on the lookout for exceptions—incidents where theories don't seem to fit the facts. This is an opportunity to perform creatively.

- [ ] Stay current. Take additional training and/or coursework. Force yourself to work on tough problems, do heavy business-related reading.

- [ ] Be thoughtful about trade-offs in making difficult decisions that often involve several contradictory factors.

- [ ] Approach complex problems with a general strategy plus the readiness to change as the situation unfolds or new factors develop.

- [ ] Think more about task accomplishment than about hours spent accomplishing it. Professionals aren't clock watchers. They're driven by goals that they've set for themselves. And because these are, in large part, their own goals, they're motivated to attain them.

- [ ] Be responsible for developing subordinates. You'll end up with better people, increase loyalty and motivation and experience the pride of seeing someone you've trained advance from neophyte to polished performer.

- [ ] Understand that excellence isn't an end state. It's a process of continuously striving to meet more challenging goals, learn new things and become more adept at solving difficult problems. Suppress the temptation to take destructive shortcuts or gain selfish advantage.

Source: Dr. Leonard Sayles, Center for Creative Leadership, Greensboro, NC.

Personal mistakes managers make

- [ ] The worst mistake made by talented managers in their early years is to underrate the boss. *The danger:* Bosses will almost always detect that attitude. And it's the kind of offense that's hard to forgive. The young manager makes an enemy. Or, even more likely, the boss writes the manager off as yet another of those fad followers who's not really so bright after all.

- [ ] Young managers often fail to understand how the boss receives information best. Communication depends as much on the recipient as it does on the sender. *Typical:* The young manager sends along a brilliant 64-page analysis and plan of action, doesn't get a reaction and blames the boss. What the subordinate has failed to recognize is that the boss is a listener, not a reader.

☐ The first big promotion—especially one to headquarters or to a position close to senior management—often presents the opportunity for the third big mistake: Trying to do too many things. Enthusiastic, and with bountiful reserves of energy, managers at this level splinter themselves. They mistake busyness for progress and performance.

☐ *The right thing to do:* Concentrate on performance, not on credibility.

☐ Don't assume that everyone understands what it is they have to accomplish. *Winning tactic:* At least every nine months ask: "On whom do I depend for information and support? And who depends on me?" Make sure each of these people is kept up to date on what you're doing and what you need.

☐ A top manager must use two basic ways of gathering information—reading analytical reports and walking around. Managers can rise to the top because they're excellent at either one of these techniques. But once there, they must force themselves to do both. Report readers will lose touch with the urgent realities of running the business. And managers who rely on their perceptions often fail to check those perceptions against hard analysis. Either one comes to grief, sooner or later.

☐ *The most fatal flaw of all in top managers:* Compromising before understanding what the right decision really is. At the top, managers won't succeed if they substitute energy and a coach's half-time exhortations for making hard decisions.

Source: Dr. Peter F. Drucker, a leading consultant to top companies around the world and author of *Innovation and Entrepreneurship,* Harper & Row, New York.

How to prevent mistakes in decision making

☐ Never make unnecessary decisions. All decisions involve risk. It can occasionally be wiser to leave well enough alone.

☐ Identify recurring problems. Resolve them once and for all.

☐ Don't develop grandiose schemes to solve simple problems. Evaluate solutions in terms of costs.

☐ Don't delay the decision. Moving quickly allows more time to correct the decision if it turns out wrong. And it frees you to tackle other problems.

Source: Don Caruth and Bill Middlebrook, Caruth Management Consultants, Carrollton, TX, authors of *Supervisory Management,* Saranac Lake, NY.

Preparing for a crisis

You may not be able to plan for a crisis, but you can prepare.

☐ Be alert. The best way to handle a crisis is to anticipate it.

☐ Stay flexible. Make a commitment to change swiftly, if necessary. Make provisions ahead of time for doing so.

☐ Know the options. Options must be developed before a crisis interrupts a personal routine.

☐ Establish clear communications with all those involved to reduce panic, ease tension and make quick changes possible.

☐ Recognize a crisis. It may create opportunities as well as problems. Play up any such advantages, rather than being content simply to survive.

Source: Walter Johnson, president of Quadrant Marketing Counselors, Ltd., New York.

New projects: Keep them exciting

New ideas have a way of exciting people, then fading away. To maintain interest:

☐ Pump in emotion and excitement by remaining personally involved.

☐ Organize schedules so that people working together have a sense of directed action.

☐ Remind everyone of the target. Make it stand out clearly as the common goal.

☐ Show respect for all participants by continuing to listen to their comments and ideas to improve ongoing projects.

Source: Craig S. Rice, author of *Secrets of Managing People,* Prentice-Hall, Englewood Cliffs, NJ.

What makes committed employees

Committed people get a great deal of personal satisfaction from their accomplishments. They totally immerse themselves in a project and often need a brief break to recover emotionally before a new assignment.

In addition, they:

☐ Assess the feasibility of a task and speak up when they think the odds are bad. Uncommitted people take on anything without caring whether it is possible.

☐ Back up and cover for coworkers and supervisors without concern for who is responsible.

☐ Understand the underlying plans and objectives of a project. Know how to proceed without checking with supervisors at every point.

☐ Feel apprehension and anxiety at the possibility of failure. Unhesitatingly ask for help from supervisors when it seems necessary.

Source: W.C. Waddell, author of *Overcoming Murphy's Law*, AMACOM, New York.

Characteristics of a good helper

☐ Works well with colleagues.

☐ Is systematic. Sets priorities well.

☐ Gives a stable and predictable work performance.

☐ Accepts direction well.

☐ Shows up regularly and punctually.

☐ Detects problems in advance and refers to them when necessary.

MBA schools as talent sources

Chief executive officers of the country's largest companies ranked business schools as sources of talent for their own companies in the following order (the percentage indicates how many chose that school as number one):

☐ Harvard (33%).

☐ Stanford (18%).

☐ Pennsylvania/Wharton (7%).

☐ Michigan (5%).

☐ Dartmouth/Tuck (5%).

☐ Chicago (4%).

☐ Texas (4%).

☐ Northwestern (3%).

☐ MIT/Sloan (3%).

☐ Purdue (2%).

☐ Columbia (1%).

Source: Arthur Young Executive Resource Consultants, *The Chief Executive: Background and Attitude Profiles*, New York.

Hiring tips

For jobs that require judgment, initiative and good sense, seek the following personality traits in potential employees:

☐ Ability to anticipate what might go wrong and to plan for it.

☐ Readiness to listen to and accept good ideas from others.

☐ High energy and perseverance.

☐ Flexibility in communicating with a variety of people.

Hiring secrets

☐ Write a clear job description. Keep this information in hand along with the applicant's résumé before he or she is interviewed.

☐ Let the candidate do about 85% of the talking in a 60- or 90-minute interview. Untrained interviewers fall into the trap of doing most of the talking themselves.

☐ Avoid talking too much yourself by working with a detailed interview guide to remind you where there are blanks in information.

☐ Don't interview anyone who hasn't filled out the company's own application form. Trained interviewees are taught to stall on the forms, hoping to present themselves in their own way first. Don't fall for that routine.

Learn how to spot the "pros" who have been professionally coached. Clues:

☐ Knowing "too much" about the company and positioning their pitch exactly to show how they could make a contribution there.

☐ Trying to take control of the interview, especially from an untrained interviewer.

☐ Asking what happened to the last person who had the job.

☐ Expecting a question-and-answer type of interview and having prepared answers to such questions as, "What are the reasons we should hire you?" or, "Why didn't you make better grades in college?"

□ Don't assume that applicants who do any one of these things have necessarily been coached. But if they give themselves away in several areas, the chances are good that they've been professionally trained.

□ Assume control with some broad lead-off statements, such as: "Begin by telling me about your previous jobs, starting with the first one and working up to the present." "Tell me about your education."

Source: Richard A. Fear, a consultant with the Selection Systems Division of Mainstream Access, Inc., a New York consulting firm specializing in outplacement, and author of *The Evaluation Interview*, McGraw-Hill, New York.

Why managers fail ...and succeed

People who fail in business usually have no trouble finding external reasons for their failure—economic conditions, discrimination, politics, uncooperative employees.

Although these play a part, internal factors are frequently as important.

In my psychiatric practice, I have observed that powerful unconscious issues affect work just as they do other areas of life. Our interactions are guided by a whole spectrum of beliefs and behavior styles developed over many years.

What we learned growing up influences the way we react to challenges in adulthood. Understanding and grappling with these issues can make a significant difference in job performance.

Personality style is one of the major internal factors in managerial performance. Three leadership styles are responsible for the most serious managerial problems...

The narcissistic leader

Characteristics: Narcissists are drawn to leadership positions by a deep need for power and prestige. They are often highly talented, hard-working and charismatic. But feelings of inferiority lead to self-aggrandizement and the need for constant, unconditional affirmation and positive feedback from others. Narcissists also tend to have a low tolerance for frustration.

Consequences: The narcissist inspires people to action but can't always follow through. By surrounding himself/herself with yes-men—people who idealize him and reflect back exactly what he wants to hear—he is unlikely to anticipate and prepare for potential trouble spots as his ideas are executed. The narcissist's need to be in the spotlight makes it hard for him to build an effective team. He may resent and even sabotage employees whose creativity threatens to overshadow his own.

Most dangerous, the narcissist fails to encourage balance and diversity of opinion. The result can be disastrous, both to him and the company, as he inspires others to pour resources into implementing his brilliant—but unworkable—ideas.

Issues: The narcissist is likely to have grown up in an environment where nothing he did was ever quite good enough. He never developed a strong sense of self-esteem. To mask this sense of inferiority, he learned to rely on self-aggrandizement and seeks out only those people who will reassure him that he's wonderful.

The narcissist needs to develop a more complete sense of self—one that is not dependent on others' perceptions or on always being the best. He needs to recognize the value of clear, attainable goals that are reached step by gradual step. Skills to develop…

□ Share credit. Use the words "we" and "us" rather than "I" and "me."

□ Be generous in giving praise instead of always expecting to receive it.

□ Rather than relying on coworkers for affirmation, explore ways to meet that need outside work. Put time into developing family relationships and satisfying hobbies.

The authoritarian leader

Characteristics: The authoritarian personality has an obsession with order, with being right and in control. This type of manager is poorly attuned to the emotional needs of employees. He relies on a competitive, rather than affiliative, model of work relationships.

Consequences: Though corporations and departments do need an authority figure in order to function efficiently, the authoritarian's excessive need for control can lead to numbing bureaucracy and a rule-bound, by-the-book decision-making style.

Autonomy and creativity are stifled—which can spell disaster when a crisis arises that requires quick, effective decisions.

The authoritarian manager is unlikely to build loyalty or team spirit among staff. He may appear petty and defensive… employees respond with feelings of dislike and by doing the bare minimum required of them.

Issues: Authoritarians learn this style by growing up in families where control and rules are valued…and emotions are ignored or denied. The authoritarian leader must work to become more aware of how he feels, not just what he does…and recognize that intellect and emotion can work together. Skills to develop…

☐ Learn to listen carefully, without interrupting or becoming defensive.

☐ Practice seeing things from a subordinate's point of view. You may come across more harshly than you mean to.

☐ Welcome criticism instead of rejecting or punishing it. Invite feedback from others.

☐ Share credit for positive results.

The emotionally isolated leader

Characteristics: The emotionally isolated manager is so uncomfortable with social interaction that he becomes almost invisible—business is carried out via subordinates, other managers or committees.

This type of leader is so afraid of making a mistake that he'll avoid taking action or making a commitment—which could turn out to be the greatest mistake of all.

Consequences: Subordinates may form small groups or pairings, seeking the direction and support that is lacking from above. Since each group is likely to have its own agenda, the organization may become fragmented. This is not an environment that fosters lively, productive collaboration and interchange.

In some cases, a more socially skilled peer or subordinate will act as a kind of buffer between the manager and the rest of the organization, helping to create a responsive climate for employees. Having a gifted coworker interpret and carry out the leader's ideas may be enough. But the leader risks being left behind as the department or company grows beyond him.

Issues: Emotionally isolated leaders lack confidence in their ability to lead or even communicate with others. They are uncomfortable with the concept and enactment of power. Some dislike people and prefer the world of ideas… others are simply shy.

Many of them have been high intellectual achievers all their lives—but received little modeling or encouragement from their parents in getting along with peers. Skills to develop…

☐ Read about and take courses in assertiveness training to become more comfortable with collaboration, leadership and basic social skills.

☐ Learn to see mistakes as a way of finding out what is and isn't effective. Errors can be corrected.

☐ Fight inaction by recognizing that there's always more information to be gathered—but that's no reason to postpone action indefinitely. *Helpful:* Set deadlines. Resolve to stop research and to make decisions based on data gathered by that date.

Source: David W. Krueger, MD, clinical professor of psychiatry at Baylor College of Medicine and author of *Emotional Business: The Meaning and Mastery of Work, Money and Success,* Avant Books, Slawson Communications, Inc., 165 Vallecitos de Oro, San Marcos, California 92069.

How to avoid errors in hiring

Many mistakes in hiring are obvious and can be avoided easily, specifically: Failing to describe jobs adequately to prospective candidates.

Other mistakes, however, are less obvious and therefore harder to avoid:

☐ Hiring overly qualified people.

☐ Too little information in help-wanted ads. Include required skills, duties, type of business and location, benefits, advancement opportunities and name of specific person to contact.

☐ Failure to prescreen applicants before scheduling interviews. This can result in time wasted interviewing unsuitable candidates, while good prospects are overlooked.

☐ Inadequate interviewing. This is a task for someone with plenty of skill and time. Interviewers should explain the interview's purpose and company policies and encourage applicants to ask questions.

☐ Unchecked references. This applies especially to those who claim success in previous jobs.

☐ Rejection because the applicant might not stay a long time. Good employees benefit the company even in short stays.

☐ Delays in making the hiring decision. If an applicant is going to be rejected anyway, the company should use its time to find other prospects. If the applicant is going to be hired, delay cuts productivity.

☐ Hiring friends or relatives who are not qualified. A uniform hiring policy boosts morale among those already employed.

Source: Alan Leighton, vice president, Cole Associates, management consultants, Short Hills, NJ.

How to be a better interviewer

When interviewing a job candidate:

☐ Spend a few minutes in small talk.

☐ Use ideas from the résumé or the application form to frame your questions.

☐ Speak softly. This encourages applicants to take center stage, where they should be.

☐ Look responsive. Most people don't use nearly enough facial expression. Raising one eyebrow a little and smiling slightly gives an expectant look that makes an interviewer seem receptive. Eye contact and a calculated pause will invite the speaker to elaborate.

☐ Give reinforcement. Some people call it stroking or giving a pat on the back. Comments such as "Very impressive!" or "Excellent!" can be dropped into the discussion without interrupting the flow.

☐ Maintain control. If someone runs on too long, interrupt gently after a thought seems to be complete but before the applicant actually finishes the sentence and starts another one.

☐ Follow up and probe. If someone fails to explain the reasons for leaving a job, bring this up in the form of a casual follow-up question. If an applicant indicates that detail work is less satisfying, probe to find out how strongly that applicant dislikes detail work.

☐ To find out why people liked or disliked a previous job, use soft phrases such as "How did you happen to…?" "What prompted your decision to…?"

☐ Use double-edged questions to get at

people's shortcomings. *Example:* "What about tact? Do you have as much of that as you would like, or is this something you could improve a little bit?" Most applicants find it much easier to discuss things that they could improve rather than qualities that they lack.

Source: Richard A. Fear, a consultant with the Selection Systems Division of Mainstream Access, Inc., a New York consulting firm specializing in outplacement, and author of *The Evaluation Interview,* McGraw-Hill, New York.

Getting essential information from a job candidate

☐ Even more important than finding out what people liked or disliked about a previous job is finding out why.

☐ Focus on asking people what they would like to improve. Most applicants find it much easier to discuss improving themselves than admitting they lack essential qualities or skills.

Questions to ask a job candidate— legally

Five questions to avoid:

☐ What is your religion?

☐ Do you have school-age children?

☐ How long have you been living at your current address?

☐ Are you married?

☐ Were you ever arrested?

What to ask instead:

☐ Will there be any problems if you have to work on a weekend?

☐ Are there any reasons why you might not be able to make an overnight business trip?

☐ What is your address?

☐ Defer questions on marital status until after the employee has been hired. Then they are completely proper if asked in connection with such purposes as insurance, etc.

☐ Were you ever convicted of a felony? (Ask only if the question is job-related.)

Source: Hunt Personnel, Ltd., New York.

What to ask a job applicant about his previous job

☐ What problems came up at your last job?

☐ How did you plan for them?

☐ What did you do?

☐ Raise a contrary point of view and observe whether the applicant thinks it through or simply responds with a knee-jerk acceptance or rejection.

☐ Identify a candidate as one with high energy if he talks comfortably and zestfully.

Source: Dr. Leonard R. Sayles, Center for Creative Leadership, Greensboro, NC.

The art of checking references

Checking references is becoming more difficult because many companies, as a matter of policy, no longer give out information other than dates of employment. This is because of the danger of being sued by a disappointed job-seeker. You'll have to be more subtle and tenacious than in the past, but you should aim to:

☐ Avoid vague questions that can be met with equally vague answers. Instead of asking, "What kind of guy is Ed?" ask for concrete instances of what Ed did. For a marketing director applicant, ask "What was Ed's contribution to any new products put out during his tenure?"

☐ Listen carefully to the former supervisor's tone of voice over the phone. Hesitations or false heartiness may be warning signs. But do not jump to this conclusion. Many managers are unused to giving recommendations and they respond awkwardly.

☐ Try not to settle for a reference from the personnel department. It knows almost nothing about the applicant's day-to-day performance.

☐ For key positions, take the reference source to lunch, if possible. Frankness is likelier in a face-to-face situation.

☐ Do not solicit references by letter or request written responses. Very few companies are willing to put much in writing these days.

☐ Double-check an overly negative response to a reference call, since the supervisor may personally dislike the applicant.

Making best use of subordinates

☐ Ask the secretary to keep a list of things to be done so she can check on your progress. (Especially good for chief executives; it gives them someone to "report to.")

☐ To make sure a typist picks up all corrections, always make them in color.

☐ Discourage excessive reporting by subordinates. Most memos contain information you don't need. One solution is to have subordinates report only when results deviate from a plan you have both approved.

☐ Have a secretary or assistant sit in at meetings; take minutes of action items; distribute to those concerned; follow up to make sure action items are actually completed; report to you if they aren't.

How to deal with excuse-makers

People who make excuses chronically aren't lazy. They're troubled—driven by a fragile sense of self-worth and fearful of any error or criticism.

To deal with habitual excuse-makers:

☐ Stress their importance to the organization (or family) and the repercussions of their irresponsibility.

☐ Refuse to hear out their recital of excuses.

☐ Keep a record of missed or late assignments.

☐ Get tough with excuse-makers if it finally becomes necessary.

Source: *Executive Productivity.*

How not to waste time on committees

It is usually flattering to be asked to serve on a committee. What it takes to turn down such invitations is a clear sense of personal direction and a strong sense of security. If you're asked:

☐ Accept appointments only to committees that are doing work you believe in.

☐ Restrict your contribution to the area of your expertise.

☐ Whenever possible, delegate time-consuming chores to paid committee assistants.

Source: Lillian Vernon, president, Lillian Vernon Corp., Mount Vernon, NY.

Forming a successful committee

Some helpful suggestions to point a committee in the right direction:

☐ Three or four members can function effectively. More participants mean members won't feel personally responsible for results. Fewer limits the input.

☐ Assign definite responsibility to each member.

☐ Rotate membership on standing committees periodically. That provides a steady flow of ideas and breaks up stagnant thinking patterns.

☐ Balance membership between experienced participants and relative newcomers.

☐ Set goals. To solve a problem (rather than merely move it elsewhere), aim for specific results. A committee that isn't expected to produce a substantial result won't.

☐ Review level of cooperation. A committee dominated by one member often produces insignificant results and frustrates other members.

☐ Set a time limit for work to be completed.

☐ Get periodic progress reports if the assignment is a multistage one.

☐ If committee proposals are rejected, the reasons for that rejection should be explained carefully.

☐ If the proposals are accepted, implement them promptly, so the committee can see the effects of its efforts.

How to create a committee that really works

☐ Give the committee the power to act on their own decisions.

☐ Make membership voluntary.

☐ Encourage members to speak freely.

☐ Match members' skills to problems. Don't make automatic appointments to subcommittees or task groups.

☐ Choose members of somewhat equal status. Otherwise, the powerful dominate, and the less powerful agree or don't participate.

Employee fraud

More companies than ever are being victimized by employee fraud—

dishonest acts going far beyond petty theft or embezzlement. And experience indicates that the loss from employee fraud is continually increasing. The best estimates are that the cost of employee dishonesty now amounts to as much as 5% of the Gross Domestic Product.

The varieties of fraud

To help deal with employee fraud, first learn the various forms it can take. The types of fraud haven't changed much over the years. There's nothing new in stealing—just variations on old methods. Some of the most common techniques employees use to steal from a business:

☐ Lapping. The employee diverts money from the account of a customer. Checks from that customer may go into a bank account maintained by the employee. The employee may steal from a second customer to cover up the first theft.

This type of theft is widespread. But while the computer has made lapping easier to carry out, it also has made it easier to detect.

☐ Accounts-payable fraud. The employee may falsify payments to real vendors, or may create phony vendor addresses to which company checks are sent. Alternatively, an employee may intentionally overpay an invoice, take the refund from the supplier and pocket it.

☐ Payroll ghosts. With so many people being discharged from companies, it is simple for someone in a company that is downsizing to keep a discharged employee on the payroll for a week or two after departing.

The stolen pay goes on the discharged employee's W-2 form, but it never gets noticed. The average worker doesn't know whether he/she has worked 27 or 30 weeks.

☐ Kickbacks. The employee takes bribes or kickbacks from suppliers and vendors.

This is almost impossible to find, because there are no records—the deals are made in cash.

☐ Inventory fraud. The employee uses company money to place a phony order, or to order more than the company needs. The merchandise is then sold for the employee's gain.

These days, inventory fraud is more likely to be fraud by management trying to make the financials look better than they are.

☐ Penny-ante fraud. This is all small stuff—submitting phony invoices, inflating personal expense items, etc.

The amounts involved are small, but it is the most common type of employee fraud—and the type that is growing most rapidly.

Mounting a defense

The most serious problem at most businesses is the ease with which employees commit fraud and get away with it. When people see they can steal and not get caught, they continue to do it.

The best defense against employee dishonesty is to have an experienced fraud auditor or accountant conduct audits for abnormalities on a regular basis. An ordinary audit is done in enough detail so the accountant can determine that the financial statements fairly represent the company's financial condition and results of operations.

A fraud audit is extremely detailed, covering cash, payables and inventory on an item-by-item basis. It is done by someone trained in fraud auditing, for the specific purpose of searching out employee fraud.

Not every accountant can do a fraud audit. Look for someone who is a certified fraud examiner (CFE). Most big CPA firms have CFEs on staff, or know how to locate one. Or contact the National Association of Certified Fraud Examiners (716 West Ave., Austin, Texas 78701; 800-245-3321).

The trouble with a fraud audit is that its emphasis on detail makes it too costly for many businesses. It's very expensive to go through the books, transaction by transaction. Some very large companies have internal auditors who continually watch for employee dishonesty. The average middle-sized company—doing under $100 million per year in business—ordinarily doesn't have the wherewithal to retain its own auditor.

Whether a company conducts audits or not, it shouldn't ignore additional defense measures such as sound business practices, rigidly maintained internal controls, fidelity bonding for all employees and insurance coverage that protects against the full range of possible fraud.

Even this, however, won't completely eliminate employee dishonesty.

Nothing will do that. But these steps will give the company some degree of protection.

Preventing fraud

Basic to controlling fraud is understanding that it can exist anywhere—in the shipping room, the accounting office or anyplace where there is something that can be taken and turned into cash.

The key to employee theft is conversion. People must be able to convert the fruits of their labor into dollars. They can do that by simply taking merchandise and reselling it. Or they can do it by falsifying records. The opportunities for employee dishonesty are almost limitless.

Problem: Spotting an employee likely to turn bad is nearly impossible. It's tough to screen out a new employee who might have been fired elsewhere for stealing. Very seldom will someone intentionally give a negative reference.

Usually, the guilty party is an existing employee with an unblemished reputation. Something happens in his/her life that creates a desperate need for money—maybe an illness or some sort of financial pressure. So the employee steals—usually not a lot of money, just a small amount. Then he/she sees how easy it is. Even when the need passes, the employee continues to steal because it was so simple.

Similarly, the company may inadvertently "invite" otherwise honest employees to steal. By leaving a computer unattended or forgetting to secure a cash drawer, the company may tempt even the most well-meaning employees to take what doesn't belong to them.

Caution: Don't rely on supervisors to control employee fraud because frequently it is supervisors, with their more detailed knowledge of the business, who are the perpetrators.

How to cope

There are many things you can do—short of a full-scale fraud audit—to combat employee fraud…

☐ Create a business culture that discourages employee fraud. Implement rigid controls, closely monitor the sensitive parts of the business and let employees know they are being monitored.

□ Don't break the rules of sound business practice. Management must set the example of honesty if it expects its employees to act accordingly. It takes very little for this example to be compromised.

Example: If you "open" the warehouse on Saturdays—selling to friends or relatives for cash, off the books, that's a secret that can't be kept. That becomes an invitation for employees to steal.

□ Know your employees. Watch for signs that an employee is spending more than his/her salary would seem to allow.

□ Get fraud insurance in order. The most important thing you can do to protect the company is to buy a fidelity bond. Be sure all your employees are bonded.

Source: Norman W. Lipshie, senior partner, Weber Lipshie & Co., certified public accountants and certified fraud examiners, New York.

How to negotiate more effectively

□ Don't allow the negotiations to be hurried by the other side. Clarify everything that seems fuzzy.

□ Have the facts to back up every objective. If no facts are available, use opinions from experts as support.

□ Maintain flexibility in every position. It avoids making the other side overly aggressive and always leaves a way out of dead ends.

□ Look for the real meaning behind the other person's words. Body language tells a lot. Looking away when discussing a key point can indicate a lack of commitment.

□ Don't focus only on money. Loyalty, ego, pride and independence can be more important than dollars to many people.

□ Be alert to the other side's priorities. Don't assume that the two sides are going to have the same priorities. Bending on a point that's important only to an adversary is one of the fastest ways to speed the process.

Key negotiation phrases

□ *Please correct me if I'm wrong.* (Shows you're open to persuasion by objective facts...defuses confrontations.)

□ *Could I ask you a few questions to see if my facts are right?* (Questions are less threatening than statements.)

□ *Let me see if I understand what you're saying.* (Once a person feels understood, he or she can relax and discuss the problem constructively.)

□ *One fair solution might be...*(Keep it open-ended and worthy of joint consideration.)

□ *Let me get back to you.* (Resist psychological pressure to give in right away.)

Source: Roger Fisher, author of *Getting to Yes*, Houghton Mifflin, Boston.

How to answer questions while negotiating

Knowing what to say and *not* to say is the key. Correct answers aren't necessarily good answers and may be foolish. Rules for good answers:

□ Take time to think. Never answer until you clearly understand the question.

□ Stall on the basis of incomplete knowledge or failure to remember.

□ Evade by answering a different question. Or answer only part of a question.

□ Prepare by writing down in advance those questions most likely to come up during negotiations.

□ Use an associate as devil's advocate.

Source: Dr. Chester L. Karrass, Karrass Seminars, Santa Monica, CA.

Patience as a negotiating tool

Patience is the most powerful tactic in negotiating. Don't rush to finish things quickly. Take the time to:

□ Divide the other side's team.

□ Lower their expectations.

□ Tire them out.

□ Bring new problems to the surface.

□ Buy time to find their weaknesses.

Source: Dr. Chester L. Karrass, Karrass Seminars, Santa Monica, CA.

Signs that the other side is ready to make a deal

It's valuable to know as early as possible that the other side is preparing to settle. It allows strong points to be pressed home and helps avoid overkill. Clues to look for:

☐ The discussion shifts focus from the points of contention to the areas of agreement.

☐ The two sides are significantly closer together.

☐ The opposition starts to talk about final arrangements.

☐ A personal social invitation is made. At this point, agreement is almost always just a formality.

☐ Other side starts to make notes. Follow through at once, even if nothing but a napkin or envelope is at hand to write on.

☐ Don't handle the signing of the formal agreement through the mail. Both parties should sign it together. This adds importance to the event and helps cement the ties that were formed during the final stage of negotiation.

Source: D.D. Seltz and A.J. Modica, co-authors, *Negotiate Your Way to Success,* Farnsworth Publishing Co., Rockville Centre, NY.

Using an ultimatum

This is a risky tactic. For it to succeed, especially in the latter stages of a negotiation, an ultimatum must be:

☐ Presented as softly and palatably as possible.

☐ Backed by documentation or some form of legitimacy.

☐ Phrased so it leaves the other side with very few alternatives except to accept or walk away.

Reneging as a negotiating tool

Going back on a deal right after it's made and demanding a higher price is a common, very effective and somewhat unethical negotiating tactic. The trick, called *escalation,* works because the other side has come too far to walk away.

Best defense: Anticipate such a move and plan for it.

☐ Get a large security deposit or performance bond.

☐ Ask the other side for other assurances against escalation.

☐ Persuade as many high-level people as possible to sign the agreement, which will make it more difficult to escalate the terms.

Source: Dr. Chester L. Karrass, Karrass Seminars, Santa Monica, CA.

Planning tips for office routine

Make your office run smoother with these techniques:

☐ Arrange routing lists alphabetically. This avoids hierarchical irritations that arise when one person's name is placed below someone else's.

☐ If there is a way to avoid written memoranda, use it. Eyeball-to-eyeball response is important in gauging how information is received and how it will be acted upon.

☐ Brevity is the essence of good communications.

☐ Boil down ideas and reports to less than one minute, if possible.

☐ Try not to hire assistants, even when the work load gets heavy. Assistants add a layer of bureaucracy, which reduces contact between managers and subordinates. They rarely expedite matters since they cannot make decisions in the boss's absence.

☐ Consider secretarial pools rather than personal secretaries. That way, letters can be dictated either to a machine or a person.

Source: Robert Townsend, author of *Robert Townsend Speaks Out,* Advanced Management Reports, Inc., New York.

Cutting telephone chitchat

☐ Preset time limit: "Yes, Tom. I can talk for three minutes."

☐ Foreshadow ending: "Bill, before we hang up…"

☐ When calling a long-winded party, time the call for just before he goes out to lunch or leaves for the day. Give him a reason to keep the call short.

☐ Never hold the phone waiting for someone.

☐ Eliminate "hello" from telephone answering habits. It just wastes time and adds confusion. Answer by identifying yourself instead—it starts conversation with no lost motion.

☐ Don't return all calls the minute you get back to the office. Spot the crucial ones. Half the rest will be from people who've already solved their problems; the rest will get back to you soon enough.

☐ When asking someone to call back later, suggest the best time. This avoids repeated interruptions at inconvenient moments.

When your secretary places a call

When a secretary places a call, tell her in advance:

☐ If there's anyone else to ask for if the person wanted isn't there.

☐ Whether to ask that the call be returned.

☐ To find out the best time of day to place the call again.

☐ To suggest the other party call back at a specified time.

Minimizing paper problems

Neither sloppiness nor quantity is the root cause of office paper gluts. The real problem is a shortfall in decision-making. The solution is to decide which of these four categories a piece of paper belongs to:

☐ Toss. Figure out the worst thing that could happen if you threw the paper away. Toss liberally.

☐ Refer. Many documents fall into the bailiwick of secretary, boss, subordinate, colleague or specialist. Make individual "discuss" folders for key colleagues. (For general referrals, use the "out" box.)

☐ Act. These are your own tasks—writing letters, planning, etc. Put them in an "action" basket or a designated location on your desk. Process the "action" basket daily.

☐ File. For future reference. Jot a "toss" date on papers that will become obsolete.

This is the TRAF system of paper management, shorthand for the key concept of traffic—what moves in must move out.

Source: Stephanie Winston, president of The Organizing Principle and author of *The Organized Executive,* W.W. Norton & Co., New York.

Thoughts on problem-solving

The process involves the question of priorities and available time.

☐ Convoluted decisions consume time and energy.

☐ Do not shy away from sticky problems, but be realistic about investing effort in either the trivial or the intractable.

Political view:

☐ Association with certain decisions determines your track record, but not all decisions will stick in others' minds.

☐ Beware of involvement in messy problems that have no good solutions—but that others are likely to remember.

Source: *Whatever It Takes* by Morgan W. McCall, Jr., Center for Creative Leadership, Greensboro, NC. Prentice-Hall, Englewood Cliffs, NJ.

Antiques: Spotting the real thing

Guidelines to help you get the antique you think you're paying for:

☐ Wedgwood. The only way to determine if a piece of Wedgwood is old or recent (assuming it bears the impressed mark of Wedgwood) is by close examination of the raised relief molding. The earlier works have greater depth and more delicacy.

☐ Porcelain. The Chinese made porcelain a thousand years before anyone else. Pieces that were copied at a later date may have had the original identifying marks copied also. Only a real expert can distinguish between the old and the very old.

☐ Pewter. The alloy of tin and other metals is easily identified by its color and appearance, which are more mellow and subtle than silver or silver plate. If a piece called pewter is marked Dixon or Sheffield, with a number on its underside, it is not pewter at all but Britannia metal, a substitute.

☐ Ironstone. Mason's ironstone, found largely in jugs made for the home and in dinner service, is the original only if the words "Mason's Patent Ironstone China" appear in capital letters on the bottom.

☐ Enamels. The term "Battersea enamel" has come to be used for old enamels made mostly in Battersea and other English towns in the 18th century. However, the piece could also have been produced within recent years in a factory in Birmingham, or even in the Czech Republic. The originals are of copper, surfaced with an opaque glass that was then hand-decorated with inked paper transfers taken from copper plates.

☐ Silver. Old Sheffield plate will show the copper where the silver plating has worn off. This generally means that the piece was made before 1850. Once a piece has been resilvered by modern electroplating methods, it is just about impossible to differentiate it from other kinds of silver.

☐ China. The patterns are not always an indication of age since copyright is a relatively new idea. In years gone by, one porcelain maker cheerfully borrowed the pattern of a predecessor. The only way to cope with the resultant identification problem, say the experts, is to look carefully until you become savvy enough to recognize a Staffordshire printed earthenware plate by the flowers of its border.

Antique auction do's and don'ts

Even inexperienced auction goers can find quality items—and not pay too much for them—if they know what to look for and how to proceed. Some simple guidelines:

☐ Examine the items carefully at the presale exhibition. Take along a tape measure and flashlight.

☐ Beware of wooden furniture with legs of a different wood. Chances are it has been put together from two or more pieces.

☐ When an item catches your interest, ask the attendant what price it is likely to bring—usually a pretty good estimate of what it will go for.

☐ If you can narrow your choice down to one item of each type, you don't have to attend the auction. Simply decide on the maximum you are willing to pay and place your bid in advance. If a piece isn't bid up to your price, the auctioneer will execute it for you at the next level of bidding.

☐ Understand auction terminology. Antique means only that an object is 100 years old or older. Style means only that; it does not mean it's from that period.

☐ Buyers do best in June, July, August and December, slow months at auction houses.

☐ Auctioneers never take anything back. They are not responsible for bidders' errors. If in doubt, take an expert along.

☐ Don't be overeager. It encourages bids from "phantom" buyers, bidding you up. Best not to open the bidding.

☐ Don't worry about bidding against dealers. They have to buy low enough to cover their overhead and make a profit.

Collecting firearms

Firearms are among the oldest and most distinguished collectibles. (Henry VIII was a keen collector, as were George Washington and Thomas Jefferson.) And because firearms have been made since the 14th century, the field is vast. No individual can be expert in every aspect.

☐ Most US collectors concentrate on Americana. For the past 40 years, they have tended to specialize—even down to a single gun series. A collector might choose the Colt Single Action Army group, the guns you see in Western movies, for example. They were called "the peacemakers" and "the thumb busters." The US Army adopted this series as a standard sidearm in 1873.

The criteria for collecting

☐ Aesthetics play a great role. The finer guns are exquisite. The engraving can be compared with the work of Faberge.

☐ Historical relevance is important, and so is condition.

☐ But quality and maker count more. Even excellent condition cannot make an ugly gun desirable.

☐ The big four are *Colt*, founded in 1836; *Remington*, founded in 1816; *Winchester*, founded in 1866 but really dating back to 1852, the same year as *Smith & Wesson*. (The last two companies trace their origin to the same firm.)

☐ Pairs are more valuable than singles. Also triplets: A rifle, a revolver and a knife made as a set, for example.

☐ Some collectors specialize in miniatures. These tiny weapons were a test of the gunsmith's art, and they were made for fun. (You can fire the little guns, though it's not advisable.) A society of miniature collectors exists.

☐ Modern engraved guns are also very collectible. In the last ten years, they've become a $15-million-per-year business. Colt, Remington and Winchester (among others) make them. The craftsmanship is magnificent. Some are the equal of anything done in the past. These are not replicas, and owners do not discharge them. One reason for collecting modern firearms is assurance of authenticity. However, after 1840, most US firearms were given serial numbers. If you own a weapon made after that date, a factory may have it on record.

Caring for a collection

☐ Rust is the great enemy. Try a light film of oil. Put on a pair of white cotton gloves, spray oil on the palm of one glove and rub the gun with it. If you use a rag, sweat from your hand will eventually mingle with the oil.

☐ Never fire a fine weapon. Well, hardly ever—only if the antique arm is not of much value. Black powder, outdated in the 1890s, is still available for shooting today. It is corrosive to metal and scars wood.

Do you need a license?

☐ Generally not, if they were made before 1898, the federal cutoff. But check with local authorities.

Source: R.L. Wilson, historical consultant for Colt Firearms Division.

The best books on restoring antiques

The care and repair of fine treasures from the past is a craft in itself and a satisfying hobby to many collectors. The following books are excellent guides to repair techniques. Most are out of print but can be found in large public libraries and museum libraries.

☐ *China Mending and Restoration: A Handbook for Restorers* by Cual & Parsons, London, 1963.

☐ *The Painter's Methods and Materials* by A.P. Laurie, New York, 1960.

☐ *Pigments and Mediums of the Old Masters* by A.P. Laurie, London, 1914.

☐ *Antiques, Their Restoration and Preservation* by A. Lucas, London, 1932.

☐ *The Artist's Handbook of Materials and Techniques* by Ralph Mayer, New York, 1957.

☐ *The Care of Antiques* by John Fitzmaurice Mills, Hastings House, New York, 1964.

☐ *Care and Repair of Antiques* by Thomas H. Ormsbee, Medill McBride Co., New York, 1949.

☐ *The Preservation of Antiques* by H.J. Plenderleith, New York, 1956.

☐ *The Art and Antique Restorer's Handbook* by George Savage, Praeger, New York, 1967.

☐ *Restoring and Preserving Antiques* by Frederick Taubes, Watson-Guptill, New York, 1963.

☐ *Handbook of American Silver and Pewter Marks* by C. Jordan Thorn, Tudor Publishing Co., 1949.

☐ *How to Restore China, Bric-a-Brac and Small Antiques* by Raymond F. Yates, Harper, New York, 1953.

Source: David Rubin, antique expert, Springfield, MA.

How to hang an investment-quality oriental rug

Done the wrong way, hanging may distort the shape and diminish the value of a valuable rug. To do it right:

☐ Top-stitch two rows of the hook side of hook-and-loop Velcro fabric fastener to the back of one end of the rug.

☐ Hot-glue the loop side to a board cut to match the rug's width.

☐ Bolt (not nail) the board to the wall.

The Velcro will hold the rug evenly without letting it stretch out of shape.

Book collecting: A time-tested hedge against inflation

As with other investments, book values act according to the laws of supply and demand. But over the years, quality books almost always appreciate in value. In addition, like art, books offer a return in aesthetic pleasure above and beyond monetary investment.

Investors who know what they're doing often have collections that appreciate in value by 20% annually.

Four principal ways to invest:

☐ First-edition classics. Collecting these books is much like collecting art masterpieces. You are competing against professionals and prices are very high. The likelihood of finding bargains is remote.

☐ First-edition nonclassics. Try to anticipate which of today's first editions will be highly valued in the future. Because these books are not yet classics, the investor risks only the book's current market price. Look for authors or subjects you like. If the book doesn't appreciate, at least you have an enjoyable item.

☐ Specialize in books by or about one author or subject. By choosing a slightly unusual author or topic, one can build a valuable collection even though it isn't in first editions. And the cost isn't exorbitant.

☐ Book clubs. These make for a much less time-consuming way to collect. You don't have to have great hunches or compete against professionals. But you must be sure to join the right club. *Recommended:* The Limited Editions Club (551 Fifth Ave., New York 10017). Because it prints only 2,000 copies of the 12 books it puts out each year (a member is required to buy all 12), each book is automatically rare. It also gets top artists to illustrate them. They are all autographed by the authors or artists. Membership is limited to 2,000, so you may have to be put on a waiting list.

Basic investment guidelines:

☐ Only invest if you love books. Book collecting is not a sure thing for everyone, and an investor must get pleasure from his books in noneconomic ways.

☐ Don't follow the crowd. If you decide to collect books by or about an author or subject, be sure to avoid the obvious choices. Shakespeare and the Civil War are two examples of subjects so popular and widely printed that it's unlikely most collections will appreciate. Don't invest more than 10% of your investable assets.

Source: Louis Ehrenkrantz, Ehrenkrantz & King, New York.

Caring for fine books

Proper care is essential to preserve them, but it need not be a burden. Some basic information:

☐ Store them in a bookcase that is protected from direct sunlight. Sunlight fades the print and can cause the printing to transfer.

☐ Keep them in a room that is cool and not too dry. Overheating warps books and yellows the pages.

☐ Bookworms are not a serious problem. If they turn up, seal the book in a large plastic bag with some paradichlorobenzine mothballs for a month. (Put the mothballs in a small cardboard box with holes in it, so that the mothballs don't touch the book itself.)

☐ Dust the books regularly.

☐ Use bookmarks.

☐ Never lay a book face down—that cracks the binding.

Source: Louis Ehrenkrantz, Ehrenkrantz & King, New York.

Getting started investing in art

The art market isn't out of the small investor's price range. There are still investment-quality prints going at auction for a few hundred dollars. Some 16th- and 17th-century oils attributed to known artists can be had for around $5,000. Lesser-known American Impressionists' paintings run $1,000–$2,000.

Collect what's appealing. Become an expert on a period, an artist or a school. How to do it:

☐ Visit museums, art shows and galleries. To find an artist to your taste, flip through a museum's print collection.

☐ Ask curators about the artist, which galleries sell the paintings and their recent selling prices.

☐ Buy two or three works right away. Plunging in speeds learning. Bargains are the artist's early work, drawings, watercolors, smaller canvases and, frequently, posters announcing an exhibition of the artist's work.

☐ Develop relationships with galleries. Use business trips to visit major dealers in other cities. Many galleries have work by living artists that's not on display but worthy of attention. Ask to see it.

☐ Visit auctions and begin to bid. *Remember:* Dealers mark up by 100% the art they buy at auctions. Overbidding a dealer by a few dollars results in a big saving.

☐ Avoid mail-order prints. They may be part of multiple editions with only minor variations, which have little, if any, real investment potential.

Finding bargains in art

Primary advice: Buy what you like, but buy quality—the best examples that you can find and afford.

☐ Because of the preference for oil paintings in today's art market, drawings and sculpture are better buys.

☐ Less popular subjects—some portraits, animals, religious paintings, violence—are often less expensive.

☐ Paintings that are under or over the most popular size (two feet by three feet to three feet by four feet) tend to cost less.

☐ Works that are not in an artist's most typical or mature style are usually less expensive.

☐ Avoid the currently stylish. Investigate the soon-to-be-stylish.

☐ Works of western art that are not attributed or authenticated can be cheap, but they are bad investments. A work with an authentic signature and date is always worth more than one without them.

Source: Steven Naifeh, author of *The Bargain Hunter's Guide to Art Collecting,* New York.

Insuring paintings

☐ If you have art holdings valued at over $5,000, insure them separately. The standard homeowners' policy does not list artworks individually, and valuation isn't made until after the object has been lost, making it difficult to settle a claim. *Also:* Standard policies do not take into account the tendency of art to appreciate rather than depreciate in value.

☐ A fine-art floater can be purchased as an extension of your regular policy. This will list each object at its appraised value, providing all-risk coverage that includes all loss and damage.

☐ Have your art collection reappraised every two or three years. Change the policy accordingly.

☐ Buy all-risk insurance, including loss and damage.

☐ If you plan to lend a work, get "wall-to-wall" coverage, which insures the work from the moment it leaves your custody until its return.

☐ *Standard exclusions in art policies:* Damages from wear and tear or stemming from restoration, moths, normal deterioration, war and nuclear disaster.

Source: "Investor's Guide to the Art Market," *ART Newsletter,* New York.

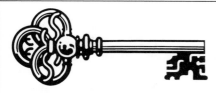

Collecting bronze sculpture

In the world of our grandparents and great-grandparents, no home was without its bronzes. Even families with modest incomes could afford these commercially produced pieces.

A recent revival of interest in sculpture of all kinds has created a lively market in old bronzes as well. They are plentiful, decorative and easy to take care of (with a feather duster).

Collecting categories

☐ Academic or salon sculpture. These realistic 19th-century bronzes from Europe and America were cast in a variety of subjects—portrait busts, prancing putti of India, laboring peasants and nudes. They provide a good starting point for beginners. *Important sculptors:* Jean Baptiste Carpeaus, Jules Dalou, Achille d'Orsi.

☐ Animal sculpture. A school of French artists led by Antoine-Louis Bayre produced sculptures of horses, dogs, lions and hunting scenes that are prized for their fine modeling and realistic movement. *Important artists:* Pierre-Jules Mene, Georges Gardet, Emanuel Fremiet, Alfred Dubucand. Attractive pieces are available starting at about $100, though name artists command more.

☐ Art Nouveau and Art Deco. Popular with collectors who specialize in all designs of these periods, these styles are subject to current fashion. Modest Art Nouveau and Art Deco pieces, particularly by American designers, can be found for $500–$5,000. Many Deco bronzes are of athletes. ("Pushing men" bookends are typical and popular.)

☐ American West sculpture. The peak of this craze has passed, but prices are still very high for this area of Americana. Frederic Remington's work is out of most collectors' reach. Western sculpture by other artists is a less secure investment, but, of course, it is also less expensive.

☐ Impressionist and Early Modern. Bronzes by established artists of this era are considered fine art rather than decorative objects and are available only through auctions and galleries. Works by Rodin, Daumier, Degas, Maillol, Picasso, Henry Moore, Brancusi, etc., have proven to be sound investments, but they are extremely expensive —from $100,000 to well over a million dollars.

☐ Museum specialties. Medieval, Renaissance, baroque, oriental and African bronzes require study and connoisseurship and attract only a few independent collectors. Expert advice is essential if you consider buying one of these.

Factors that affect value

☐ Fame of artist or founder. Signatures or foundry marks should be crisp and clear. (Fakes abound.)

☐ Edition. A rare and limited edition is more valuable than a common one. But records of most 19th-century bronzes are sketchy. Many pieces then were cast in thousands. And the records vary for established artists.

☐ Condition. Original condition is preferable. However, it is acceptable to have 19th-century bronzes repatinated or repaired in a reputable foundry if necessary.

☐ Size. This is a matter of fashion. In recent years, the demand (and prices) is greatest for very large pieces appropriate for outdoor settings.

Spotting fakes

☐ A piece slightly smaller than an original (made from a cast of the original) is probably a forgery. Fakes also may vary in color, weight and clarity of detail.

☐ Bronzes that have been epoxied to a marble base so you can't check the hollow interior.

☐ An unnaturally even "Hershey-bar brown" color.

☐ Color that can be removed with nail-polish remover or scratched with a fingernail.

☐ A ghost impression around the signature or foundry mark.

☐ Air bubbles, bumps and craters around the base (good 19th-century craftsmen would have hand-finished such imperfections).

Source: Alice Levi-Duncan, Jody Greene and Christopher Burge, Christie's, New York.

Collecting coins for investment

Collector-investors approach their coins with a higher level of commitment than hobbyists. *Main difference:* They spend significant amounts of money in the hope of reaping financial rewards.

Salient facts about the market

☐ The market for US Treasury-minted coins was once fairly steady, since only collectors bought and sold. But starting in the mid-1960s, noncollecting investors began to move cash in and out of the market, buying and selling coins as speculative investments much as they might stocks and bonds. This injection of volatile money transformed a relatively steady market into one of cycles, with booms and busts.

☐ Experienced collector-investors and dealers sometimes use their expertise to take advantage of the novice investor and stick him with junk.

How to avoid being skinned

☐ Study before making major money investments. Background knowledge helps keep you from being cheated. There are a number of books about each major US coin series. These volumes discuss the historical background of the coins. *Examples:* How well the coins were struck and the condition of the dies when the coins were made. The rare years and common years for the coins and dozens of variations that make each coin distinct from others.

☐ Check prices. The coin books often give values for the coins, but these are usually out of date. For the latest figures, consult coin collectors' newsletters.

☐ Learn from dealers. Get acquainted with several to gain a sense of them as people. Be alert to their willingness to protect beginners from their own errors.

☐ But do not depend on the advice of dealers for long. To wean yourself away, spend lots of time at coin shows and auctions. Learn to identify and grade individual coins and note their sale prices. Subscribe to and study the literature read by professionals.

Other guidelines

☐ Sell part of your collection every year. This shows you whether or not you knew what you were doing when you bought. Sell duplicates for which you have better samples, coins from periods that no longer interest you and samples that have lost their fascination.

☐ Take good care of your coins. The value of a coin does not depend entirely on the market cycle. It can drop rapidly from poor handling or cleaning or even from coughing on the coin. Avoid plastic holders made from polyvinylchloride (PVC). This material breaks down with time and releases an oil that oxidizes the copper in coins, turning them green and oily. (Although damaged coins can be cleaned, they never look the same to an experienced eye.)

Source: Dr. Martin G. Groder, consultant to a coin dealership in Durham, NC.

Collecting movie posters

Movie posters shouldn't be purchased primarily as investment items. They are fun items for movie fans rather than graphic art collectors.

☐ By 1911 there were 10,000 movie theaters, with posters promoting films of scenery, exotic places, romance, comedy and sexy dances. These historical posters are rare and expensive.

☐ Pick a movie type. Epics, adventure stories, comedies, Western melodramas, "problem" stories, romance/sex subjects, literary classics, mysteries and crime are each a popular collecting category. Movie studios began to produce features, five-reel films that ran for over an hour, in 1912. (The first epic, *The Birth of a Nation*, appeared in 1915.)

☐ The silent films produced in the era following WWI are a relatively untapped area for poster collectors.

☐ Favorite movie stars may be the major reason collectors go hunting for posters. When a star has caught the imagination of many, the supply of posters becomes scarce.

☐ The impact of television in the past two decades has caused the number of new movies and the theaters showing them to dwindle drastically, greatly reducing the number of posters produced. Particularly scarce are posters for blockbuster movies such as *Star Wars* and the gory horror pictures that appeal to teenagers, who quickly gobble up the supply. Contemporary posters may grow in value if the trend continues.

☐ Prices of movie posters do not necessarily increase with age as they do with other paper collectibles. Supply and demand determine cost, which can run from $10 to $1,000.

☐ Perfect condition raises prices.

☐ Reproductions costing $6–$10 are available for some of the most popular films of the past, but these are not valuable.

☐ New York and Los Angeles have the largest supply of movie memorabilia. Ads in film magazines can provide leads to local stores and mail-order sources.

Source: Ernest Burns, owner of Cinemabilia, which sells movie memorabilia.

Collecting color posters

Posters caught the public's fancy in the 1880s and have retained a fascination for collectors ever since.

☐ *Categories for collectors:* Circus, theater, ballet, movies, music halls and both World Wars.

☐ *Posters in constant demand:* Those connected to avant-garde art that combine strong typographic design with photomontage.

☐ *Rare finds:* Work from the 1920s associated with the Bauhaus, the Dada movement and Russian Constructivism. Constructivist film posters made in 1925–31 most often measure about 40 inches by 28 inches. *Classic example:* Any of the few advertising the film *The Battleship Potemkin.*

☐ *Best buys:* Automobile posters (except those for American cars, which are not of very good quality). *Star:* The Peugeot poster by French artist Charles Loupot.

☐ Beginners should look at Japanese posters made from the mid-1970s to the present. *Also recommended:* Post-World War II Swiss posters for concerts and art exhibits. Posters of note since World War II include those of Ben Shahn and the San Francisco rock posters of the 1960s.

☐ *Best:* Stick to recent foreign posters made in limited editions and not distributed beyond their place of origin.

☐ *Poster condition:* Creases and small tears in the margin are acceptable. (The quality standards are not quite as stringent for posters as they are for prints.)

Source: Robert Brown, co-owner of Reinhold Brown Gallery, New York.

Collecting bottles

Collecting bottles is one of the most popular pastimes in the field of antiques. Besides the age-old allure of glass itself, bottles offer a collector a wide variety of types to choose from, generally moderate prices and a range of sizes and colors.

Prime sources of collectible bottles include attics and basements, barns, flea markets and antique dealers.

Although there are many subdivisions to specialize in, most bottles available to a collector fall into the following categories:

☐ Spirits bottles. Large, crude, dark-colored bottles in which whiskey was shipped to the American colonies from England; "seal" bottles to hold smaller quantities of liquor; ribbed and swirled pint-sized flasks made by the Pitkin Glassworks in Connecticut in the 1780s; 18th- and 19th-century decanters.

☐ Medicinal bottles. 19th-century patent-medicine bottles; bitters bottles; pharmaceutical bottles, including the deep blue ones that held poisons.

☐ Household bottles. Late 19th- and early 20th-century bottles that held everything from mineral water to soda pop to vinegar to ink. Milk bottles are especially popular.

☐ Personal bottles. Late 19th- and early 20th-century bottles for such substances as cologne, smelling salts and ammonia.

Tips for collecting:

☐ Because prices vary widely, consult a reputable dealer before buying.

☐ Keep in mind that condition is a major determinant of price.

☐ Guides to collecting, including price guides, are available at libraries and bookstores.

☐ The Corning Glass Museum in Corning, NY, is a superb place to see a wide variety of bottles.

☐ Subscribe to a newsletter, such as *Antique Bottle World*, Chicago.

Source: William Delafield, Bottles Unlimited, New York 10021.

Collecting seashells

Seashell collecting is a just-for-the-fun-of-it hobby, not something to do if you have investment appreciation in mind.

Begin by collecting as many types of shells as appeal to you. This way you can learn their names and become familiar with the distinctive qualities of each type. Most collectors are eventually drawn to one or two species and narrow their scope.

Prices within every species range from 25¢ to several thousand dollars. But it is easy to put together a very broad collection of several thousand shells for $1–$10 apiece, with an occasional splurge into the $20–$25 range.

Most popular species:

☐ Cones (Conus). Cone-shaped shells that exhibit an astonishing variety in pattern and color.

☐ Cowries (Cypraea). Very rounded shells, with lips rolled inward to reveal regularly spaced teeth. Naturally so smooth, hard and glossy that they appear to have been lacquered, they are often considered the most pleasurable shells to handle.

☐ Murexes. Swirling shells favored for their pointy spines, though many are delicate and hard to store.

☐ Scallops (Pectens). Shaped like ribbed fans in surprisingly intense reds, oranges, yellows and purples.

☐ Volutes (Voluta) and Olives (Oliva). Equally popular species.

Other hints:

☐ Stay away from lacquered shells.

☐ Avoid ground lips (an edge that has been filed will feel blunt rather than sharp).

☐ Get a label to accompany each shell, with its scientific name and location information.

Source: Jerome M. Eisenberg, The Galleries at La Jolla, and William Gera, The Collectors' Cabinet, New York.

Art appraisal: Some definitions

What's it worth? In an art appraisal, the word "value" can have several different meanings.

☐ Fair market value: The price at which an item would change hands between a willing and informed seller and a willing and informed buyer.

☐ Replacement value: The amount it would cost to replace the item with a similar one.

☐ Estimated value: Fair market value, but taking into account local conditions at the time of the sale (i.e., is the item "hot" right now?)

☐ Liquidation value: An item's value if it had to be sold today. Often the lowest determinable value.

A new hobby

Postcard collecting is an intriguing, low-budget hobby. Many thrift shops and flea markets sell cards for less than 25 cents apiece—and ephemera (collectibles such as posters and tickets that are not intended to have lasting value) shows have many dealers offering large selections. The cards touch on many subjects. Most hobbyists focus on themes such as early baseball, social history, small-town America or specific publishers or geographic areas.

Source: Kenneth W. Rendell, a leading collector of historical letters and documents and founder of the Kenneth W. Rendell Galleries in Beverly Hills, New York and Tokyo.

Surviving the over-the-counter stock market

Over-the-counter (OTC) stocks, being small and often not well followed by many brokers, are especially susceptible to rumors and false reports. Stockbrokers and underwriters flourish on heavy trading and are usually themselves the source of misleading reports. *Basic wisdom:* When a company sounds too good—its product will replace toothpaste—watch out!

☐ *Rule of thumb:* If you don't know why you own a stock—or why you're buying—or why you're selling—then you're in someone else's hands. This makes you more vulnerable to the caprices of the market.

☐ OTC stocks, particularly new issues, are usually short-term plays. One should never buy without having a sell target in mind.

☐ If the selling price is reached, even within a week of buying, stick to the sell decision unless there is some major mitigating factor you hadn't considered before.

☐ About 80% of all new issues will be selling below their issue price within 18 months. *Reason:* Most new issues are overpriced in relation to existing companies. But they are all destined to become just another existing company within a year.

☐ In evaluating a new issue, find out who the people involved are. If the underwriter is or has been the target of the Securities and Exchange Commission's investigations, this is often mentioned in the prospectus. The SEC prints a manual of all past violators. Avoid underwriters that have had lots of SEC problems. The strong companies rarely use them to go public.

☐ Check out the auditors of a new-issue company. (They will be named in the prospectus.) If the auditor is not well-known or is in trouble with the SEC, question the numbers in the financial reports.

☐ A danger in over-the-counter stocks is a key market maker who crosses buy and sell orders among its own brokerage customers so that the market price is artificial. If such a broker collapses, so will its main stocks. This illustrates the danger of buying a stock dependent on only a single market maker. To avoid such a problem, invest in stocks quoted on NASDAQ, where by definition there are at least two strong market makers, and hopefully a lot more.

☐ Spot companies just before they decide to go onto NASDAQ. When they do, their price inevitably rises because of the increased attention. Very often the managements will simply tell you if they have NASDAQ plans or not. *Tip-off:* If they've just hired a new financial man, it's often a sign of a move to NASDAQ.

Source: Robert J. Flaherty, editor of *The OTC Review*, Oreland, PA.

Techniques for evaluating over-the-counter stocks

☐ Growth potential is the single most important consideration. Earnings increases should average 10% over the past six years when acquisitions and divestitures are factored out.

☐ Cash, investments, accounts receivable, materials and inventories should be twice the size of financial claims due within the next year.

☐ Working capital per share should be greater than the market value of the stock (an $8 stock should be backed by $10 per share in working capital).

☐ Long-term debt should be covered by working capital, cash or one year's income.

☐ The balance sheet should show no deferred operating expenses and no unreceived income.

The criteria for final selections include:

☐ Ownership by at least ten institutions reported in *Standard & Poor's Stock Guide*.

☐ Public ownership of between 500,000 and one million shares, with no more than 10% controlled by a single institution.

☐ Continued price increases after a dividend or split.

☐ Strong likelihood of moving up to a major exchange. (A good sign is strong broker and institutional support.)

Avoid companies that are expanding into unrelated fields, where they lack the required management experience and depth and have stock selling at prices far below recent highs. This sign of loss of investor support can take months to overcome.

Source: C. Colburn Hardy, *Physician's Management.*

Takeover fever

If you own stock in a target company: Wait 24 to 48 hours to see how the stock price is affected by the takeover announcement. *If the price is near or just below proposed offer:* Bidding is at a fair price—sell all stock and take your profits. *If stock exceeds offer price within 48 hours:* Bidding will probably go higher—sell 20% to 50% of holdings to hedge against the deal falling through. *Advice for non-holders of target stocks:* Don't buy after the announcements. Individuals don't have access to the information needed to evaluate the high risks.

Source: A round-up of portfolio managers quoted in *The New York Times*.

Pointers from professional traders

Here's a collection of suggestions from some of Wall Street's savviest traders:

☐ If the market has already risen for five to six weeks, it is almost always too late to make new purchases with safety. *Possible exception:* The first months of a fresh bull market.

☐ *Strongest short-term market periods:* Last trading day of each month and first four trading days of the subsequent month. Days before holidays often show good market strength, too.

☐ If a stock has not made a new high within a five- to six-week period, there is a good chance that its intermediate trend is about to turn down.

☐ If a stock fails to make a new low five to six weeks after a decline, there's a good chance its intermediate trend is about to turn up.

☐ Count the weeks from one significant market bottom to another and from one significant market top to another. Strong market advances often start at intervals of from 20 to 26 weeks. Severe declines often start at the same intervals.

☐ Before buying preferred stocks of blue-chip companies, investors should consider that the same company's bonds may yield ¼% to ½% more.

Reading index futures for stock-market signals

Trading in stock-index futures contracts is too volatile for many investors. But they can be used as a reliable forecaster of short-term market swings and, therefore, can be valuable.

How index futures relate to day-to-day trading:

☐ Index futures generally lead the stock market. If the market is down for the day but the price of contracts is up, expect the market to swing upward. Conversely, if the market is up but index futures are down, expect the market to turn down within a day or two.

☐ When the *Value Line* and *Standard & Poor's* indexes gain more than the contracts, the market is bearish. If the indexes lose less than the contracts, the market is bullish.

☐ If futures contracts continue to rise after the stock market closes, expect a good opening for stocks the next day. If they fall after the stock market closes, expect the market to open mixed or down the next day.

☐ The market will often change direction when the premium paid for futures contracts exceeds or falls below the actual market indexes by about 2.5% to 3%. If the stock market rises but premiums for futures contracts decrease, expect a downside market reversal within a day or two.

☐ *Caution:* These trends apply to short-term market swings only.

Stock-market advisory letters

If you buy market letters, first look carefully at their performance record. Checking their investment philosophy is also extremely important.

Bear in mind:

☐ Stocks most recommended by investment advisers as a group consistently underperform the Dow Jones industrial and *Standard & Poor's 500* averages. This has proven true in all time periods checked.

☐ Stocks that are recommended by the best-performing market letters slightly outperform the averages.

☐ Equities owned by investment advisers—as distinct from those they merely recommended—consistently outperform market averages.

☐ Even when advisory-letter recommendations drive up the price of a stock, as they often do, the odds of making a profit favor those who sell those stocks within three months of the original recommendation. After that, stocks decline from lack of interest or are overtaken either by events or by more recent recommendations. *Caution:* Investors should not necessarily dump a premier growth stock based on market-letter recommendations. There are always other fundamentals to consider.

☐ Investors who buy a stock they know little about just because a market letter is pushing it should be aware that the push soon dissipates. Moreover, advisers often fail to tell subscribers when a previous pick goes sour.

☐ Low-priced issues (those under $10) outperform high-priced stocks.

☐ Stocks with a high price/earnings ratio outperform low p/e ratio stocks. This finding goes against traditional Wall Street wisdom. *Possible explanation:* Stocks for which investors have high enough hopes to pay a premium generally tend to fullfill those hopes.

☐ Market letters have a huge bias toward buy advice as opposed to sell recommendations. This is particularly true of market letters published by big brokerage houses. These letters are highly edited to make sure they don't offend clients in other areas of the firm's business.

☐ Limit stock purchases to issues recommended by the top-performing advisers in industries recommended by the best-performing forecasters.

Source: George H. Wein, president, *Select Information Exchange*, New York.

Following insider stock trading

No one knows a company better than those who run it—the officers, directors and, usually, owners of large chunks of stock, too. Fortunately for investors, the law requires these insiders to report stock trades within their own companies. Investors who follow those insider trades generally outperform the market significantly over time. But watching insider trading is a sophisticated art, full of pitfalls for the unwary.

☐ Widespread insider buying in the open market (not through the exercise of stock options) is a clearer market signal than insider selling. That's because people have many reasons for selling. They might need cash for their children's college tuition or a down payment on a home. But they buy largely for one specific reason—they have inside information that leads them to believe that the price of company stock will go up.

☐ About 35% of insider transactions on the open market are usually buys, and 65% are sells. When this ratio changes significantly, it's an important signal for investors to follow the same trend.

☐ Share or dollar volume of insider trading is far less important than the number of insiders that are buying or selling. Unanimity among insiders—all buyers or all sellers—is very significant.

☐ Look at who is buying and who is selling. In general, trades made by the company president or its chairman are most significant.

☐ Insider trading is easier to read in smaller companies than in big ones.

☐ Insider trading is valid as an indicator for all industries except the brokerage industry. *Reason:* It has so many insiders with so many kinds of private purchases that there are normally very few buyers and lots of sellers. This makes data too confusing to interpret.

☐ Insider trading is not an infallible indicator of future stock prices. Over the entire market, it's accurate about 75% of the time. *Important:* Insider buying will push stock prices relatively higher than insider selling will cause a price drop.

☐ Stock moves generally follow insider trading gradually over 12 to 24 months. Investors can often climb aboard even if they're acting on information that's several months old.

☐ Insider trading can also be used to anticipate broad trends across the entire market, not just for individual stocks.

☐ As an aggregate indicator, insider trading is usually early by several months.

Source: Norman Fosback, publisher of the twice-a-month newsletter, *The Insiders*, Fort Lauderdale, FL.

How to spot a market decline before it starts

Strong market moves frequently end in one- or two-day reversal spikes. Those spikes often provide advance warning of significant market turning points. Checkpoints that show when a market decline may be coming:

☐ The market will rise sharply in the morning on very high volume running at close to 15 million shares during the first hour of trading.

☐ From 10:30 AM (Eastern time) on, the market will make little or no progress despite heavy trading throughout the day.

☐ By the end of the first day, almost all the morning's gains will have been lost, with the market closing clearly toward the downside. Occasionally, this process will be spread over a two-day period.

☐ *Steps to take:* When you see the pattern, either sell immediately or await the retest of the highs that were reached during that first morning. Such a retest often takes place within a week or two, on much lower trading volume. This may prove to be the last opportunity to sell into strength.

How bear-market rallies can fool you

Bear-market rallies are often sharp. They're fueled, in part, by short sellers rushing to cover shares. However, advances in issues sold short often lack durability once short covering is completed.

Here is what you need to know about bear-market rallies:

☐ They tend to last for no more than five or six weeks.

☐ Advances often end rapidly—with relatively little warning. If you are trading during a bear market, you must be ready to sell at the first sign of weakness.

☐ The first strong advance during a bear market frequently lulls many analysts into a false sense of security, leading them to conclude that a new bull market is underway. The majority of bear markets don't end until pessimism is widespread and until the vast majority are convinced that prices are going to continue to decline indefinitely.

☐ Although the stock market can remain "overbought" for considerable periods of time during bull markets, bear-market rallies generally end fairly rapidly, as the market enters into "overbought" conditions.

☐ Price/earnings multiples for the group soar far above historical norms.

☐ Heavy short-selling appears. Early short sellers of the stocks are driven to cover by sharp rallies. Their covering of shorts adds fuel to late rallies within the group. (Short sellers who enter the picture later, however, are likely to be amply rewarded.)

Trading tactics that work for professionals:

☐ Exercise extreme caution, first and foremost.

☐ Place close stop orders on any long and/or short positions taken.

☐ Enter into short sales only after these issues have shown signs of fatigue and of topping out, and then only after recent support levels have been broken.

☐ Wait for a clear sign that the uptrend has ended before selling out.

Spotting the bottom of a bear market

Here's how sophisticated investors recognize that a bear market is near its last phase:

☐ Downside breadth increases. That is, market declines become broader, including even stocks that have been strong before. More issues are making new lows.

☐ "Oversold" conditions (periods in which the market seems to decline precipitously) extend for longer periods of time. Technical recoveries are relatively minor.

☐ Pessimism spreads, but analysts and bullish advisories still discuss "bargains" and "undervalued issues."

☐ Stocks continue to be very sensitive to bad news. The market becomes very unforgiving of poor earnings reports and monetary difficulties.

☐ Trading volume remains relatively dull. Prices seem to fall under their own weight, the result of a lack of bids rather than urgent selling.

Important: The bear market isn't likely to end until pessimism broadens into outright panic, and until public and institutional selling become urgent. One of the most reliable nontechnical signals that the bear market is over is when the mass media begin to headline the fact that the stock market is hitting its bottom.

How to make money in market declines

Mistake: Most investors tend to place capital into the stock market following important market advances. This increases your risks.

Instead:

☐ Adopt a planned strategy of making investments in phases as the market declines. Market declines of greater than 10% are relatively unusual during bull markets and investors should look upon them as an opportunity.

☐ Don't take quick profits early in intermediate advances and reinvest quickly into new stocks. You miss the really good moves and simply incur additional commission costs.

☐ Prepare for market advances during periods of market decline. Determine which groups are best resisting market decline, and plan to purchase into such groups upon a 10% market decline. Hold for a minimum of several weeks, preferably months.

☐ Don't chase stocks that have already risen sharply in price, particularly when the price rise has been based upon speculative expectation.

☐ Try to ferret out true value—stocks in companies that feature solid balance sheets, regular earnings growth, increasing dividend payout.

☐ Avoid stocks with institutional followings. They tend to underperform the market.

☐ Study the market on days when trading is quiet. If such days show positive closing action, you can presume that the professionals are positioning themselves for market advance.

How to buy stock in an up market

Basic rule (expressed in exaggerated form here): There is never a second chance to buy a good stock. However, if the stock is genuinely strong, any downward correction is usually minor, so the longer you wait the more you'll pay. Don't be too concerned about getting in at the lowest price. If it's a good stock (and a steady rise in price

confirms that), it will probably be good even if you have to pay a bit more by not jumping in.

To handle that dilemma of either waiting for a correction or chasing it up:

☐ Consider that a stock has gotten "too far away" if it has already advanced three days in a row or gained 15% in price or both. You should have acted before the rise. But if you missed that point, wait.

☐ Stocks typically fall back by about 50% after a strong rally. (If the stock has grown from 25 to 30, a 50% retracement of that five-point gain would mean back to about 27⅔.)

☐ In order not to miss a stock you really want (one that didn't dip back to the buy-order level), jump on it the moment the stock shoots up past 30 (its prior high point) because that usually means the stock is on its way up again.

Knowing when to wait before buying

Investors often think they are buying stock at a bargain price, only to see it fall further because of an overall market falloff. Signs that such a falloff is ahead:

☐ Just before the decline, the market advance becomes very selective. Gains are recorded in just a few industry groups rather than across the board.

☐ Speculative interest runs high in the American Stock Exchange and over-the-counter markets.

☐ During the first phase of the decline, the stocks that failed to participate at the end of the previous advance show the most severe declines. The strongest industry groups tend to keep rising on short-term rallies. This pattern traps unwary traders who believe that stocks are at bargain levels.

☐ During the second phase of the decline, most groups participate, but the previously strong groups decline only slightly.

☐ During the final stages, even the once strong industry groups fall sharply. Odds are that the decline will soon come to an end. Wait for evidence that all segments of the market have declined before stepping in to buy.

☐ As a general rule, groups that were strongest during the previous rally will advance sharply when the market starts to recover, although they may not remain in the forefront throughout the next market cycle.

- ☐ Strong market rallies often take place at quarterly intervals.
- ☐ Leaders of one quarter often do not maintain leadership in the next upward cycle.

How to avoid selling too soon

If you're nervous about the direction of stock-market movement, adopt the following method to avoid selling securities just as the market may be gathering upside momentum:

- ☐ Each week, record the number of issues making new highs for that week on the New York Stock Exchange. (These and other key data are record-ed in *Barron's,* among other sources.)
- ☐ Maintain a moving four-week total of the number of issues making new highs on the NYSE.
- ☐ Presume that the intermediate uptrend is intact for as long as the four-week total of issues making new highs continues to expand. Investors can hold long positions in most issues without fear until the four-week total turns down.

Source: *Timing and Tactics*, Ventura, CA.

Selecting stocks: A disciplined approach

- ☐ Consistency. You want to see six consecutive years of 10% earnings growth in adjusted pretax earnings. To do this, eliminate interest income and gain or loss from the sale of property, plant or equipment. If accounting procedures change, adjust earnings so performance is comparable over the years. You are trying to strip away all illusion and get to the real numbers.
- ☐ Magnitude. Over the six-year period, adjusted pretax earnings (exclusive of acquisition and divestiture) must have shown a 20% annually compounded growth rate.
- ☐ Working capital. Look for very strong ratios and require:
- ☐☐ Two-to-one or better current ratio.*
- ☐☐ One-to-one or better quick asset ratio.**

*The ratio of current assets to current liabilities. The ratio determines how able the company is to pay its near-term debts (those due in a year or less).

**The ratio between existing liabilities and quick assets (cash and receivables without inventory). This is another measure of how able a firm is to pay off its liabilities rapidly with available funds.

- ☐☐ Working capital in excess of market valuation (shares outstanding multiplied by current market price).
- ☐ Corporate liquidity. Long-term debt must be covered by working capital, by cash and equivalents or by the latest 12-month cash flow.
- ☐ Accounting procedures. Eliminate companies if they follow deceptive, unconservative accounting practices. *Examples:* They defer operating expenses or prematurely realize revenues.
- ☐ Owner diversification. Investment-company ownership should be no more than 10% of outstanding shares.
- ☐ Price/earnings multiple. This must be under ten times estimated earnings for the current fiscal year.

Source: Barry Ziskin, *The Opportunity Prospector*, Brooklyn, NY.

Questions to ask before buying a stock

You'll want a "yes" answer to just about every one of these questions before taking a long position in a stock.

- ☐ Is the price/earnings ratio of the stock (price divided by latest 12-month earnings) well below the price/earnings ratio of the average listed issue?
- ☐ Have earnings of the company been rising at a steady rate over a period of years, preferably at a rate exceeding the rate of inflation?
- ☐ Has the company had a recent history of steadily rising dividend payouts?
- ☐ Has the stock recently risen above a clearly defined trading range that lasted for at least five weeks?
- ☐ If not, has a recent sharp decline ended with the stock trading on extremely high volume for that issue, without the price falling further?
- ☐ Have insiders of the company purchased more shares of the company than they have sold?
- ☐ Has the company recently purchased its own shares on the open market?
- ☐ Has the stock remained relatively undiscovered by the advisory services and brokerage houses? (One sign that an issue is near the end of a rise is that many advisory services suddenly begin to recommend its purchase.)

Source: Gerald Appel.

Blue chips

Buying cheap stocks, as measured by low stock prices in relation to the earnings per share, is a classic contrarian method of buying cheap, out-of-favor issues. *The big hope:* As the market recognizes the stock as a substantial performer, or earnings begin to rise, the market "votes" it a higher multiple. Therefore the stock price rises.

Applying the technique to blue-chip stocks:

☐ Stick with low-priced blue-chip companies that offer high yields and are strong financially. These issues give you a better chance of being well-positioned for a market rally and also provide a strong defensive position in case the market falls.

☐ When the market declines, blue-chip low price/earnings-ratio issues tend to go down less than the high flyers. While many fast-track investors may be down 20% or even 40% during a market pullback, most low p/e-ratio portfolios decline considerably less than the *Standard & Poor's 500* as a whole.

☐ Preserving capital during a bear market is at least as important as enhancing it during bull markets. Investors who stay fully vested, with their capital basically intact, are ready for the next market move upward. That prepares the low p/e-ratio investor to take advantage of the strong beginnings of a market rally.

Source: David Dreman, author of *The New Contrarian Investment Strategy* and managing director of Dreman, Gray & Emby, a New York-based investment firm.

Scam-avoidance checklist

Don't be a participant in your own financial downfall. Avoid…

☐ Anything that requires up-front cash to get rich quick.

☐ Anything that requires you to pay for the secrets of someone else's success.

☐ Anything that promises to make you or your house the envy of your neighbors.

☐ Anything that costs you money in order to save you money.

☐ Anyone who tells you that rather than working for your money, you should let your money work for you.

☐ Anyone who doesn't tell you in plain English what it is you're putting your money into.

☐ Anyone who doesn't have the time, inclination or willingness to let you get a second opinion about the proposed investment idea.

Source: Jonathan Pond, president, Financial Planning Information, Nine Galen St., Watertown, MA 02172, and author of *The New Century Family Money Book,* Bantam Doubleday Dell, New York.

How professionals spot a low-priced stock that is ready to bounce back

A top-quality large company selling at a high price/earnings multiple is less attractive than a lesser-quality company selling at a depressed price in terms of its past and future earning power, working capital, book value and historical prices.

What to look for:

☐ Stocks that have just made a new low for the last 12 months.

☐ Companies likely to be liquidated. In the liquidation process, shareholders may get paid considerably more than the stock is selling for now.

☐ Unsuccessful merger candidates. If one buyer thinks a company's stock is a good value, it's possible others may also come to the same conclusion.

☐ Companies that have just reduced or eliminated their dividends. The stock is usually hit with a selling wave, which often creates a good buying opportunity.

☐ Financially troubled companies in which another major company has a sizable ownership position. If the financial stake is large enough, you can be sure that the major company will do everything it can to turn the earnings around and get the stock price up so that its investment will work out.

There are also opportunities in stocks that are totally washed out—that is, situations where all the bad news is out. The stock usually has nowhere to go but up.

How to be sure a stock is truly washed out:

☐ Trading volume slows to practically nothing. If it's an over-the-counter stock, few if any dealers are making a market.

☐ No Wall Street research analysts are following the company any more.

☐ No financial journalists, stock-market newsletters or advisory services discuss the company.

☐ Selling of the stock by company's management and directors has stopped.

Signs of a turnaround:

☐ The company plans to get rid of a losing division or business. If so, learn whether the company will be able to report a big jump in earnings once the losing operation is sold.

☐ The company is selling off assets to improve its financial situation and/or reduce debt.

☐ A new management comes on board with an established track record of success with turnaround situations.

☐ Management begins buying the company's stock in the open market.

☐ Form 13d statements are filed with the SEC. (A company or individual owning 5% or more of a public company must report such holdings to the Securities and Exchange Commission.) If any substantial company is acquiring a major position in a company, it's possible a tender offer at a much higher price is in the wind.

Source: Robert Ravitz, director of research, David J. Greene & Co., New York.

Looking west for investments

Investors are looking to California today in spite—or because—of the publicity given to its economic problems. When the New England economy was described as being in collapse, shares in regional banks and savings-and-loans were available at bargain prices. Now that the New England economy has recovered, those who bought when prices were low have made a profit. A similar situation exists in California, where half the S&Ls are selling below book value. There's no reason to think the same script won't be played out, presenting profit opportunities for forward-thinking investors.

Source: Peter Lynch, legendary former manger of the Fidelity Magellan mutual fund.

Protect yourself

Rebalance your portfolio periodically to protect against market swings. If you put 60% of your portfolio into stocks, 30% into bonds and 10% into money-market funds—and the stock market chugged steadily up—your stock position could easily turn into 75% of your holdings. *Result:* You would be more vulnerable in a market decline than if you had kept only 60% in stocks. *To rebalance:* Add to lagging positions while trimming holdings that have done well.

Source: Kenneth Gregory, editor, *No-Load Fund Analyst,* Four Orinda Way, Suite 230-D, Orinda, CA 94563.

Picking small-company stocks

Most investors prefer recognized names and are willing to pay a big premium for them. Smaller, less-well-known companies can sell at a substantial discount from their private worth.

A company's private worth is what another company would pay to buy it outright.

Small companies have more room to grow. And because they are more likely to be controlled by the original owners, management's interests coincide with shareholders'.

☐ *Main investment criterion:* Cash flow in excess of what it needs in the business. Excess cash flow builds up pressure in the company—pressure to repurchase stock or go private, to make acquisitions, to increase dividends or to be taken over. *Point:* All of those are factors that can cause the private worth of the company to be realized.

☐ Buy many different stocks (at least 20), and be prepared to hold them for as long as three to five years. When you buy stock in an undervalued small company, you cannot be sure what will be the trigger that causes private worth to be realized…and how long it will take to happen.

☐ Look for above-average return on assets, combined with a below-average ratio of price to book value.

☐ Small does not necessarily mean high-tech. Investors traditionally overpay for high-growth, high-technology stocks. Mundane companies are much more likely to be undervalued.

☐ Don't pay much attention to earnings. They're only one component of cash flow. Down earnings can mask a fundamental positive change going on underneath.

☐ Don't bother trying to "get a feel for management." Management either produces decent results or it doesn't.

☐ Don't waste time trying to understand all the minutiae of a company before investing. Even little companies are extremely complex, and situations can change very rapidly.

☐ Don't try to time the market. No one out there has a long-term investing record built on market-timing alone. The investors who have made money over the long term are the ones who have made broad economic bets based on value.

Source: Charles M. Royce, president, Pennsylvania Mutual Fund, Inc. and Royce Value Fund, Inc., New York.

How to spot a small growth company—I

An analyst with an exceptional performance record tells how he spots attractive small companies. They usually have these specifics:

☐ Unconventional managers willing to take risks. Strong chief financial officer, marketing manager, research director. Executives who can and do play devil's advocate to the boss's ideas.

☐ A focus on where the company is going rather than where it has been. Be sure that the company is spending heavily from current revenues on the development of new projects.

☐ A company in a period of healthy transition. *Good sign:* Rising earnings after several years of flat results due to heavy R&D and marketing expenses.

What to avoid:

☐ Companies run by lawyers. To grow, a young company needs a chief executive who is willing to take risks. Such an approach is anathema to most legal minds.

☐ A management that responds to tough questions in a vague way.

Source: Bob Detwiler, partner, Fechtor Detwiler, Boston.

How to spot a small growth company—II

When you want a small growth company, look for:

☐ Current ratio (current assets to current liabilities) of 2:1 or better, a large amount of cash and little debt. Keep a wary eye on long-term lease obligations, which are, in effect, a form of indebtedness. Learn how heavy such obligations are and whether they will put an undue burden on the financial resources of the company.

☐ No recent accounting changes that artificially boost earnings.

☐ Inventories accounted for on the most conservative basis (LIFO rather than FIFO).

☐ Fast inventory turnover.

☐ Small number of shares outstanding. This will prevent institutional investors from taking a position in the stock, which can be disastrous if they decide to sell all at once.

☐ A return on equity of at least 17% and profit margins that are high in relation to industry norms.

☐ The company's tax rate. Be sure that if the company is paying less than the usual 35% tax rate, an increase in the rate isn't likely for several years. A big tax bill could wipe out any earnings gains for the year.

☐ Company annual reports for four to ten years. See if actual results live up to management's predictions.

Source: Charles Allmon, publisher, *Growth-Stock Outlook,* Bethesda, MD.

Picking the right industry at the right time

In addition to studying individual stocks, you should know which industries are likely to prosper and which are likely to suffer at various stages of the economic cycle.

When inflation fears predominate:

☐ *Strong groups:* Metals, gold, silver, natural-resource stocks, oil and gas and timber.

☐ *Weak groups:* Utilities, banks, finance companies and other interest-sensitive groups. Long-term debt instruments are dangerous.

When recession fears predominate:

☐ *Strong groups:* Drugs, insurance and basic food stocks.

☐ *Weak groups:* Autos, chemicals, steel, auto parts, textiles, appliance manufacturers and other cyclical industries.

When a recession is many months old:

☐ *Strong groups:* Autos, chemicals and other cyclical industries that usually move upward in anticipation of an economic turnaround.

☐ *Weak groups:* Defensive stocks.

At a time of strong economic recovery marked by sharply falling interest rates —the most favorable market climate of all—the most volatile industry groups usually do their best.

Stocks that benefit when oil prices fall

☐ Airlines. Fuel prices will be lower.

☐ Homebuilders. Interest rates fall because lower oil prices add liquidity to the system. Lower interest rates boost home-building activity.

☐ Restaurants. The nondiscretionary portion of the average paycheck is 86%. With more discretionary income, people will eat out more.

☐ Motel chains. There will be more auto travel.

☐ Automobiles. Lower gasoline prices.

☐ Retail industry. Another area buoyed by more discretionary spending.

☐ Brokerage industry. People may invest some of that extra money.

☐ Interest-rate-sensitive stocks. As rates fall, these companies benefit.

☐ Japan. The yen will rise and the Japanese economy becomes healthier due to lower oil prices.

Source: Barry Sahgal, managing director of research, Ladenburg Thalmann & Co., New York.

Investing in biotechnology companies

☐ Look at the company's valuation relative to its science and potential products. Does the company have a sound scientific staff working on products that address a solid market? Do the scientists have a good publishing track record in their field?

☐ Look at the competition. Is the company just another "me-too" firm trying to get a piece of an already heavily sliced pie?

☐ Look at the management. Who's running the company? Well-meaning scientists or skilled executives with a scientific background? Read what management says in the press, in annual reports and during meetings. If managers are talking through their hats, they probably won't be able to pull rabbits out of them.

☐ Look for staying power. Does the company have the cash to stay in the game for the long haul—through R&D (as well as a few years of clinical trials, in the case of human pharmaceuticals)? Does the company have at least four times its R&D budget as cash in the bank?

☐ Look at the price of the stock. The higher the price, the more difficult it will be for investors to recoup their investment—and then make a profit.

☐ Look at trends in the industry. Biotech abhors a vacuum. If there is a need, the industry will fill it.

☐ Look at the company's joint ventures. Biotech R&D burns up cash quickly. Joint ventures with big companies are pipelines to money—and staying power. *Remember:* The big companies had a good, inside look at the company before forming a partnership. If they were impressed by what they saw, it might be worth your time to consider investing in that firm, too.

Questions to ask before buying utility stocks

Utility stocks, more than most issues, are purchased for reliable income by conservative investors who may require current income from investment holdings.

Here are some guidelines to help avoid unpleasant surprises:

☐ Is the utility located in a state with a favorable regulatory climate? Some states make it very difficult for utilities to pass along rising costs to consumers; some states are more permissive. Typically, a state will grant the utility approximately two thirds of the rate increase requested.

☐ Does the utility have ample earnings from which to pay interest on any bonds outstanding? Utility companies are generally heavy borrowers of capital for expansion. Should a cash-flow bind develop, dividend payouts may have to be suspended, since bondholders hold first call on company assets. Earnings for the company should amount to at least 2.5 times the interest payments due on corporate notes, preferably more.

□ Does the utility have earnings sufficient to cover projected dividend payouts?

□ What is the relationship of the price of the shares to book value? If the company has plans to issue more shares, the price should be no lower than book value. Otherwise, shareholder equity will be diluted by such distribution.

□ Is the company paying out too high a percentage of earnings in dividends? Approximately 65% to 70% is average. The lower a percentage of earnings in dividend payout, the more protected the dividend.

□ Does the utility have excessive debt? Check the balance sheet for favorable asset-to-liability ratios.

Your broker should be able to provide the above information either via in-house research or access to *Standard & Poor's* ratings of corporations and corporate debt.

Buying new stock issues

□ Don't expect general stockbrokers and wire houses to service you on new issues as well as they do on conventional stock transactions. Find a source that specializes in such stocks by monitoring the formal announcements of new issues (called tombstone ads) that appear in *The Wall Street Journal*.

□ Identify the lead underwriter (the first name listed among the brokers handling a new issue), and keep track of what happens to the issues brought out by that underwriter over time. If prices in the aftermarket hold a premium above the issue price on a fairly consistent basis, call that underwriter directly.

□ Ask for the firm's biggest producer. When an issue is really hot, you can buy only so much. The superstar's allotment, however, is bigger. Tell him that you want to be on his primary mailing list for prospectuses. *Aim:* To get them as soon as they are issued.

□ Read the prospectuses carefully. Note people or firms (lawyers, accountants, etc.) where you have contacts. Ask them about the company. While they probably will not say much directly helpful, with experience you can do some very valuable reading between the lines.

□ Don't buy at the new-issue broker, hold the stock for a short time as the price runs up and then sell it through a wire house. If everyone runs out after the first day or week, the reputations of both the stock and the original underwriter are hurt. *Suggestion:* Tell the broker that you need some liquidity as soon as possible, and ask what you can sell in a short time without hurting the market. *A common practice:* Sell enough to get back the original investment at the issue price, and hold onto the rest for a free ride.

□ The best profit opportunities are in a down market. Companies that do go public then are usually stronger and will probably outperform, on average, companies brought out in a frothy market.

Source: Patrick Rooney, president of Rooney Pace, Inc., New York.

Balanced funds benefit you

Balanced funds own common stocks and a large percentage of interest-bearing securities—preferred stocks and bonds. Fund types:

□ Regular balanced funds are more heavily weighted toward stocks than bonds.

□ Income-oriented funds favor bonds.

□ Asset allocation, or asset manager, funds vary the blend of stocks, bonds and cash as circumstances dictate.

Benefits

□ Balanced funds offer diversification.

□ You only have to make one minimum initial purchase to get wide diversification.

Drawbacks

□ Investors seeking income might be better served by tax-free bond funds. Almost all balanced funds hold taxable, rather than tax-free, bonds.

□ Because they have significant portions of their assets in bonds, and sometimes in cash, balanced funds are likely to underperform stock funds over the long haul.

Young investors should probably not have a sizable portion of their assets in balanced funds, which are more appropriate for older investors with more conservative goals. Balanced funds also may be desirable for short-term investment needs.

Source: Sheldon Jacobs, publisher, *The No-Load Fund Investor*, Box 318, Irvington, NY 10533.

Dividend reinvestment plans

Some 1,000 corporations now offer stockholders special inducements to reinvest their dividends. *Important:* Dividend reinvestment plans should only be considered by an investor with a high degree of confidence in the future outlook of the issuing company.

What an investor should know about such offers:

☐ Some companies offer a 5% price discount. Buying additional stock this way eliminates brokerage commissions, although a few plans have a small service charge.

☐ Stockholders may be able to invest additional cash, saving more on commissions and price discounts.

☐ Reinvestment plans provide investment discipline for those who would otherwise fritter away small amounts.

☐ The agent for the plan will hold original shares for safekeeping and send a regular statement to the stockholder.

☐ One slight drawback is tax treatment. A private ruling* by the IRS states that any administrative service charges and brokerage fees that are subsidized by company reinvestment plans may be treated as additional dividend income to the investor.

☐ Reinvested dividends are still subject to income tax ($100 dividend exclusion could partially offset income-tax consequences. If some shares are put in a spouse's name, the exclusion is boosted to $200.)

*7830104, July 24, 1978.

Source: Ernest Sando, Georgeson & Co., New York.

Misperceived companies: An opportunity to make money

☐ Companies with excess assets against which an acquiring company can borrow. These are generally the most attractive companies for potential buyers or raiders. And that buying effort could raise the price of the stock.

☐ Firms with very little debt and very good borrowable assets. *Ideal:* A company with a lot of cash, inventory and salable real estate but very little bank debt. Make an estimate of how much an investor could borrow against these assets. If the borrowing power less the bank debt divided by the number of shares works out to be less than the price of the stock, look more closely at the company.

☐ Firms with undervalued real estate. One clue is the date real estate was purchased. Sometimes the book value of the real estate will appear in a financial footnote.

☐ Company assets that could be sold or spun off for substantial values.

☐ Companies with overfunded pension funds—i.e., funds with more assets than their liabilities to employees and retirees. An overfunded pension fund makes the company a more attractive buyout candidate.

Source: Norman Weiner, Oppenheimer & Co., Inc., New York.

What every mutual-fund investor must know now

Investors are pouring money into mutual funds at an unprecedented rate. Many are buying funds for the first time. Here are ten basic facts that mutual-fund investors should know:

1. Government-bond funds aren't risk-free. These days, a lot of people are moving money out of certificates of deposit (CDs) and into government-bond funds. They see "government" in a fund's name and think the returns are somehow guaranteed. While they are safer than nongovernment funds during periods of rising interest rates, even well-run government bond funds have posted double-digit losses.

The same holds true for municipal-bond funds. Just because a fund owns bonds issued by state and/or local governments doesn't mean there isn't a risk.

2. Money-market funds aren't investments. They masqueraded as investments during the early 1980s, when 10%-plus yields were available. But that was an aberration. Money-market funds are really just a temporary parking place for cash. Once you add taxes and inflation, you probably won't make any money with these funds. You would be much better off in stock and bond funds, providing you have a reasonably long-time horizon—seven or more years.

3. Everyone should own stock funds. That includes retirees. If you've made it to age 65, the actuarial tables indicate there's a good chance you'll live another 20 years. That's plenty of time to successfully invest in stocks. The idea that you retire, buy bonds and clip coupons for the rest of your life is very dangerous. Because of the threat to your standard of living from inflation, you've got to own some stock funds.

4. Load funds don't perform better. Just because a fund charges a sales commission, or "load" as it's known in mutual-fund lingo, doesn't mean you're going to get superior performance. The commission is there to compensate the broker who sells you the fund. If you don't need that service, you can save some money by going the no-load route and buying funds that don't charge a sales commission.

5. High expenses can mean low returns. In the 1990s, investment returns are likely to continue lower than they were in the 1980s. As a result, it's critical that you don't shortchange your investment returns by buying funds with high annual expenses. Right now, stock funds charge average annual expenses of 1.5%, taxable bond funds levy an average of 1% and municipal-bond funds and money-market funds charge about 0.75% annually. Any time you see a fund with above-average expenses—beware.

6. Fund investment minimums aren't set in stone. Many of the top-notch no-load fund groups will waive their minimums if you sign up for an automatic investment plan—so that every month at least $50 is withdrawn from your bank account and put directly into a fund.

Other fund groups offer similar services. *Warning:* If you use automatic invest-

ment plans, it becomes tougher to figure out your capital gain or loss when you sell your fund shares, so be prepared for some tax headaches.

7. Selling a mutual fund isn't always painless. Unless you're selling a money-market fund, you can never be sure what share price you are going to get. You might need a signature guarantee from a bank before you can redeem your shares. And you may have to pay certain fees when you sell—a back-end sales charge.

8. Good funds can have bad fund managers. Before buying a fund, you should find out how much of the fund's record is attributable to the current fund manager. Some funds are run by individual managers, and some are run by committee. If a fund is run by a single portfolio manager, a change of manager may have a big impact on how the fund performs.

9. No fund performs well all the time. That's why you should own a mix of different funds. A lot of people look at the lists of leading fund performers and buy a bunch of funds just because they've been at the top of the performance charts for the past year or the past three years.

But if you do that, you are likely to end up buying funds that have been on a hot streak—and that have all used essentially the same investment style. If that style goes out of favor, all your funds could get battered at the same time.

Most investors should own a variety of funds that use different investment styles. To find out how a fund manages money, look at its annual report and see what sort of securities the fund buys. Alternatively, talk to one of the fund's phone representatives or look in the financial press and see if you can find an interview with the fund's portfolio manager.

10. There are some top-notch funds you may want to avoid. These funds may take more risk than you're comfortable with.

In addition to knowing how well a fund can perform, it is also important to know how badly the fund can do. Even the best funds go through rough patches. The severity of these losses can affect your ability to stick with a fund and thus enjoy the wonderful returns that it boasts about in its advertising. Look at the fund's year-by-year results and see how much you could have lost—and how long it took for the fund to recoup those losses. If the fund's past losses seem unbearable, don't buy it.

Source: Don Phillips, publisher of *Morningstar Mutual Funds,* a newsletter that evaluates and ranks mutual funds, Chicago.

Stock options as an alternative to buying on margin

Aggressive investors who think the market will advance often buy options instead of buying stock on margin.

Advantages:

☐ The choice of options avoids margin-interest charges, which can be very high when the prime rate is high.

☐ There's a much smaller loss if the stock drops sharply.

☐ If the stock goes up as expected, the profit will be almost as big as with buying on margin.

Disadvantages:

☐ Loss to the investor is larger if the stock doesn't move at all.

☐ Profits will be taxed as a short-term gain rather than long-term.

How to read a mutual-fund prospectus

A mutual-fund prospectus is not easy reading. The way to pry out the information needed to make a good investment decision is to focus on the following questions:

☐ Does the fund's portfolio mesh with your investment goals? Some funds have highly volatile portfolios and employ leverage or margin-selling to enhance return, but at greater risk.

☐ What's the fund's performance record? Select a fund that has matched or surpassed *Standard & Poor's 500* during periods of both rising and falling markets. Most prospectuses include several years' performance data. Best performers are usually funds with less than $50 million in assets.

☐ What are the minimum initial and subsequent investments? The lower the better.

☐ Is there a switch privilege? It is highly desirable to pick a fund that allows investors to switch back and forth between a firm's equity and money-market funds by phone. (Some funds charge for switching, but the charges usually don't amount to much, except for the frequent trader.)

☐ Are there fees for opening and closing an account? There is no reason to pay such fees.

☐ Is it a load (i.e., sales commission) fund or a no-load? As a group, no-load funds, those without sales commissions, perform pretty much as well as those with fees.

☐ What are the limitations on how the fund can invest money? Some funds must diversify their portfolios, while others allow management to concentrate highly on one or more industry groups. As a general rule, diversification reduces risk.

☐ Does the fund have a policy of moving into cash during bear markets? While a fund can cut losses this way, it may also delay reinvestment in equities when the market starts to rise. Long-term holders often adopt the strategy of investing in funds that have a record of increasing cash positions by selling equities before bear markets or at least at their earliest stages.

Source: *Switch Fund Advisory*, MD.

Evaluating a mutual fund

Before taking a position in a mutual fund, answer these questions:

☐ Does the fund suit your tolerance for risk? Certain funds are extremely volatile in price action. They suit investors with risk capital better than those who cannot afford to run the risk of a sharp decline in their capital. Secure a price history on the fund, either from the fund itself or by visiting the public library of a financial publication. Analyze the fund's historical ups and downs.

☐ Does the fund have a good track record during declining markets? Does the management make an attempt to reduce portfolio exposure during down markets or does the fund generally stay fully invested? Don't expect helpful answers to questions like these from a commissioned salesperson for the fund.

☐ Has the fund's management altered policies in the past counter to your own investment objectives? Certain funds are steadily increasing redemption charges to discourage trading. Or they're imposing restrictions that may not suit your purposes. Verify the facts in the current prospectus. Inquire if any changes are contemplated.

Fitting your psychology to a mutual fund

Techniques useful to investors for evaluating performance…

For aggressive investors:

☐ Each week that the market rises, divide the closing price of the mutual fund at the end of the week by the closing level of either the *Standard & Poor's 500* Stock Index or the NYSE Index. Plot the results on a graph for comparison. If the fund is indeed stronger than the average during a rising market, it will show up clearly, indicating that it is suitable for an aggressive investor.

☐ Remember that since such funds also frequently decline more sharply than the averages during falling market periods, they may be suitable only for investors with an accurate sense of market timing.

For safety-oriented investors:

☐ Each week the market declines, divide the closing price of the mutual fund at the end of the week by the closing level of one of the averages. If your fund resists the downtrend more than the average stock during a falling market, the plotted results will show the fund's line declining less than that of the average.

☐ Don't be disappointed when mutual funds advance less than more aggressive funds during rising market periods.

For investors who want to try to beat the averages:

☐ At the end of each week divide the price of the mutual fund (rising or falling) by the price of one of the broad market averages, and plot the results. The result will demonstrate the relative strength curve of the fund, indicating whether it is outperforming the broad market, regardless of the price trend.

☐ To protect yourself, as soon as your fund's relative strength curve begins to show weakness, consider switching your holdings to a better-performing vehicle.

Guidelines for investing in closed-end funds

A closed-end fund is like a mutual fund, in that it invests in a number of other securities. But unlike mutual (or open-end) funds, it doesn't constantly sell new shares and redeem shares at net asset values. Rather, the shares of a closed-end fund trade in the open market, just like stocks of individual corporations.

Most closed-end funds sell at a 15% to 30% discount from their net asset value. In a rising market, closed-end funds generally outperform other securities. And in a declining market, if shares were purchased at a heavy discount from net asset value, a decline in the portfolio should have relatively little, if any, effect on the price of the fund's shares.

Criteria for selecting the right closed-end funds:

☐ Find out the fund's discount from net asset value over the last year. Shares that sell at 5% below their normal value are a good buy, although 10% below the normal discount would be even better.

☐ Be selective. Some funds are selling at a heavy discount for a good reason. The assets in the portfolio may be illiquid or unmarketable.

☐ Don't buy a fund "at the market." These funds can be fairly volatile. Instead, put in the order to buy at a specific price.

☐ Avoid funds with bylaws that require a supermajority of shareholders (usually two thirds) to change the fund's status from a closed-end fund to an open-end fund. *Reason:* If a fund becomes open-end, the shareholders get an immediate step-up in the value of some 20% to 30%, depending on the actual discount of the fund from net asset value.

How to hedge with closed-end funds: Buy a stock fund and then sell naked (uncovered) options against the largest holdings in the fund.

☐ *If the stock market declines:* Options will make a lot of money, while the closed-end fund may not decline at all because it is already selling at a large discount from net asset value.

☐ *If the stock market rallies:* Gain in the price of the fund should more than offset losses in the options.

Source: Thomas J. Herzfeld, executive vice president, Bishop, Rosen & Co., Inc., South Miami, FL.

Ten laws of venture-capital investments

Many people are intrigued by the prospect of investing in start-up companies, especially those on the leading edge of technological development.

But before plunging into the brave new world of venture capital, be sure you understand these "laws":

☐ The probability that a company will succeed is inversely proportional to the amount of publicity received before it began to manufacture its first product.

☐ An investor's ability to talk about winners is an order of magnitude greater than the ability to remember the losers.

☐ If a venture-capital investor does not think he has a problem, he has a big problem.

☐ Happiness is a positive cash flow. Everything else will come later.

☐ The probability of a small firm's success is inversely proportional to the president's office size.

☐ Would-be entrepreneurs who pick up the check after luncheon discussions are usually losers.

☐ The longer the investment proposal, the shorter the odds of success.

☐ There is no such thing as an over-financed company.

☐ Managers who worry a lot about voting control usually have nothing worth controlling.

☐ There is no limit on what a person can do or where he can go if he does not mind who gets the credit.

Source: Frederick R. Adler, senior partner, Adler & Shaykin, New York.

Selecting a full-service stockbroker

Be sure that you do the interviewing. Don't let the prospective broker turn the tables and interview you. If you are reluctant to ask all these questions, select at least some of them and have the answers supplemented with a résumé.

☐ Where did he study? What?

☐ How long has he been with the brokerage firm? How long has he been in the securities industry?

☐ What was his prior employment? Why did he leave his last place of employment?

☐ From where does he get his investment recommendations? His firm's research department? Company contacts? Friends in the business? His own research? A combination?

☐ Can he supply a certified history of his firm's and his own research recommendations?

☐ Does he have any client references?

☐ What is his theory on giving sell advice and profit taking?

☐ How many clients does the account executive service? (You want your telephone calls to be answered promptly.)

☐ How diversified is the brokerage firm? Does it have, for example, a bond department? How about an economist? An in-house market technician (essential for timing)? Money-market experts? Commodity department? Option department? Tax-shelter experts?

☐ How many industries does his firm's research department follow? How many companies? How many senior analysts does the firm have?

☐ Will you get weekly, monthly or only occasional printed research reports?

☐ What fees, if any, will be charged for such services as securities safekeeping?

☐ What is the firm's commission structure? What discounts is it willing to offer?

☐ Can the investor talk directly to the investment-research analyst to get first-hand clarifications and updates on research reports? Must everything be funneled through the account executive?

☐ What is the financial condition of the brokerage firm? (You want the latest annual and quarterly financial statements.)

☐ How many floor brokers does the firm have at the various stock exchanges? (You want prompt order execution.)

☐ Is the potential broker willing to meet personally on a regular basis (monthly or quarterly, depending on portfolio size and activity) to discuss progress?

☐ What kind of monthly customer statements are prepared? (More and more firms now offer tabulation of monthly dividend income, portfolio valuation and annual portfolio yield estimate.)

Using discount brokers

Discount brokers generally charge 35% to 85% less in commissions than full-service houses. Savings are particularly good on trades involving large numbers of shares, but discounters generally don't give investment advice. Otherwise, confirmations, monthly statements and account insurance are generally the same for discounters as they are for full-service brokerage firms.

Investors who can benefit by using discounters:

☐ Investors liquidating market holdings.

☐ Investors buying on margin. Margin rates are generally better, but this matters only if you're borrowing a substantial amount.

☐ Beneficiaries of estates who are moving inheritance from stocks and bonds to other kinds of investments.

☐ Employees whose only holdings are stocks in the companies they work for, who sell these stocks occasionally.

☐ Lawyers, accountants and other professionals who believe their personal contacts and own market analyses make for better guidance than what brokers are offering.

☐ Retired persons or other investors with free time to do their own market research.

Who should not use discounters?

☐ Investors interested in commodity trading. Discount houses handle stocks, bonds and options only.

☐ Investors who need mortgages, tax shelters, special bonds.

☐ Those with less than $2,000 to invest. Savings on discount commissions at this level do not outweigh the plus of free advice from full-service houses.

☐ Individuals without stock-market experience.

Source: J. Bud Feuchtwanger, financial consultant, New York.

How to place orders with a stockbroker

Most investors are familiar with the basic forms of execution orders which they may give to their stockbrokers. The most common are limit orders (orders to buy and/or sell at the best available price) and stop-loss orders (orders to buy and/or sell at the best available price if specified price levels are crossed).

Far fewer investors are familiar with other instructions:

☐ Fill or kill orders. These are either executed immediately or canceled.

The investor wants to buy and/or sell immediately in light of current market conditions.

☐ Clean-up basis. Buy an amount of stock at the asked price only if the purchase "cleans up" all available stock at that price. If the order is executed, the investor has reasonable assurance that no other heavy seller exists at the price range at which he purchased the shares. So price is unlikely to drop rapidly.

☐ Not held. The investor provides the floor broker with full authority to use his judgment in the execution of the order, which may mean a more advantageous price. But if the floor broker makes an error in judgment, the investor has no recourse.

☐ All or none. When buying or selling multiple lots, the investor requests that his entire position or none be sold at a limit price. He can often save on commissions by trading in large lots.

☐ Short, short exempt. If the investor holds securities or bonds which may be converted into common stock, he can sell short the amount of stock into which these convertible issues may be converted without waiting for an uptick. To do this, he places a "short, short exempt" order. *Advantages:* The market for many convertible securities is thinner than the market for the underlying common. He will often get superior executions by selling the common short and then turning the convertible security into common, which is then employed to cover the short sale.

Source: Irving Waxman, R.F. Lafferty & Co., New York.

When not to listen to your broker

The few words the average investor finds hardest to say to his broker are, "Thanks for calling, but no thanks." There are times when it is in your own best interest to be able to reject a broker's blandishments.

☐ When the broker's hot tip is that a certain stock is supposed to go up because of impending good news. Ask yourself: If the "news" is so superspecial, how come you (and/or your broker) have been able to learn about it in the nick of time? Often insiders have been buying long before you get the hot tip. After you buy, when the news does become "public," who'll be left to buy?

☐ When the market is sliding. When your broker asks, "How much lower can they go?" the temptation can be very great to try to snag a bargain. But before you do, consider: If the stock, at that price, is such a bargain, wouldn't some big mutual funds or pension funds be trying to buy up all they could? If that's the case, how come the stock has been going down?

☐ Don't fall for the notion that a stock is "averaging down." It's a mistake for the broker (or investor) to calculate that if he buys more "way down there," he can get out even. Stock-market professionals average up, not down. They buy stocks that are proving themselves strong, not ones that are clearly weak.

How to protect yourself in disputes with stockbrokers

☐ Keep a diary of all conversations with stockbrokers that involve placing of orders, purchase recommendations and other important matters. A detailed record adds credibilty if the dispute goes to court, arbitration or the broker's boss.

☐ Note the exact time of conversation, as well as the date. The brokerage firm is liable if it fails to place an order promptly and you lose money as a result of the delay.

☐ If necessary, complain to the head of the brokerage firm. That's sure to get attention.

☐ If that doesn't get results, write a complaint letter to the SEC, which regularly examines such letters.

☐ If none of these work, get a new broker.

Source: Nicholas Kelne, attorney, American Association of Individual Investors, Chicago.

When not to pay a stockbroker's commission

It's not necessary to use a broker and pay a commission to make a gift of stock. Or if a sale of stock is negotiated privately.

How to transfer stock ownership to another person:

☐ Enter the other person's name, address and Social Security number on the back of the certificate.

☐ Sign the back of the certificate and have the signature guaranteed by a commercial bank.

☐ Send it by registered mail to the transfer agent, whose name is on the certificate.

☐ Allow two to six weeks for the other person to receive the new certificate. There will be no charge, although in some states the seller, or donor, has to pay a small transfer tax.

Investing in gold

Almost all the advisers who pushed gold several years ago continue to believe every portfolio should contain some gold as a protection against inflation or economic collapse. Here are some shrewd ways to invest:

☐ Stay away from the gold futures market. Diversify holdings among gold coins, bullion and stocks of South African gold mines.

☐ Pick the mines with the most marginal, high-cost production. These companies are traded internationally, and their reserves are known. As the price of gold goes up, their production becomes economic and they offer very high yields.

☐ Keep in mind that, as a rule, the price of mining shares moves with the price of gold, although the swings are more exaggerated. Calling the turn in the gold market is difficult because gold is a very emotional investment. The political stability of gold-mining countries is a factor to consider.

☐ When buying or selling, remember that gold prices are generally strong on Fridays and lower on Mondays. This is because investors are reluctant to carry short positions over weekends, when central banks sometimes make announcements that affect prices.

☐ Prices are also stronger toward the end of the year and weaker in summer. The supply decreases toward the end of the year because laborers on short-term contracts to South African gold mines return home to harvest crops. Demand decreases in summer, when the European gold-jewelry industry closes.

Guidelines for investing in diamonds

Diamonds are complex—no field for tyros looking for a safe investment. Diamond prices fluctuate as supply and demand conditions change, and the swings can be sharp. Invest only funds not needed for three to five years. That's how long it takes for the wholesale price (at which you can sell) to catch up with the retail price (at which you buy). Thus, even if prices continue steadily upward, it may take three years or more to break even.

☐ If liquidity is your most important consideration, buy the same grades that jewelers do. That is, diamonds worth less than $2,000 (roughly the maximum amount most people are willing to pay for an engagement ring).

☐ Look for a GIA (Gemological Institute of America) color grade not lower than J (K and lower grades have traces of yellow visible to the naked eye). The GIA clarity grade should be no lower than VS (very slight imperfection) or SI (slight imperfection).

☐ For maximum appreciation, buy high-quality diamonds, which are the rarest. Top grade is D (pure white) Flawless (no imperfections). Also accepted as high-quality are diamonds with color grades down to about F and clarity grades down to VVS (very very slight imperfection).

☐ Buy the finest diamonds at major jewelers, diamond investment firms and auction houses as well as through private investors.

☐ Check the reputation of a firm carefully before doing business. Talk to the firm's banker, and get the latest Dun & Bradstreet report. Ask the local Better Business Bureau if it has received any complaints about the company.

☐ Shop around before choosing your firm. Markups range from 20% to 100%. Ask diamond investment firms, jewelers and diamond brokers (who sell to jewelers) what they would charge for a diamond of a specific weight, cut, color and clarity.

☐ Insist on a grading certificate from a major independent laboratory. Don't rely solely on a certificate from the seller. Diamonds graded by the Gemological Institute of America are the most salable and can command a 15% to 20% premium. *Other laboratories whose certificates are widely accepted:* American Gemological Laboratories, United States Gemological Services.

☐ Avoid buying on margin plans. Some firms have misappropriated investor funds.

☐ Insist on prompt delivery. If diamonds are ordered by phone or mail, the contract should specify that the diamonds will be sent within ten days after the firm receives good funds.

☐ Make sure you get a satisfaction guarantee. Thirty days is a reasonable guarantee period, although not every firm offers that much. Use the guarantee period to check whether the diamond that was ordered matches the diamond that was received. *Note:* The guarantee should remain in force even though a laboratory report is received after the guarantee period has expired.

☐ Have the diamonds reappraised every six months. The longer the delay, the greater the uninsured risk. Use an appraisal firm linked via computer to diamond cutters and dealers across the country. *Two such firms:* International Gemological Institute, New York, 212-753-7100; United States Gemological Services, Santa Ana, California, 714-838-8747.

☐ Follow news affecting diamond investments by reading *Diamond Registry Bulletin*, New York, 212-575-0444.

Why rubies, emeralds and sapphires are a safer investment than diamonds

When prices of investment-grade diamonds plunged as much as 30%, colored gemstones magically held on to heady price gains. *Reason:* Scarcity. Only some $200 million in rubies, emeralds and sapphires were sold in the US in a recent year, a fraction of the amount of diamonds sold.

The areas where the finest stones come from: Cambodia, Thailand, Ceylon, Burma and parts of Africa. *Scarcity factor:* These areas are politically unstable and, therefore, are not reliable sources.

☐ Grading. Although techniques in grading colored stones are less advanced than those for diamonds, tests under microscopes and refractometers allow gemologists to distinguish synthetic stones from real ones. They can often tell you the origin of the stone. Certain countries of origin command higher prices. *Example:* Burma rubies.

☐ Flaws. Although all stones have flaws, gross flaws ruin the stone.

☐ Setting. Determine whether the setting does justice to the stone. Does it overwhelm the stone?

☐ Color. It is the most important determinant of price once the stone is adjudged authentic. Never view a single stone. Compare it with several others. *Why:* The clarity of the redness of a ruby and the absence of orange, pink, purple or brown is what makes it most valuable. The variation is best seen by looking at several stones.

☐ A family-owned jewelry retailer with an excellent reputation is the best place to buy. *Leaders:* Van Cleef & Arpels or Harry Winston. They are willing to risk their own money investing in fine gems from around the world. Larger chains of jewelers can't afford to invest. They custom order.

☐ In small towns without direct access to a large selection of colored gemstones, go to reputable retail jewelers and commission them to find the kind of stone you like and can afford. Many fine jewelers have connections with the American Gem Society, which will send them a selection of stones for conditional purchase. The jewelers receive a commission for their advice and service.

☐ The best gems to buy are stones over one carat that are free of externally visible flaws. Buy one that will look good mounted in jewelry. That way, if the investment does not gain in value, at least you will have a remarkable piece of jewelry, not just a stone in a glass case.

☐ Expect to keep a colored gem for at least five years when buying for investment. Then evaluate what the stone would go for on the dealers' (wholesale) market. *Alternative:* Put stones up for auction at Sotheby Parke Bernet or Christie's. Although you cannot be sure of a definite sales price, you can put a minimum price on your item.

Penny-stock traps

☐ Avoid a company that is not generating unit growth, that has high debt or whose management doesn't have a good track record.

☐ Stay away from companies in very competitive situations.

☐ Don't get caught up in other investors' stories.

☐ Be leery of companies with 20 million shares outstanding of a penny stock.

Source: Stephen Leeb, president of Money Growth Institute, Jersey City, NJ. The company publishes *Penny-Stock Ventures, The Speculator* and *The Investment Strategist.*

Stockbroker traps

Watch out for:

☐ Recommendations for a stock you've never heard of.

☐ An investment strategy that depends on exceptionally heavy trading.

☐ Transactions involving investments such as low-activity, over-the-counter stocks or Ginnie Mae securities, for which up-to-the-minute prices are rather difficult to obtain.

☐ Pressure to use the company's cash-management account.

Source: *Fortune.*

How to choose a prime growth stock

Prime growth stocks should meet all or most of the following characteristics:

☐ A dominant position in a growth industry.

☐ A long record of rising earnings and high profit margins.

☐ Superb management.

☐ A commitment to innovation and a good research program.

☐ The ability to pass on cost increases to the consumer.

☐ A strong financial position.

☐ Ready marketability of the stock.

☐ Relative immunity to consumerism and government regulation.

Source: *Preserving Capital* by John Train, Clarkson N. Potter Publishers, New York.

What to ask a financial planner

The probing questions to ask:

☐ *What's your specialty?* If the planner lists specialties—say, hard assets or insurance or stocks or tax shelters—scratch him/her from your list. *What you should be looking for:* A generalist with a professional staff.

☐ *What percentage of your income comes from fees and how much from commissions?* If much of the income is generated by commissions, also scratch him.

☐ *What are your educational background and professional experience?* If he passes the background test, call his references.

☐ *Are you affiliated with any other firm?* Some planners are affiliated with an insurance company, a stockbroker or even a marketer of tax shelters. You should eliminate them.

☐ *Can you quantify what you can do for me?* Eliminate planners who jump to that bait and start reeling off numbers.

☐ *How much will it cost?* If he immediately quotes you a package price, go on the next candidate.

Source: Connie S.P. Chen, a former financial consultant at Merrill Lynch's Personal Financial Planning Group and for the last seven years head of Chen Planning Consultants, New York.

What to look for in good-quality stock

☐ A price/earnings ratio that's lower than the market average. Right now the *S&P 500* index has a p/e ratio of 18. I'm buying stocks with p/e's of no more than 14—and preferably no more than 12. When their p/e's rise to market levels, it's usually time to sell.

☐ A solid track record. The growth of its earnings and dividends over the past five to ten years should have outpaced the *S&P 500.*

☐ Above-average return on equity compared with the *S&P 500* for the past five to ten years. This shows that the company really knows how to use capital intelligently to create higher profits.

☐ A strong balance sheet. A good company can have long-term debt, but it should not exceed the company's equity. In recent years we've seen far too many companies struggling to get out from under debt that has prevented them from growing and prospering as they otherwise would have done.

Source: David Dreman, chairman, Dreman Value Management, which manages $2.7 billion in stocks, bonds and mutual funds for individual and institutional clients, Ten Exchange Place, Jersey City, New Jersey 07302.

A selling plan

Before buying a stock or mutual fund, have a plan for selling it. Set both a target price, at which you'll take profits …and a bailout price, at which you'll sell if the shares drop in value. The discipline imposed by a predetermined selling strategy will help you avoid mistakes that can result from short-term fear or greed. *Key:* Don't buy shares if a sudden drop in their price will cause you to panic. *Remember:* The person selling the shares to you is either taking profits or bailing out. Have a good, long-term reason for buying the shares in light of this fact.

Source: John Dessauer, editor, *Investor's World*, 7811 Montrose Rd., Potomac, Maryland 20854.

Growth-stock warning signal

Consider selling a growth stock when its relative strength declines steadily over a period of months. Relative strength is the stock's price performance compared to that of the *S&P 500* or another broad market index. *Key:* A high price/earnings (p/e) ratio by itself is not a warning sign concerning a growth stock. *Reason:* A growth stock has a high p/e. But the high p/e must be justified by above-average performance. A slippage in performance as measured by relative strength is a warning sign that there may be earnings problems ahead and also warns that growth-oriented investors may soon be bailing out of the stock, depressing its price.

Source: Arnold Kaufman, editor, *The Outlook*, 25 Broadway, New York 10004.

The selling question

Before selling a stock because you think it is overpriced, ask yourself this question: "Would I buy it today at today's price?" Say you bought a stock at $30 a share and now it is $50 a share. Would you buy it at $50? If not, it may be time for you to sell. If you think it still looks attractive at $50, why sell? Why not buy more? The next question—why are you keeping a stock that you wouldn't want to buy? And if the stock is not worth buying today, why not sell it? It's never a mistake to clean up your portfolio…to weed out anything that's too aggressive …doesn't make sense…or never belonged there in the first place.

Source: Esther M. Berger, CFP, first vice president, Paine Webber, Inc., Beverly Hills. She is the author of *Money Smart: Take The Fear Out of Financial Planning*, Avon Books, 1350 Avenue of the Americas, New York 10019.

Rules of stock picking

The key rules for making profitable stock investments…

☐ Buy a stock only if it is priced at less than you think it is worth now…and only if you believe it will be worth more tomorrow. Buying at a low price is absolutely fundamental to making profits.

☐ Buy on bad news that temporarily depresses a stock's price.

☐ When a stock seems like a bargain, investigate further to be sure it actually is. Understand why the rest of the market has priced it low and why you think its price will go up nonetheless.

☐ Quantify the bargain you see. Don't buy a stock because it "seems" like a good deal. Figure out the stock's value in dollar terms considering factors such as cash flow and future earnings.

☐ Investing is hard work. If you take short cuts you can expect to get second-rate results.

Source: *Global Investing the Templeton Way*, as told by John Templeton to Norman Berryessa, money manager, and Eric Kirzner, associate professor of finance, University of Toronto. Irwin Professional Publishing, 1333 Burr Ridge Pkwy., Burr Ridge, Illinois 60521.

Investment scams

Beware of "innovative" securities that brokers may try to sell on the promise that they safely provide more income than can be obtained from bonds, Treasury bills or CDs.

Examples: ARPS, adjustable rate preferred stocks…CMOs, collateralized mortgage obligations…MITTS, market index target term securities…etc.

Key: While any of these can be a good investment for an informed investor, they all carry risk that is likely to be minimized by a broker. *Vital:* Never make an investment you don't understand.

When a broker explains to you how a "new" security can make money, insist that he explain how it can lose money. Only with this knowledge can you make an informed decision.

Source: Charles B. Carlson, CFA, editor, *Dow Theory Forecasts*, 7412 Calumet Ave., Hammond, Indiana 46324.

Five signs of a good stock

☐ Earnings per share show an upward trend over five years.

☐ Increasing earnings are accompanied by increasing dividends.

☐ A *Standard & Poor's* rating of A- or better for the firm's financial strength.

☐ At least 10 million shares of stock outstanding, to assure liquidity if you decide to sell.

☐ A price/earnings ratio that has not been bid up to much above market averages—which would indicate that investors have already discovered the stock and run up its price so that it is no bargain.

Source: *How to Invest $50–$5,000* by Nancy Dunnan, financial analyst. HarperPerennial, Ten E. 53 St., New York 10022.

Raising money on property

Selling property and leasing it back may be a better way to raise money than taking out a mortgage loan.

The biggest advantage is immediate cash amounting to 100% of current value of the property. A mortgage loan would probably produce only 75%.

The seller (lessee):

☐ Continues to use the property for term of lease, including renewal options.

☐ Pays rent which is fully deductible.

☐ Realizes taxable gain or loss on sale.

The buyer (lessor):

☐ Puts up the cash, maybe borrowing some of the amount needed.

☐ Receives taxable rental income.

☐ Takes depreciation deductions.

When the lease runs out:

☐ There is usually an option to repurchase the property. Generally, this must provide for purchase at fair market value at the time.

☐ The IRS will look very carefully at sale-leasebacks. It's sure trouble if there's an option to repurchase for $1. In that case, the IRS may claim it isn't really a sale, but a sham with no real change of ownership, really a disguised mortgage loan. Then the "rent" will not be deductible, but only the part of it considered to be "interest" on the "loan."

What you should know about real-estate agents

Knowing your legal rights and responsibilities when selling your home yourself or through a real-estate broker can save you thousands of dollars.

☐ Shop around to find a broker who is knowledgeable about your community and with whom you feel comfortable.

☐ Be sure to read the legal documents pertaining to brokers' contracts to avoid misunderstandings.

☐ Be aware that commissions paid by the seller to the broker are no longer established by any state agency or private trade association (by federal law). Individual brokers set fees for their own offices.

☐ Try to negotiate the commission rate. Some brokers will; others will not. The law does not require them to.

☐ Understand the listing agreement before you sign it. It is a legal document that outlines the understanding between you and the broker about how your home will be listed for sale. It includes your name, the broker's name, the address of the property, the asking price and other details about the home, as well as the amount of time you are giving the broker to find a buyer (30, 60 or 90 days is usual).

☐ The most common type of listing offered by a broker is the exclusive right to sell. This means that you will pay full commission to the listing broker, regardless of which real-estate office brings in the buyer—even if the seller brings in the buyer.

☐ Signing a contract and accepting a buyer's "earnest" money commit you to the sale—unless the buyer reneges and therefore forfeits the money, or some contingency to the sale negates the contract.

☐ If you've signed a contract and then refuse to follow through, you could face a lawsuit should the buyer want to initiate one. In any event, you may still be responsible for the broker's commission.

Source: John R. Linton, vice president, legal affairs, National Association of Realtors.

Getting a higher price for an old house

An old house (built between 1920 and 1950) can be sold as easily as a new one. The right strategy and a few improvements can raise the selling price significantly.

☐ Invest in a complete cleaning, repainting or wallpapering. Recarpet or have the rugs and carpets professionally cleaned.

☐ Get rid of cat and dog odors that you may be used to but potential buyers will notice.

☐ With the trend to smaller families and working couples, it may be desirable to convert and advertise a four-bedroom house as two bedrooms, library and den.

☐ The exterior of the house is crucial. It's the first thing a buyer sees. Clean and repair porch and remove clutter. Repaint porch furniture.

☐ Landscaping makes a great difference and can sell (or unsell) a house.

Get expert advice on improving it.

☐ Good real-estate agents are vital to a quick sale. There are one or two top people in every agency who will work hard to show houses and even arrange financing. Multiple listings let these super salespeople from different agencies work for the seller.

Tax-saving tactics for home sellers

A person who purchases a new primary residence but can't sell the old one can be in the expensive position of carrying two homes at once. To rent out the old home until it can be sold:

☐ Give the tenant of the old house a month-to-month lease requiring him to move when the house is sold. It's also possible to lease the house to a prospective purchaser before a sale agreement is finalized.

☐ Use the cash earned to offset the cost of carrying two houses.

☐ Deduct expenses related to the old home (such as insurance, utilities and repairs) up to the amount of rental income received. (Rents collected are sheltered from tax.)

☐ When the old home is sold, the sale proceeds will still qualify for tax-deferred treatment when applied against the cost of the new home (as long as the old home is sold within two years after the new home was bought).

☐ *Rule:* The homeowner's primary goal must always be to sell the old home, rather than rent it.

Source: *Stephen Bolaris,* 81 TC No. 52.

Best sale—spruce it up first

Your house doesn't have to be perfect to sell it, just spacious and neat, clean and well cared for.

Most people want to buy a house—not take on a part-time job as a painter, plumber or handyman. So ease of care and low maintenance are attributes buyers seek out.

Pay attention to the "curb appeal" of your house. A broken fence, for example, will send visitors scurrying away. To at least get people out of their cars to look, you can…

☐ Plant fresh flowers or healthy new shrubs.

☐ Put down fresh blacktop sealer if you have a blacktop driveway.

☐ Touch up the paint job on the exterior of the house (painting the entire exterior is worth it if needed, but will cost more).

☐ Install new hardware around the front door.

On the inside: Pay special attention to the kitchen and bathroom. In sprucing up the interior, you can…

☐ Put new hinges and knobs on kitchen and bathroom cabinets.

☐ Install brighter light bulbs and make sure your window dressings let in the maximum natural light.

☐ Paint the walls off-white or any light neutral color to give a feeling of space.

Eliminate clutter by following the three Rs—Remove, Rearrange and Reorganize. A tidy and organized closet, for example, seems more spacious. Placing furniture around the perimeter of a room can create a sense of space.

☐ Keep kitchen counters as clear as possible.

☐ Bathrooms should be spotless and dripless. Replace the shower curtain.

Source: Michael C. Murphy, author of *How to Sell Your Home in Good or Bad Times,* Sterling Publishing, New York.

How to sell your home fast

If you need or want to sell your home on your own quickly, you can get a great price in just five days.

Steps to take…

☐ Lower your asking price. To attract a large number—between 20 and 40—of serious buyers and show that you are flexible, price your home 10% below the price of similar homes in your area. The goal is to price your home as attractively as possible when your ad first appears in the local paper. Free enterprise—having potential buyers bid against one another—will take care of the rest.

☐ Plan to hold an open house—and offer critical information. Get your home in tip-top shape and gather all the information that will answer buyers' questions over the phone or in person.

This information includes a detailed description of your home, an independent inspection report, a radon report and a copy of your property survey. Expect to hear from between 50 and 100 people.

☐ Run your newspaper ad for the three days before and the two days during the open house. This will attract the maximum number of buyers. The content of the ad is critical. It should mention…

…the location of the home.

…a brief description of the home.

…the asking price.

…you're selling it yourself.

…you'll accept the best reasonable offer.

…the times of the open house.

…you plan on selling the home by the next week.

…your phone number.

When interested buyers call, say your home will be sold to the highest bidder.

☐ Hold the open house on Saturday and Sunday. On Saturday morning, put up signs in your neighborhood to help guide those who saw your ad for the open house. These signs may also attract some walk-in traffic.

Be absolutely honest about all of your home's flaws. This is not only ethical but smart. Getting interested buyers to make high bids is only part of the reason. You also don't want them to withdraw their bids after they learn the truth about your property.

☐ Conduct round-robin bidding. You will probably receive many offers. The only way to settle on one offer is to accept the highest bid.

Source: William G. Effros, a Greenwich, Connecticut-based computer consultant who sold his own home quickly one year ago using this method. He is author of *How to Sell Your Home in Five Days,* Workman Publishing, New York.

Mortgage-refinancing trap

☐ "Points," or finance charges that are paid to obtain a mortgage loan, are generally tax-deductible in the year in which they are paid—provided the mortgage is taken out for the "purchase or improvement" of a taxpayer's principal residence.

☐ *Trap:* The IRS has now ruled, however, that points paid in order to *re*finance a

mortgage loan are *not* currently deductible, because the new mortgage is *not* used for purchase of a residence, but for repayment of an existing debt. As a result, the usual rule on prepaid interest applies—the points must be amortized and deducted at an even rate over the entire period of the loan.

☐ *Example:* Jones pays $3,000 in points to refinance a $100,000 mortgage over 20 years. He cannot deduct the $3,000 this year. Jones can deduct only $150 a year over the 20-year period.

Rules on mortgage-interest deductions

Under the 1986 Tax Reform Act, you could deduct the interest on mortgage debt up to the cost of the house and improvements, plus any additional amounts borrowed for medical or educational expenses up to the current market value of the house. *Note:* Additional amounts might be deducted if the mortgage was taken out on or before August 16, 1986.

New law: You can deduct the interest on up to $1 million of *acquisition debt,* used to purchase, construct or improve the residence, *plus* an additional $100,000 of *home-equity debt,* used for any purpose whatsoever.

Important saving: Interest on mortgages taken out before October 14, 1987, is *fully deductible without regard to the dol-lar limits.* The amount of the old mort-gage must be subtracted from the amount of new *acquisition debt* still avail-able but does not affect home-equity debt.

Getting personal tax benefits from depreciated business property

A taxpayer who owns property (a building or medical equipment, for instance) that is used for a business but which has used up most or all of its depreciation, can arrange, with expert advice, to get personal tax benefits by arranging a gift-leaseback with lower-income family members.

□ The business owner makes a gift of the property to a family member and immediately leases it back.

□ The rental payments are treated as expenses to the business.

□ The rental payments are income to the lower-income family members who now own the building.

□ The donor must not retain the same control over the physical property that he had before the gift-leaseback arrangement.

□ The lease must be in writing and the leaseback rental must be reasonable.

□ The donor may not continue to own substantial equity in the property after the gift-leaseback arrangement.

□ Expert tax and law advice is essential in setting up this tax-saving arrangement. If the gift-leaseback is successfully challenged by the IRS, the business owner will be denied the rental deduction and the person or persons who received the rental payments may be required to pay income tax on those distributions.

Winning with large loss real-estate tax shelters

The major impact the Tax Reform Act of 1986 has had on real-estate investing is the restriction placed on the use of passive-activity losses and passive-activity income.*

Losses from passive activities, such as most rental-property investments and limited partnerships, are now deductible only if taken against income from other passive activities. (Unused losses can be carried forward, however, to offset future income in the activity or partnership.) Losses cannot be used as deductions against ordinary income—wages or portfolio income (interest and dividends).

These changes have made for some interesting opportunities.

Opportunities

□ Real-estate losses not taken in one year as a result of restrictions on passive-activity income can be carried forward indefinitely.

□ *Benefit:* Losses can be used to offset passive-activity income in future years

*Passive activity is any business or trade in which the investor does not materially participate. The investment could take the form of a sole proprietorship, a limited or general partnership or an S corporation.

…or even taken against gains made on sale of the properties from which the losses originated.

□ Find investments that generate passive-activity income to be sheltered by your passive-activity losses.

□ *Best bet:* Real estate purchased for all cash or with very little debt that has a large annual cash flow.

□ Look for properties (or partnerships buying properties) with established occupancy levels and attractive locations to guarantee adequate rental income after operating expenses. *A reasonable rate of return:* 7%–8%.

□ Some investors in rental real estate will be able to deduct up to $25,000 in losses each year. Such an investor must have an adjusted gross income of below $100,000 (because of the phase-out between $100,000 and $150,000)… must "actively participate" in the property's management…and must have more than a 10% direct interest in the investment.

Source: Robert A. Stanger, chairman, Robert A. Stanger & Co., publisher of *The Stanger Report: A Guide to Partnership Investing,* 1129 Broad St., Shrewsbury, NJ 07701.

Traps in real-estate tax shelters

The key to a valid tax shelter is economic substance, the shelter's value as an investment. If you don't understand how the deal works, you can't judge its investment merit.

Test the assumptions:

□ If the cash-flow projections are based on an apartment house being rented 100% of the time, watch out. How likely is this to happen? A 95% occupancy rate in a low-vacancy area is optimistic. That leaves a 5% difference between the assumption and reality. That 5% comes off the projected cash flow, diminishing the return on your investment.

□ Rental-income projections may also be inflated. To find out a reasonable rent projection for a given area, check with real-estate brokers.

Check management fees:

□ In addition to fees for continuing to manage the property, does the shelter management company get fees for selling the project to the group and for selling the property at the end?

☐ Does the shelter management get a piece of the profit on final sale?

☐ Are the managing partners getting too big a share of the profit on sale? Has too large a fee been built into the selling price?

☐ Are the fees reasonable? Continuing management fees should not be more than 5% to 6% of the gross rents.

☐ Does the total amount that the managers get from the project seem "fair"? This is something you must decide for yourself—at what point does the managers' return affect your opinion of the whole deal?

☐ Do the managers get most of their fees up front? *Better:* Managers ride along with the investors and get their fees as they go along. That gives them a continuing stake in the property.

Source: Herbert C. Speiser, partner, Deloitte & Touche, New York.

What to investigate in a real-estate investment

☐ Find out who the high-paying tenants are. One may be the building owner, and the others may be affiliated with the seller. Or the owner may have offered the tenants a free month's rent or a delayed increase to sign a lease at the higher rates. It may be hard to raise rents any higher.

☐ Low operating expenses. Sellers may be operating the building themselves to avoid a management fee. If buyers cannot take care of the building personally, this fee must be added to real operating expenses.

☐ Reasonable property tax. If the building has not been assessed for several years, the buyer may have a substantial tax bite on the next reassessment.

☐ Assessments. Ask the local assessment office for the tax card or listing sheet. It will show the building's assessment and when it was assessed. If it was assessed a year and a half ago and there has been no significant addition to the building, reassessment may not hurt the buyer. But if it has not been assessed for eight years, there could be a significant tax boost.

☐ Check the owner's property description against the one listed on the card. If the owner says that 20,000 square feet are being sold, but the tax card says 15,000 square feet, there has been some addition to the structure that has not been recorded and, therefore, has not been assessed. Or there may be an assessment error that, when corrected, will raise costs.

☐ Low insurance premiums. Is coverage in line with the structure's current value? What does the policy cover? Ask to see the policy. If coverage is insufficient, how much more will proper coverage cost?

☐ Energy efficient. Verify the owner's claim with the local utility to determine actual energy costs. *Also:* Check with regulatory commissions to see whether utility companies are scheduled to increase their tariffs.

Source: Thomas L. O'Dea, O'Dea & Co., Inc., investment real-estate consultants, Winston-Salem, NC, and senior editor *Rental House and Condo Investor.*

Before investing in condos or co-ops

Despite the recent drop in housing starts, many investors are turning again to condominium and cooperative apartment houses, especially in big cities. Smart investors today can profit from errors made in the last decade. Now they know that:

☐ It's best to avoid investing in the development of condos or co-ops that are surrounded by rental apartments. *Best investment:* Co-ops and condos that are next to single-family housing.

☐ People who buy individual apartment units like buildings where apartments cost less than comparable single-family housing nearby. *Rule of thumb:* Apartments should sell for 25% less than the lowest-priced houses in the area.

☐ Apartment buyers also avoid units in outlying areas. For psychological reasons, people don't mind commuting 20 to 30 miles to work from a suburban house, but many dislike an apartment in a remote area.

☐ It's easier to overbuild the apartment market than standard housing because the cost per unit is cheaper for apartments. When there's a housing glut, a co-op or condo can have high vacancy rates for many months or even years.

☐ Factors that make houses cheaper will almost always make apartments difficult to sell. *Examples:* Lower interest rates. Oversupply. Changes in zoning or building codes that favor house construction.

Source: Vincent Mooney, real-estate consultant on condominium building and conversion and president of Condominium Home Realtors, Tulsa, OK, and author of *Condoeconomics*.

Investing in a single-family house

☐ Make sure there is an active rental market for homes in the area you choose. Know the odds of finding a good tenant, keeping the tenant and getting the price you need on rent.

☐ Leverage for a single-family home is more expensive than financing for other real-estate investments. Home mortgages may be several percentage points higher than financing for commercial properties.

☐ Single-family homes bought as rental properties are usually either 100% rented or 100% vacant. That means significant risk and a cash drain if the house goes empty for months.

☐ Don't discount mortgage payments because they are tax-deductible. Tax benefits should always be looked at as incidental to the investment. The investment should make economic sense without tax benefits.

Investing in multi-family buildings or condos

☐ Multifamily apartment houses are less risky than single-family homes if the location is satisfactory. If one of four apartments is vacant, the property is still 75% leased.

☐ This type of property is management-intensive. Floors must be swept and lightbulbs changed. There are emergency repairs. Either the owner must be handy and have free time, or he should hire a professional manager—which means less profit.

☐ Condos are less management-intensive than straight rentals, since the condo association cares for day-to-day maintenance.

☐ Resort condos are more risky than condos in a well-populated area within a driving radius of your own home. If the property can't be rented in season, the investor is in serious trouble. *Another minus:* Resort properties typically are remote, far from the investor's area, so

he can't inspect or manage them. He must depend on the condo operator.

Investing in a shopping center

☐ Shopping centers are for wealthy investors.

☐ They can be an easy real-estate operation. Outside contractors are hired for management duties, and tenants have responsibility for most of the maintenance.

☐ For an existing property with all space leased on a three- to five-year basis, the key question is, "How are the tenants doing?" If well, they will renew their leases and rents will go up. The increase in rent increases the property's income and value.

☐ Ask what existing leases are going for and what new leases can go for in that area.

☐ Quantify the difference. That is what you can capture when the current leases expire.

The smart way to buy a condominium

Experience in buying and selling several single-family homes doesn't alert you to all the things to look for in a good condo deal. Basic guidelines:

☐ Don't buy on impulse.

☐ Make sure your lawyer reads the covenant of condominium (also called the master deed or declaration of condominium).

☐ Be aware that clauses in a covenant are non-negotiable. All participants must have the same wording.

If you spot any of these traps, consider walking away from the whole deal:

☐ Resale restrictions. The condo association may have a 30-, 60- or 90-day right of first refusal. That delay could cost you a sale. Be advised that FHA, VA and other government-insured mortgages are not available when there are certain resale restrictions. Your resale market could be cut significantly.

☐ Use restrictions. Does the covenant permit owners to rent their units? If you are buying the condo as an investment, you must be able to rent. But, if you are planning to live in a unit, you may want this restriction. Other use restrictions may concern children, pets, window decorations, even the type of mailbox you can put up.

☐ **Sweetheart deals.** The most common one is when the developer owns the common areas and leases them back to the association. Such leases are usually long-term and include escalator clauses and pass-alongs that could cause big jumps in your monthly association fees. In other cases, the developer does not own the common areas, but has a long-term contract to manage them.

The best deal for the buyer is when the condo association owns all the common areas. All management agreements with the condo association should strictly control costs and contain termination provisions.

Potential problems that won't show up in the covenant:

☐ **Subsidized fees.** Developers of newly-built condos often manage common areas for a fee until most of the new units are sold. To speed sales, the developer may keep the management fee below cost. Then, when the condo association assumes management, the owners' monthly costs soar. Compare fees charged by similar condo associations in the same area.

☐ **Construction problems.** Before you buy, have an engineer inspect the entire property, if feasible, not just your unit. If the condo association has to make repairs, you will be assessed for the cost.

If you are buying a unit in a converted building, ask the condo salesperson for the engineer's report. Most converted buildings need one to obtain financing.

☐ *Other tips:* The best times to buy are when prices are lowest during the pre-construction sale of new units, or early in the conversion of a building.

☐ But if you buy too soon, you could end up as one of the few owners. As long as units remain unsold, your investment will not appreciate. Check the price and demand for similar units in the area.

Source: Thomas L. O'Dea, O'Dea and Co., Inc., Winston-Salem, NC.

How to avoid condominium (and co-op) unhappiness

Investment differences between apartments and houses are far greater than most individual buyers realize.

What the experts know:

☐ Apartments are more volatile in price than houses are. Apartments can easily be overbuilt, and that's when it's best to buy them.

☐ Anything that makes houses easier to buy hurts apartment sales. *Examples:* Lower interest rates, lower inflation, an oversupply of houses and changes in building codes or in zoning laws that make houses less expensive to build.

☐ For the best chance at resale, buy an apartment priced 25% lower than the starting prices on houses in the same area. Apartments that cost the same or more than the average one-family house will appeal only to prospects who prefer an apartment over a house. These people are only 30% of all condominium/co-op buyers.

☐ Ideally, neighboring houses should cost an average of twice what an apartment costs. It's a matter of psychology. Apartment buyers are often looking for an inexpensive way to live in an expensive neighborhood.

☐ Prices of condos and co-ops are very sensitive to rental vacancies. They're difficult to sell when rental units are cheap. *Advice:* Buy when vacancy rates are high, sell when they're low. Ironically, most investors do just the opposite because they want to buy an apartment only when it's hard for them to find one to rent.

☐ Don't buy an apartment in an area where there are many rental apartments. Buy in neighborhoods of single-family houses.

☐ Try to get an assumable loan. If you're forced to sell in a down market, the only way you may be able to attract buyers is by letting them take over the payments on your loan.

Source: Vince Mooney, real-estate consultant and president of Condominium Home Realtors, Tulsa, OK, and author of Condoeconomics.

When you rent out your vacation house or resort apartment

☐ Use a comprehensive lease. The Blumberg form available at most stationery stores is a fine starting point.

☐ Check the standard lease and take out all sections that are not acceptable to you.

☐ Have the lease witnessed or notarized, preferably by a lawyer or real-estate agent.

□ Add to the lease a list of all household property and the condition of each item.

□ Tell the renter about any recurrent problems, such as summer floods, insect or rodent infestations or anything else that affects the habitability of the house or apartment. Failure to do so is grounds for the renter to break the lease and get his money back.

□ Ask for business and personal references and check them out thoroughly. Don't rely only on the appearance of the renters.

□ Make clear, in writing, if the renter is to be responsible for care and watering of plants and lawn, for raking the beach or for any other regular maintenance.

□ Make sure your insurance will cover any burglary, accident or damage to the house and grounds while renters occupy it.

How to buy property with little or no money down

As hard as it is to believe, it's not only possible to buy property with no money down, it's not even that hard to do— provided you have the right fundamental information.

Note: No money down doesn't mean the seller receives no down payment. It means the down payment doesn't come from your pocket.

Success strategies

□ **Paying the real-estate agent.** If a seller uses a real-estate agent on the sale, he's obligated to pay the agent's commission. *Strategy:* You, the buyer, pay the commission, but not up front. You approach the agent and offer a deal. Instead of immediate payment, suggest that the agent lend you part of the commission. In return, you offer a personal note guaranteeing to pay the money at some future date, with interest. If you make it clear that the sale depends on such an arrangement, the agent will probably go along with the plan. If he balks, be flexible. Negotiate a small monthly amount, perhaps with a balloon payment at the end. You then subtract the agent's commission from the expected down payment.

□ **Assuming the seller's debts.** Let's say, as so often happens, that the seller is under financial pressure. *Strategy:* With the seller's cooperation, contact all his creditors and explain that you, not the seller, are going to make good on the outstanding debts. In some cases, the relieved creditors will either extend the due dates or, if you can come up with some cash, they'll likely agree to a discount. Deduct the face amount of the debts you'll be assuming, pocketing any discounts, from the down payment.

□ **Prepaid rent.** Sometimes you, the buyer, are in no rush to move in and the seller would like more time to find a new place to live—but you'd both like to close as soon as possible. *Strategy:* Offer to let the seller remain in the house or apartment, setting a fixed date for vacating. Then, instead of the seller paying the buyer a monthly rent, you subtract from the down payment the full amount of the rent for the entire time the seller will be living there.

□ **Satisfying the seller's needs.** During conversations with the seller, you learn that he must buy some appliances and furniture for a home he's moving into. *Strategy:* Offer to buy those things— using credit cards or store credit to delay payment—and deduct the lump sum from the down payment.

Source: Robert G. Allen, a real-estate insider and author of the bestseller, *Nothing Down.* He's also publisher of the monthly newsletter *The Real-Estate Advisor,* Provo, UT.

How to make your money work

☐ Earn up to 21% risk-free by paying off charge-card balances early. You may not realize that carrying a $500 balance on a bank card can cost as much as $105 per year.

☐ Make contributions to your IRA or Keogh plan as early in the year as possible.

☐ Borrow money from your corporate profit-sharing or pension plan rather than from a bank. You may still claim the interest expense as a deduction.

☐ Shift income to your children with trusts or custodial accounts. The money will be taxed at their low rate.

☐ Increase your insurance deductibles.

☐ Don't rely on your accountant to find the best possible tax deductions for you. Invest in a good self-help manual.

☐ Prepay your mortgage. An extra $100 a month will dramatically shorten your term and total interest expenses.

Source: Dr. Paul A. Randle, professor of finance, Utah State University, writing in *Physicians' Management*, New York.

Stretching due dates on bills

Due dates on bills can be stretched—but not far—without risk. *Typical grace periods:* Telephone companies, eight days. Gas and electric utilities, ten days. Banks and finance companies, ten days. Even after a late charge is imposed on an unpaid bill your credit rating should be safe for 30 days.

Source: Terry Blaney, president of Consumer Credit Counseling Service of Houston and the Gulf Coast Area.

Money strategies... for your 20s, 30s, 40s...and beyond

When managing your money, you should learn to act your age. These are key strategies for investors in three different age groups—those in their 20s and 30s...those in their 40s and 50s...and those who are retired.

20s and 30s:

☐ Buy a home. It may turn out to be your single best investment, especially if you buy a single-family home rather than a condominium.

☐ Invest for growth. Those in their 20s and 30s should put 70% of their long-term investment money into stocks and/or stock mutual funds. The remainder should go into bonds or bond funds.

☐ Plan now if you want to retire early. Almost half of all working-age people hope to retire before age 65. Many of them do it—but they actually can't afford to. Successful early retirees typically established that goal in their 20s and 30s, when they still had plenty of time to accumulate wealth. They sacrificed early by saving 20% or 25% of their income and living in cheaper housing than they could afford.

40s and 50s:

☐ Keep investing for growth. You should have 50% to 60% of your investment portfolio in stocks and the remainder in bonds. When you're within 10 years of retirement, keep that same mix but change the types of securities you own to reduce your risk somewhat.

☐ Avoid taxes. Make full use of tax-deferred savings vehicles, including 401(k) plans, Individual Retirement Accounts (IRAs) and variable annuities. Your 40s and 50s are your peak earning years and, hence, your peak tax years, so tax-favored savings are critical.

☐ Project your retirement income and expenses. Do this once a year, so you know how much you need to be saving and when you can retire.

☐ Review estate plans every few years.

☐ Keep loved ones informed.

Source: Jonathan D. Pond, president of Financial Planning Information Inc., 9 Galen St., Watertown, Massachusetts 02172. He is author of numerous books on personal finance, most recently, *The New Century Family Money Book*, Dell Publishing, New York.

How to find money you didn't know you had

Few people take full advantage of the capital at their disposal. There are a myriad of simple ways to optimize your personal financial resources:

☐ Convert passbook savings accounts, savings bonds, etc., into better investments. American still have $300 billion sitting in low-interest passbook savings accounts when they could be so easily transferred to CDs at nearly double the yield! Review your portfolio now, particularly bonds that have recently registered nice gains. Should you still be owning what you do? People often hold investments long after they've forgotten why they originally made them.

☐ Borrow on life insurance (such low interest rates aren't being offered today). Many folks who bought life insurance back in the 1960s and 1970s (term insurance is more prevalent today) could borrow back the money and reinvest it at a higher rate.

☐ Pay real-estate taxes directly instead of through the bank. Most banks withhold an amount on monthly mortgage payments for paying the homeowner's real-estate taxes. Yet, in most towns, real-estate tax bills are sent annually. The bank is earning interest on your money. *Caution:* You must make the payments on time. Banks can call in your mortgage if the taxes are delinquent, and they'd just love to do it if you are fortunate enough to have a low-interest mortgage.

☐ Prepay mortgage principal. Making a monthly $25 prepayment of principal from day one on a $75,000, 30-year, 13% mortgage would save $59,372, and the mortgage would be paid off in 23 years and four months. (Most mortgages allow prepayment.)

☐ Conduct a garage sale. Turn unwanted items into cash. (Sotheby's or another auction house will appraise a possible collectible free.)

If you are self-employed:

☐ Keep good records of travel and entertainment expenses and of the business use of cars, computers and other property used for both business and personal purposes. Taxpayers who can't back up their deductions with good records will lose the deductions and may be charged negligence penalties.

☐ Reward yourself first. Plan for your future by putting money into your tax-deferred retirement plan now. Too many entrepreneurs wait until they're successful before taking money out of the business and risk receiving nothing.

Source: William E. Donoghue, publisher of several investment newsletters, including *Donoghue's Moneyletter,* Holliston, MA.

Smart borrowing

Even many supersuccessful business people find themselves short of cash at times, whether in paying a child's college tuition or in taking advantage of an irresistible investment.

Once you have decided on a sound reason and a sound plan for borrowing, you naturally want to find the best possible interest rate. There are a variety of ways to avoid the high unsecured loan rates being offered at most banks and thrifts across the country:

☐ Insurance policy loan. Particularly attractive if you have an old policy that provides for low interest rate loans. It is especially good if the policy has been in effect for more than seven years. *Reason:* There is a legal provision that policyholders must have paid four out of the first seven payments to get a tax-deductible loan. If the policy has been in effect for seven years, there is no question about tax deductibility. *Safety valve:* Many people fear borrowing on their life insurance policies because this reduces the coverage in case of death. *Solution:* You can use the dividends on the policy to buy additional term insurance to keep the insurance level at face value. That permits you to borrow and to maintain the death value.

☐ Qualified savings plan. Many corporate savings plans, including 401(k) plans, permit employees to borrow the savings that they (and their employer) have put into the plan. Typically, the borrowing rate on savings plans is lower than bank rates, although each company has its own rules. Ask your personnel office about your company's policies. *Caution:* Do not confuse this with IRAs or Keoghs. You cannot borrow against them. And although some firms permit employees to borrow against their pension funds, it isn't advisable.

☐ Brokerage house loan. The current big thing in the brokerage houses is cash-management accounts (in their various guises)—and home-equity accounts. Cash-management accounts let you borrow against stocks and bonds. Home-equity accounts include the value of your home as collateral against loans. Brokerage houses have the resources to appraise your home, and they permit you to borrow at a fairly good rate—the broker loan rate. *Problem:* Margin loans against stock can be called if the stock market goes down sharply and the collateral loses value.

☐ Second mortgage. Exercise extreme caution when using this technique. You are giving someone a lien on your home. You might lose your job, or your business might falter. It is a dangerous way to get into a bind—and you could end up losing your home.

Source: Thomas Lynch, senior vice president, Ayco/American Express, a financial consulting group that advises corporate personnel about financial and tax matters.

The best places to borrow money

There are now more ways to borrow money than ever before. By carefully shopping around, you may be able to save big dollars while establishing valuable new credit lines. But where you borrow the money from can have a great effect on the final cost to you. *Important:* Be sure to consider all the costs associated with the loan, including application fees, title searches, points and so on. *Most important:* The tax law has greatly changed the types of interest that are deductible on your tax return. If the interest is tax-deductible, the tax savings can reduce the cost of your loan.

Before you start looking, determine how much money you will need, how long you will need the loan for and how you will be able to pay it back.

Where to seek funds:

☐ Interest-free loans from the company have been a favorite perk for key executives for years. The bookkeeping is now more complicated and the tax outcome is quite different. The company will be very much in the same position as if it had not made the loan. It will have interest income on the loan, but will be able to take a deduction for salaries representing the value of the loan to the executive. The executive, however, will have to recognize salary income and be left with interest expense. But this interest is known as consumer interest and, typically, will not be deductible by the executive. He or she will owe tax on the value of the loan. *Note:* The interest must be treated as if it had been paid even if in reality no money ever changes hands.

☐ Family members and friends may all be good sources of loans. But chances are the interest you pay will not be deductible. And even if you don't pay interest, the law requires all the parties to handle the transaction *as if interest were being paid.* That means your parents, friends or employer will have to pick up interest income, while chances are you still won't get the deduction.

☐ If the amounts of the loan are large enough, or you need the money for an extended term, you are probably better off putting a mortgage on your home. You can replace your present mortgage and draw out as much as $100,000 above the present amount of the mortgage, or you can seek a home-equity credit line of up to $100,000. With either of the two, interest on this loan will be tax-deductible *and* you will probably get a lower interest rate than you would on unsecured loans. The set-up costs can be considerable, however, and may not be canceled out by the savings. You will have to make some calculations to determine which is best for you.

Preferred financing terms are often provided by banks to the employees of major commercial accounts. *Typical benefit:* Home mortgages at a half point or full point lower than the standard mortgage rate.

☐ Home-equity loans. When the original mortgage on a house has been largely paid off, and/or the house has gone up in value, a borrower may be able to get a loan at about one-and-a-half to two points over the prime rate. *Caution:* There are drawbacks to using your house as collateral. First, you're establishing a lien against your home. Second, there are charges involved—often a one-time fee of around 2% on the credit line, plus an annual maintenance fee of $25 to $100, and perhaps a mortgage recording tax. Nevertheless, bargains are around and it pays to shop.

If the amount you are seeking isn't so large as to warrant a mortgage or home-equity loan, you may wish to look at these options:

☐ Company pension plans frequently contain provisions that allow employees to borrow against their plan accounts. Many plans allow loans to be made at a reasonable interest rate in order to help finance the purchase of a new primary residence or to meet specified emergencies. Employees can typically borrow as much as half the value of their nonforfeitable retirement benefits, up to a maximum of $50,000.

☐ Credit unions are usually a cheap source of funds for their members. Because they have less overhead than banks and are looking to break even rather than to make a profit, they lend at rates lower than commercial rates. *Typical:* Personal loans of up to half your salary. Many credit unions also have insurance programs.

☐ Bank loans. It's important to shop around for the best terms. Remember that as a borrower you don't have to worry about the bank's solvency. You can safely take advantage of unusual terms offered by a bank that's desperate for business.

☐ Credit and debit cards may be the most expensive form of financing (typically charging interest rates of 18% to 20%), but they also offer the most convenient source of cash around. *Danger:* Letting charges pile up. *Rule of thumb:* Monthly loan payments, exclusive of the home mortgage, should total no more than 10% to 15% of net income.

☐ Merchant financing may represent a better deal than the average bank loan. *Typical case:* An auto purchase loan. While a local bank may offer auto loans at a percent or two lower than other types of loans, many auto dealers helped out by funds from the major manufacturers can extend credit at even lower rates. But watch out. You may get a better price or a rebate if you don't go for the low-interest loan. It may be smarter to take the rebate and seek your financing elsewhere, such as a home-equity loan, particularly if you already have a line of credit.

Tax break: Interest on a home-equity loan may also be tax-deductible. The loan from the auto dealer won't be.

☐ Brokerage accounts. A margin or brokerage account can provide an easy way to obtain funds. Normally, the cost to borrow from a brokerage account is the broker call rate.

Source: David S. Rhine, partner, BDO Seidman, 330 Madison Ave., New York 10017.

How to beat the banks before they beat you

Since deregulation, banks vary widely in their services and in the costs of those services. In order to turn the best profit, banks depend on the fact that customers don't know what to ask for. How you can get the most for your banking dollar:

☐ Deal with the smallest bank you can find. After deregulation, most large banks decided to get rid of smaller depositors. They find it cheaper to serve one corporate account than ten individual accounts. Smaller banks, on the other hand, are more responsive to individual depositors because they need this business.

Ask about checking accounts:

☐ What is the minimum-balance requirement? How does the bank calculate it? Watch out for a minimum-balance calculation that uses the lowest balance for the month. A figure based on the average daily balance is best.

☐ Does the balance on other accounts count toward the checking-account minimum balance?

☐ What is the clearing policy for deposits? This is especially important if you have a NOW account.

☐ What is the overdraft charge? Often it is outrageous. In parts of the Midwest, for example, most banks charge $20.

☐ Don't buy loan insurance from the bank. Credit life or disability insurance is often routinely included on loan forms and added to the cost of your loan. Don't sign any such policy when you take out a loan. This insurance benefits the bank—not you. It covers the bank for the balance of your loan should you die or become disabled. You can get more coverage from an insurance agent for half (or even less) of what the bank charges.

☐ Avoid installment loans. These loans are front-end loaded—even though your balance is declining, you're still paying interest on the original balance throughout the term of the loan. Ask for a single-payment note with simple interest and monthly payments. If you do have an installment loan, don't pay it off early—this actually adds to its real cost.

☐ Pay attention to interest computations. Most people compare rates and assume higher is better. Look for interest figured on a day-of-deposit-to-day-of-withdrawal basis, compounded daily.

☐ Avoid cash machines. The farther bankers can keep you from their tellers and loan officers, the more money they'll make and the less responsive they'll be to your needs. Bankers like machines because people can't argue with them.

☐ Negotiate interest rates. This sounds simple, but it means combating banks' tendencies to lump loans in categories—commercial, mortgage, retail, etc. For example, banks offer a long-time depositor the same interest rate on a car loan as they do a complete newcomer. But often all it takes to get a better rate is to say, "I think my car loan should be 2% lower. I've been banking here for 15 years and I have $10,000 in my savings account."

☐ Forget FDIC security. Given the option of a higher interest rate investment with a secure major corporation that probably has more reserves than the FDIC, many people will still automatically opt for the bank investment because of FDIC insurance. But the FDIC has only $16 billion in reserves. That's a miniscule portion of the money it's insuring. Now that more and more banks are closing every year, the FDIC may soon find itself in big trouble.

☐ Ignore the bank's amortization schedule for mortgages. When you make your monthly payment, especially in the early part of your mortgage, very little goes toward the principal. However, if you choose to pay a small amount extra every month, this will go toward the principal and save you an enormous amount of money.

☐ Don't put all your money in one certificate of deposit. Now that you can deposit as little as $1,000 for the money-market rate, split your deposits so that you get the same interest rate and more liquidity. If you put your money into a $10,000 or $20,000 CD and then find you need to take out $1,000 or $2,000, you will have to pay a horrendous penalty. Instead buy ten or twenty $1,000 CDs.

Source: Edward F. Mrkvicka, Jr., a former bank president and author of *The Bank Book: How To Revoke Your Bank's License To Steal,* Harper-Collins, New York.

Bank-ad deception

The high-yield certificates of deposit advertised by many banks are often not what the ads say they are. *Trap:* The annual yield is meaningless when you buy a three-month CD. And— "effective annual yield" doesn't mean compounded annual yield. Many advertised CDs are so-called simple interest securities that aren't compounded. *Advice:* Don't buy CDs from a bank. Buy shares in money-market mutual funds. They shop for the best CDs.

Source: William E. Donoghue, publisher, *Donoghue's Moneyletter,* Box 6640, Holliston, MA 01746.

Prime-rate secret

Banks calculate their lending rate in arbitrary ways that differ from institution to institution. Your rate may be based on the prime rate set by large money center banks, but it will be calculated and applied by the bank's own formula, which will almost always be higher. *Self-protection:* Before taking out any loan, read and be sure you understand the fine print that spells out the interest-rate adjustment formula. Then make comparisons from bank to bank.

Source: Edward F. Mrkvicka, Jr., president of Reliance Enterprises, a financial consulting company, Box 413, Marengo, IL 60152 and editor of *Money Insider,* a monthly newsletter.

Offshore banking

An offshore bank is any bank that operates outside the jurisdiction of US regulators. Major Swiss banks in Switzerland or elsewhere around the world are offshore banks. So are the Bank of Montreal in Canada, Barclay's Bank in London and the vast world of well-capitalized foreign banks. Those banks may also have branches in the US where they follow US regulations in every way— here. But overseas and in their own countries, they follow the regulations of their host country. And—at times they pay rates to depositors that are better than those obtainable in the US.

Offshore banks are not illegal. There are even facilities of major US banks within the US called International Banking Facilities (IBFs) that are restricted to taking deposits only from overseas customers and making overseas loans. They may not deal with domestic customers. Many major US banks have IBFs. It is really an accounting system in which foreign accounts stay segregated.

☐ Offshore banks offer more privacy to depositors. The privacy feature is useful for law-abiding citizens who would like to keep their assets and records away from a snooping ex-spouse, a business colleague or some other prying investigator.

☐ Only if the money deposited in an offshore bank is undeclared income is there any criminal activity. For the average person who has reported his income and already paid his taxes, it is not illegal to put that money in an off-shore bank either for secrecy reasons or to get a higher return than is obtainable in the US.

☐ Don't do business with a private off-shore bank that's trying to lure you with tax avoidance schemes. Check out the institution in *Polk's Directory of Interna-*

tional Banks (found in most libraries). Each bank listed must submit its financial statement and the names of its officers and explain its operating procedures.

☐ Report any interest that accrues on an overseas account. Offshore banks report your interest earnings directly to you only. They do not report them to the IRS. It is your responsibility to report that income on your tax return. Although it is tempting not to report the interest, since it would be difficult for US authorities to find small bits of interest earnings overseas, it is illegal.

☐ Mailing your deposits overseas and writing checks on overseas accounts are not dissimilar to using a money-market account. When you want to make a withdrawal, just write a check to a local domestic bank on your foreign account. Deposits work similarly. The transfer of funds overseas between banks is very rapid.

☐ Hold an offshore account in dollars unless you are a very sophisticated currency trader. You need professional intelligence in the currency markets to try to guess which currencies will appreciate.

Source: J. F. Straw, publisher and editor of *Offshore Banking News*, Dalton, GA.

How to be richer a year from now

1. Pay down your credit cards. This is the single easiest way to boost your wealth. Paying off credit-card balances—on which you may be paying interest rates of as much as 19% to 21%—is like finding a riskless 30% investment. Not only is the interest on credit-card balances no longer tax-deductible, but you're repaying that money in after-tax dollars.

2. Pay yourself first. If you can live on your present salary, you can also live on 95% of it. Arrange to save 5% of your gross income each pay period—perhaps through an automatic payroll-deduction program with your bank or mutual fund. What you don't see, you won't spend.

3. Boost your withholding to reflect your home mortgage expense. The interest that homeowners pay to the financial institutions that hold their mortgages is tax-deductible. To ease the strain on their budgets, homeowners should adjust their withholding at work and claim exemptions to reflect these deductible expenses and property taxes.

4. Refinance your old mortgage. Even though mortgage rates have crept up and many people have already refinanced, there are still millions of people who are needlessly paying interest on their old mortgages of 12% or more. Even those who have refinanced may find that they can benefit if they refinance a second time.

5. Maximize your contributions to your 401(k) plan. A 401(k) plan is one of the best ways to save for retirement, especially if your employer matches your contributions. The employer's contribution provides an instant return on your money, even before you take into account the tax-deferred compounding you get on your investment earnings. The maximum you can contribute for 1994 is $9,240.

Don't be too conservative and confine yourself to safe but low-yielding bonds or Guaranteed Investment Contracts (GICs). Remember, this is long-term money that you won't need until you retire, so invest in no-load stock funds that offer opportunities for capital appreciation.

6. Don't overlook your Individual Retirement Account (IRA). Even if your income is too high (more than $35,000 a year if single…$50,000 if married) to deduct your IRA contribution or you are already covered by a retirement plan at work, the power of tax-deferred compounding will allow your IRA investment to multiply faster than through a similar investment outside the IRA. Manage your IRA assertively, and don't be too conservative. Avoid fixed-income investments…concentrate on equity investments instead.

7. Lighten up on bonds and bond funds. While we've already had a shakeout, I think the weakest point is still coming. I expect yields to rise and prices to tumble again. If you need income, look into investing for growth—by purchasing stock funds, and then systematically liquidate a portion of your principal to produce spendable cash. Sell off holdings that have increased in price. When people say they need income, they really need cash. Whether that comes from bond interest or principal appreciation in the stock market is irrelevant. By keeping a

money-market fund in your growth portfolio and withdrawing from that, you end up with more spendable cash and let stock-fund profits run.

8. Invest in international stock funds. Domestic growth funds are not the best place to be. We have an aging, tired bull market in the US that is going through a correction. Foreign markets are surprisingly independent of the American stock market. And recent declines simply mean foreign funds will be much better buys during this period. They tend to get ahead of themselves, correct and start up again.

9. Liberate the lemons. Get rid of assets that no longer fit in with your goals or desires.

10. Don't forget that wealth is measured in ways other than just money. The greatest riches of all come from your relationships with family and friends. Nurture them with the same care you give your investments.

Source: William E. Donoghue, author of *William E. Donoghue's Mutual Fund Superstars: Invest with the Best, Forget About the Rest,* Elliott & James, Seattle.

Withholding credit-card payments

You may be able to withhold payments on a credit card used to purchase goods or services that proved substandard. This is the result of a little-known provision of the Fair Credit Billing Act, which enables the credit-card companies to reclaim disputed amounts from merchants after credit-card slips are signed.

You must meet four conditions to be entitled to withhold credit-card payments:

□ The amount of the charge must be more than $50.

□ The charge must be made within the customer's home state, or within 100 miles of the customer's home.

□ The customer must first attempt to settle the dispute with the merchant directly.

□ The customer must give the bank that issued the card written notice that the attempt to settle has failed.

When the bank receives your notice, it credits your account with the amount of the charge. It then charges this amount back to the bank that serves the merchant. That bank then charges the merchant.

Prevent credit-card rip-offs

Here's a simple trick: Pick a number and if possible—make sure that all your credit-card charges end in that number. *For example:* Say you choose the number 8 and your dinner bill comes to $20.00. Instead of adding a $3.00 tip, add $3.08. When your bill comes at the end of the month, check to see if all the charges have 8 as the last digit. If they don't, compare them against your receipts and report discrepancies to the card issuer.

Beware of low credit-card rates

In many cases, bank cards with the lowest rates (11%–14%) can cost much more than cards with traditional 18%–21% charges. *Reason:* A growing number of banks begin tacking on interest charges the minute a transaction is posted to their books. This interest charge accrues until the charge amount and the interest are paid in full. Even if you pay your charges off as soon as you receive the bill each month, you'll still have to pay an interest charge. *Solution:* If you pay in full whenever you use a credit card, choose a bank that charges interest only on balances that are still outstanding following the payment due date on the bill.

Source: *Money.*

20 easy ways to save hard dollars...year in...year out

Small changes in your lifestyle can add up to significant savings over the course of a year. If you adopt just half of these suggestions, you'll save over $1,000 a year…

□ Switch from a bank to a credit union. The average checking account now costs $185 a year in service charges to maintain. Credit unions are nonprofit organizations that return surplus funds to members in the form of low-cost services. Larger credit unions offer free checking, low or no annual fees on credit cards and excellent rates on car loans.

Disadvantages: Fewer branch offices, and the branches may not have automatic teller machines. But, remember, not very long ago, we all survived without ATMs.

☐ Buy your home heating oil in the summer. In my area, prices drop 20¢ a gallon during the off-season, so filling a 275-gallon tank in the summer saves $55. If you are a do-it-yourselfer with extra space, you can buy a used second tank, so you'll have two tanks that can be filled in the off-season. Check local laws about installation and inspection of the second tank. You will have to monitor prices for some weeks to get the best deal in your area, but the bottom should hit sometime between July and early September.

Caution: Don't wait until November, when prices go back up, to get your first fill-up.

☐ Change the oil in your car yourself.

☐ Review your insurance policies. Take higher deductibles where you can afford them, and eliminate coverage you don't need for your lifestyle.

Examples: Many people past childbearing age are still paying for maternity benefits. Most car insurance policies cover car-rental reimbursement when the car is in the shop—but will you use this? Maybe you have a second car or friends who will help out. Are there extra drivers listed on your insurance who no longer live with you? Many homeowners' policies cover furs, jewelry, computers or other items you may not own.

Also, check with your agent to make sure you are getting any discounts you qualify for.

Examples: Nonsmoking on health insurance, alarm systems or safe-driving records on car insurance, owning multiple policies with one company.

☐ Make your own popcorn. A family that pops two batches of traditional generic popcorn a week instead of an equivalent amount of microwave popcorn will save $100 in a year. And it can take less time to make popcorn in a hot-air popper than in a microwave.

☐ Reduce your smoking by three cigarettes a day. (Or give up smoking altogether and save even more.)

☐ Rent videos instead of going to the movies. Even better, check them out of the library.

☐ Make pizza from scratch instead of having it delivered.

☐ Give personal services rather than store-bought presents. Offer to garden, clean bathrooms or baby-sit for your friend in the hospital. Bring your hostess potted herbs from your kitchen or a homemade casserole. Give the new graduate "free résumé service" or 100 pages of thesis typing. Fill out change-of-address forms for your friend who just moved. Refinish a chest of drawers for newlyweds. And don't forget to make your own greeting cards.

☐ Share a newspaper subscription with your neighbor. Are you finished with the paper before you leave for work in the morning? Does your neighbor read the paper before supper? Share magazine subscriptions, too. Many public libraries microfilm, then discard, magazines every six months. Request the outdated issues be held for you. Raid recycling bins.

☐ Hang four loads of laundry a week instead of running the dryer.

☐ Drink four fewer cans of soda per week—saves $100 a year.

☐ Tape ten pieces of music from the radio rather than buying commercially recorded audiotapes.

☐ Cut your family's hair yourself. A child's haircut costs as much as $8 to $10 every six weeks. An adult haircut at $25 every six weeks adds up to $217 a year. If you learn to trim it yourself you will only need to have a professional job at the hairdresser half the time. This will save you $100.

☐ Bake one batch of bread (two loaves) once a week.

☐ Write one good letter a month instead of making an $8 long-distance telephone call.

☐ Use half your usual amount of cleaning and personal-care products. Find the minimum effective level of shampoo, conditioner, laundry detergent, bleach, dishwasher detergent, toothpaste, shaving cream, lotion, perfume, etc. You may find you can make do with less than half your usual amount.

☐ Buy articles of clothing from thrift shops and yard sales rather than paying store prices. This is also a fun way to shop.

☐ Barter for one regular service. Handy with graphics? Arrange to make fliers and do an advertising layout for your massage therapist in return for monthly sessions. Want help cleaning? Offer to take your cleaning person's kids for a weekly activity in return for two hours of housecleaning. Are you an accountant? Trade tax preparation for lawn care or TV repair.

Consider three-party trades to get what you need.

Example: You want ten $10 computer lessons, the computer instructor needs a $100 repair on her car, so you prepare the mechanic's tax return in exchange for fixing the car, in exchange for your lessons.

Be creative!

☐ Use dry milk. A gallon of whole milk costs up to $2.59 per gallon. Dry milk, purchased in the 20-quart store-brand box, costs $1.60 per gallon. Dry milk is 100% fat-free, while whole milk contains 4% fat. By mixing the two kinds of milk half and half, you can make your own 2% milk. If you use a gallon of milk every three days, you will easily save $100 in a year by substituting dry milk in cooking, homemade cocoa mix and in using the half-and-half mixture for drinking.

Source: Amy Dacyczyn—"The Frugal Zealot." She is the author of *The Tightwad Gazette,* a book of excerpts from her newsletter of the same name, Villard Books, New York. *The Tightwad Gazette* is published monthly, RR1, Box 3570, Leeds, Maine 04263.

Reducing taxable gains when you sell your house

If you sell your home and then do not use the proceeds to buy another one, you are taxed on any gain realized from the deal (unless you're over 55 and gain is less than $125,000—and you can only do this once). Gain, in general, is the difference between your cost basis and the selling price, less selling expenses.

It's important then to understand: (1) How your cost basis is computed, and (2) what selling expenses are deductible. It's essential to keep an accurate record of those items which will help to reduce your tax liability.

Cost basis includes:

☐ Price paid in cash or property and by mortgage obligation assumed or mortgage to which property is subject.

☐ Attorney's fees and expenses in connection with the purchase contract and its closing or settlement; also the cost of searching, defending or perfecting title.

☐ Costs of appraisal, recording of deed and mortgage, survey.

☐ Title search and title insurance.

☐ Cost of getting cash for purchase (mortgage broker's fees, lender's origination fee, title search and/or title insurance, legal fees for drafting bond and mortgage), but not "points."

☐ Architectural and engineering fees, plus termite inspection.

☐ Restoration of building or improvements prolonging its useful life or increasing its value which are in the nature of capital investment and long-term improvements. *Example:* Owner replaces the roof when house is sold.

☐ The cost of improvements outside the building(s), such as landscaping, grading, driveways, wells, kitchens, walks, patio.

☐ Real-estate taxes of the seller assumed by the buyer as part of the purchase price.

☐ Purchasing commissions.

☐ Insurance during construction.

☐ "Rent" paid while occupying under option to purchase and applied to purchase price on exercise of option.

Deductible selling expenses include:

☐ Broker's commission.

☐ Legal expenses and attorney's fees.

☐ Advertising.

☐ Sales tax, if applicable.

☐ Title abstract.

☐ "Points" paid by the seller to enable buyer to obtain financing.

☐ Fixing-up expenses if incurred within 90 days of the sale contract and paid within 30 days after sale.

Float can work both ways

The textbook definition of float is "converting a negotiable instrument into cash or the transit period required to turn a contingency into an asset." This means, on the one hand, the time lapse between your deposit and the date the bank allows you to use those funds or, on the other hand, the time lapse between when you make a payment by check or other draft and the date that debit is charged to your account.

Assuming that the money in question is "working," using float is a way of "creating money."

Perhaps the first step in dealing with float is to minimize its use against you. Find a bank with a reasonable "hold" policy (the delay in crediting deposits to customer accounts).

Once you have arranged to make your deposits work as long and hard as possible, you might give some attention to making float work to positive financial advantage. If you have a NOW account or a money-market account, by making payment by mail on the last possible day, you may keep that money earning as much as a week longer than otherwise, given mail delivery time and time for the draft to clear through the system. (A postmarked mailing is the legal equivalent of making payment in person on the same date.)

There are ways to use float in your savings program, too. There are still banks that offer an in-by-the-tenth, earning-from-the-first policy. You can routinely turn this to your advantage by the simple expedient of opening a second account in a day-of-deposit-to-day-of-withdrawal bank (we'll call it Bank 2) and playing one bank against the other: Withdraw funds from Bank 2 on the tenth of the month, depositing them in Bank 1, thus earning an extra ten days' interest on the sum every month. On the last day of the month, simply transfer funds back to Bank 2 and begin again. (*Note:* Some in-by-the-tenth banks offer this privilege only on a quarterly basis. Still, that's 40 days' double interest per year.)

Source: Edward F. Mrkvicka, Jr., founder and president of Reliance Enterprises, Inc., PO Box 413, Marengo, IL 60152.

Cashing CDs before maturity

Many investors don't realize that they can also buy bank CDs through Merrill Lynch and other brokers. *Benefit:* Merrill Lynch maintains a market in CDs, so it's possible to sell them back before maturity.

Don't collect credit cards

Owning six or more credit cards can get you turned down for additional credit, even if you don't use them. Some lenders consider not only how much debt you have but also how much credit is available to you when you apply. That's because they recognize the danger of temptation. *Strategy:* When you switch to an issuer that offers a good deal, close out an older account and ask the issuer to report to the credit bureau that the account is closed. That way, it won't count against you as available credit.

Source: Gerri Detweiler, consumer credit consultant in Dale City, Virginia, and author of *The Ultimate Credit Handbook*, Good Advice Press, Box 780, Elizaville, New York 12523.

Bankruptcy and you

If facing possible bankruptcy, try to pay off at least one major credit card. A credit card that is paid off before a bankruptcy filing does not have to be included in the bankruptcy and can be used to help re-establish credit afterward. Use the credit card only for small purchases that you can pay off each month to show a positive payment pattern.

Source: Deborah McNaughton, founder, Professional Credit Counselors, Orange County, California, and author of *Everything You Need to Know About Credit*, Thomas Nelson Publishers, Box 141000, Nashville 37214.

Your pension payout: The partial distribution option

When it comes time to collect your company pension benefits, there are a bewildering range of payout options. An option that is less used, but could have benefits to you under certain circumstances, is to take some of the money out of the pension plan in a lump sum and leave the rest in. Make sure to get good tax advice before electing a partial distribution, however.

☐ If you have big tax deductions, it may be to your advantage to take some of the distribution as income and roll over the balance into an IRA or another company plan. The deductions will offset the distribution, so you may wind up with some tax-free income.

☐ You may also want to take a partial distribution if you have to pay the alternative minimum tax (AMT). *Reason:* The most tax you can pay on the extra income is 28%—the top AMT tax rate.

☐ You can roll over any qualifying portion of a lump-sum distribution into an IRA or into another qualified company pension plan. But you cannot roll over any nondeductible voluntary contributions you may have made to the plan over the years.

Tax loopholes to finance your retirement nest egg

The tax laws are peppered with loopholes designed to help us live comfortably in retirement. Eight to spice up your retirement financial plan:

☐ Tax-free home sales. If you or your spouse is 55 or older when you sell your house, and you've lived in it for three of the last five years, you have an optional tax break on the first $125,000 of profit on the sale.

If you're about to remarry and one partner has already used the home sales exclusion, the one who hasn't should sell his house *prior* to the marriage to take the exclusion. The right will be revoked after the marriage.

☐ Gifts to grandchildren. Before selling appreciated assets, such as securities, to give cash gifts to your descendants, give the actual securities and let the kids sell them. A gift of the property will save tax (and create a bigger gift) if the recipient is in a lower tax bracket than you. The recipient will pay less tax on the gain than you would.

Reverse the strategy if the recipient intends to retain the property. In this case, give cash now and let the intended recipient inherit the appreciated property. *Reason:* The recipient will inherit the property at a stepped-up basis, that is, its value at the date of your death. He or she won't have to pay capital-gains tax on the property's increase in value.

☐ Rent a condominium from your children. Get Uncle Sam to subsidize the cost of supporting an elderly parent by getting the children to buy the parent's retirement condominium and rent it to the parent. At the very least, the children will get tax deductions for mortgage interest and property taxes. These deductions will produce a greater tax benefit to high-income children than they would to a low-bracket retired parent. And if the children charge the parent fair market rent, they will also be able to take depreciation deductions on the condo.

You can deduct up to $25,000 of losses if your adjusted gross income is less than $100,000. This loss allowance is phased out between $100,000 and $150,000 of adjusted gross income.

☐ Plan in advance for nursing-home care. Before the government will pay your nursing-home bills, you have to use up the money that's in your name. *Strategy:* Put your money into a trust that pays you income but which doesn't allow you to touch the principal. Then only the income would be lost to nursing-home care—you won't lose the principal. *Caution:* In most states, a trust that is set up within two years of a person's entering a nursing home *won't* be effective. Check with an attorney about your state's laws.

☐ IRS vs. remarriage. A married couple, both age 65 or over, will pay more tax on a joint return than the combined tax they would pay if they were single. *Another consideration:* If income (including tax-exempt income) plus one-half Social Security benefits exceed certain levels, the Social Security benefits are taxable. *The levels are:* $25,000 for a single person, or $32,000 for a married couple. Combining incomes on a joint return may force taxation of Social Security benefits that would completely escape taxation if the couple did not marry.

☐ IRA strategy. Now, arrange for IRA certificates of deposit (CDs) to mature at the same time, so you can then re-invest the accumulated funds *together* in a single, higher-yielding investment. *Example:* Put this year's IRA in a five-year CD, next year's in a four-year CD and so on. *General rule:* The larger your IRA, the better your return.

Then, as you approach age 70½, don't lock up all accounts in certificates of deposit that won't be accessible at that age. *Reason:* You are required by law to begin taking distributions from your IRA by April 1 of the year following the year in which you become 70½…even if that entails paying an early-withdrawal penalty.

☐ Collecting Social Security early can pay off. Even though benefits are re-duced, they'll usually add up to more in the long run. *Example:* If full benefits are $750 per month for retiring at age 65, you can get reduced benefits of $600 a month by retiring at age 62. You'd have to collect full benefits for 12 years to make up the $21,600 you'd receive dur-ing the three years of early payments.

☐ Retirement-plan distributions. You must start taking money out of your Individual Retirement Account by April 1 following the year in which you reach age 70½. *Loophole:* You may be able to slow the distribution down (take less in the early years) by using actuarial tables. Check with the IRA trustee to see if a slower distribution schedule can be used for your payouts.

Source: Edward Mendlowitz, partner, Mendlowitz Weitsen, Two Pennsylvania Plaza, New York 10121.

What it takes

Comfortable retirement requires about 50%–75% of the final working year's income.

Source: *CPA Digest,* Milwaukee.

Which Keogh is best for you?

☐ The defined-benefit type works best if you are within, say, 20 years of retirement. This type can produce a larger Keogh fund, from bigger tax-deductible contributions, than the other types. Also, inflation and mediocre investment performance matter less with this type.

☐ The money-purchase type is favored if you have a Midas touch with your investments, or if you start your Keogh relatively early in life.

☐ Profit-sharing plans are much like money-purchase plans, though easier to set up and operate. But since the 1984 law change that liberalized defined-benefit and money-purchase Keoghs, profit-sharing plans now lag behind in tax benefits. The top deduction in a profit-sharing Keogh is only 60% of what's possible with a money-purchase Keogh, and only 15% of what's possible (though not typical) with defined-benefit Keoghs.

For economic reasons, you might have to settle for a plan that's less than the best for you, if you have employees who must be included in your plan.

IRA vs. deferred annuities: A checklist

One of the most attractive investment products around is the insurance industry's deferred annuities.

☐ Deferred annuities are an alternative for individuals whose incentive to continue to make IRA contributions was devastated by tax reform.

Although contributions to a deferred an-nuity are not tax-deductible, earnings accumulate tax-deferred. *Advantage over an IRA:* There is no limit to the amount of money you can invest in an annuity.

☐ Variable annuities are the ideal re-placement for investments that used to receive the benefit of favorable long-term capital-gains treatment. *Reason:* Long-term gains from investments in stocks, which are now taxed as ordinary income, can be sheltered in a variable annuity. That income is not taxed until you withdraw your money.

☐ When you buy an annuity from an insurance company you pay in a lump sum or a series of payments over time. In return, the insurance company guar-antees that the funds will grow at a certain tax-free rate. On a specified date you begin to receive regular income payments for the rest of your life.

☐ Payments depend on the amount of money contributed to the account, the length of time the funds are left in it and the rate of return earned on the funds.

☐ Another factor in determining the size of the payments is whether you include your spouse and other heirs as beneficiaries.

☐ Different options enable you to have payments continue to your wife, or to your children, or for a minimum of, say, 20 years, regardless of who is there to receive them after you die.

☐ Deferred annuities are part insurance and part investment. If you are willing to part with at least $5,000 (the minimum amount can differ from company to company) for five years or longer, you can be guaranteed a competitive, tax-free return on your funds. Because the earned income is not taxed until you begin withdrawing the money (presumably at a much lower tax rate), your funds accumulate much faster than they would if they were taxed. The insurance component, of course, is guaranteed regular monthly income payments for the rest of your life—taking the worry and risk out of budgeting for your retirement income.

☐ Should you die before you begin receiving payments, your heirs are guaranteed to receive the full amount of your original principal.

Source: Alexandra Armstrong, Armstrong, Welch & MacIntyre, Washington, DC.

Making voluntary contributions to a company pension plan

Making voluntary payments to your company's pension plan, in addition to the contributions your employer already makes for you, makes tax sense.

☐ The voluntary contribution isn't deductible but the interest it earns accumulates tax-free.

☐ You won't be taxed on what the contribution earns until you take it out at retirement.

☐ When you make a withdrawal from the plan, that part of the withdrawal that is attributable to your voluntary contributions is tax-free. (The percentage is figured by a complex formula set by law. Check with your tax advisor before making a withdrawal.)

☐ *Voluntary contribution limit:* 10% of your salary.

How safe is your pension?

Whether you are examining pension information of public or private firms, you are seeking the same sort of basic information.

How to check on the safety of your retirement income:

☐ *For employees of public companies:* Basic information is included in the firm's annual report. Usually the size of a firm's unfunded pension liability and the size of its past service liability are disclosed in footnotes. More detailed information is available in the financial section of the firm's 10K report, filed with the Securities and Exchange Commission.

☐ *For employees of private companies:* Everyone who is in a qualified plan (one approved by the IRS under the Code) has the right to obtain information about his pension from the trustees of the plan. They may be either internal or external trustees. The average person may not be able to decipher the information. If you can't, then take it to a pension expert, actuary, lawyer or accountant for an analysis.

☐ The size of a company's liability for retirement payouts is not as important as the assumptions about funding these liabilities. Like a mortgage, these obligations don't exist 100% in the present. Concern yourself with how the company expects to fund its liabilities.

Types of liabilities:

☐ Unfunded pension liabilities. The amount a firm expects to need over the next 20 to 30 years to supply vested workers with promised pension benefits. These figures are derived from various actuarial assumptions.

☐ Past service liabilities. Created when a company raises its pension compensation. For instance, a company may have been planning to provide 40% of compensation as a pension. One year, they may raise that to 45% and treat it retroactively.

Trouble signs:

☐ A poor record on investing. Compare the market value of the assets in the pension with their book value. If book value is more than market value, the trustees have not been investing wisely. *Point:* If the fund had to sell those assets today, there would be a loss. *Another bad sign:* The fund is still holding some obscure bonds or other fixed-income obligations issued at low rates years ago.

☐ Funding assumptions are overstated. Actuaries have a myriad of estimates on how long it takes to fund pension plans and what rate of return a company will get.

What to look at:

☐ Time frame. This should not be too long. If the firm is funding over 40 years, find out why and how; 10 to 20 years is more customary. Assumptions made on 40 years may not hold up at all.

☐ Rate of return. If a company assumes a conservative 6% to 7% or less right now, you can be comfortable. If the assumed rate is 10% or more, question how they are going to meet that expectation for the entire fund over the long run.

☐ Salary and wage scales. The company should be assuming an increase in compensation over years. Most plans have such provisions.

☐ Assumptions about the employee turnover rate. These should be consistent with the historically documented turnover of the company. If a firm has a very high turnover rate and assumes a 4% turnover, the company will be underfunded at some time. Estimates should be conservative.

☐ To assess your own status in a corporate pension plan, see how many years you have been vested. Many people have the illusion that they are fully vested for maximum pensions after a few years. In truth, companies couldn't afford to vest people fully with such short service. With so much job-hopping in the past two decades, an individual's pension-fund status may be much less than imagined.

☐ Employees of troubled or even bankrupt companies need not panic. Trustees of the plan have an obligation to the vested employees. The assets of the plan are segregated, and no creditor can reach them. In fact, as a creditor, the corporate pension plan can grab some corporate assets under certain circumstances. And if there has been gross mismanagement of pension funds, stockholders of a closely held company can be held personally liable.

Source: James E. Conway, president of The Ayco Corporation, Albany, NY.

New job opportunities for retirees

Finding a job after retirement requires a different kind of strategy from the career tactics you used earlier in life. For many, the key move is taking advantage of the vast, but often little-known, resources that can lead to satisfying jobs.

The inside track:

Many companies hire retirees, but a few actively seek older people to employ. Applying to the "seekers" can be a shortcut to employment:

☐ Days Inns of America

☐ Hewlett-Packard

☐ Kentucky Fried Chicken

☐ Travelers Corp.

☐ Walt Disney

Of Travelers' 34,000 employees, for example, 6,500 are retirees.

Groups that track these companies and offer other employment help to retirees include:

☐ American Association of Retired Persons, 601 E St. NW, Washington, DC 20049, 202-434-2277.

☐ Forty Plus, 1718 P St. NW, Washington, DC 20036, 202-387-1582.

☐ Operation Able, 180 N. Wabash Ave., Suite 802, Chicago 60601, 312-782-3335. Able also holds "job fairs" that put employers together with job-seeking retirees. Increasingly, employment and temporary agencies attend the fairs.

☐ Senior Career Planning & Placement Service, 257 Park Ave. S., New York 10010, 212-529-6660. This group has had great success in helping retired managers find jobs at companies such as Polaroid and Seagram's.

It generally makes more sense to apply to small rather than large businesses. Small companies often have difficulty finding the type of expertise that comes only with years of experience.

Best places to look:

Today's hot businesses for retirees: Financial services, health care, the hotel and hospitality industry, pharmaceuticals, restaurants and catering, sales and marketing, travel.

Many retirees overlook nonprofit corporations because of the mistaken belief that they rely chiefly on volunteers. As a matter of fact, most nonprofits have a good track record of hiring retirees, especially in part-time and temporary positions.

Try to take advantage of the network you built up during your earlier career. Many retired network members may be working again. If they are, some are likely to know of positions for other retirees.

Unconventional opportunities:

☐ International Executive Service Corps. This group places retired American executives as volunteer consultants to overseas businesses and governments. Box 10005, Stamford, Connecticut 06904, 203-967-6000.

☐ Peace Corps. Some 12% of the Corps is over 50—the oldest is 81. Like the Service Corps, the Peace Corps can be more emotionally than monetarily rewarding. 1990 K St. NW, Washington, DC 20526, 800-424-8580.

Upgrading skills:

To make yourself more marketable, be prepared to beef up your skills with additional training. That's especially necessary in jobs where new technology, such as word processing, has been introduced.

Other types of training may be needed to help you use old knowledge in new ways.

Example: Many people who worked with a product during their earlier career may now be able to find a job selling the product, provided they acquire training in sales.

Where to go for training: The same groups that help retirees find jobs are usually excellent resources in recommending local organizations and schools that offer training courses to retirees.

Companies that offer training to older workers include AT&T, GE and Pitney Bowes.

Playing to strength:

In your résumé and job interviews, show how you can help a company meet two of today's biggest needs in employees—experience and stability:

☐ Stress experience by highlighting specific accomplishments in previous jobs.

☐ Use words that convey how your past performance has contributed to profit and growth—launched, pioneered, created, generated, streamlined, tripled, expanded.

☐ Omit your age and irrelevant dates on the résumé, but be frank about your background. (It's illegal for employers to ask your age.)

☐ Frame your responses to an interviewer's questions in terms of your seasoned judgment and lifetime experience of working with people. When asked about your last job, for instance, talk about projects that demanded your ability to get along with others. Cite examples of your good judgment.

☐ Avoid self-deprecating comments about old age. The most common are, "When you get to be my age"…and "Back then we did things differently."

☐ Never set limits on how many years you plan to work. Some companies believe that retirees are only interested in working for a year or two.

☐ Dress well for interviews, but don't try to look younger than you are. Rehearse for interviews with a friend.

☐ If an interviewer says you're overqualified, say something like this, "If overqualified means I have a lot of experience, you're right. But I'm willing to work at the going rate and would enjoy bringing my experience and skill to the job."

Your rights:

Sadly, "overqualified" is often used as a euphemism for "too old." Under the federal Age Discrimination in Employment Act, it's illegal (with several exceptions) to discriminate against workers on the basis of age.

If you believe that a prospective employer is guilty of discrimination, you might want to contact an office of the US Equal Employment Opportunity Commission. To find the nearest office, phone 800-669-4000.

The self-employment trap:

Don't be tempted to go into business for yourself if you lack the right combination of skills to make it a success.

To be a successful freelance consul-tant, for instance, you first have to be a good salesperson. And running your own company also requires a broad range of skills including administrative skills.

Frequent solution: Team up with other people, one who's talented in administration and another who's skilled at selling. Many regional Forty Plus offices are especially good at building entrepreneurial teams of retirees with different skills.

Advantages:

The advantage to health in finding a job after retirement can be surprising. Not only do employed older people live longer, but studies show they also recover faster from ailments. And keeping active may even improve your looks and attitude.

Source: Robert S. Menchin, former vice president of the Chicago Board of Trade and author of *New Work Opportunities for Older Americans,* Prentice Hall, Englewood Cliffs, NJ. He's now president of Wall Street Marketing, 401 N. Franklin St., Chicago 60610, consultants in selling to older consumers.

Early IRA withdrawals

Although the Tax Reform Act clobbered the IRA deduction for many taxpayers, it created a penalty-free way to withdraw money from the account before you reach age 59½.

☐ *Old law:* You had to pay an additional 10% penalty tax on distributions from IRA accounts before age 59½.

☐ *New law:* You won't pay the extra 10% penalty tax if you convert the account to an annuity and receive the money in a scheduled series of substantially equal payments over your life or your life expectancy.

Managing your own IRA account

With a brokerage house account or a no-load family of mutual funds for an IRA, the investor can change his mind about an investment without penalty.

At a bank or S&L, the investor who changes his mind about a five-year certificate of deposit pays an early-withdrawal penalty. But the only penalty for changing an IRA investment at a brokerage house is commission.

☐ Investors should not take chances with their IRA money. They should buy high-yielding instruments or equities with the ability to pay a dividend (whether they actually do or not) and the potential for high growth.

☐ The big mistake made in self-directed IRAs is overtrading. Some people think there is a magical way for them to double their money in a very short time, especially in an IRA, and they buy highly speculative securities. In volatile,

aggressive stocks, investors can lose money at least as easily as they can make it. And any dollar in an IRA is worth even more to the investor than a regular dollar, since the money it earns is tax-free. The account can turn into a sizable amount without risk.

☐ If you lose money in an IRA account, you get no tax help from the government—it gives you no tax deduction for such a loss.

☐ There is usually a custodial fee ($30 or so a year) for self-directed IRAs. Although the custodial fee is tax-deductible, it is difficult for an investor with only a $2,000 account to justify it. It is easier to justify the custodial fee when there is $5,000 or more in an account. And when the account reaches a significant size, the investor can buy a greater number of instruments and increase diversification.

☐ *Favorite investments for IRAs in recent years:* Zero-coupon bonds, Ginnie Mae bonds, convertible bonds and common stocks (particularly oil companies and utility issues).

Source: Robert L. Thomas, executive vice president, Advest, Hartford, CT.

IRA-investment traps

The April 15 tax deadline for personal income taxes is also the deadline for making IRA contributions. Everyone who is eligible to should make the maximum contribution the law allows. But before you invest:

☐ Read the fine print. Watch for set-up charges, management fees and early withdrawal penalties that institutions charge (over and above the tax-law penalties). The penalties can be steep and fees vary widely. Shop around.

☐ Make IRA contributions in cash or check only. That's the law. You won't get a deduction for a transfer of stock from your investment account into an IRA.

☐ Stay within the contribution limits. If you exceed the limit, you're liable for a nondeductible excise tax (6% of the excess amount) for each year the excess remains in your account. To avoid the penalty, you must withdraw the excess along with the earnings attributable to such excess before your return is due (including extensions).

☐ Don't put your IRA in an investment that already provides tax-exempt income, such as municipal bonds or a municipal investment trust. *Reason:* Tax-exempt bonds typically yield less than taxable bonds because the tax exemption is of value to investors. By law, the income earned in an IRA builds up tax-free until withdrawn. Thus, tax-free interest on municipal bonds is of no value to an IRA.

☐ Don't invest your IRA in the federal government's Individual Retirement Bonds. *Problem:* With other IRA investments you can take your money out over a period of years, starting when you're 59½. But you must take the whole Individual Retirement Bond out in one piece. (You can't redeem just a part of the bond.)

Source: Brett D. Yacker, tax partner, and Leonard J. Senzon, tax manager, Price Waterhouse, New York.

Better retirement benefits for the self-employed

Businesses no longer have to be incorporated for the owners to obtain maximum benefits from a tax-favored retirement plan. Keogh-type plans for self-employed persons and unincorporated businesses have been liberalized to provide larger benefits.

☐ The maximum deductible contribution has been increased to $30,000 or 25% of income—whichever is less.

Working after retirement

Many retirees would like to keep working after retirement, at least part-time. But those who want to work for financial reasons should be aware of the drawbacks and some alternatives.

☐ You can earn up to $11,280 a year (for 1995) if you're age 65 to 69 and still collect full Social Security benefits. But for every $3 earned above that amount,

you lose $1 in benefits. When you add your commuting costs, job-related expenses and payroll deductions, you may find part-time work doesn't pay off.

☐ If you continue working part-time for the same company, you may not be eligible to collect your pension. One way around this, if the company will go along, is to retire as an employee and return as a consultant or freelancer. Since you're now self-employed, your pension won't be affected.

☐ Although most employees can't legally be compelled to retire before age 70, companies still set up retirement ages of 65 or under. You can work past that age, but you won't necessarily earn further pension credits. And you lose Social Security and pension benefits while you continue to work.

☐ A very attractive alternative to working part-time is to start your own business. Professionals such as lawyers can often set up a practice, setting their own hours. Or you might turn a hobby into a business.

Source: William W. Parrott, a chartered financial consultant at Merrill Lynch, Pierce, Fenner & Smith, Inc., New York.

Five kinds of pay that are exempt from Social Security taxes

☐ Wages paid to your child under 18, when the business is a proprietorship. Wages paid by a corporation are subject to tax.

☐ Loans taken out from the company by an employee or shareholder. But be sure the loan is fully documented, so that there is no doubt about its legitimacy. If the IRS concludes that the loan will not be paid back, tax will be imposed. The loan must carry an interest rate equal to 110% of the applicable federal rate at the time of the loan. The IRS announces this rate twice each year.

☐ Health-insurance payments made

into an employee accident, health or medical-reimbursement plan.

☐ Educational benefits which add to employee's on-the-job skills.

☐ Moving-expense reimbursements when a move is job-related, covers more than 50 miles and the worker stays at the new job site at least 39 weeks during the next year.

Tax considerations for expatriate retirees

Before you retire abroad, be prepared for many more complex variables than there are in US retirement communities.

☐ All American citizens are subject to US income tax, regardless of where they live. But they get US tax credit for income taxes paid to the other government. However, they won't get a refund from the US if local tax rates are higher than US rates, and that's often the case. In fact, some foreign countries tax US Social Security income as well.

☐ Only by renouncing US citizenship can an individual escape US income taxes. Dividends and other passive income are taxed at their source. However, if the IRS can prove that US citizen-ship has been renounced within the last ten years with the principal reason being to escape income taxes, the individual will be taxed as a US citizen.

☐ *Test of foreign residency for US income tax:* Living abroad for a full calendar year or having a physical presence outside the US for 12 of 13 consecutive months. Foreign residents are, however, exempt from state and local taxes in the US.

☐ *Good idea:* Americans who can arrange to earn income while residing abroad (through a personal company, for example) qualify for a US tax ex-

emption on the first $70,000 of earned income plus a living-allowance exclusion, provided they meet the residency or presence test above. For someone locating in a country without an income tax, that can amount to quite a windfall.

☐ Some retirees prefer to maintain their US home either as a place to stay while visiting or as an investment that can be rented and depreciated to tax advantage while they live abroad. The US government won't consider it a principal place of residence if it's used as a permanent abode for fewer than 183 days a year.

☐ The once-in-a-lifetime tax-free gain of $125,000 on the sale of a principal residence can be applied to a foreign home, provided it's been used as a principal residence for three out of the last five years.

☐ A person moving abroad has four years, not just two as in the US, to buy a home of equivalent value after the sale of the principal residence and qualify for the tax deferral on the gain.

☐ *Reason to rent rather than buy a home:* Currency restrictions and capital-gains rules vary from country to country. As a general rule, it's easier to invest abroad than it is to repatriate dollars after a sale.

Source: Israel Press, partner, and Alan Brad, manager, tax department, Financial Services Center, Deloitte & Touche, New York.

Before you replace a life-insurance policy

Before replacing a life-insurance policy, ask, "Will you have full protection during the transition period?" A gap in coverage could put your family at risk. "Will the new policy fully protect dependents?" If you swap a term policy for a cash-value policy, you're likely to get less protection at the same price in early years before the policy builds up cash value. "Are you still insurable?" Illness or advancing age may cause a new insurer to charge you much more than you paid for the old policy. "Does the swap help you or the insurance agent?" An agent who is anxious for a commission may try to talk you into borrowing against an old policy to buy a new one—leaving you with a loan to repay that will eat up policy proceeds.

Source: Jersey Gilbert, financial reporter, *Money Magazine*, and author of *Life-Insurance Handbook*, Consumer Reports Books, 101 Truman Ave., Yonkers, New York 10703.

Medigap-insurance basics

First decide which benefits you're most likely to need. Policies cover a variety of services, including nursing-home copayments, foreign-travel emergencies, prescription drugs, etc. Be sure to understand the premium structure for policies offering similar benefits as well as the pricing structure and what can or will happen to premiums during the next several years. *Consider:* Does the company offer "crossover billing?" This means Medicare will automatically send bills to the Medigap insurer and ensures that you won't pay the bill yourself and then forget to file for reimbursement. Also explore group policies offered by social or professional organizations… get free counseling, pamphlets or actual rate comparisons by contacting a senior health-insurance counseling program available in most states or through a professional health-insurance agent.

Source: Charles Ratner, national director of personal insurance counseling, Ernst & Young, Cleveland.

Insurance traps and opportunities

☐ Don't buy travel insurance at airports. Coverage is much more expensive and rates vary from city to city. Instead, buy directly from the insurance company.

☐ A fire or burglar alarm should entitle you to a reduction in insurance premiums. The saving on homeowners' premiums is about 2% to 10% a year. Addition of a smoke detector should lower premiums another 3%.

☐ Bargain policy picks up when major medical runs out. The cost of really complicated illness today can exceed major medical coverage. To protect yourself, buy an "excess" major medical policy with deductible equal to maximum benefit under your current plan. *Features to shop around for:* Guaranteed renewability; five-year benefit period; coverage of children from birth to age 18 or 21; payment of "reasonable" or "usual" hospital costs rather than specified daily rate.

☐ Don't buy insurance that pays off a loan or installment debt if you die or are disabled. Instead, buy decreasing term-life insurance for the duration of the installments. Saves up to 44%.

How much insurance is enough

It's conventional wisdom that you need life insurance equal to five or seven times your annual income. That's OK as a general rule, but following it too closely can be costly. The danger of over- or underinsuring is especially great as your asset base changes.

Before deciding how much life insurance to carry, look at:

☐ Cash needs for settling the estate and paying uninsured medical costs and funeral expenses.

☐ Outstanding debts. It's nice to give the family greater financial freedom by paying off the mortgage, car loans, outstanding installment debt and credit-card balances.

☐ Educational goals for children.

☐ Surviving family income fund. The amount of insurance needed is the difference between expenses and income, including Social Security. Always include a cushion for emergencies.

☐ Inflation protection. Figure 9% inflation a year to protect current purchasing power. Be prepared to alter your coverage as inflation expectations change.

☐ Accumulated assets. The same assets that can provide income for your heirs can be wiped out unless you have adequate liability coverage. Never settle for $1 million—because you can get $5 million for very little more. Here, the sky is almost the limit.

☐ Present age. Insurance is most essential for people who haven't yet accumulated substantial assets. It's important to start young, even if you can afford only term insurance. The danger with term insurance is that as it becomes more expensive with age, it's increasingly tempting to drop it.

☐ Instead of a raise, ask the company for more disability insurance. It's deductible for the company, and the premiums aren't considered income to you for tax purposes. But unless the company plan is adequate, be prepared to buy substantially more disability coverage.

☐ Set a definite time each year—preferably twice a year—to review your financial plan and insurance coverage. For business owners, these reviews are especially useful because the business will be growing and changing, too. Then act. Change your financial plan and insurance coverage to reflect the current situation.

Source: J. Gary Sheets, chairman, CFS Financial Corp., financial planners, Salt Lake City, UT.

How not to buy insurance coverage that you don't need

While so many people worry about being underinsured, we should all be concerned instead about having too much insurance.

The most common insurance mistakes are wasting money on the wrong kind of insurance…and on insurance that duplicates coverage already provided by another policy.

Myth: By purchasing all of your insurance from the same agent, you'll get coordinated at the best value.

Reality: For personal insurance, you'll very often pay more by using an agent. According to one authoritive study, the best price and service was delivered by Amica Mutual Insurance and United Services Auto Association, both of which sell direct. Some of the biggest and best-known companies were the worst buys.

Best: Carefully determine your own needs, then shop around. Get quotes both from agents and from direct insurance writers. Compare the rates and coverages and pick the best value.

Coverage you don't need

The biggest insurance trap is being sold insurance you don't need. If you're single and have no dependents, for example, you really have no need for life insurance. And there's no financial reason to buy life insurance on a child who does not contribute to the family's income. Other insurance you don't need:

☐ Flight insurance. Many people buy flight insurance as a kind of good-luck charm, but it is grossly overpriced. Take the money you would spend to buy insurance on a two-hour flight and use it, instead, to buy more term-life insurance that covers you 365 days a year, around the clock, wherever you are.

☐ Cancer insurance. This is very expensive and protects you against only that one disease. You're much better off buying good comprehensive health insurance that covers all illnesses.

☐ Mortgage insurance. In a recent study, we found that bank mortgage insurance was more than twice as expensive as plain term-life insurance. And if you die, your family might be better off not repaying the mortgage—if, for example, they can invest their money to earn a rate of return that exceeds the after-tax cost of deductible mortgage interest. *Best strategy:* Buy enough life insurance from one company to cover all your family needs. Don't be talked into buying extra insurance that is for the benefit of the bank, not you.

☐ Credit-card life insurance. If you are being charged premiums for life insurance to cover your unpaid credit-card balance, ask that it be eliminated or switch to a credit-card company that doesn't burden you with insurance that is only for the benefit of the credit-card company.

☐ Liability duplication. If you have an umbrella liability policy, be sure not to duplicate liability coverage with your auto insurance.

Example: If your automobile insurance policy includes $300,000 of liability, and the umbrella liability policy kicks in after the first $100,000, you don't need the extra $200,000 of coverage on your auto policy.

You may also find there's duplication under your homeowners' policy.

Also…if you have good comprehensive health insurance, you don't need to buy additional coverage in your auto insurance.

Buying smart

☐ Generally speaking, with liability and health insurance it's smart to take the largest possible deductibles to hold premiums down.

Put aside the money you save in a family savings account that earns interest. You can use it to pay whatever deductibles do arise under your policies, and in the end you—not the insurance company—will probably have a nice nest egg.

With homeowners' insurance, you should get coverage for the full replacement cost of your property. Even then, the biggest mistake many people make is not keeping an adequate inventory of what they have and how much it is all worth. You can have the finest insurance in the world, but if you don't have any proof of loss to show the insurance company, you will not get a fair settlement. Most of us could never remember everything that's in our homes, especially after the trauma of a fire.

Solution: Take time now to make a room-by-room inventory on paper. Back this up with photos and receipts or appraisals. Keep all of this material in your safe-deposit box or with a friend—but not in your house.

Source: J. Robert Hunter, president of the National Insurance Consumer Organization, 121 N. Payne St., Alexandria, Virginia 22314.

Jewelry-insurance savings

Insure valuable jewelry at less cost by keeping it in a safe-deposit box and asking your insurer for in-vault valuable-articles coverage. Typical cost is just 30 cents per $100 of insured value, plus a small charge for each day you keep the jewelry outside of the safe-deposit box. This is much less than the typical $2 to $4 per-$100-of-coverage cost you'll pay if you keep the jewelry in your home and insure it under your homeowners' policy.

Source: Lew Altfest, CPA, CFP, president of L.J. Altfest & Co., 140 William St., New York 10038, and author of *Lew Altfest Answers All Your Questions About Money,* McGraw-Hill, New York.

How much life insurance you need

After the death of its principal income-producer, a family requires 75% of its former after-tax income to maintain its standard of living, and at least 60% to get along at all.

Here is the amount of life insurance (in terms of annual earnings multiples) needed at different ages to provide this income (taking into account Social Security benefits and assuming the insurance proceeds were invested to produce an after-inflation return of 5% a year, with the entire principal consumed over survivor's life expectancy).

	Current Income				
Your age	$15K	$23.5K	$30K	$40K	$65K
☐ 25 years					
75%	4.5	6.5	7.5	7.5	7.5
60%	3.0	4.5	5.0	5.0	5.5
☐ 35 years					
75%	6.5	8.0	8.0	8.0	7.5
60%	6.0	6.5	6.5	6.0	6.0
☐ 45 years					
75%	8.0	8.5	8.5	8.0	7.5
60%	6.0	6.5	6.5	6.0	6.0
☐ 55 years					
75%	7.0	7.5	7.0	7.0	6.5
60%	5.5	5.5	5.5	5.5	5.0

The chart implicitly shows capital requirements. These requirements can be met by life insurance or through savings and investments, employee benefits or inheritance. Thus, to the extent that the independent capital resources are built up, insurance needs diminish.

Don't be disabled by your disability insurance

When buying a disability policy, the policy's definition of what constitutes a "disability" is critical. You want the broadest definition of disability possible —certainly one that covers any illness or injury that keeps you from performing your current line of work.

Beware of policies that consider an injury or illness to be a disability only if it keeps you from doing *any* kind of work… and policies that adopt a more limited definition of disability after a certain period of time passes, effectively forcing you to enter a new line of work.

Source: David L. Scott, PhD, professor of accounting and finance, Valdosta State University, Georgia, and author of *The Guide to Buying Insurance,* Globe Pequot Press, Old Saybrook, CT.

Preparing for your insurance physical

☐ Have the test done at your convenience. Do it when you feel best.

☐ If it suits you, arrange for an early morning exam. Most people are relaxed then, you don't lose too much time out from a busy workday and it's easier to fast if blood tests are required.

☐ If you have to be tested in the afternoon, avoid caffeine and don't eat heavily during the day. If you must have coffee, make it decaffeinated.

☐ Limit your intake of salt for several days before the physical. Avoid alcohol for at least 24 hours. Both can raise your blood pressure.

☐ If you're a nonsmoker, make sure the examining physician knows it, because premiums are lower for nonsmokers who meet a specific height and weight standard. (If you do smoke, go "cold turkey" for two hours or more before the exam.)

☐ See your personal doctor before the exam to make sure there'll be no surprises. If there is any sensitive medical or physical information in your records, ask your doctor exactly what you should tell the insurance company.

☐ If you feel tired or ill before the physical, cancel it. Don't worry about delaying the process. The most important thing is to feel relaxed and healthy when you take the physical exam.

Source: Benjamin Lipson, Benjamin Lipson Insurance Agency, Boston, MA.

When to surrender or change your life-insurance policy

A change might be in order if:

☐ You have an old life-insurance policy with a cash value that is 30% or more of its face value, and you are in good health (meaning you will have no trouble getting a standard life-insurance policy).

☐ You have an old policy that you have borrowed against fully at the guaranteed low rates. You have no intention of paying back the loan and you are not in a high tax bracket. (Replacing your policy in this case probably has attractive tax advantages for you.)

☐ Your present policy is "rated" for health reasons (you are paying higher premiums because of the risks of your

illness), but your health has improved. You may be eligible for a less expensive policy or the "rate" (higher premium) may be removed from the policy.

☐ Your insurance needs have changed …your income has increased or decreased dramatically, your mortgage is paid off or your children are through college.

☐ You are paying on several small policies. Consolidation may be cost-effective.

☐ *Caution:* Because new life-insurance products are coming on the market at a rapid pace, there are many high-pressure salespeople at work to persuade you to turn in your old policy without reason. Many of the new policies are better. But sometimes the old policy may be upgraded internally through company changes. Most are offering upgrades without commission.

Source: Arthur Schechner, president, Schechner Corp., insurance consultants, Millburn, NJ.

Saving on house insurance

☐ Save on title insurance. Many title insurers have a special reissue rate for property on which they've written a policy within the past five years. *Advantage:* A full title search is not necessary. Savings can be considerable. Companies usually don't mention the special rate unless a customer asks for it.

☐ Poor lock can lose insurance claim. Most insurers won't pay if lock was opened by key (even if it was a stolen key).

☐ Collecting when insurance company says "no." Even insurance agents and claims investigators are sometimes unaware of the policy's full coverage. Claimant who's told he's not covered should always ask to speak to the disclaimer's manager. If the answer is still "no," there is plenty of time to check with a lawyer.

Boat-insurance guidelines

☐ The policy should cover ice, freezing and racing damage.

☐ It should include protection and indemnity coverage. A boat can be sued much like a corporation ashore. Personal homeowners' insurance won't protect it from confiscation to satisfy an award against it.

□ The policy should cover use of the boat in all planned geographic areas.

□ Ask about discounts based on owner experience, Power Squadron courses, automatic fire-extinguishing systems, diesel engine, etc.

How to get your health insurance company to pay up

Don't give up if you have trouble getting a fair claims settlement from your health insurance company. There are a number of steps you can take to fight the insurer's decision to refuse your claim.

First: Resubmit another medical insurance claim form about 30 days after the refusal. Very often, a company randomly denies a claim…and just as randomly approves the same claim when it comes in again. It does no harm to try for reimbursement of a doctor's bill by submitting your insurance forms a second time.

Second: If that does not work, contact the insurer and request, in writing, a full explanation of the refusal to pay. Sometimes the denial-of-benefits statement is filled with numeric or alphabetic codes that are undecipher-able by a layperson. Request a clear explanation. There should be no ambiguity as to why a health insurer will not pay the benefits that you think are called for in the contract.

Third: Once you are given the insur-ance company's rationale for turning you down, you have a couple of other weapons in your arsenal…

…The insurer cannot give you an alternative reason for the refusal after you refute the initial one.

…When the refusal is based on a rule against paying for experimental treatment, you can marshal evidence from your doctor and others that the treatment was, in fact, the treatment of choice—and therefore should be covered by the policy.

Fourth: If it becomes necessary to appeal, start within the company. Write directly to the president—whose name can be found in insurance directories at your local library…or call the company and ask.

Enclose copies of all relevant documents…claims forms, medical receipts, responses from the insurer, notes of telephone conversations and any backup materials.

Caution: Never send any originals, since you may need them for future action.

Fifth: If you get nowhere at the company level, write to your state insurance department. Every state now has a section set up to assist con-sumers with complaints. You can reach them by checking directory assistance for a toll-free number.

With the correct department and ad-dress, again mail copies of the relevant documents and ask for a response. The insurance department won't take your side in every dispute, but it can obtain an answer from your insurance company in situations where you have been stonewalled or treated unfairly.

Ultimate weapon: File a suit against the insurer in small claims court, or in a regular court if the amount at stake is too large to be handled by the small claims court. If you go to regular court you'll need a lawyer, preferably one who takes the case on a contingency basis, where the fee is a percentage of what you recover. You can handle a small claims case yourself. If the insurer's behavior is particularly abusive, you may be able to collect punitive damages from such a suit.

Real case: A man was conned into trading in his health policy for another on the basis that the second policy was substantially improved. Yet when he filed a claim, he found the new policy paid 40% less in benefits than the old one. He sued the insurance company for fraud…and wound up collecting over $1 million in punitive damages.

Bottom line:

Carefully review your policy before filing claims for illness or injury.

Go to your corporate benefits manager or insurance agent with any questions about coverage and costs. By knowing exactly what you can expect from your policy, you won't be surprised when the reimbursement check arrives. And in the event that the insurer sends you the wrong amount, you will be ready to take whatever action is necessary to obtain the money you deserve.

Source: Robert Hunter, insurance commissioner for the State of Texas and former president, National Insurance Consumer Organization, Alexandria, VA.

Collecting for disability

Who can collect—and how much

There are two disability programs under Social Security.

☐ Supplemental Security Income Program is basically a nationalization of welfare benefits for the unemployable.

☐ Old Age and Survivors Disability Insurance (OASDI) applies to working people and is the basic insurance program that you pay into as the FICA tax.

☐ Disability criteria for acceptance are the same under both programs.

☐ You don't have to prove financial need for OASDI. You're eligible if you've worked and paid into the system for 20 quarters out of the last 40 (five years out of the last ten) and have the necessary years of work credit, depending upon your age.

☐ If your last day in the system was ten years ago or more, you're not eligible for disability benefits now, though you may be eligible eventually for retirement benefits.

☐ Benefits are based on what you've paid into the system, since dependents are taken into account.

How the system works

☐ *The first step:* File an application with your local Social Security office. You'll be interviewed by a claims representative, who will ask you basic questions about your disability. The interviewer will also note any evidence of your disability that he observed.

☐ This material is sent to a trained disability examiner at a state agency, who will contact your medical sources.

☐ If the medical information you have submitted isn't sufficient, the agency will send you to a consulting specialist, at the government's expense. This information becomes part of your file.

☐ If you've met the medical disability requirements (which are extremely stringent), you'll be granted benefits.

☐ You can still be found disabled even if you don't meet the medical requirements. Age, past work experience and education are also taken into account. The approach is individualized throughout the process.

☐ The final eligibility decision is made and signed by the disability examiner,

together with a physician who works for the state (not the consulting physician).

☐ If benefits are denied, you can appeal the decision or reapply.

Proving your disability

☐ *Social Security's definition of medical disability:* The inability to do any substantial, gainful activity by reason of any medically determinable physical or mental impairment which can be expected to result in death, or which has lasted, or can be expected to last, for a continuous period of not less than 12 months. To meet the definition you must have a severe impairment that makes you unable to do your previous work or any other gainful work that exists in the national economy.

☐ It's crucial that your doctor submit very precise medical information, including all test results—the same kind of information a doctor would use in coming up with a diagnosis and treatment plan. Social Security won't accept your doctor's conclusions. It wants the medical evidence that led to the conclusion.

☐ Social Security has a long list of impairments under which your disability should fall. The listing, broken down into 13 body systems, covers about 99% of the disabilities that people apply for. *Recommended:* You and your doctor should take a look at the listings before you apply. If your doctor answers in enough detail, you might avoid a visit to the agency's consulting physician.

Filing an appeal

☐ When benefits are denied, a notice is sent. A brief paragraph explains the reason in general terms. At that point you can go back to the Social Security office and file for a reconsideration, which is simply a review of your case.

☐ If the reconsideration is denied, you can take your case to an administrative law judge within Social Security's Office of Hearings and Appeals. You don't need a lawyer for this hearing, but many people do have one. At the hearing you present your case, review the evidence in your file, add other relevant evidence and personally impress the judge. The reversal rate at this level is fairly high (40% to 60%).

☐ If denied at this hearing, you can go to the Appeals Council and then up through the courts. The chances of reversal improve at each level. Most people just go up to the administrative-law-judge level. If they're turned down there, they file a new claim and start all over.

Source: Dan Wilcox, Disability Program Specialist, Social Security Administration, Disability Programs Branch, New York.

Photographic proof

To speed up an insurance claim in case of fire, flood or other damage to your home, a photographic record of your possessions is the best means of establishing proof of loss.

Check your policy. Furnishings (for example, sofas and silverware) are usually covered under the heading of actual cash value (ACV).

Guidelines for photographing household possessions:

☐ Use an instant-copy camera, to get the job done to your satisfaction in a day.

☐ Photograph everything you own. Open cupboards to show contents. Even objects that appear to be inexpensive and ordinary may be costly to replace.

☐ Don't forget the boiler, water heater and pump.

☐ Mark the backs of the photos with model and serial numbers and other pertinent information.

☐ Unstack pots and pans and group small appliances when shooting kitchen appliances.

☐ Put silver and bric-a-brac on black velvet material to make them look as valuable as they are. Shoot them with color film.

☐ Don't neglect the bicycles, tools and barbecues in the garage.

☐ Get exterior shots of shrubbery and other landscaping, which are generally covered by insurance.

☐ File the pictures, along with receipts and related documents, categorizing them by room.

Reducing home and auto insurance

Do you qualify for any of these insurance discounts?

Home

☐ No smokers.

☐ Personal articles (jewelry, etc.) are kept in a vault.

☐ Protective devices (burglar alarms, fire alarms, smoke alarms, dead-bolt locks and other locking devices).

☐ Near a fire department or a source of water.

Some companies give discounts to retirees, and in some states co-op owners are entitled to homeowners' insurance. Or consider taking a higher deductible to keep premiums down.

Auto

☐ Equipped with antitheft locks and alarms.

☐ One of the drivers insured on the policy is away from home (at college, for instance).

☐ "No fault" insurance laws reduce payments in some states.

How to cut auto insurance

Cut auto insurance costs by:

☐ Raising deductibles from $100 to $500 or even $1,000. That saves 35%–60% on premiums.

☐ Dropping collision coverage on cars over five years old.

☐ Finding out whether the car qualifies for discounts on autos less likely to be stolen or less costly to repair.

☐ Discontinuing medical coverage if it's duplicated by your employer's health plan.

☐ Reconsidering extras such as coverage for towing or car rentals during repair.

Source: National Consumer Insurance Organization, as reported in *Money*.

Buying disability insurance

What to aim for when you buy disability insurance:

☐ The policy is noncancelable. That means the company cannot cancel the policy for medical condition or number of claims or change the premium before the individual's 65th birthday. *Not as good:* A guaranteed renewable policy. Premiums on such a policy may be increased.

☐ Benefits are payable over a long period. The first choice is a lifetime policy. *Second choice:* One that covers you until you reach the age of 65. Anything less than that leaves a major gap.

☐ The policy will pay benefits as long as you cannot practice your "own occupation." Policies that use the phrase "own occupation" will pay you a benefit as long as you cannot work full-time at the type of work you did full-time before the disability. With such a policy you can "double dip" by working at a position that pays less than you earned before and collect full benefits. Less attractive policies will stop paying benefits if you can do any work, even if that work brings far less income. *Compromise:* A residual policy. This is true income-replacement insurance, and it is satisfactory for many people. *How it works:* If the disability results in your being able to work, but in a position that brings in, for example, only 50% of your former income, you will receive 50% of your total benefit.

☐ The insuring company has a good reputation for paying claims. Your broker's knowledge and sophistication are critical in choosing a company that you won't have trouble with.

☐ The benefits are subject to cost-of-living adjustments. This feature is worth the extra cost in premiums.

When both spouses have health insurance

More employees are being asked to pay more of the cost of health-care coverage at work as health costs keep rising.

But working couples—where each spouse has health coverage—have options. While they can keep their separate health plans, they may save money if they opt for the spouse's plan that offers the most for the family.

Doing the arithmetic

How to do the economic analysis to determine if switching plans makes economic sense for you…

Using a legal pad, compare the four key costs of health coverage for each plan:

1. Annual premium cost. How much will it cost a year for everyone in the family to be covered?

2. Maximum deductible. How much must you pay before the plan starts to kick in?

3. Co-insurance. What percentage of each bill will the plan pay, and how much must you pay?

4. Plan cap. What's the most you will have to pay out-of-pocket for medical bills each year?

Example: It would cost $500 a year for the family to join John's health plan and $1,000 to join Jane's plan. But the out-of-pocket cap for Jane's plan is $1,000, while John's cap is $3,000.

Maximum possible total cost: $2,000 with Jane's plan, $3,500 with John's plan.

Other considerations

☐ Opt-out opportunities. Many companies pay a cash payment if you drop your coverage and shift to your spouse's plan.

Example: Your employer will pay $500 if you don't join your company's medical plan. You can use the money to pay the higher premium required to get family coverage under the spouse's plan.

☐ What is covered? Money isn't always the only consideration. Consider switching if one plan offers considerably more liberal coverage for services important to your family, such as outpatient psychiatric or dental care, or chiropractic services.

Important: Paying extra to keep both plans seldom makes economic sense today. Working couples once could get 100% coverage for treatment by co-ordinating plans. Now most plans have a "nonduplication of benefits" provision that makes the employee's plan the primary provider.

Example: Before, your plan might have paid 80% of a $1,000 claim, while your spouse's plan would pay the remaining $200. That's rare today.

Key: Before you switch, determine if the family can rejoin your plan if your spouse is laid off or fired. Most employers will count it as a "change in family status," and let you back in. But double check, just to be certain.

Source: Tom Beauregard, health-care consultant, Hewitt Associates, 40 Highland Ave., Rowayton, Connecticut 06853.

How to get what you need from your accountant

The biggest mistake people make in dealing with the professionals they hire to work on their tax returns is to drop everything in the professional's lap and walk away. To get the most from your accountant, you must take an active role in the preparation of your returns… even if you pay hundreds of dollars in preparation fees to the most prestigious firm in town. Not only must you help your accountant find everything that will save you tax dollars, but you must also understand how every figure that's reported on the return was arrived at.

☐ Organize the information. This saves his time and your money.

☐ Bring to his attention any out-of-the-ordinary deductions…job-hunting expenses, child care or dependent care, unreimbursed business travel, etc.

☐ Be complete. The more last-minute changes you call in after your return has been prepared, the bigger your bill will be.

☐ Mention changes in essential personal and financial data. If, for example, you don't tell your accountant that you're supporting aged parents, he isn't likely to know about the dependency exemptions or possible medical deductions for them, or to recommend a multiple-support agreement with your brothers and sisters.

☐ Discuss your audit tolerance. If you want a return that will save you top tax dollars, you must take aggressive positions on your various financial dealings. The more aggressive you are, the more likely your return will be audited. If you want to cut your audit risk, you must take a more conservative approach to the way you handle your return. You can't have it both ways.

☐ Assume that your return will be audited. Using a tax professional doesn't lessen that likelihood. Your accountant isn't responsible to the IRS for your return. You are. The IRS auditor will ask you how your charitable contributions were calculated, how your interest was calculated or when depreciable assets were purchased.

☐ Keep worksheets detailing the calculations for each figure on your tax return.

Source: Paul N. Strassels, a former IRS tax-law specialist.

Prudent accountant-client communications

Be careful of what you say to your accountant…if you have something to hide. Suppose that for years you consistently neglected to tell your accountant about a certain source of income. If you now tell the accountant about it, he can be called on by the government to testify against you in court, since accountant-client communications aren't privileged. But conversations you have with an attorney are privileged. An attorney can't be compelled to testify against a client who has admitted that he committed a crime. *Best advice for someone in this position:* Hire an attorney, who can then hire the accountant and include him under his umbrella of privilege.

Source: Ms. X, Esq., a former IRS agent, who is still well-connected.

Should you file a joint or separate tax return?

The effect of a joint tax return is to treat a married couple as one taxpayer, no matter which spouse realized the income. Filing a joint return will usually result in tax savings because the joint-return rates are generally more favorable than the rates for married persons filing separately.

☐ Credit for child-care expenses is only available on a joint return.

☐ Keep in mind that when a couple files a joint return, both parties are liable for the full amount of tax due, regardless of who earned the income.

But there are some advantages to filing separately:

☐ In community property states, all community income and deductions are reported one half on each return. This can result in lower tax-bracket filings.

☐ Some married couples file separate returns so they won't have to disclose to their spouse the source and extent of their earnings.

☐ Filing separate returns may make sense if one of the spouses has extraordinary medical expenses. These expenses are deductible only to the extent that they exceed 7½% of the combined income of both spouses. Therefore, the smaller income on a separate return might result in a deduction that would be reduced or eliminated on a joint return because of the larger combined income.

☐ In certain states, the income-tax saving from filing separate returns can be greater than the federal tax saving from filing a joint return.

Source: *Family: The Best Tax Shelter*, Boardroom Books, Greenwich, CT.

Before mailing in a tax return

Getting the details right the first time can save the time and trouble of dealing with the IRS later. Checklist:

☐ Sign the return.

☐ Did your preparer sign?

☐ Did you answer every question on the return?

☐ Put your Social Security number on every page and every attachment, including your check.

☐ Put your tax-shelter registration number on the return.

☐ Make copies of your return.

☐ Compare your return with last year's to make sure you didn't overlook anything.

☐ Put the return away for a few days or a week so that you can look at it with a fresh eye before mailing it.

☐ Send it by certified mail so there will be no question that your return was filed on time. Mailed on time is considered to be filed on time by the IRS.

☐ Use a separate envelope for each return.

☐ Put your children's returns or estimated payments in separate envelopes.

☐ Attach your W-2.

☐ Include your check if you owe money to the IRS.

☐ Include any receipts and forms required to prove your charitable contributions.

☐ Include a check for the tax you owe if you are filing an extension request.

Top filing mistakes... according to the IRS

☐ Miscalculating medical and dental expenses. This deduction is based on your adjusted gross income—AGI. Carefully complete up to the AGI line on your 1040 before attempting to figure your medical expenses.

☐ Taking the wrong amount of earned-income credit. Use the worksheet in the instruction booklet to avoid mistakes.

☐ Entering the wrong amount of tax. Use the right tax tables.

☐ Confusion about income tax withheld. Don't confuse this with the Social Security tax that was withheld from your pay.

☐ Unemployment-compensation errors. Use the special formula in the IRS instruction booklet to calculate the amount of taxable unemployment.

☐ Mistakes in calculating child and dependent care expenses. Use Form 2441 and double-check your math.

☐ Errors in tax due. Believe it or not, taxpayers often err in determining the bottom line of their tax return—are they entitled to a refund or do they owe the IRS? Carefully compare the tax you owe with the amount you have paid through withholding or estimated tax payments.

☐ Overlooking credits. Read all IRS instructions carefully.

☐ Adding income incorrectly. Mistakes are frequently made by taxpayers when adding the income section of Form 1040.

Source: *IRS Publication 910.*

Filing late

Reasons for getting an extension:

☐ You don't have all the information you need to fill out the return.

☐ You need time to find the cash to make a contribution to your Keogh account. (Unlike IRAs, which must be made by April 15, Keogh contributions can be made up to the extended due date of your return—as late as October 15.)

☐ You have a complicated transaction that you need time to ponder.

Timetable:

☐ First extension. April 15 is the due date for tax returns. But you can get an automatic four-month extension by filing Form 4868 by April 15. If you pay late you'll owe late-payment penalties, plus interest on the tax paid late. *Trap:* You must make estimated tax payments on Form 1040-ES by April 15. You can't get an extension of time to make quarterly estimated payments.

☐ Second extension. It's possible to get a second filing extension of two months. But the second extension isn't automatic; you must have a valid reason for requesting it, such as a death in the family or loss of your records. *Loophole:* It has been my experience that the closer you file to October 15 (after August 15) the less chance there is that you'll be audited. A second extension may be the way to get off the audit treadmill if you've been audited every year for the last few years.

Source: Edward L. Mendlowitz, partner, Mendlowitz Weitsen, New York.

To avoid late-filing penalties

A person who files a late tax return without getting a prior extension faces stiff penalties. It's possible to avoid these penalties, but you must convince the IRS that you had a good excuse for filing late.

Situations in which the IRS has said it may accept a late return without penalty:

☐ The return was postmarked on time, even if it had insufficient postage.

☐ The return was filed on time but in the wrong IRS district or office.

☐ The return was filed late because of inaccurate information received from an IRS employee.

☐ A filing delay was caused by the destruction of the taxpayer's records in a fire, flood or other casualty.

☐ An individual couldn't get proper tax forms from the IRS, in spite of asking for them at a reasonable time.

☐ The filer was not able to get necessary information from an IRS official, despite a personal visit to an IRS office.

☐ The taxpayer died, was seriously injured or was forced to be away from home for a reason that was unexpected and beyond his or her control.

☐ The taxpayer was ignorant of the law, in that he or she never had to file a particular kind of form or return before.

☐ The death or illness of an immediate family member.

☐ Incapacitating illness of the taxpayer himself.

☐ A competent and informed tax adviser told the taxpayer that a tax return was not necessary.

How to proceed: Make your request for abatement of the penalty in writing to your local IRS Service Center. Give a detailed explanation of your reason for filing late. Use the term "reasonable cause" both at the beginning and the end of the letter. To speed up the process, attach your letter to the return you are filing late. Don't wait until you get a penalty notice—that could take months.

Not-so-safe amendments

Filing an amended return to take a deduction for the following may result in an audit because of the high susceptibility of these items to audit:

☐ Travel and entertainment expenses.

☐ Unreimbursed business expenses.

☐ Casualty losses.

☐ Transactions with relatives.

☐ Charitable donations of property.

☐ Home-office deductions.

Audit triggers

Red flags most likely to bring on an audit:

☐ Deductions that are excessively high in relation to your income. A return that shows $50,000 of income and $40,000 of itemized deductions is almost certain to be pulled for an audit. Keep your deductions reasonable. But don't cheat yourself just because you're afraid of an audit. Attach an explanation to your return for an item that you believe the IRS may question. When your return gets kicked out of the computer that screens all returns for possible audit, an IRS official will read your explanation. If he's satisfied, he will probably put the return back into the processing system without sending it on to be audited.

☐ Undocumented charitable gifts. Attach a statement to your return showing the date of all property contributions, the fair market value and the name of the charity. If you don't automatically supply this statement, the IRS will pull your return to look for it—increasing your chance of audit. You must now attach an independent appraisal for charitable gifts of property worth more than $5,000.

☐ Overstated casualty losses. Many audits are triggered because taxpayers exceeded the legal limits on casualty-loss deductions. Use the IRS worksheet, Form 4684. You can deduct only the part of your loss that exceeds 10% of your adjusted gross income. And then you deduct only the lesser of what you paid for the item or the decrease in its value as a result of the casualty.

☐ Overstated medical deductions. To be deductible, medical expenses must exceed 7½% of your adjusted gross income.

☐ Tax shelters with very large losses. These almost always trigger an audit. Avoid tax shelters unless you get professional advice. Make sure it's a legitimate shelter.

☐ Inclusion of Schedule C. Self-employed individuals must file a Schedule C with their tax returns. It shows all business-related income and deductions. *Warning:* It is also a red flag for an audit. Prepare it carefully, and have the records to back it up.

☐ Home-office deductions. These must meet stringent IRS guidelines. The office must be used regularly and exclusively for business purposes. If your family watches television there when it's not in use as an office, you lose the deduction. The office must be your principal place of business. If you have an office at the company where you are employed, you can't deduct the home office. But if you freelance in a different business at night, the office is deductible.

☐ Overstated business expenses. The IRS will scrutinize these deductions. Keep your travel and entertainment deductions reasonable. (And be very careful to stay within the tax law's limits for deducting your business car and computer.)

☐ Sloppy returns. Simple errors cause many tax returns to be kicked out of the IRS computers This means the chances for audit are greater because the return is now in human hands. Don't make these mistakes on your return:

☐☐ Errors in simple mathematics.

☐☐ Failure to transfer totals correctly from one page to the next.

☐☐ Use of the wrong rate tables for your filing status (single, joint, head-of-household, etc.).

☐☐ Failure to follow IRS instructions.

☐☐ Failure to answer all questions. A blank space where there should be an answer will wake up the computer.

☐☐ Failure to attach W-2s or other required statements.

Source: Michael L. Borsuk, tax partner and managing partner of the Long Island office of Coopers & Lybrand, Melville, NY.

When it pays to ask for an audit

☐ When someone dies, the heirs can count only on sharing in the after-tax proceeds of the estate. So the sooner the IRS examines matters to settle things the better.

☐ When you close down a business, its records and the key personnel who can explain its tax strategies may soon disappear. An IRS examination at a much later date could prove awkward and costly.

☐ When you ask for a prompt assessment of taxes that are due, the IRS must act within 18 months. Otherwise it has up to three years to conduct an examination of the year's return.

☐ Use Form 4810 to ask for the prompt assessment. You don't have to use this form, but if you don't use it, be sure to eliminate any possible confusion by mentioning in your letter to the IRS that your request for an examination is made under Code Section 6501(d).

Tax-saving ideas for last-minute filers

Here's a list of tax-saving ideas for your personal tax return.

Saving ideas:

☐ Claim parents as dependents. If you provide more than half of a parent's support, you may be able to claim the parent as a dependent even if the parent does not live with you.

If you and other family members jointly support a parent or other individual, with no one person providing more than half the support, you can file a *Multiple Support Declaration,* IRS Form 2120, to obtain a dependency exemption that can be assigned to one among those providing support. The exemption can be assigned to a different person each year.

☐ Claim head-of-household status. If you are single with a child or other dependent, you may be able to claim head-of-household status and pay lower tax rates than on a single return.

To do this, you must have maintained a household for more than half of 1994 for a child or dependent relative who lives with you. However, having a dependent parent not living with you may enable you to claim head-of-household filing status.

☐ Claim the dependent-care tax credit. If you and your spouse both work, or you are single and work, and you have children or other dependents who have to be cared for while you work, you may be eligible for the child-care tax credit.

Rules: You must have dependent children younger than age 13, or some other dependent who is incapable of caring for him/herself, who you maintain in your home and who must be cared for so that you and your spouse can work or go to school.

The credit equals 20% to 30% of the amount you pay for care—depending on your income level—and is worth a maximum of $720 for one dependent or $1,440 for two.

☐ Shift the exemption for a child. It can make sense for divorced or separated parents to shift the dependency exemption for a child from the custodial to the noncustodial parent if the noncustodial parent is in a higher tax bracket. Remember, however, that exemptions are phased out for some higher-income taxpayers. Do this by filing IRS Form 8332, *Release of Claim to Exemption for Child of Divorced or Separated Parents.*

☐ File separate returns. This can make sense if you and your spouse both have income and one of you has large deductions that are subject to a percentage-of-Adjusted-Gross-Income (AGI) limitation.

Example: Medical expenses, which are deductible only to the extent that they exceed 7.5% of AGI.

Point: Combining AGI on joint returns will reduce the deduction. Filing separate returns reduces the impact of the AGI limit on the deduction, since only part of your joint income will be counted.

Separate filings can have many tax repercussions, so work through the figures both ways.

☐ Take advantage of joint-filer tax rates if you are a qualifying widow or widower. You can do this for two years after the death of a spouse, provided you continue to maintain a home for a dependent child.

☐ Deduct medical expenses of dependents. If you paid the medical bills of a dependent—including a person for whom you have filed a multiple support declaration—you can deduct those costs. If you paid the medical bills for a former spouse before getting divorced during the year, you can deduct those, too, even though you are no longer married.

☐ Claim all medical expenses. These are deductible only to the extent that their total exceeds 7.5% of AGI, which can be a high hurdle to jump. However, many surprising items qualify for the deduction.

Examples: Health insurance, the cost of travel to and from a doctor's office or hospital—no matter how far—eyeglasses and contact lenses, prescription birth control, schools for the handicapped and many other items.

Appliances acquired for medical reasons—such as air conditioners and dehumidifiers—can be deducted. So can some medically justified home improvements—such as elevators, central air conditioning and special bathrooms—to the extent that their cost exceeds any increase in value that they add to the home.

☐ Cut home taxes. If you sold a home in the past year, file IRS Form 2119 to defer your gain on the sale of the home, even if you have not yet acquired a replacement residence. This gives you two years to acquire such a replacement.

Also, you can use Form 2119 to elect the once-in-a-lifetime $125,000 exclusion for gain on a home sale if you are 55 or older.

If you did not sell your home during the year, keep records of all the improvements you made to it during the year—new locks, screen doors, mailboxes, telephone outlets, light fixtures, garbage disposals and anything else that is attached permanently to your home and adds to its value.

You can add the cost of these items to your home's basis (cost), which reduces your profit when you sell your home or its final replacement. Over a lifetime, these items can accumulate to generate huge tax savings.

☐ Make deductible retirement-plan contributions. Contributions to IRAs, Keogh plans and Simplified Employee Pension plans (SEPs) made for 1994—before you file your return—provide a double tax benefit.

They provide a deduction directly…and they reduce your AGI—which can indirectly increase other deductions on your return.

How: Deductions for medical bills, theft and casualty losses and miscellaneous expenses are allowed only to the extent that they exceed set percentages of your AGI. Also, high-income individuals have their total deductions and personal exemptions cut back to the extent that their AGI exceeds certain limits.

Thus, reducing your AGI can increase the tax benefit you gain from all these items.

☐ Get Social Security numbers for infants. These are now required for all children. The penalty for failing to report a Social Security number for a child has been increased to $50.

To get a Social Security number, file Form SS-5 with your local Social Security office. You can ask for one over the phone. If you file your return before the card arrives, write "applied for" on the space on the return where it is requested.

☐ Examine "kiddie tax" filing options. Children younger than age 14 who have investment income generally must file their own tax returns to report it.

However, you may be able to avoid the inconvenience of filing multiple returns for children who have income less than $5,000 by reporting their income on your own return. File IRS Form 8814 with your return to do this.

Catch: Reporting a child's income on your own return increases your AGI, which may reduce the availability of certain other deductions, as mentioned above. It may also eliminate the child's ability to take a personal exemption for him/herself on a state tax return. So compare the impact of filing both ways.

☐ Deduct self-employment tax if you have self-employment income. Fifty percent of self-employment taxes is deductible as an AGI-reducing adjustment to income—one of the most frequently overlooked deductions, according to the IRS.

☐ Deduct 25% of self-employed medical premiums. The new tax law reinstated this deduction for self-employed persons. Even better, it did so retroactively to June 30, 1992—when this provision previously expired. So you may also be able to file an amended return to claim this deduction for 1992 and obtain a tax refund.

☐ Avoid estimated-tax penalties. If you underpaid your estimated taxes for 1995, or failed to pay them in equal installments, you can expect the IRS to add a penalty to your tax bill. But you may be able to defeat the penalty…

☐ If your underpayment resulted solely from the new tax law's retroactive application of higher tax rates, you owe no penalty.

☐ If you received a disproportionate amount of your income late in the year, you can avoid the penalty for failing to make equal quarterly payments by showing that your payment for each quarter was proportionate to the quarter's income.

Demonstrate that these exceptions apply to you by filing IRS Form 2210, Underpayment of Estimated Tax, with your return.

☐ Defer increased taxes. If your taxes were increased in 1993 by the retroactive application of higher tax rates, you need pay only one-third of the increase this April 15. The rest can be paid in equal installments on April 15 of 1995 and 1996 with no interest due.

Limit: The amount you can pay through installment payments is reduced to the extent that your Alternative Minimum Tax calculation on Form 6251, filed with your tax return, exceeds the tax you would have owed if old tax rates had stayed in effect.

☐ Get an extension. An automatic four-month filing extension, IRS Form 4868, can give you extra time to find tax-saving strategies and make deductible contributions to a Keogh or SEP.

Remember though, an extension does not give you extra time to pay taxes. You must estimate what you will owe for the year and make a corresponding payment with your extension.

☐ Collect records. Protect against the risk of a future audit by collecting, organizing and attaching explanations to your records now, while filing strategies are fresh in your mind.

Remember, an audit is likely to occur

two or more years after you file, when you may not remember the reasons for actions you took. So have well-organized receipts and records that make things clear.

Source: Jeff Keyser, national director–personal tax, Deloitte & Touche, Cincinnati.

To make your family's wealth IRS-proof

Family wealth is increasingly difficult to shelter from the IRS. The new tax law increases the top income-tax rates, reduces the maximum retirement benefits that can be earned from pension plans, cuts the amount that many of us can save for retirement through Keogh plans and 401(k) savings plans and increases the top estate-tax rate to 55%.

In addition, the $600,000 exemption for estate taxes loses value to inflation every year. If your wealth grows in dollar terms by 10% a year due to a combination of inflation and real growth, the value of the exemption is cut in half every 7.2 years.

In 22 years—if the $600,000 exemption remains in place—your exemption will protect only one-eighth as much of your estate as it does today.

However, with smart planning you can make your wealth immune to the IRS—obtaining current deductions to cut taxes, increasing future retirement income and protecting the assets you wish to leave to your heirs from estate tax.

A combined strategy of charitable giving, intrafamily gifts and life-insurance planning can make this possible.

Self-defense strategy:

The most important tool is the Charitable Remainder Trust (CRT).

How it works: You place assets that will pass to a charity upon your death in a trust. As a result, you retain the income earned from the assets. And you get an income-tax deduction now for the value of the gift that will pass to the charity when you die. The amount of the deduction is determined from IRS tables according to the size of the gift and your life expectancy.

Keys:

☐ You must elect to take an annual percentage payout from the trust. The trust's terms, however, may state that this will be paid only out of current income, plus a makeup factor, enabling the payouts to be delayed if the trust invests in low-yield, appreciating assets.

☐ The trust is tax-exempt, so investment earnings compound tax-free.

☐ You can be the trustee of the trust and control its investments.

These rules make it possible to use a CRT as a tax-favored retirement plan.

Then, when you retire, you switch the CRT to high-yield investments. At that point, the CRT begins making 8% payments to you plus makeup payments for past years—giving you a large retirement benefit for the rest of your life.

No limits: Contributions to a CRT are not subject to the dollar limits that apply to other retirement contributions—such as the $2,000 annual limit for an IRA or the $9,500 limit that applies to a 401(k) savings plan in 1996. CRTs are also not subject to the maximum accumulation or distribution limits that apply to other types of retirement plans.

Even better: If you fund the CRT with appreciated property, you avoid paying capital-gains tax on the property.

Bottom line: The CRT's big benefit is capital-gains tax savings and tax-saving deductions now…plus higher retirement income later. The cost is that the property left in the CRT ultimately goes to charity instead of to your heirs. But this does not mean that your heirs lose out. Why not?

☐ With your estate subject to estate tax, 37% to 55% of the assets left to your heirs—instead of to charity—would actually go to the IRS.

☐ Life insurance, if placed in a properly structured trust arrangement, is free from estate tax. And you can use the current tax savings and increased income derived from the CRT to buy life insurance that will pay your heirs an amount equal to what they would have received after taxes from your estate. The insurance proceeds will be free not only of estate and local inheritance taxes but also of various administration fees that apply to property that passes through an estate.

Bottom line: A CRT can enable everyone to come out ahead—including the charity that ultimately receives a valuable bequest.

The big give-away:

The CRT will protect only part of your family's wealth. You will, of course, have other assets that may be subject to estate tax and that you will want to protect from the IRS.

Key to planning in this area: Remember that while your wealth increases each year due to both real earnings and inflation, the basic tax devices you can use to cut future estate taxes lose value every year to inflation. The basic tax devices:

☐ The lifetime unified estate-and-gift-tax credit for $600,000 of assets.

☐ The $10,000 per-recipient annual gift-tax exemption ($20,000 when gifts are made by a married couple).

The simplest strategy to cut future estate taxes is to make gifts of appreciating property to the next generation today, so that their growing value is not taxed in your estate when you die.

Every family can use the $10,000 (or $20,000) annual exemption to make such gifts. However, it may pay to use the full $600,000 exemption to make a large gift now and protect it from tax, even though it means your heirs won't be able to use the $600,000 exemption when you die.

Life-insurance trust:

Of course, you may not be willing or able to make large gifts directly to the next generation—perhaps because assets are in the form of a family business or you wish to assure the financial security of your spouse first.

In such cases, the best idea is to establish a life-insurance trust that will pay estate taxes for your estate, leaving the estate's assets intact to pass to heirs.

Trap: Don't rely on the unlimited marital estate-tax deduction to protect assets that are left to a spouse from tax. Although the assets will escape tax when they pass to your spouse, they will be fully taxable when your spouse dies.

Smart use of insurance may enable you to pass on a multiple of the $600,000 estate-tax exemption amount free of estate tax.

Of course, families with lesser needs can use their $10,000 (or $20,000) annual gift-tax exemption to obtain the same insurance benefit on a smaller scale.

Example: At the time of his death, Malcolm Forbes was reputed to be one of the most heavily insured people in America, having used an insurance trust to pass his $1 billion publishing empire intact to his children.

Planning:

While these tax-saving strategies can provide powerful protection for family wealth, they must be implemented with care and an expert's help. Many technical rules apply. Examples:

☐ A CRT is irrevocable. While you can change the charitable beneficiary, you cannot withdraw contributions to the trust principal after they have been made.

☐ Life-insurance trusts are also irrevocable and must meet technical requirements to be free of estate tax.

☐ Second-to-die insurance is cheaper than conventional insurance, but it is also less flexible. If you might want to withdraw funds from the policy before your spouse dies, consider other insurance options.

Also, while you can serve as the trustee of your own CRT, you will need to hire a third-party administrator to handle the technical paperwork associated with trust management.

Problem: The typical third-party bank trust department will not be willing to act as third-party administrator for you unless it can act as the trustee of the CRT—exercising control and collecting the related fees.

Source: Arthur A. Wood, CLU and chartered financial consultant in private practice in Kent, New York. He is the author of How To Create Tax-Exempt Wealth, Kent Publishing Co., Kent, NY.

Putting family members on the payroll of a family-owned business

There are numerous ways business income can be shifted to family members. One of the easiest methods is putting family members who perform services for the business on the payroll. Some of the advantages, however, are not immediately obvious. Some things to consider:

☐ Putting family members on the payroll of an incorporated company may incur the cost of Social Security, unemployment and self-employment taxes, but the income-tax savings from income splitting will usually more than offset this cost.

☐ Family members on the payroll must perform services and their compensation must be reasonable in relation to the services performed. If the payments are considered excessive by the IRS, the amounts could be reclassified as earnings of the parent and a gift to the child.

☐ A spouse on the payroll may not reduce tax on income for the business owner since a joint return is usually filed.

☐ If a child or other family relative performs services for the business, the income can be effectively split and shifted to lower tax brackets.

☐ A child in college who works during the summer for his or her parents can use the earnings for college and, essentially, fund the cost with pre-tax dollars.

☐ In order to split business income among family members who do not actually perform services for the business, an interest in the business must be shifted to that family member. The transfer of a business interest is often accomplished through the use of a family partnership or a corporation. There are exceptions to this rule, so check with your tax lawyer.

How Social Security is taxed

Social Security benefits are taxable if the individual's total income for the year exceeds these dollar limits…

☐ $25,000 if you are single.

☐ $32,000 if you are married and file a joint return.

☐ $25,000 if you are married, do not file a joint return and do not live with your spouse.

☐ Zero if you are married, do not file a joint return and did live with your spouse at any time during the year.

Trap: Total income includes adjusted gross income (AGI), tax-exempt interest and half of your Social Security benefits.

If you are likely to exceed the limit, consider these strategies…

☐ Invest in assets that appreciate in value without producing current income, such as Series EE savings bonds or growth stocks.

☐ Time the recognition of income (IRA withdrawals, etc.) so that you receive it, for instance, in alternate years, or when you have deductions that reduce your adjusted gross income.

☐ Divorce…while a married couple filing jointly will have a $32,000 income limit, two single people can take $25,000 each, or $50,000 together.

Source: *Ernst & Young's Arthur Young Tax Guide.*

Compensation loopholes: deferring pay

The compensation package you get from your employer probably includes some form of deferred compensation whereby money is put away for you but is not available until some time in the future. This form of compensation boosts your pay and offers significant tax advantages.

Loopholes:

☐ Pension and profit-sharing plans. Your employer contributes money to a retirement plan on your behalf and the money accumulates on a tax-deferred basis. You don't pay a current tax on the contribution or on the interest the money earns. No tax is due until you receive a distribution of money from the plan. More:

Loophole: Take a tax-free loan from the pension or profit-sharing plan. Borrowing is not a taxable transaction. You can only do this if the plan permits borrowing—not all do. Plans that allow borrowing usually make it easy on the participant—there's no need to justify why the loan is needed.

Tax law limits: The amount you can borrow is limited to your vested balance in the plan up to the greater of $10,000 or one-half of your vested balance, with a maximum of $50,000.

Loophole: Put some of your own money into the plan—many plans allow employees to make voluntary contributions. Such contributions are not tax-deductible, but the money accumulates on a tax-deferred basis.

Loophole: If your company's plan is inactive—no additions are being made and no benefits are accruing on your behalf—you are eligible to contribute to an IRA.

☐ 401(k) plans. You contribute part of your salary to a company-sponsored savings program. You pay no income tax on the money you contribute until you make withdrawals. Interest, dividends and other earnings accumulate tax-deferred until you take them out.

Many companies "match" employees' contributions by putting additional money into the plan for the employee.

Loophole: Though the amount you can contribute each year is limited by the tax law, it's far more than you can put into an IRA. Maximum 401(k) contribution for 1996: $9,500.

☐ Company-paid life insurance. As long as the coverage doesn't exceed $50,000 worth of insurance, you are not taxed on the premiums the employer pays. But if it is more than $50,000, you are taxed on part of the premiums.

Loophole: The taxable amount is figured from IRS tables and is less than the actual premiums the employer pays. You pay some tax for the extra coverage, but it is far less than it would cost you to buy similar life insurance coverage outside the company.

☐ Survivor's tax-free benefit. The first $5,000 of death benefits paid by an employer to an employee's surviving spouse or other beneficiary is tax-free. The benefit can come out of deferred salary payments or retirement-plan distributions.

Limit: $5,000 is the maximum amount that can be paid out tax-free regardless of how many beneficiaries there are. The $5,000 can be allocated among any number of beneficiaries.

☐ Stock options. When a company gives an employee an option to purchase stock that does not qualify as an incentive stock option (more relevant information below), the employee must pay tax when the option is exercised. The taxed amount is the difference between the option price and the fair market value of the stock at the time the option is exercised.

Loophole: There is no tax paid when the option is granted. Stock options are a form of deferred compensation. The employee benefits on a tax-deferred basis from the growth in value of the company stock.

☐ Incentive stock options. These are options that qualify under the Tax Code for special treatment. No tax is levied when the options are issued to the employee.

Loophole: No tax is levied when the options are exercised. Tax isn't payable until the options are sold.

Trap: The difference between the option price and the fair market value at the time the option is exercised is a "preference item" that is subject to the Alternative Minimum Tax (AMT). Employees should be careful not to exercise so many incentive stock options that they fall into the AMT. The exercise of these options must be carefully timed.

☐ Restricted stock. Sometimes an employer issues stock to an employee that is subject to a "substantial risk of forfeiture." The most common situation: The employee will have to give up the stock if he/she doesn't continue working for the company for a specified number of years.

When the restriction lapses, the employee is taxed on the difference between the stock's fair market value at that time and the price paid for the stock.

Loophole: The employee can make an election under Section 83(b) of the Internal Revenue Code to pay tax on the value of the stock when it is originally issued. Then, there is no tax when the restriction lapses. (Tax on any gain is payable when the employee ultimately disposes of the stock.) Employees should make the Section 83(b) election in instances where they expect the company's stock to appreciate considerably.

☐ Phantom stock, also called stock appreciation rights, is sometimes issued to employees. No actual stock is given, but payments are made as if actual stock had been issued. If any dividends are paid to stockholders, they are also paid to the phantom stockholders. And when the employee leaves the company he/she is compensated for his/her phantom shares. Payments to the employee are taxed as compensation, rather than tax-favored capital gains.

Loophole: The employee doesn't pay tax until there is an actual payment to him as a phantom stockholder. No tax is payable when he first receives the phantom stock. So phantom stock is another form of deferred compensation.

Source: Edward Mendlowitz, partner, Mendlowitz Weitsen, CPAs, Two Pennsylvania Plaza, New York 10121. He is the author of *New Tax Traps, New Opportunities,* Boardroom Special Reports, P.O.Box 2614, Greenwich, CT 06836.

Biggest estate planning mistakes... and how to avoid them

A good estate plan can slash your estate-tax bill so you can leave more to your heirs and less to Uncle Sam. As you fine-tune your estate plan, watch out for these common mistakes:

☐ Mistake: Failing to use the annual $10,000 gift-tax exclusion. The IRS lets you give away up to $10,000 a year per donee free of gift tax to an unlimited number of people. Spouses who make joint gifts can give each donee $20,000 a year.

Solution: Set up an annual gifting program to reduce the size of your estate. Consider making gifts at the beginning of the year so that the income being produced by the sum will no longer be your tax problem.

☐ Mistake: Overusing the estate-tax marital deduction. The IRS lets spouses leave each other property free from estate tax. But leaving everything to your spouse increases the family's estate-tax bill. You forfeit one of the $600,000 estate-and-gift-tax exclusions available to you when you die.

Example: Jack leaves property worth $1.2 million to his wife, Mary. No estate tax will be owed because of the estate-tax marital deduction. When Mary dies, one-half of her property will be sheltered by her $600,000 exclusion. Taxes owed on the other $600,000 will be about $250,000.

Solution: Jack puts $600,000 for Mary into a trust that does not qualify for the estate-tax marital deduction. When Jack dies, no estate tax will be owed because the $600,000 remaining in his estate will be sheltered by his $600,000 lifetime exclusion. Mary will receive income from the trust for life and when she dies, the children will receive the property in the trust. No estate tax will be due on Mary's estate because the $600,000 she owns outright will be sheltered by her exclusion.

☐ Mistake: Making no plans to shelter taxable life insurance proceeds. Many people are not aware that life insurance proceeds in their estate are taxable if they push the estate over $1.2 million. After taxes, your heirs receive the remainder.

Solution: Transfer ownership of the insurance policy to your children or other beneficiaries, or if you are planning to buy an insurance policy, make your heirs the owners. Another option: You can fund a trust with a life insurance policy. Your spouse can receive income for life, and the trust proceeds can pass to your children when your spouse dies.

Important: If you die within three years of transferring an insurance policy, that asset is still considered part of your taxable estate. So make any necessary changes as soon as possible.

☐ Mistake: Making gifts to someone who uses the money to pay for medical or educational expenses. When you pay a medical or educational institution directly on someone else's behalf, you can exceed the $10,000 annual limit on tax-free gifts.

Solution: By paying medical or educational costs yourself, you can reduce the size of your estate by more than the $10,000 allowance—without owing any gift taxes.

☐ Mistake: Setting up a living trust to reduce your estate-tax bill. Living trusts—trusts set up during your lifetime—have no impact on estate-tax liability.

Solution: Understand that estates of people who have living trusts bypass probate, thereby eliminating those costs. Living trusts also prevent the public inspection of your estate. But don't rely on them to save estate taxes.

☐ Mistake: Saving the unified credit to shelter estate assets at your death. The $600,000-per-person estate-tax exclusion also applies to gifts that are made during your lifetime.

Solution: In some cases, it makes more sense to make large gifts of property during your lifetime than after your death. This will shelter gifts from taxes by reducing the $600,000 lifetime estate-and-gift-tax exclusions.

The reason for making such gifts is that you can remove all future appreciation on the gifted property from your taxable estate. Good assets to consider: Interest in a family-owned business, partnership shares, real estate, growth-oriented stocks and mutual funds.

☐ Mistake: Not keeping your beneficiary designations up-to-date. Beneficiaries must be named on many assets. Examples: Life insurance, retirement plans, bank and brokerage accounts.

That's why it is easy to inadvertently leave valuable insurance proceeds to a former spouse, for instance.

Solution: Check beneficiary designations whenever there have been major changes in your life. Examples: Marriage, death, birth of a child.

Sources: David Gerson, tax partner and regional director of estate planning, and Charles R. Cangro, senior tax manager, Ernst & Young, New York.

Tax traps in divorce

Divorcing couples often fall into tax traps that prove costly for both spouses. Family-law attorneys and judges often don't understand the tax law, and in many states judges aren't required even to consider taxes when rendering decisions.

Divorcing couples are likely to do much better, taxwise, by reaching a voluntary agreement that benefits both of them. Planning points:

☐ *Dependency exemptions:* The exemption goes to the parent with custody, unless that parent agrees in writing to give up the exemption. If there are several children, the parents can agree to divvy up the exemptions. Normally, an exemption is most valuable to the parent in the higher tax bracket.

☐ Lower tax rates are available to a parent who qualifies for head-of-household tax status. To get this, a parent must have at least one child living with him or her. Otherwise, the divorced parent must file as a single person and pay higher tax rates, even if that parent is making large support payments and claims the dependency exemption.

☐ Alimony is deductible by the spouse who pays and taxed to the spouse who receives it, while child support isn't deductible by or taxable to either spouse. But if a divorce decree requires regular payments covering both, without making an allocation between them, all the payments are treated as alimony unless there's a clear indication to the contrary. For example, if a monthly payment of $1,000 for a mother and child is to be reduced to $700 when the child reaches age 18, it's clear that $300 of the monthly payment is intended as child support. This can produce net savings if the paying spouse is in a much higher tax bracket than the receiving one.

☐ Year-end divorces should be timed to have favorable tax impact. One's marital status on December 31 determines his or her filing status.

New-job loophole

Roll a pension-plan distribution from your old company over into the qualified plan at your new firm.

☐ You won't pay any tax on the distribution now. Taxes are deferred until you receive a distribution from your new company's pension plan.

☐ *Even better:* You'll preserve the right to use five-year averaging on the distribution, a very special tax-saving method used to figure the tax on retirement distributions.

☐ *Danger:* Don't make the mistake of rolling your pension-plan distribution over into your IRA. That makes it ineligible for five-year averaging.

☐ There are many different tax strategies available when you receive a distribution from a retirement plan. Examine them all to see which one is best for you.

Advantage: Ownership

Excellent tax-saving opportunities occur when people own real estate or equipment used by their own company or business, even if that business is only a sideline. Advantages of personal ownership:

☐ Tax shelter. Personal ownership lets depreciation deductions be claimed on the owner's personal tax return. Further, the investor controls the investment. Deductions aren't acquired by investing in an unfamiliar tax-shelter business that is managed by someone else.

☐ Liquidity. The owner may be able to use the property to obtain cash in a tax-favored way. *Examples:* If the value of real estate goes up, it can be refinanced to obtain a tax-free cash in-flow. When property is no longer needed by the company, it can be sold for the owner's personal account. If property is leased to a family-owned company, the owner gets cash flow from the rental payments.

☐ Estate-planning flexibility. More options are available for the disposal of your property. For example, a building can be given to a spouse or child to insure their financial well-being, without giving up a controlling interest in the business.

Tax loopholes for those over 50

Believe it or not, as we grow older, tax loopholes become easier to find…

☐ Loophole: Escaping a stiff penalty tax on distributions from retirement plans by delaying distributions. If you withdraw money from a tax-qualified retirement plan, such as an IRA, Keogh or 401(k) plan, before the magic age of 59½, you are subject to a 10% penalty tax on early distributions from the plan. By postponing distributions until after that age, you avoid the penalty. However, any money you take out is considered taxable income.

More: Avoid tax on large distributions from retirement plans by speeding up withdrawals. The law imposes a stiff 15% penalty tax on withdrawals from retirement plans that are considered excessive. What's excessive? Annual payments of more than $150,000 and lump-sum payments of more than $750,000. One way around this is to start taking money from your retirement plans as soon as possible after you reach age 59½, in order to reduce the size of your plans and limit your exposure to the penalty.

…and more: If you use some of the distribution money to buy life insurance policies through a life insurance trust, the insurance proceeds will not be subject to estate taxes.

☐ Loophole: Not paying tax on $125,000 in profits from the sale of your house. If you are age 55 or older when you sell your primary residence and you have lived in it for three of the last five years, the first $125,000 of profit is totally tax-free. But since this tax break can be taken only once during your lifetime, it's important to wring the maximum tax advantage from it. Two situations in which you should pass up the exclusion:

☐ If you're planning to buy another house within two years of the sale. Reason: This enables you to defer tax on your profits from the initial sale and preserves your right to claim the $125,000 exclusion on the sale of the second house.

☐ If the profit on the sale of your home is relatively small. Reason: Since the exclusion can be taken only once, you may be better off paying capital-gains tax now on the modest gain—perhaps because you were forced to sell in a depressed real-estate market—and preserving the exclusion for the future, when market values may have rebounded.

More: If you're planning to remarry, and if both you and your prospective spouse are 55 or older, you can make double use of the exemption if you each sell your house before you tie the knot. Reason: The exemption can be used only once. If one spouse has taken it previously, it can't be taken again by a newly married couple, even if the other spouse has never used it. So by each using the exemption before marriage, the couple can escape tax on as much as $250,000 in gains on the sale of their separate homes.

☐ Loophole: Making full use of the $10,000 annual gift-tax exemption to reduce estate taxes. The maximum federal tax on estates is 55%. If you live in a state that imposes estate taxes as well, your beneficiaries may wind up getting no more than 40% of what you leave them. One of the easiest ways to cut estate taxes is to give away property during your lifetime.

You can give up to $10,000 a year ($20,000 if you and your spouse make a joint gift) to each of any number of recipients without having to pay gift tax. The advantage of making such lifetime gifts is that they remove assets that otherwise would be included in your taxable estate.

More: Make larger gifts that are subject to gift tax now—to reduce estate taxes in the future. This is a good technique if you don't need all the income from your assets.

Example: You want to make a gift of $25,000 to your grandchild. The gift tax on that would be 50%, or $12,500. So your total cost of the gift would be $37,500. If, instead, you left your grandchild that same $25,000 in your will, the total cost of delaying the $25,000 bequest would be $50,000. Reason: When you pay gift tax on a transfer made during your life, the tax itself reduces the size of your estate. But if the transfer does not take place until after death, the estate tax becomes part of your estate. Caution: Gift tax on gifts made within three years of death will be added back to your taxable estate.

□ Loophole: Getting the government to help share the cost of your job-hunting expenses, if you're an executive who has been hit by corporate downsizing. The cost of looking for a job in the same field you're already in is deductible as a miscellaneous expense—once you've exceeded the threshold of 2% of your Adjusted Gross Income. This means you can write off the expenses of retaining an outplacement firm, preparing and printing a résumé, telephone calls, traveling to job interviews and lunches and dinners (subject to the new 50% limit) related to your search.

□ Loophole: Transferring appreciated assets from an ill spouse to the healthy one to cut capital-gains taxes. The healthy spouse transfers assets that have a large unrealized gain, such as stocks, to the sick spouse. (There's no tax on transfers between spouses.) The sick spouse bequeaths the assets in his/her will to the healthy one. After the sick spouse dies, the healthy spouse inherits the assets with the tax cost (or basis) increased to their value as of the date of death. The healthy spouse can then turn around and sell the assets without having to pay capital-gains-tax on the appreciation.

Caution: The gift from one spouse to the other must be made more than one year before the date of death or the stepped-up basis will be denied.

Source: Edward Mendlowitz, a partner in the New York certified public accounting firm of Mendlowitz Weitsen. He is the author of several books, including *New Tax Traps/New Opportunities,* Boardroom Books, Greenwich, CT.

New tax break for small-business investors

As an incentive to channel capital into new small businesses, the 1993 Tax Act created a tax break for investors.

One-half of the gain from investments in certain small businesses is tax-free when the following IRS criteria are met…

□ Shares must be bought in an initial offering, not on the secondary market. Exceptions: Shares acquired by gift or death of the purchaser, or distributed by a partnership (in either case acquired as an initial offering).

□ Shares must be held for at least five years to qualify for the tax break.

Impact: In most cases, one-half of the profit when the stock is sold will not be subject to capital-gains tax.

Example: You buy shares for $5,000 and sell them for $20,000 six years later. One-half of your $15,000 gain—or $7,500—is tax-free. Because the top tax rate on capital gains is 28%, the net effective tax rate on your profit equals only 14%—a big savings.

Limit: You cannot exclude from taxation more than $10 million ($5 million for married filing separately) or ten times the tax cost (basis) in your shares—whichever is more. The limit is applied separately to each eligible company in which you invest.

Caution: One-half of the amount of the excluded capital gain will be a tax preference item in calculating the Alternative Minimum Tax (AMT).

Example: You buy shares for $5,000 and sell them for $20,000 six years later. You can exclude $7,500 from capital-gains tax, but $3,750 is a tax preference item for AMT purposes. Because the top AMT rate today equals 28%, the net tax rate is potentially 21%.

Nearly all types of regular corporations can issue shares that qualify for this tax break. They must be active businesses, meaning that at least 80% by value of their assets must be used in the active conduct of their trade or business and no more than 10% of their assets can be tied up in securities or real estate.

Exceptions: Financial companies, real-estate investment trusts, personal-service corporations, S corporations, "possessions" corporations and oil and gas producers, among others.

When a company issues stock, its cash plus its adjusted basis in other property (including the amount of the stock issue) must be $50 million or less.

To qualify, shares must be issued after August 10, 1993, the date the new Tax Act was signed into law.

Note: The tax break applies to newly issued stock of an existing company as well as stock issued by a new company.

Downside: New start-ups of small companies are extremely risky investments. The risk is magnified because if you bail out of your shares when you see signs of trouble in the business, you forfeit the tax break.

Source: Richard J. Shapiro, tax partner, Goldstein Golub Kessler, New York.

After filing your income-tax return

Don't relax too quickly after filing your income-tax return. Post–April 15 problems and what to do about them:

☐ If you haven't received your refund, and it's 12 weeks since you filed your return, contact the taxpayer service representative at the Internal Revenue Office where you filed your return. If you write, include your name, address and Social Security number. (As a general rule, the closer to the April 15 deadline you filed, the longer it will take you to get your refund.)

☐ If your refund check is bigger or smaller than you expected, request a transcript of your account from the IRS. A computer printout shows all payments you've made to the IRS for the past few years and how much of your tax liability has been paid. The transcript will help you determine where the extra refund came from or why the refund wasn't as large as you thought it would be.

☐ If you receive a refund that's too big, get it straightened out with the IRS. *Reason:* You are responsible for interest on the extra amount, even if it is the IRS's fault. So don't spend the portion that you aren't entitled to. *Strategy:* Deposit the check in your own account rather than return it to the IRS uncashed. There's less chance of a mix-up, and you won't be stuck waiting for the portion of the money that you are entitled to have now. Contact the IRS for the correct amount and then send a check for the difference.

☐ If your refund check is too small, you can safely cash the check without giving up any of your rights to contest the amount.

☐ You are entitled to interest from the IRS if you filed on time but didn't receive your refund until after May 30.

☐ If you didn't file your return on time, file as quickly as possible to limit the interest you will owe the IRS on the amount that's overdue. *Escape hatch:* You won't owe a penalty for late filing if you filed a valid extension application and submitted a check by April 15 for at least 90% of the tax you owe, subject to certain conditions. However, you will owe interest for any additional tax due with the return when it is filed.

☐ If the IRS sends you a notice stating that you didn't report all your income, don't automatically assume that the IRS is right and pay the extra tax. Make sure you understand the notice itself, and carefully go over your records and your return.

☐ If you made a mistake on your return that you didn't realize until after you filed: The general rule is that you have three years from the original due date of the return to file an amended return. It's not wise to wait this long, however, especially if you *owe* tax. Interest and penalties just keep adding up. If the income that you forgot to report was reported to the IRS on a 1099 form, it will be just a matter of time until the IRS catches up with you anyway. *Better:* Amend your return as soon as possible to avoid the extra payment or claim your refund.

☐ If a financial institution reported your tax-exempt interest as taxable income to the IRS, contact the institution and have the correct amount reported to the IRS.

Source: Arnold H. Koonan, tax partner in charge, Coopers & Lybrand, CPAs, Washington, DC.

What the IRS double-checks

You will receive a W-2 wage and tax statement and 1099 statements from the sources listed below, showing the amount of income you received from each. Make sure you include every dollar of this income on your return. The IRS matches all 1099s with your return…by computer. If the figures don't agree, you will be contacted by the IRS.

☐ Interest and dividends. The 1099-INT and 1099-DIV statements show income from bank accounts, certificates of deposit and credit unions and dividends from securities.

☐ State tax refunds. The 1099-G shows the amount you received as a state tax refund last year. If you took an itemized deduction for state and local taxes in the previous year and obtained a full tax benefit, report the amount of any refund as income on your current tax return.

☐ Stock sales income. Your 1099-B shows the sales price of stock you sold last year. Part of the amount shown on 1099-B may be attributable to transfer taxes and brokers' commissions rather than to income from the sale itself. Exclude these nonincome items and show the IRS why you aren't including the whole 1099-B amount in your income by reconciling it carefully on Schedule D.

☐ Social Security income. Your SSA 1099 shows all Social Security income you received last year. Depending on your income from other sources and the amount of Social Security you receive, it could be taxable. Use the worksheet in the IRS instructions to calculate your tax.

☐ IRS interest refund. The 1099-C shows the amount of interest income you must report from an IRS refund.

☐ W-2 wage and tax statements. These statements show your salary and amounts withheld for the year. Make sure you know the reason for every entry on your W-2, and be sure the information agrees with the amounts shown on your December 31 pay stub.

☐ All of the above statements should be correct and in agreement with your records. If they aren't, contact the source immediately and have a new statement issued. If there isn't enough time to get a new statement, attach a note to your return showing why there is a discrepancy between the information return and the amounts you actually report. You alone are responsible for making sure all these statements are correct.

☐ If you didn't receive a 1099 from a source who paid you money last year, be sure to arrange to get one. Chances are the income is being reported to the federal government whether you received the statement or not.

Source: Lester A. Marks, partner, Ernst & Young, New York.

IRS bell-ringers

Discuss the proper handling of any of the following immediately with your tax adviser:

☐ Any out-of-the-blue request, penalty or demand.

☐ Any notice containing errors, even "little" mistakes.

☐ All IRS correspondence relating to tax shelters.

IRS communications

☐ Audit notices. Normally, no written response is required for notices of office or field audits. Information Document Requests (IDRs), for field audits, simply list what records the agent wants to examine. You may need to prepare schedules, etc., to respond to an IDR. You do need to reply to a so-called correspondence audit. What's needed is clearly spelled out.

☐ Agreement forms received following an audit generally require you to sign only if you agree with the specified changes on your return. However, a no-change letter requires no action on your part.

☐ Tax bill. Termed "Notice and Demand," this is to be treated like any bill. Pay it on time, or accept the consequences.

☐ Penalty notice. Related to a specific penalty (e.g., Form 2210 for underpayment of estimated taxes). The reason for it, amount due and what's required of you are noted. Many penalties can be abated by proper action.

☐ 30-day letter. Gives you 30 days to submit a written protest against the IRS adjustments specified in the letter or pay the amount noted. Protest-filing instructions and details regarding an appeals hearing accompany the letter. (If your tax involves $2,500 or less, a written protest is not required.)

☐ 90-day letter. This statutory notice of deficiency gives you 90 days to file a petition with the Tax Court, or else you must pay the amount specified.

☐ Request to extend the statute of limitations. Sign only if you agree. *Pitfall:* If you don't agree, you'll probably receive a 90-day letter.

☐ Tax-shelter notices. A prefiling notification states that a shelter's benefits are nondeductible and, if claimed, will subject you to penalties. No response is required. And you may receive a shelter questionnaire (sometimes conducted during an audit) requesting various information.

☐ *Important:* Consult your tax adviser before acting on any IRS document that you receive.

Handling mail from the IRS

The types of written IRS communications that most taxpayers receive are generally cut-and-dried.

Never ignore any IRS communication. If you're not certain about what to do, consult your tax adviser…the sooner, the better.

When documents are requested (as in a correspondence audit), send only copies, never originals.

Send all replies and payments by certified mail, return receipt requested. Certification provides legal proof of time of mailing. The return-receipt procedure gives you an early warning of possible nondelivery, alerting you to follow up.

Tag every piece of paper with your name and Social Security number to speed IRS processing and help guard against misfiling.

For multipage documents, provide internal numbering (e.g., "page 1 of 10"). For multidocument replies, number each item and supply a finding list. This checklisting helps you organize and ensures that you omitted nothing.

Strictly observe time limits for your reply. Even if your adviser is handling the reply, verify that all was mailed on time (check the receipt). It's always your responsibility to meet IRS deadlines.

When the IRS claims you didn't report income

One of the most troubling IRS communications a taxpayer can get these days is a "matching notice"—a long, confusing computer printout summarizing income that you failed to report and recalculating your tax. In the IRS matching program, a computer matches the 1099 information forms that report income from various sources with the income taxpayers declare on their returns. Although it's good, the program isn't sophisticated enough to deal with some fairly common situations. Here are a few examples:

☐ Custodial accounts. You have a custodial account for your child. But your Social Security number, not the child's, is on the account. You get a matching notice saying that you failed to report the interest on the account. *What to do:* Send a copy of the bank passbook to the IRS, together with a letter explaining that the money in the account is your child's and that you will see to it that your child gets a Social Security number.

☐ *Hidden items:* When you prepared your return you may have included some income on a schedule. For example, you may have reported some self-employment income on Schedule C. The computer may not find that income,

in which case it will generate a notice saying you failed to report it. *Defense:* Write back to the IRS, showing how the 1099 income is included in the gross receipts on Schedule C.

☐ Incorrect 1099s. The IRS assumes that income reported on a 1099 is correct and that you are wrong if you declare some other figure. But your broker may have made a mistake. The broker's computer may have incorrectly listed nontaxable income as taxable income. *Defense:* Send copies of bank or brokerage statements explaining the discrepancy. Show which part of the 1099 income was not taxable.

Contesting IRS penalties: Problems to watch out for

Always check penalty notices from the IRS carefully to make sure you really are liable for the penalty. You may not be. But it's up to you to get yourself off the hook.

Possible problems:

☐ Estimated tax. When withholding estimated-tax payments don't total at least 90% of the tax owed, the IRS automatically assesses a penalty on the underpayments. You may, however, qualify for one of the tax law's exceptions to the penalty. (For example, you may be able to base your payments on "annualized income" if you earned most of your income late in the year.) *To avoid the penalty:* Fill out Form 2210 (*Underpayment of Estimated Tax by Individuals*), indicating which of the exceptions applies. Send the form back to the IRS, together with a copy of the penalty notice.

☐ Late filing. Penalties are assessed automatically when you file a tax return late. But you may have a legitimate excuse for late filing. Send the IRS a letter, explaining why you had "reasonable cause" for filing late and should, therefore, be excused from the penalty. Send a copy of the notice along with your letter.

☐ If you didn't file a return, it is possible to get a letter from the IRS asking why a return wasn't filed, even though none was required. This often happens when a trust or a company becomes inactive. Send the IRS a statement saying that the company or trust had insufficient income to warrant filing a return.

☐ If the IRS slips up and sends you a refund check even though you asked that overpayment be applied to next year's tax, this can be a problem if your accountant intended the overpayment to cover your first estimated-tax installment. If you keep the refund check, you'll be short on your estimated payments and liable for a penalty. Always confirm refunds with your accountant.

☐ If you can't get action from the IRS Service Center or District Office, take the matter to the IRS's Problem Resolution Office. This special section of the IRS is staffed by people whose job is to cut through IRS red tape. Call the Problem Resolution Office directly. Each IRS district has one. You can get the number by calling your local taxpayer service office. *Suggestion:* Call early in the morning. All lines are busy by noon.

If you can't pay your taxes

Most creditors must have a court order before they can seize your property. All that's required of the IRS is that it present you with a bill for unpaid tax and wait ten days. After that, if you still haven't paid, it can seize your bank accounts, garnish your wages and even sell your house. Fortunately, the IRS seizes property only as a last resort in the collection process. Before invoking its enforcement powers, the IRS generally gives financially strapped taxpayers a chance to try to work out a payment agreement.

Here's how to proceed when there's no cash to pay the bill:

☐ File a tax return. The worst thing you can do when you owe the IRS money is not file a tax return. Owing money to the IRS that you simply can't pay is not a crime. The IRS can't put you in jail for not having the money. But it is a crime not to file a tax return—a crime for which you can go to jail. By filing, you also avoid the big penalties for late filing. If you don't get your return in on time (or don't have a valid extension), you'll incur a late-filing penalty of 5% a month (or any fraction of a month), up to a maximum of 25% of the tax you owe.

☐ Pay what you can when you file your return. Keep to a minimum your penalties for late payment and interest on the tax you owe. *Trap:* If you file for an extension, you must send the IRS 90% of the tax you expect to owe or they'll charge you late-payment penalties. And if you lie on the extension form and say you expect to owe no tax, you can be charged with perjury.

☐ Six to eight weeks after you've filed, you'll get a bill for the unpaid balance. The bill will include interest and penalties. Don't ignore it. If you're still short of money, arrange a meeting at your local IRS office to work out an installment-payment arrangement.

☐ Be prepared to submit a financial statement showing that you don't have assets that can be liquidated to pay your tax. Don't expect the IRS to give you extra time to pay if you have certificates of deposit in the bank that you simply don't want to cash in early.

☐ Go easy on the hard-luck stories when asking for an installment arrangement. The IRS has heard them all. Concentrate on negotiating, in a businesslike manner, a series of monthly payments that you'll be able to manage.

☐ When you give the IRS an analysis of your monthly income and expenses, show that there's money left over for tax payments. If you come up broke each month, the IRS will be less inclined to agree to installment payments. Where will you find the money to make the payments?

☐ The IRS likes to see a tax bill paid up in a year or less. If you can figure out a way to pay the debt in less than a year, you have a better shot at getting an installment agreement than if you say you need five years to pay.

☐ File all your delinquent tax returns before you negotiate an installment agreement. Establish all your tax liabilities, and have them all covered by the agreement. *Trap:* If you agree to a payment plan for one year and then get a bill for other years' back taxes, you'll be in default on the agreement. The IRS will then demand payment in full.

☐ Never miss a payment without first talking to a revenue officer. You're technically in default of the agreement when you miss just one payment. And when you're in default, you have to start over again, trying to negotiate a new agreement.

□ *If you can't make a payment:* Meet with a revenue officer. Explain the unusual circumstances that make it impossible for you to pay and hope that the officer will alter the terms of your agreement.

Source: Randy Bruce Blaustein, Esq., partner, Blaustein, Greenberg & Co., New York, and author of *How to Do Business With the IRS*, Prentice-Hall, Inc., Englewood Cliffs, NJ.

What the IRS cannot seize if you fail to pay your taxes

The IRS is vested with the power to seize your property without a court order. The only requirement is that it have a valid assessment, give notice with a demand for payment (which has to be sent to your last known address) and give notice of intent to seize.

In addition to seizing your property, the IRS can also place a levy on your bank accounts and on your salary. This means that both your bank and your employer must turn over to the IRS all funds being held for you, to the extent of the levy. (*Note:* Special rules apply to salary.)

Property exempt by law from levy:

□ Apparel and schoolbooks. (Expensive items of apparel such as furs are luxuries and are not exempt from levy.)

□ Fuel, provisions, furniture and personal effects, not to exceed $1,650 in value (for the head of a household).

□ Books and tools used in your trade, business or profession, not to exceed $1,100 in value.

□ Unemployment benefits.

□ Undelivered mail.

□ Certain annuity and pension payments (including Social Security benefits).

□ Workers compensation.

□ Salary, wages or other income subject to a prior judgment for court-ordered child-support payments.

□ A minimum amount of wages, salary and other income—$75 per week—plus an additional $25 for each legal dependent.

The IRS is now seizing personal residences more frequently. After a Notice of Seizure is placed on the front door of your house, you have ten days to come up with the money you owe, or there is an excellent chance that it will be sold at auction to satisfy the tax bill. The house may be redeemed at any time within 180 days after the sale by paying the purchaser the amount paid for the property, plus interest. By law, the purchaser must sell.

Excuses that work with the IRS

Suppose you filed your tax return late and did not obtain an extension. Worse still, you also owe the IRS money. The IRS has sent you a bill for the tax you owe plus interest and penalties. You know that the tax and interest must be paid but feel that you have "reasonable cause" for filing your return late. If one of the following situations honestly applied to you, you may be able to persuade the IRS to drop the penalties:

□ You were seriously ill or there was a death or serious illness in your immediate family. In the case of failure to pay a previous penalty, the death or serious illness must be of an individual having the sole authority to make payment.

□ Your place of business or business records were destroyed by fire or other disaster.

□ You were unavoidably absent from home or business.

□ You were unable to obtain records necessary to determine the amount of tax due, for reasons beyond your control.

□ Your ability to pay was materially impaired by civil disturbances.

□ You were in a combat zone.

□ You have exercised ordinary business care and prudence in providing for payment of taxes and have posted a bond or acceptable security, coupled with a collateral agreement showing that paying the tax when due would have caused undue hardship.

□ Any other reason showing that you exercised ordinary care and prudence but still were unable to pay the tax when due.

□ Seasonal changes resulted in sudden increases in your tax liability, even though you are not ordinarily required to make deposits. (This excuse applies to penalties for late payment or nonpayment of payroll taxes.)

□ Failure to file a tax return upon the advice of a reputable accountant or attorney whom you selected with reasonable and ordinary prudence and whom you furnished in good faith with information you reasonably believed was sufficient.

☐ **Late filing by tax preparer.** When a taxpayer has relied on an accountant or attorney to prepare a tax return, which was then not filed on a timely basis, the IRS usually allows this as an acceptable excuse. Technically, such an excuse is not reasonable cause, but it usually works, particularly when the accountant or attorney admits blame to the IRS in writing.

☐ **Absence of key employees.** When a business has had heavy employee turnover or when an important financial executive such as a vice president or controller is no longer employed by the business, it can be considered reasonable cause for late filing and late payment.

☐ **Change of CPA firm.** If you recently fired a CPA firm because it was not taking care of things properly and on time and the problem wasn't discovered until new accountants were retained, it may be reasonable cause to abate a penalty.

☐ **Lost or misplaced records.** This usually works if the information needed to prepare the tax return in question was misfiled or lost and had to be reconstructed.

Excuses that don't work with the IRS...

Excuses probably won't work if:

☐ You made the same mistake on a previous return.

☐ You filed a negligent return and you are an accountant or lawyer.

☐ You didn't keep proper records and you are a CPA. (Professionals are less likely to escape a penalty because the IRS thinks they should know better than nonprofessionals.)

Source: Peter A. Weitsen, partner, Mendlowitz Weitsen, New York.

Negotiation tactics

☐ **Provide only the information requested.** *For an office audit:* Take with you only the documentation relating to the requested items.

☐ If the agent requests support for other items, suggest, diplomatically, that since this would require yet another meeting, perhaps such information could be mailed in.

☐ **Involve a supervisor only if necessary.** If you've reached an impasse—because of an honest disagreement or a personality conflict—enlist the agent's help by asking, "Would you discuss this with your supervisor?" Communicate through—not around—the agent.

☐ **Avoid a change of agents, if possible.** You'll avoid the double audit that results from starting afresh.

☐ **Know your appeal rights,** and let the agent know that you do. Use this knowledge to achieve agreements. Agents like to close cases "agreed."

☐ **Sign an agreement form only if you truly agree** with all the proposed adjustments. Never allow yourself to cave in to pressure. If unsure, ask for time to consider and to consult your tax adviser.

Dealing personally with the IRS

Taxpayers sometimes choose to deal personally with the IRS on routine matters. Here are some pointers to help you deal productively with the Service:

☐ **Be prepared.** It's to your advantage to organize and summarize all requested information. Have an adding machine tape to show how you calculated each questioned deduction. This will expedite the review and let the reviewer know you're in control.

☐ **Be honest.** Don't try to disguise a problem area, such as lack of certain types of documentation. Never risk arousing IRS suspicion. *Best:* Explain the problem in terms of what proof you have. If that's not sufficient, then ask if you can gather additional proof to satisfy the IRS.

☐ **Be businesslike.** Use good-sense rules of courtesy and tact in all your dealings with the IRS.

☐ **Be prudent.** Limit your involvement to nontechnical, routine matters. Don't get in over your head. Do only what, and as much as, you feel comfortable doing. *Alarm bells:* Uncertainty, anxiety, frustration and anger are the signs that professional help is needed.

☐ Office audits held at a local IRS office are typically used to determine if income and deductions claimed are properly supported by documentation. They are usually limited to several items, and are not likely to involve technical or legal issues.

☐ Field audits held at the taxpayer's business and/or residence are generally used to scrutinize a variety of IRS concerns—in many cases related to business returns—often involving technical or legal issues. Discuss how best to handle such an audit with your tax adviser. In most cases, it's wise to have your adviser represent you at the audit.

Source: Roy B. Harrill, tax partner in charge of firmwide practice for IRS procedures and administration, Arthur Andersen & Co., Chicago.

Recent taxpayer victories that could be valuable to you

Use these recent taxpayer victories over the IRS to help plan your tax-cutting strategies for next year…

☐ IRS loses. Travel deductible. A self-employed person traveled daily to several work locations. He deducted his travel costs as a business expense, but the IRS said it was nondeductible commuting expenses. Court: The individual also worked at home an average of three hours a week. Although this was a small amount of time, it made his home his one regular, permanent work location. Since the cost of travel between two work sites is deductible, the individual could deduct all the costs of traveling between home and the other work locations.

Philip Alan Boice, TC Memo 1993-498.

☐ IRS loses. Smart business owner. Richard Hansen figured out a way to depreciate land used in his business, even though the Tax Code says land is not depreciable. How: Instead of having his company buy the land outright, he had it buy a 30-year "right-to-use" the land while he personally bought the remainder interest—which gave him full ownership of the land when the 30 years were up.

Because the right-to-use had a fixed price and a limited term, the company said it could deduct the price over the term, effectively creating annual depreciation deductions for the cost of the land. IRS objection: The deal was set up this way solely to create tax deductions that wouldn't be there if the company had bought the land outright. Court: It is perfectly legal to structure a property purchase to maximize tax benefits. The deductions were allowed.

Richard Hansen Land, Inc., TC Memo 1993-248.

☐ IRS concedes. Smart investor. An individual who took out a loan on his home and used the money to make an investment was allowed to deduct the interest on the loan as investment interest rather than mortgage interest. The investment interest paid on the loan could then be deducted against investment income, sheltering it from tax. Point: This strategy makes sense if further borrowing against a home will not produce deductible mortgage interest because of the $100,000 limit on deductible home-equity financing. By treating the mortgage interest as investment interest, you obtain a second way to deduct it.

IRS Letter Ruling 9335043.

☐ IRS loses. Refund is paid. When Peter McConaughy hadn't received a refund more than a year after requesting it with supporting documents, he was allowed to sue the IRS to compel its payment and he won—and then also collected reimbursement from the IRS for the legal expenses he incurred in the process.

Peter McConaughy, D. Md., No. WN-91-2874.

☐ IRS loses. Late amended claim is allowed. A refund claim was filed just before the filing deadline. After the deadline, the taxpayer discovered that the refund had been underestimated and filed an amended claim for a larger amount. But the IRS said it was too late. Court: The new claim was simply an adjustment of the original, timely claim, so it was allowed.

Mutual Assurance Inc., ND Ala., No. CV-93-H-0952-S.

☐ IRS loses. Pay rent to yourself. D. Sherman Cox ran his business from an office located in a building that he owned with his wife. He paid himself an annual rent of $18,000—which he deducted as a business expense on Schedule C of his tax return.

He also reported it as rental income on Schedule E—producing a net tax benefit, since passive losses from other real-estate properties could be used to shelter the rental income from tax. But the IRS disallowed the transaction, saying one can't pay rent to oneself. Court: Half the rent Cox paid became the legal property of his wife, since she was co-owner of the building. He could claim rental treatment for the $9,000 that accrued to her—even though she filed a joint tax return with him.

D. Sherman Cox, TC Memo 1993-326.

☐ IRS loses. Inferred theft. A couple followed the advice of their broker and put $300,000 in an investment, which turned out to be a Ponzi scheme.* When the IRS allowed them only a $3,000 capital-loss deduction, they claimed a theft-loss deduction for their full investment. The IRS answered that they hadn't been defrauded because they never had any direct contact with the investment operators—they had simply taken bad advice from their broker. Court: The couple had been the victims of fraud, if only indirectly. The theft-loss deduction was allowed.

David Jensen, TC Memo 1993-393.

*A Ponzi scheme is an investment swindle in which some early investors are paid off with money put up by later ones in order to encourage more and more risk.

Which court to appeal a tax case to

A taxpayer who wants to appeal an IRS decision has the choice of three courts:

☐ Tax Court. A proceeding in Tax Court (of which the Small Case Division is part) is a direct appeal from the IRS's decision. The taxpayer need not pay the disputed tax until the case is decided. If he loses, however, he has to pay interest on any judgment. To prevent interest from piling up, he can pay the disputed amount to the court in advance. Then, if he wins or compromises the case, he gets all or part of the money back.

☐ Claims Court or District Court: The taxpayer must pay the disputed amount and sue for a refund. In effect, though not in form, he is appealing the IRS's decision.

☐ Which court to use is a matter of legal strategy to be discussed with your lawyer or tax adviser. Disputed or unsettled legal issues have often been decided differently by different courts, so there can be a distinct advantage in picking the right one.

Taking your own case to tax court

Taxpayers who want to challenge an IRS decision can save time, trouble and legal fees by using the Small Case Division of the Tax Court

☐ The Division's streamlined procedures are now available in all disputes of up to $10,000 (formerly $5,000). The Division handles estate- and gift-tax cases, as well as income-tax ones.

Advantages

☐ Paperwork is simplified and kept to a minimum. Trials are informal. The strict rules of evidence are relaxed.

☐ You can have a lawyer if you want, but you don't need one. Most taxpayers appear for themselves.

☐ Cases are reached and disposed of much faster than cases in the regular Tax Court. In addition, over half the cases are settled before trial, by agreement between the IRS and the taxpayer.

☐ The Division's judges travel to over 100 cities around the country, including cities where the regular Tax Court does not hold sessions. You can pick whichever city is most convenient.

Rules

☐ Decisions of the Small Case Division are final. Neither party may appeal. Furthermore, no decision may be used as a precedent in deciding any other case, even one involving the same taxpayer.

☐ In rare instances, a case may be transferred from the Small Case Division to the regular Tax Court. This might happen if the case presented a new or unusual legal issue and it was desirable to get a decision that could be used as precedent for future cases.

☐ Get all the forms you need by writing the Clerk of the Court, US Tax Court, 400 Second St. NW, Washington, DC 20217. You'll receive a simplified petition (Form 2), a form for designating the place of trial and a booklet explaining how the Division works and including a list of cities it visits.

☐ You must file your petition, along with a $60 filing fee, within 90 days of the date the IRS mails you a notice of deficiency. (The date is shown at the top of the notice.) The time limit is absolute. *Caution:* 90 days does not mean three months. If, for example, a notice of deficiency is mailed to you on October 10, you must file your petition by January 8—not January 10.

☐ Use registered or certified mail. That way, you'll have proof of the date of mailing.

Procedure

☐ In your petition, state your disagreement with the IRS as clearly as possible, including your reasons for disagreeing. You don't have to use legal language and you won't be penalized, even if you forget something. But the clearer your statement, the faster the case can be handled and the greater the possibility of a settlement.

☐ A copy of your petition will be sent to the IRS, and the Service will probably contact you soon afterward. Be prepared to discuss a settlement arrangement. Most cases are settled at this stage of the proceedings.

☐ If no settlement is reached, you will receive notice of trial about 60 days in advance. Depending on the Division's workload and its schedule of cities to be visited, you can expect to receive notice about seven to ten months after filing your petition.

☐ At the trial, you can testify, call witnesses, argue your case orally or in writing and submit any evidence you have to support your case. Documentary evidence is particularly important; bring everything you can. Some legal questions depend entirely on documentary evidence. The tax status of payments to an ex-spouse, for example, may depend on the wording of the divorce decree.

☐ The more documents and records that you have to support the accuracy of your tax return, the more likely it is that the court will believe your testimony on disputed or undocumented matters. *Caution:* Documents already submitted to the IRS are not automatically a part of the record. Be sure to request the Service, in writing, to bring them to the trial. Play safe and spell out exactly what documents you want.

Source: Charles Casazza, Clerk of the Court, US Tax Court, Washington, DC.

Lending money to a friend

☐ No matter how friendly a loan, draw up a note stating terms and conditions.

☐ Be businesslike. Include a provision for reasonable interest.

☐ Be prepared to document the loan, so that you can take a tax deduction on any loss.

Collecting on a judgment

After getting a judgment, many people find that they have spent much time and money and gone to a lot of trouble to get a worthless piece of paper. According to one lawyer, less than 25% of all judgments are collected. To make winning a judgment worthwhile, it is important to know what to do and what to avoid.

☐ Don't sue a firm just because its name is on a sign outside a place of business, and don't sue the person you assume owns the business. Check with the local county clerk's office, business-licensing bureau, department of consumer affairs or police department to find out the real name in which the business is registered.

☐ Sue where the assets are. The service person who did the damage, the franchise owner, the corporate owner or the parent corporation may all be liable if you can prove wrongful involvement. Sue whichever entity or entities have enough assets to pay your judgment. You can sue more than one.

☐ If you have ever received a check from or given a check to the debtor, you may have a clue to the whereabouts of the debtor's bank account.

☐ If you have a judgment against someone who owns a home, check the county's homeownership records in that area of residence.

☐ If you have won a judgment against a business, go personally to the business location to see what equipment and machinery are on the site.

☐ If the judgment is large enough, hire an agency to do an asset search. Before paying for a professional search, find out what the agency is actually going to do to uncover assets and what results you can realistically expect.

☐ To avoid creditors, an unscrupulous company will often go out of business in one name and start up the same business the next day with a different name—on the same location and with the same equipment. To collect on your judgments, you will need a lawyer to prove that the transfer of assets took place for the purposes of fraud.

☐ Judgments can be forcibly collected only by an enforcement officer (a local marshal, sheriff or constable) or sometimes the court clerk. You are responsible for informing the officer where to find the debtor's assets.

☐ The enforcement officer may seize any property that is not exempt and sell it at auction to pay the debt.

☐ The enforcement officer may garnishee a debtor's salary. You can collect 10%–25% of take-home pay, depending on state law. (You must tell the officer where the debtor works.)

☐ *Generally exempt from collection*:* Household and personal items, including furniture, stove, refrigerator, stereo, TV, sewing machine, clothing, cooking utensils, tools of a person's trade.

☐ *Generally collectible items*:* Motor vehicles, valuable jewelry, antiques, real estate, bank accounts, business equipment, stocks, bonds and the like.

☐ A home lived in by the debtor is exempt up to a certain amount (which varies from state to state). *The major problem in collecting on a home:* If a judgment is obtained against only the wife, for instance, the house can't be touched if it's also in her husband's name. But if only the debtor owns it, you can have it seized, sell it and return the exempt amount.

☐ Legal help is recommended if you are suing for an amount over the small-claims-court limit. After you win the judgment, your lawyer may arrange an asset search for you or recommend an agency to do one.

☐ Collection agencies are not recommended. They deal mostly with large accounts and not with one-shot cases. *Also:* A collection agency can only dun a debtor in a formal, legalistic way to convince him to pay voluntarily. After assets have been uncovered, only an enforcement officer can actually collect.

*These are general guidelines. Details vary from state to state. Check with the local marshal or other enforcement officer for more information.

Source: Kenneth D. Litwach, director, bureau of city marshals, New York City Department of Investigation.

Liability lawsuits: Beware

You may be even more vulnerable to personal liability lawsuits than you fear. In some states, for example, you can be held liable for injuries sustained by firefighters battling a blaze in your house… or by a pedestrian who falls on a public sidewalk abutting your property.

☐ Your first line of defense is homeowners' insurance with liability coverage. Most people get adequate protection from standard policies.

☐ If you have a large income or sizable assets, an additional "umbrella" policy may be necessary. Umbrella policies provide extra liability coverage for virtually any litigious incident (including libel and slander). They are surprisingly inexpensive.

☐ By the time a liability suit reaches court, there is seldom any question over the occurrence of the alleged wrong. What is under dispute is where the blame should fall.

☐ Most juries today are instructed by the judge to use a single criterion in deciding liability cases: Did the defendant (property owner) exercise "reasonable care" in guarding against injury and property damage? Although this may sound straightforward, the ways juries interpret "reasonable care" vary widely.

☐ In some states, the identity of the wronged person helps determine the meaning of "reasonable care." A person who is invited onto your property, for example, is entitled to more care than a trespasser. And someone hired to work for you is entitled to more consideration than a friend.

☐ Increasingly, states are adopting a so-called "single standard of care," which means that every person who ventures onto your property is entitled to the same level of protection. *Impact:* Homeowners must be careful to protect not only guests but anyone who happens onto their property. This includes children who cut through your yard on the way home from school, neighbors soliciting for charity or door-to-door salespeople.

The increasing reliance on the single-standard-of-care doctrine makes it significantly more difficult for homeowners to fight lawsuits. It is more and more important to maintain your home in such a way that you will not be sued in the first place. Some suggestions:

☐ Hire cautiously. Hire only fully bonded, insured contractors. Keep an eye out for potentially hazardous work conditions.

☐ Cover your chimney. Homeowners have been held liable for fires and smoke damage caused by sparks that escaped from uncovered chimneys. A chimney cover can prevent sparks from flying. Don't burn anything that might produce noxious fumes or dense soot, other potential sources of litigation.

☐ Get rid of vicious pets. Many pet owners assume they can limit their liability for dog bites by posting a "Beware of dog" sign in plain view. Not true. In fact, posting such a sign indicates to authorities that you are aware of your pet's "vicious propensities."

☐ Eliminate potential hazards. Swimming pools, trampolines, uncovered ditches and "attractive nuisances" that are likely to draw children must be made safe. Fence them in—well. Make and enforce strict rules as to their use: No diving in the pool…No jumping on the trampoline without "spotters" or adult supervision.

☐ Keep trees healthy and trimmed. If a bolt of lightning knocks a well-cared-for tree on your property onto a neighbor's house or car, you probably will not be liable. (There is no way to protect against such an event.) However, if the tree that falls is obviously diseased, or if it was leaning precariously, that's another matter.

☐ Clear snow and ice carefully. If you clear a public sidewalk of snow and someone falls and is injured there, you could be held liable. And what if a local ordinance requires you to clear the sidewalk in front of your house and you don't? In most cases, if someone does fall, the worst that can happen is that you would be fined for failing to clear the sidewalk. Chances are you would not be held liable for any injuries suffered in the fall. *Rule of thumb:* If there's a public sidewalk in front of your property, clear it very, very carefully—or don't clear it at all.

☐ Perform routine maintenance. Any loose brick on a staircase or pothole in your driveway can mean trouble.

Source: Melvin M. Belli, Sr., and Barry G. Saretsky. Belli, the well-known "king of torts" and father of "demonstrative evidence" (dramatic visual aids in the courtroom), heads the law firm Belli & Belli, San Francisco. Saretsky is a partner with Bower & Gardner, a firm that specializes in defending negligence cases, New York.

How liable are you for your child's mischief?

The issue of who is to blame when your child damages someone else's property or endangers another person is complicated. The growing number of homes where both parents work and depend on day-care centers or makeshift supervision of their children after school contributes to the problem. The legal issue is clouded by joint custody of divorced parents and by children's-rights concepts that are concerned with stemming child abuse and neglect.

□ No federal law directly holds a parent responsible for a child's actions simply because he is the child's parent. However, if it can be proved that a child was acting as the agent of a parent when he committed his crime, the parent is tried as though he had committed the crime himself. (This would apply, for example, to the burglar who used his small child to get through a tiny opening into a house.)

□ Although statutes differ, case law decisions seem to have established the age of 12 as the point at which a child can be tried in juvenile court. Younger children usually cannot be tried. At 17 or 18, a young person is considered to be an adult and is therefore tried as an adult.

□ A parent can be held responsible for a child's mischief if it can be proved that the parent neglected to exercise reasonable control over his child's behavior. This concept comes from state laws called *vicarious liability statutes*. Almost every state has some form of vicarious liability law that requires a parent to pay for damages to property up to a certain maximum ($200 to $10,000, depending on the state) if it can be proved that the parent neglected to control the child's behavior. About half the states hold parents liable for personal injuries their child may have inflicted on others.

□ Several states with large urban populations have implemented laws to deal specifically with the vandalization of public buildings and transit systems. *New Jersey law:* If it can be shown that the parents failed to supervise the child, they are liable for up to $1,000 worth of damage done by that child to a public utility, plus court costs. The penalty is levied in lieu of charging juvenile delinquency. Many parents pay just to keep their children from having a police record.

Bottom line: If your child gets into trouble by vandalizing property, your best bet is to pay the damages yourself. That keeps the problem out of court and in the family. For more serious crimes, you need a lawyer.

Source: David Schechner, partner, Schechner and Targan, lawyers, West Orange, NJ.

The business side of divorce

Divorce law has entered a new era. The new laws on divorce say, in effect, that no one is at fault when a marriage breaks up and that there is no victor to whom the spoils should belong. State legislatures now view marriage as an economic partnership and divorce as the dissolution of that partnership. Details to be aware of for negotiations:

Equitable distribution versus community property

□ Community property, a system that has been around since the turn of the century, simply means that all property acquired during a marriage is split 50–50 upon divorce, no matter who holds title. There are less than a dozen community-property states that retain this system.

□ The new game in divorce law is equitable distribution. Unlike community property, which is fairly clear-cut, equitable distribution means that all property acquired during a marriage must be distributed equitably (fairly). Enormous problems have arisen with equitable distribution because nobody knows exactly what fairness is. Fairness, it seems, is in the eye of the beholder. Case law is coming down from day to day, defining the parameters of equitable distribution, but no clear-cut guidelines have yet emerged.

□ The only thing that is crystal clear about equitable distribution is that negotiation between the parties is crucial. The cost of a full-blown equitable-distribution trial can be enormous.

Men versus women

The women's movement opposed equitable distribution because it foresaw that women would get the short end.

☐ The split in equitable distribution has been running about 70–30 in favor of the men.

☐ Since under equitable distribution a woman gets property, she can get alimony only for a fixed time, whereas previously she often got it for life. She can come back to court to ask for an extension, but this puts her in the supplicant position.

☐ The working wife comes out behind in many equitable-distribution cases because she usually doesn't get alimony. She can wind up being penalized for having worked, even though she might have earned only a fraction of what her husband made.

☐ The man who suffers under equitable distribution is usually not the one with a six-figure income. It's the one who makes $32,000 a year and has a wife, four kids and a house. His wife, who usually stays home with the kids, gets their only asset—the house. He often winds up with nothing but support payments.

New trends

☐ Equitable distribution has encouraged a whole new movement toward mediation of divorce. Mediation can be particularly good for the average middle-class divorce, where huge sums of money aren't involved. *Problem:* A lot of unqualified people have set themselves up as mediators. *Recommended:* A large mediation service with access to business experts, psychiatrists and other support staff. Mediation works only if both sides are equally informed. If one side is financially sophisticated and the other is not, the agreement will not be fairly mediated. It might not stand up in court.

☐ Custody. There's a national trend toward joint custody of the children, but most judges will order it only if there's an amicable agreement between the spouses. *Another recent trend:* Many fathers seek custody of the children.

☐ Blue-chip involvement. Divorce used to be considered a slightly seedy legal area, better left to single practitioners. But now, many major law firms that previously wouldn't touch a divorce action are actively involved. *Reason:* Their clients are getting divorced, and in community-property or equitable-distribution states, the outcome of a divorce can seriously affect the continuation of a business or the ownership of stock. *Also:* Big firms can provide the team approach, with tax, estate and other relevant services available "in-house."

Negotiating effectively

☐ Detach yourself from the emotional issues. Under equitable distribution, the party who tries to get revenge can do himself in financially. *Strongly recommended:* Psychotherapy, at least on a short-term basis, to resolve the emotional problems.

☐ Develop a business support system. Hire an accountant and bring in real-estate appraisers and other experts if necessary, especially if the valuation of a business is involved.

☐ Make them an offer they can't refuse. For the person with substantial assets (usually the husband) who doesn't want both the IRS and the spouse's lawyer snooping through business records, it pays to be generous. Remember, there's a third partner to every divorce of people with substance: The IRS. There's no reason to make the IRS a full partner if it can be avoided. *Example:* The man who says, "I won't give her a dime in alimony," should keep in mind that alimony is tax-deductible. *Also:* People who fail to take a businesslike approach to divorce frequently find themselves getting reported to the IRS a year or two later by an "innocent" spouse.

☐ Separate the financial issues from the custody issue. Divorce is hard enough for children. Don't make it worse.

Source: Marilyn S. Lashin, an attorney specializing in divorce law, New York.

Dealing with divorce lawyers

☐ Never ask your company's lawyer to handle a divorce. There is one question that you should ask him, however (and, even then, check out his answer independently): "Who's the best divorce lawyer around?"

☐ Don't use a general-purpose lawyer. The corporate lawyer knows he doesn't know divorce law. The general lawyer thinks he does. And you will pay for that mistake.

☐ To find a good divorce lawyer, just ask around. The best names in the area will come up automatically.

☐ As good as the recommendation is, check the lawyer out personally. Interview him. See if you two can communicate. Do you understand him? Does he swamp you with details?

☐ Discuss fee arrangements. Tell him you'd like the arrangement in writing. Don't feel that the fee isn't negotiable; it frequently is.

☐ Make sure the lawyer understands that you want to be kept abreast of everything he does (every document and every conference on your case). It's not that you'll necessarily be able to make any legal contributions (although you may). It's just that you must deal with your peace of mind. Divorce is so mind-shattering that you don't want to make it even more disconcerting by feeling you don't know what is going on—a common complaint.

☐ Expect to be emotionally upset much of the time when dealing with the divorce proceeding. It's important, however, that your lawyer doesn't make you feel worse. (If he does, consider someone else.)

☐ Don't waste time (and money) putting a notice in the newspapers saying you're not responsible for your spouse's debts. Instead, send a certified letter to every creditor your spouse has dealings with. (Prepare a list of those credit cards before the divorce proceedings get under way.)

☐ Never let your spouse become a party to any agreement without his or her own lawyer providing advice. In many states, weakness becomes strength; the law holds that any disagreement over interpretation must be construed in favor of the party who entered the agreement without any legal advice.

Writing a will that works

☐ Include a simultaneous-death clause that dictates how property will be disposed of in the event both you and your spouse die simultaneously in a common disaster. This prevents acrimony among the beneficiaries as well as potential litigation.

☐ Consider a no-contest clause to prevent a disappointed beneficiary from suing to have your will overturned. Such a clause says that any beneficiary who challenges the will must forfeit his share under the will.

☐ Tailor bequests to the beneficiary. Leave property to each beneficiary in the form he can best handle it. This may mean outright transfers. But depending on the beneficiary's age, experience, financial sophistication and personal inclinations, a trust or a custodianship or some other form of management may be more appropriate.

☐ Avoid giving complicated or risky investments, such as tax shelters, to financially unsophisticated beneficiaries who may not have your desire to fight the IRS.

☐ Don't leave property in joint ownership when one of the co-owners is likely to be dominated by the other.

☐ Don't give undivided fractional interests in property to beneficiaries who have very different ideas about the management or selling price of the property. Instead, transfer the property to a corporation and give the beneficiaries voting shares.

☐ Consider percentage bequests to favored beneficiaries, rather than absolute dollar amounts. In inflationary times, an estate can turn out to be worth far more than anticipated. A bequest of a dollar amount, no matter how generous it seemed at the time you made it, may be embarrassingly small in relation to the size of the inflated estate.

Source: Dr. Robert S. Holzman, professor emeritus of taxation at New York University and author of *Estate Planning: The New Golden Opportunities*, Boardroom Books, Greenwich, CT.

Limits on estate planning

Any will or estate plan must take into account the legal limits that govern the allocation of inherited property. The principal ones:

☐ Under varying state laws, a spouse has the right to a minimum portion of the partner's estate. A particular state's law may specify, for example, 35%. If the survivor is left a smaller amount, he or she can sue. In a few states, minor children are allowed specified percentages of a parent's estate.

☐ If a person dies without a will, his property will be distributed according to the intestacy laws of his state. These apportion his assets to the next of kin (spouse, children, siblings, etc.), according to definitions that vary from state to state. Even when a person has a will, if it is legally flawed, the laws of intestacy override the stated wishes of the deceased. *Most common flaw:* The will lacks the minimum number of witnesses specified by state law.

☐ An individual may have left property to persons who die before he does. Unless the decedent makes provisions for contingent or successor beneficiaries, the property will go to the "remainderman" (the person named to get what is left after all specific bequests have been honored). This could leave the remainderman with far more than had been intended.

☐ A person may write a will with the intention of leaving the bulk of the property to favored beneficiaries and very little to the remainderman. But inflation could raise the value of the person's properties far above his expectations. Specific dollar bequests to favored beneficiaries account for a small part of the estate, and the remainderman becomes the chief beneficiary. To avoid this, make bequests in percentages rather than in dollar amounts to self-adjust for inflation.

☐ The laws of some states place restrictions upon certain bequests. A state may provide, for example, that bequests to tax-exempt organizations, such as hospitals or churches, are void if made within 30 days of death. The laws are intended to discourage "bequests under pressure." But they can prevent a person's intentions from being carried out.

☐ Joint or mutual wills (usually by husband and wife) can ensure that upon the death of the second spouse, property that had been owned by the first spouse to die will go, under a prearranged plan, to relatives or friends of each spouse. *Result:* The second spouse to die must leave property according to the terms of the joint or mutual wills. But check with your tax adviser first. There can be heavy tax penalties for restrictions on property left to a surviving spouse.

☐ Many corporations purchase group insurance for employees in which the policy specifies that proceeds have to go to the surviving spouse (or to the children if there is no surviving spouse, or to the parents if there should be no children and the like). This limits the ability of the employee to designate who will benefit financially from his death.

☐ The Internal Revenue Service can make a prior claim against an estate. For example, if the deceased owed back taxes, the IRS can attach the cash-surrender value of any insurance policies on the decedent's life which he owned or in which he had a significant incident of ownership.

Source: Dr. Robert S. Holzman, author, *Encyclopedia of Estate Planning*, Boardroom Books, Greenwich, CT.

Revoking a will

It sounds fairly simple to do, but many individuals who try to revoke their wills don't succeed, and others have discovered that their wills have been revoked—by law—against their wishes. How these unwanted consequences can occur:

☐ In the aftermath of a death, no one is sure that the will was revoked. Testator (person making the will) may have destroyed it alone or in the presence of a witness who has also died. Much time and effort can be wasted looking for a document that no longer exists. Worse yet, a serious mistake may be made. In some states, a copy of a will may be accepted when the original can't be found and there's no indication it was revoked.

☐ In many states, a will is automatically revoked—wholly or partly—whenever certain events occur in the lifetime of a testator, such as marriage, divorce, birth of a child or death of a major beneficiary.

What to do:

☐ Write a separate document spelling out revocation. Keep it where the will would have been.

☐ Check with a lawyer whenever a family event could trigger automatic revocation.

Source: Paul P. Ashley, author of *You & Your Will*, McGraw-Hill, New York.

Advance-directive legislation and the right to die

Doctors are ambivalent about terminally ill patients. The Hippocratic oath tells them to preserve life, but it also directs them to relieve suffering. These two goals too often conflict. American courts and legislatures are still in the process of confronting the legal issues of the right to die, but guidelines are emerging.

Typically, states have approached these issues by enacting living will and/or medical durable power-of-attorney statutes. Although both forms of legislation allow you to plan in advance for the type of medical treatment you want to receive, each does so in a different manner.

Living wills allow you to specify your treatment wishes in writing. Subject to some statutory limitations, these laws allow you to give instructions concerning the use or withdrawal of artificial life support. Laws often require the attending physician to certify that a patient's condition is not expected to improve before the advance directive can be implemented. Every state except Massachusetts, Michigan and New York has passed legislation authorizing the use of living wills.

The medical durable power of attorney allows you to appoint agents to make medical treatment decisions for you in the event you are incapacitated. Every state except Alabama and Alaska has legislation authorizing the use of these documents. The majority of these statutes require the agent to make health-care decisions according to the patient's wishes, if known, or in the patient's best interests.

Here is a checklist of issues to consider if you are a concerned relative or appointed agent acting for someone who is seriously ill:

☐ Make sure a copy of the living will or durable power of attorney for health care is on the patient's medical record.

☐ Initiate a discussion with the physician about the removal of life support if it is clear there is no hope of recovery and the advance directives indicate that the patient would not want life-sustaining measures under these conditions.

☐ Do not give permission for additional life-sustaining procedures. Ask for interim measures. Try to get a "do not resuscitate" order placed on the chart, which will prevent aggressive cardio-pulmonary resuscitation if the patient's heart or breathing stops.

☐ If the doctor refuses to do what you want, find out why. Then talk to the hospital patient representative or ombudsman, if there is one.

☐ If the doctor is uncooperative, try to get a more cooperative doctor assigned to the case. Failing that, try to get the patient transferred to another hospital.

☐ Ask for an ethics-committee meeting. Most hospitals have committees that attempt to sort through these issues without resort to the courts. If the hospital remains uncooperative, alert the hospital attorney and administration that the patient is receiving treatments he or she did not want. If the physician and hospital continue to treat against the expressed wishes of the patient, they may be liable for assault and battery.

☐ Consider other resources such as hospices. A hospice provides comfort care in a home setting.

☐ Stay calm and clear about your requests. No matter how desperate you feel, do not "pull the plug" yourself.

☐ Call Choice In Dying at 800-989-WILL with your questions and concerns. They can give you information relevant to your state and advise you about the steps you should take.

Source: Choice In Dying, Inc., an educational council, 200 Varick St., New York 10014.

How to choose a guardian for your children

Whom do you want to take care of your children in the event you and your spouse die in the same accident? If you don't appoint a guardian, a probate judge will. And you are likely to make a better choice than the judge.

To do the job right, follow these guidelines:

☐ Prepare a list of possible guardians. Rate each individual or couple according to their degree of responsibility, accessibility, lifestyle, moral tenets, opinions on child raising, personal compatibility with your children, the candidates' ages, whether they have children and the ages of their children.

☐ Have meetings with the candidates. Assess their willingness to become your children's guardians.

☐ Select only individuals who satisfy all your criteria. And remember to provide for alternates in case your first choices become unable or unwilling to be your children's guardians.

☐ Keep in touch with the guardians you have appointed. Meet with them from time to time to fill them in on the current needs and plans for your children. These meetings will also give the guardians a chance to voice changes in their own lives that might have a dramatic impact on your children. You might use these sessions to let your children and other guardians get to know each other.

☐ Prepare a memorandum of instructions for the guardians, and keep it up to date. Include a list of things important to your children's well-being, such as their allergies, medical requirements, family medical history, personality traits and behavior responses. State your personal opinions about allowances, dating, schooling, driving, drinking and other areas of parental discretion.

☐ Provide direction about spending funds to achieve short-range and long-range goals. Indicate which goals have priority, such as a college education, and which are secondary, such as a car or a vacation in Europe.

☐ Set a minimum monthly allowance to be paid to the guardians for the children's day-to-day spending needs. Review this amount from time to time for reasonableness. Give your trustee the power to increase the allowance if necessary.

☐ Project your estate's future cash flow.

Source: Alan Gold, CPA.

When you rent a holiday home

It's important to be clear about the respective responsibilities of landlords and renters. As a rule:

☐ Be prepared to give business and personal references when you rent a summer place. *References commonly requested:* Your place of business and length of time employed. A current or former landlord as a personal reference. Your phone and utility account numbers (to check your payment record). A credit reference (some owners are now subscribing to services that check the credit rating of prospective tenants).

☐ Expect to pay all the rent plus the security (which is as much as half the rent) in advance. Installment payments are generally unacceptable. Your security will be returned when the outstanding bills have been paid. The best way to insure that you will get your security back in full is to check the house thoroughly before the lease is signed. Make sure everything is listed so you can't be accused of taking something that wasn't there.

☐ Improvements you plan to make must be noted in the lease, along with the owner's approval and any reimbursement agreement.

☐ Expect to pay for heat, hot water, electricity and telephone for the rental period. You may be asked to install a phone in your own name.

☐ The renter is generally responsible for the care and watering of the plants and lawn, raking the beach, keeping the place reasonably clean and other standard household maintenance. Responsibility for expensive or highly technical maintenance, such as pool cleaning or skilled gardening, should be discussed and outlined in the lease. (Owners often include items such as pool maintenance as part of the rental price.)

☐ The house must be left in the same condition you found it in. If you damage something, you must replace it with a similar item. *Recommended:* Attempt to work things out amicably with the owner. Offer to pay for anything you have broken before the owner discovers the problem.

☐ The owner must repair any essential items that break down in midseason (such as the refrigerator or the plumbing). If he is unavailable, you can pay for repairs and bill him.

☐ The owner must tell the renter about climatic changes (such as summer floods), insect or rodent infestation or anything else that affects the house's habitability. Failure to do so is grounds for breaking the lease and getting your money back.

☐ Your summer house should be covered by your landlord's homeowner's policy for burglary, accident, damage to the house and grounds, fire and flood. However, if you caused the damage, you can be held responsible.

☐ Insure your own property. Your jewelry and other valuables will not be covered by your landlord's homeowners' policy.

Source: Jacqueline Kyle Kall, City Island, NY, realtor specializing in resort properties in the US and worldwide.

Forming a tenants' organization

The most effective method of confronting a landlord about problems with rented apartments is through a tenant organization. If you are having problems with your landlord, the other tenants in your building probably are, too. If you approach the problem as a group, your chances of success improve immeasurably.

How to go about it:

☐ Speak with the tenants in your building and distribute flyers calling a meeting. At the meeting, elect a committee of tenants to lead the group.

☐ Pass out questionnaires to all tenants, asking them to list needed repairs in their apartments.

☐ After the questionnaires have been collected and reviewed, call the landlord and suggest a meeting with him to negotiate complaints. Many landlords will comply with this request, since the specter of all their tenants withholding rent can be a frightening prospect. Negotiation is always preferable to litigation.

☐ If negotiation fails, organize a rent strike. That's a procedure whereby tenants withhold rent collectively, depositing the money each month in an escrow fund or with the court until repairs are made. If your tenant organization is forced to go this route, you will need a good lawyer. Be prepared for a long court battle.

If you become disabled

Delegate power of attorney to someone with financial expertise to handle your business and financial affairs. But be aware of the drawbacks:

☐ The power ends in some states if you become legally incompetent.

☐ It ends in all states when you die.

☐ You are personally liable for any acts the proxy commits in your name.

☐ Some third parties may be reluctant to deal with the proxy for fear he may be exceeding his mandate.

Additional hints:

☐ Set up a standby trust triggered by a specific event, like an illness. The trust ends when the disability ceases. This avoids probate.

☐ Declare yourself a trustee of all or part of your property. If you become incapacitated, a substitute trustee automatically steps in. This type of trust also avoids probate. (But the trust can be overridden in some cases, so discuss this with your lawyer.)

☐ Avoid a judicial guardianship. It's complex and expensive because the courts require a periodic accounting from the trustee.

Filing a claim for bodily injury

Claims against insurance companies for bodily injury can be the most complicated and negotiable type of claim, especially when based upon pain and suffering. Be aware:

☐ In a no-fault state, you are limited to out-of-pocket expenses in a nonserious injury. This includes lost wages. In a fault-governed state, you can negotiate for more.

☐ Don't miss damages. Start at the top of your head and go down to your toes, to include every part that's been hurt.

☐ Photograph your injury. In addition to medical reports, photos are the best documentation of suffering.

☐ Consider every aspect of your life affected by your injury. Include your career, sports, hobbies, future interests and family relationships.

☐ Ask the insurance company what a lawyer would ask—at least twice the actual expenses when there has been no permanent disability. Where liability is clear, the insurance company will be likely to give you what you ask, if it believes that you really had difficulties and were out of work for a few weeks. However, where there has been permanent disability, multiples of expenses do not apply. *Example:* Your medical bills for a lost eye might have been only $3,000, but a jury might award you 50 times that amount.

Source: Dan Brecher, a New York City attorney.

Financial aid for the mugging victim

Financial compensation programs for mugging victims exist in more than 30 states. Compensation can cover both medical expenses and lost earnings. However, most of these programs utilize a means test that effectively eliminates all but lower-income victims. Additionally, the victim's own medical and unemployment insurance must be fully depleted before state compensation is granted.

If you are mugged, check the following:

☐ Workers' compensation may cover you if you were mugged on the job or on your way to or from company business during your workday. It will not cover you while commuting.

☐ Homeowners' policies may cover financial losses suffered during a mugging.

☐ Federal crime insurance insures up to $10,000 against financial losses from a mugging. This program is for people who have had difficulty purchasing homeowners' insurance privately.

☐ Mugging insurance is now available in New York. It covers property loss, medical care and mental anguish. If successful, it may spread rapidly to other states.

☐ A lawsuit may be successful if you can prove that the mugging was the result of negligence.

Source: Lucy N. Friedman, executive director, Victim Services Agency, New York.

Before you sign a contract with a health club

☐ Inspect the club at the time of day you'd be most likely to attend. Check on how crowded the pool, sauna and exercise rooms are.

☐ Make certain all facilities that are promised are available.

☐ Avoid clubs that require long-term contracts.

☐ Once you sign a contract, if you wish to terminate, it's usually possible to avoid liability for the full term of the contract by notifying the club by registered mail and paying for services already rendered and a small cancellation fee. Check your local consumer protection agency for rules.

☐ *Most important:* Don't be pushed into a hasty decision by a low-price offer. Specials are usually repeated.

If the dry cleaner loses or ruins a garment

☐ You should be reimbursed or given a credit. Most dry cleaners are neighborhood businesses where reputation is vital. You can hurt a cleaner's reputation by giving the cleaner bad word of mouth. You might remind the store of this fact if there is resistance to satisfying your complaint.

☐ If your cleaner fails to remove a stain you were told could be removed, you still have to pay for the cleaning job.

☐ If your cleaner dry-cleans a garment with a "do not dry-clean" label, the store is responsible for ruining the garment.

☐ If your cleaner ruins a garment that should not be dry-cleaned but lacks the "do not dry-clean" label, responsibility is a matter of opinion. The cleaner may reimburse you to keep your goodwill, or you may have to complain to an outside agency.

☐ The amount you will be reimbursed is always up for bargaining. You will have to consider original value and depreciation, and whether you have a receipt.

☐ If you cannot get satisfaction from your cleaner voluntarily, most states have dry-cleaners associations to arbitrate complaints. These associations go under various names in different states, so check with your local Department of Consumer Affairs. Make sure to keep all dry-cleaning receipts and other relevant information to substantiate your complaint.

When to use small-claims court

Suing in small-claims court can bring both spiritual and material satisfaction when you feel that you have been wronged. Although the monetary stakes are low—most states limit small-claims settlements to no more than $1,000—the rewards can be high.

Take a case to small-claims court when you:

☐ Have the time. Usually it takes a month for a case to be called and you'll have to spend at least a few hours in court during the hearing.

□ Value justice over a monetary settlement.

□ Want a public hearing of your grievance.

□ Feel the money involved represents a significant sum to you.

Social Security number secret

Few people know it, but the first three digits of a Social Security number are a code for the state in which the card was issued. This code, which can be used to confirm a place of birth or an employment history, is not public knowledge. However, many private detectives have the key to the code and will crack the Social Security number for a fee.

Source: Milo Speriglio, director and chief of Nick Harris Detectives, Inc., Van Nuys, CA, the second-oldest private detective agency in the US, and administrator of Nick Harris's Detective Academy.

Hiring a private detective

Times have changed for private detectives. They're no longer breaking down hotel doors to snap incriminating photos for divorce cases.

The modern private eye's bread and butter lies in serving the business world, in both security and personnel matters.

□ Consider hiring a private detective to track down runaway children. A missing persons bureau may have to worry about 30 cases at a time; a private eye can focus and coordinate the leads for a single client, giving the matter undivided attention. Be cautious, however. If the detective can't find a hard lead within three days but is eager to continue, he may be "milking" you.

□ Use a detective to devise a home security plan that will satisfy any insurance company, including itemized lists, photographs, locks and alarms. This should take three hours.

□ Before hiring a detective, get a résumé. After reviewing it, interview the person for at least 20 minutes to discuss your needs and how they'll be met.

□ Be sure the detective is licensed and bonded. A bond larger than the minimum bond might be advisable for a broad investigation covering several states or even a foreign country.

□ To make certain the private eye's record is clean, check with the appropriate state division on licensing (usually the Department of State). Ask the detective for the names of previous clients. Check with them. The best gauge is frequently word of mouth—reputations are hard won in the private-eye business.

Source: James Casey, private investigator and former New York City police detective, East Northport, NY.

Divorce or separation deadline

If a divorce or separation is in the works, it can pay to make it legal by December 31. *Reason:* Spouses who are divorced or separated by court decree at year-end file single rather than joint tax returns covering the whole year. They avoid the "marriage tax" that increases the tax bill of two-income married couples, and avoid future liability for each other's taxes. Spouses who aren't divorced or legally separated at year-end must file as married individuals. *Safety:* Still-married spouses moving toward divorce can use the "married filing separately" status. This results in a higher tax bill than joint filing but eliminates liability for the other spouse's tax bill.

Source: Ed Mendlowitz, partner, Mendlowitz Weitsen, CPAs, New York.

Name confusion in credit reports

If you are a "Junior" or "Senior," or have a common last name, someone else's credit information may be put in your file. Even if the other person has a perfect credit record, your loan application may be rejected if his/her borrowing added to your own puts you over your limit. *Self-defense:* When applying for credit, use your full middle or maiden name—or both—to be sure your file isn't confused with another.

Source: *All About Mortgages* by Julie Garton-Good, real-estate broker, Coral Gables, Florida. Real-Estate Education Company, 520 N. Dearborn St., Chicago 60610.